Meeting the Ethical Challenges of Leadership

Fifth Edition

To my students

Meeting the Ethical Challenges of Leadership

Casting Light or Shadow

Fifth Edition

Craig E. Johnson

George Fox University

Los Angeles | London | New Delhi
Singapore | Washington DC

Los Angeles | London | New Delhi
Singapore | Washington DC

FOR INFORMATION:

SAGE Publications, Inc.
2455 Teller Road
Thousand Oaks, California 91320
E-mail: order@sagepub.com

SAGE Publications Ltd.
1 Oliver's Yard
55 City Road
London EC1Y 1SP
United Kingdom

SAGE Publications India Pvt. Ltd.
B 1/I 1 Mohan Cooperative Industrial Area
Mathura Road, New Delhi 110 044
India

SAGE Publications Asia-Pacific Pte. Ltd.
3 Church Street
#10-04 Samsung Hub
Singapore 049483

Acquisitions Editor: Patricia Quinlin
Associate Editor: Maggie Stanley
Assistant Editor: Katie Guarino
Production Editor: Olivia Weber-Stenis
Copy Editor: Judy Selhorst
Typesetter: C&M Digitals (P) Ltd.
Proofreader: Pam Suwinsky
Indexer: Marilyn Augst
Cover Designer: Glenn Vogel
Marketing Manager: Liz Thornton

Printed in the United States of America

Library of Congress Cataloging-in-Publication Data

Johnson, Craig E. (Craig Edward), 1952–

Meeting the ethical challenges of leadership: casting light or shadow / Craig E. Johnson, George Fox University. — Fifth edition.

pages cm
Includes bibliographical references and index.

ISBN 978-1-4522-5918-5 (alk. paper)

1. Leadership--Moral and ethical aspects. I. Title.
HM1261.J64 2014
303.3′4—dc23   2013033339

This book is printed on acid-free paper.

Certified Chain of Custody
Promoting Sustainable Forestry
www.sfiprogram.org
SFI-01268
SFI label applies to text stock

14 15 16 17 18 10 9 8 7 6 5 4 3 2 1

Contents

PART 3. ETHICAL STANDARDS AND STRATEGIES

PART 4. SHAPING ETHICAL CONTEXTS

Preface

You have chosen an excellent time to study ethical leadership. Interest in the topic is greater than ever, generating a constant stream of new books, articles, and research studies. As a result, you have a rapidly growing body of knowledge to draw from in your efforts to become a more ethical leader and follower.

This edition of *Meeting the Ethical Challenges of Leadership* incorporates the latest developments in the field but, like previous versions, is guided by seven principles. First, there are few topics as important as leadership ethics. To highlight that fact, I've adopted Parker Palmer's metaphor of light and shadow as the book's central metaphor. Palmer reminds us that leaders have the power to do significant benefit or substantial harm. In extreme cases, leaders literally make the difference between life and death for their followers.

Second, we need to recognize the reality of bad leadership. Understanding why and how leaders cast shadows can help us prevent destructive behaviors and promote positive leadership. At the same time, we can also learn a great deal from the example of good leaders. Models of ethical and unethical leadership are found throughout the text.

Third, there are important ethical demands associated with the leadership role. Those who want to serve as leaders have a responsibility to exercise their authority on behalf of others. There are also ethical challenges associated with the follower role.

Fourth, the study of leadership ethics must draw from a wide variety of academic disciplines and traditions. Philosophers have been interested in the moral behavior of leaders for centuries. In the modern era they have been joined by social scientists, resulting in significant advances in our understanding of moral and immoral leadership. As a consequence, material for this text is drawn not only from philosophy but also from political science, psychology, neuroscience, management, business ethics, communication, education, sociology, and other fields. This multidisciplinary approach introduces readers to (1) how moral decisions are made (what scholars describe as the descriptive perspective on ethics) and (2) how to lead in a moral manner (the prescriptive or normative perspective).

Fifth, both theory and practice are essential to learning. I try to balance presentation of important concepts and research findings with opportunities for application through self-assessments, case analyses, and exploration exercises.

Sixth, texts should be readable. My objective is to write in an informal, accessible style. I don't hesitate to bring in my own experiences and, in some cases, my biases, in the hope of engaging readers and sparking discussion and disagreement.

Seventh, improvement is the bottom line. The ultimate goal of teaching and writing about ethics is to produce more ethical leaders. I believe that ethical development is part of leadership (and followership) development. Leaders and followers can develop their ability to make and carry through on their moral decisions, just as they develop their other competencies. *Meeting the Ethical Challenges of Leadership* is designed to help students build their ethical expertise through theoretical understanding, skill development, case and film analysis, group and class discussions, personal assessment and reflection, research projects, and writing assignments.

Key Features

Examples and Case Studies

Whatever their specific contexts, leaders face similar kinds of ethical choices. For that reason, I draw examples from a wide variety of settings: business, medicine, coaching, education, government, nonprofit organizations, and the military. Cases continue to play an important role in this edition. Discussion probes at the end of each case encourage readers to reflect on key ethics issues and concepts and to apply what they have learned from the preceding chapters to these narratives.

Leadership Ethics at the Movies

Each of these short summaries introduces a feature film (new to this edition) that illustrates principles related to the chapter discussion. This feature is designed to encourage students to (1) identify the important ethical principles portrayed in the film, (2) analyze and evaluate how the characters respond to moral dilemmas, and (3) draw ethical implications and applications from the movie. I provide three discussion questions for each film to get you started.

Self-Assessments

The self-assessments are designed to help students measure their performance with respect to important behaviors, skills, or concepts discussed in the chapters. Two self-assessments are now found at the end of each chapter.

Focus on Follower Ethics

This feature addresses the ethical challenges facing followers. Followers are critical to the success of any enterprise. The "Focus on Follower Ethics" box in each chapter helps students recognize and master the ethical demands of the follower role.

Implications and Applications

This section, found immediately after the body of each chapter, reviews key ideas and their ramifications for readers.

For Further Exploration, Challenge, and Self-Assessment

This feature encourages interaction with chapter content. Activities include brainstorming exercises, small-group discussions, conversational dyads, debates, self-analysis, personal reflection, and application and research projects.

What's New to This Edition?

This edition features new and expanded coverage of the following:

- Ethical leadership and effectiveness

- Bad/destructive leadership

- Bad followership

- Moral disengagement

- Character virtues

- Pragmatism

- Moral exclusion

- Apology

- Moral emotions and intuition (the dual-process approach to ethical decision making)

- Ethical blind spots

- Aesthetic leadership

- Responsible leadership

- Authentic followership

- Escalation of commitment

- Minority influence

- Ethical intergroup leadership

- Characteristics of healthy ethical organizational climates

- Organizational corruption

- The Universal Declaration of Human Rights

- Crisis myths

- Crisis leadership competencies

Most of the case studies from previous editions have been replaced. New cases in this edition involve the Secret Service, Rupert Murdoch, the Fukushima Nuclear Power Plant, Lance Armstrong, Wangari Maathai, the New England Compounding Center, North Korea, drone warfare, the Patagonia clothing company, WikiLeaks, in extremis leadership, a climbing disaster on K2, marijuana in the workplace, Yahoo!, Dominique Strauss-Kahn, and the New Delhi rape case that made international headlines. Cases retained from the fourth edition have been updated, including those dealing with payment for college athletes, Siemens, Greg Mortenson, Asian carp, and Google in China.

Ancillaries

Instructor Teaching Site

A password-protected instructor's manual is available at **www.sagepub.com/johnsonmecl5e** to help instructors plan and teach their courses. These resources have been designed to help instructors make the classes as practical and interesting as possible for students:

- **Overview for the Instructor** offers the author's insights on how to use this book most effectively in a course on leadership ethics.

- **Chapter tests** offer a variety of questions to assist with assessment of student learning.

- **PowerPoint slides** capture key concepts and terms for each chapter for use in lectures and review.

- **Leadership Ethics Sample Course Syllabus** provides a model for structuring a course.

- **Leadership Seminar Sample Syllabus** is an additional course option for a seminar format.

- **Teaching Strategies** offers ideas and insights into various approaches to teaching and learning.

- **Assignments and Projects** provide unique and highly creative activities for meaningful involvement in learning.

- **Learning From SAGE Journal Articles** gives access to full journal articles that instructors can assign and use as further teaching tools in class.

Student Study Site

An open-access student study site can be found at **www.sagepub.com/johnsonmecl5e**. The site offers **Learning From SAGE Journal Articles**, with access to recent, relevant full-text articles from SAGE's leading research journals. Each article supports and expands on the concepts presented in the book. This feature also provides discussion questions to focus and guide student interpretation.

Acknowledgments

Colleagues and students provided practical and emotional support during the writing of this edition, just as they did for earlier versions. Research librarians helped locate sources and double-check facts. Phil Smith clarified my understanding of several philosophical theories. Michelle Shelton reviewed references. Students enrolled in my leadership seminar, doctoral leadership seminar, business ethics, and leadership communication classes shaped this and earlier editions by responding to chapter content, exercises, and cases. My special thanks go to instructors from around the country who adopted the first four editions of *Meeting the Ethical Challenges of Leadership,* which made this fifth edition possible. Five anonymous reviewers provided input that guided my revisions. Editor Patricia Quinlin ably picked up where her predecessors at SAGE left off. Finally, I want to once again thank my wife, Mary, who continues to encourage my writing efforts.

Introduction

Leaders: The Bad News and the Good News

When it comes to leaders, there is both bad news and good news. The bad news is that wherever we turn—business, military, politics, medicine, education, or religion—we find leaders toppled by ethical scandals. Nearly all have sacrificed their positions of leadership and their reputations. Many face civil lawsuits, criminal charges, and jail time. The costs can be even greater for followers. Consider, for example:

- The world continues to recover from a global economic crisis sparked by leaders in the financial industry who downplayed risks and engaged in fraud in order to generate short-term profits.

- Millions of cycling fans and cancer victims were disillusioned when seven-time Tour de France winner and cancer survivor Lance Armstrong had his wins vacated because of a blood-doping scandal.

- The Gulf of Mexico oil spill, one of the greatest environmental disasters in U.S. history, was the product of a series of poor decisions by leaders at BP who ignored safety warnings and had no strategy in place for capping deepwater oil leaks. The company agreed to pay $7.6 billion to compensate individuals and businesses damaged by the disaster.

- Owners and managers of a Massachusetts pharmacy allegedly failed to sterilize a pain drug shipped to hospitals and other health care providers, triggering a meningitis outbreak.

- Efforts to build schools for children in Pakistan and Afghanistan were endangered when Central Asia Institute founder and best-selling author Greg Mortenson misspent donor funds.

- British reporters and private detectives invaded the privacy of murder victims and their families by secretly hacking into their cell phones to access their voice mail.

- Dozens of children in Pennsylvania and Britain suffered sexual abuse at the hands of former Pennsylvania State University football coach Jerry Sandusky and British music promoter Jimmy Savile. Officials at both Penn State and the BBC (Savile's employer) were accused of covering up the men's crimes.

- 400,000 women caught in Congo's civil war were raped in one 12-month period as military leaders engaged in a campaign of sexual terrorism.

- U.S. senators accused Apple of avoiding $9 billion in taxes by shifting profits to foreign subsidiaries, a strategy that increased the federal budget deficit as well as the tax burden for other businesses and average Americans.

- More than 1,000 Bangladeshi garment workers died when their factory building collapsed. Company bosses had ordered them back to work even though the building had been declared unfit for occupation the day before.

- Executives at Toyota were slow to respond to sudden acceleration problems in some of the company's car models, putting the lives of hundreds of thousands of drivers in danger.

- A West Virginia coal mine explosion took the lives of 29 miners after officials at Massey Energy failed to follow basic safety procedures.

The misery caused by unethical leaders drives home an important point: Ethics is at the heart of leadership.[1] When we assume the benefits of leadership, we also assume ethical burdens. I believe that, as leaders, we must make every effort to act in such a way as to benefit rather than damage others, to cast light instead of shadow. Doing so will significantly reduce the likelihood that we will join the future ranks of fallen leaders.

Fortunately, we can also find plenty of examples of leaders who brighten the lives of those around them. That's the good news. Consider these examples:

- Managers and employees at the Fukushima Nuclear Power Plant in Japan risked massive radiation exposure to prevent a meltdown following a tsunami that severely damaged the facility.

- Kenyan activist Wangari Maathai and her followers established the Green Belt Movement, which plants trees and fosters economic development and democracy in rural communities in Africa.

- Relief organizations and government agencies rushed to help the victims of Hurricane Sandy.

- Pakistani teenager Malala Yousafzai promotes schooling for girls while opposing the Taliban. She continues to speak out despite having been shot and seriously injured by a Taliban gunman.

- Sudanese billionaire Mo Ibrahim offers a $5 million prize to African leaders who promote democracy, don't steal public funds, and peacefully leave office when their terms end.

- On his 81st birthday, CEO Robert Moore passed ownership of his company, Bob's Natural Foods, to his 200 Oregon employees.

- The 2012 winners of the annual CNN Heroes Award are involved in a variety of community efforts, ranging from caring for the children of Nepalese prisoners and teen moms in Colombia to helping victims of sexual violence in Haiti to teaching African American children to swim in Ohio.

- Teachers at Sandy Hook Elementary School in Newtown, Connecticut, led their students to safety and comforted them during a gunman's murderous rampage; six adults died while protecting their students. First responders rushed into the building as the killer was still shooting.

- At 8 years old, Makenzie Snyder started an organization that provides duffel bags (each with a stuffed animal) for foster children to use as they move from home to home.

- As chair of the U.S. Commodity Futures Trading Commission, Gary Gensler is cleaning up the banking industry, successfully bringing suit against HSBC, Barclays, and other financial institutions for manipulating interest rates.

- US Airways pilot Captain Chesley Sullenberger saved the lives of all of his crew and passengers by safely landing his damaged plane in New York's Hudson River.

You should find this book helpful if you are a leader or an aspiring leader who (1) acknowledges that there are ethical consequences associated with the leadership role, (2) wants to exert positive influence over others, (3) seeks to make more informed ethical choices and to follow through on your decisions, and (4) desires to foster ethical behavior in others. You will also find useful insights if you are a follower who wants to behave ethically and bring out the best in your leaders.

There is no guarantee that after reading this book you will act in a more ethical fashion in every situation. Nor can you be sure that others will reach the same conclusions as you do about what is the best answer to an ethical dilemma or that you will succeed in improving the ethical climate of your group or organization. Nevertheless, you can increase your ethical competence and encourage others to do the same. This book is dedicated to that end.

Defining Terms

Because this is a book about leadership ethics, we need to clarify what both of these terms mean. Leadership is the exercise of influence in a group context.[2] Want to know who the leaders are? Look for the people having the greatest impact on the group or organization. Leaders are change agents engaged in furthering the needs, wants, and goals of leaders and followers alike. They are found wherever humans associate with one another, whether in social movements, sports teams, task forces, nonprofit agencies, state legislatures, military units, or corporations.

No definition of leadership is complete without distinguishing between leading and following. Generally leaders get the most press. The newfound success of a college football team is a case in point. The head coach gets most of the credit for changing a losing team into a winner, but the turnaround is really the result of the efforts of many followers. Assistant coaches work with offensive and defensive lines, quarterbacks, and kicking teams; trainers tend to injuries; academic tutors keep players in school; athletic department staff members solicit contributions for training facilities; and sports information personnel draw attention to the team's accomplishments. (In Chapter 5 we will see that followers in all fields are more important than ever.)

In truth, leaders and followers function collaboratively, working together toward shared objectives. They are relational partners who play complementary roles.[3] Whereas leaders exert a greater degree of influence and take more responsibility for the overall direction of the group, followers are more involved in implementing plans and doing the work. During the course of a day or week, we typically shift between leader and follower roles, heading up a project team at work, for example, while taking the position of follower as a student in a night class. As a result, we need to know how to behave ethically as both leaders and followers.

Moving from a follower role to a leadership role brings with it a shift in expectations. Important leader functions include establishing direction, organizing, coordinating activities and resources, motivating, and managing conflicts. Important follower functions include carrying out important group and organizational tasks (engineering, social work, teaching, accounting), generating new ideas about how to get jobs done, working in teams, and providing feedback.[4]

Viewing leadership as a role should put to rest the notion that leaders are born, not made. The fact that nearly all of us will function as leaders at some point if we haven't already done so means that leadership is not limited to those with the proper genetic background, income level, or education. Ordinary people emerged as leaders during the shooting that seriously injured Arizona congresswoman Gabby Giffords and killed six others in 2012, for instance. An intern on the congresswoman's staff applied pressure to Giffords's head wound, saving her life. One member of the crowd prevented the killer from reloading his weapon by grabbing a loaded magazine he had dropped, and another clubbed the shooter in the back of his head with a folding chair. One of the wounded, a 74-year-old army colonel, tackled the gunman, and he and other bystanders subdued him. A doctor and nurse shopping at the Safeway where the attack occurred provided treatment for victims.

Leadership should not be confused with position, although leaders often occupy positions of authority. Those designated as leaders, such as a disillusioned manager nearing retirement, don't always exert a great deal of influence. On the other hand, those without the benefit of a title on the organizational chart can have a significant impact. Václav Havel was a Czech playwright who served time in prison for opposing his country's government. Later he went on to help lead the Velvet Revolution, which overthrew the country's Communist regime, and became the new Czech Republic's first democratic president. Erin Brockovich was a poor single mother in California without legal training who helped victims of chemical poisoning reach a multimillion-dollar legal settlement with Pacific Gas and Electric. Mohamed Bouazizi was a Tunisian fruit vendor who burned himself alive to protest political oppression and lack of economic opportunity. His dramatic act launched the Arab Spring, a popular uprising that toppled several dictatorships in the Middle East. (See Case Study 0.1 at the end of this introduction for another example of an unlikely leader.)

Human leadership differs in important ways from the pattern of dominance and submission that characterizes animal societies. The dominant female hyena or male chimpanzee rules over the pack or troop through pure physical strength. Each maintains authority until some stronger rival (often seeking mates) comes along. Unlike other animals, which seem to be driven largely by instinct, humans consciously choose how they want to influence others. We can rely on persuasion, rewards, punishments, emotional appeals, rules, and a host of other means to get our way. Freedom of choice makes ethical considerations an important part of any discussion of leadership. The term *ethics* refers to judgments about whether human behavior is right or wrong. We may be repulsed by the idea that a male lion will kill the offspring of the previous dominant male when he takes control of the pride. Yet we cannot label his actions as unethical because he is driven by a genetic imperative to start his own bloodline. We can and do condemn the actions of leaders who decide to lie, belittle followers, and enrich themselves at the expense of the less fortunate.

Some philosophers distinguish between *ethics,* which they define as the systematic study of the principles of right and wrong behavior, and *morals,* which they describe as specific standards of right and wrong ("Thou shall not steal"; "Do unto others as they would do unto you"). Just as many scholars appear to use these terms interchangeably, I will follow the latter course.

The practice of *ethical leadership* is a two-part process involving personal moral behavior and moral influence.[5] Ethical leaders earn that label when they act morally as they carry out their duties and shape the ethical contexts of their groups, organizations, and societies. Both components are essential. Leaders must demonstrate such character traits as justice, humility, optimism, courage, and compassion; make wise choices; and master the ethical challenges of their roles. In addition, they are responsible for the ethical behavior of others. (Complete Self-Assessment 0.1 to determine how well your leader fills each of these roles.) These dual responsibilities intertwine. As we'll see later in the book, leaders act as role models for the rest of the organization. How followers behave depends in large part on the example set by leaders. Conversely, leaders become products of their own creation. Ethical climates promote the moral development of leaders as well as that of followers, fostering their character and improving their ability to make and follow through on ethical choices. Ethical organizational environments are marked by humility, integrity, justice, trust, a concern for how goals are achieved, and a sense of social responsibility. They also have safeguards that keep both leaders and followers from engaging in destructive behaviors.

There is a widespread misconception that ethics and effectiveness are incompatible. Many believe that in order to be effective leaders have to sacrifice their ethical standards. They are convinced of the truth of the old adage "Nice guys (or gals) finish last." However, investigators report that ethical leaders are frequently more, not less, effective than their unethical colleagues. For example:[6]

- Ethical leaders are rated as more promotable and effective.

- Those working for ethical leaders are more satisfied and are more committed to their organizations and their managers. They work harder, are more willing to report problems to management, and are more productive.

- Members of work groups led by moral leaders are less likely to engage in theft, sabotage, cheating, and other deviant behaviors.

- Ethical leadership enhances organizational trust levels, fostering perceptions that the organization is competent, open, concerned for employees, and reliable. Such trust leads to improved organizational performance and greater profitability.

- Employees who consider their leaders to be moral persons and moral managers also believe that their organizations are effective.

- Ethical leadership fosters an ethical organizational climate, which, in turn, increases job satisfaction and commitment to the organization.

- Followers in both Western and non-Western cultures want leaders of high character who respect the rights and the dignity of others.

In sum, while unethical leaders can prosper, a growing body of evidence suggests that if you strive to be an ethical leader, you are more likely to be a successful one as well.

Overview of the Book

Part I of this book, "The Shadow Side of Leadership," examines the important topic of leadership's dark side. Chapter 1 outlines common shadows cast by leaders: abuse of power and privilege, mismanagement of information, misplaced and broken loyalties, inconsistency, and irresponsibility. Chapter 2 explores the reasons leaders often cause more harm than good and then outlines strategies for stepping out of the shadows and into the light.

After identifying the factors that cause us to cast shadows as leaders, the discussion turns to mastering them. To do so we will need to look inward. Part II, "Looking Inward," focuses on the inner dimension of leadership. Chapter 3 examines the role of character development in overcoming our internal enemies and faulty motivations, and Chapter 4 explores the nature of evil, forgiveness, apology, and spirituality.

Part III, "Ethical Standards and Strategies," addresses moral decision making and provides the theory and tactics we need to develop our ethical expertise. Chapter 5 surveys a wide range of ethical perspectives that can help us set moral priorities, while Chapter 6 describes the process of ethical decision making as well as formats that we can use to make better moral choices and follow through on our decisions. Chapter 7 introduces theories specifically developed to guide the ethical behavior of leaders.

Part IV, "Shaping Ethical Contexts," looks at ways in which leaders can shed light in a variety of situations. Chapter 8 examines ethical group decision making. Chapter 9 describes the creation of ethical organizational climates. Chapter 10 highlights the challenges of ethical diversity. Chapter 11 provides an overview of ethical leadership in crisis situations.

Expect to learn new terminology along with key principles, decision-making formats, and important elements of the ethical context. This information is drawn from a number of different fields of study—philosophy, communication, theology, history, psychology, neuroscience, sociology, political science, and organizational behavior—because we need insights from many different disciplines if we are to step out of the shadows. You can anticipate reading about and then practicing a variety of skills, ranging from information gathering to listening and conflict management.

With these preliminaries out of the way, let's begin with Chapter 1, which takes a closer look at some of the ethical hurdles faced by leaders.

CASE STUDY 0.1

Leading With a Blink of the Left Eye

Jean-Dominique Bauby led a charmed life. The 43-year-old editor of the French fashion magazine *Elle* moved in the highest levels of society, attended fashion shoots, dined at the best restaurants, drove fine automobiles, traveled extensively, attracted the attention of beautiful women, and was the doting father of two children. All that changed in December 1995 when Bauby (nicknamed Jean-Do by his friends) had a massive stroke. After 20 days of intensive treatment, he awoke in a hospital to find that he suffered from "locked-in syndrome." In this rare condition, the mind remains healthy but is locked into a body that no longer works. Bauby could move only his neck, and his only way of communicating was by blinking his left eye (the other was sewn shut). He was fed through an intravenous tube. This once active, proud, handsome, and highly independent man was reduced to a drooling shadow of his former self, totally dependent on others. Here is how Jean-Dominique describes what he saw when he noticed his reflection in a glass case:[1]

Reflected in the glass I saw the head of a man who seemed to have emerged from a vat of formaldehyde. His mouth was twisted, his nose damaged, his hair tousled, his gaze full of fear. One eye was sewn shut, the other goggled like the doomed eye of Cain. For a moment I stared at that dilated pupil, before I realized it was only mine.

Whereupon a strange euphoria came over me. Not only was I exiled, paralyzed, mute, half deaf, deprived of all pleasures, and reduced to the existence of a jellyfish, but I was also horrible to behold. (p. 25)

A speech therapist introduced Bauby to an alphabet based on frequency of usage (the letters *E*, *S*, and *A* appear first in this system). Each letter was given a number ($E = 1, S = 2, A = 3$), and Bauby would blink the assigned number of times to select the letters he wanted to use. He employed this system to construct words and sentences when conversing with visitors and to create letters he mass-mailed to friends and acquaintances. Later, with the help of a book editor, Bauby went on to write his memoir. He would wake early in the morning, mentally compose and rehearse what he wanted to say, and then blink out the text when the editor arrived. (The project took an estimated 200,000 blinks to complete.)

Bauby titled his work *The Diving Bell and the Butterfly.* The image of a diving bell captures his feeling of being shut up in his body, and the butterfly refers to his imagination. Bauby's imagination set him free to sample delicious meals, to travel to distant locations, and to move back and forth in time despite all of his physical limitations. He was motivated to write about his experience, in part, because of reports that gossips in Paris had called him a "total vegetable," relegating him to "a vegetable stall and not to the human race." Bauby concluded, "I would have to rely on myself if I wanted to prove that my IQ was still higher than a turnip's" (p. 82).

The former editor's testament reveals a man who had been deepened by his tragic circumstances. Bauby, as many observers have noted, was far from a saint before his stroke. Quick-tempered, he had a number of mistresses and left the mother of his children to live with a fellow journalist. In his memoir he speaks of his regrets and admits that he was ashamed of "playing at being editor in chief in the frothy world of fashion magazines" when a journalistic colleague was held hostage for several years in the Middle East. He makes peace with his current condition, however, noting, "I have indeed begun a new life, and life is here, in this bed, that wheelchair, and those corridors. Nowhere else" (p. 129).

Bauby died of heart failure caused by pneumonia just two days after his book was released and 10 years before the film based on the book brought his story to the attention of a wider international audience. Millions have been moved by his experience. The stricken editor demonstrated that it is possible to lead with the blink of an eye. He provided insight into the inner lives of those who are locked into their bodies and helped the rest of us better meet their needs. A month before he died he established the Association for Locked-In Syndrome to help patients and their families deal with this condition and search for a cure. This organization reflects the hope found in the final words of Jean-Dominique's memoir: "Does the cosmos contain keys for opening up my diving bell? A subway line with no terminus? A currency strong enough to buy my freedom back? We must keep looking" (p. 132).

Discussion Probes

1. What enabled Bauby to overcome his condition and emerge as a leader?

2. How do you think Bauby was "deepened" by his personal tragedy?

3. Did Jean-Do exert more influence before or after his massive stroke?

4. What have you learned from Bauby's story?

5. Can you name other leaders who have undergone significant hardships that have helped them become more ethical and effective?

Note

1. All quotations come from Bauby, J.-D. (1997). *The diving bell and the butterfly: A memoir of life in death.* New York: Vintage Books.

Sources

Mallon, T. (1997, June 15). In the blink of an eye [Review of *The diving bell and the butterfly*, by J.-D. Bauby]. *The New York Times*. Retrieved from http://www.nytimes.com/books/97/06/15/reviews/970615.mallon.html

Swardson, A. (2007, March 11). A tale of courage, told in a blink of an eye. *The Washington Post*, p. A01.

Webster, P. (1997, March 7). Memoir unlocks medical enigma. *The Guardian*, p. 15.

SELF-ASSESSMENT 0.1

Ethical Leadership Scale

Instructions: In responding to the following items, think about your CEO (top leader) at work. Indicate your level of agreement with the statements in the next section by circling your responses.

1 = strongly disagree

2 = disagree

3 = neutral

4 = agree

5 = strongly agree

My organization's CEO (top leader)

1. listens to what employees have to say.

   1   2   3   4   5

2. disciplines employees who violate ethical standards.

   1   2   3   4   5

3. conducts his or her personal life in an ethical manner.

   1   2   3   4   5

4. has the best interests of employees in mind.

   1   2   3   4   5

5. makes fair and balanced decisions.

   1   2   3   4   5

6. can be trusted.

1   2   3   4   5

7. discusses business ethics or values with employees.

1   2   3   4   5

8. sets an example of how to do things the right way in terms of ethics.

1   2   3   4   5

9. defines success not just by results but also by the way that they are obtained.

1   2   3   4   5

10. when making decisions, asks, "What is the right thing to do?"

1   2   3   4   5

Scoring

Add up your responses to the 10 items. Total score can range from 10 to 50. The higher the score, the more ethical you believe your leader to be.

SOURCE: Brown, M. E., Trevino, L. K., & Harrison, D. A. (2005). Ethical leadership: A social learning perspective for construct development and testing. *Organizational Behavior and Human Decision Processes, 97*, 117–134. Used by permission.

NOTES

1. See Ciulla, J. B. (Ed.). (2004). *Ethics, the heart of leadership* (2nd ed.). Westport, CT: Praeger.
2. Bass, B. M. (1990). *Bass and Stogdill's handbook of leadership* (3rd ed.). New York: Free Press.
3. Hollander, E. P. (1992). The essential interdependence of leadership and followership. *Current Directions in Psychological Science, 1,* 71–75.
4. Johnson, C. E., & Hackman, M. Z. (1997). *Rediscovering the power of followership in the leadership communication text.* Paper presented at the annual convention of the National Communication Association, Chicago.
5. Brown, M. E., & Trevino, L. K. (2006). Ethical leadership: A review and future directions. *Leadership Quarterly, 17*, 595–616.

6. Brown, M. E., & Trevino, L. K. (2006). Socialized charismatic leadership, values congruence, and deviance in work groups. *Journal of Applied Psychology, 91*, 954–962; Brown, M. E., Trevino, L. K., & Harrison, D. A. (2005). Ethical leadership: A social learning perspective for construct development and testing. *Organizational Behavior and Human Decision Processes, 97,* 117–134; Neubert, M. J., Carlson, D. S., Kacmar, K. M., Roberts, J. A., & Chonko, L. B. (2009). The virtuous influence of ethical leadership behavior: Evidence from the field. *Journal of Business Ethics, 90,* 157–170; Khuntia, R., & Suar, D. (2004). A scale to assess ethical leadership of Indian and public sector managers. *Journal of Business Ethics,*

49, 13–26; Johnson, C. E., Shelton, P. M., & Yates, L. (2012). Nice guys (and gals) finish first: Ethical leadership and organizational trust, satisfaction, and effectiveness. *International Leadership Journal, 4*(1), 3–19; Davis, A. L., & Rothstein, H. R. (2006). The effects of the perceived behavioral integrity of managers on employee attitudes: A meta-analysis. *Journal of Business Ethics, 67*, 407–419; Rubin, R. S., Dierdorff, E. C., & Brown, M. E. (2010). Do ethical leaders get ahead? Exploring ethical leadership and promotability. *Business Ethics Quarterly, 20*, 215–236; Resick, C. J., Hanges, P. J., Dickson, M. W., & Mitchelson, J. K. (2006). A cross-cultural examination of the endorsement of ethical leadership. *Journal of Business Ethics, 63*, 345–359; Johnson, C. E. (2007). Best practices in ethical leadership. In J. A. Conger & R. E. Riggio (Eds.), *The practice of leadership: Developing the next generation of leaders* (pp. 150–171). San Francisco: Jossey-Bass.

The Shadow Side of Leadership

The Leader's Light or Shadow

We know where light is coming from by looking at the shadows.

—Humanities scholar Paul Woodruff

What's Ahead

This chapter introduces the dark (bad, toxic) side of leadership as the first step in promoting good or ethical leadership. The metaphor of light and shadow dramatizes the differences between moral and immoral leaders. Leaders have the power to illuminate the lives of followers or to cover them in darkness. They cast light when they master ethical challenges of leadership. They cast shadows when they (1) abuse power, (2) hoard privileges, (3) mismanage information, (4) act inconsistently, (5) misplace or betray loyalties, and (6) fail to assume responsibilities.

A Dramatic Difference/The Dark Side of Leadership

In an influential essay titled "Leading From Within," educational writer and consultant Parker Palmer introduces a powerful metaphor to dramatize the distinction between ethical and unethical leadership. According to Palmer, the difference between moral and immoral leaders is as sharp as the contrast between light and darkness, between heaven and hell:

> A leader is a person who has an unusual degree of power to create the conditions under which other people must live and move and have their being, conditions that can be either as illuminating as heaven or as shadowy as hell. A leader must take special responsibility for what's going on inside his or her own self, inside his or her consciousness, lest the act of leadership create more harm than good.[1]

For most of us, leadership has a positive connotation. We have been fortunate enough to benefit from the guidance of teachers or coaches, for example, or we admire noteworthy historical leaders. As we saw in the introduction, ethical leaders brighten the lives of those around them significantly by building trust, commitment, and satisfaction; by reducing negative behavior; and by increasing individual and collective performance. However, Palmer urges us to pay more attention to the shadow side of leadership. Political figures, parents, clergy, and business executives have the potential to cast as much shadow as they do light. Refusing to face the dark side of leadership makes abuse more likely. All too often, leaders "do not even know they are making a choice, let alone how to reflect on the process of choosing."[2]

Recently other scholars have joined Palmer in focusing on the dark or negative dimension of leadership. Claremont Graduate University professor Jean Lipman-Blumen uses the term *toxic leaders* to describe those who engage in destructive behaviors and who exhibit dysfunctional personal characteristics.[3] These behaviors and qualities (summarized in Table 1.1) cause significant harm to followers and organizations.

Harvard professor Barbara Kellerman believes that limiting our understanding of leadership solely to good leadership ignores the reality that a great many leaders engage in destructive behaviors.[4] Overlooking that fact, Kellerman says, undermines our attempts to promote good leadership: "I take it as a given that we promote good leadership not by ignoring bad leadership, nor by presuming that it is immutable, but rather by attacking it as we would a disease that is always pernicious and sometimes deadly."[5]

According to Kellerman, bad leaders can be ineffective, unethical, or ineffective and unethical. She identifies seven types of bad leaders:

Incompetent. These leaders don't have the motivation or the ability to sustain effective action. They may lack emotional or academic intelligence, for example, or be careless, distracted, or sloppy. Some cannot function under stress, and their communication and decisions suffer as a result. Former International Olympic Committee president Juan Antonio Samaranch (1961–2000) is one example of an incompetent leader. Toward the end of his tenure he turned a blind eye to commercialism, drug scandals, and corruption in the Olympic movement.

Rigid. Rigid leaders may be competent, but they are unyielding, unable to accept new ideas, new information, or changing conditions. Thabo Mbeki is one such leader. After becoming president of South Africa in 1999, he insisted that HIV does not cause AIDS and withheld antiretroviral drugs from HIV-positive pregnant women. These medications would have dramatically cut the transmission of the disease to their babies.

Table 1.1   The Behaviors and Personal Characteristics of Toxic Leaders

Destructive Behaviors	Toxic Qualities
Leaving followers worse off	Lack of integrity
Violating human rights	Insatiable ambition
Feeding followers' illusions; creating dependence	Enormous egos
Playing to the basest fears and needs of followers	Arrogance
Stifling criticism; enforcing compliance	Amorality (inability to discern right from wrong)
Misleading followers	Avarice (greed)
Subverting ethical organizational structures and processes	Reckless disregard for the costs of their actions
Engaging in unethical, illegal, and criminal acts	Cowardice (refusal to make tough choices)
Building totalitarian regimes	Failure to understand problems
Failing to nurture followers, including successors	Incompetence in key leadership situations
Setting constituents against one another	
Encouraging followers to hate or destroy others	
Identifying scapegoats	
Making themselves indispensable	
Ignoring or promoting incompetence, cronyism, and corruption	

SOURCE: Adapted from Lipman-Blumen, J. (2005). *The allure of toxic leaders: Why we follow destructive bosses and corrupt politicians—and how we can survive them.* Oxford, England: Oxford University Press, pp. 19–23.

Intemperate. Intemperate leaders lack self-control and are enabled by followers who don't want to intervene or can't. The political career of Marion Barry, Jr., demonstrates intemperate leadership in action. Barry served as mayor of Washington, D.C., from 1979 to 1991. He ignored widespread corruption in his administration, perhaps in part because he was busy cheating on his wife and doing drugs. Barry was convicted of possessing crack cocaine and served six months in jail. After being released from prison, he was elected to the city council in 1992 and was reelected as mayor in 1994. During his administrations, the district's schools and public services deteriorated while the murder rate soared.

Callous. The callous leader is uncaring or unkind, ignoring or downplaying the needs, wants, and wishes of followers. Former hotel magnate Leona Helmsley personifies the callous leader. She earned the title "the Queen of Mean" by screaming at employees and firing them for minor infractions such as having dirty fingernails. Helmsley later served time in prison for tax evasion. (She once quipped, "Only the little people pay taxes.")

Corrupt. These leaders and at least some of their followers lie, cheat, and steal. They put self-interest ahead of the public interest. Former United Way of America chief William Aramony is an exemplar of this type of leader. Aramony used United Way funds to buy and furnish an apartment for his girlfriend and to pay for vacations. His top financial officers helped him hide his illegal actions. Aramony and his colleagues were convicted on fraud-related charges.

Insular. The insular leader draws a clear boundary between the welfare of his or her immediate group or organization and outsiders. Former U.S. president Bill Clinton behaved in an insular manner when he didn't intervene in the Rwandan genocide that took the lives of 800,000 to 1 million people in 1994. He later traveled to Africa to apologize for failing to act even though he had reliable information describing how thousands of Tutsis were being hacked to death by their Hutu neighbors.

Evil. Evil leaders commit atrocities, using their power to inflict severe physical or psychological harm. Foday Sankoh is one example of an evil leader. He started a civil war in Sierra Leone in 1991. His army, which included many boy soldiers, carried out a campaign of rape and murder. The rebels were also known for chopping off the legs, hands, and arms of innocent civilians.

Lipman-Blumen and Kellerman developed their typologies based on case studies of prominent leaders. Now investigators are shifting the focus to ordinary leaders. They are interested in measuring destructive leader behavior and then determining the impact of bad leadership on followers. In one project, researchers at Bond University in Australia asked employees to explain why they would label someone as a bad leader, describe how a bad leader made them feel, and describe the impact bad leaders had on them and the organization as a whole.[6] Respondents reported that bad leaders are incompetent (they are unable to use technology, for example, and can't work with subordinates or plan strategy) and unethical (they demonstrate poor ethics as well as poor personal and interpersonal behavior). Such leaders made respondents angry and frustrated while lowering their self-esteem. Individual and collective performance suffered as a result. Those working under bad leaders reported feeling more stress at home. They had trouble sleeping, for instance, and felt fatigued. Negative emotions toward their leaders consumed their thoughts and hurt their family relationships. According to the survey, bad leaders often go unpunished; instead, many are promoted or rewarded.

Using information generated by this study, the Australian researchers developed a tool to measure destructive organizational leadership. They discovered that demonstrating just a couple of bad behaviors was enough to label a leader as destructive, even though he or she might also have lots of positive qualities. The Bond scholars identified seven clusters of destructive leader behaviors:[7]

Cluster 1: This type of leader makes poor decisions (often based on inadequate information), lies and engages in other unethical behavior, cannot deal with new technology, and typically fails to prioritize and delegate.

Cluster 2: This type of leader lacks critical skills. She or he is unable to negotiate or persuade and cannot develop or motivate subordinates.

Cluster 3: This type of leader makes good decisions and has the necessary leadership skills but is overly controlling and micromanages followers.

Cluster 4: This type of leader can't deal with conflict but plays favorites and behaves inconsistently.

Cluster 5: This type of leader isn't all that bad but isn't all that good either. Leaders in this category don't seek information from others, don't change their minds, and don't do a good job of coordinating followers.

Cluster 6: This type of leader isolates the group from the rest of the organization.

Cluster 7: This type of leader creates a situation of "significant misery and despair." Leaders in this group are brutal and bullying, frequently lying and engaging in other unethical behavior.

Ståle Einarsen and his Norwegian colleagues offer an alternative classification of bad leadership based on its negative effects either on the organization or on followers. Destructive leaders can be antiorganization, antisubordinates, or both.[8] *Tyrannical leaders* reach organizational goals while abusing followers. *Supportive-disloyal leaders* care for the welfare of subordinates at the expense of organizational goals. They may tolerate loafing or stealing, for example. *Derailed leaders* act against the interests of both subordinates and the organization. At the same time they bully, manipulate, deceive, and harass followers, they may be stealing from the organization, engaging in fraudulent activities, and doing less than expected. *Laissez-faire leaders* engage in passive and indirect negative behavior. They occupy leadership positions but don't exercise leadership, therefore hurting followers and their organizations. *Constructive leaders,* on the other hand, care about subordinates and help the organization achieve its goals while using resources wisely. Einarsen and his fellow researchers found a high incidence of bad leadership in Norwegian organizations, with 61% of respondents reporting that their immediate supervisors engaged in ongoing destructive behavior over the past six months. Laissez-faire behavior was by far most common form of bad leadership, followed by supportive-disloyal leadership, derailed leadership, and tyrannical leadership.[9] (Turn to Self-Assessment 1.1 at the end of this chapter to determine whether your leader engages in destructive leadership behavior.)

While empirical research into bad leadership is just beginning, initial results suggest that Palmer was right to emphasize the importance of the shadow side of leadership. Followers have lots of firsthand experience with bad leaders and report that such leaders cause significant damage. It takes only a few destructive behaviors to overcome a leader's positive qualities. In addition, the shadows cast by destructive leaders extend beyond the workplace. Not only do their subordinates report that they are less motivated and less effective at work, but they also acknowledge that their home lives suffer as well.

The Leader's Shadows

When we function as leaders, we take on a unique set of ethical burdens in addition to a set of expectations and tasks. These involve issues of power, privilege, information, consistency, loyalty, and responsibility. How we handle the challenges of leadership determines whether we cause more harm than good or, to return to Palmer's metaphor, whether we cast light or shadow. Unless we're careful, we're likely to cast one or more of the shadows described in this section. (For a list of the ethical challenges faced by those in the follower role, see "Focus on Follower Ethics: The Ethical Challenges of Followership.)

The Ethical Challenges of Followership

Followers, like leaders, face their own set of ethical challenges. Followers walk on the dark side when they fail to meet the moral responsibilities of their roles. Important ethical challenges confronted by followers include those described below.

The Challenge of Obligation. Followers contribute to a shadowy atmosphere when they fail to fulfill their minimal responsibilities by coming to work late, taking extended breaks, not carrying out assignments, undermining the authority of their leaders, stealing supplies, and so on. However, they can also contribute to an unethical climate by taking on too many obligations. Employees forced to work mandatory overtime and salaried staff at many technology and consulting firms work 70–80 hours a week, leaving little time for family and personal interests. They experience stress and burnout, and their family relationships suffer.

Followers also have ethical duties to outsiders. Carpenters and other trades-people involved in home construction have an obligation to buyers to build high-quality houses and to meet deadlines, for example. Government employees owe it to taxpayers to spend their money wisely by working hard while keeping expenses down.

These questions can help us sort out the obligations we owe as followers:

- Am I doing all I reasonably can to carry out my tasks and further the mission of my organization? What more could I do?

- Am I fulfilling my obligations to outsiders (clients, neighbors, community, customers)? Are there any additional steps I should take?

- Am I giving back to the group or organization as much as I am taking from it?

- Am I carrying my fair share of the workload?

- Am I serving the needs of my leaders?

- Am I earning the salary and benefits I receive?

- Can I fulfill my organizational obligations and, at the same time, maintain a healthy personal life and productive relationships? If not, what can I do to bring my work and personal life into balance?

The Challenge of Obedience. Groups and organizations couldn't function if members refused to obey orders or adhere to policies, even the ones they don't like. As a result, followers have an ethical duty to obey. However, blindly following authority can drive followers to engage in illegal and immoral activities that they would never participate in on their own. Obeying orders is no excuse for unethical behavior. Therefore, deciding when to disobey is critical. To make this determination, consider the following factors: Does this order appear to call for unethical behavior? Would I engage in this course of action if I weren't ordered to? What are the potential consequences for others, and for myself, if these directions are followed? Does obedience threaten the mission and health of the organization as a whole? What steps should I take if I decide to disobey?

The Challenge of Cynicism. There is a difference between healthy skepticism, which prevents followers from being exploited, and unhealthy cynicism, which undermines individual and group performance. Followers darken the atmosphere when they become organizational cynics. That's because cynicism destroys commitment and undermines trust. Collective performance suffers as a result. Few give their best effort when they are disillusioned with the group. Cynical employees feel less identification with and commitment to their employers while being more resistant to change. The greater the degree of cynicism, the more effort is directed toward attacking the organization at the expense of completing the task at hand.

The Challenge of Dissent. Expressing disagreement is an important ethical duty of followership. Followers should take issue with policies and procedures that are inefficient, harmful, or costly and with leaders who harm others or put the organization at risk. Doing so serves the mission of the organization while protecting the rights of its members and the larger community. Although followers contribute to a shadowy environment when they fail to speak up, they can go too far by generating a constant stream of complaints. Ethical followers know when to speak up (not every issue is worth contesting) and when to wait until a more important issue comes along. They must also determine whether the problem is significant enough to justify going outside the organization (becoming a whistle-blower) if leaders don't respond.

The Challenge of Bad News. Delivering bad news is risky business. Followers who tell their bosses that the project is over budget, that sales are down, or that the software doesn't work as promised may be verbally abused, demoted, or fired. Organizations and leaders pay a high price when followers hide or cover up bad news, deny responsibility, or shift blame. Leaders can't correct problems they

(Continued)

(Continued)

don't know exist. Failure to address serious deficiencies such as accounting fraud, cost overruns, and product contamination can destroy an organization. Leaders who don't get feedback about their ineffective habits—micromanaging, poor listening skills, indecisiveness—can't address those behaviors. When leaders deny accountability and shift blame, this undermines trust and diverts people's focus from solving problems to defending themselves.

To avoid contributing to a shadowy environment, followers must deliver bad news and accept responsibility for their actions. They also need to pay close attention to how they deliver bad tidings, selecting the right time, place, and message channel. Significant problems should be brought to the leader's attention immediately, when he or she is most receptive, and delivered face-to-face whenever possible, not through e-mail, faxes, and other less personal channels.

SOURCE: Adapted from Johnson, C. E. (2012). *Organizational ethics: A practical approach* (2nd ed.). Thousand Oaks, CA: Sage, Ch. 9.

Additional Sources

Bedian, A. G. (2007). Even if the tower is "ivory," it isn't "white": Understanding the consequences of faculty cynicism. *Academy of Management Learning and Education, 6,* 9–32.

Dean, J. W., Brandes, P., & Dharwadkar, R. (1998). Organizational cynicism. *Academy of Management Review, 23,* 341–352.

Hajdin, M. (2005). Employee loyalty: An examination. *Journal of Business Ethics, 59,* 259–280.

Roloff, M. E., & Paulson, G. D. (2001). Confronting organizational transgressions. In J. M. Darley, D. M. Messick, & T. R. Tyler (Eds.), *Social influences on ethical behavior in organizations* (pp. 53–68). Mahwah, NJ: Erlbaum.

Schrag, B. (2001). The moral significance of employee loyalty. *Business Ethics Quarterly, 11,* 41–66.

Stanley, D. J., Meyer, J. P., & Topolnytsky, L. (2005). Employee cynicism and resistance to organizational change. *Journal of Business and Psychology, 19,* 429–459.

The Shadow of Power

Power is the foundation for influence attempts. The more power we have, the more likely others are to comply with our wishes. Power comes from a variety of sources. One typology, for example, divides power into two categories: hard and soft.[10] *Hard power* uses inducements (bonuses, raises) and threats (arrests, firings) to get people to go along.

Soft power is based on attracting others rather than forcing them or inducing them to comply. Leaders use soft power when they set a worthy example, create an inspiring vision, and build positive relationships with subordinates. Typically those without formal authority rely more heavily on soft power, but even those in formal leadership positions, such as military officers, try to attract followers by acting as role models and emphasizing the group's mission. Effective leaders combine hard and soft power into *smart power* to achieve their goals. For instance, a manager may try to persuade an employee to follow a new policy while at the same time outlining the penalties the subordinate will face if he or she does not comply.

The most popular power classification system identifies five power bases.[11] *Coercive power* is based on penalties or punishments such as physical force, salary reductions, student suspensions, or embargoes against national enemies. *Reward power* depends on being able to deliver something of value to others, whether tangible (bonuses, health insurance, grades) or intangible (praise, trust, cooperation). *Legitimate power* resides in the position, not the person. Supervisors, judges, police officers, instructors, and parents have the right to control our behavior within certain limits. A boss can require us to carry out certain tasks at work, for example, but in most cases he or she has no say in what we do in our free time. In contrast to legitimate power, *expert power* is based on the characteristics of the individual regardless of that person's official position. Knowledge, skills, education, and certification all build expert power. *Referent (role model) power* rests on the admiration one person has for another. We're more likely to do favors for a supervisor we admire or to buy a product promoted by our favorite sports hero.

Leaders typically draw on more than one power source. The manager who is appointed to lead a task force is granted legitimate power that enables her to reward or punish. Yet in order to be successful, she'll have to demonstrate her knowledge of the topic, skillfully direct the group process, and earn the respect of task force members through hard work and commitment to the group. ("Leadership Ethics at the Movies: *Lincoln*" describes one leader who skillfully uses his power to achieve a worthy objective.)

LEADERSHIP ETHICS AT THE MOVIES • • • • • • • • •

Lincoln

Key Cast Members: Daniel Day-Lewis, Sally Field, David Strathairn, Joseph Gordon-Levitt, Tommy Lee Jones, Hal Holbrook

(Continued)

(Continued)

Synopsis: In January 1865 the Civil War is nearing its conclusion. President Abraham Lincoln (played by Day-Lewis) has already freed the slaves through his Emancipation Proclamation but is worried that slavery could be reinstituted when the defeated Confederate states reenter the Union. He decides to push for congressional passage of the 13th Amendment to the U.S. Constitution, which would permanently ban slavery. However, Lincoln faces opposition from factions in his own Republican Party as well from Democrats. Some representatives want to negotiate for peace first; others oppose abolition; still others fear that banning slavery will be the first step toward racial equality. With the help of Secretary of State William Seward (Strathairn), Lincoln manages to put together a winning coalition. In April, he is assassinated.

Rating: PG-13 for intense war scenes

Themes: types of power, use and abuse of power, deception, politics, courage, humility, justice

Discussion Starters

1. What types of power do Lincoln and Seward use to secure passage of the 13th Amendment? Are any of these strategies unethical?

2. Does the end (the passage of the amendment) justify the means (the use of patronage, delaying the peace process)?

3. What aspects of Lincoln's character do you admire? What character weaknesses do you note?

The use of each power type has advantages and disadvantages. For instance, the dispensing of rewards is widely accepted in Western culture but can be counterproductive if the rewards promote the wrong behaviors (see Chapter 9) or go to the wrong people. Researchers report that U.S. workers are more satisfied and productive when their leaders rely on forms of power that are tied to the person (expert and referent) rather than forms of power that are linked to the position (coercive, reward, and legitimate).[12] In addition, positional power is more susceptible to abuse. Coercive tactics have the potential to do the most damage, threatening the dignity as well as the physical and mental health of followers. Leaders, then, have important decisions to make about the types of power they use and when. (Complete Self-Assessment 1.2 to determine the types of power you prefer to use.)

The fact that leadership cannot exist without power makes some Americans uncomfortable. Harvard business professor Rosabeth Kanter goes so far as to declare that *power* is "America's last dirty word."[13] She believes that, for many of us, talking about money and sex is easier than discussing power. We admire powerful leaders who act decisively but can be reluctant to admit that we have and use power.

Our refusal to face up to the reality of power can make us more vulnerable to the shadow side of leadership. Cult leader Jim Jones presided over the suicide–murder of 909 followers in the jungles of Guyana. Perhaps this tragedy could have been avoided if cult members and outside observers had challenged Jones's abuse of power.[14] Conversely, ignoring the topic of power prevents the attainment of worthy objectives, leaving followers in darkness. Consider the case of the community activist who wants to build a new shelter for homeless families. He can't help these families unless he skillfully wields power to enlist the support of local groups, overcome resistance of opponents, raise funds, and secure building permits.

I suspect that we treat *power* as a dirty word because we recognize that power has a corrosive effect on those who possess it. We've seen how U.S. president Richard Nixon used the power of his office to order illegal acts against his enemies and how Russian president Vladimir Putin punishes those who protest his policies. (Another example of the corrosive effects of power can be seen in Case Study 1.1 later in this chapter.) Many corporate leaders have been intoxicated by their power, using their positions to abuse their subordinates. One such boss kept an employee in an all-day meeting even as her mother was dying. Another called the paramedics when an employee had a heart attack and then ordered everyone else to go back to work even as the victim was still lying on the floor. Yet another berated and humiliated a subordinate who suffered an emotional breakdown and had to be hospitalized. His response? "I can't help it if she is overly sensitive."[15]

Unfortunately, abuse of power is an all-too-common fact of life in modern organizations. In one survey, 90% of those responding reported that they had experienced disrespect from a boss at some time during their working careers; 20% said they were currently working for an abusive leader. "Brutal" bosses regularly engage in the following behaviors, some of which will be discussed in more detail later in the chapter:[16]

- *Deceit:* lying and giving false or misleading information

- *Constraint:* restricting followers' activities outside work, such as telling them whom they can befriend, where they can live, with whom they can live, and the civic activities they can participate in

- *Coercion:* making inappropriate or excessive threats for not complying with the leader's directives

- *Selfishness:* blaming subordinates and making them scapegoats

- *Inequity:* supplying unequal benefits or punishments based on favoritism or criteria unrelated to the job

- *Cruelty:* harming subordinates in such illegitimate ways as name-calling or public humiliation

- *Disregard:* ignoring normal standards of politeness; obvious disregard for what is happening in the lives of followers

- *Deification:* creating a master–servant relationship in which bosses can do whatever they want because they feel superior

The cost of the petty tyranny of bad bosses is high. Victims suffer low self-esteem and psychological distress, are less satisfied with their jobs and lives, are less productive, and are more likely to quit. The work unit as a whole is less trusting and cohesive, reducing collective performance.[17] The majority of employees in one study reported spending 10 or more hours every month complaining about abusive and other kinds of bad bosses or listening to the complaints of fellow workers.[18] In addition to complaining, workers respond to tyranny by surrendering their personal beliefs, keeping a low profile, engaging in revenge fantasies, taking indirect revenge (i.e., not supporting the boss at a critical moment), challenging the supervisor directly, or bringing in outsiders, such as the human resources department or the boss's boss, to get help in dealing with the abusive leader.[19]

The greater a leader's power, the greater the potential for abuse. This prompted Britain's Lord Acton to observe that "power corrupts, and absolute power corrupts absolutely." The long shadow cast by absolute power, as in the case of North Korea's Kim Jong Il and, until recently, the military junta in Burma, can be seen in censorship, repression, torture, imprisonment, murder, and starvation. Businesses and other organizations foster centralization of power through top-down structures that emphasize status differences, loyalty, dependence, fear, and obedience while celebrating "tough" bosses and business practices like hard bargaining and aggressive marketing tactics.[20]

Psychologists offer several explanations for why concentrated power is so dangerous.[21] First, power makes it easier for impulsive, selfish people to pursue their goals without considering the needs of others. They are likely to justify their actions by claiming that their personal rights and interests take priority over obligations to others. Second, those in power protect their positions by attacking those they perceive as threats. Third, powerful leaders are prone to biased judgments.[22] They generally make little attempt to find out how followers think and feel. As a result, they are more likely to hold and act on faulty stereotypes that justify their authority. Powerful people believe that they deserve their high status because powerless people aren't as capable as they are. Fourth, possessing power makes individuals more resistant to feedback from others.

Power deprivation exerts its own brand of corruptive influence.[23] Followers with little power become fixated on what minimal influence they have, becoming cautious, defensive, and critical of others and new ideas. In extreme cases, they may engage in sabotage, such as when one group of fast-food restaurant employees took out their frustrations by spitting and urinating into the drinks they served customers.

To wield power wisely, leaders have to wrestle with all the issues outlined here. They have to consider what types of power they should use and when and for what purposes. They also have to determine how much power to keep and how much to give away. Finally, leaders must recognize and resist the dangers posed by possessing too much power while making sure that followers aren't corrupted by having too little. Fortunately, there is evidence, when it comes to power, that a number of leaders are casting light rather than shadow. They recognize that sharing power prevents power abuses and improves organizational performance. Top officials at Johnsonville Sausage, Patagonia, Harley-Davidson, McCormick & Company, and other successful organizations have relinquished much of their legitimate, coercive, award, and expert power bases to lower-level leaders. At a great many other companies, self-directed work teams have taken over functions (hiring, scheduling, quality control) that used to be the province of mid- and lower-level managers.[24]

The Shadow of Privilege

Leaders almost always enjoy greater privileges than followers do. The greater the leader's power, generally the greater the rewards he or she receives. Consider the perks enjoyed by corporate CEOs, for example. Top business leaders in the United States are the highest paid in the world. Over the past 30 years, the average pay for chief executives of large U.S. firms skyrocketed to $14.5 million (including salary, bonuses, stock, and stock option grants).[25] A growing number make more than $50 million a year, including Apple's Tim Cook ($378 million), Walt Disney's Robert Iger ($452 million), and Qualcomm's Paul Jacobs ($50.6 million).[26] The paycheck of the average American was left in the dust. Typical U.S. workers now make less, when adjusted for inflation, than did their counterparts in the 1970s.[27] The top 1% of Americans make approximately 22% of all income, which exceeds the share made by the bottom 50% of the population.[28]

Abuse of privilege is particularly evident in the financial industry. U.S. banking executives received generous pay packages in 2007 even as the country entered the worst financial crisis since the Great Depression. Nine banks paid out an estimated $32 billion in

bonuses at the same time they were being bailed out with $175 billion from the federal government. Five thousand employees received bonuses of $1 million or more. Merrill Lynch paid out $3.6 billion just before declaring $15 billion in losses and merging with Bank of America. Goldman Sachs awarded nearly $1 billion to 200 of its workers.[29] As the recession continues, Wall Street pay packages continue to be 5.5 times greater than the rest of the private sector. New York securities firms paid employees an estimated $20 billion in year-end cash compensation in 2011.[30]

Nonprofit leaders can also abuse the perks that come from their positions of influence. Senators criticized the Boys & Girls Clubs of America for paying the organization's president nearly $1 million a year and spending more than $4 million on travel expenses for 350 staff members even as some branches were forced to close. A number of senior U.S. military officers suffer from "rank excess." Many have their own cooks and drivers and travel around in private jets and armored limousines. General David Petraeus had his staff prepare sliced fresh pineapple for him before bedtime when he was traveling. A U.S. Army general in charge of the Africa Command had his staff run personal errands and plan his parties. He spent $750 for a hotel suite for himself and his wife to use during a refueling stop in Bermuda. When he was head of NATO, Admiral James Stavridis took family members on taxpayer-funded private plane trips, stopping on one occasion to attend a wine gathering in France.[31]

Leader excess is not a new phenomenon. Ancient Chinese philosophers criticized rulers who lived in splendor while their subjects lived in poverty. Old Testament prophets railed against the political and social elites of the nations of Israel and Judah, condemning them for hoarding wealth, feasting while the poor went hungry, and using the courts to drive the lower classes from their land.

The passage of time hasn't lessened the problem but has made it worse. There are an estimated 950 billionaires in the world, with a combined wealth of $3.5 trillion. At the same time, the poorest of the poor are deprived of such basic necessities as food, shelter, clean water, and health care. The AIDS epidemic is fueled in large part by poverty. Little money is available in the developing world for prevention efforts or HIV/AIDS medicines. While wealthy nations generally provide such medications for their citizens, individuals in poor countries are unable to get the drugs they need to save their lives. The problem appears to be getting worse as governments and nongovernmental organizations cut back on funding for AIDS programs as a result of the worldwide recession. According to the Joint United Nations Programme on HIV/AIDS, two people are becoming infected with HIV for each new person entering treatment. Infection rates are highest in the poor countries of sub-Saharan Africa, with as many as one in five adults living with the virus in some nations.[32]

Most of us would agree that leaders deserve more rewards than followers do because leaders assume greater risks and responsibilities; many would also agree that some leaders get more than they deserve. Beyond this point, however, our opinions are likely to diverge. Americans are divided over questions such as these: How many additional privileges should leaders have? What should be the relative difference in pay and benefits between workers and top management? How do we close the large gap between the world's haves and the have-nots? We will never reach complete agreement on these issues, but the fact remains that privilege is a significant ethical burden associated with leadership. Leaders must give questions of privilege the same careful consideration as questions of power. The shadow cast by the abuse of privilege can be as long and dark as that cast by the misuse of power. Conversely, sharing privilege can cast significant light. Every year, for example, thousands of Americans (often members of religious congregations) leave their comfortable homes to spend their vacations serving in developing nations. There they build schools and homes, dig wells, and provide medical care.

The Shadow of Mismanaged Information

Leaders have more access to information than do others in an organization. They are more likely to participate in decision-making processes, network with managers in other units, review personnel files, and formulate long-term plans. Knowledge is a mixed blessing. Leaders must be in the information loop in order to carry out their tasks, but possessing knowledge makes life more complicated. Do they reveal that they are in the know? When should they release information and to whom? How much do they tell? Is it ever right for them to lie?

No wonder leaders are tempted to think ignorance is bliss! If all these challenges weren't enough, leaders face the very real temptation to lie or hide the truth to protect themselves. For instance, government and industry officials denied that the Rocky Flats nuclear facility outside Denver posed a health risk even as the facility continued to release plutonium and toxic chemicals into the air and water.[33] The U.S. Army, hoping to prevent bad publicity and build support for the war in Iraq, lied to cover up the fact that former National Football League star Pat Tillman was killed by friendly fire.[34]

The issues surrounding access to information are broader than deciding whether to lie or to tell the truth. Although leaders often decide between lying and truth telling, they are just as likely to be faced with questions related to the release of information. Take the case of a middle manager who has learned about an upcoming merger that will mean layoffs. Her superiors have asked her to keep this information to herself for a couple of weeks until the deal is completed. In the interim, employees may make financial commitments—such as home and car purchases—that they would postpone if they knew that major changes were in the works. Should the manager voluntarily share information about the merger with such employees despite her orders? What happens when a member of her department asks her to confirm or deny the rumor that the company is about to merge? (Turn to Case Study 1.2 for a description of how one group of leaders made a controversial decision to release information.)

Privacy issues raise additional ethical concerns. E-commerce firms routinely track the activity of Internet surfers, collecting and selling information that will allow marketers to target their advertisements more efficiently. Supermarkets use "courtesy" or "club" cards to track the purchases of shoppers. Hundreds of thousands of video cameras track our movements at automated teller machines, in parking lots, at stores, and in other public places (and even in not-so-public places, such as high school bathrooms and hospital rooms). Children use popular apps for smartphones and tablets to share personal information without their parents' knowledge.[35] Employers are also gathering more and more information about employee behavior both on and off the job.[36] Technology allows supervisors to monitor computer keystrokes and computer screens, phone calls, website use, voice-mail, and e-mail. Employers also monitor worker behavior outside the workplace. Employees have been fired for posting offensive comments and pictures on blogs and social networking sites. Employers use personal information on Facebook and other social networking sites to screen out job applicants. In a few cases, companies have asked applicants to provide their social media user names and passwords or to log on to their accounts during job interviews so interviewers can look over their shoulders as they scroll through their sites. Applicants can refuse these requests, but many may not because they fear they won't get hired.

Companies have a right to gather information in order to improve performance and eliminate waste and theft. Organizations are also liable for the inappropriate behavior of members, such as when they send sexist or racist messages using their companies' e-mail systems. However, efforts to monitor employee behavior are often done without the knowledge of workers and are inconsistent with organizational values such as trust and community. Invading privacy takes away the right of employees to determine what they reveal about themselves; unwanted intrusion devalues their worth as individuals.[37]

In sum, leaders cast shadows not only when they lie but also when they mismanage information and engage in deceptive practices. Unethical leaders

- deny having knowledge that is in their possession,

- withhold information that followers need,

- use information solely for personal benefit,

- violate the privacy rights of followers,

- release information to the wrong people, and

- put followers in ethical binds by preventing them from releasing information that others have a legitimate right to know.

Patterns of deception, whether they take the form of outright lies or the hiding or distortion of information, destroy the trust that binds leaders and followers together. Consider the popularity of conspiracy theories, for example. Many Americans are convinced that the U.S. Air Force is hiding the fact that aliens landed in Roswell, New Mexico. Many also believe that law enforcement officials are deliberately ignoring evidence that John F. Kennedy and Martin Luther King, Jr., were the victims of elaborate assassination plots. More than one-third of Americans polled (and the majority of respondents between the ages of 18 and 29) believe that the George W. Bush administration either planned the attacks on the World Trade Center in 2001 or did nothing after learning in advance of the terrorist plot. These theories may seem illogical, but they flourish in part because government leaders have created a shadow atmosphere through deceit. It wasn't until after the first Gulf War that we learned that our "smart bombs" weren't really so smart and missed their targets. The president and other cabinet officials overstated the danger posed by Saddam Hussein in order to rally support for the second Gulf War.

University of California, Davis, history professor Kathryn Olmsted argues that many Americans believe that the government is out to get them in large part because government officials have previously engaged in secret conspiracies.[38] In 1962, for example, the Joint Chiefs of Staff cooked up a plan to get citizens to support a war on Castro's Cuba by sending a drone plane painted to look like a passenger airliner over the island to be shot down. Fortunately, this plot (dubbed "Operation Northwoods") never went into effect. However, many others were implemented. According to Olmsted:

> By the height of the cold war, government agents had consorted with mobsters to kill a foreign leader, dropped hallucinogenic drugs into the drinks of unsuspecting Americans in random bars, and considered launching fake terrorist attacks on Americans in the United States.

Public officials had denied potentially life-saving treatment to African American men in medical experiments, sold arms to terrorists in return for American hostages, and faked documents to frame past presidents for crimes they had not committed. . . . Later, as industrious congressmen and journalists revealed these actual conspiracies by the government, many Americans came to believe that the most outrageous conspiracy theories about the government could be plausible.[39]

Leaders must also consider ethical issues related to the image they hope to project to followers. In order to earn their positions and to achieve their objectives, leaders carefully manage the impressions they make on others. Impression management can be compared to a performance on a stage.[40] Leader-actors carefully manage everything from the setting to their words and nonverbal behaviors in order to have the desired effects on their follower audiences. For example, presidential staffers make sure that the chief executive is framed by visual images (Mount Rushmore, the Oval Office) that reinforce his messages and his presidential standing. Like politicians, leaders in charge of such high-risk activities as mountain climbing and whitewater kayaking also work hard to project the desired impressions. In order to appear confident and competent, they stand up straight, look others in the eye, and use an authoritative tone of voice.

Impression management is integral to effective leadership because followers have images of ideal leaders called prototypes.[41] We expect that the mountain climbing guide will be confident (otherwise we would cancel the trip!), that the small-group leader will be active in group discussions, and that the military leader will stay calm under fire. The closer the person is to the ideal, the more likely it is that we will select that person as leader and accept her or his influence. Nonetheless, some people (including a number of students) find the concept of impression management ethically troubling. They particularly value integrity and see such role-playing as insincere because a leader may have to disguise his or her true feelings in order to be successful.

There is no doubt that impression management can be used to reach immoral ends. Disgraced financier Bernie Madoff, for example, convinced investors that he was a financial genius even as he was stealing their money in a gigantic fraud scheme. Careerists who are skilled at promoting themselves at the expense of others are all too common.[42] It would be impossible to eliminate this form of influence, however. For one thing, others form impressions of us whether we are conscious of that fact or not. They judge our personality and values by what we wear, for instance, even if we don't give much thought to what we put on in the morning. Most of us use impression management to convey our identities accurately, not to conceal them or to manipulate others.

When considering the morality of impression management, we need to consider its end products. Ethical impression managers meet group wants and needs, not just the needs of the leaders. They spur followers toward highly moral ends. These leaders use impression management to convey accurate information, to build positive interpersonal relationships, and to facilitate good decisions. Unethical impression managers produce the opposite effects, subverting group wishes and lowering purpose and aspiration. These leaders use dysfunctional impression management to send deceptive messages, to undermine relationships, and to distort information, which leads to poor conclusions and decisions.[43]

The Shadow of Inconsistency

Leaders deal with a variety of constituencies, each with its own set of abilities, needs, and interests. In addition, they like some followers better than others. Leader–member exchange (LMX) theory is based on the notion that a leader develops a closer relationship with one group of followers than with others.[44] Members of the "in-group" become the leader's advisers, assistants, and lieutenants. High levels of trust, mutual influence, and support characterize their exchanges with the leader. Members of the "out-group" are expected to carry out the basic requirements of their jobs. Their communication with the leader is not as trusting and supportive. Not surprisingly, members of in-groups are more satisfied and productive than members of out-groups. For that reason, LMX theorists have begun to explore ways in which leaders can develop close relationships with all of their followers.

Situational variables also complicate leader–follower interactions. Guidelines that work in ordinary times may break down under stressful conditions. A professor may state in a syllabus that five absences will result in a student's flunking the class, for instance. However, she may have to loosen that standard if a flu epidemic strikes the campus.

Diverse followers, varying levels of relationships, and elements of the situation make consistency an ethical burden of leadership. Should we, as leaders, treat all followers equally even if some are more skilled and committed or closer to us than others? When should we bend the rules and for whom? Shadows arise when leaders appear to act arbitrarily and unfairly when faced with questions such as these, as in the case of a resident assistant who enforces dormitory rules for some students but ignores infractions committed by friends. Of course, determining whether a leader is casting light or shadow may depend on where you stand as a follower. If you are the star player on your team, you may feel justified taking it easy during practices. If you are less talented, you probably resent the fact that the team's star doesn't have to work as hard as you.

Issues of inconsistency can also arise in a leader's relationships with those outside the immediate group or organization. Misgivings about the current system of financing political elections stem from the fact that large donors can buy access to elected officials and influence their votes. Laws often favor those who have contributed the most, as in the case of climate change–related legislation. Midwestern congressional representatives who received significant contributions from the Farm Bureau and ethanol producers were able to weaken a bill aimed at cutting greenhouse gas emissions by gaining exemptions in the bill for farmers, ranchers, and biodiesel refineries and by making other changes to the proposed legislation. This group (dubbed the "Agracrats") has been successful in convincing Congress to retain farm subsidies as well.[45] The power of political donations can also be seen in the battle over health insurance reform. Many of the senators and representatives who oppose revisions to health insurance law are major recipients of money from pharmaceutical companies and health care providers.

The Shadow of Misplaced and Broken Loyalties

Leaders must weigh a host of loyalties or duties when making choices. In addition to their duties to employees and stockholders, they must consider their obligations to their families, their local communities, their professions, the larger society, and the environment. Noteworthy leaders put the needs of the larger community above selfish interests. For example, outdoor clothing manufacturer Timberland receives praise for its commitment to community service and social responsibility. Company leaders pay employees for volunteer service, partner with community groups, and support nonprofit organizations through the sale of selected products. In contrast, those leaders who appear to put their own interests first are worthy of condemnation. Executives at United Airlines were harshly criticized for profiting at the expense of employees and travelers. The company filed for bankruptcy, which allowed the executives to dump pension funds, void labor contracts, and cut costs. A quarter of the workforce was laid off, and those remaining took significant pay cuts. Customer service suffered as a result. When United emerged from bankruptcy, 400 executives (some of whom had helped mismanage the airline into bankruptcy) ended up with 8% of the new firm, estimated to be worth more than $300 million. CEO Glenn Tilton alone received $40 million in stock and stock options.[46]

Loyalties can be broken as well as misplaced. If anything, we heap more scorn on those who betray our trust than on those who misplace their loyalties. Many of history's villains are traitors: Judas Iscariot, Benedict Arnold, Vidkun Quisling (he sold out his fellow Norwegians to the Nazis), and Tokyo Rose, a U.S. citizen who broadcast to American troops on behalf of the Japanese during World War II. More recent examples of leaders who violated the trust of followers include Enron CEO Kenneth Lay, who assured workers that the firm was in good shape even as it was headed toward collapse, and the leaders of Lehman Brothers, who told investors that the firm was strong even as it was struggling to raise money to stave off bankruptcy during the financial crisis.[47]

Employees are often victimized by corporate betrayal motivated by the bottom line. Individuals commonly develop deep loyalties to their coworkers and to their employers. As a consequence, they may do more than is required in their job descriptions, turn down attractive job offers from other employers, and decide to invest their savings in company stock.[48] Unfortunately, companies and their leaders often fail to respond in kind. During economic downturns they are quick to slash salaries and benefits and to lay off even the most loyal workers. Even if business is good, they don't hesitate to shut down domestic plants and research facilities in order to move their operations overseas, where labor costs are lower. It's no wonder that leaders who stick by their workers shine so brightly. One such leader is Bob Moore, who turned over ownership of his Red Mill Natural Foods company to his employees on his 81st birthday.[49]

As egregious as corporate examples of betrayal appear, they pale in comparison to cases where adults take advantage of children. Catholic priests in Massachusetts, Oregon, New Mexico, Brazil, Ireland, Germany, and elsewhere used their positions as respected spiritual authorities to gain access to young parishioners for sexual gratification.[50] Church leaders, bishops and cardinals, failed to stop the abusers. In far too many instances they let offending priests continue to minister and to have contact with children. Often church officials transferred pedophile priests without warning their new congregations about these men's troubled pasts. Officials at Pennsylvania State University turned a blind eye to evidence that assistant football coach Jerry Sandusky was abusing young boys. In another example involving the betrayal of children, two Pennsylvania juvenile court judges sentenced undeserving young offenders to for-profit detention centers in return for cash payments.

The fact that I've placed the loyalty shadow after such concerns as power and privilege is not intended to diminish its importance. Philosopher George Fletcher argues that we define ourselves through our loyalties to families, sports franchises, companies, and other groups and organizations.[51] Fellow philosopher Josiah Royce contends that loyalty to the right cause produces admirable character traits like justice, wisdom, and compassion.[52] Loyalty is a significant burden placed on leaders. In fact, well-placed loyalty can make a significant moral statement. Such was the case with Pee Wee Reese. The Brooklyn Dodger never wavered in his loyalty to Jackie Robinson, the first Black player in baseball's major leagues. In front of one especially hostile crowd in Cincinnati, Ohio, Reese put his arm around Robinson's shoulders in a display of support.[53]

Pay particular attention to the shadow of loyalty as you analyze the feature films highlighted in the "Leadership Ethics at the Movies" boxes in each chapter. In most of these movies, leaders struggle with where to place their loyalties and how to honor the trust others have placed in them.

The Shadow of Irresponsibility

Earlier we observed that breadth of responsibility is one of the factors distinguishing between the role of leader and that of follower. Followers are largely responsible for their own actions or, in the case of a self-directed work team, for those of their peers. This is not the case for leaders. They are held accountable for the performance of entire departments or other units. However, determining the extent of a leader's responsibility is far from easy. Can we blame a college coach for the misdeeds of team members during the off-season or for the excesses of the university's athletic booster club? Are clothing executives responsible for the actions of their overseas contractors who force workers to labor in sweatshops? Do employers owe employees a minimum wage level, a certain degree of job security, and safe working conditions? If military officers are punished for following unethical orders, should those who issue those orders receive the same or harsher penalties? Rabbis and pastors encourage members of their congregations to build strong marriages. Should they lose their jobs if they have affairs?

Leaders act irresponsibly when they fail to make reasonable efforts to prevent misdeeds on the part of their followers, ignore or deny ethical problems, don't shoulder responsibility for the consequences of their directives, deny their duties to followers, or hold followers to higher standards than themselves. We don't hold coaches responsible for everything their players do. Nonetheless, we want them to encourage their athletes to obey the law and to punish any misbehavior. Most of us expect the Gap, Apple, Old Navy, and Banana Republic to make every effort to treat their overseas labor force fairly, convinced that the companies owe their workers (even the ones employed by subcontractors) decent wages and working conditions. When a company's employees break the law or make mistakes, we want the CEO to take accountability. That was the case at JPMorgan Chase when a London trader lost more than $3 billion in risky trades. CEO Jamie Dimon first called the crisis a "tempest in a teapot," a statement that drew heavy criticism from financial analysts. Only later did he take responsibility, saying, "I am absolutely responsible. The buck stops with me."[54] (As Case Study 1.3 demonstrates, failure to take responsibility can sometimes have tragic consequences.)

We generally believe that officers giving orders are as culpable as those carrying them out, and we have little tolerance for religious figures and others who violate their own ethical standards. For that reason, a number of well-known American politicians from both major parties have been labeled as hypocrites for preaching family values while cheating on their spouses. The list includes (but is not limited to) (1) former vice presidential candidate John Edwards, who had an affair with a campaign videographer while his wife battled cancer; (2) Eliot Spitzer, former New York attorney general and governor who prosecuted prostitution rings while regularly meeting with a hooker; (3) conservative Christian Senator John Ensign of Nevada, who had an extramarital affair with a staffer; and (4) Senator David Vitter of Louisiana, who frequented an escort service run by the woman known as the DC Madam.[55]

Many corporate scandals demonstrate what can happen when boards of directors fail to live up to their responsibilities. Far too many boards in the past functioned only as rubber stamps. Made up largely of friends of the CEO and those doing business with the firm, they were quick to approve executive pay increases and other management proposals. Some board members appeared interested only in collecting their fees and made little effort to understand the operations or finances of the companies they were supposed to be directing. Other members were well-intentioned but lacked expertise. Now federal regulations require that the chair of a corporation's audit committee be a financial expert. The compensation, audit, and nominating committees must be made up of people who have no financial ties to the organization. These requirements should help prevent future abuses, but only if board members take their responsibilities seriously.

These, then, are some of the common shadows cast by leaders faced with the ethical challenges of leadership. Identifying these shadows raises two important questions: (1) *Why is it that, when faced with the same ethical challenges, some leaders cast light and others cast shadows?* (2) *What steps can we take as leaders to cast more light than shadow?* In the next chapter we will explore the forces that contribute to the shadow side of leadership and outline ways to meet those challenges.

IMPLICATIONS AND APPLICATIONS

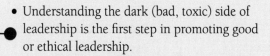

- Understanding the dark (bad, toxic) side of leadership is the first step in promoting good or ethical leadership.

- The contrast between ethical and unethical leadership is as dramatic as the contrast between light and darkness.

- "Toxic" or "bad" leaders engage in destructive behaviors. They may be ineffective, unethical, or both. Common types of bad leaders include incompetent, rigid, intemperate, callous, corrupt, insular, and evil. Destructive leaders are common and have negative impacts on followers and organizations.

- Certain ethical challenges or dilemmas are inherent in the leadership role. If you choose to become a leader, recognize that you

accept ethical burdens along with new tasks, expectations, and rewards.

- *Power* may not be a dirty word, but it can have a corrosive effect on values and behavior. You must determine how much power to accumulate, what forms of power to use, and how much power to give to followers.

- If you abuse power, you will generally overlook the needs of followers as you take advantage of the perks that come with your position.

- Leaders have access to more information than do followers. In addition to deciding whether or not to tell the truth, as a leader you'll have to determine when to reveal what you know and to whom, how to gather and use information, and so on.

- A certain degree of inconsistency is probably inevitable in leadership roles, but you will cast shadows if you are seen as acting arbitrarily and unfairly.

- As a leader you'll have to balance your needs and the needs of your small group or organization with loyalties or duties to broader communities. Expect condemnation if you put narrow, selfish concerns first.

- Leadership brings a broader range of responsibility, but determining the limits of accountability may be difficult. You will cast a shadow if you fail to make a reasonable attempt to prevent abuse or to shoulder the blame, deny that you have a duty to followers, or hold others to a higher ethical standard than you are willing to follow.

- Followers face their own set of ethical challenges. When filling a follower role, you will need to determine the extent of your obligations to the group, decide when to obey or disobey, combat cynicism, offer dissent, and deliver bad news to your leaders.

FOR FURTHER EXPLORATION, CHALLENGE, AND SELF-ASSESSMENT

1. Create an ethics journal. In it, describe the ethical dilemmas you encounter as a leader and as a follower, how you resolve them, how you feel about the outcomes, and what you learn that will transfer to future ethical decisions. You may also want to include your observations about the moral choices made by public figures. Make periodic entries as you continue to read this text.

2. Harvard professor Rosabeth Kanter argues that "powerlessness corrupts and absolute powerlessness corrupts absolutely." Do you agree? What are some of the symptoms of powerlessness?

3. What does your score on the Destructive Leader Behavior Scale (Self-Assessment 1.1) reveal about your leader? How can you use this information to become a more effective follower?

4. What factors do you consider when determining the extent of your loyalty to an individual, a group, or an organization?

5. Debate the following propositions in class:
   - The federal government should set limits on executive compensation.
   - Married politicians who have extramarital affairs should be forced to resign.
   - Employers have the right to monitor the behavior of workers when the workers are not on the job.

6. Evaluate the work of a corporate or nonprofit board of directors. Is the board made up largely of outside members? Are the members qualified? Does the board fulfill its leadership responsibilities? Write up your findings.

7. Which shadow are you most likely to cast as a leader? Why? What can you do to cast

light instead? Can you think of any other ethical shadows cast by leaders?

8. Look for examples of unethical leadership behavior in the news and classify them according to the six shadows. What patterns do you note? As an alternative, look for examples of ethical leadership. How do these leaders cast light instead of shadow?

9. What is the toughest ethical challenge of being a follower? How do you meet that challenge?

STUDENT STUDY SITE _____

Visit the student study site at **www.sagepub.com/johnsonmecl5e** to access full SAGE journal articles for further research and information on key chapter topics.

CASE STUDY 1.1

Rupert Murdoch: Down but Not Out

Australian billionaire Rupert Murdoch is one of the world's most powerful men. Murdoch holds controlling interest in the News Corporation, which owns media outlets around the world, including U.S.-based Fox News Network, the 20th Century Fox movie studio, and *The Wall Street Journal.* Murdoch's influence has been greatest in Great Britain, where the U.K. News Corporation controls 40% of the British newspaper market through its ownership of *The Sun, The Times of London,* and *The Sunday Times.* The firm also owns British Sky Television.

Murdoch's dominance over such a large portion of the British media market provided him with political clout. Politicians were afraid to speak out against Murdoch and his company for fear of retaliation. Candidates courted his favor, and his endorsement helped elect the last four British prime ministers. His influence reached its zenith after the 2010 victory of Prime Minister David Cameron (elected after Murdoch swung his endorsement from the Liberal Party to the Conservative Party). Murdoch was Cameron's first visitor at 10 Downing Street following his election, and Andy Coulson, a former U.K. News Corporation editor, was appointed as Cameron's media director. A News Corporation lobbyist had a close relationship with the British culture minister, who had the authority to approve News Corp's bid for BSkyB, Britain's largest and most profitable cable television network. Murdoch protégé Rebekah Brooks, *News of the World* editor and head of the company's British newspaper division, was a neighbor of Cameron's and socialized with him as well as with other prominent government officials.

The first serious challenge to Murdoch's power came in 2011, when *The Guardian* newspaper broke the story that editors at the *News of the World* had hacked into the cell phone of a 13-year-old murder victim. Employees listened to voice-mail messages left by distraught relatives trying to find the missing girl and then deleted them. Their actions hindered the murder investigation. Later police discovered 4,700 instances of hacking by U.K. News Corp employees and private investigators hired by the company. Victims included not only British royals and celebrities but also ordinary citizens. As the investigation continued, authorities uncovered a broad pattern of corruption. News Corp employees had bribed police and government officials for inside information, including, for example, gossip about celebrities and the phone directory containing contact information for the royal family. To date, 50 editors, reporters, police officers, and government officials have been arrested in connection with the scandal, including Brooks and Coulson.

In response to the crisis, Murdoch fired Brooks and closed the *News of the World.* He withdrew his bid to acquire BSkyB and divided his company into two separate firms, one focusing on newspapers, the other on entertainment. Murdoch retains control of both operations, however, serving as chief executive for each. Despite being known for his hands-on management style (he admitted at one point, "I interfere a bit too much"), Murdoch claimed to be a victim of a "culture of cover-up" at the *News of the World.* He accused corporate officials, including his son James, who ran News Corp's U.K. operations, with keeping him in the dark about what was really going on at the paper.

Prime Minister Cameron, while denying that he had made any deals with Murdoch, did admit that the relationship between politicians and the country's newspapers had been "too close." Media observers and members of the British Parliament were highly critical of the connections between News Corporation officials and governmental leaders. One critic noted that the company's power provided it with "political cover" as it bribed officials and intimidated others. According to a national commission appointed to investigate newspaper ethics, while there was no evidence of hidden deals between Murdoch and any British prime minister, Murdoch and his editors nevertheless exerted a great deal of political influence.

> Sometimes the greatest power is exercised without having to ask. Just as Mr. Murdoch's editors knew the basic ground rules, so did the politicians. The language of trades and deals is far too crude in this context. In their discussions with him, politicians knew that the prize was personal and political support in his mass-circulation newspapers.[1]

A parliamentary panel condemned Murdoch as "not a fit person" to be in charge of a large multinational corporation and claimed that he and his son James engaged in "willful blindness" by not acting sooner to stop the phone hacking by News Corp employees and outside contractors.

There can be little doubt that Murdoch's power has been dealt a serious blow in England. However, the corruption scandal may prove to be only a temporary, minor setback. Few outside the United Kingdom appeared to be troubled by the scandal, and the company remains highly profitable. "Rupert has his mojo back," said one media analyst in 2012.[2] A number of financial experts applauded the decision to divide the company. They had been pushing the firm to divide for some time, noting that television and film are much more profitable than newspapers. The media entertainment company has plans to buy the Yes television network in New York. The newspaper division may acquire more papers, such as the *Los Angeles Times* and *Chicago Tribune.* Rupert Murdoch has little to fear from his board of directors either. News Corporation board members, many of them family members and senior company executives, gave Murdoch a vote of confidence despite the scandal and the criticisms of members of Parliament and media regulators.

Discussion Probes

1. How did leaders cast the shadow of power in this case?

2. Can you think of other examples where corporate money and influence have corrupted the political process?

3. What other leadership shadows do you see cast in the News Corp phone hacking and bribery scandal?

4. Should Rupert Murdoch be held accountable for the scandal?

5. Should there be limits on how many media outlets one company can own?

6. Should the News Corporation be prevented from purchasing more newspapers or television networks in the United States?

7. Is the scandal only a temporary, minor setback for Rupert Murdoch?

Notes

1. Burns, J. F., & Cowell, A. (2012, November 30). Hacking report says new regulatory system needed for British newspapers. *The New York Times,* p. A8.

2. Cowell, A., & Burns, J. F. (2012, November 21). Ex-leaders at News Corp. face new round of charges. *The International Herald Tribune,* News, p. 3.

Sources

Benjamin, M., & Calabresi, M. (2012, August 13). News Corp's U.S. hacking problem. *Time,* pp. 43–45.

Burns, J. F. (2012, May 2). Cameron stands to lose much as scandal wears on. *The New York Times.* Retrieved from http://www.nytimes.com

Burns J. F., & Cowell, A. (2012, April 12). Murdoch case shifts to a minister. *The New York Times,* p. A1.

Burns, J. F., & Cowell, A. (2012, November 30). Hacking report says new regulatory system needed for British newspapers. *The New York Times,* p. A8.

Carr, D. (2012, May 7). News Corp. board's cozy compliance. *The New York Times,* p. B1.

Cowell, A., & Burns, J. F. (2012, November 21). Ex-leaders at News Corp. face new round of charges. *The International Herald Tribune,* p. 3.

Marquand, R. (2011, July 22). The metamorphosis of "Murdochgate." *The Christian Science Monitor.*

Marquand, R. (2012, February 13). Murdoch media crisis deepens with five new arrests. *The Christian Science Monitor.*

Marquand, R. (2012, July 24). Phone hacking scandal: Two UK media leaders charged with conspiracy. *The Christian Science Monitor.*

Reece, D. (2012, September 20). Ofcom delivers the final blow to James Murdoch's UK years. *The Telegraph.*

Rushton, K. (2012, December 2). Rupert Murdoch to split News Corp early to limit fallout from hacking. *The Telegraph.*

Saunders, D. (2012, April 25). Rupert Murdoch says sorry, but takes no blame for scandal. *The Globe and Mail*, p. A3.

Wolff, M. (2012, November 26). Murdoch may not be out of the woods yet. *USA Today*, p. 1B.

CASE STUDY 1.2

The Gun Owner Next Door

Shortly after the massacre at Sandy Hook Elementary School in Newtown, Connecticut, *The Journal News,* a suburban newspaper published in White Plains, New York, published the names and addresses of all handgun permit holders in its market. The paper provided an interactive online map that allowed readers to zoom in on dots providing information about individual gun holders. Some 44,000 individuals appeared on the map, approximately 1 in every 23 adults in two counties.

Publication of the firearms database unleashed a torrent of criticism as news of the map spread via social media and national media outlets. Gun owners complained that their privacy rights were being violated and that they were being stigmatized like sex offenders. They worried that thieves would use the information to target them for burglaries. (Editors at *The Commercial Appeal* in Memphis generated a similar response in 2009 when that paper published the names and zip codes of everyone with a permit to carry a concealed weapon in Tennessee.) Some argued that such information could endanger abused women by revealing that they were not armed. One angry blogger retaliated by publishing an interactive map with the names and addresses of *Journal News* employees. Other critics complained that the newspaper had published the map to promote an antigun agenda. According to a faculty member at the Poynter Institute, a school for journalists:

It is journalistic arrogance to abuse public record privilege, just as it is to air 911 calls for no reason or to publish the home addresses of police and judges without cause. Unwarranted publishing of the names of permitted owners just encourages gun owners to skip the permitting.[1]

In its defense, the paper noted that the names and addresses of gun owners are public information available through county clerks' offices in New York. (The county clerk in one county refused to provide the names and addresses to the paper.) In fact, the editors wanted to publish data on what kinds of weapons area residents possessed and how many guns they owned, but records of this information were not available under a Freedom of Information request. The online map included only those who applied to own handguns—they may not actually have purchased them—and did not have data on rifles or shotguns, which can be bought without a permit.

Janet Hasson, president of the Journal News Media Group, offered this defense of the company's decision to publish the firearms records:

> One of our roles is to report publicly available information on timely issues, even when unpopular. We knew publication of the database (as well as the accompanying article providing context) would be controversial, but we felt sharing information about gun permits in our area was important in the aftermath of the Newtown shootings.[2]

Discussion Probes

1. As a gun owner, how would you respond if your name and address were included in a list of gun owners published in a newspaper or online? Would it make any difference to you if this information was already available to the public through some other source?

2. Did the publication of the database violate the privacy rights of gun owners?

3. Does the public have the right to know who owns guns? Would you want to know if your neighbor owns a gun?

4. By publishing the database, did the newspaper cross the line from journalism to advocacy?

5. Are there certain types of personal information that should never be released to the public?

6. Was the publication of the database ethical? Why or why not?

Notes

1. Maas, K. C., & Levs, J. (2012, December 27). Newspaper sparks outrage for publishing names, addresses of gun permit holders. CNN. Retrieved from http://www.cnn.com

2. Maas & Levs.

Sources

Grossman, C. L. (2012, December 27). N.Y. gun-owner database draws ire. *USA Today*, p. 3A.

Howerton, J. (2012, December 27). NY paper broke no laws with gun owner map—but is it ever ethical to publish personal info to push an agenda? The Blaze. Retrieved from http://www.theblaze.com

Surico, J. (2012, December 27). The *Journal News* gun owner database debacle. *The Village Voice*, Guns blog.

Weiner, R. (2012, December 27). *Journal News'* gun-owner database draws criticism. Lohud.com. Retrieved from http://www.lohud.com

CASE STUDY 1.3

Drug Compounding and the FDA

A shipment of contaminated drugs sparked a meningitis outbreak in the United States in 2012. Thirty-nine people died and 620 more were sickened when 14,000 people received spinal injections of a steroid designed to relive chronic neck and back pain. The product, manufactured by the New England Compounding Center (NECC), was contaminated with a black fungus. Others injected with the steroid developed spinal infections or abscesses that required surgery. The antifungal drugs prescribed to treat the spinal infections can cause liver, kidney and heart problems as well as hallucinations.

Inspectors found a variety of sterilization violations at the NECC plant, including dirty mats and hoods, a greenish-yellow residue on equipment, inadequate time to sterilize products, a leaky boiler, an air conditioner designed to control temperature and humidity that was shut off at night, and possible environmental contamination from a recycling center located next door. In several vials the presence of mold and fiber was visible to the naked eye. Said one sterility expert, "In all my time in the pharmaceutical industry, which is 45 years, I've never seen one this bad."[1]

The company's owner and chief pharmacist, Gary Cadden, lost his license, as did three other co-owners. NECC then filed for bankruptcy. Ameridose, another firm owned by Cadden and members of his family, was also closed due to safety violations. Some employees reported that executives at Ameridose and NECC continually pushed for speedy production to increase profits. Cadden and the other owners enjoyed lavish lifestyles, which included multimillion-dollar homes (one with a home theater and indoor saltwater pool) and luxury cars.

Following the outbreak, journalists, congressional representatives, and others wondered why NECC was allowed to stay in operation despite ongoing safety concerns. In 2003 the U.S. Food and Drug Administration (FDA) had warned about "potential for serious public health consequences" because of the company's poor sterilization procedures. While the FDA recommended that NECC be shut down, the agency deferred to Massachusetts regulators, who reached a settlement with the company that kept it open. The Massachusetts Pharmacy Board investigated NECC 12 times between 1998 and 2012 and issued four advisory letters. Yet the firm continued to ship medications to hospitals, pain clinics, and medical centers around the United States.

In a congressional hearing titled "The Fungal Meningitis Outbreak: Could It Have Been Prevented?," House Energy and Commerce Subcommittee members blamed FDA Commissioner Dr. Margaret Hamburg for lax oversight. Representative John Dingell of Michigan charged that the FDA and the Massachusetts Pharmacy Board "have dropped the ball." The FDA administrator defended her agency, arguing that while the FDA has jurisdiction over drug manufacturers, it does not have authority to regulate drug compounders. Compounders, companies that mix drugs in small amounts for specific patients with special needs, don't have to register with the FDA, share their records, open their facilities to inspections, or report adverse effects from the products they make. They are regulated by the states instead. Hamburg asked for expanded authority to oversee compounding pharmacies.

Committee members were not impressed with Hamburg's testimony. They pointed out that NECC had clearly been mass-producing drugs and shipping them all over the nation, which made the company a drug manufacturer, not a drug compounder. The FDA raided the NECC production facility after the outbreak and seized computers and drug samples, which indicated to the subcommittee that the FDA did have jurisdiction over its operations. Even if the FDA's authority to act was unclear, Representative Henry Waxman of California claimed that he would have intervened had he headed the agency. "I would have assumed jurisdiction," he said. "I would have acted on it."[2]

The state of Massachusetts proposed new regulations to monitor drug compounders, including strict licensing requirements and fines for safety violations. Nevertheless, there is nothing to keep these operations from moving across state lines. And other compounders have had safety problems as well. Nine patients at an Alabama hospital died in 2011 after receiving a feeding solution that was contaminated with bacteria from a Birmingham compounder. A South Carolina pharmacy caused five cases of fungal meningitis in 2002.

Determining who has regulatory responsibility for compounding pharmacies is critical, since compounders make up a rapidly growing segment of the medical market,

accounting for 2–3% of all prescriptions written in the United States. Not only do compounders offer specialized products, but their prices can be lower as well. Then, too, patient and doctor demand for compound medications is increasing. Pain clinics are prescribing more of the kinds of steroid shots involved in the meningitis outbreak, for example. Patients are desperate for pain relief, and the shots are highly profitable to administer. However, pain experts argue that steroids, while effective for some patients, are overused in the United States. More often than not they are ineffective. Some of the patients who contracted meningitis should not have been getting steroid injections in the first place.

Discussion Probes

1. How much blame should be placed on the FDA for failing to prevent the meningitis outbreak? How much responsibility belongs to the state?

2. Should FDA Commissioner Hamburg have shut down the NECC plant even though she lacked clear jurisdiction to do so? What might have been the consequences had she done so?

3. What principles should guide leaders when they are deciding whether or not to act when their authority is unclear?

4. Should the FDA be given more power to regulate the drug compounding industry?

5. Should doctors refuse to provide treatments that may not work for patients who demand those treatments?

Notes

1. Tavernise, S., & Pollack, A. (2012, October 27). F.D.A. details contamination at pharmacy. *The New York Times*, p. A1.

2. Grady, D. (2012, November 20). Deaths stir a dispute on powers of the F.D.A. *The New York Times*, p. D5.

Sources

Goodnough, A., Tavernise, S., & Pollack, A. (2012, October 25). Spotlight put on founders of drug firm in outbreak. *The New York Times*, p. A18.

Grady, D. (2012, December 22). Dangerous abscesses add to tainted drug's threat. *The New York Times*, p. A3.

Grady, D., & Tavernise, S. (2012, November 13). F.D.A. finds safety problems at company supplying drugs. *The New York Times*, p. A13.

McVeigh, K. (2012, November 13). Meningitis outbreak: Pharmacy flagged by FDA as early as 2003. *The Guardian.*

Pollack, A., & Tavernise, S. (2012, November 22). Oversight failures documented in meningitis outbreak. *The New York Times*, p. A27.

SELF-ASSESSMENT 1.1

Destructive Leader Behavior Scale

Instructions: Think of a leader, supervisor, or manager you have worked with in the past five years. Rate this individual on each of the following items. A rating of 1 indicates that this person *never* engages in this behavior; a rating of 5 indicates that he or she engages in this behavior *very often.*

1	2	3	4	5
Never				Very Often

1. Avoids addressing important issues

2. Denies subordinates things they are entitled to (e.g., lunch breaks, vacation time)

3. Disciplines subordinates a long time after the rule infraction occurs

4. Discounts feedback or advice from subordinates

5. Fails to defend subordinates from attacks by others

6. Fails to give subordinates credit for jobs requiring a lot of effort

7. Falsely accuses or punishes subordinates for something they were not responsible for

8. Ignores phone calls and/or e-mails

9. Inadequately explains performance reviews

10. Insults or criticizes subordinates in front of others

11. Invades subordinates' privacy

12. Is confrontational when interacting with subordinates

13. Says one thing and does another

14. Shows no clear standards for administering rewards and punishments

15. Accepts financial kickbacks

16. At times appears to be under the influence of alcohol or recreational drugs while at work

17. Breaks the law while at work

18. Falsifies documents

19. Lets violations of company policy slide

20. Litters the work environment

21. Steals company funds

22. Steals company property and resources

23. Tells people outside the job what a lousy place he or she works for

24. Uses company property for personal use

25. Violates company policy/rules

26. Brings inappropriate sexual material to work (e.g., pornography)

27. Engages in romantic and/or sexual relationships with others from work

28. Hints that sexual favors will result in preferential treatment

Scoring

Possible score ranges from 28 to 140. The higher the score, the greater your leader's destructive behavior. You can also determine the leader's tendency to engage in three types of destructive behavior. Items 1–14 measure subordinate-directed behavior. Items 15–25 measure organization-directed destructive behavior. Items 26–28 measure sexual harassment behaviors.

SOURCE: Thoroughgood, C. N., Tate, B. W., Sawyer, K. B., & Jacobs, R. (2012). Bad to the bone: Empirically defining and measuring destructive leader behavior. *Journal of Leadership & Organizational Studies, 19,* 230–255. Used by permission of the publisher.

Personal Power Profile

Instructions: Below is a list of statements that describe possible behaviors of leaders in work organizations toward their followers. Read each statement carefully while thinking about *how you prefer to influence others.* Mark the number that most closely represents how you feel.

I prefer to influence others by	Strongly Disagree	Disagree	Neither Agree nor Disagree	Agree	Strongly Agree
1. increasing their pay level.	1	2	3	4	5
2. making them feel valued.	1	2	3	4	5
3. giving undesirable job assignments.	1	2	3	4	5
4. making them feel like I approve of them.	1	2	3	4	5
5. making them feel that they have commitments to meet.	1	2	3	4	5
6. making them feel personally accepted.	1	2	3	4	5
7. making them feel important.	1	2	3	4	5
8. giving them good technical suggestions.	1	2	3	4	5
9. making the work difficult for them.	1	2	3	4	5
10. sharing my experience and/or training.	1	2	3	4	5
11. making things unpleasant here.	1	2	3	4	5
12. making work distasteful.	1	2	3	4	5
13. helping them get a pay increase.	1	2	3	4	5

	Strongly Disagree	Disagree	Neither Agree nor Disagree	Agree	Strongly Agree
14. making them feel they should satisfy job requirements.	1	2	3	4	5
15. providing them with sound job-related advice.	1	2	3	4	5
16. providing them with special benefits.	1	2	3	4	5
17. helping them get a promotion.	1	2	3	4	5
18. giving them the feeling that they have responsibilities to fulfill.	1	2	3	4	5
19. providing them with needed technical knowledge.	1	2	3	4	5
20. making them recognize that they have tasks to accomplish.	1	2	3	4	5

Scoring

Record your responses to the 20 questions in the corresponding numbered blanks below. Total each column, then divide the result by 4 for each of the five types of influence.

	Reward	Coercive	Legitimate	Referent	Expert
	1	3	5	2	8
	13	9	14	4	10
	16	11	18	6	15
	17	12	20	7	19
Total					
Divide by 4					

Interpretation

A score of 4 or 5 on any of the five dimensions of power indicates that you prefer to influence others by using that particular form of power. A score of 2 or less indicates that you prefer not to employ this particular type of power to influence others. Your power profile is not a simple addition of each of the five sources. Some combinations are more synergistic than the simple sum of their parts. For example, referent power magnifies the impact of other power sources because these other influence attempts are coming from a "respected" person. Reward power often increases the impact of referent power because people generally tend to like those who can give them things. Some power combinations tend to produce the opposite of synergistic effects. Coercive power, for example, often negates the effects of other types of influence.

SOURCE: Modified version of Hinken, T. R., & Schriesheim, C. A. (1989). Development and application of new scales to measure the French and Raven (1959) bases of social power. *Journal of Applied Psychology, 74,* 561–567. Reprinted with permission.

NOTES

1. Palmer, P. (1996). Leading from within. In L. C. Spears (Ed.), *Insights on leadership: Service, stewardship, spirit, and servant-leadership* (pp. 197–208). New York: John Wiley.
2. Palmer, p. 200.
3. Lipman-Blumen, J. (2005). *The allure of toxic leaders: Why we follow destructive bosses and corrupt politicians—and how we can survive them.* Oxford, England: Oxford University Press.
4. Kellerman, B. (2004). *Bad leadership: What it is, how it happens, why it matters.* Boston: Harvard Business School Press; Kellerman, B. (2008). Bad leadership—and ways to avoid it. In J. V. Gallos (Ed.), *Business leadership* (2nd ed., pp. 423–432). San Francisco: Jossey-Bass.
5. Kellerman (2004), p. xvi.
6. Erickson, A., Shaw, J. B., & Agabe, Z. (2007). An empirical investigation of the antecedents, behaviors, and outcomes of bad leadership. *Journal of Leadership Studies, 1*(3), 26–43.
7. Shaw, J. B., Erickson, A., & Harvey, M. (2011). A method for measuring destructive leadership and identifying types of destructive leaders in organizations. *Leadership Quarterly, 22,* 575–590.
8. Einarsen, S., Aasland, M. S., & Skogstad, A. (2007). Destructive leadership behaviour: A

definition and conceptual model. *Leadership Quarterly, 18,* 207–216.
9. Aasland, M. S., Skogstad, A., Notelaers, G., Nielson, M. B., & Einarsen, S. (2010). The prevalence of destructive leadership behavior. *British Journal of Management, 21,* 438–452. For a closely allied approach, see Thoroughgood, C. N., Tate, B. W., Sawyer, K. B., & Jacobs, R. (2012). Bad to the bone: Empirically defining and measuring destructive leader behavior. *Journal of Leadership & Organizational Studies, 19,* 230–255.
10. Nye, J. S. (2008). *The powers to lead.* Oxford, England: Oxford University Press.
11. French, R. P., & Raven, B. (1959). The bases of social power. In D. Cartwright (Ed.), *Studies in social power* (pp. 150–167). Ann Arbor: University of Michigan, Institute for Social Research.
12. Hackman, M. Z., & Johnson, C. E. (2013). *Leadership: A communication perspective* (6th ed.). Prospect Heights, IL: Waveland, Ch. 5.
13. Kanter, R. M. (1979, July–August). Power failure in management circuits. *Harvard Business Review,* pp. 65–75.
14. Pfeffer, J. (1992). Understanding power in organizations. *California Management Review, 34*(2), 29–50.

15. Examples taken from Caudron, S. (1995, September 4). The boss from hell. *Industry Week*, pp. 12–16; Terez, T. (2001, December). You could just spit: Tales of bad bosses. *Workforce*, pp. 24–25.

16. Hornstein, H. A. (1996). *Brutal bosses and their prey*. New York: Riverhead.

17. Ashforth, B. E. (1997). Petty tyranny in organizations: A preliminary examination of antecedents and consequences. *Canadian Journal of Administrative Sciences, 14*, 126–140; Burton, J. P., & Hoobler, J. M. (2006). Subordinate self-esteem and abusive supervision. *Journal of Managerial Science, 3*, 340–355; Tepper, B. J. (2000). Consequences of abusive supervision. *Academy of Management Journal, 43*, 178–190; Tepper, B. J. (2007). Abusive supervision in work organizations: Review, synthesis, and research agenda. *Journal of Management, 33*, 261–289.

18. Bad bosses drain productivity. (2005, November). *Training & Development*, p. 15.

19. For a complete typology of responses to abusive supervisors, see Bies, R. J., & Tripp, T. M.(1998). Two faces of the powerless: Coping with tyranny in organizations. In R. M. Kramer & M. A. Neale (Eds.), *Power and influence in organizations* (pp. 203–219). Thousand Oaks, CA: Sage.

20. Vega, G., & Comer, D. R. (2005). Bullying and harassment in the workplace. In R. E. Kidwell, Jr., & C. L. Martin (Eds.), *Managing organizational deviance* (pp. 183–203). Thousand Oaks, CA: Sage.

21. Keltner, D., Langner, C. A., & Allison, M. L. (2006). Power and moral leadership. In D. L. Rhode (Ed.), *Moral leadership: The theory and practice of power, judgment, and policy* (pp. 177–194). San Francisco: Jossey-Bass; Kipnis, D. (1972). Does power corrupt? *Journal of Personality and Social Psychology, 24*, 33–41.

22. Bailon, R. R., Moya, M., & Yzerbyt, V. (2000). Why do superiors attend to negative stereotypic information about their subordinates? Effects of power legitimacy on social perception. *European Journal of Social Psychology, 30*, 651–671; Fiske, S. T. (1993). Controlling other people: The impact of power on stereotyping. *American Psychologist, 48*, 621–628.

23. Smith, P. K., Jostmann, N. B., Galinsky, A. D., & van Dijk, W. W. (2008). Lacking power impairs executive functions. *Psychological Science, 19*, 441–447.

24. See, for example, Ray, D., & Bronstein, H. (1995). *Teaming up: Making the transition to a self-directed, team-based organization*. New York: McGraw-Hill; Harper, B., & Harper, A. (1992). *Succeeding as a self-directed work team*. Mohegan Lake, NY: MW Corporation.

25. Popper, N. (2012, June 16). C.E.O. pay is rising despite the din. *The New York Times*.

26. Strauss, G. (2012, January 24). More CEOs rake in $50m and up. *USA Today*, p. 1A.

27. Greenstone, M., & Looney, A. (2012, October 12). The uncomfortable truth about American wages. *The New York Times*, Economix blog.

28. Upper 1 percent of Americans are rolling in the dough. (December 12, 2012). *The Oregonian*, p. A2.

29. Dickson, D. M. (2009, July 31). Doing well—regardless; billions in bonuses paid employees despite losses. *The Washington Times*, p. A10; Hamilton, W. (2009, July 31). Payouts lavish despite bailout. *Los Angles Times*, p. A1; Story, L. (2008, December 18). Wall St. profits were a mirage, but huge bonuses were real. *The New York Times*, p. A1.

30. Roose, K. (2012, March 2). Wall St. bonuses don't shrink as much as bank profits. *The International Herald Tribune*, Finance, p. 23.

31. Thompson, M. (2012, December 24). General disorders: Why some senior military officers are going off the rails. *Time*, p. 16.

32. Income disparity statistics taken from Sachs, J. (2007, May 27). Sharing the wealth. *Time*, p. 81. Data about the AIDS epidemic taken from Joint United Nations Programme on HIV/AIDS. (2012). *2012 UNAIDS report on the AIDS global epidemic*. Retrieved from http://www.unaids.org

33. Iversen, K. (2012). *Full body burden: Growing up in the nuclear shadow of Rocky Flats*. New York: Crown.

34. Krakauer, J. (2009). *Where men win glory: The odyssey of Pat Tillman*. New York: Doubleday.

35. Moses, A. (2012, December 23). Privacy concern as apps share data from kids left to their own devices. *Sunday Age* (Melbourne, Australia), News, p. 3.

36. See, for example, Armour, S. (2006, November 8). Employers look closely at what workers do on job. *USA Today,* pp. B1–B2; Patel-Predd, P. (2009, January). The all-seeing employer. *IEEE Spectrum,* p. 23; Rosenberg, T. (2011, November 24). An electronic eye on hospital hand-washing. *The New York Times,* Opinionator blog; Rainey, M. (2012, April/May). Fired before you're hired. *INSIGHT into Diversity,* pp. 18–21.

37. Hubbartt, W. S. (1998). *The new battle over workplace privacy.* New York: AMACOM.

38. Olmsted, K. S. (2009). *Real enemies: Conspiracy theories and American democracy, World War I to 9/11.* Oxford, England: Oxford University Press.

39. Olmsted, pp. 8–9.

40. Brissett, D., & Edgley, C. (1990). The dramaturgical perspective. In D. Brissett & C. Edgley (Eds.), *Life as theater: A dramaturgical sourcebook* (2nd ed., pp. 1–46). New York: Aldine de Gruyter.

41. Brown, D. J., Scott, K. A., & Lewis, H. (2004). Information processing and leadership. In J. Antonakis, A. T. Cianciolo, & R. J. Sternberg (Eds.), *The nature of leadership* (pp. 125–147). Thousand Oaks, CA: Sage.

42. Bratton, V. K., & Kacmar, K. M. (2004). Extreme careerism: The dark side of impression management. In W. Griffin & K. O'Reilly (Eds.), *The dark side of organizational behavior* (pp. 291–308). San Francisco: Jossey-Bass.

43. Rosenfeld, P., Giacalone, R. A., & Riordan, C. A. (1995). *Impression management in organizations: Theory, measurement, practice.* London: Routledge.

44. For more information on LMX theory, see Graen, G. B., & Graen, J. A. (Eds.). (2007). *New multinational network sharing.* Charlotte, NC: Information Age; Graen, G. B., & Uhl-Bien, M. (1998). Relationship-based approach to leadership. Development of leader–member exchange (LMX) theory of leadership over 25 years: Applying a multi-level multi-domain perspective. In F. Dansereau & F. J. Yammarino (Eds.), *Leadership: The multiple-level approaches* (pp. 103–158). Stamford, CT: JAI Press; Schriesheim, C. A., Castor, S. L., & Cogliser, C. C. (1999). Leader–member exchange (LMX) research: A comprehensive review of theory, measurement, and data-analytic practices. *Leadership Quarterly, 10,* 63–114; Vecchio, R. P. (1982). A further test of leadership effects due to between-group variation and in-group variation. *Journal of Applied Psychology, 67,* 200–208.

45. Morgan, D. (2009, August 16). Democratic dissenters. *The Oregonian,* p. D5; Samuelson, R. J. (2013, January 7). Can't we kill farm subsidies? *The Oregonian,* p. A9.

46. Shared sacrifice? Not for these airline executives. (2006, February 2). *USA Today,* p. 14A.

47. Berman, D. K. (2008, October 28). The game: Post-Enron crackdown comes up woefully short. *The Wall Street Journal,* p. C2.

48. Rosanas, J. M., & Velilla, M. (2003). Loyalty and trust as the ethical bases of organizations. *Journal of Business Ethics, 44,* 49–59.

49. Tims, D. (2010, February 17). Bob gives Red Mill to workers. *The Oregonian,* pp. A1, A5.

50. Ghosh, B. (2010, March 29). Sins of the fathers. *Time,* pp. 34–37; Pogatchnik, S. (2010, March 14). Abuse scandals hit Catholic Church across Europe. *The Oregonian,* p. A11.

51. Fletcher, G. (1993). *Loyalty: An essay on the morality of relationships.* New York: Oxford University Press.

52. Royce, J. (1920). *The philosophy of loyalty.* New York: Macmillan.

53. Rampersad, A. (1997). *Jackie Robinson.* New York: Alfred A. Knopf.

54. Goldfarb, A. Z. (2012, June 12). JPMorgan CEO Jamie Dimon apologizes for trading losses in Hill testimony. *The Washington Post.*

55. The cheat sheet. (2009, July 9). *The Boston Globe,* p. G23; William, J., & Blood, M. R. (2012, September 28). Arnold Schwarzenegger affair: Ex-governor says maid affair was "stupidest thing." Huffington Post.

Stepping Out
of the Shadows

Darkness is most likely to get a "hold" when you are safely settled in the good and righteous position, where nothing can assail you. When you are absolutely right is the most dangerous position of all, because, most probably, the devil has already got you by the throat.

—Psychotherapist Edward Edinger

What's Ahead

In this chapter, we look at why leaders cast shadows instead of light and how they can master these forces. Shadow casters include (1) unhealthy motivations; (2) faulty thinking caused by mistaken assumptions, failure of moral imagination, and moral disengagement; (3) lack of ethical expertise; and (4) contextual (group, organizational, societal) pressures that encourage people to set their personal standards aside. To address these shadow casters, we need to look inward to address our motivations, improve our moral decision making, acquire ethical knowledge and skills, and resist negative situational influences as we create healthy ethical environments. Ethical development, like other forms of leader development, incorporates assessment, challenge, and support. We can track our progress by adopting the skills and strategies used by ethical experts.

Only humans seem to be troubled by the question "Why?" Unlike other creatures, we analyze past events (particularly the painful ones) to determine their causes. The urge to understand and to account for the ethical failures of leaders has taken on added urgency with the recent spate of corporate and political scandals. Observers wonder: Why would bright, talented CEOs make fraudulent loans, lie to investors, and engage in insider trading? Why can't multimillionaire executives be satisfied with what they already have? Why do they feel they need more? Why do politicians lose sight of the fact that they are public servants? How can they urge others to behave ethically at the same time they enrich themselves at taxpayer expense and cheat on their spouses? (See Box 2.1 for one set of answers to these questions.)

• • • BOX 2.1 THE DARK SIDE OF SUCCESS: THE BATHSHEBA SYNDROME • • •

Management professors Dean Ludwig and Clinton Longenecker believe that top managers often become the victims of their own successes, leading even highly moral individuals to abandon their principles. Having achieved their goals after years of service and hard work, these competent, popular, and ethical leaders destroy their careers by engaging in behavior they know is wrong. Ludwig and Longenecker refer to this pattern as the "Bathsheba syndrome," named for the story of King David reported in both the Bible and the Torah. King David, described as a "man after His [God's] own heart" in I Samuel 13:14, expanded the national borders of ancient Israel by vanquishing the country's enemies. Yet, at the height of his powers, he began an affair with Bathsheba. After she got pregnant, he tried to cover up his actions by calling her husband, Uriah, back from the battlefield to sleep with her. When Uriah refused to enjoy the comforts of home while his comrades remained in battle, David sent Uriah back to the front lines to be killed. As Ludwig and Longenecker note, "David's failings as a leader were dramatic even by today's standards and included an affair, the corruption of other leaders, deception, drunkenness, murder, the loss of innocent lives . . ." (p. 265). The fallout from David's immoral behavior was devastating. He lost the child he fathered with Bathsheba, his top military commander, Joab, betrayed him, and one of his sons temporarily drove him from office.

There are four by-products of success that put otherwise ethical leaders in a downward spiral. First, personal and organizational success encourages leaders to become complacent and to lose their strategic focus. They begin to shift their attention to leisure, entertainment, and other self-centered pursuits and fail to provide adequate supervision. David's problems began, for example, when he stayed home instead of going to war with his men. Second, success leads to privileged access to information and people, which the leader uses to fulfill personal desires (like having sex with Bathsheba) instead of serving the organization. Third, success leads to the control of resources, which the leader then uses selfishly. David employed his power to begin the affair, to call Uriah back from the battlefield, and then to order Joab to put Uriah in the thick of the battle and to withdraw, leaving Uriah and his colleagues to be killed. Fourth, control of resources is often tied to an inflated belief in one's ability to control the outcomes of a situation. David was confident that he could cover up his actions, but the prophet Nathan later revealed his sins.

Professors Ludwig and Longenecker offer advice to successful leaders to keep them from becoming victims of the Bathsheba syndrome. Be humble—what happened to David and to other successful leaders can happen to any leader no matter how smart or skilled. Keep in touch with reality by living a balanced life filled with family, relationships, and interests outside of work. Never be satisfied with current direction and performance. Recognize that privilege and status equip leaders for providing a strategic vision and executing strategy; they are not the reward for past performance or for personal gratification. Assemble a team of ethical managers to provide challenge or support as needed. Finally, recognize that ethical leadership is a component of good leadership. Ethical, effective leaders serve as role models, make wise use of resources, build trust, and make good decisions.

SOURCE: Ludwig, D. C., & Longenecker, C. O. (1993). The Bathsheba syndrome: The ethical failure of successful leaders. *Journal of Business Ethics, 12,* 265–273.

Coming up with an explanation provides a measure of comfort and control. If we can understand *why* something bad has happened (broken relationships, cruelty, betrayal), we may be able to put it behind us and move on. We are also better equipped to prevent something similar from happening again. Such is the case with shadows. If we can identify the reasons for our ethical failures (what I'll call "shadow casters"), we can then step out of the darkness they create.

The first section of this chapter identifies common shadow casters; the second section outlines strategies for meeting these challenges. Keep in mind that human behavior is seldom the product of just one factor. For example, leaders struggling with insecurities are particularly vulnerable to external pressures. Faulty decision making and inexperience often go hand in hand; we're more prone to make poor moral choices when we haven't had much practice. To cast more light and less shadow, we need to address all the factors that undermine ethical performance.

Shadow Casters

Unhealthy Motivations

Internal Enemies or Monsters

Parker Palmer believes that leaders project shadows out of their inner darkness. That's why he urges leaders to pay special attention to their motivations, lest "the act of leadership create more harm than good." Palmer identifies five internal enemies or "monsters" living within leaders that produce unethical behavior.[1] I'll include one additional monster to round out the list.

Monster 1: Insecurity. Leaders often are deeply insecure people who mask their inner doubts through extroversion and by tying their identities to their roles as leaders. Who they are is inextricably bound to what they do. Leaders project their insecurities on others when they use followers to serve their selfish needs.

Monster 2: Battleground Mentality. Leaders often use military images when carrying out their tasks, speaking of "wins" and "losses," "allies" and "enemies," and "doing battle" with the competition. For example, former IBM chief Lou Gerstner inspired hatred of Microsoft by projecting a picture of Bill Gates on a large screen and telling his managers, "This man wakes up hating you."[2] Acting competitively becomes a self-fulfilling prophecy; competition begets competitive responses in return. This militaristic approach can be counterproductive. More often than not, cooperation is more productive than competition (see Chapter 8). Instead of pitting departments against each other, for instance, a growing number of companies use cross-functional project teams and task forces to boost productivity.

Monster 3: Functional Atheism. Functional atheism is a leader's belief that she or he has the ultimate responsibility for everything that happens in a group or an organization. As Palmer describes it, "It is the unconscious, unexamined conviction within us that if anything decent is going to happen here, I am the one who needs to make it happen."[3] This shadow destroys both leaders and followers. Symptoms include high stress, broken relationships and families, workaholism, burnout, and mindless activity.

Monster 4: Fear. Fear of chaos drives many leaders to stifle dissent and innovation. They emphasize rules and procedures instead of creativity and consolidate their power instead of sharing it with followers.

Monster 5: Denying Death. Our culture as a whole denies the reality of death, and leaders, in particular, don't want to face the fact that projects and programs should die if they are no longer useful. Leaders also deny death through their fear of negative evaluation and public failure. Those who fail should be given an opportunity to learn from their mistakes, not be punished. Only a few executives display the wisdom of IBM founder Thomas Watson. A young executive entered his office after making a $10 million blunder and began the conversation by saying, "I guess you want my resignation." Watson answered, "You can't be serious. We've just spent $10 million educating you!"[4]

Monster 6: Evil. There are lots of other demons lurking in leaders and followers alike—jealousy, envy, rage—but I want to single out evil for special consideration, making it the focus of Chapter 4. Palmer doesn't specifically mention evil as an internal monster, but it is hard to ignore the fact that some people seem driven by a force more powerful than anxiety or fear. Evil may help us answer the question "Why?" when we're confronted with monstrous shadows such as those cast by the Holocaust and the genocides in Serbia and Sudan.

Selfishness

A great deal of destructive leadership behavior is driven by self-centeredness, which manifests itself through pride, greed, narcissism, and Machiavellianism. Self-centered leaders are proud of themselves and their accomplishments. They lack empathy for others and can't see other points of view or learn from followers. They are too important to do "little things" such as making their own coffee or standing in line, so they hire others to handle these tasks for them.[5] Their focus is on defending their turf and maintaining their status instead of on cooperating with other groups to serve the common good. Ego-driven leaders ignore creative ideas and valuable data that come from outside their circles of influence.

Greed is another hallmark of self-oriented leaders. They are driven to earn more (no matter how much they are currently paid) and to accumulate additional perks. Greed focuses attention on making the numbers—generating more sales, increasing earnings, boosting the stock price, collecting more donations. In the process of reaching these financial goals, the few often benefit at the expense of the many, casting the shadow of privilege described in Chapter 1.

The recent international financial crisis, which stemmed from the collapse of the U.S. housing market, can largely be attributed to greed.[6] Mortgage brokers generated higher commissions and profits by making risky and fraudulent loans. Borrowers often took on too much credit, buying homes or consumer items they couldn't afford. Wall Street banks, eager to make money off of the mortgage market, repackaged mortgages and sold them to investors as "low-risk" products in the United States, in Europe, and elsewhere. AIG and other insurers generated revenue by guaranteeing what turned out to be toxic investments. The financial system nearly collapsed when housing prices dropped and consumers defaulted on their loans, putting lenders, investment bankers, investors, and insurers at risk.

Narcissism is another manifestation of self-centeredness. The word *narcissism* has its origins in an ancient Greek fable. In this tale, Narcissus falls in love with the image of himself he sees reflected in a pond. Like their ancient namesake, modern-day narcissists are self-absorbed. They like attention, constantly seek positive feedback, and feel entitled to their power and positions. They also have an unrealistic sense of what they can accomplish.[7]

Narcissistic leaders engage in a wide range of unethical behaviors. They claim special privileges, demand admiration and obedience, abuse power for their personal ends, fail to acknowledge the contributions of subordinates, are dishonest, ignore the welfare of others, and have an autocratic leadership style. In extreme cases (Adolf Hitler and Joseph Stalin, for example), they can be hyperaggressive, exploitative, and sadistic. Narcissists put their groups, organizations, and countries at risk because their dreams and visions are unrealistic and can't be implemented. For example, Napoleon stretched France's resources beyond the breaking point. Jean-Marie Messier, a modern French business leader, followed in Napoleon's footsteps by overextending his financial empire.[8] Messier spent $100 billion trying to build Vivendi—originally a French water and sewage provider—into the largest media and entertainment company in the world by buying phone companies, Internet ventures, cable networks, and Seagram's (which owned Universal Studios and Universal Records). His grandiose ambitions outstripped his ability to bring them to fruition. Losses from his collection of mismatched companies mounted, and he was forced out. The result was the greatest financial loss in French corporate history.

Machiavellianism is the fourth indication that a leader is more self- than other-focused. Psychologists Richard Christie and Florence Geis first identified this personality factor in 1970. Christie and Geis named this trait after Italian philosopher Niccolò Machiavelli, who argued in *The Prince* that political leaders should maintain a virtuous public image but use whatever means necessary—ethical or unethical—to achieve their ends.[9] Highly Machiavellian individuals are skilled at manipulating others for their own ends. They have a better grasp of their abilities and reality than narcissists but, like their narcissistic colleagues, engage in lots of self-promotion, are emotionally cold, and are prone to aggressive behavior. Machiavellian leaders often engage in deception because they want to generate positive impressions while they get their way. They may pretend to be concerned about others, for example, or assist in a project solely because they want to get in good with the boss. Machiavellians often enjoy a good deal of personal success—organizational advancement, higher salaries—because they are so skilled at manipulation and at disguising their true intentions. Nonetheless, Machiavellian leaders put their groups in danger. They may be less qualified to lead than others who are not as skilled as they in impression management. They are more likely to engage in unethical practices that put the organization at risk because they want to succeed at any cost. If followers suspect that their supervisors are manipulating them, they are less trusting and cooperative, which can make the organization less productive.[10] (See "Focus on Follower Ethics: The Susceptible Follower" for more information on what motivates subordinates to follow leaders who cast shadows.)

FOCUS ON FOLLOWER ETHICS

The Susceptible Follower

Most researchers interested in studying the impact of destructive leadership concentrate on the traits and behaviors of the leaders. They want to know why these individuals engage in selfish, unethical behavior that undermines the organization and harms others. Focusing solely on the leader, however, can obscure the fact that destructive leadership requires the participation of followers. For example, a medical clinic operator can't overbill insurance companies for treatments without the cooperation of administrative staff, accountants, and (perhaps) nurses and physicians.

A group of scholars from Pennsylvania State University argues that we can gain a better understanding of the process of destructive leadership by identifying the factors that make followers susceptible to the influence of destructive superiors. They place susceptible subordinates into two categories: conformers and colluders. Conformers engage in destructive behavior while obeying their leaders. Colluders actively support or contribute to their leaders' destructive missions.

Conformers: Lost Souls. Lost souls are needy individuals. They are vulnerable to destructive leaders because they have basic unmet needs (for love and affection, for example), may be experiencing high levels of distress (e.g., flunking out of college, losing a parent), lack a clear sense of self, and have low self-esteem. They comply because they identify with the leader, who offers them a sense of direction, community, and a stronger sense of self and self-esteem.

Conformers: Authoritarians. Authoritarians believe that leaders have a right to demand obedience, and it is their belief in the legitimacy of the leader that triggers their obedience. They reflect an unconditional respect for authority, prefer a simple, well-defined environment, and believe in a just world where people get what they deserve.

Conformers: Bystanders. Bystanders, perhaps the largest group of susceptible followers, are generally passive and motivated by fear. They let destructive leaders have their way because they think they will be punished if they object. Bystanders generally have negative self-evaluations that convince them that they can't resist, believe that have to submit to whoever is in power, and often see themselves as victims. Highly sensitive to elements of the situation, they remain passive in order to avoid punishment. These individuals are often introverts who lack a courageous, prosocial orientation.

Colluders: Opportunists. Opportunists carry out the destructive directives of their leaders because they believe that they will be rewarded for doing so. Opportunists are ambitious, greedy, and manipulative, lacking in self-control. Rewards—money, status, power—are the key to motivating them to participate in unethical and illegal behaviors.

(Continued)

(Continued)

Colluders: Acolytes. Acolytes are "true believers." They actively partner with the leader because they share the leader's goals and values. They are largely self-motivated. Collaborating with the destructive leader helps them fulfill their personal identities, which have toxic qualities.

SOURCE: Thoroughgood, C. N., Padilla, A., Hunter, S. T., & Tate, B. W. (2012). The susceptible circle: A taxonomy of followers associated with destructive leadership. *Leadership Quarterly, 23,* 897–917.

See also:

Barbuto, J. E. (2000). Influence triggers: A framework for understanding follower compliance. *Leadership Quarterly, 11,* 365–387.

Padilla, A., Hogan, R., & Kaier, R. B. (2007). The toxic triangle: Destructive leaders, susceptible followers, and conducive environments. *Leadership Quarterly, 18,* 176–194.

Faulty Decision Making

Identifying dysfunctional motivations is a good first step in explaining the shadow side of leadership. Yet well-meaning, well-adjusted leaders can also cast shadows, as in the case of Shell UK. In 1995, company officials decided to dispose of the Brent Spar, a large floating oil storage buoy in the North Sea, by sinking it in deep water.[11] This was the least expensive option for disposing of the structure, and the British government signed off on the project. However, Shell and British government leaders failed to give adequate consideration to the environmental impact of their proposal. Greenpeace activists, who were trying to curb the dumping of waste and other contaminants into the world's oceans, argued that deepwater disposal set a bad precedent. They worried that the sinking of the Brent Spar would be the first of many such sinkings; Greenpeace members twice occupied the Brent Spar in protest. Consumers in continental Europe began boycotting Shell gas stations, and representatives of the Belgian and German governments protested to British officials. Shell withdrew its plan to sink the buoy, and it was towed to Norway instead, where it was cut apart and made part of a quay. Shell later noted that this was a defining event in the company's history, one that made it more sensitive to outside groups and possible environmental issues.

Blame for many ethical miscues can be placed on the way in which decisions are made. Moral reasoning, though focused on issues of right and wrong, has much in common with other forms of decision making. Making a wise ethical choice involves many of the same steps as making other important decisions: identifying the issue, gathering information, deciding on criteria, weighing options, and so on. A breakdown anywhere along the way can derail the process. Problems typically stem from (1) unsound assumptions and (2) failure of moral imagination.

Decision-making experts David Messick and Max Bazerman speculate that many unethical business decisions aren't the products of greed or callousness but stem instead from widespread weaknesses in how people process information and make decisions. In particular, executives have faulty theories about how the world operates, about other people, and about themselves.[12]

Theories About How the World Operates. These assumptions have to do with determining the consequences of choices, judging risks, and identifying causes. Executives generally fail to take into account all the implications of their decisions (see Box 2.2). They overlook low-probability events, fail to consider all the affected parties, think they can hide their unethical behavior from the public, and downplay long-range consequences. In determining risk, decision makers generally fail to acknowledge that many events happen by chance or are out of their control. America's involvement in Vietnam, for example, was predicated on the mistaken assumption that the United States could successfully impose its will in the region. Other times, leaders and followers misframe risks, thus minimizing the dangers. For instance, a new drug seems more desirable when it is described as working half of the time rather than as failing half of the time.

● ● ● BOX 2.2 DECISION-MAKING BIASES ● ● ●

Theories of the World

- Ignoring low-probability events even when they could have serious consequences later

- Limiting the search for stakeholders and thus overlooking the needs of important groups

- Ignoring the possibility that the public will find out about an action

- Discounting the future by putting immediate needs ahead of long-term goals

- Underestimating the impact of a decision on a collective group (e.g., industry, city, profession)

(Continued)

(Continued)

- Acting as if the world is certain instead of unpredictable

- Failing to acknowledge and confront risk

- Framing risk differently than followers

- Blaming people when larger systems are at fault

- Excusing those who fail to act when they should

Theories About Other People

- Believing that our group is normal and ordinary (good) whereas others are strange and inferior (bad)

- Giving special consideration and aid to members of the in-group

- Judging and evaluating according to group membership (stereotyping)

Theories About Ourselves

- Rating ourselves more highly than other people

- Underestimating the likelihood that negative things will happen to us, such as divorce, illness, accidents, and addictions

- Believing that we can control random events

- Overestimating our contributions and the contributions of departments and organizations

- Overconfidence, which prevents us from learning more about a situation

- Concluding that the normal rules and obligations don't apply to us

SOURCE: Messick, D. M., & Bazerman, M. H. (1996, Winter). Ethical leadership and the psychology of decision making. *Sloan Management Review, 37*(2), 9–23. See also Bazerman, M. H. (1986). *Management in managerial decision making.* New York: John Wiley.

The perception of causes is the most important of all our theories about the world because determining responsibility is the first step to assigning blame or praise. In the United States, we're quick to criticize the person when larger systems are at fault. We may criticize salespeople for trying to sell us extended warranties that are generally a waste of money.

However, executives should be blamed for requiring their employees to push these products. Messick and Bazerman also point out that we're more likely to blame someone else for acting immorally than for failing to act. We condemn the executive who steals, but we are less critical of the executive who doesn't disclose the fact that another manager is incompetent.

Theories About Other People. These are "our organized beliefs about how 'we' differ from 'they'" (competitors, suppliers, managers, employees, ethnic groups). Such beliefs, which we may not be aware of, influence how we treat other people. Ethnocentrism and stereotyping are particularly damaging. *Ethnocentrism* is the tendency to think that we are better than they, that our way of doing things is superior to theirs. We then seek out (socialize with, hire) others who look and act like us. Military leaders often fall into the trap of ethnocentrism when they underestimate the ability of the enemy to resist hardships. For example, commanders have no trouble believing that their own citizens will survive repeated bombings but don't think that civilian populations in other nations can do the same. Such was the case in World War II. The British thought that bombing Berlin would break the spirit of the Germans, forgetting that earlier German air raids on London had failed to drive Britain out of the war. Similar reasoning fed into the FBI's decision to storm the Branch Davidian compound in Waco, Texas, in 1993. FBI officers underestimated the commitment of cult leader David Koresh and his followers to their cause. They thought that Koresh was afraid of physical harm and would surrender rather than risk injury. Instead, he led his followers in a mass suicide when federal authorities rushed the compound.[13]

Stereotypes, our beliefs about other groups of people, are closely related to ethnocentrism. These theories (women are weaker than men, the mentally challenged can't do productive work) can produce a host of unethical outcomes, including sexual and racial discrimination. (We'll take a closer look at ethnocentrism and stereotyping in Chapter 10.)

Theories About Ourselves. These faulty theories involve self-perceptions. Leaders need to have a degree of confidence to make tough decisions, but their self-images are often seriously distorted. Executives tend to think that they (and their organizations) are superior, are immune to disasters, and can control events. No matter how fair they want to be, leaders tend to favor themselves when making decisions. Top-level managers argue that they deserve larger offices, more money, and stock options because their divisions contribute more to the success of the organization. Overconfidence is also a problem for decision makers because it seduces them into thinking that they have all the information they need, so they fail to learn more. Even when they do seek additional data, they're likely to interpret new information according to their existing biases.

Unrealistic self-perceptions of all types put leaders at ethical risk. Executives may claim that they have a "right" to steal company property because they are vital to the success of the corporation. Over time they may come to believe that they aren't subject to the same rules as everyone else. University of Richmond leadership studies professor Terry Price argues that leader immorality generally stems from such mistaken beliefs.[14] Leaders know right from wrong but often make exceptions for (justify) their own behavior. They are convinced that their leadership positions exempt them from following traffic laws or from showing up to meetings on time, for example. As Case Study 2.1 illustrates, they often disregard sexual norms as well.

Leaders may justify immoral behavior such as lying or intimidating followers on the grounds that it is the only way to protect the country or to save the company. Unethical leaders may also decide, with the support of followers, that the rules of morality apply only to the immediate group and not to outsiders. Excluding others from moral considerations—from moral membership—justified such unethical practices as slavery and colonization in the past. In recent times, this logic has been used to deny legal protections to suspected terrorists. (Turn to Chapter 4 for an in-depth look at moral exclusion.)

The loftier a leader's position, the greater the chances that he or she will overestimate his or her abilities. Powerful leaders are particularly likely to think they are godlike, believing they are omniscient (all-knowing), omnipotent (all-powerful), and invulnerable (safe from all harm).[15] Top leaders can mistakenly conclude they know everything because they have access to many different sources of information and followers look to them for answers. They believe that they can do whatever they want because they have so much power. Surrounded by entourages of subservient staff members, these same officials are convinced that they will be protected from the consequences of their actions. Former Hewlett-Packard CEO Mark Hurd believed that he could get away with billing the company for unauthorized travel expenses for a female employee who may have been his lover. Former South Carolina governor Mark Sanford thought he could tell constituents he was hiking the Appalachian Trail to hide the fact that he was in Argentina with his mistress.

Failure of Moral Imagination

According to many ethicists, moral imagination—sensitivity to moral issues and options—is key to ethical behavior and works hand in hand with moral reasoning in the decision-making process.[16] University of Virginia professor Patricia Werhane offers a three-part definition of moral imagination. *Reproductive imagination* is being aware of elements of the context (participants, setting, and so on), what schemas (scripts, ways of thinking) are operating, and what ethical conflicts are present. *Productive imagination* is reframing the problem from a variety of perspectives and revamping one's current schemas. *Creative imagination* is coming up with new and morally sound solutions that can be justified to outsiders. Those with moral imagination are sensitive to ethical dilemmas but can also detach themselves from the immediate situation in order to see the bigger picture. They recognize their typical ways of thinking and set aside these normal operating rules to come up with creative solutions that are "novel, economically viable, and morally justifiable."[17] (You can determine your level of moral imagination by completing Self-Assessment 2.1.)

Werhane cites former Merck CEO Roy Vagelos as one example of a leader with a vivid moral imagination. He proceeded with the development of the drug Mectizan, which treats the parasite that causes river blindness in Africa and South America, even though developing the product would be expensive and there was little hope that patients in poor countries could pay for it.[18] When relief agencies didn't step forward to fund and distribute the drug, Merck developed its own distribution systems in poor nations. Lost income from the drug totaled more than $200 million, but the number of victims (who are filled with globs of worms that cause blindness and death) dropped dramatically. In contrast, NASA engineer Roger Boisjoly recognized the ethical problem of launching the space shuttle *Challenger* in cold weather in 1985 but failed to generate a creative strategy for preventing the launch. He stopped objecting and deferred to management (normal operating procedure). Boisjoly made no effort to go outside the chain of command to express his concerns to the agency director or to the press. The *Challenger* exploded soon after liftoff, killing all seven astronauts aboard. Failure of moral imagination also contributed to the crash of the space shuttle *Columbia* seventeen years later as lower-level employees once again failed to go outside the chain of command to express safety concerns.

Moral imagination facilitates ethical reasoning because it helps leaders step away from their typical mental scripts or schemas and to recognize the moral elements of events. Unfortunately, our scripts can leave out the ethical dimension of a situation. Shell officials failed to take into account the ethical considerations of their decision to sink the Brent Spar, for instance. To them, this was a routine business decision, largely based on cost, that would solve an oil industry problem—how to dispose of outdated equipment cheaply. Or consider the case of Ford Motor Company's failure to recall and repair the gas tanks on the Pintos it manufactured between 1970 and 1976. The gas tank on this subcompact was located behind the rear axle. It tended to rupture during any rear-end collision, even at low speed. When this happened, sparks could ignite the fuel, engulfing the car in flames. Fixing the problem would have only cost $11 per vehicle, but Ford refused to act. The firm believed that all small cars were inherently unsafe and that customers weren't interested in safety. Furthermore, Ford managers conducted a cost–benefit analysis and determined that the costs in human life were less than what it would cost the company to repair the problem.

The National Highway Traffic Safety Administration finally forced Ford to recall the Pinto in 1978, but by that time the damage had been done. The company lost a major lawsuit brought by a burn victim. In a trial involving the deaths of three Indiana teens in a rear-end crash, Ford became the first major corporation to face criminal, not civil, charges for manufacturing faulty products. The automaker was later acquitted, but its image was severely tarnished.

Business professor Dennis Gioia, who served as Ford's recall coordinator from 1973 to 1975, blames moral blindness for the company's failure to act.[19] Ethical considerations were not part of the safety committee's script. The group made decisions about recalls based on the number of incidents and cost–benefit analyses. Because there were only a few reports of gas tank explosions and the expense of fixing all Pinto tanks didn't seem justified, members decided not to act. At no point did Gioia and his colleagues question the morality of putting a dollar value on human life or of allowing customers to die in order to save the company money.

Moral imagination also enhances moral reasoning by encouraging the generation of novel alternatives. Recognizing our typical problem-solving patterns frees us from their power. We are no longer locked into one train of thought but are better able to generate new options. However, Werhane cautions that moral imagination must always be grounded in solid logic and reasoning and have an evaluative component. In fact, she notes that creative imagination can become overactive when leaders and followers focus on novelty at the expense of ethical common sense. For example, managers and employees at personal computer disk manufacturer MiniScribe tried to meet impossible sales goals in the 1980s by double shipping to customers, making up accounts, altering auditors' reports, and, at one point, shipping bricks in disk drive cartons. These were highly creative but highly immoral responses to an ethical dilemma. Audi had to recall its 5000 series German automobile when drivers and the media claimed that the vehicle suffered from an acceleration problem. As it turned out, deaths purportedly linked to a mechanical defect were really the product of drivers accidentally putting their feet on the accelerator instead of the brake. Hyperactive moral imagination created a false scenario that cost Audi 80% of its market share.

Moral Disengagement

While moral decision making has much in common with other forms of reasoning, it does have unique features. Most important, morality involves determining right and wrong based on personal ethical standards. Normally we feel guilt, shame, and self-condemnation if we violate our moral code by lying when we believe in truth telling, telling a racist joke when we believe in treating others with dignity, and so on. According to Stanford University social psychologist Albert Bandura, we frequently turn off or deactivate these self-sanctions through the process of moral disengagement. Moral disengagement helps account for the fact that individuals can have a clear sense of right and wrong yet engage in immoral activities.

As a result, they are able to commit unethical behavior with a clear conscience. Using the following mechanisms, they convince themselves that their immoral conduct is moral, minimize their role in causing harm, and devalue the victims of their destructive behavior.[20]

Turning Immoral Conduct Into Moral Conduct

1. *Moral justification.* Moral justification is a process of self-persuasion. Leaders persuade themselves that their harmful behavior is actually moral and beneficial. Team captains justify cheating and dirty play as a way of protecting team members or team honor. Hiding product defects is defended as a way to keep sales up and thus save the company and jobs.

2. *Euphemistic labeling.* Euphemistic language has a sanitizing function, making harmful behavior appear more respectable and reducing personal responsibility. Examples include referring to civilians accidently killed in war as "collateral damage" and using the term "disfellowshipped" to describe those kicked out of some Christian churches. Leaders may also try to exonerate themselves by speaking as if what they did was the product of nameless outside forces. For instance, instead of saying "I laid employees off," they say, "There were layoffs." Or they may use language associated with legitimate enterprises to lend an aura of respectability to illegitimate ones. Members of the Mafia call themselves "businessmen" instead of criminals, for example, to make their activities appear more acceptable.

3. *Advantageous comparison.* Contrast involves comparing unethical or criminal acts with even worse activities, thus making them appear more tolerable. In sports, coaches and players excuse their use of bad language by comparing this offense to more serious violations like fighting with opponents. Defenders of Bill Clinton minimized his sexual affairs by noting that he didn't get the nation into war as did his successor George W. Bush.

Minimizing Harm

4. *Displacement of responsibility.* Individuals are most likely to sanction themselves for bad behavior if they acknowledge their role in causing harm. Therefore, they often put the blame on someone else so as to minimize their responsibility for doing damage to others. Followers may claim that they were following orders when they inflated sales figures, for instance. Leaders often distance themselves from illegal activities by remaining "intentionally uninformed." They don't go looking for evidence of wrongdoing and, if wrongdoing occurs, dismiss these cases as "isolated incidents" caused by followers who didn't understand corporate policies.

5. *Diffusion of responsibility.* Diffusing or spreading out responsibility also lessens personal accountability for immoral behavior. In large organizations, division of labor reduces

responsibility. Each individual's job may appear to be harmless, but the collective labor of workers can produce significant damage. Consider a tobacco company, for example. The efforts of marketing, human resources, quality control, and other departments are worthy on their own merits. Nevertheless, the firm as a whole produces a deadly product that shortens the lives of users.

6. *Disregard or distortion of consequences.* Hiding suffering is one way to disregard the consequences of harmful actions and reduce the likelihood of self-recrimination. For example, in drone warfare (see Chapter 8), plane operators cause death and destruction thousands of miles away. Such physical separation makes it easier to kill without remorse. Organizational hierarchies also hide destructive consequences as middle and upper managers may not see the outcomes of their choices. They may never visit their oppressive overseas manufacturing facilities, for example, or watch toxic waste being released by their plants.

Devaluing Victims

7. *Dehumanization.* It is easier to mistreat others if they are seen as less than fully human. In extreme cases, dehumanization leads to rape, genocide, and other acts of atrocity. Viewing outsiders as "savages," "degenerates," or "fiends" encourages brutality. Dehumanization can be much more subtle, however. Many societal forces, such as urbanization, mobility, and technology, make it hard to relate to others in personal ways. When people are strangers, they are more likely to be targeted for mild forms of exclusion such as disparaging comments and unfair comparisons.

8. *Attribution of blame.* Blaming others is an expedient way to excuse unethical behavior. In a conflict, each party generally blames the other for starting the dispute and each side considers itself faultless. Blaming the victim is also common. If the victim is to blame, then the victimizer is freed from guilt. Some sexual harassers, for instance, excuse their behavior by saying that certain women invite sexual harassment by the way that they dress. Sadly, some victims come to accept the definition put on them by their victimizers.

Moral disengagement is a progressive, gradual process occurring over time. Take the case of ecoterrorists. They generally start out protecting the environment through prosocial tactics like protests and lawsuits. After becoming bitter and disillusioned, they turn to more radical methods, such as burning luxury cars, lumber yards, Forest Service buildings, and ski resorts. They justify their acts by calling them essential to saving the planet, claiming that the damage they cause is minor compared to the damage caused by corporations and political officials. In addition, moral disengagement is the product of personal and social forces. Society helps determine personal standards (e.g., it is wrong to cheat or to hurt innocent people), but groups and organizations commonly weaken sanctions for violating personal values. As noted above, leaders who engage in unethical acts often declare that such behavior is essential to achieving worthy goals. They help displace responsibility when they order followers to engage in illegal activities. When some group members dehumanize outsiders, others in the group are more likely to do the same.

Using scales like the one found in Self-Assessment 2.2, researchers have discovered a strong link between moral disengagement and unethical behavior in a variety of settings.[21] Disengaged children are more likely to be aggressive and delinquent. Disengaged high school and college athletes are more prone to antisocial behaviors, such as trying to injure opponents and breaking the rules of the game. At the same time, they are less likely to demonstrate such prosocial behaviors as helping injured opponents or congratulating them for good play. In the work setting, the tendency to morally disengage increases the likelihood of lying, deception, cheating, stealing, computer hacking, favoring the self at the expense of others, damaging company property, using illegal drugs, and making racist remarks. Citizens with a propensity for moral disengagement show higher support for military aggression. (An extreme example of moral disengagement is described in "Leadership Ethics at the Movies: *Lord of War*.")

LEADERSHIP ETHICS AT THE MOVIES • • • • • • • • • •

Lord of War

Key Cast Members: Nicolas Cage, Jared Leto, Bridget Moynahan, Ethan Hawke, Ian Holm

Synopsis: Ukrainian immigrant Yuri Orlov (Nicolas Cage) discovers that his calling in life is gun running, which propels him beyond his humble Brooklyn roots. Using bribery, deception, and a near-total disregard for the consequences of his actions, Orlov becomes a world-class arms dealer, supplying small arms, assault rifles, grenades, tanks, and armored helicopters to combatants in Africa, the Balkans, and elsewhere. Wealth comes at a price, however, costing Yuri his family and whatever moral standards he might once have had. Ethan Hawke plays the Interpol agent who relentlessly pursues Orlov only to discover that the U.S. government considers the arms dealer a necessary evil.

Rating: R for graphic violence, sexuality, language

Themes: moral disengagement, selfishness, greed, pride, deception, corruption, ambition

(Continued)

Lack of Expertise

Leaders may unintentionally cast shadows because they lack the necessary knowledge, skills, and experience. Many of us have never followed a formal, step-by-step approach to solving an ethical problem in a group. Or we may not know what ethical perspectives or frameworks can be applied to ethical dilemmas. When you read and respond to Case Study 2.2, for example, you may have a clear opinion about whether or not you would produce and market the sneaker (most of my students would). You may be less clear about the standards you use to reach your conclusion, however. You might use a common ethical guideline ("Companies are solely responsible to stockholders"; "Consumers should be free to decide how they spend their money") but not realize that you have done so.

Emotions are critical to ethical decision making and action, as we'll see in Chapter 6. And it is possible to blunder into good ethical choices. Nevertheless, we are far more likely to make wise decisions when we are guided by some widely used ethical principles and standards. These ethical theories help us define the problem, highlight important elements of the situation, force us to think systematically, encourage us to view the problem from a variety of perspectives, and strengthen our resolve to act responsibly.

Contextual Pressures

Not all shadow casters come from individual forces like unhealthy motivations, faulty decision making, and lack of expertise. Ethical failures are the product of group, organizational, and cultural factors as well. Conformity is a problem for many small groups. Members put a higher priority on group cohesion than on coming up with a well-reasoned choice. They pressure dissenters, shield themselves from negative feedback, keep silent when they disagree, and so on.[22] Members of these shadowy groups engage in unhealthy communication patterns that generate negative emotions while undermining the reasoning process.

Organizations can also be shadow lands. For instance, car dealerships are known for their deceptive practices, and cell phone retailers have largely earned the same reputation. Although working in such environments makes moral behavior much more difficult, no organization is immune to ethical failure. Top managers at some organizations may fire employees who talk about ethical issues so that they can claim ignorance if followers do act unethically. This "don't ask, don't tell" atmosphere forces workers to make ethical choices on their own, without the benefit of interaction. They seldom challenge the questionable decisions of others (see Case Study 2.3) and assume that everyone supports the immoral acts.

Obedience is a particularly strong conformity pressure. Even in highly individualistic cultures like the United States, people appear programmed to follow orders. In one of the most vivid examples of this tendency, psychologist Stanley Milgram asked research subject "teachers" to administer electric shocks to "learners" (who were really confederates and were not hurt) who failed to answer questions correctly. More than 60% of the participants in his 1960s studies were fully obedient. They turned up the power to maximum level at the request of an experimenter dressed in a lab coat, even though the cries and protests of the "learners" grew louder with each increase in voltage. Replications of Milgram's studies 40 years later revealed the same pattern, with subjects just as willing to follow the orders of the experimenters.[23]

Socialization is another process that encourages employees to set their personal codes aside. Organizations use orientation sessions, training seminars, mentors, and other means to help new hires identify with the group and absorb the group's culture. Loyalty to and knowledge of the organization are essential. Nonetheless, the socialization process may blind members to the consequences of their actions. This may have happened at Google. Google employees believe that their company can be trusted with customer data and recently instituted a new policy that combines user information across the company's many platforms. However, outsiders are not as convinced that the company is trustworthy. Twenty-seven European Union regulators criticized Google's plans to consolidate customer information. In another case, the company paid a $22.5 million fine in the United States for evading the privacy settings on Apple's Safari Web browser.[24] Some organizations deliberately use the socialization process to corrupt new members, as we'll see in Chapter 9.

Cultural differences, like group and organizational forces, can also encourage leaders to abandon their personal codes of conduct. (We'll examine this topic in more depth in Chapter 11.) A corporate manager from the United States may be personally opposed to bribery. Her company's ethics code forbids such payments, and so does federal law. However, she may bribe customs officials and government officials in her adopted country if such payments are an integral part of the national culture and appear to be the only way to achieve her company's goals.

So far, our focus has been on how external pressures can undermine the ethical behavior of leaders and followers. However, this picture is incomplete, as we will explore in more depth in the last section of the text. Leaders aren't just the victims of contextual pressures but are the architects of the unethical climates, structures, policies, and procedures that cause groups and organizations to fail in the first place. Corporate scandals are typically the direct result of the actions of leaders who not only engage in immoral behavior but also encourage subordinates to follow their example. They are poor role models, pursue profits at all costs, punish dissenters, reward unethical practices, and so on.

Stepping Out of the Shadows

Now that we've identified the factors that cause us to cast shadows as leaders, we can begin to master them. To do so we will need to look inward to address our motivations; improve our ethical decision making; acquire ethical knowledge, strategies, and skills; and resist negative contextual influences at the same time we create healthy ethical climates.

I hope you will view your ethical development as part of your overall development as a leader. According to researchers at the Center for Creative Leadership (CCL), we can expand our leadership competence, and the skills and knowledge we acquire (including those related to ethics) will make us more effective in a wide variety of leadership situations, ranging from business and professional organizations to neighborhood groups, clubs, and churches.[25] CCL staff members report that leader development is based on assessment, challenge, and support. Successful developmental programs provide plenty of feedback that lets participants know how they are doing and how others are responding to their leadership strategies. Assessment data provoke self-evaluation ("What am I doing well?" "How do I need to improve?") and provide information that aids in self-reflection. Simply put, a leader learns to identify gaps between current performance and where he or she needs to be and then closes those gaps. The most powerful leadership experiences also stretch or challenge people. As long as people don't feel the need to change, they won't. Difficult and novel experiences, conflict situations, and high goals force leaders outside their comfort zones and give them the opportunity to practice new skills. To make the most of feedback and challenges, leaders need support. Supportive comments ("I appreciate the effort you're making to become a better listener"; "I'm confident that you can handle this new assignment") sustain the leader during the struggle to improve. The most common source of support is other people (family, coworkers, bosses), but developing leaders can also draw on organizational cultures and systems. Supportive organizations believe in continuous learning and staff development, provide funds for training, reward progress, and so on.

All three elements—assessment, challenge, and support—should be part of your plan to increase your ethical competence. You need feedback about how well you handle ethical dilemmas, how others perceive your character, and how your decisions affect followers. You need the challenges and practice that come from moving into new leadership positions. Seek out opportunities to influence others by engaging in service projects, chairing committees, teaching children, or taking on a supervisory role. You also need the support of others to maximize your development. Talk with colleagues about ethical choices at work, draw on the insights of important thinkers, and find groups that will support your efforts to change.

Wright State University ethics professor Joseph Petrick argues that we need to develop three broad types of ethical competencies.[26] *Cognitive decision-making competence* encompasses all the skills needed to make responsible ethical choices, including moral awareness, moral understanding, moral reasoning and dialogue, and the resolution of competing arguments and demands. *Affective prebehavioral disposition competence* describes the motivation needed to act on ethical choices. To match our words with our deeds, we need to be morally sensitive, empathetic, courageous, tolerant, and imaginative. *Context management competence* focuses on creating and shaping moral environments. Essential context management skills involve managing formal compliance and ethics systems, overseeing corporate governance, and exercising global citizenship.

University of Notre Dame psychologists Darcia Narvaez and Daniel Lapsley offer the novice–expert continuum as one way to track our ethical progress.[27] They argue that the more we behave like moral experts, the greater our level of ethical development. Ethical authorities, like experts in other fields, think differently than novices. First, they have a broader variety of schemas to draw from, and they know more about the ethical domain. Their networks of moral knowledge are more developed and connected than those of beginners. Second, they see the world differently than novices. While beginners are often overwhelmed by new data, those with expertise can quickly identify and act on relevant information, such as what ethical principles might apply in a given situation. Third, experts have different skill sets. They are better able than novices to define the moral problem and then match the new dilemma with previous ethical problems they have encountered. "Unlike novices," Narvaez and Lapsley say, "they know *what* information to access, *which* procedures to apply, *how* to apply them, and *when* it is appropriate."[28] As a result, they make faster, better moral decisions.

Narvaez and Lapsley argue that to become an ethical expert, you should learn in a well-structured environment (like a college or university) where correct behaviors are rewarded, and where you can interact with mentors and receive feedback and coaching. You will need to master both moral theory and skills (see Box 2.3). You should learn how previous experts have dealt with moral problems and how some choices are better than others. As you gain experience, you'll not only get better at solving ethical problems but also be better able to explain your choices. Finally, you will have to put in the necessary time and focused effort. Ethical mastery takes hours of practice wrestling with moral dilemmas.

Darcia Narvaez developed the following list of ethical skills that should be incorporated into the training offered in ethical education programs. These are also the abilities that we need to develop as leaders and are addressed in this text. Narvaez developed the list after surveying moral exemplars like Martin Luther King, Jr., and virtue theory, as well as scholarship in morality, moral development, positive psychology, and citizenship. Taken together, these skills help us function well in a pluralistic democracy while promoting the health of society as a whole.

Ethical Sensitivity (recognition of ethical problems)

Understanding emotional expression

Taking the perspective of others

Connecting to others

Responding to diversity

Controlling social bias

Interpreting situations

Communicating effectively

Ethical Judgment (decision making)

Understanding ethical problems

Using codes and identifying judgment criteria

Reasoning generally

Reasoning ethically

Understanding consequences

Reflecting on process and outcome

Coping and resilience

Ethical Focus (motivation to act ethically)

Respecting others

Cultivating conscience

Acting responsibly

Helping others

Finding meaning in life

Valuing traditions and institutions

Developing ethical identity and integrity

Ethical Action (following through on moral decisions)

Resolving conflicts and problems

Asserting respectfully

Taking initiative as a leader

Implementing decisions

Cultivating courage

Persevering

Working hard

SOURCE: Narvaez, D. (2006). Integrative ethical education. In M. Killen & J. Smetana (Eds.), *Handbook of moral development* (pp. 717–728). Mahwah, NJ: Erlbaum, p. 717. Used by permission of the publisher.

It is important to note that making and implementing ethical decisions takes communication as well as critical thinking skills, as the list in Box 2.3 illustrates. We must be able to articulate our reasoning, convince other leaders of the wisdom of our position, and work with others to put the choice into place. For instance, a manager who wants to eliminate discriminatory hiring practices will have to listen effectively, gather information, formulate and make arguments, appeal to moral principles, and build relationships. Failure to develop these skills will doom the reform effort.

IMPLICATIONS AND APPLICATIONS

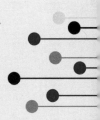

- Unethical or immoral behavior is the product of a number of factors, both internal and external. You must address all of these elements if you want to cast light rather than shadow.

- Unhealthy motivations that produce immoral behavior include internal enemies (insecurity, battleground mentality, functional atheism, fear, denying death, evil) and selfishness (pride, ego, narcissism, Machiavellianism).

- "Good" leaders can and do make bad ethical decisions because of defective reasoning.

- Beware of faulty assumptions about how the world operates, about other people, and about yourself. These can lead you to underestimate risks and overestimate your abilities and value to your organization. Avoid the temptation to excuse or justify immoral behavior based on your leadership position.

- Exercise your moral imagination: Be sensitive to ethical issues, step outside your normal way of thinking, and come up with creative solutions.

- Be alert to the process of moral disengagement, which involves persuading yourself that immoral conduct is actually moral, minimizing the harm you cause, and devaluing the victims of your destructive actions.

- Leaders may unintentionally cast shadows because they lack the necessary knowledge, skills, and experience.

- Contextual or situational pressures encourage leaders and followers to set aside their personal standards to engage in unethical behavior. Conformity will encourage you to put cohesion above ethical choices. Obedience may override your personal moral code.

- Make your ethical development part of your larger leadership development plan. The three key elements of any development strategy are (1) assessment or feedback that reveals any gaps between current and ideal performance, (2) challenging (difficult, new, demanding) experiences, and (3) support in the form of resources and other people.

- Key ethical competencies involve making responsible ethical decisions, being motivated to follow through on moral choices, and shaping the moral environment.

- To become more of an ethical expert, learn in a well-structured environment, master moral theory and skills, and devote the necessary time and effort to the task of ethical improvement.

FOR FURTHER EXPLORATION, CHALLENGE, AND SELF-ASSESSMENT

1. In a group, identify unhealthy motivations to add to the list provided in this chapter.

2. Evaluate a well-publicized ethical decision you consider to be faulty. Determine whether mistaken assumptions and/or lack of moral imagination were operating in this situation. Write up your analysis.

3. Complete Self-Assessment 2.2, the Propensity to Morally Disengage Scale. What do your results reveal about your tendency to excuse your unethical behavior? What steps can you take to avoid this form of faulty reasoning?

4. Rate your ethical development based on your past experience and education. Where would you place yourself on the continuum between novice and expert? What in your background contributes to your rating?

5. Analyze a time when you cast a shadow as a leader. Which of the shadow casters led to your unethical behavior? Write up your analysis.

6. How much responsibility do followers have for supporting destructive leaders? Record your conclusions.

7. Does your employer pressure you to abandon your personal moral code of ethics? If so, how? What can you do to resist such pressure?

8. Create a plan for becoming more of an ethical expert. Be sure that it incorporates assessment, challenge, and support. Revisit your plan at the end of the course to determine how effective it has been.

STUDENT STUDY SITE

Visit the student study site at **www.sagepub.com/johnsonmecl5e** to access full SAGE journal articles for further research and information on key chapter topics.

CASE STUDY 2.1

A Modern-Day Libertine

In France, multiple marriages, multiple affairs, and serial seduction don't usually mean the end of a political or business career. The French are less concerned about the personal lives of powerful people than are citizens in the United States. Particularly in the case of male public figures, affairs and seduction are often seen as signs of strength and virility and thus are admired rather than condemned.

This laissez-faire attitude toward the private sex lives of the political elite may be changing thanks to the excesses of Dominique Strauss-Kahn (known as DSK). A French economist, DSK was head of the International Monetary Fund and was favored to become France's next president. But he lost his job and any chance of winning the French presidency when he was charged with sexually assaulting a New York hotel maid in 2011. He was cleared of criminal charges in the New York rape case but reached a financial settlement with the victim. Later he admitted to participating in a series of upscale sex parties costing around $13,000 each. These events began with formal dinners and ended in orgies. Strauss-Kahn reportedly wanted to have sex with three or four women at each of these parties. To meet his needs, event organizers sometimes hired prostitutes when they couldn't recruit enough other female participants. While prostitution is not a crime in France, employing prostitutes is. DSK has been accused of being part of a prostitution ring. He denies that he had anything to do with arranging the parties, noting that he generally arrived late. By that time most of the women were naked and he had no idea who was a prostitute and who was not.

DSK has been described as a modern-day libertine. Libertinism, which dates back to 16th-century Europe, is a philosophy based on the pursuit of "a life without moralistic limits." Its best-known advocate was Giacomo Casanova, who believed that as long as he lived within the law he should be able to do whatever he wanted. The former IMF chief operated according to the same philosophy, at least when it came to sex. In a magazine interview, DSK admitted: "I long thought I could lead my life as I wanted. And that includes free behavior between consenting adults. I was too out of step with French society. I was wrong."[1]

While Strauss-Kahn kept the dark side of his sexual proclivities secret, his sexual appetite was public knowledge. He was called the "Great Seducer," the "hot rabbit," and the "frisky Frenchman" before he took over the IMF. His third wife (who has since left him) even argued, "It's important for a man in politics to be able to seduce."[2] At the IMF, he admitted to having an affair with a subordinate.

Entitlement, not lust, may be the best explanation of DSK's libertine behavior. Members of France's elite have long ignored the sexual restrictions put on the middle and lower classes. However, the link between power and sex isn't limited to France. Powerful men and women are more likely than their less powerful counterparts to engage in sexual infidelity no matter what their nationality. They are more confident and have access to more partners. At the same time, they are less bound by societal rules and have a greater tendency to fail to exercise self-restraint. Commenting on Strauss-Kahn, one political science professor noted:

> For powerful people, it's part of the thrill that they can get things that other people can't get. They are usually surrounded by sycophantic people, and after a while they come to believe that they have a right to be surrounded by attractive men and women. There is a sense of entitlement that is a general attribute of power.[3]

The same night DSK was arraigned for the alleged New York attack, another powerful man, former California governor Arnold Schwarzenegger, admitted to having fathered a child with a member of his household staff. He kept the affair and his son secret from his wife, Maria Shriver, for a decade.

Discussion Questions

1. What other powerful leaders can you name who have apparently engaged in sexual misconduct out of a sense of entitlement?

2. What can followers do to prevent their leaders from feeling entitled?

3. What other factors, aside from power, might encourage leaders to believe

they are entitled to ignore the rules that apply to everyone else?

4. Do you think that powerful men are more likely than powerful women to engage in sexual infidelity? Why or why not?

5. Does being a libertine automatically disqualify someone from becoming a good leader?

6. How much should citizens be concerned about the private lives of their political leaders?

Notes

1. Carvajal, D., & de Blume, M. (2012). Strauss-Kahn says sex parties went too far, but lust is not crime. *The New York Times*, p. A1.

2. Gibbs, N. (2011, May 11). Men behaving badly: What is it about power that makes men crazy? *Time*, pp. 16–30.

3. Politics, power and sex. (2011, May 21). *Belfast Telegraph*, p. 20.

Sources

Davis, B., & Gauthier-Villars, D. (2008, October 22). IMF chief facing fresh claim of abusing power. *The Australian*, World, p. 12.

Lammers, J., Stoker, J. I., Pollman, M., & Stapel, D. A. (2011). Power increases infidelity among men and women. *Psychological Science, 22*, 1191–1197.

Moutet, A. (2011, May 7). "I love women, et alors?" *The Daily Telegraph*, p. A3.

Wolff, L. (2012, October 17). Free to be a sexual predator? *The New York Times,* Op-Ed.

CASE STUDY 2.2

The $300 Sneaker

LeBron James is the world's best basketball player. Perhaps it only stands to reason, then, that his namesake basketball shoe would be the world's most expensive. Nike's LeBron X sneaker is the latest item in the Miami Heat star's signature shoe line. The Plus version of the product, retailing for around $300, is equipped with motion sensors that allow wearers to measure their vertical leap and quickness. The less expensive version, costing $180, comes without the sensors.

Two groups make up the primary market for the LeBron X Plus: high school students seeking the latest fashion and "sneakerheads." Sneakerheads like to collect shoes, sometimes never taking them out of the box. African American youth make up a significant proportion of both groups. There have been reports of young people in minority communities being beaten up and their expensive athletic shoes stolen. Mark Morial, president of the National Urban League, an organization that promotes African American economic development, urged Nike to withdraw the shoe. "To release such an outrageously overpriced product while the nation is struggling to overcome an unemployment crisis is insensitive at best," he said. "It represents twisted priorities and confused values."[1] For its part, Nike denies that it is arbitrarily raising prices and claims that the sensors in the shoe provide valuable information to players who want to improve their performance.

While it refused to discontinue the LeBron X, Nike did put new safety rules in place for the day of its release. Retailers were not allowed to open at midnight to start selling the new model; they had to wait until 8:00 a.m. This move was made in response to the chaos that had occurred during the earlier release of Nike's Air Jordan XI, a replica of the original Air Jordan shoe. Police had to break up crowds in malls and other outlets in Seattle, Atlanta, Louisville, Houston, San Antonio, and Spokane. Morial noted that these incidents cost taxpayers money because they required the intervention of law enforcement, and he further asserted that the release of the LeBron X was a contradiction of Nike's stated values: "Nike has tremendous influence in this country,

and they promote the values of teamwork, responsibility and good ethics, and I think the launch is inconsistent with Nike's projected and professed values."[2]

Imagine that you are a top-level Nike executive. Would you produce and market the LeBron X Plus?

Notes

1.   Martin, J. (2012, August 22). $300 sneaker rankles some. *USA Today*, p. 1C.

2.   Kaplan, B. (2012, August 29). Footloose and fanciful. *National Post*, p. AL8.

Sources

Jonsson, P. (2011, December 23). Concord pandemonium: "Sneakerheads" flock to grab Air Jordans. *The Christian Science Monitor.*

Stoda, G. (2012, August 25). Don't blame LeBron James for $300 sneaker. *Palm Beach Post.*

CASE STUDY 2.3

Death by Peanuts

Nothing scares consumers more than the thought that the food they eat may not be safe. And rightfully so. Every year, 325,000 people are hospitalized in the United States as the result of eating contaminated food; 5,000 die. Some survivors suffer organ damage. In recent years, recalls have been issued for tainted almonds, cantaloupes, jalapeño peppers, tomatoes, spinach, pistachios, and other food products. Fifty Europeans died in 2011 from eating fenugreek sprouts tainted with a rare form of *E. coli* bacteria.

One of the most serious breaches of food safety in the United States to date involved the Peanut Corporation of America (PCA), which had plants in Georgia and Texas. The firm's peanut paste and peanut butter were used in an estimated 4,000 products, ranging from Thai food, granola bars, and peanut butter crackers to frozen cookie dough and ice cream. General Mills, Kellogg's, PetSmart, Kroger, Nutrisystem, and Clif Bar & Company used PCA as a supplier. PCA shipped directly to schools and nursing homes as well. In fact, authorities issued a recall of all products using PCA ingredients when an elderly woman in a rehabilitation facility in Minnesota died after eating tainted peanut butter.

The form of salmonella found in the PCA products comes from the feces of rats and birds and causes diarrhea, fever, and abdominal cramps lasting four to seven days. After eating the contaminated products, 644 consumers in 44 states and one Canadian province reportedly fell ill, and 8 died. As many as 20,000 may have been sickened but did not get tested or see a physician.

U.S. Food and Drug Administration inspectors discovered a host of unsanitary conditions at PCA's facility in Blakely, Georgia, including leaky roofs, moldy walls and ceilings, and holes that allowed birds, rodents, and other animals into the plant. Raw and roasted products were stored together, which increased the likelihood of cross-contamination, and workers washed their hands in the same sink that was used for cleaning utensils and mops.

Further investigation revealed that plant owner Stewart Parnell and plant manager Sammy Lightsey knowingly shipped contaminated products. On 12 separate occasions they received positive test results for salmonella. If they received word that a sample had tested positive for the bacteria, Parnell and Lightsey would forward the sample to another laboratory in the hope of getting a negative result. (Regulators recommend that products be destroyed after one positive test.) Five times the plant managers shipped the product even before additional test results came back, according to the FDA.

Parnell's primary concern was keeping costs down by getting product out the door as quickly as possible. In one instance, after being alerted that a sample had tested positive, he sent an e-mail replying that "the time lapse, besides the cost is costing us huge $$$$$ and causing obviously a huge lapse in time."[1] In another instance plant worker Mary Wilkerson wrote, "This lot is presumptive on SALMONELLA!!!!" Parnell replied, "Thanks Mary, I go thru this about once a week . . . I will hold my breath . . . again."[2] Later Parnell would tell employees that the firm had "never found any salmonella at all."[3]

Parnell and Lightsey may face criminal charges for deliberately putting contaminated products into the nation's food system, and the Peanut Corporation of America has since gone out of business as a result of the recall. State and private inspectors, along with the FDA, have come under fire for failing to identify the problems at the plant. Congress passed a food safety law to prevent future outbreaks, and the FDA moved to implement new rules designed to prevent contamination of both produce and processed foods. Much less attention has been focused on the culpability of PCA employees. Workers at the plant in Georgia were well aware of the deplorable conditions. Employees told reporters that they had to step over puddles of water after rainstorms and saw roaches and rats every day. They only deep cleaned the plant before scheduled inspections and had little time to clean after completing their regular tasks. Buckets of outdated product received updated labels and then were shipped. According to David James, who worked in the shipping department, "It was filthy and nasty all around the place."[4] One cook at the plant said that he refused to eat the peanut butter he made or serve it to his kids.

Employees apparently talked about the plant's failings among themselves but were afraid to complain to management or to inspectors for fear of losing their jobs. Employment is hard to come by in rural Georgia, and even minimum-wage positions like those at the plant are coveted in an area with an average annual household income of $26,000. PCA also relied heavily on part-time workers and often left important positions, such as that of quality manager, unfilled for long periods of time. Since the plant passed inspections, some employees convinced themselves that their concerns were overblown.

While the workers may have had good reasons for keeping their concerns to themselves, lives might have been saved if they had spoken up. Former employee James acknowledged that keeping silent had tragic consequences. "I'm not surprised this [the outbreak] happened," he said. "I just hate that people died."[5]

Discussion Probes

1. What factors described in the chapter contributed to PCA's top management's decision to ship contaminated products?

2. What factors encouraged plant workers to keep silent about conditions at the plant?

3. Were employees justified in keeping their concerns to themselves?

4. Should former PCA employees face criminal charges for failing to report the conditions at the plant to outside authorities? Why or why not?

5. How can leaders encourage followers to report unethical and illegal behavior?

6. What advice would you offer to employees who must decide whether or not to report unethical behavior or situations?

7. What leadership/followership ethics lessons do you take from this case?

Notes

1. Owner won't talk. (2009, February 12). *Newsday*, p. A08.

2. Owner won't talk.

3. Harris, G. (2009, February 12). Peanut foods shipped before testing came in. *The New York Times*, p. A24.

4. Glanton, D. (2009, February 9). Ex-peanut plant workers tell of rats, filth, mold. *The Oregonian*, p. A1.

5. Glanton, p. A4.

Sources

Charges possible in outbreak. (2009, February 15). *Newsday*, p. A50.

Glanton, D. (2009, February 8). Peanut recall puts town "in hot water." *Los Angeles Times*, p. A28.

Harris, G. (2009, January 31). Peanut plant recall leads to criminal investigation. *The New York Times*, p. A17.

Layton, L. (2009, January 29). Every peanut product from Ga. plant recalled. *The Washington Post*, p. A01.

Layton, L. (2009, April 3). FDA hasn't intensified inspections at peanut facilities, despite illness. *The Washington Post*, p. A04.

Layton, L. (2009, May 28). House calls for closer watch on food supply. *The Washington Post,* p. A17.

Making the food supply safer. (2009, August 10). *The Oregonian,* p. A10.

Maugh, T. H., & Engel, M. (2009, February 7). FDA says firm lied about peanut butter. *Los Angeles Times,* p. A1.

Moss, M. (2009, February 9). Peanut case shows holes in food safety net. *The New York Times,* p. A1.

Moss, M., & Martin, A. (2009, March 6). Food safety problems elude private inspectors. *The New York Times,* p. A1.

Neuman, W. (2011, September 28). Deaths rise in outbreak of listeria. *The New York Times,* p. B1.

Ricks, D. (2009, January 22). Salmonella scare spreads. *Newsday,* p. A10.

Salmonella shipped. (2009, February 7). *Newsday,* p. A09.

Schmit, J. (2009, April 27). Broken system hid peanut plants' risks. *USA Today,* p. 1B.

Schmit, J., & Weise, E. (2009, January 29). Peanut butter recall grows. *USA Today,* p. 1B.

Strom, S. (2013, January 5). F.D.A. proposes broad new rules on food safety. *The New York Times,* p. A1.

Weise, E. (2009, April 2). Nuts. *USA Today,* p. 1B.

Weise, E., & Schmit, J. (2009, February 10). Health risks may reach far beyond reported victims. *USA Today,* p. 1A.

Zhang, U. (2009, February 14). Peanut corporation files for bankruptcy. *Wall Street Journal Abstracts,* p. A3.

SELF-ASSESSMENT 2.1

Moral Imagination Scale

The following survey is designed to provide you with feedback on all three components of moral imagination: reproductive, productive, and creative. Respond to each of the following items on a scale of 1 (*strongly disagree*) to 7 (*strongly agree*).

1	2	3	4	5	6	7
Strongly Disagree						Strongly Agree

1. I like to imagine how the consequences of my behavior affect others.   1 2 3 4 5 6 7

2. I anticipate any moral problems that threaten our organization.   1 2 3 4 5 6 7

3. I am not able to imagine similarities and differences between the situation at hand and other situations where I could apply the same rule.*   1 2 3 4 5 6 7

4. I have the ability to recognize which ideas are morally worth pursuing and which are not.   1 2 3 4 5 6 7

5. When I find myself uncertain about how to act in a morally ambiguous situation, I change my understanding of the moral concepts that might be involved.

1 2 3 4 5 6 7

6. I resist any regulations detrimental to the environment, even if I have to risk my current position in the organization.

1 2 3 4 5 6 7

7. I have systematically investigated the factors that may affect the moral decisions of my organization.

1 2 3 4 5 6 7

8. I am careful about condemning past decisions made under entirely different circumstances.

1 2 3 4 5 6 7

9. I accept new regulations of the organization without any justification.*

1 2 3 4 5 6 7

10. In general, when there is a discussion about moral issues, everyone tends to listen to me.

1 2 3 4 5 6 7

11. My moral imagination heightens my ability to perceive morally relevant situations.

1 2 3 4 5 6 7

12. I have the ability to revise my existing moral beliefs so as to adapt to changing conditions.

1 2 3 4 5 6 7

13. My imagination enables me to look at myself from the point of view of another person.

1 2 3 4 5 6 7

14. It would be a waste of time for me to ask the opinion of those who disagree with me when I make a decision.*

1 2 3 4 5 6 7

15. It is difficult for me to bridge the gap between sensory data and intelligent thought.*

1 2 3 4 5 6 7

16. I can put myself in the place of others.

1 2 3 4 5 6 7

17. I do not have enough ability to compare and contrast my own culture with that of others.*

1 2 3 4 5 6 7

18. I can create alternative solutions to new moral situations.

1 2 3 4 5 6 7

19. I discipline all my capacities and inclinations in order to achieve self-control.

1 2 3 4 5 6 7

20. I do not have moral responsibility for what I imagine in terms of affecting others.*

1 2 3 4 5 6 7

21. Once I have generated reasons supporting my belief, I find it difficult to generate contradictory reasons.* 1 2 3 4 5 6 7

22. I have trouble understanding others' culture and values.* 1 2 3 4 5 6 7

Scoring

Reverse scoring on items marked with an *.

Reproductive imagination. Add up scores for items 1, 2, 4, 5, 7, 10, 12, 13, 18, 19 (Range 10–70)

Productive imagination. Add up scores for items 6, 11, 14, 16, 17, 22 (Range 7–42)

Creative imagination. Add up scores for items 3, 8, 9, 15, 20, 21 (Range 7–42)

SOURCE: Adapted from Yurtsever, G. (2006). Measuring moral imagination. *Social Behavior and Personality, 34*, 205–220, pp. 212–213. Used by permission.

SELF-ASSESSMENT 2.2

Propensity to Morally Disengage Scale

Instructions: Respond to each item below on a scale of 1 (*strongly disagree*) to 7 (*strongly agree*).

| 1 | 2 | 3 | 4 | 5 | 6 | 7 |

Strongly
Disagree

Strongly
Agree

1. It is okay to spread rumors to defend those you care about.

2. Taking something without the owner's permission is okay as long as you're just borrowing it.

3. Considering the ways people grossly misrepresent themselves, it's hardly a sin to inflate your own credentials a bit.

4. People shouldn't be held accountable for doing questionable things when they were just doing what an authority figure told them to do.

5. People can't be blamed for doing things that are technically wrong when all their friends are doing it too.

6. Taking personal credit for ideas that were not your own is no big deal.

7. Some people have to be treated roughly because they lack feelings that can be hurt.

8. People who get mistreated have usually done something to bring it on themselves.

Scoring

Add up your scores on the eight scale items. Possible total score ranges from 8 to 56. The higher the score, the greater your propensity for or likelihood of participating in the process of moral disengagement.

SOURCE: Moore, C., Detert, J. R., Trevino, L. K. Baker, V. L, & Mayer, D. M. (2012). Why employees do bad things: Moral disengagement and unethical organizational behavior. *Personnel Psychology, 65,* 1–48. Used by permission.

NOTES

1. Palmer, P. (1996). Leading from within. In L. C. Spears (Ed.), *Insights on leadership: Service, stewardship, spirit, and servant-leadership* (pp. 197–208). New York: John Wiley.
2. Bing, S. (2000). *What would Machiavelli do? The ends justify the meanness.* New York: HarperBusiness.
3. Palmer, p. 205.
4. Garvin, D. A. (1993, July–August). Building a learning organization. *Harvard Business Review,* pp. 78–91.
5. Nash, L. L. (1990). *Good intentions aside: A manager's guide to resolving ethical problems.* Boston: Harvard Business School Press.
6. Michaelson, A. (2009). *The foreclosure of America: The inside story of the rise and fall of Countrywide Home Loans, the mortgage crisis, and the default of the American dream.* New York: Berkley Books; Wilmers, R. G. (2009, July 27). Where the crisis came from. *The Washington Post,* p. A19.
7. McFarlin, D. B., & Sweeney, P. D. (2010). The corporate reflecting pool: Antecedents and consequences of narcissism in executives. In B. Schyns & T. Hansbrough (Eds.), *When leadership goes wrong: Destructive leadership, mistakes, and ethical failures* (pp. 247–284). Charlotte, NC: Information Age; Higgs, M.

(2009). The good, the bad and the ugly: Leadership and narcissism. *Journal of Change Management, 9,* 165–178; Lubit, R. (2002). The long-term organizational impact of destructively narcissistic managers. *Academy of Management Executive, 18,* 127–183; Padilla, A., Hogan, R., & Kaiser, R. B. (2007). The toxic triangle: Destructive leaders, susceptible followers, and conducive environments. *Leadership Quarterly, 18,* 176–194.
8. Johnson, J., & Orange, M. (2003). *The man who tried to buy the world: Jean-Marie Messier and Vivendi Universal.* New York: Portfolio.
9. Christie, R., & Geis, F. L. (1970). *Studies in Machiavellianism.* New York: Academic Press.
10. Becker, J. A. H., & O'Hair, H. D. (2007). Machiavellians' motives in organizational citizenship behavior. *Journal of Applied Communication Research, 35,* 246–267; Paulus, D. L., & Williams, K. M. (2002). The dark triad of personality: Narcissism, Machiavellianism, and psychopathy. *Journal of Research in Personality, 36,* 556–563; Boyle, E. H., Jr., Forsyth, D. R., Banks, G. C., & McDaniel, M. A. (2012). A meta-analysis of the dark triad and work behavior: A social exchange perspective. *Journal of Applied Psychology, 97,* 557–579.

11. Jourdan, G. (1998). Indirect causes and effects in policy change: The Brent Spar case. *Public Administration, 76,* 713–770; Zyglidopoulus, S. C. (2002). The social and environmental responsibilities of multinationals: Evidence from the Brent Spar case. *Journal of Business Ethics, 36,* 141–151.

12. Messick, D. M., & Bazerman, M. H. (1996, Winter). Ethical leadership and the psychology of decision making. *Sloan Management Review, 37*(2), 9–23.

13. Verhovek, S. H. (1993, April 22). Death in Waco: F.B.I. saw the ego in Koresh, but not a willingness to die. *The New York Times,* p. A1.

14. Price, T. L. (2006). *Understanding ethical failures in leadership.* Cambridge, England: Cambridge University Press. See also De Cremer, D., & Van Dijk, E. (2005). When and why leaders put themselves first: Leader behaviour in resource allocations as a function of feeling entitled. *European Journal of Social Psychology, 35,* 553–563.

15. Sternberg, R. J. (2002). Smart people are not stupid, but they sure can be foolish. In R. J. Sternberg (Ed.), *Why smart people can be so stupid* (pp. 232–242). New Haven, CT: Yale University Press.

16. See Guroian, V. (1996). Awakening the moral imagination. *Intercollegiate Review, 32,* 3–13; Johnson, M. (1993). *Moral imagination: Implications of cognitive science for ethics.* Chicago: University of Chicago Press; Kekes, J. (1991). Moral imagination, freedom, and the humanities. *American Philosophical Quarterly, 28,* 101–111; Tivnan, E. (1995). *The moral imagination.* New York: Routledge, Chapman, and Hall.

17. Werhane, P. H. (1999). *Moral imagination and management decision-making.* New York: Oxford University Press, p. 93. See also Bowie, N. E., & Werhane, P. H. (2005). *Management ethics.* Malden, MA: Blackwell.

18. Useem, M. (1998). *The leadership moment: Nine stories of triumph and disaster and their lessons for us all.* New York: Times Books.

19. Gioia, D. A. (1992). Pinto fires and personal ethics: A script analysis of missed opportunities. *Journal of Business Ethics, 11,* 379–389.

20. Bandura, A., Barbaranelli, C., Caprara, G. V., & Pastoreli, C. (1996). Mechanisms of moral disengagement in the exercise of moral agency. *Journal of Personality and Social Psychology, 71,* 364–374; Bandura, A. (1999). Moral disengagement in the perpetration of inhumanities. *Personality and Social Psychology Review, 3,* 193–209; Bandura, A. (2002). Selective moral disengagement in the exercise of moral agency. *Journal of Moral Education, 31,* 101–119.

21. Bandura et al. (1996); Boardley, I. D., & Kavussanu, M. (2007). Development and validation of the Moral Disengagement in Sport Scale. *Journal of Sport & Exercise Psychology, 29,* 608–628; Boardley, I. D., & Kavussanu, M. (2008). The Moral Disengagement in Sport Scale—Short. *Journal of Sports Sciences, 26,* 1507–1517; Moore, C., Detert, J. R., Trevino, L. K., Baker, V. L., & Mayer, D. M. (2012). Why employees do bad things: Moral disengagement and unethical organizational behavior. *Personnel Psychology, 65,* 1–48; Barsky, A. (2011). Investigating the effects of moral disengagement and participation on unethical work behavior. *Journal of Business Ethics, 104,* 59–75; Shu, L. L., Gino, F., & Bazerman, M. H. (2009). *Dishonest deed, clear conscience: Self-preservation through moral disengagement and motivated forgetting.* Harvard Business School Working Paper 09-078.

22. Janis, I. (1971, November). Groupthink: The problems of conformity. *Psychology Today,* pp. 271–279; Janis, I. (1982). *Groupthink* (2nd ed.). Boston: Houghton Mifflin; Janis, I. (1989). *Crucial decisions: Leadership in policymaking and crisis management.* New York: Free Press; Janis, I., & Mann, L. (1977). *Decision making.* New York: Free Press.

23. Milgram, S. (1965). Some conditions of obedience and disobedience to authority. *Human Relations, 18,* 57–76; Milgram redux. (2008, September). *Psychologist,* p. 478; Navarick, D. J. (2009). Reviving the Milgram

obedience paradigm in the era of informed consent. *Psychological Record, 59,* 155–170.

24. O'Brien, K. J. (2012, December 8). Dismayed at Google's privacy policy, European group is weighing censure. *The New York Times,* p. B3; Cowley, S. (2012, July 11). Google to pay $22.5 million fine for Safari privacy evasion. CNNMoney. Retrieved from http://money.cnn.com

25. McCauley, C. D., & Van Velsor, E. (Eds.). (2004). *The Center for Creative Leadership handbook of leadership development* (2nd ed.). San Francisco: Jossey-Bass, p. 4.

26. Petrick, J. A. (2008). Using the business integrity capacity model to advance business ethics education. In D. L. Swanson & D. G. Fisher (Eds.), *Advancing business ethics education* (pp. 103–124). Charlotte, NC: Information Age.

27. Narvaez, D., & Lapsley, D. K. (2005). The psychological foundations of everyday morality and moral expertise. In D. K. Lapsley & F. C. Power (Eds.), *Character psychology and character education* (pp. 140–165). Notre Dame, IN: University of Notre Dame Press.

28. Narvaez & Lapsley, p. 151.

Looking Inward

The Leader's Character

The course of any society is largely determined by the quality of its moral leadership.

—Psychologists Anne Colby and William Damon

Virtue is better than wealth.

—Kenyan proverb

What's Ahead

This chapter addresses the inner dimension of leadership ethics. To shed light rather than shadow, we need to develop strong, ethical character made up of positive traits or virtues. We promote our character development through direct interventions or indirectly by finding role models, telling and living collective stories, learning from hardship, establishing effective habits, determining a clear sense of direction, and examining our values.

Elements of Character

In football, the best defense is often a good offense. When faced with high-scoring opponents, coaches often design offensive game plans that run as much time as possible off the clock. If they're successful, they can rest their defensive players while keeping the opposing team's offensive unit on the sidelines. By building strong, ethical character, we take a similar proactive approach to dealing with our shadow sides. To keep from projecting our internal enemies and selfishness on others, we need to go on the offensive, replacing or managing our unhealthy motivations through the development of positive leadership traits or qualities called *virtues*. Interest in virtue ethics dates at least as far back as Plato, Aristotle, and Confucius. The premise of virtue ethics is simple: Good people (those of high moral character) make good moral choices. Despite its longevity, this approach has not always been popular among scholars. Only in recent years have modern philosophers turned back to it in significant numbers.[1] They've been joined by positive psychologists who argue that there is more value in identifying and promoting the strengths of individuals than in trying to repair their weaknesses (which is the approach of traditional psychologists).[2]

Character plays an important role in leadership. CEOs Franklin Raines (Fannie Mae), John Thain (Merrill Lynch), Angelo Mozilo (Countrywide Financial), and Martha Stewart (Martha Stewart Living Omnimedia) cast shadows due to greed, arrogance, dishonesty, ruthlessness, and other character failings. Their lack of virtue stands in sharp contrast to such widely admired leaders as Costco cofounder Jim Sinegal, and Southwest Airlines president emeritus Colleen Barrett. These leaders serve followers and customers and create organizational climates that foster caring and equality. (Turn to Box 3.1 to see how virtues are essential when leading in life-and-death situations.)

Proponents of virtue ethics start with the end in mind. They develop a description or portrait of the ideal person (in this case a leader) and identify the admirable qualities or tendencies that make up the character of this ethical role model. They then suggest ways in which others can acquire these virtues.

Virtues have four important features. First, they are woven into the inner lives of leaders; they are not easily developed or discarded but persist over time. Second, virtues shape the way leaders see and behave. Being virtuous makes leaders sensitive to ethical issues and encourages them to act morally. Third, virtues operate independent of the situation. A virtue may be expressed in different ways, depending on the context (what is prudent in one situation may not be in the next). Yet virtuous leaders will not abandon their principles to please followers. Fourth, virtues help leaders live better (more satisfying, more fulfilled) lives.[3] Important virtues for leaders include courage, temperance, wisdom, justice, optimism, integrity, humility, reverence, and compassion. Each of these is discussed below.

Courage

Of all the virtues, courage is no doubt the most universally admired.

—Philosopher Andre Comte-Sponville

Courage is overcoming fear in order to do the right thing.[4] Courageous leaders acknowledge the dangers they face and their anxieties. Nonetheless, they move forward despite the risks and costs. The same is true for courageous followers (see "Focus on Follower Ethics: Courageous Followership"). Courage is most often associated with acts of physical bravery and heroism, such as saving a comrade in battle or rescuing a drowning victim. Nevertheless, most courageous acts involve other forms of danger, such as when a school principal faces the wrath of parents for suspending the basketball team's leading scorer before the state tournament or when a manager confronts his boss about unauthorized spending even though he could lose his job for speaking up.[5] Such acts demonstrate moral courage, which involves living out one's personal values even when the price for doing so may be high. One common way in which leaders put moral courage into action is by intervening on behalf of others who are being victimized. For example, the human rights attorney representing jailed dissidents under a repressive regime risks persecution and jail.[6]

FOCUS ON FOLLOWER ETHICS

Courageous Followership

Ira Chaleff, who acts as a management consultant to U.S. senators and representatives, believes that courage is the most important virtue for followers. Exhibiting courage is easier for followers if they recognize that their ultimate allegiance is to the purpose and values of the organization, not to the leader. Chaleff outlines five dimensions of courageous followership that equip subordinates to meet the challenges of their role:

The Courage to Assume Responsibility. Followers must be accountable both for themselves and for the organization as a whole. Courageous followers take stock of their skills and attitudes, consider how willing they are to support and challenge their leaders, manage themselves, seek feedback and personal growth, take care of themselves, and care passionately about the organization's goals. They take initiative to change organizational culture by challenging rules and mindsets and by improving processes.

The Courage to Serve. Courageous followers support their leaders through hard, often unglamorous work. This labor takes a variety of forms, such as helping leaders conserve their energies for their most significant tasks, organizing communication to and from leaders, controlling access to leaders, shaping leaders' public images, presenting leaders with options during decision making, preparing for crises, mediating conflicts between leaders, and promoting performance reviews for leaders.

The Courage to Challenge. Inappropriate behavior damages the relationship between leaders and followers and threatens the purpose of the organization. Leaders may break the law, scream at or use demeaning language with employees, display an arrogant attitude, engage in sexual harassment, abuse drugs and alcohol, and misuse funds. Courageous followers need to confront leaders who act in a destructive manner. In some situations, just asking questions about the wisdom of a policy decision is sufficient to bring about change. In more extreme cases, followers may need to disobey unethical orders.

The Courage to Participate in Transformation. Negative behavior, when unchecked, often results in a leader's destruction. Leaders who act destructively may deny that they need to change, or they may attempt to justify their behavior. They may claim that whatever they do for themselves (e.g., embezzling, enriching themselves at the expense of stockholders) ultimately benefits the organization. To succeed in modifying their behavior patterns, leaders must admit they have a problem and acknowledge that they should change. They need to take personal responsibility and visualize the outcomes of the transformation: better health, more productive employees, higher self-esteem, restored relationships. Followers can aid in the process of transformation by drawing attention to what needs to be changed; suggesting resources, including outside facilitators; creating a supportive environment; modeling openness to change and empathy; helping contain abusive behavior; and providing positive reinforcement for positive new behaviors.

The Courage to Leave. When leaders are unwilling to change, courageous followers may take principled action by resigning from the organization. Departure is justified when a leader's behaviors clash with his or her self-proclaimed values or the values of the group, or when the leader degrades or endangers others. Sometimes leaving is not enough. In the event of serious ethical violations, followers must bring the leader's misbehavior to the attention of the public by going to the authorities or the press.

SOURCE: Chaleff, I. (2003). *The courageous follower: Standing up to and for our leaders* (2nd ed.). San Francisco: Berrett-Koehler.

People must have courage if they are to function as ethical leaders. Ethical leaders recognize that moral action is risky but continue to model ethical behavior despite the danger. They refuse to set their values aside to go along with the group, to keep silent when customers may be hurt, or to lie to investors. They strive to create ethical environments even when faced with opposition from their superiors and subordinates. They continue to carry out the organization's mission even in the face of dangers and uncertainty.

Temperance

To use things, therefore, and take pleasure in them as far as possible—not, of course, to the point where we are disgusted with them, for there is no pleasure in that—this is the part of a wise man.

—Dutch philosopher Baruch Spinoza

Moderation is key to practicing temperance, which is the ability to control emotions and pleasure.[7] The temperate person takes the middle ground between self-disgust/self-denial and self-indulgence. That means enjoying life's pleasures but not being controlled by them—for example, enjoying food without falling into gluttony, drinking but not becoming addicted to alcohol, enjoying sex without becoming trapped by desire. Temperance also means knowing one's limits and living within one's means.

Unfortunately, a great many leaders are intemperate. They are unable to control their anger and rail at subordinates, appear to have an insatiable desire for money and power, and fall victim to their need for pleasure. They may overreach by trying to know and control all that goes on in their organizations. Intemperate leaders also set unrealistically high goals for themselves and their followers and fail to live within their budgets no matter how inflated their salaries. Professional athletes far too often demonstrate the dangers of intemperance. Many end up broke at the end of their playing careers, after spending all their money on expensive cars, mansions, jewelry, homes for friends and family members, luxury clothing, and other items.

Wisdom and Prudence (Practical Wisdom)

We judge a person's wisdom by his hope.

—American poet Ralph Waldo Emerson

The goal of human life is to be good. Prudence assists us in getting there.

—Baldwin-Wallace College professors Alan Kolp and Peter Rea

Wisdom draws upon knowledge and experience to promote the common good over both the short term and the long term. Wise organizational leaders engage in six practices.[8] First, they are skilled at thinking. They are smart, drawing from a broad base of knowledge to engage in complex decision making. Second, wise leaders demonstrate high emotional capacity. They are empathetic and sensitive, recognizing differences and respecting them. Third, wise leaders are highly collaborative. These individuals work well with others and seek their benefit. Fourth, wise leaders are engaged with their organizations and their worlds. They are proactive, constantly experimenting, forming networks, and adapting to changing circumstances. Fifth, wise leaders are reflective, demonstrating depth. They are keenly aware of their values, needs, and emotions and have a sound sense of self. Sixth, wise leaders are aspiring. Well-intentioned, they pursue principled objectives and hope to make themselves, their organizations, and their world better places.

Prudence is a form of wisdom that enables individuals to discern or select the best course of action in a given situation.[9] Thomas Aquinas argued that this virtue governs the others, determining when and how the other qualities should be used. For example, prudence reveals what situations call for courage or compassion and helps us determine how to act justly. Foresight and caution are important elements of practical wisdom. Prudent leaders keep in mind the long-term consequences of their choices. As a result, they are cautious, trying not to overextend themselves and their organizations or to take unnecessary risks. Billionaire investor Warren Buffett is one example of a prudent leader. Buffett, the head of Berkshire Hathaway, sticks to a basic investment strategy, searching for undervalued companies that he can hold for at least 10 years. His lifestyle is modest as well (he still lives in the home he bought for $31,500 and earns $100,000 a year). When Buffett and his wife die, 99% of their estate will go to a charitable foundation.

Justice

> And what does the Lord require of you? To act justly, and to love mercy. And to walk humbly with your God.
>
> —Old Testament prophet Micah

Justice has two components. The first is a sense of obligation to the common good. The second is the fair and equal treatment of others.[10] A just person feels a sense of duty and strives to do his or her part as a member of the team, whether that team is a small group, an organization, or society as a whole. A just person supports equitable rules and laws. In addition, those who are driven by justice believe that all people deserve the same rights, whatever their skills or status.

Although justice is a significant virtue for everyone, regardless of her or his role, it takes on added importance for leaders. To begin, leaders who don't carry out their duties put the group or organization at risk. Furthermore, leaders have a moral obligation to consider the needs and interests of the entire group and to take the needs of the larger community into account. The rules and regulations they implement should be fair and should benefit everyone. In fact, employees often complain about injustice, and their performance suffers when they believe they are being treated unfairly.[11] Leaders also need to guarantee to followers the same rights they enjoy. They should set personal biases aside when making choices, judging others objectively and treating them accordingly. Leaders also have a responsibility to try to correct injustice and inequality caused by others. (You can rate your level of courage, temperance, prudence, and justice by completing Self-Assessment 3.1)

Optimism

Hope is not the conviction that something will turn out well, but the certainty that something makes sense, regardless of how it turns out.

—Former Czech Republic president Václav Havel

Optimists expect positive outcomes in the future even if they are currently experiencing disappointments and difficulties.[12] They are more confident than pessimists, who expect that things will turn out poorly. People who are hopeful about the future are more likely to persist in the face of adversity. When faced with stress and defeat, optimists acknowledge the reality of the situation and take steps to improve. Their pessimistic colleagues, on the other hand, try to escape problems through wishful thinking, distractions, and other means.

Optimism is an essential quality for leaders. As we'll see later in the chapter, nearly every leader experiences hardships. Those who learn and grow from these experiences will develop their character and go on to greater challenges. Those who ignore unpleasant realities stunt their ethical growth and may find their careers at an end. At the same time, leaders need to help followers deal constructively with setbacks, encouraging them to persist. Followers are more likely to rally behind optimists who appear confident and outline a positive image or vision of the group's future.

Integrity

Integrity lies at the very heart of understanding what leadership is.

—Business professors Joseph Badaracco and Richard Ellsworth

Integrity is wholeness or completeness. Leaders possessing this trait are true to themselves, reflecting consistency between what they say publicly and how they think and act privately. They live out their values and keep their promises. In other words, they practice what they preach. They are also honest in their dealings with others.[13]

Nothing undermines a leader's moral authority more quickly than lack of integrity. Followers watch the behavior of leaders closely, and one untrustworthy act can undermine a pattern of credible behavior. Trust is broken, and cynicism spreads. In an organizational setting, common "trust busters" include inconsistent messages and behavior, inconsistent rules and procedures, blaming, dishonesty, secrecy, and unjust rewards.[14] (You can measure the integrity of one of your leaders by completing Self-Assessment 3.2, the Perceived Leader Integrity Scale.) Employees at United Airlines were particularly outraged by the bonuses given to executives described in Chapter 1 because these officials had consistently promoted "shared sacrifice" during the company's bankruptcy. Performance suffers when trust is broken. Trust encourages teamwork, cooperation, and risk taking. Those who work in trusting environments are more productive and enjoy better working relationships.[15] (I'll have more to say about trust in Chapter 9.)

Humility

Let us be a little humble; let us think that the truth may not be entirely with us.

—Indian prime minister Jawaharlal Nehru

The failure of many celebrity CEOs makes a strong argument for encouraging leaders to be humble. In the 1990s, many business leaders, such as Carly Fiorina of Hewlett-Packard, Revlon's Ron Perelman, Disney's Michael Eisner, WorldCom's Bernie Ebbers, and Tyco's Dennis Kozlowski, seemed more like rock stars than corporate executives.[16] These charismatic figures became the public faces of their corporations, appearing on magazine covers and cable television shows and in company commercials. Within a few years, however, most of these celebrity leaders were gone because of scandal (some are in jail) or poor performance. Quiet leaders who shunned the spotlight replaced them and, in many instances, produced superior results.

Management professors J. Andrew Morris, Celeste Brotheridge, and John Urbanski argue that true humility strikes a balance between having an overly low and having an overly high opinion of the self.[17] It does not consist of low self-esteem, as many people think, or of underestimating one's abilities. Instead, humility is made up of three components. The first of these is self-awareness. A humble leader can objectively assess her or his own strengths and limitations. The second element is openness, which is a product of knowing one's weaknesses. Possessing humility means being open to new ideas and knowledge. The third component is transcendence. Humble leaders acknowledge that there is a power greater than the self. This prevents them from developing an inflated view of their importance while increasing their appreciation for the worth and contributions of others.

Humility has a powerful impact on ethical behavior. Humble leaders are less likely to be corrupted by power, claim excessive privileges, engage in fraud, abuse followers, and pursue selfish goals. They are more willing to serve others instead, putting the needs of followers first while acting as role models. Humility encourages leaders to build supportive relationships with followers that foster collaboration and trust. Because they know their limitations and are open to input, humble leaders are more willing to take advice that can keep them and their organizations out of trouble.

Reverence

It's not wise to lift our thoughts too high; We are human and our time is short.

—Ancient Greek playwright Euripides

University of Texas humanities professor Paul Woodruff argues that reverence, which was highly prized by the ancient Greeks and Chinese, is an important virtue for modern leaders.[18] Reverence has much in common with humility. It is the capacity to feel a sense of awe, respect, and even shame when appropriate. Awe, respect, and shame are all critical to ethical leadership, according to Woodruff. Ethical leaders serve higher causes or ideals. They are concerned not about power struggles or winners and losers but about reaching common goals. They respect the input of others, rely on persuasion rather than force, and listen to followers' ideas. Ethical leaders also feel shame when they violate group ideals. Such shame can prompt them to self-sacrifice—accepting the consequences of telling the truth, for example, or supporting unpopular people or ideas.

Reverence and humility are critical to preventing executive hubris. Hubris is the feeling of invincibility that often comes with assuming the top power position in an organization.[19] CEOS who suffer from hubris have a highly inflated view of themselves. They also believe that they are superior to the rest of humanity and that the normal rules and laws don't apply to them because of their lofty positions. Hubris has much in common with narcissism (see Chapter 1). However, hubris is specifically tied to positions of power. Those who suffer from it often equate themselves with organizational status. Organizations, followers, and society all pay a high price when leaders fall victim to hubris. For example, overconfident business leaders pay too much to acquire other companies, which then underperform. They take on too much debt and engage in more risk taking. Arrogant leaders become cruel tyrants ruling by fear and intimidation. They reject the rules of society and express contempt for any authority except their own. Former Bear Stearns CEO Jimmy Cayne was one leader who appeared to suffer from hubris. He bragged about intimidating critics. He spent much of his time out of the office playing bridge and golf while his firm was collapsing. Even after he was fired, Cayne remained convinced of his abilities, claiming that he received standing ovations from employees and board members on his final day at the office.[20]

Humility and reverence both remind leaders that they are not gods. Both emphasize that there is a power greater than the self and that we all share a common humanity. Both foster sound decisions because they remind leaders that they have limited knowledge and power. And both encourage respect for followers and the development of healthy relationships.

Compassion (Kindness, Generosity, Love)

All happiness in the world comes from serving others; all sorrow in the world comes from acting selfishly.

—Leadership expert Margaret Wheatley

Compassion and related concepts such as concern, care, kindness, generosity, and love all refer to an orientation that puts others ahead of the self.[21] Those with compassion value others regardless of whether they get anything in return from them. Compassion is an important element of altruism, an ethical perspective addressed in more detail in Chapter 5. An orientation toward others rather than the self separates ethical leaders from their unethical colleagues.[22] Ethical leaders recognize that they serve the purposes of the group. They seek power and exercise influence on behalf of followers. Unethical leaders put their own self-interests first. They are more likely to control and manipulate followers and subvert the goals of the collective. In extreme cases, this self-orientation can lead to widespread death and destruction.

Eunice Shriver provides an outstanding model of compassionate leadership.[23] Born into the wealthy and powerful Kennedy family, which included brother John, who became president of the United States, and brothers Robert and Ted, who became senators, she used her money and political clout on behalf of those with mental limitations. When John Kennedy became president, she convinced him to set up a committee to study developmental disabilities, which led to the creation of the National Institute of Child Health and Human Development. She started a camp for the intellectually disabled at her estate and cofounded the Special Olympics. The first Special Olympics meet had 1,000 contestants. Now more than 2.5 million athletes in 80 countries take part. Shriver's efforts played a major role in changing public attitudes toward those facing Down syndrome, mental retardation, and other intellectual challenges. They used to be viewed as outcasts and warehoused in mental facilities. Shriver encouraged Americans to see that, with adequate training, those with intellectual limitations could live productive lives and contribute to society.

Concern for employees plays a central role in paternalistic leadership, a leadership style popular in many parts of the world, including Asia, Latin America, Mexico, Turkey, and the Middle East.[24] In paternalism, leaders act as parental figures who demonstrate concern for the welfare of their workers both on and off the job. They may lend money to their subordinates, attend the weddings of their children, find them housing, and so on. Paternalistic leaders also set a moral example through selflessness, self-discipline, a strong work ethic, and other positive behaviors. Researchers distinguish between exploitative and benevolent paternalistic leaders. Exploitative paternalists abuse their authority and mistreat followers. In contrast, benevolent paternalists are genuinely interested in the well-being of their employees, who then pay back their supervisors with loyalty and respect. Followers of benevolent, moral paternalistic leaders are more committed to their organizations and obey company rules and procedures as well as professional and legal standards. Like their leaders, they demonstrate concern for others both inside and outside their organizations.[25] Paternalistic leadership is most effective in societies that (a) value the group over the individual, (b) accept large differences in power between leaders and followers, and (c) demonstrate low tolerance for uncertainty. (See Chapter 10 for more information on these important cultural differences.) Nonetheless, even followers in more individualistic, egalitarian societies such as the United States appreciate considerate leaders, suggesting that the benefits of benevolent paternalism may generalize across cultures.[26]

Identifying important leadership virtues is only a start. We then need to blend desirable qualities together to form a strong, ethical character—to develop what moral psychologist Augusto Blasi calls *moral identity*.[27] Those with moral identity place ethics at the center of their being. They are motivated to take moral action (e.g., be just, demonstrate compassion) because they want to act in a way that is consistent with their core identity. Developing ethical character or moral identity is far from easy, of course. At times, our personal demons will overcome even our best efforts to keep them at bay, and we will fail to live up to our ideals. We're likely to make progress in some areas while lagging in others. We may be courageous yet arrogant, reverent yet pessimistic, optimistic yet unjust. No wonder some prominent leaders reflect both moral strength and weakness. Martin Luther King, Jr., showed great courage and persistence in leading the civil rights movement but engaged in extramarital relationships. Franklin Roosevelt was revered by many of his contemporaries but had a long-standing affair with Lucy Mercer. In fact, Mercer (not Eleanor Roosevelt) was present when he died. Longtime Penn State football coach Joe Paterno's legacy was tarnished when he apparently failed to stop one of his staff from molesting boys. (See Case Study 3.2 for another example of a leader who demonstrates both moral strength and weakness.)

The poor personal behavior of political and business leaders has sparked debate about personal and public morality. One camp argues that the two cannot be separated. Another camp makes a clear distinction between the public arena and private life. According to this second group, we can be disgusted by the private behavior of politicians such as those who engage in extramarital affairs (e.g., Bill Clinton, Rudy Giuliani, former New York governor Eliot Spitzer, Nevada senator John Ensign) but vote for them anyway based on their performance in office.

I suspect that the truth lies somewhere between these extremes. We should expect contradictions in the character of leaders, not be surprised by them. Private lapses don't always lead to lapses in public judgment. On the other hand, it seems artificial to compartmentalize private and public ethics. Private tendencies can and do cross over into public decisions. Arizona State business ethics professor Marianne Jennings points out that many fallen corporate leaders (e.g., Richard Scrushy, Dennis Kozlowski, Scott Sullivan, Bernie Ebbers) cheated on their wives or divorced them to marry much younger women.[28] She suggests that executives who are dishonest with the most important people in their lives—their spouses—are likely to be dishonest with others who aren't as significant: suppliers, customers, and stockholders. Furthermore, conducting an affair distracts a leader from his or her duties and provides a poor role model for followers. That's why the Boeing board fired CEO Harry Stonecipher when members discovered that he was having an affair with a high-ranking employee.[29]

In the political arena, Franklin Roosevelt tried to deceive the public as well as his wife and family. He proposed expanding the number of Supreme Court justices from 9 to 15, claiming that the justices were old and overworked. In reality, he was angry with the Court for overturning many New Deal programs and wanted to appoint new justices who would support him. Roosevelt's dishonest attempt to pack the Supreme Court cost him a good deal of his popularity. Bill Clinton's personal moral weaknesses overshadowed many of his political accomplishments. (Turn to "Leadership Ethics at the Movies: *The Iron Lady*" to see how character played a role in the successes and failures of another political figure.)

LEADERSHIP ETHICS AT THE MOVIES • • • • • • • • •

The Iron Lady

Key Cast Members: Meryl Streep, Jim Broadbent, Alexandra Roach, Anthony Head

Synopsis: Meryl Streep won an Academy Award for her portrayal of Margaret Thatcher, the longest-serving British prime minister of the 20th century. Thatcher, a grocer's daughter, overcame great odds to become leader of the elitist, male-dominated Conservative Party and then of the nation. Near the end of her life, the former prime minister struggles with the loss of her husband, Denis

(Continued)

(Continued)

(played by Broadbent), as well as dementia. In a series of flashbacks she revisits key moments in her tumultuous political career. Her austerity policies as prime minister made her the target of domestic riots as unemployment soared; she survived one bombing carried out by the Irish Republican Army. Thatcher led Britain to victory over Argentina for possession of the Falkland Islands, a war that many considered unnecessary. Eventually she lost the support of her party (and her job as prime minister) after humiliating her cabinet members and refusing to listen to their advice.

Rating: PG-13 for some violent images and brief nudity

Themes: courage, determination, persistence, ethical decision making, the cost of power, abuse of power

Discussion Starters

1. What character traits helped Thatcher to become prime minister and to remain in office? What character traits ultimately led to her downfall?

2. What price did Thatcher pay for her rise to power?

3. At one point, Thatcher says that ideas are more important to her than feelings. Did this trait make her less sensitive to the impacts of her policies and to the opinions of her colleagues?

Fostering character is a lifelong process requiring sustained emotional, mental, and even physical effort. Strategies for developing leadership virtues can be classified as direct or indirect. Direct approaches are specifically designed to promote virtues. For example, many schools have character education programs.[30] Instead of deliberate moralizing (telling children how to behave), the best of these programs foster character development though debate, dialogue, case studies, self-evaluation, and problem solving. In psychological interventions, therapists help clients become less egocentric (and therefore more humble) by encouraging them to develop more realistic assessments of their strengths and weaknesses. Counselors suggest that their counselees convert pessimism into optimism by identifying their negative cognitions ("I am a failure") and then transforming them into more positive thoughts ("I may have failed, but I can take steps to improve"). Psychologists have also found ways to help people deal with their fears while building their courage. They first expose clients to low levels of threat and then, once the clients have mastered their initial fears, introduce them to progressively greater dangers.[31]

Although direct methods can build character, more often than not virtues develop indirectly, as by-products of other activities. In the remainder of this chapter, I will introduce a variety of indirect approaches or factors that encourage the development of leadership virtues. These include identifying role models, telling and living out shared stories, learning from hardship, cultivating good habits, creating a personal mission statement, and clarifying values.

Character Building

Finding Role Models

Character appears to be more caught than taught. We often learn what it means to be virtuous by observing and imitating exemplary leaders. That makes role models crucial to developing high moral character.[32] Eunice Shriver is one such role model; William Wilberforce, who led the fight to abolish the British slave trade, is another.

Government ethics expert David Hart argues that it is important to differentiate between different types of moral examples or exemplars.[33] Dramatic acts, such as rescuing a child from danger or landing a plane safely, capture our attention. However, if we are to develop worthy character, we need examples of those who demonstrate virtue on a daily basis. Hart distinguishes between *moral episodes* and *moral processes.* Moral episodes are made up of *moral crises* and *moral confrontations.* Moral crises are dangerous, and Hart calls those who respond to them "moral heroes." Oskar Schindler, a German industrialist, was one such hero. He risked his life and fortune to save 1,000 Jewish workers during World War II. Moral confrontations aren't dangerous, but they do involve risk and call for "moral champions." Marie Ragghianti emerged as a moral champion when, as chair of the state parole board in Tennessee, she discovered that the governor and his cronies were selling pardons and reported their illegal activities to the FBI.

Moral processes consist of *moral projects* and *moral work.* Moral projects are designed to improve ethical behavior during a limited amount of time and require "moral leaders." A moral leader sets out to reduce corruption in government, for example, or to introduce a more effective medical treatment, or to improve the working conditions of migrant farmworkers. In contrast to a moral project, moral work does not have a beginning or an end but is ongoing. The "moral worker" strives for ethical consistency throughout life. This moral exemplar might be the motor vehicle department employee who tries to be courteous to everyone who comes to the office or the neighbor who volunteers to coach youth soccer.

Hart argues that the moral worker is the most important category of moral exemplar. He points out that most of life is lived in the daily valleys, not on the heroic mountain peaks. Because character is developed over time through a series of moral choices and actions, we need examples of those who live consistent moral lives. Those who engage in moral work are better able to handle moral crises when they arise. For instance, André and Magda Trocmé committed themselves to a life of service and nonviolence as pastors in the French village of Le Chambon. When the German occupiers arrived in France in 1940, the Trocmés didn't hesitate to protect the lives of Jewish children and encouraged their congregation to do the same. This small community became an island of refuge to those threatened by the Holocaust.[34]

Anne Colby and William Damon studied 23 moral workers to determine what we can learn from their lives.[35] They found three common characteristics in their sample:

- *Certainty:* Moral exemplars are sure of what they believe and take responsibility for acting on their convictions.

- *Positivity:* Exemplars take a positive approach to life even in the face of hardship. They enjoy what they do and are optimistic about the future.

- *Unity of self and moral goals:* Exemplars don't distinguish between their personal identity and their ethical convictions. Morality is central to who they are. They believe they have no choice but to help others and consider themselves successful if they are pursuing their mission in life.

What sets exemplars apart from the rest of us is the extent of their engagement in moral issues. We make sure that our children get safely across the street. Moral exemplars, on the other hand, "drop everything not just to see their own children across the street but to feed the poor children of the world, to comfort the dying, to heal the ailing, or to campaign for human rights."[36]

Colby and Damon offer some clues about how we might develop broader moral commitments like the exemplars in their study. They note that moral capacity continues to develop well beyond childhood—some in their sample didn't take on their life's work until their 40s and beyond. Given this fact, we should strive to develop our ethical capacity throughout our lives. The researchers also found that working with others on important ethical tasks or projects fosters moral growth by exposing participants to different points of view and new moral issues. We too can benefit by collaborating with others on significant causes, such as working for better children's health care, building affordable housing, or fighting the spread of AIDS. The key is to view these tasks not as burdens but as opportunities to act on what we believe. Adopting a joyful attitude will help us remain optimistic in the face of discouragement. (See Box 3.1 for additional information on how to become a more compassionate leader.)

• • • BOX 3.1 THE JOURNEY TO HUMANITARIAN LEADERSHIP • • •

Humanitarian leaders spearhead efforts to feed the homeless, fight sex trafficking, educate street children, bring medical care to poor rural villages, and so on. Researchers Frank LaFasto and Carl Larson wondered why some individuals "take charge of helping people in need" while most of us do not. They conducted interviews with 31 humanitarian leaders ranging from age 16 to 88 from a variety of educational and social backgrounds. The investigators found that, despite their differences, their subjects followed a common path. Seven choice points marked this journey to helping others.

Choice 1: Leveraging Life Experiences. Humanitarian leaders reflect on their life stories. They develop empathy for the needs of others through (1) role models (parents, teachers, religious leaders, friends) and positive values, such as caring for the poor or serving others; (2) troubling awareness about a societal problem like sex abuse or lack of clean water; or (3) traumatic personal experiences, such as the death of parents or a cancer diagnosis.

Choice 2: Having a Sense of Fairness. Humanitarians are convinced that the world is divided into those who are fortunate and those who are not. The disadvantaged are victims of circumstance and are therefore worthy of help. To make the world fairer, the humanitarian leader believes in providing opportunities for those who have been denied such access by fate.

Choice 3: Believing That We Can Matter. Those out to assist others aren't overwhelmed by the need. Instead, they focus on helping individuals. Meeting the needs of one person is the first step to addressing the broader problem—whether that is poverty, substandard housing, or disease. Humanitarian leaders believe that they have something to offer and know what they can and cannot do to contribute. They try to make the future better for those in need.

(Continued)

(Continued)

Choice 4: Being Open to Opportunity. Compassionate leaders are inclined to say yes to possibilities instead of automatically saying no. They have an external focus. They are attuned to the needs of others, and their impulse is to respond because they have a clear sense of life's direction. Unlike many people, humanitarian leaders align their actions with their convictions.

Choice 5: Taking the First Small Step. Every leader interviewed by LaFasto and Larson reported a pivotal or defining moment when he or she first responded to the impulse to help. Humanitarian leaders don't let the size of the problem discourage them; rather, they do something, no matter how small. While they don't know where their efforts will lead, they still make the commitment to act. Take the case of Ryan Hreljac. Ryan started his humanitarian career as a 6-year-old by trying to raise $70 to provide one well for a village in a developing nation. This small step led to the creation of the Ryan's Well Foundation, which has provided sanitation and clean water for three-quarters of a million people around the world.

Choice 6: Persevering. Those who tackle difficult social problems can expect to encounter a great deal of frustration. But they believe in what they are doing and are convinced that reaching their goals is worth the cost. Humanitarian leaders are also adaptable, often turning obstacles into opportunities. If funding sources dry up, they find new, more stable ones, for example. They maintain their positive focus by taking heart in short-term victories and remaining convinced they can make a difference.

Choice 7: Leading the Way. The passion of humanitarian leaders draws others to their causes. Their enthusiasm, energy, and optimism are contagious. Others join in, and movements are born.

LaFasto and Larson conclude that we all have the potential to become humanitarian leaders. However, to start down the path to socially responsible leadership, we must first answer yes to this question: Do I feel a sense of responsibility for helping others?

SOURCE: LaFasto, F., & Larson, C. (2012). *The humanitarian leader in each of us: Seven choices that shape a socially responsible life.* Thousand Oaks, CA: Sage.

Telling and Living Collective Stories

Character building never takes place in a vacuum. Virtues are more likely to take root when nurtured by families, schools, governments, and religious bodies. These collectives impart values and encourage self-discipline, caring, and other virtues through the telling of narratives or stories. Shared narratives both explain and persuade. They provide a framework for understanding the world and, at the same time, challenge us to act in specified ways. For example, one of the most remarkable features of the American political system is the orderly transition of power from president to president.[37] George Washington set this precedent by voluntarily stepping down as the country's first leader. His story, told in classrooms, books, and films, helps explain why the current electoral system functions smoothly. Furthermore, modern presidents and presidential candidates follow Washington's example, as in the case of the 2000 election. Although he garnered more of the popular vote than George W. Bush, Al Gore conceded defeat after the Supreme Court rejected his court challenge.

Character growth comes from living up to the roles we play in the stories we tell. According to virtue ethicist Alasdair MacIntyre, "I can only answer the question 'What am I to do?' if I can answer the prior question, 'Of what story or stories do I find myself a part?'"[38] Worthy narratives bring out the best in us, encouraging us to suppress our inner demons and to cast light instead of shadow.

In the introduction to this text, I argued that we could learn about leadership ethics from fictional characters as well as from real-life ones. Ethics professor C. David Lisman offers several reasons the ethical models contained in literature can provide a moral education that helps us to nurture our virtues.[39] Lisman focuses on literature, but his observations also apply to other forms of fiction (films, plays, television shows). In Lisman's estimation, fiction helps us understand our possibilities and limits. We can try to deny the reality of death, the fact that we're aging, and that there are factors outside our control. However, novels and short stories force us to confront these issues.

Literature explores many common human themes, such as freedom of choice, moral responsibility, conflict between individual and society, conflict between individual conscience and society's rules, and self-understanding. Fiction writers help us escape our old ways of thinking and acting. Their best works expand our emotional capacity, enabling us to respond more fully to the needs of others. They also provide us with opportunities to practice moral reflection and judgment by evaluating the actions of important characters.[40] In sum, almost any story about leaders, whether real or fictional, can teach us something about ethical and unethical behavior. Moral exemplars can be found in novels, television series, and feature films as well as in news stories, biographies, documentaries, and historical records.

Learning From Hardship

Hardship and suffering also play a role in developing character. The leaders we admire the most are often those who have endured the greatest hardships. Nelson Mandela, Václav Havel, and Aleksandr Solzhenitsyn served extended prison terms, for instance, and Moses endured 40 years in exile and 40 in the wilderness with his people.

Perhaps no other American leader has faced as much hardship as did Abraham Lincoln. He was defeated in several elections before winning the presidency. Because of death threats, he had to slip into Washington, D.C., to take office. He presided over the slaughter of many of his countrymen and -women in the Civil War, lost a beloved son, and was ridiculed by Northerners (some in his cabinet) and Southerners alike. However, all these trials seemed to deepen both his commitment to the Union and his spirituality. His second inaugural address is considered to be one of the finest political and theological statements ever produced by a public official. (Turn to Case Study 3.3 for another example of a leader who faced and overcame hardship.)

Trainers at the Center for Creative Leadership have identified hardship as one of the factors contributing to leadership development. Leaders develop the fastest when they encounter situations that stretch or challenge them. Hardships, along with novelty, difficult goals, and conflict, challenge people. CCL staffers Russ Moxley and Mary Lynn Pulley believe that hardships differ from other challenging experiences because they are unplanned, are experienced in an intensely personal way, and involve loss.[41]

Research conducted by the CCL reveals that leaders experience five common categories of hardship events. Each type of hardship can drive home important lessons.

- *Business mistakes and failures:* Examples of this type of hardship event include losing an important client, failed products and programs, broken relationships, and bankruptcies. These experiences help leaders build stronger working relationships, recognize their limitations, and profit from their mistakes.

- *Career setbacks:* Missed promotions, unsatisfying jobs, demotions, and firings make up this hardship category. Leaders faced with these events lose control over their careers, their sense of self-efficacy or competence, and their professional identity. Career setbacks function as wake-up calls, providing feedback about weaknesses. They encourage leaders to take more responsibility for managing their careers and to identify the type of work that is most meaningful to them.

- *Personal trauma:* Examples of personal trauma include divorce, cancer, death, and difficult children. These experiences, which are a natural part of life, drive home the point that leaders (who are used to being in charge) can't run the world around them. As a result, they may strike a better balance between work and home responsibilities, learn how to accept help from others, and endure in the face of adversity.

- *Problem employees:* Troubled workers include those who steal, defraud, can't perform, or perform well only part of the time. In dealing with problem employees, leaders often lose the illusion that they can turn these people around. They may also learn how important it is to hold followers to consistently high standards and become more skilled at confronting subordinates about problematic behavior.

- *Downsizing:* Downsizing has much in common with career setbacks, but in this type of hardship leaders lose their jobs through no fault of their own. Downsizing can help leaders develop coping skills and force them to take stock of their lives and careers. Those carrying out the layoffs can also learn from the experience by developing greater empathy for the feelings of followers.

Being exposed to a hardship is no guarantee that you'll learn from the experience. Some ambitious leaders never get over being passed over for a promotion, for instance, and become embittered and cynical. Benefiting from adversity takes what Warren Bennis and Robert Thomas call "adaptive capacity." Bennis and Thomas found that, regardless of generation, effective leaders come through *crucible moments* that have profound impacts on their development.[42] These intense experiences include failures such as losing an election but also encompass more positive events, such as climbing a mountain or finding a mentor. They generally fall into three categories. *New territory crucibles,* like taking an overseas assignment or serving in a new organizational role, put leaders into stretching experiences. *Reversal crucibles* involve loss, defeat, or failure. *Suspension crucibles* involve extended periods of reflection or contemplation, such as between promotions and jobs. The accomplished leaders Bennis and Thomas sampled experienced just as many crises as everyone else but were able to learn important principles and skills from their struggles. This knowledge enabled them to move on to more complex challenges.

Successful leaders see hard times as positive high points of their lives. In contrast, less successful leaders are defeated and discouraged by similar events. To put it another way, effective leaders tell a different story than their ineffective counterparts. They identify hardships as stepping stones, not as insurmountable obstacles. We too can enlarge our adaptive capacity by paying close attention to our personal narratives, defining difficult moments in our lives as learning opportunities rather than as permanent obstacles. To see how you can learn from a specific failure, take the following steps:

1. Identify a significant failure from your professional or personal life and summarize the failure in a sentence (be sure to use the word *failure*).

2. Describe how you felt and thought about the failure immediately after it happened.

3. Move forward in time to identify any positive outcomes that came out of the failure, including skills you acquired, lessons you learned, and any relationships you established.

4. Identify how the failure changed or shaped you as a person, noting any new traits or attitudes you have adopted and whether you are any more mature now than you were before the failure event.[43]

Developing Habits

One of the ways in which we build character is by doing well through the development of habits.[44] Habits are repeated routines or practices designed to foster virtuous behavior. Examples of good habits include working hard, telling the truth, giving to charity, standing up to peer pressure, and always turning in original work for school assignments. Every time we engage in one of these habits, it leaves a trace or residue. Over time, these residual effects become part of our personality and are integrated into our character. We also become more competent at demonstrating virtues. Take courage, for example. To develop the courage and skill to confront our bosses about their unethical behavior, we may first need to practice courage by expressing our opinions to them on less critical issues such as work policies and procedures.[45]

Business consultant Stephen Covey developed the most popular list of positive habits. Not only did he author the best-selling book *The Seven Habits of Highly Effective People,* but thousands of businesses, nonprofit groups, and government agencies have participated in workshops offered by the Covey Center for Leadership.[46] In his best-seller, Covey argues that effectiveness is based on such character principles as integrity, fairness, service, excellence, and growth. The habits are the tools that enable leaders and followers to develop these characteristics. Covey defines a habit as a combination of knowledge (what to do and why to do it), skill (how to do it), and motivation (wanting to do it). Leadership development is an "inside-out" process that starts within the leader and then moves outward to affect others. The seven habits of effective and ethical leaders are as follows:

> *Habit 1: Be Proactive.* Proactive leaders realize that they can choose how they respond to events. When faced with career setbacks, they try to grow from these experiences instead of feeling victimized by them. Proactive people also take the initiative by opting to attack problems instead of accepting defeat. Their language reflects their willingness to accept rather than avoid responsibility. A proactive leader makes statements such as "Let's examine our options" and "I can create a strategic plan." A reactive leader, in contrast, makes comments such as "The organization won't go along with that idea," "I'm too old to change," and "That's just who I am."
>
> *Habit 2: Begin With the End in Mind.* This habit is based on the notion that "all things are created twice." First we get a mental picture of what we want to accomplish, and then we follow through on our plans. If we're unhappy with the

current direction of our lives, we can generate new mental images and goals, a process Covey calls "rescripting." Creating personal and organizational mission statements is one way to identify the results we want and thus control the type of life we create. (I'll talk more about how to create a mission statement in the next section.) Covey urges leaders to center their lives on inner principles such as fairness and human dignity rather than on such external factors as family, money, friends, or work.

Habit 3: Put First Things First. A leader's time should be organized around priorities. Too many leaders spend their days coping with emergencies, mistakenly believing that urgent means important. Meetings, deadlines, and interruptions place immediate demands on their time, but other less pressing activities, such as relationship building and planning, are more important in the long run. Effective leaders carve out time for significant activities by identifying their most important roles, selecting their goals, creating schedules that enable them to reach their objectives, and modifying plans when necessary. They also know how to delegate tasks and have the courage to say no to requests that don't fit their priorities.

Habit 4: Think Win–Win. Those with a win–win perspective take a cooperative approach to communication, convinced that the best solution benefits both parties. The win–win habit is based on these dimensions: character (integrity, maturity, and a belief that the needs of everyone can be met), trusting relationships committed to mutual benefit, performance or partnership agreements that spell out conditions and responsibilities, organizational systems that fairly distribute rewards, and principled negotiation processes in which both sides generate possible solutions and then select the one that works best.

Habit 5: Seek First to Understand, Then to Be Understood. Ethical leaders put aside their personal concerns to engage in empathetic listening. They seek to understand, not to evaluate, advise, or interpret. Empathetic listening is an excellent way to build a trusting relationship. Covey uses the metaphor of the emotional bank account to illustrate how trust develops. Principled leaders make deposits in the emotional bank account by showing kindness and courtesy, keeping commitments, paying attention to small details, and seeking to understand. These strong relational reserves help prevent misunderstandings and make it easier to resolve any problems that do arise.

Habit 6: Synergize. Synergy creates a solution that is greater than the sum of its parts and uses right-brain thinking to generate a third, previously undiscovered alternative. Synergistic, creative solutions are generated in trusting relationships—those with full emotional bank accounts—where participants value their differences.

Habit 7: Sharpen the Saw. "Sharpening the saw" refers to the continual renewal of the physical, mental, social or emotional, and spiritual dimensions of the self. Healthy leaders care for their bodies through exercise, good nutrition, and stress management. They encourage their mental development by reading good literature and writing thoughtful letters and journal entries. They create meaningful relationships with others and nurture their inner or spiritual values through study or meditation and time in nature. Continual renewal, combined with the use of the first six habits, creates an upward spiral of character improvement.

Developing Mission Statements

Developing a mission statement is the best way to keep the end or destination in mind. Leaders who cast light have a clear sense of what they hope to accomplish and seek to achieve worthwhile goals. For example, Abraham Lincoln was out to preserve the Union, Nelson Mandela wanted to abolish apartheid, and Mother Teresa devoted her whole life to reducing suffering.

Author and organizational consultant Laurie Beth Jones asserts that, to be useful, a mission statement should be short (no more than a sentence long), easily understood and communicated, and committed to memory.[47] According to Jones, developing a personal mission statement begins with personal assessment. Take a close look at how your family has influenced your values and interests. Identify your strengths and determine what makes you unique (what Jones calls your "unique selling point"). Once you've isolated your gifts and unique features, examine your motivation. What situations make you excited or angry? Chances are, your mission will be related to the factors that arouse your passion or enthusiasm (teaching, writing, coaching, or selling, for example).

Jones outlines a three-part formula for constructing a mission statement. Start with the phrase "My mission is to" and record three action verbs that best describe what you want to do (e.g., *accomplish, build, finance, give, discuss*). Next, plug in a principle, value, or purpose that you could commit the rest of your life to (joy, service, faith, creativity, justice). Finish by identifying the group or cause that most excites you (real estate, design, sports, women's issues). Your final statement ought to inspire you and should direct all your activities, both on and off the job.

Leadership consultant Juana Bordas offers an alternative method or path for discovering personal leadership purpose based on Native American culture. Native Americans discovered their life purposes while on vision quests. Vision cairns guided members of some tribes. These stone piles served both as directional markers and as reminders that others had passed this way before. Bordas identifies nine cairns or markers for creating personal purpose.[48]

Cairn 1: Call Your Purpose; Listen for Guidance. All of us have to be silent in order to listen to our intuition. Periodically you will need to withdraw from the noise of everyday life and reflect on such questions as "What am I meant to do?" and "How can I best serve?"

Cairn 2: Find a Sacred Place. A sacred place is a quiet place for reflection. It can be officially designated as sacred (e.g., a church or meditation garden) or merely a spot that encourages contemplation, such as a stream, park, or favorite chair.

Cairn 3: See Time as Continuous; Begin With the Child and Move With the Present. Our past has a great impact on where we'll head in the future. Patterns of behavior are likely to continue. Bordas suggests that you should examine the impact of your family composition, gender, geography, cultural background, and generational influences. A meaningful purpose will be anchored in the past but will remain responsive to current conditions such as diversity, globalization, and technological change.

Cairn 4: Identify Special Skills and Talents; Accept Imperfections. Take inventory by examining your major activities and jobs and evaluating your strengths. For example, how are your people skills? Technical knowledge? Communication abilities? Consider how you might further develop your aptitudes and abilities. Also take stock of your significant failures. What did they teach you about your limitations? What did you learn from them?

Cairn 5: Trust Your Intuition. Sometimes we need to act on our hunches and emotions. You may decide to turn down a job that doesn't feel right, for instance, in order to accept a position that seems to be a better fit.

Cairn 6: Open the Door When Opportunity Knocks. Be ready to respond to opportunities that are out of your control, such as a new job assignment or a request to speak or write. Ask yourself whether this possibility will better prepare you for leadership or fit in with what you're trying to do in life.

Cairn 7: Find Your Passion and Make It Happen. Passion energizes us for leadership and gives us stamina. Discover your passion by imagining the following scenarios: If you won the lottery, what would you continue to do? How would you spend your final six months on Earth? What would sustain you for a hundred more years?

Cairn 8: Write Your Life Story; Imagine a Great Leader. Turn your life into a story that combines elements of reality and fantasy. Imagine yourself as an effective leader and carry your story out into the future. What challenges did you overcome? What dreams did you fulfill? How did you reach your final destination?

Cairn 9: Honor Your Legacy, One Step at a Time. Your purpose is not static but will evolve and expand over time. If you're a new leader, you're likely to exert limited influence. That influence will expand as you develop your knowledge and skills. You may manage only a couple of people now, but in a few years you may be responsible for an entire department or division.

Researchers at the Gallup Organization offer a tool for determining your strengths, a step that both Jones and Bordas argue is key to determining your purpose.[49] They report that people who concentrate on developing their abilities, instead of addressing their weaknesses, are much more engaged with their jobs and report a higher quality of life. Using the StrengthsFinder instrument, Gallup researchers have isolated 34 common talents. Representative talents include empathy, connector, discipline, learner, achiever, ideation, and self-assurance. But talent alone is not enough. In order to turn a natural talent into a strength, which is the ability to perform consistently at a high level, you must develop the talent by acquiring new information, practicing, and developing new skills. The Gallup investigators cluster talents into four domains of leadership strength.[50] Chances are, as a leader, you will find yourself strongest in (1) executing (implementing, making ideas reality), (2) influencing (helping your team reach a wider audience through speaking up and persuading), (3) relationship building (holding the group together), or (4) strategic thinking (focusing on the future).

Identifying Values

If a mission statement identifies our final destination, then our values serve as a moral compass to guide us on our journey. Values provide a frame of reference, helping us to set priorities and to distinguish between right and wrong. There are all sorts of values. For example, I value fuel economy (I like spending less on gas), so I drive a small, fuel-efficient pickup truck. However, ethical decision making is concerned primarily with identifying and implementing moral values. Moral values are directly related to judgments about what is appropriate or inappropriate behavior. I value honesty, for instance, so I choose not to lie. I value privacy, so I condemn Internet retailers who gather personal information about me without my permission.

There are two ways to identify or clarify the values you hold. You can generate a list from scratch, or you can rate the values in a list supplied by someone else. If brainstorming a list of important values seems a daunting task, you might try the following exercise developed by James Kouzes and Barry Posner. The "credo memo" asks you to spell out the important values that underlie your philosophy of leadership.

> Imagine that your organization has afforded you the chance to take a six-month sabbatical, all expenses paid. You will be going to a beautiful

island where the average temperature is about eighty degrees Fahrenheit during the day. The sun shines in a brilliant sky, with a few wisps of clouds. A gentle breeze cools the island down in the evening, and a light rain clears the air. You wake up in the morning to the smell of tropical flowers.

You may not take any work along on this sabbatical. And you will not be permitted to communicate to anyone at your office or plant—not by letter, phone, fax, e-mail, or other means. There will be just you, a few good books, some music, and your family or a friend.

But before you depart, those with whom you work need to know something. They need to know the principles that you believe should guide their actions in your absence. They need to understand the values and beliefs that you think should steer their decision making and action taking. You are permitted no long reports, however. Just a one-page memorandum.

If given this opportunity, what would you write on your one-page credo memo? Take out one piece of paper and write that memo.[51]

Examples of values that have been included in credo memos include "operate as a team," "listen to one another," "celebrate successes," "seize the initiative," "trust your judgment," and "strive for excellence." These values can be further clarified through dialogue with coworkers. Many discussions in organizations (e.g., how to select subcontractors, when to fire someone, how to balance the needs of various stakeholders) have an underlying value component. Listen for the principles that shape your opinions and the opinions of others.

Working with a list of values can also be useful. Psychologist Gordon Allport identifies six major value types. People can be categorized based on how they organize their lives around each of the following value sets.[52] Prototypes are examples of occupations that fit best into a given value orientation.

- *Theoretical:* Theoretical people are intellectuals who seek to discover the truth and pride themselves on being objective and rational. Prototypes: research scientists, engineers.

- *Economic:* Usefulness is the most important criterion for those driven by economic values. They are interested in production, marketing, economics, and accumulating wealth. Prototype: small business owners.

- *Aesthetic:* Aesthetic thinkers value form and harmony. They enjoy each event as it unfolds, judging the experience based on its symmetry or harmony. Prototypes: artists, architects.

- *Social:* Love of others is the highest value for social leaders and followers. These "people persons" view others as ends, not means, and are kind and unselfish. Prototype: social workers.

- *Political:* Power drives political people. They want to accumulate and exercise power and enjoy the recognition that comes from being in positions of influence. Prototypes: senators, governors.

- *Religious:* Religious thinkers seek unity through understanding and relating to the cosmos as a whole. Prototypes: pastors, rabbis, Muslim clerics.

Identifying your primary value orientation is a good way to avoid situations that could cause you ethical discomfort. If you have an economic bent, you will want a job (often in a business setting) where you solve real-life problems. On the other hand, if you love people, you may be uncomfortable working for a business that puts profits first.

Some well-meaning writers and consultants make values the be-all and end-all of ethical decision making. They assume that groups will prosper if they develop a set of lofty, mutually shared values. However, having worthy values doesn't mean that individuals, groups, or organizations will live by these principles. Other factors—time pressures, faulty assumptions, corrupt systems—undermine their influence. Values, though critical, have to be translated into action. Furthermore, our greatest struggles come from choosing between two good values. Many corporate leaders value both good customer service and high product quality, but what do they do when reaching one of these goals means sacrificing the other? Pushing to get a product shipped to satisfy a customer may force the manufacturing division into cutting corners in order to meet the deadline. Resolving dilemmas such as these takes more than value clarification; we also need some standards for determining ethical priorities. With that in mind, I will identify ethical decision-making principles in Chapters 5 and 6. But first we need to confront one final shadow caster—evil—in Chapter 4.

IMPLICATIONS AND APPLICATIONS

- Character is integral to effective leadership, often making the difference between success and failure.

- Virtues are positive leadership qualities or traits that help us manage our shadow sides.

- As a leader, strive to to develop courage (overcoming fear in order to do the right thing), temperance (self-control), wisdom (drawing on knowledge and experience to pursue the common good) and prudence (practical wisdom), justice (obligation to the common good, treating others equally and fairly), optimism (expectation of positive outcomes in the future), integrity (wholeness, completeness, consistency), humility (self-awareness, openness, a sense of transcendence), reverence (a sense of awe, respect, and shame), and compassion (kindness, generosity, love).

- Strive for consistency but don't be surprised by contradictions in your character or in the character of others. Become more tolerant of yourself and other leaders. At the same time, recognize that a leader's private behavior often influences his or her public decisions.

- Indirect approaches that build character include identifying role models, telling and living out shared stories, learning from hardship, cultivating habits, creating a personal mission statement, and clarifying values.

- Never underestimate the power of a good example. Be on the lookout for real and fictional ethical role models.

- Shared narratives nurture character development, encouraging you to live up to the role you play in the collective story.

- Hardships are an inevitable part of life and leadership. The sense of loss associated with these events can provide important feedback, spur self-inspection, encourage you to develop coping strategies, force you to reorder your priorities, and nurture your compassion. However, to benefit from them you must see challenges as learning opportunities that prepare you for future leadership responsibilities.

- Adopting positive habits can speed the development of character. Seek to be proactive, begin with the end in mind, organize around priorities, strive for cooperation, listen for understanding, develop synergistic solutions, and engage in continual self-renewal.

- Having an ultimate destination will encourage you to stay on your ethical track. Develop a personal mission statement that reflects your strengths and passions. Use your values as a moral compass to keep you from losing your way.

FOR FURTHER EXPLORATION, CHALLENGE, AND SELF-ASSESSMENT

1. Which virtue is most important for leaders? Defend your choice.

2. Can the private and public morals of leaders be separated? Try to reach a consensus on this question in a group.

3. What steps can you take to develop a more positive outlook about future events?

4. Brainstorm a list of moral exemplars. What does it take to qualify for your list?

How would you classify these role models according to the types described in this chapter?

5. Reflect on the ways in which a particular shared narrative has shaped your worldview and behavior. Write up your conclusions.

6. Interview a leader you admire. Determine his or her crucible moment and capacity to learn from that experience.

7. Rate yourself on each of the seven habits of effective people and develop a plan for addressing your weaknesses. Explore the habits further through reading and training seminars.

8. Develop a personal mission statement using the guidelines provided by Jones or Bordas.

9. Complete the credo memo exercise above if you haven't already done so. Encourage others in your work group or organization to do the same, and then compare your statements. Use this as an opportunity to engage in a dialogue about values.

STUDENT STUDY SITE

Visit the student study site at **www.sagepub.com/johnsonmecl5e** to access full SAGE journal articles for further research and information on key chapter topics.

CASE STUDY 3.1

Virtue and In Extremis Leadership

In extremis leaders provide followers with purpose and direction in combat, firefighting, hostage rescue, mountain climbing, wildlife photography, skydiving, and other life-and-death situations. Such leaders voluntarily put themselves in extreme danger. They are successful when they help their teams emerge alive and healthy. To determine the characteristics of leaders who operate at "the point of death," Colonel Thomas Kolditz of the U.S. Military Academy at West Point and his colleagues participated in high-risk activities and conducted interviews with in extremis leaders. They visited Iraq to interview U.S. soldiers and Iraqi prisoners of war and jumped with parachute teams. In addition, they talked to SWAT team chiefs from the New York City Police Department and the San Francisco FBI office, mountain climbing guides, and others. Kolditz and his team

discovered that in extremis contexts are inherently motivating because of their risk. Hostile conditions demand a learning orientation because only those who continually scan the environment and respond will survive. Not surprisingly, competence is critical in dangerous situations. Followers demand that their leaders know what they are doing; competence is the foundation for trusting leader–follower relationships.

Kolditz reports that character, like competence, is also essential to the survival of in extremis leaders and followers. The leaders he studied demonstrated several virtues:

- *Courage:* In extremis leaders choose to put themselves in danger and take on more than their fair share of risks. Said one SWAT team leader, "If you put the plan together and you're not comfortable being up there with a foot through the door, then what the hell is up?"[1]

- *Optimism:* Both optimism and fear are contagious. Successful leaders offer hope that keeps the group going. Ineffective leaders allow their groups to wallow in despair, which saps the will to survive.

- *Integrity:* Followers in high-risk situations want consistent leaders who are transparent about the challenges facing the group. They are quick to note inconsistencies in leaders' behavior.

- *Loyalty:* In extremis leaders are intensely loyal to their followers, constantly looking out for their welfare. They may deny themselves rations so that subordinates may eat, for example. At other times they share in the discomfort of followers. One Christmas morning, the commander of the U.S. 25th Infantry Division military unit left the comfort of headquarters in Bagram, Afghanistan, and flew to a remote military base. When he arrived, he sent two junior officers stationed at the base back to Bagram to enjoy the holiday. He stayed, spending the day in the back of a truck with soldiers on patrol. Said one soldier, "To sit in a cav truck in one of the worst seats and ride with us, to come and pull guard with us ... makes lower enlisted soldiers like myself feel good about him as our leader."[2]

- *Humility:* In extremis leaders generally live modestly and don't earn that much more than their followers. They are motivated by their commitment to the group's mission, not wealth. Their humility is particularly apparent when a team member dies. Leaders treat the fallen, no matter how lowly their status or rank, with respect. They recognize that when someone is killed or seriously injured, "the leader has to be small so the focus of the activity can make the decedent or the hospitalized person big."[3]

Kolditz argues that we can apply lessons from in extremis leadership to other contexts. Business, education, government, and nonprofit leaders can become more effective through communicating optimism, sharing risk with followers, putting the needs of others before their own safety and comfort, living modestly, and so on. Even leaders who don't seek danger may discover that danger finds them. Nearly all organizations face crises—natural disasters, crime, accidents—that threaten the health of members and the group as a whole (see Chapter 11). When disaster strikes, executives need to demonstrate the virtues of successful in extremis leaders if their organizations are to survive.

Discussion Probes

1. Have you ever followed someone in a life-or-death situation? If so, what qualities (competencies, virtues) did you look for in your leader?

2. Have you ever been an in extremis leader? If so, what qualities (competencies, virtues) did you demonstrate?

3. Do you want a career in a high-risk occupation such as law enforcement, the military, or firefighting? If so, why are you interested in pursuing a dangerous profession?

4. Have you ever been part of an organization that experienced a crisis and/or the death or serious injury of one or more its members? If so, how did leaders respond to the crisis or tragedy? What virtues did they demonstrate?

5. How can we prepare ourselves to function effectively in high-risk situations?

Notes

1. Kolditz, T. A. (2005, Fall). The in extremis leader. *Leader to Leader,* pp. 6–18, p. 11.

2. Kolditz, T. A., & Brazil, D. M. (2005). Authentic leadership in *in extremis* settings: A concept for extraordinary leaders in exceptional situations. In W. L. Gardner, B. J. Avolio, & F. O. Walumbwa (Eds.), *Authentic leadership theory and practice: Origins, effects and development* (pp. 345–356). Amsterdam: Elsevier, p. 346.

3. Kolditz, T. A. (2007). *In extremis leadership: Leading as if your life depended on it.* San Francisco: Jossey-Bass. p. 143.

CASE STUDY 3.2

The Spectacular Rise and Fall of a Humanitarian Hero

For much of the past decade Greg Mortenson was an American hero. Mortenson, a former nurse and mountain climber, founded the Central Asia Institute (CAI), which builds schools, primarily for girls, in Afghanistan and Pakistan. His book *Three Cups of Tea* tells the story of how Mortenson survived a harrowing mountain descent with the help of the townspeople of the Afghan village of Korphe. He then decided to build a school in honor of his disabled sister to repay the villagers. Later, according to the book, Mortenson was held captive by the Taliban and continued to build schools throughout one of the harshest and most remote regions on earth. The book's title comes from the fact that effective humanitarian work in Central Asia takes community buy-in. Relationships must be built first; business cannot be conducted until the third cup of tea is shared.

Three Cups of Tea spent 220 weeks on *The New York Times* nonfiction best-seller list from 2007 to 2011, selling an estimated 4 million copies. Some colleges made the book required reading, as did the U.S. military, which adopted Mortenson's methods in Central Asia. Sales of the book, as well as its sequel, *Stones Into Schools,* made Mortenson a celebrity. He appeared on *The Oprah Winfrey Show, Charlie Rose,* and other national television programs, spoke at the Pentagon, and crisscrossed the nation giving presentations. He made more than 400 speeches in 140 cities in one eight-month period alone. The humanitarian hero was awarded Pakistan's Silver Star (the nation's third-highest civilian honor) and was nominated for the Nobel Peace Prize. President Barack Obama, who received the Nobel Peace Prize in 2009, contributed $100,000 from the award to CAI.

While Mortenson's public popularity soared, there were indications of trouble behind the scenes. Three CAI board members were ousted in a power struggle over

Mortenson's management of the charity in 2002, and a financial manager resigned after only a year on the job due to clashes over a lack of financial controls. Events reached a crisis point in 2011 when author Jon Krakauer, a former CAI board member and donor, published an e-book titled *Three Cups of Deceit*. Krakauer alleges that many of the events described in *Three Cups of Tea* never happened. For example, Mortenson never spent time recovering in the village of Korphe after his climb but stayed in a hotel instead. He was never held captive by the Taliban; rather, he was the guest of friendly villagers. (The Taliban was not operating in the area at the time.) Mortenson claimed that he held the hand of Mother Teresa, but at the time this purportedly happened, she had already been dead for three years.

60 Minutes, the television newsmagazine, ran an exposé of Mortenson and CAI. The show's producers visited 30 schools supposedly funded by the charity and found that some hadn't been constructed while others stood empty or were being used to store hay. The attorney general of Montana, where CAI is headquartered, charged Mortenson with misappropriating funds. CAI purchased copies of *Three Cups of Tea*, paying full price instead of getting a discount so that the royalties went to Mortenson. He was supposed to donate the equivalent of the royalties he received to CAI but did not. Greg bought luxury items and vacations for himself and his family using CAI credit cards. He also engaged in double-dipping, billing CAI for travel expenses for events at which he was paid up to $30,000 to speak. The Montana attorney general found that CAI invested only 40% of the donations it received to building schools, spending 60%

on promoting Mortenson's book and on administrative expenses.

Mortenson agreed to repay $1 million to the charity and lost his position as director of CAI, although he remains a CAI employee. The Montana attorney general forced CAI to expand its board of directors by adding seven new members (by 2009 the board had shrunk to just Mortenson and two loyal supporters).

It would be easy to blame Mortenson's ethical fall on underlying character flaws like lack of integrity, greed, and what Krakauer calls "an apparently insatiable hunger for esteem."[1] And Mortenson admits that he has a number of faults, including extreme shyness, chronic disorganization, and a near- total lack of managerial skills. However, CAI's founder also has a number of admirable qualities, such as compassion, justice, optimism, and persistence. He has labored since 1996 to help the children of Central Asia. There is no doubt that a number of CAI schools are operating, benefiting local communities. Reporters for *The Christian Science Monitor*, for instance, found that CAI was active building schools and providing computers in the Badakhshan province of Afghanistan. Local teachers in the region expressed their gratitude to "Mister Greg."

Mortenson may have been partially the victim of his own success. He likely would have remained an obscure humanitarian had the United States not gone to war in Afghanistan. The nation was looking for a feel-good story against the background of the difficult war and Mortenson provided it. The flood of popularity, fame, and funds generated by book sales overwhelmed the charity and its founder. CAI was small and then ballooned rapidly, seeing contributions skyrocket. Mortenson may have felt the need to embellish details to keep the donations pouring in. (He admits that some events in *Three Cups of Tea* were compressed and blames his coauthor, David Oliver Relin, who later committed suicide, for taking too many liberties with his story.) Maybe he felt that he was so important to the cause that his expenditures were justified.

Greg Mortenson's rise and fall may have as much to say about American culture as it does about CAI's founder. We make celebrities out of "do-gooders" just as we do out of athletes and actors, tempting humanitarians with lucrative book contracts, television appearances, and speaking engagements. In search of heroes, we are all too willing to overlook the fact that even saints have flaws. Mortenson was never as perfect as the public made him out to be. Perhaps he is not as imperfect as many now believe.

Discussion Probes

1. How much was Mortenson's failure the result of poor character and how much was the product of other factors?

2. Which poses the greater danger to a leader's character, success or failure?

3. Why do we often have difficulty acknowledging that our heroes have flaws?

4. Is Mortenson now completely discredited as a spokesperson for building schools in Central Asia?

5. As a donor, what ethical responsibility do you have when deciding which charities to support?

6. Has Mortenson done more good than harm?

Note

1. Lamb, C. (2011, April 24). Beautiful fantasy of a fallen hero. *The Sunday Times*, Features, pp. 2–3.

Sources

Bestselling author owes charity $1M. *The Toronto Star*, p. A12.

Courchane, C. (2011, June 27). *Three cups of tea's* bitter taste. *Washington Times*, p. C10.

Gose, B. (2012, April 15). $1-million settlement in "Three cups" scandal offers warning to boards. *Chronicle of Philanthropy*.

Martin, C. E., & Cary, J. (2011, April 24). Greg Mortenson and our false ideas about social change. *The Christian Science Monitor*.

McGeough, P. (2012, July 22). When charity bites the hand that feeds it. *The Sun Herald*.

Peter, T. A., Ahmend, A., & Arnoldy, B. (2011, April 18). Greg Mortenson's "Three cups of tea": Will CBS report harm aid work? *The Christian Science Monitor*.

Rubin, T. (2011, May 1). Waiting for author Greg Mortenson to explain himself. *Lewiston Morning Tribune*.

Sides, H. (2011, May 2). Shattered faith: What the fall of Greg Mortenson tells us about America's irrepressible longing for heroes. *Newsweek*, p. 5.

Wong, E. (2011, April 24). Two schools, one complicated situation. *The New York Times*, p. WK5.

CASE STUDY 3.3

Wangari Maathai: Unbowed and Unbroken

Kenya's Wangari Maathai compiled an impressive résumé over the course of her life. Maathai, who died in 2011, was the first woman from East and Central Africa to earn a doctorate and the first woman to secure a professorship at the University of Nairobi. Later she became an international advocate for human rights, spoke regularly at the United Nations (which appointed her a minister of peace), and was awarded the Nobel Peace Prize in 2004.

Maathai is best remembered as the founder of the Green Belt Movement, an organization that encourages poor rural women and men to plant trees to fight deforestation. But tree planting is just the start. The Green Belt Movement also addresses a broad range of issues plaguing the poor, including lack of fuel, food and water shortages, soil erosion, powerlessness, and poor leadership. Maathai used the image of the traditional three-legged African stool to demonstrate how democracy, respect for human rights, and the proper management of resources work together to support the development of just and stable societies:

The first leg stands for democratic space, where rights are respected, whether they are human rights, women's rights, children's rights, or environmental rights. The second represents sustainable and equitable management of resources. And the third stands for cultures of peace that are deliberately cultivated within communities and nations. The basin or seat represents society and its prospects for development. Unless all three legs are in place, supporting the seat, no society can thrive.[1]

The Green Belt Movement currently operates nurseries in nearly 4,000 communities in Kenya, planting more than 8 million seedlings annually. Unlike many other nongovernmental organizations operating in Africa, it is managed by Africans, not by aid workers from other countries.

Maathai's accomplishments are all the more noteworthy because they came in the face of setbacks and fierce opposition. When she was employed at the University of Nairobi, women were paid less than men holding the same positions and received no benefits. Her husband divorced her in part because she had more education than he. After Maathai lost her first bid for a seat in the Kenyan Parliament, she was fired from her university position. Foresters opposed the Green Belt Movement, arguing that only professionals could plant and care for trees. During most of Maathai's career, Kenya was under the corrupt one-party rule of Daniel Moi. Maathai and her friends and associates opposed Moi's attempts to seize public parks and forestland to give to his cronies. She was repeatedly threatened, beaten, and imprisoned as a result.

At times only intervention from officials overseas saved Maathai from further persecution. Through it all, she refused to give up. She viewed failure both as temporary and as an opportunity to try something different. Despite the criticism and violence directed toward her, she remained unbowed (the title of her autobiography). In her book about the Green Belt Movement, she sums up her determination and commitment this way: "Those of us who understand the complex concept of the environment have the burden to act. We must not tire, we must not give up, we must persist."[2]

Maathai's determination paid off. Many of the most egregious land grabs were scuttled. The Moi government was replaced with a multiparty system. When democracy was reinstituted in Kenya, Maathai was elected to Parliament and served as deputy minister of the environment. Most important, the Green Belt Movement continues to lay the foundation for peace and justice in Kenya.

Discussion Probes

1. What did Maathai have in common with other moral exemplars?

2. What character traits did Maathai exhibit?

3. What role did hardship play in her ultimate success?

4. Can you develop character without experiencing failure?

5. What leadership/followership ethics lessons do you take from this case?

Notes

1. Maathai, W. (2007). *Unbowed.* New York: Anchor Books, p. 294.

2. Maathai, W. (2004). *The Green Belt Movement: Sharing the approach and the experience.* New York: Lantern Books, p. xii.

Source

Green Belt Movement website. (2012). http://www.greenbeltmovement.org

---

SELF-ASSESSMENT 3.1

The Leadership Virtues Questionnaire (LVQ)

Instructions: Ask someone else to rate you on the following items or select one of your leaders and rate that individual. Scale: 1 = not at all, 2 = once in a while, 3 = sometimes, 4 = fairly often, 5 = frequently, if not always. Reverse scoring where indicated. You will generate a score for each individual virtue and a total perceived character score.

1. Does as he/she ought to do in a given situation.

2. Does not carefully consider all the information available before making an important decision that impacts others.

3. Boldly jumps into a situation without considering the consequences of his/her actions.

4. Does not seek out information from a variety of sources so the best decision can be made.

5. Considers a problem from all angles and reaches the best decision for all parties involved.

6. Would rather risk his/her job than to do something that was unjust.

7. May have difficulty standing up for his/her beliefs among friends who do not share the same views.

8. Fails to make the morally best decision in a given situation.

9. May hesitate to enforce ethical standards when dealing with a close friend.

10. Ignores his/her "inner voice" when deciding how to proceed.

11. Seems to be overly concerned with his/her personal power.

12. Is not overly concerned with his/her own accomplishments.

13. Wishes to know everything that is going on in the organization to the extent that he/she micromanages.

14. Gives credit to others when credit is due.

15. Demonstrates respect for all people.

16. May take credit for the accomplishments of others.

17. Respects the rights and integrity of others.

18. Would make promotion decisions based on a candidate's merit.

19. Does not treat others as he/she would like to be treated.

Prudence	Courage (Fortitude)
1. _____	6. _____
2. _____ (Reverse score)	7. _____ (Reverse)
3. _____ (Reverse)	8. _____ (Reverse)
4. _____ (Reverse)	9. _____ (Reverse)
5. _____	10. _____ (Reverse)
_____ out of 25	_____ out of 25

Temperance   Justice

11. _____ (Reverse)   14. _____

12. _____   15. _____

13. _____ (Reverse)   16. _____ (Reverse)

                                        17. _____

_____ out of 15   18. _____

                                        19. _____ (Reverse)

                                        _____ out of 30

Total _____ out of 95

SOURCE: Riggio, R. E., Zhu, W., Reina, C., & Maroosis, J. A. (2010). Virtue-based measurement of ethical leadership: The Leadership Virtues Questionnaire. *Consulting Psychology Journal: Practice and Research, 62*(4), 235–250.

SELF-ASSESSMENT 3.2

Perceived Leader Integrity Scale

Instructions: You can use this scale to measure the integrity of your immediate supervisor or, as an alternative, ask a follower to rate you. The higher the score (maximum 124), the lower the integrity of the leader rated.

The following items concern your immediate supervisor. You should consider your immediate supervisor to be the person who has the most control over your daily work activities. Circle responses to indicate how well each item describes your immediate supervisor. Response choices: 1 = not at all, 2 = somewhat, 3 = very much, 4 = exactly.

1. Would use my mistakes to attack me personally   1 2 3 4

2. Always gets even   1 2 3 4

3. Gives special favors to certain "pet" employees but not to me   1 2 3 4

4. Would lie to me   1 2 3 4

5. Would risk me to protect himself or herself in work matters   1 2 3 4

6. Deliberately fuels conflict among employees   1 2 3 4

7. Is evil   1 2 3 4

8. Would use my performance appraisal to criticize me as a person   1 2 3 4

9. Has it in for me   1 2 3 4

10. Would allow me to be blamed for his or her mistake   1 2 3 4

11. Would falsify records if it would help his or her work reputation   1 2 3 4

12. Lacks high morals   1 2 3 4

13. Makes fun of my mistakes instead of coaching me as to how to do my job better   1 2 3 4

14. Would deliberately exaggerate my mistakes to make me look bad when describing my performance to his or her superiors   1 2 3 4

15. Is vindictive   1 2 3 4

16. Would blame me for his or her own mistake   1 2 3 4

17. Avoids coaching me because she or he wants me to fail   1 2 3 4

18. Would treat me better if I belonged to a different ethnic group   1 2 3 4

19. Would deliberately distort what I say   1 2 3 4

20. Deliberately makes employees angry at each other   1 2 3 4

21. Is a hypocrite   1 2 3 4

22. Would limit my training opportunities to prevent me from advancing   1 2 3 4

23. Would blackmail an employee if she or he could get away with it   1 2 3 4

24. Enjoys turning down my requests   1 2 3 4

25. Would make trouble for me if I got on his or her bad side   1 2 3 4

26. Would take credit for my ideas   1 2 3 4

27. Would steal from the organization   1 2 3 4

28. Would risk me to get back at someone else   1 2 3 4

29. Would engage in sabotage against the organization   1 2 3 4

30. Would fire people just because she or he doesn't like them if she or he could get away with it   1 2 3 4

31. Would do things that violate organizational policy and then expect subordinates to cover for him or her   1 2 3 4

Total Score _____

SOURCE: Bartholomew, C. S., & Gustafson, S. B. (1998). Perceived leader integrity scale: An instrument for assessing employee perceptions of leader integrity. *Leadership Quarterly, 9,* 143–144. Used by permission.

NOTES

1. Johannesen, R. L. (2002). *Ethics in human communication* (5th ed.). Prospect Heights, IL: Waveland, Ch. 1.

2. Snyder, C. R., & Lopez, S. J. (2005). *Handbook of positive psychology.* Oxford, England: Oxford University Press; Aspinwall, L. G., & Staudinger, U. M. (Eds.). (2002). *A psychology of human strengths: Fundamental questions about future directions for a positive psychology.* Washington, DC: American Psychological Association.

3. Johannesen, R. L. (1991). Virtue ethics, character, and political communication. In R. E. Denton (Ed.), *Ethical dimensions of political communication* (pp. 69–90). New York: Praeger; Annas, J. (2006). Virtue ethics. In D. Copp (Ed.), *The Oxford handbook of ethical theory* (pp. 515–536). Oxford, England: Oxford University Press; Timmons, M. (2002). *Moral theory: An introduction.* Lanham, MD: Rowman & Littlefield.

4. Peterson, C., & Seligman, M. E. P. (2004). *Character strengths and virtues: A handbook and classification.* Oxford, England: Oxford University Press; Comte-Sponville, A. (2001). *A small treatise on the great virtues: The uses of philosophy in everyday life.* New York: Metropolitan.

5. Kidder, R. M. (2005). *Moral courage.* New York: William Morrow.

6. Osswald, S., Greitemeyer, Fischer, P., & Frey, D. (2010). What is moral courage? Definition, explication, and classification of a complex construct. In C. L. S. Pury & S. J. Lopez (Eds.), *The psychology of courage: Modern research on an ancient virtue* (pp. 149–164). Washington, DC: American Psychological Association; Lopez, S. J., Rasmussen, H. N, Skorupski, W. P., Koetting, K., Petersen, S. E., & Yang, Y. (2010). Folk conceptualizations of courage. In C. L. S. Pury & S. J. Lopez (Eds.), *The psychology of courage: Modern research on an ancient virtue* (pp. 23–45). Washington, DC: American Psychological Association.

7. Comte-Sponville; Riggio, R. E., Zhu, W., Reina, C., & Maroosis, J. A. (2010). Virtue-based measurement of ethical leadership: The Leadership Virtues Questionnaire. *Consulting Psychology Journal: Practice and Research, 62*(4), 235–250.

8. Kessler, E. H., & Bailey, J. R. (2007). Introduction: Understanding, applying, and developing organizational and managerial wisdom. In E. H. Kessler & J. R. Bailey (Eds.), *Handbook of organizational and managerial wisdom* (pp. xv–lxxiv). Thousand Oaks, CA: Sage.

9. Kolp, A., & Rea, P. (2006). *Leading with integrity: Character-based leadership.* Cincinnati, OH: AtomicDog; Comte-Sponville.

10. Peterson & Seligman; Comte-Sponville; Smith, T. (1999). Justice as a personal virtue. *Social Theory & Practice, 25,* 361–384; Solomon, R. C. (1990). *A passion for justice: Emotions and*

the origins of the social contract. Reading, MA: Addison-Wesley.

11. Viswesvaran, C., & Ones, D. S. (2002). Examining the construct of organizational justice: A meta-analytic evaluation of relations with work attitudes and behaviors. *Journal of Business Ethics, 38,* 193–203; Cohen-Charash, Y., & Spector, P. E. (2001). The role of justice in organizations: A meta-analysis. *Organizational Behavior and Human Decision Processes, 86,* 278–321.

12. Carver, C. S., & Scheier, M. F. (2005). Optimism. In C. R. Snyder & S. J. Lopez (Eds.), *Handbook of positive psychology* (pp. 231–243). Oxford, England: Oxford University Press.

13. Simons, T. L. (2002). Behavioral integrity: The perceived alignment between managers' words and deeds as a research focus. *Organization Science, 13,* 18–35; Palanski, M. E., & Yammarino, F. J. (2007). Integrity and leadership: A multi-level conceptual framework. *Leadership Quarterly, 20,* 405–420.

14. See Bruhn, J. G. (2001). *Trust and the health of organizations.* New York: Kluwer/Plenum; Elangovan, A. R., & Shapiro, D. L. (1998). Betrayal of trust in organizations. *Academy of Management Review, 23,* 547–566.

15. See Dirks, K. T. (1999). The effects of interpersonal trust on work group performance. *Journal of Applied Psychology, 84,* 445–455; Kramer, R. M., & Tyler, T. R. (Eds.). (1996). *Trust in organizations: Frontiers of theory and research.* Thousand Oaks, CA: Sage.

16. Crosariol, B. (2005, November 21). The diminishing allure of rock-star executives. *The Globe and Mail,* p. B12; Varachaver, N. (2004, November 15). Glamour! Fame! Org charts! *Fortune,* pp. 76–85.

17. Morris, J. A., Brotheridge, C. M., & Urbanski, J. C. (2005). Bringing humility to leadership: Antecedents and consequences of leader humility. *Human Relations, 58,* 1323–1350. See also Tangney, J. P. (2000). Humility: Theoretical perspectives, empirical findings and directions for future research. *Journal of Social and Clinical Psychology, 19,* 70–82.

18. Woodruff, P. (2001). *Reverence: Renewing a forgotten virtue.* Oxford, England: Oxford University Press.

19. Petit, V., & Bollaert, H. (2012). Flying too close to the sun? Hubris among CEOS and how to prevent it. *Journal of Business Ethics, 108,* 265–283.

20. Gladwell, M. (2009, July 27). Cocksure. *The New Yorker,* pp. 24ff.

21. Peterson & Seligman.

22. Howell, J., & Avolio, B. J. (1992). The ethics of charismatic leadership: Submission or liberation? *Academy of Management Executive, 6,* 43–54.

23. Smith, J. Y. (2009, August 12). The Olympian force behind a revolution. *The Washington Post,* p. A07; Hodgson, G. (2009, August 12). Eunice Kennedy Shriver; mental health campaigner who founded the Special Olympics. *The Independent,* Obituaries, p. 26.

24. Pellegrini, E. K., & Scandura, T. A. (2008). Paternalistic leadership: A review and agenda for future research. *Journal of Management, 34,* 566–593.

25. Erbin, G. S., & Guneser, A. B. (2007). The relationship between paternalistic leadership and organizational commitment: Investigating the role of climate regarding ethics. *Journal of Business Ethics, 82,* 955–968; Cheng, B. L., Wu, T., Huang, M., & Farh, J. (2004). Paternalistic leadership and subordinate responses: Establishing a leadership model in Chinese organizations. *Asian Journal of Social Psychology, 7,* 89–117; Otken, A., & Cenkci, T. (2012). The impact of paternalistic leadership on ethical climate: The moderating role of trust in leader. *Journal of Business Ethics, 108,* 525–536.

26. Pellegrini, E. K., Scandura, T. A., & Jayaraman, V. (2010). Cross-generalizability of paternalistic leadership: An expansion of leader–member exchange theory. *Group & Organization Management, 35,* 391–420; Pellegrini & Scandura.

27. Blasi, A. (1984). Moral identity: Its role in moral functioning. In W. M. Kurtines & J. L. Gewirtz (Eds.), *Morality, moral behavior, and moral development* (pp. 128–139). New York: John Wiley.

28. Jennings, M. M. (2006). *The seven signs of ethical collapse: How to spot moral meltdowns in companies . . . before it's too late.* New York: St. Martin's Press.

29. Wayne, L. (2005, March 8). Boeing chief is ousted after admitting affair. *The New York Times,* p. A1.

30. Devine, T., Seuk, J. H., & Wilson, A. (2001). *Cultivating heart and character: Educating for life's most essential goals.* Chapel Hill, NC: Character Development.

31. Tangney; Carver & Scheier; Cavanagh, G. F., & Moberg, D. J. (1999). The virtue of courage within the organization. In M. L. Pava & P. Primeaux (Eds.), *Research in ethical issues in organizations* (Vol. 1, pp. 1–25). Stamford, CT: JAI Press.

32. MacIntyre, A. (1984). *After virtue: A study in moral theory* (2nd ed.). Notre Dame, IN: University of Notre Dame Press; Hauerwas, S. (1981). *A community of character.* Notre Dame, IN: University of Notre Dame Press.

33. Hart, D. K. (1992). The moral exemplar in an organizational society. In T. L. Cooper & N. D. Wright (Eds.), *Exemplary public administrators: Character and leadership in government* (pp. 9–29). San Francisco: Jossey-Bass.

34. Hallie, P. (1979). *Lest innocent blood be shed: The story of the village of Le Chambon and how goodness happened there.* New York: Harper & Row.

35. Colby, A., & Damon, W. (1992). *Some do care: Contemporary lives of moral commitment.* New York: Free Press; Colby, A., & Damon, W. (1995). The development of extraordinary moral commitment. In M. Killen & D. Hart (Eds.), *Morality in everyday life: Developmental perspectives* (pp. 342–369). Cambridge, England: Cambridge University Press.

36. Colby & Damon (1995), p. 363.

37. Burns, J. M. (2003). *Transforming leadership: A new pursuit of happiness.* New York: Atlantic Monthly Press, Ch. 5.

38. MacIntyre, p. 216.

39. Lisman, C. D. (1996). *The curricular integration of ethics: Theory and practice.* Westport, CT: Praeger.

40. Lisman's arguments are echoed by Goldberg, M. (1997). Doesn't anybody read the Bible anymo'? In O. F. Williams (Ed.), *The moral imagination: How literature and films can stimulate ethical reflection in the business world* (pp. 19–32). Notre Dame, IN: University of Notre Dame Press; Ellenwood, S. (2006). Revisiting character education: From McGuffey to narratives. *Journal of Education, 187,* 21–43.

41. Moxley, R. S., & Pulley, M. L. (2004). Hardships. In C. D. McCauley & E. Van Velsor (Eds.), *The Center for Creative Leadership handbook of leadership development* (2nd ed., pp. 183–203). San Francisco: Jossey-Bass.

42. Bennis, W. G., & Thomas, R. J. (2002). *Geeks and geezers: How era, values, and defining moments shape leaders.* Boston: Harvard Business School Press; Thomas, R. J. (2008). *Crucibles of leadership: How to learn from experience to become a great leader.* Boston: Harvard Business Press.

43. Dotlich, D. L., Noel, J. L., & Walker, N. (2008). Learning for leadership: Failure as a second chance. In J. V. Gallos (Ed.), *Business leadership* (2nd ed., pp. 478–485). San Francisco: Jossey-Bass.

44. Aristotle. (1962). *Nichomachean ethics* (M. Ostwald, Trans.). Indianapolis: Bobbs-Merrill.

45. Cavanagh & Moberg.

46. Covey, S. R. (1989). *The seven habits of highly effective people.* New York: Simon & Schuster.

47. Jones, L. B. (1996). *The path: Creating your mission statement for work and for life.* New York: Hyperion.

48. Bordas, J. (1995). Becoming a servant-leader: The personal development path. In L. Spears (Ed.), *Reflections on leadership* (pp. 149–160). New York: John Wiley.

49. Rath, T. (2007). *StrengthsFinder 2.0.* New York: Gallup Press.

50. Rath, T., & Conchie, B. (2008). *Strengths based leadership.* New York: Gallup Press.

51. Kouzes, J. M., & Posner, B. Z. (2003). *Credibility: How leaders gain and lose it, why people demand it.* San Francisco: Jossey-Bass, pp. 62–63. Used by permission of the publisher.

52. Allport, G. (1961). *Pattern and growth in personality.* New York: Holt, Rinehart & Winston; Guth, W. D., & Tagiuri, R. (1965, September–October). Personal values and corporate strategy. *Harvard Business Review,* pp. 123–132.

Combating Evil

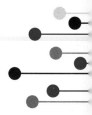

Evil, in whatever intellectual framework, is by definition a monster.

—Essayist Lance Morrow

Without forgiveness there is no future.

—South African archbishop Desmond Tutu

What's Ahead

In this chapter, we wrestle with the most dangerous of all unhealthy shadow casters: evil. The first section surveys some of the forms or faces of evil. The second section examines the role of forgiveness, both giving and seeking, in breaking cycles of evil. The third section probes the relationship between spirituality and leadership, highlighting how spiritual practices can equip us to deal with evil and to foster more ethical, productive workplaces.

The Faces of Evil

The mass shootings in Connecticut, Colorado, and Wisconsin; the systematic rape of hundreds of thousands of women in the Congo; suicide bombings and prisoner abuse in the Middle East; the Boston Marathon attack; human rights violations in North Korea (see Case Study 4.1); and global sex trafficking—all serve as powerful reminders of the existence of evil. While recognizing the presence of evil is an important first step, we can't combat this powerful force until we first understand our opponent. Contemporary Western definitions of evil emphasize its destructiveness.[1] Evil inflicts pain and suffering, deprives innocent people of their humanity, and creates feelings of hopelessness and despair. Evildoers do excessive harm, going well beyond what is needed to achieve their objectives. The ultimate product of evil is death. Evil destroys self-esteem, physical and emotional well-being, relationships, communities, and nations.

We can gain some important insights into the nature of evil by looking at the various forms or faces it displays. In this section, I'll introduce six perspectives on evil. In the next section, I'll talk about how understanding these perspectives can help us better deal with this powerful, destructive force.

Evil as Dreadful Pleasure

University of Maryland political science professor C. Fred Alford defines evil as a combination of dread and pleasure. Alford recruited 60 respondents of a variety of ages and backgrounds to talk about their experiences with evil. He discovered that people experience evil as a deep sense of uneasiness, "the dread of being human, vulnerable, alone in the universe and doomed to die."[2] They do evil when, instead of coming to grips with their inner darkness, they try to get rid of it by making others feel "dreadful." Inflicting this pain is enjoyable. Part of the pleasure comes from their being in charge, of being the victimizers instead of the victims.

Evil can also be a product of chronic boredom.[3] Boredom arises when people lose their sense of meaning and purpose. They no longer enjoy life and try to fill the emptiness they feel inside. Ordinary distractions such as television, movies, surfing the Internet, social media, shopping, and sports don't fill the void, so people turn to evil instead. Evil is an attractive alternative because it engages the full energy and attention of perpetrators. For example, a serial killer has to plan his crimes, locate victims, keep his actions secret, and outsmart law enforcement.

Evil as Exclusion

In moral exclusion, group members draw a mental circle.[4] Those inside the circle (the *moral community* or *scope of justice*) are treated with respect, are considered deserving of sacrifice from other members, and get their fair share of resources. If those within the circle are harmed, other group members come to their rescue. Those outside the circle, on the other hand, are seen as undeserving or expendable. As a result, "harming them appears acceptable, appropriate, or just."[5]

Mild forms of exclusion are part of daily life and include, for example, making sexist comments, applying double standards when judging the behavior of different groups, and making unflattering comparisons to appear superior to others. (Mild exclusion can also include ignoring or allowing such behaviors.) However, moral exclusion can also take extreme forms, resulting in such evils as human rights violations, torture, murder, and genocide. For instance, during World War II, Japanese soldiers viewed the Chinese with contempt. Murdering them was like "squashing a bug or murdering a hog."[6] This mindset allowed Japanese soldiers to rape, torture, and slaughter civilians in the Chinese city of

Nanking (now known as Nanjing), killing an estimated 300,000 residents. Other examples of evil exclusion include the Russian oppression of Chechen rebels, genocide in Guatemala, Serbian atrocities, attacks on villages in the Darfur region of Sudan, and the abuse of suspects in the War on Terror.[7] Box 4.1 presents a list of the symptoms of moral exclusion.

● ● ● BOX 4.1 SYMPTOMS OF MORAL EXCLUSION ● ● ●

Symptom	Description
Double standards	Having different norms for different groups
Concealing effects of harmful outcomes	Disregarding, ignoring, distorting, or minimizing injurious outcomes that others experience
Reducing moral standards	Asserting that one's harmful behavior is proper while denying one's lesser concern for others
Utilizing euphemisms	Making and sanitizing harmful behavior and outcomes
Biased evaluation of groups	Making unflattering between-group comparisons that bolster one's own group at the expense of others
Condescension and derogation	Regarding others with disdain
Dehumanization	Denying others' rights, entitlements, humanity, and dignity
Fear of contamination	Perceiving contact or alliances with other stakeholders as posing a threat to oneself
Normalization and glorification of violence	Glorifying and normalizing violence as an effective, legitimate, or even sublime form of human behavior while denying the potential of violence to damage people, the environment, relationships, and constructive conflict resolution processes
Victim blaming	Placing blame on those who are harmed
Deindividuation	Believing one's contribution to social problems is undetectable
Diffusing responsibility	Denying personal responsibility for harms by seeing them as the result of collective rather than individual decisions and actions
Displacing responsibility	Identifying others, such as subordinates or supervisors, as responsible for harms inflicted on victims

SOURCE: Opotow, S., Gerson, J., & Woodside, S. (2005). From moral exclusion to moral inclusion: Theory for teaching peace. *Theory Into Practice 44*, 303–318. Used by permission.

Dispute resolution expert Susan Opotow believes that moral exclusion progresses through the following five states or elements, which reinforce one another and can become a vicious cycle that ends in death and destruction.[8]

1. *Conflicts of interest are salient.* Moral exclusion is often set in motion during zero-sum conflicts where one group wins at the expense of the others. As tensions increase, members distance themselves from their opponents, focusing on differences based on company, job function, religion, education, hometown, ethnic background, social status, skin color, and other factors. Competition for resources can even set adults against children. Under the Communist regime in Romania, families were forced to have four children when there was little to eat. As a result, survival took priority over the welfare of children, who were seen as competition for food; many children were placed in orphanages. One Romanian cab driver summed up the attitude of many of his countrymen this way: "With so many decent people struggling to get along, why do you bother with the kids? They are not good; they are trash."[9] Only recently have Romanian citizens begun to address the problem of neglected children.

2. *Group categorizations are salient.* The characteristics of competing groups are given negative labels, helping to divide the world into those who deserve empathy and assistance and those who don't. These derogatory labels excuse unfair treatment and negative consequences. In much of Europe, for example, Romanies (often called Gypsies) are described as "lazy," "dirty," and "thieves."[10]

3. *Moral justifications are prominent.* Hurting outsiders is justified and even celebrated as a way to strike a blow against a corrupt enemy. These exclusionary moral claims can be identified by their self-serving nature. They justify doing harm and reinforce moral boundaries by denigrating outsiders. Nazis blamed Jews for causing Germany's defeat in World War I and subsequent economic collapse. Jews were seen as a threat to the nation's racial purity and Aryan superiority. First they were excluded from economic, political, and social life, and then, with their humanity denied, they were sent to concentration camps.[11]

4. *Unjust procedures are described as expedient.* The damage done by moral exclusion is often disguised because it administered through technical or rational means (see the discussion of evil as bureaucracy below). Unjust procedures often hurt the very people they are supposed to benefit. For example, government bureaucrats in the United States and Australia claimed to be helping native peoples even as they stole their lands and tried to eradicate their cultures.

5. *Harmful outcomes occur.* Exclusion has damaging physical and psychological effects. Members of excluded groups may suffer physical harm like abuse, sickness, and death. At the same time, they suffer from a loss of self-esteem and identity as they internalize the

negative judgments of the dominant group. Perpetrators also pay a high price. They have to spend significant energy and resources to deal with conflicts, excuse their behavior, and maintain group boundaries. Excluders also suffer psychologically, as the harm they cause threatens to overshadow any good they do. This was the case under apartheid in South Africa, where Afrikaners could not overcome the "stain" of racism.

Evil as Deception

Psychiatrist Scott Peck identifies evil as a form of narcissism or self-absorption.[12] Mentally healthy adults submit themselves to something beyond themselves, such as God or love or excellence. Submission to a greater power encourages them to obey their consciences. Evil people, on the other hand, refuse to submit and try to control others instead. They consider themselves above reproach and project their shortcomings on others, attacking anyone who threatens their self-concepts. Evil people are consumed with keeping up appearances. Peck calls them "the people of the lie" because they deceive themselves and others in the hope of projecting a righteous image. Peck believes that truly evil people are more likely to live in our neighborhoods than in our jails. They generally hide their true natures and appear to be normal and successful. In contrast, those who land in prison often do so because they've been morally inconsistent or stupid.

Evil as Bureaucracy

The twentieth century was the bloodiest period in history. More than 100 million people died as the direct or indirect result of wars, genocide, and other violence. According to public administration professors Guy Adams and Danny Balfour, the combination of science and technology is what made the 1900s so destructive.[13] Scientific and technological developments (tanks, airplanes, chemical warfare, nuclear weapons) made killing highly efficient. At the same time, belief in technological progress encouraged government officials to take a rational approach to problems. The integration of these factors produced administrative evil. In administrative evil, organizational members commit heinous crimes while carrying out their daily tasks as "good," "responsible" professionals. Adams and Balfour argue that the true nature of administrative evil is masked or hidden from participants. Officials are rarely asked to engage in evil; instead, they inflict pain and suffering while fulfilling their job responsibilities, often believing that they are engaged in a worthy cause.

The Holocaust provides the most vivid example of administrative evil in action. Extermination camps in Germany would not have been possible without the willing cooperation of thousands of civil servants engaged in such functions as collecting taxes, running municipal governments, and managing the country's social security system. These duties may seem morally neutral, but in carrying them out public officials condemned millions to death. Government authorities defined who was undesirable and then seized their assets. Administrators managed the ghettos, built concentration camp latrines, and employed slave labor. Even the railway authority did its part. The Gestapo had to pay for each prisoner shipped by rail to the death camps. Railroad officials billed the SS at third-class passenger rates (one way) for adult prisoners, with discounts for children. Guards were charged round-trip fares.

Evil as a Choice

Any discussion of good and evil must consider the role of human choice. Just how much freedom we have is a matter of debate, but a number of scholars argue that we become good or evil through a series of small, incremental decisions. In other words, we never remain neutral but are always moving toward one pole or another. Scholar C. S. Lewis draws on the image of a road to illustrate this point.[14] On a journey, we decide which direction to take every time we come to a fork in the road. We face a similar series of decisions throughout our lives. We can't correct a poor decision by continuing on but must go back to the fork where we went wrong and take the other path.

Psychologist Erich Fromm makes the same argument as Lewis. Only those who are very good or very bad do not have a choice; the rest of us do. However, each choice we make reduces our options:

> Each step in life which increases my self-confidence, my integrity, my courage, my conviction also increases my capacity to choose the desirable alternative, until eventually it becomes more difficult to choose the undesirable rather than the desirable action. On the other hand, each act of surrender and cowardice weakens me, opens the path for more acts of surrender, and eventually freedom is lost. Between the extreme when I can no longer do a wrong act and the other extreme when I have lost my freedom to right action, there are innumerable degrees of freedom of choice. In the practice of life the degree of freedom to choose is different at any given moment. If the degree of freedom to choose the good is great, it needs less effort to choose the good. If it is small, it takes a great effort, help from others, and favorable circumstances.[15]

Fromm uses the story of the Israelites' exodus from ancient Egypt to illustrate what happens when leaders make a series of evil choices. Moses repeatedly asks Pharaoh to let his people go, but the Egyptian ruler turns down every request. Eventually his heart is "hardened," and he and his army are destroyed.

Evil as Ordinary

The evil-as-ordinary perspective focuses on the situational factors that cause otherwise ordinary or normal people to become evildoers. Although it may be comforting to think that evildoers must be heartless psychopaths or deranged killers, we know that in many cases perpetrators look and act a lot like the rest of us. Social philosopher Hannah Arendt pointed this out in her analysis of the trial of Nazi officer Adolf Eichmann in 1961.[16] Eichmann was responsible for the deportation of millions of Jews to concentration and extermination camps. What struck Arendt was how ordinary Eichmann seemed. Half a dozen psychiatrists examined him and certified him as "normal." Arendt used the phrase the "banality of evil" when describing Eichmann to point out that the sources of evil are not mysterious or demonic but commonplace. If that is the case, then any one of us can commit heinous crimes. The Rwandan genocide depicted in "Leadership Ethics at the Movies: Beyond the Gates" supports Arendt's thesis. Thousands of ordinary Rwandan Hutus literally went next door or across the street to hack and beat their Tutsi neighbors to death with machetes and other farm implements. Interviews with one group of young killers revealed a chilling routine. They would have a hearty breakfast (running down Tutsis took a lot of energy), meet at the soccer field to get their assignments to kill or loot, march off singing, find and murder victims until the final whistle blew, and then relax with beer and food after a hard day's work.[17]

LEADERSHIP ETHICS AT THE MOVIES • • • • • • • • • •

Beyond the Gates

Key Cast Members: John Hurt, Hugh Dancy, Dominique Horwitz, Clare-Hope Ashitey, Nicola Walker

Synopsis: At the beginning of the Rwandan genocide in April 1994, 2,500 Tutsis flee to a Catholic school run by Father Christopher (John Hurt) to avoid death at the hands of their Hutu countrymen. Father Christopher, young teacher Joe Connor (Dancy), and a garrison of United Nations peacekeepers manage to keep the crowd safe as a mob of Hutu killers gathers outside the school gates. After a few days, though, the garrison's commander (played by Dominique Horwitz) is ordered to withdraw. Father Christopher and Joe must decide whether to die with their flock or flee to safety with the rest of the Europeans.

Rating: Not rated but contains extreme violence and intense themes

(Continued)

Philip Zimbardo and other social psychologists have identified a number of situational factors that can turn otherwise "nice" people into torturers and murderers.[18] Zimbardo discovered firsthand the power of the system to promote unethical behavior through his famous Stanford Prison Experiment. In this study, he created a mock prison in the basement of the building housing Stanford University's psychology department and randomly assigned student volunteers to roles as prisoners and guards. It didn't take long for both groups to get caught up in their roles. Soon the prisoners revolted and the guards retaliated. The jailers strip-searched prisoners, forced them into prolonged exercise, put them into solitary confinement, denied them bathroom privileges (they had to urinate and defecate in their cells), and made them clean toilets by hand. Two prisoners suffered significant emotional trauma and had to be immediately released from the experiment. Zimbardo, who served as the prison warden, also got caught up in the role play. At one point, he tried to transfer the experiment to an empty cell at the local police station to ensure more security and he got angry when the police refused his request. Zimbardo ended the experiment early after a visitor (who would later become his wife) complained about the disgusting conditions at the "jail." Of the 50 outsiders who visited the mock prison while the experiment was being conducted, she was the only person to object.

Zimbardo went on to analyze the role of situational variables in real-life cases of evil, such as the widespread torture of political opponents in Brazil and prisoner abuse at Iraq's Abu Ghraib prison. According to Zimbardo, ordinary people, such as the military guards at Abu Ghraib, are motivated to do evil when they feel peer pressure to participate in such acts, obey authority, remain anonymous, are given permission to engage in antisocial behavior, and dehumanize others (treat them as less than fully human). Evil is likely to continue when others fail to intervene to stop it.

Facing Evil

Each of the perspectives just described provides insights into how we as leaders can come to grips with evil. The dreadful pleasure approach highlights both the origins of evil and the attraction of doing evil, forcing us to examine our motivations. We need to ask ourselves: Am I projecting my insecurities onto others? Am I punishing a subordinate because of her or his poor performance or because exercising coercive power makes me feel strong? Am I making a legitimate request or merely demonstrating that I have the authority to control another person? Am I tempted to harm others just to fill the emptiness I feel inside?

Evil as exclusion highlights the dangers of putting other groups outside our circle of concern. However, combating moral exclusion is difficult because it is often subtle and hard to detect. Further, group members often deny or ignore their exclusionary behavior to protect themselves from guilt or anxiety.[19] Being alert to the symptoms outlined in Box 4.1 is a good place to start. Pay particularly close attention to the language used by group members. Negative labels, critical comments, unfair comparisons, and other verbal strategies narrow the scope of justice. Biased speech also paves the way for more extreme behaviors. Adopting a pluralistic perspective can help leaders deter moral exclusion at each stage of its development.[20] Pluralism acknowledges the legitimacy of a variety of groups. This approach sees conflicts not as win–lose battles but as opportunities to integrate the interests of all parties. Members of pluralistic groups enlarge the definition of the moral community by viewing all persons as worthy of justice. Pluralism encourages group members to be skeptical of self-serving claims and moral justifications for destructive acts, to develop fair procedures for distributing resources, and to support dissenters.

The evil-as-deception viewpoint makes it clear that people aren't always as they seem. On the surface, evil people appear to be successful and well-adjusted. In reality, they exert tremendous energy keeping up appearances. (Turn to Case Study 4.2 for a chilling example of how two young evildoers were able to mislead their families and authorities until it was too late.) Deceit and defensiveness can serve as warning signs. If we routinely lie to protect our images, refuse constructive feedback, and always blame others, we may be engaged in evil. The same may be true of other leaders and followers who display these behaviors. Peck, like Parker Palmer, believes that to master our inner demons we must first name them. Once we've identified these tendencies, we can begin to deal with them by examining our will. We should determine whether we're willing to submit to a positive force—an ideal, authority—that is greater than we are. Peck urges us to respond to the destructive acts of others with love. Instead of attacking evildoers, we can react with goodness and thereby "absorb" the power of evil.

The administrative evil perspective introduces a new type of evil, one based on technology and logic. In today's world, evil has increased capacity for destruction. The impacts of evil, once contained by distance and technological limitations, can now extend to the entire world. Globalization and the miniaturization of nuclear and biochemical weapons mean that just one person can wreak as much havoc as infamous world leaders such as Caligula and Stalin did in the past.[21] Furthermore, the face of evil may be masked or hidden from those who participate in it. We need to be aware of how our activities contribute to good or evil. Claiming that we were "just following orders" is no excuse.

Evil as a choice puts the ethical burden squarely on our shoulders. Group and organizational pressures may contribute to our wrongdoing, but we are the ones who make the decisions to participate in evil acts. Furthermore, the choices we make now will limit our options in the future. Every moral decision, no matter how insignificant it seems at the time, has lasting consequences.

The final perspective, evil as ordinary, is a sobering reminder that we all have the potential to become evildoers. Not only do we as followers need to resist situational influences that can turn us into brutes (see "Focus on Follower Ethics: Resisting Situational Pressures to Do Evil"), but also as leaders we should eliminate conditions that promote evil behavior in our subordinates. It is our ethical duty to intervene when we see evil behavior and to reward others who do the same.

FOCUS ON FOLLOWER ETHICS

Resisting Situational Pressures to Do Evil: A 10-Step Program

Philip Zimbardo offers the following 10-step program designed to help followers resist situational forces that promote evildoing.

"I made a mistake!" Admit your mistakes. (Say "I'm sorry"; "I apologize"; "Forgive me.") Vow to learn from your errors and move on. Don't stay the course if you are engaged in an immoral activity.

"I am mindful." Don't rely on scripts from the past. They can blind you to the tactics of influencers and key elements of the situation. Instead, pay close attention to (be mindful of) the here and now. In addition, think critically. Ask for evidence, imagine future consequences, and reject simple solutions to complex problems. Encourage others to do the same.

"I am responsible." Maintaining personal accountability increases your resistance to conformity pressures. Take charge of your decisions and actions rather than

spreading responsibility to your group, coworkers, or military unit. Remember that claiming "everyone else was doing it" is no defense in a court of law.

"I am me, the best I can be." Don't let others take away your individuality, making you anonymous. State your name, credentials, and unique features.

"I respect just authority but rebel against unjust authority." Distinguish between those in authority who deserve your respect and those who are leading others astray or promoting their own interests. Critically evaluate and disobey destructive leaders.

"I want group acceptance but value my independence." Group acceptance is a powerful force but shouldn't overpower your sense of right and wrong. Resist social pressure by stepping out of the group, getting other opinions, and finding new groups more in line with your values.

"I will be more frame-vigilant." Frames (words, pictures, slogans, logos) shape our attitudes toward issues and people, often without our being aware of their impact. For example, many politicians use the colors of the flag—red, white, and blue—on their campaign signs and other materials. Be vigilant, noting the way that the frame is designed to shape your thoughts and emotions.

"I will balance my time perspective." Living in the present increases the power of situational influences that promote evil. You are less likely to go along with abusive behavior if you consider the long-term consequences of such actions and remember the values and standards you developed in the past.

"I will not sacrifice personal or civic freedoms for the illusion of security." Reject any offer that involves sacrificing even small freedoms for the promise of future security. Such sacrifices (e.g., loss of privacy, legal protections, and freedom of speech) are immediate and real, but the promised security is often a distant illusion.

"I can oppose unjust systems." Join with others to resist systems that promote evil. Try to bring about change, blow the whistle on corruption, get away from the group or organization, resist groupthink, draw on the resources of outsiders, and so on.

SOURCE: Adapted from Zimbardo, P. G. (2007). *The Lucifer effect: Understanding how good people turn evil.* New York: Random House, pp. 451–456.

Making a Case for Forgiveness

Breaking the Cycle of Evil

Scott Peck is not alone in arguing that loving acts can overcome evil. A growing number of social scientists believe that forgiving instead of retaliating can prevent or break cycles of evil. In a cycle of evil, aggressive acts provoke retaliation followed by more aggression. When these destructive patterns characterize relations between ethnic groups (e.g., Turks versus Armenians, Serbs versus Croats), they can continue for hundreds of years. Courageous leaders can end retaliatory cycles through dramatic acts of reconciliation, however. As president of Egypt, Anwar Sadat engaged in one such conciliatory gesture when he traveled to Jerusalem to further the peace process with Israel. Pope John Paul II went to the jail cell of his would-be assassin to offer forgiveness. Archbishop Desmond Tutu and Nelson Mandela prevented a bloodbath in South Africa by creating the Truth and Reconciliation Commission. This body, made up of both Blacks and Whites, investigated crimes committed during the apartheid era and allowed offenders to confess their guilt and ask for pardon. Similar commissions were created after incidents of widespread torture and murder in Argentina, Uruguay, Peru, Guatemala, Rwanda, and elsewhere.

The concept of forgiving evildoers is controversial.[22] Skeptics assert that (1) guilty parties will get off without acknowledging they have done wrong or paying for their crimes, (2) forgiveness is a sign of weakness, (3) forgiveness is impossible in some situations, (4) forgiveness can't be offered until the offender asks for it, and (5) no leader has the right to offer forgiveness on behalf of other victims. Each of these concerns is valid. You will have to decide for yourself whether forgiveness is an appropriate response to evil deeds. However, before you make that determination, I want to describe the forgiveness process and identify some of the benefits that come from extending mercy to others.

The Forgiveness Process

There are many misconceptions about what it means to forgive another person or group of people. According to Robert Enright, professor of educational psychology and president of the International Forgiveness Institute at the University of Wisconsin, forgiveness is *not* the following:[23]

- Forgetting past wrongs to "move on"

- Excusing or condoning bad, damaging behavior

- Reconciling or coming together again (Forgiveness opens the way to reconciliation, but the person being forgiven must change or desire to reconcile.)

- Reducing the severity of offenses

- Offering a legal pardon

- Pretending to forgive in order to wield power over another person

- Ignoring the offender

- Dropping our anger and becoming emotionally neutral

Enright and his colleagues define forgiveness as "a willingness to abandon one's right to resentment, negative judgment, and indifferent behavior toward one who unjustly injured us, while fostering the undeserved qualities of compassion, generosity, and even love toward him or her."[24] This definition recognizes that the wronged party has been unjustly treated (slandered, betrayed, imprisoned); the offended person willingly chooses forgiveness regardless of the offender's response; forgiving involves emotions, thoughts, and behavior; and forgiveness is a process that takes place over time. (To measure your likelihood to forgive others, complete Self-Assessment 4.1, the Tendency to Forgive Scale.)

Enright and his fellow researchers offer a four-stage model to help people forgive. In the first phase, *uncovering*, a victim may initially deny that a problem exists. However, when the person does acknowledge the hurt, he or she may experience intense feelings of anger, shame, and betrayal. The victim invests a lot of psychic energy in rehashing the offense and comparing his or her condition with that of the offender. Feeling permanently damaged, the person may believe that life is unfair.

During the second phase, *decision*, the injured party recognizes that he or she is paying a high price for dwelling on the injury, considers the possibility of forgiveness, and commits him- or herself to forgiving.

Forgiveness is accomplished in the third stage, *work*. The wronged party tries to understand (not condone) the victimizer's background and motivation. He or she may experience empathy and compassion for the offender. Absorbing pain is the key to this stage. The forgiver decides to endure suffering rather than pass it on, thereby breaking the cycle of evil. Viewed in this light, forgiveness is a gift of mercy to the wrongdoer.

The fourth and final phase, *deepening*, consists of the outcomes of forgiving. A forgiver may find deeper meaning in suffering, realize his or her own need for forgiveness, and come to a greater appreciation for support groups—friends, congregations, classmates. In the end, the person offering forgiveness may develop a new purpose in life and find peace.

This four-stage model has been used successfully with a variety of audiences: survivors of incest, prison inmates, college students deprived of parental love, heart patients, substance abusers, youth at risk for aggressive behavior, and elderly women suffering from depression. In each case, forgivers experienced significant healing. Enright emphasizes that personal benefits should be a by-product, not the motivation, for forgiving. Nonetheless, a growing body of evidence suggests that forgiveness can pay significant psychological, physical, and relational dividends.[25] Those who forgive are released from resentments and experience less depression and anxiety. Overall, they enjoy a higher sense of well-being. By releasing their grudges, forgivers experience better physical health. Reducing anger, hostility, and hopelessness lowers the risk of heart attack and high blood pressure while increasing the body's resistance to disease. Acting mercifully toward transgressors can also help to maintain relationships among friends and family members.

The social scientific study of forgiveness is continuing, and results are extremely encouraging. Forgiving does appear to absorb or defuse evil. If this is the case, then as leaders we should practice forgiveness when we are treated unjustly by followers, supervisors, peers, or outsiders. At times, however, we will need to go further and follow the examples of Sadat and Mandela by offering forgiveness on behalf of followers in the hope of reconciling with a long-standing enemy.

Donald Shriver uses the metaphor of a cable to explain how warring groups can overcome their mutual hatred and bind together to restore fractured relationships.[26] This cable is made up of four strands. The first strand is *moral truth*. Forgiveness starts with recalling the past and rendering a moral judgment. Both parties need to agree that one or both engaged in behavior that was wrong (see the discussion of political apologies below) and unjust and caused injury. Refusal to admit the truth makes reconciliation impossible. That is why South Africa's Truth and Reconciliation Commission began the process of national healing after the abolition of apartheid by publicly airing Black victims' statements and requests for amnesty by White police officers.

The second strand of the cable is *forbearance*—that is, rejecting revenge in favor of restraint. Moral indignation often fuels new crimes as offended parties take their vengeance. Forbearance breaks this pattern and may soften enemies who expect retaliation.

The third strand is *empathy* for the enemies' humanity. Empathy doesn't excuse wrongs but acknowledges that offender and offended share much in common. This recognition opens the way for both sides to live together in peace. Union general Ulysses S. Grant demonstrated how to combine the judgment of wrong with empathy at Appomattox, where Southern troops surrendered to end the U.S. Civil War. On that occasion, Grant wrote the following in his journal: "I felt . . . sad and depressed at the downfall of a foe who had fought so long and valiantly, and had suffered so much for a cause, though that cause was, I believe, one of the worst for which a people ever fought."[27]

The fourth and final strand of the forgiveness cable is *commitment* to restore the broken relationship. Forgivers must be prepared to live and interact with their former enemies. At first, the two parties probably will coexist in a state of mutual toleration. Later, they may fully reconcile, as the United States and Germany have done since the end of World War II.

In sum, I believe that forgiveness is one of a leader's most powerful weapons in the fight against evil. Or, to return to the central metaphor of this text, forgiving is one of the ways in which leaders cast light rather than shadow. We must face our inner darkness, particularly our resentments and hostilities, in order to offer genuine forgiveness. By forgiving, we short-circuit or break the shadowy, destructive cycles that poison groups, organizations, and societies. Offering forgiveness brightens our lives by reducing our anxiety levels and enhancing our sense of well-being.[28] Requesting forgiveness, as we'll see below, opens the door for reconciliation.

Seeking Forgiveness

Just as we need to offer forgiveness, we need to seek forgiveness. In fact, some observers have called the current era the "Age of Apology." Nearly every week, it seems, a prominent figure offers an apology for his or her misdeeds. Consider sports figures, for example. Over the past few years, sprinter Marion Jones, baseball star Ryan Braun, golfing great Tiger Woods, NFL quarterback Michael Vick, basketball player Kobe Bryant, college football coach Bobby Petrino, and cyclist Lance Armstrong (see Case Study 4.3) are just a few of the athletes who have confessed to using performance-enhancing drugs, lying, engaging in dogfighting, having extramarital affairs, and other unethical activities.[29] The demand for apologies is likely to increase for several reasons.[30] First, globalization is creating more friction as cultures and values clash; apologies act as a conflict management tool. Second, digital technology reduces the likelihood that misbehavior can be kept secret. Offensive behavior is now broadcast around the world. President George W. Bush and Secretary of Defense Donald Rumsfeld were forced to apologize, for example, when photographs of prisoner abuse at Abu Ghraib were released. Third, as old regimes crumble, new leaders find that they need to acknowledge the suffering of victims under previous governments. Often past regimes did not acknowledge their guilt, so the burden falls on incoming officials. As a result, political apologies appear to be increasingly common. Examples include the following:[31]

- British prime minister Tony Blair apologized for his country's inaction during the Irish potato famine of the nineteenth century.

- The Belgian prime minister apologized to Rwandans for not stepping in to prevent the 1994 genocide.

- Germany's chancellor Gerhard Schroeder requested forgiveness from the Russian people for the damage done by his nation during World War II.

- U.S. president Bill Clinton expressed regret to Ugandans for African slavery.

- The Natal Law Society apologized for excluding Mohandas K. Gandhi from the practice of law in South Africa.

- The U.S. Senate passed a resolution apologizing for not enacting legislation that would have made lynching a federal crime.

- The Oregon state legislature held a public session to revoke and to express regret about an 1849 law that prohibited African Americans from entering Oregon territory.

- British Columbia premier Gordon Campbell apologized to aboriginal peoples for the Canadian province's failure to provide adequate support for their needs.

Businesses and religious groups, too, are have officially apologized for past wrongs. JPMorgan Chase and Wachovia banks expressed regret for their support of slavery, as did the Southern Baptist convention. The Catholic Church has issued apologies for its inaction during the Holocaust, denigration of women, and other sins and errors.

Apologies can be highly beneficial. They help restore the dignity of victims and promote healing. They acknowledge that the victims were indeed wronged and assure them of safety. Apologizing also signals a commitment to the relationship as well as to shared values. Victims see the offenders suffer through their expressions of remorse; reparations help to repair the damage. Apologizers develop a sense of integrity and greater self-awareness. By seeking forgiveness, offenders open the door to dialogue with victims.

Unfortunately, many apologies (*pseudo-apologies,* or *inauthentic* apologies) come up short. The offender, while ostensibly apologizing, refuses to admit guilt, appears insincere, blames others, and so on. For example, when attempting to apologize for a columnist who had offended Latino readers, the publisher of the *Boston Herald* stated, "To those who took offense at his words I offer my personal apology." He then backed the columnist. This was not a sincere or authentic apology because the publisher was only sorry that some were offended and had no plans to make changes. Pseudo-apologies can make a situation worse by further offending victims. Inauthentic apologies are frequently vague ("I apologize for whatever I did . . ."), use the passive voice ("Mistakes have been made . . ."), make the offense conditional ("If mistakes were made . . ."), question whether the victim was damaged ("If anyone was hurt . . .), or minimize the damage ("There's really nothing [or very little] to apologize for . . .").[32]

Apology expert John Kador argues that delivering effective apologies (and avoiding inauthentic apologies) is a critical skill for modern leaders:

Today's most urgent leadership challenges demand the ability to apologize when you make a mistake. The capacity of leaders to apologize can determine their ability to create the kinds of high-trust organizations required to navigate turbulent times. Apology is a leadership skill. And, like any skill, it can be improved with reflection and practice.[33]

Kador outlines five dimensions of an effective or authentic apology that can help us develop our ability to apologize. We can also use his "5-R" model for evaluating the apologies of others.

Recognition. An authentic apology begins with identifying the specific offenses committed (for example, lying to colleagues, abusing followers, failing to protect the safety of workers). When framing an apology, consider your answers to the following questions:

1. What am I apologizing for?

2. What was the impact of my actions on the victim?

3. What norm or value did I violate?

4. Am I apologizing to the right person?

5. Do I have cause to apologize?

6. Do I have the standing to apologize?

7. Should my apology contain an explanation?

Responsibility. Take personal responsibility for the offenses. Avoid the temptation to blame others, to make excuses, or to defend yourself.

Remorse. "I'm sorry" or "I apologize" or "I regret" should be part of admission of responsibility. These words need to be reinforced with the appropriate nonverbal cues that reflect sadness and remorse.

Restitution. Take concrete steps to aid the victim by, for example, restoring employee benefits or paying restitution for damages. Making amends helps to restore balance to the relationship and signals that you are sincere. It is not always possible to offer tangible restitution. In those cases, offer humility, community service, and other intangible reparations.

Repetition. Signal your commitment to not repeat the offensive behavior. This helps the victim overcome her or his reluctance to forgive.

Spirituality and Leadership

Coming to grips with evil is hard work. We must always be on the lookout for evil whatever form it takes; continually evaluate our motivations and choices; make a conscious effort to forgive by reshaping our thoughts, emotions, and behaviors; and have the courage to apologize. A great number of leaders turn to spirituality to help equip themselves for these tasks. If spirituality seems to be a strange topic to discuss in a book about leadership ethics, consider the recent explosion of interest in spirituality in the workplace. More and more academics are studying the link between spiritual values and practices and organizational performance.[34] One interest group in the Academy of Management, for example, focuses on the connection between spirituality and managerial practice and publishes the *Journal of Management, Spirituality & Religion*. A number of other scholarly journals (including the *Journal of Managerial Psychology, Journal of Organizational Change Management, Journal of Management Education, Leadership Quarterly,* and *Journal of Management Inquiry*) have devoted special issues to the topic.

Popular interest in spirituality is also surging. Meditation rooms and reflective gardens are part of many company headquarters. Some organizations sponsor groups for spiritual seekers, hire chaplains, and send employees to business and spirituality workshops. Tom's of Maine, Toro, BioGenex, Interstate Batteries, and Medtronic integrate spiritual values into their organizational cultures. David Whyte, James Autry, and Thomas Chappell are a few of the popular writers who encourage spiritual development at work.

The recent surge of interest in spirituality in the workplace has been fueled in large part by the growing importance of organizations. For better or worse, the corporation has replaced other groups (family, church, social groups) as the dominant institution in society. Work takes up increasing amounts of our time and energy. As a result, we tend to develop more friendships with coworkers and fewer with people outside our workplaces. Many of us want a higher return on this investment of time and energy, seeking meaningful tasks and relationships that serve higher purposes. At the same time, downsizing, restructuring, rapid change, and information overload have generated fear and uncertainty in the workplace, which prompts us to seek stability and to reexamine our lives.[35] Baby boomers, in particular, are reevaluating their priorities, shifting their focus from individual achievement toward purpose and community. (You can determine your level of spiritual well-being by completing Self-Assessment 4.2.) For their part, organizations hope to benefit because their members feel a greater sense of connection. Investigators have discovered that spirituality enhances the following:[36]

- Commitment to mission, core values, and ethical standards

- Organizational learning and creativity

- Morale

- Productivity and profitability

- Collaboration and community

- Loyalty

- Willingness to mentor others

- Job effort

- Job satisfaction

- Social support

- Sense of well-being

- Sense of purpose

- Sensitivity to ethical issues

Donde Ashmos and Dennis Duchon define workplace spirituality as "the recognition that employees have an inner life that nourishes and is nourished by meaningful work that takes place in the context of community."[37] *Inner life* refers to the fact that employees have spiritual needs (their core identity and values) just as they have emotional, physical, and intellectual wants, and they bring the whole person to work. Even industrialist Henry Ford, who only wanted human cogs for his automobile assembly line, noted this fact. "Why is it that I always get the whole person," he complained, "when all I really want is a pair of hands?"[38] *Meaningful work* refers to the fact that workers typically are motivated by more than material rewards. They want their labor to be fulfilling and to serve the needs of society. *Community* refers to the fact that organization members desire connection to others. A sense of belonging fosters the inner life. It should be noted that religion and spirituality overlap but are not identical. Religious institutions encourage and structure spiritual experiences, but spiritual encounters can occur outside formal religious channels.[39]

Interest in spiritual leadership is an offshoot of the larger workplace spirituality movement. Many leaders report that spirituality has played an important role in their character development, giving them the courage to persist in the face of obstacles, remain optimistic, demonstrate compassion, learn from hardship, and clarify their values.[40] Spiritual leadership expert Laura Reave reviewed more than 150 studies and found that leaders who see their work as a calling demonstrate a higher degree of integrity (honesty) and humility, key virtues described in Chapter 3. These character traits, in turn, build trust with followers and foster honest communication.[41] Reave also found that leaders who engage in common spiritual practices are both more ethical and more effective. These behaviors, emphasized in a variety of belief systems, include the following:

- *Demonstrating respect for others' values.* Many spiritual traditions emphasize respect for the individual. Ethical leaders demonstrate their respect for followers by including them in important decisions. By doing so, they empower followers and bring individual, group, and organizational values into alignment. When the values of leaders and followers are aligned, an organization is more likely to enjoy long-term success.

- *Treating others fairly.* Fairness is a natural outcome of viewing others with respect. Employees are very concerned about how fairly they are treated, particularly when it comes to compensation. Followers are more likely to trust leaders who act justly. Subordinates who believe that their supervisors are fair also go beyond their job descriptions to help coworkers.

- *Expressing caring and concern.* Spirituality often takes the form of supportive behavior. Caring leaders typically have more satisfied and productive followers. Concerned leaders are also more likely to build positive relationships that are the key to their personal success. Furthermore, demonstrating care and concern for the community pays dividends. Employees working for firms known for their corporate philanthropy rate their work environments as excellent and ethical, get a greater sense of achievement from their work, and take more pride in their companies.

- *Listening responsively.* Listening and responding to the needs of others is another practice promoted in many spiritual paths. Good listeners are more likely to emerge as group leaders; organizational leaders who demonstrate better listening skills are rated as more effective. Ethical leaders also respond to what they hear by acting on feedback and suggestions.

- *Appreciating the contributions of others.* Most of the world's faith traditions encourage adherents to treat others as creations of God who are worthy of praise. Praise of God's creation, in turn, becomes an expression of gratitude to God. In the workplace, recognizing and praising employee contributions generates goodwill toward the organization, creates a sense of community, and fosters continuing commitment and contribution.

- *Engaging in reflective practice.* Spiritual practice doesn't end with demonstrating fairness, caring, and appreciation to others. It also incorporates individual self-examination or communication with God. Meditation, prayer, journaling, and spiritual reading not only deepen spirituality, but they also pay practical dividends.[42] Leaders who engage in such activities are more effective because they experience less stress, enjoy improved mental and physical health, and develop stronger relationships with others. They are better equipped to rebound from crises and see a greater (transcendent) meaning in even the most stressful circumstances. Self-reflective leaders also manage their emotions more effectively and exercise greater self-discipline.

Tarleton State University (Texas) professor Louis Fry developed spiritual leadership theory to explain how leaders tap into the desire for meaning and connection to transform organizations.[43] Spiritual leadership begins with the inner life of the leader. Leaders who engage in spiritual practices develop (1) hope and faith in a vision of service to others and (2) a commitment to altruistic love. They then model altruism and develop a vision that helps organization members experience a sense of calling—the belief that life has meaning and makes a difference. This vision builds hope and faith in the future, which encourages employees to put forth their best efforts and to persevere. Spiritually focused leaders also establish cultures based on altruistic love that foster a sense of membership and connection. (I'll have more to say about altruism in Chapter 5.) Leaders and followers enjoy a sense of "ethical well-being" in which their behavior reflects their inner values. Not only are they more likely to be satisfied, committed, and productive, but the organization as a whole is also changed for the better. Fry reports that spiritual leadership improves sales and financial performance while fostering corporate social responsibility.

The path to individual and organizational spiritual transformation has its ups and downs. After the initial excitement of discovering the benefits of spirituality, individuals and organizations typically hit obstacles—frustration, financial challenges, feelings of emptiness—that demand new spiritual practices and renewed commitment to a greater purpose if growth is to continue.[44] With this in mind, you can use the following values framework to measure the spiritual climate of your workplace and to determine your organization's spiritual progress.[45]

- *Benevolence:* kindness toward others; desire to promote the happiness and prosperity of employees

- *Generativity:* long-term focus; concern about future consequences of actions for this and future generations

- *Humanism:* policies and practices that respect the dignity and worth of every employee; opportunity for personal growth when working toward organizational goals

- *Integrity:* adherence to a code of conduct; honesty; sincerity; candor

- *Justice:* evenhanded treatment of employees; impartiality; unbiased rewards and punishments

- *Mutuality:* feelings of interconnectedness and mutual dependence; employees working together to complete projects and achieve goals

- *Receptivity:* flexible thinking; open-mindedness; willingness to take calculated risks; rewards for creativity

- *Respect:* treatment of employees with esteem and value; demonstration of consideration and concern

- *Responsibility:* independent follow-through on goals despite obstacles; concern with what is right

- *Trust:* confidence in the character and truthfulness of the organization and its representatives by members and outsiders

To this point our focus has been on the positive benefits of spirituality. However, before ending discussion of the topic, I should note that spiritual leadership has a potential dark side. Noting these pitfalls can keep us from falling victim to them as leaders or followers. To begin, some leaders view spirituality solely as a tool for increasing follower commitment (obedience) and productivity. They lose sight of the fact that spirituality has value in and of itself, helping organizational members find meaning and establish connections. Other leaders try to impose their particular religious and spiritual views on followers. In the worst-case scenario, authoritarian leaders engage in spiritual abuse.[46] They use spirituality to reinforce their power, to seek selfish (often fraudulent) goals, and to foster dependence in followers. Spiritual abuse is a danger in business organizations as well as in religious ones. Common abusive tactics include (1) overemphasizing spiritual authority and forbidding challenges from followers; (2) demanding unquestioning obedience as a sign of follower loyalty, which takes away the right of subordinates to make their own choices; (3) keeping members apart from outsiders and dismissing external critics while at the same time hiding character flaws and unethical practices from the public; (4) insisting on rigid beliefs and behavior while demanding conformity and perfection; (5) suppressing follower dissent through humiliation, deprivation, and other means; and (6) using nearly absolute power to engage in fraud, sexual immorality, and other unethical practices.

IMPLICATIONS AND APPLICATIONS

- Evil takes a variety of forms or faces, including as a sense of dreadful pleasure, as exclusion, as deception, as rational administration, as a series of small but fateful decisions, and as the product of situational forces that convert ordinary people into evildoers. Whatever face it displays, evil is a destructive force that inflicts pain and suffering and ends in death.

- Moral exclusion limits members' willingness to treat outsiders fairly. Combat moral exclusion through pluralism, which encourages team members to broaden their scope of justice to include a wider variety of outside groups.

- Ultimately, the choice of whether to do or participate in evil is yours.

- Work to eliminate the situational factors—peer pressure, obedience to authority, anonymity, and dehumanization—that turn leaders and followers into evildoers. Intervene to stop evil behavior.

- Forgiveness is one way to defuse or absorb evil. As a leader, you need to seriously consider the role of forgiveness in your relations with followers, peers, supervisors, and outsiders.

- Forgiving does *not* mean forgetting or condoning evil. Instead, forgivers hold offenders accountable for their actions at the same time they offer mercy. Forgiving takes a conscious act of will, unfolds over time, and replaces hostility and resentment with empathy and compassion.

- Forgiveness breaks cycles of evil and restores relationships. However, you may gain the most from extending mercy. Forgiving can heighten your sense of well-being, give you renewed energy, and improve your health.

- Warring groups can overcome their mutual hatred by facing and judging the past, rejecting revenge in favor of restraint, feeling empathy for their enemies' humanity, and being committed to restoring the broken relationship.

- You will need to seek forgiveness in addition to offering forgiveness. An effective apology incorporates recognition of the offense, taking responsibility, expressing remorse, offering restitution, and signaling a commitment to not repeat the offensive behavior.

- Spiritual resources can equip you for the demanding work of confronting evil by contributing to your character development.

- Common spiritual practices that can make you more effective and ethical as a leader include (1) demonstrating respect for others' values, (2) treating others fairly, (3) expressing caring and concern, (4) listening responsively, (5) appreciating the contributions of others, and (6) engaging in reflective practice.

- You can foster an ethical organizational climate by acting as a spiritual leader who creates a vision that helps members experience a sense of calling and establishes a culture based on altruistic love.

- Recognize that there is a potential dark side to spiritual leadership. Be careful not to use spirituality solely as a tool to boost productivity, to force your particular beliefs onto followers, or to reinforce your power.

FOR FURTHER EXPLORATION, CHALLENGE, AND SELF-ASSESSMENT

1. Which of the perspectives on evil described in the chapter is most useful to you? How does it help you better understand and prevent evil?

2. Develop your own definition of forgiveness. Does your definition set boundaries that limit when forgiveness can be offered? What right do leaders have to offer or accept forgiveness on behalf of the group?

3. Consider a time when you forgave someone who treated you unjustly. Did you move through the stages identified by Enright and his colleagues? What benefits did you experience? Conversely, describe a time when you asked for and received forgiveness. What process did you go through? How did you and the relationship benefit?

4. Develop your own forgiveness case study based on the life of a leader who prevented or broke a cycle of evil through an act of apology, mercy, or reconciliation.

5. Analyze the apology of a well-known leader and analyze its effectiveness. Conclude with an overall evaluation and provide suggestions for how the apology could have been improved.

6. What should be the role of spirituality in leadership? Try to reach a consensus on this question in a group.

7. Define spiritual leadership. How does it differ from other forms of leadership? How can abuse of spiritual leadership be prevented?

8. Evaluate the spiritual climate of an organization using the values presented in this chapter. Share your findings with the rest of the class.

STUDENT STUDY SITE

Visit the student study site at **www.sagepub.com/johnsonmecl5e** to access full SAGE journal articles for further research and information on key chapter topics.

CASE STUDY 4.1

Repression in the Hermit State

North Korea grabbed international headlines for its efforts to develop a nuclear weapons program. It further ramped up tensions by threatening to aim missiles at South Korea and the United States. All the anxiety about North Korea's nuclear program has overshadowed the fact that the nation may be the most repressive place on earth. Discovering the true extent of the country's evil is difficult, however, because North Korea is highly secretive, earning it the label "the Hermit State."

Since it was founded in 1948, the Democratic People's Republic of Korea (DPRK) has operated under harsh Stalinist principles, ruled by a family dynasty that demands absolute obedience. Between 1948 and 1987 (under the country's first leader, Kim Il Sung), as many as 3.5 million people, including American and South Korean soldiers and civilians captured during the Korean War, were murdered or worked to death. During widespread famine in the 1990s (caused by mismanagement of the food system and the economy), 3–5% of the population died of hunger. The North Korean government withheld international food aid from some portions of the population and used it to feed the military, Communist Party members, and others supportive of the regime. Under current leader Kim Jong-un, hunger continues to threaten the population. A UNICEF report estimates that one-third of North Korean women and children are malnourished.

In the DPRK, human rights violations are the norm. Public executions are held without trials, and suspects are tortured. There are prohibitions against freedom of speech, freedom of religion, freedom of the press, freedom of movement, and freedom of assembly. Of particular note is the country's network of secret prison camps. As many as 250,000 citizens, many of them children, are locked in labor camps with no hope of release. There they are literally worked to death—25% don't survive the first year. And it is easy to get sent to these camps. Folding a newspaper so that the crease falls across a photo of the "Dear Leader" can result in imprisonment, for example. Extended family members are often punished for the missteps of distant relatives. According to law, punishment can extend to three generations of an offender's family. Thus a child can be jailed for the politically incorrect statements of a grandparent.

Few escape from the camps or from the country as a whole. If any citizens do manage to reach neighboring China, DPRK's lone ally, they are returned to North Korea. Female refugees fare the worst. They are often forced into granting sexual favors by Chinese authorities. If they become pregnant, they are coerced into mandatory abortions when they are returned to their homeland.

The Hermit State's isolation has helped spare it from international condemnation. South Korea and the United States have been more concerned with shutting down North Korea's nuclear program than with the government's human rights abuses. Then, too, North Korea has a powerful ally in China, which wants to protect a fellow Communist state and believes that its neighbor has the right to operate without outside interference. However, pressure on North Korea to change its repressive policies is likely to increase. Human rights officials at the United Nations are considering an official inquiry, and U.S. Secretary of State John Kerry has encouraged the Obama administration to speak up on behalf of North Korean political prisoners.

Discussion Probes

1. Should preventing North Korea from developing nuclear weapons take priority over efforts to stop the country's human rights abuses?

2. Should the international community provide food aid to North Korea if it is likely to divert the food to the military and to government officials as it has in the past?

3. What, if anything, can the international community do to stop the abuses in North Korea?

4. Should the United States risk its relationship with China to stop the murder and human rights violations in North Korea?

5. What faces of evil do you see reflected in this case?

Sources

Dyer, E. (2012, May 2). North Korea continues to brutalize its people and yet we do nothing. *The Telegraph*. Retrieved from http://telegraph.co.uk

Kim, H.-W. (2011, December 19). Genocide and politicide alert: North Korea. *Genocide Watch*.

150,000 N. Koreans incarcerated in Soviet-style gulag: Report. (2012, April 11). *Korea Times*.

Park, R. (2012, November 24). Genocide and crimes of humanity ongoing in North Korea. *Forbes*.

Ramzy, A. (2013, January 24). After successful missile launch, North Korea threatens new nuclear test. *Time*. Retrieved from http://www.time.com

Rogers, B. (2013, January 29). North Korea in the dark. *The New York Times*, Op-Ed.

Stein, Y., & Richter, E. D. (2010, Fall). Suspected mass killings—call them democide, politicide, or maybe genocide in North Korea. Genocide Prevention Now, no. 4. Retrieved from http://www.genocidepreventionnow.org

Turning a blind eye to North Korea's "hidden gulag." (2012, April 12). *The Washington Post*.

CASE STUDY 4.2

Evil in the Basement

On April 20, 1999, two teens dressed in long coats and armed with bombs, shotguns, and semiautomatic rifles launched an assault on Columbine High School in a suburb of Denver, Colorado. For 48 minutes seniors Eric Harris and Dylan Klebold set off homemade pipe bombs and napalm while shooting at students and teachers. At the end of their killing spree, 14 students (including the shooters) and 1 faculty member were dead (23 others were seriously injured). The carnage could have been much worse. The killers wanted to inflict a higher death toll than the bombing of the Alfred P. Murrah Federal Building in Oklahoma City in 1995, but their most powerful explosive devices failed to detonate. In addition, they seemed to get bored with murder and killed themselves well before law enforcement officials entered the building.

Many other school attacks have occurred since the Columbine tragedy, but this event remains the one of the most infamous. Other school shooters have adopted the dress and tactics of the Columbine killers and looked to them for inspiration. Virginia Tech killer Seung-Hui Cho, for example, mentioned Harris and Klebold twice in the manifesto he left after murdering 32 students and faculty. Further, the motives of Harris and Klebold are harder to explain. Unlike a number of other school shooters who could clearly be labeled as mentally ill (like Cho) or as social outcasts, the Columbine killers were highly intelligent, mainstream students from privileged backgrounds who had bright futures to look forward to after graduation. The horrific acts of these adolescents, who held part-time jobs, bowled regularly, and attended the prom, brought the reality of evil far too close to home.

Reporter and author David Cullen spent several years reconstructing what happened before, during, and after the killing spree at Columbine High School. In his book *Columbine* he describes the evolution of the shooters and how outward appearances can be deceiving. Drawing on the tapes and journals of the teens and interviews with an FBI profiler, Cullen concludes that Eric Harris, the duo's leader, was a psychopath who "just enjoyed being bad" (p. 240). He boasted of his superiority to the rest of the human race and demonstrated a total lack of empathy. He spewed forth hate on his website and in Internet chat rooms as well as in his private journal. For his part, Dylan Klebold struggled with depression and low self-worth, feeling cut off from humanity. The attack on Columbine for him was a form of murder–suicide. He took his own life after taking out his anger and self-loathing on others.

Harris and Klebold evolved into killers over time. Their criminal activities escalated from vandalism against those they particularly detested to computer hacking, to breaking into school lockers and a vehicle, to making and setting off pipe bombs, to the final assault. While they hinted at their plans to friends and on websites, their skill at deceiving school officials, law enforcement authorities, and their parents ultimately kept them from being stopped. Like other psychopaths, Harris was a master of deception. He confessed just enough of his crimes to appear sincere. For example, he admitted to his parents that he had been drinking a few times but hid the fact that he often got drunk and used pot. For his part, Klebold kept his despair to himself. His parents didn't discover the depth of his pain until after he was dead.

The duo's behavior after they were arrested for stealing equipment from a van illustrates their success in fooling adults. When faced with a felony conviction, they managed to convince a judge to approve them for a diversion program instead. They made a very positive impression on the magistrate by dressing up, acting well behaved, and treating him with respect. The judge thought they were going to do well in the program. After the murders, he admitted that he had been misled. "What's mind-boggling is the amount of deception," the judge noted. "The ease of their deception. The coolness of their deception" (p. 220). Harris, in particular, manipulated the counselors in the diversion program. He was humorous and clever, kept his grades and work performance up, and pretended to have concern for the victim of his crime. As a result, he was released early, which is achieved by only 5% of those enrolled in the program. All the while, Eric recorded his contempt for the legal system, his counselors, the van owner, and humankind in his personal notebook. He took a great deal of pleasure in conning his parents and the authorities.

Despite the duo's efforts to hide their plans, authorities came agonizingly close to preventing the massacre, according to Cullen. Parents of a former friend of Harris and Klebold complained repeatedly about the threats they made against their son. The Jefferson County sheriff's office investigated, copied Harris's Web pages, and found evidence that he was making pipe bombs. The investigator on the case drafted an affidavit for a search warrant for the Harris residence 13 months before the attack, but the affidavit was never presented to a judge. (After the assault, sheriff's officials would also engage in deception by denying that they had ever investigated the complaints or drafted an affidavit.)

Harris's parents missed several opportunities to prevent the assault as well. They believed their son's lies. When his father discovered evidence that he was making pipe bombs, Eric promised to stop and did a better job of hiding his activities from that point on. (Police did discover bomb-making materials in the Harris home after the attack.) As the day for carrying out the plot grew near, Harris and Klebold created the "Basement Tapes" while the Harris family slept upstairs. On the tapes the killers vented their rage, insulted those they considered inferior (Blacks, Latinos, women, gays), identified victims they were going to shoot, and offered apologies (but then excused their behavior). They also described how they were going to die in the final battle they called NBK, after the movie *Natural Born Killers.* Tragically, Mr. and Mrs. Harris never awoke to discover the evil festering in their suburban basement.

Discussion Probes

1. What, if anything, do you remember about the Columbine attack? Why do you think it has inspired other school shooters?

2. What forms of evil do you see reflected in the Columbine murders?

3. What steps could parents and authorities have taken to prevent Harris and Klebold from evolving into killers?

4. How can we keep from being deceived by evildoers?

5. Should Harris and Klebold be forgiven for their assault on Columbine High School? Should their parents be forgiven for not stopping the attack?

6. What leadership ethics lessons do you take from this case?

Source

Cullen, D. (2009). *Columbine.* New York: Twelve.

CASE STUDY 4.3

Forgiving Lance Armstrong

Few Americans cared about the sport of professional cycling until Lance Armstrong began winning the Tour de France, the most prestigious bike race in the world. Armstrong won the grueling two-week race a record seven times in a row. Even more impressive, he did so as a cancer survivor. In 1996 Armstrong was treated for testicular cancer that had spread to his lungs, abdomen, and brain. Rather than giving up, he recovered, winning his first Tour de France in 1998 and continuing his streak through 2005. He retired but then competed again in the Tour in 2009 and 2010. Since his retirement from cycling, he has competed in marathons and triathlons.

Armstrong served as an inspiration for other cancer victims. He founded the Livestrong Foundation in 1997 to support cancer victims and cancer research. Under his leadership the foundation raised $500 million, in part through the sale of distinctive yellow bracelets.

Throughout his career Armstrong faced accusations that he used performance-enhancing drugs. Not only did Armstrong vehemently deny these allegations, claiming that he had never tested positive for drugs, but he also attacked his accusers. He successfully sued a newspaper for defamation when it published allegations that he had been doping. He turned on former associates who claimed he had cheated. For example, Armstrong called his former masseuse a prostitute and an alcoholic. He made it difficult for former teammate Frankie Andreu to get jobs in the cycling industry and said that Betsy Andreu was "crazy." While on the victor's stand at the 2005 Tour de France, Armstrong proclaimed: "I'll say to the people who don't believe in cycling, the cynics and the skeptics, I'm sorry for you. I'm sorry that you can't dream big. I'm sorry you don't believe in miracles."[1]

In 2012, the United States Anti-Doping Agency (USADA) conducted an in-depth investigation into the allegations against Armstrong. Largely based on the testimony of fellow team riders, the USADA banned Armstrong from cycling and all other sports that follow the World Anti-Doping Code (including the Olympics) for life. He was stripped of his Tour de France titles and every other award he won from 1998 on, including a 2000 Olympic bronze medal. The USADA report claimed that Armstrong was more than a participant in the team's doping efforts, he was in charge—pressuring team members to participate, flying in doctors to administer blood transfusions, hiding injection marks with makeup, using a false doctor's prescription to cover up a positive blood test, and so on. According to the head of the USADA, Armstrong's team ran "the most sophisticated, organized and professionalized doping scheme in the history of cycling."[2] Armstrong called the USADA's case "an unconstitutional witch-hunt" but said he would not fight the charges because of the cost to his family and his cancer foundation. He then stepped down from his position as Livestrong chairman.

In early 2013, the cyclist finally admitted his drug use, appearing in a televised interview with Oprah Winfrey. During the interview he admitted to doping during his Tour de France victories by using cortisone, blood transfusions, human growth hormone, testosterone, and the blood booster EPO. He was careful to say that he did not dope when he returned to the Tour in 2009–2010 and refused to name others who were involved in his doping schemes. The cyclist blamed his actions on his "ruthless desire to win at all costs" and claimed that, at the time, doping was part of the cycling culture, like putting air in his bike tires. He didn't believe he could win without cheating. He also admitted he didn't feel any guilt, which he described as "scary." Armstrong said that he decided to confess after hearing his oldest son defend him in front of his friends. He admitted to being a narcissist and a bully. While Armstrong said he had apologized to the journalist he had successfully sued, he was not as gracious to Betsy Andreu, admitting that while had called her "crazy" and a "bitch," he never said she was "fat."

The cyclist's apology did not satisfy a number of his critics. The head of the World Anti-Doping Agency said that Armstrong gave "weasel" answers during his interview with Winfrey. Betsy Andreu reported she was "furious" with Armstrong's lack of remorse for mistreating her. Many suspected that he sought forgiveness in order to reduce the length of his lifetime ban from sports that operate under the World Anti-Doping Code, such as the Chicago Marathon. Though he stated during the interview that he had stopped cheating before 2009, at least one other cyclist claims otherwise. Cynics believe that Armstrong did not admit to doping after his return because the statute of limitations for criminal fraud has not run out. Then, too, Armstrong denied being the mastermind of a wide-scale doping operation, claiming his approach was "very conservative, very risk-averse." Questions remain about an alleged payment he made to the International Cycling Federation to stop its investigation into his use of performance-enhancing drugs.

Armstrong (who has an estimated worth of $125 million) claims that he lost $75 million in endorsements because of the scandal. But his troubles are far from over. He may face fraud charges for misusing taxpayer funds as the leader of the U.S. Postal Service's cycling team. Some sponsors will likely sue to get their money back. Even Armstrong admits that he may never regain the trust of the public. In his interview with Winfrey, he stated to the American people: "I lied to you and I'm sorry. I am committed to spending as long as I have to make amends, knowing full well that I won't get very many back."[3]

Did Lance Armstrong offer an effective apology for his actions? Why or why not?

Notes

1. Macur, J. (2013, January 17). What to ask after years of denials. *The New York Times*, p. B15.

2. Macur, J. (2013, January 18). Confessing, but continuing to fight. *The New York Times*, p. B11.

3. Lance Armstrong & Oprah Winfrey: Part two interview transcript. BBC. Retrieved from http://www.bbc.co.uk

Sources

Belson, K., & Pilon, M. (2012, October 18). Armstrong is dropped by Nike and steps down as foundation chairman. *The New York Times*, p. B17.

Chadbrand, I. (2013, January 25). Wiggins: I know Lance lied about comeback. *The Daily Telegraph*, Sport, p. 13.

Hampton, R. (2013, January 18). Can you forgive Lance Armstrong? *USA Today*, p. A1.

Lance Armstrong's interview with Oprah Winfrey: The transcript. (2013, January 18). *The Telegraph*. Retrieved from http://www.telegraph.co.uk.

Macur, J. (2012, August 24). Armstrong ends fight against doping charges. *The New York Times*, p. A1.

Macur, J. (2012, August 24). Questions and answers on the Armstrong doping case. *The New York Times*, p. A1.

Macur, J., & Austen, I. (2013, January 19). After the tears, some questions remain unanswered. *The New York Times*, p. D2.

Magnay, J. (2013, January 13). Lance Armstrong gave "weasel answers" in interview with Oprah Winfrey. *The Telegraph.* Retrieved from http://www.telegraph.co.uk.

Schrotenboer, B. (2013, January 28). USADA leader says Armstrong might still be lying. *USA Today*, p. 8C.

SELF-ASSESSMENT 4.1

Tendency to Forgive Scale

Instructions: Respond to each of the following items on a scale of 1 (*strongly disagree*) to 7 (*strongly agree*).

1	2	3	4	5	6	7
Strongly Disagree						Strongly Agree

1. "I tend to get over it quickly when someone hurts my feelings." _____
2. "If someone wrongs me, I often think about it a lot afterward." _____
3. "I have a tendency to harbor grudges." _____
4. "When people wrong me, my approach is just to forgive and forget." _____

Scoring

Reverse your scores on items 2 and 3 and then add up your responses to all four statements. The higher the score (possible scores range from 4 to 28), the more likely you are to forgive others and the less likely you are to bring up offenses from the past.

SOURCE: Brown, R. P. (2003). Measuring individual differences in the tendency to forgive: Construct validity and links with depression. *Personality and Social Psychology Bulletin, 29,* 759–771. Published by SAGE Publications on behalf of the Society for Personality and Social Psychology, Inc. Used by permission.

SELF-ASSESSMENT 4.2

Spiritual Well-Being Questionnaire

Instructions: Indicate how well each of the following statements describes your personal experience over the past six months on a scale of 1 (*very low*) to 5 (*very high*).

1	2	3	4	5
Very Low				Very High

1. Developing a love of other people

2. Developing a personal relationship with God

3. Developing forgiveness toward others

4. Developing a connection with nature

5. Developing a sense of identity

6. Developing worship of the Creator

7. Developing awe at a breathtaking view

8. Developing trust between individuals

9. Developing self-awareness

10. Developing oneness with nature

11. Developing oneness with God

12. Developing harmony with the environment

13. Developing peace with God

14. Developing joy in life

15. Developing a prayer life

16. Developing inner peace

17. Developing respect for others

18. Developing meaning in life

19. Developing kindness toward other people

20. Developing a sense of magic in the environment

Scoring

Add up total scores on each of the four dimensions and then add up the dimension totals to come up with an overall score.

Personal well-being: items 5, 9, 14, 16, 18

Transcendental well-being (connection with God and large forces): items 2, 6, 11, 13, 15

Environmental well-being: items 4, 7, 10, 12, 20

Communal well-being (relationships with others): items 1, 3, 8, 17, 19

Scores for each dimension range from 5 to 25. Total score can range from 25 to 100. The higher the score, the greater your sense of well-being on each dimension and your overall sense of spiritual well-being.

SOURCE: Gomez, R., & Fisher, J. W. (2003). Domains of spiritual well-being and development and validation of the Spiritual Well-Being Questionnaire. *Personality and Individual Differences, 35,* 1975–1991. Used by permission.

NOTES

1. Definitions of evil can be found in the following sources: Hallie, P. (1997). *Tales of good and evil, help and harm.* New York: HarperCollins; Katz, F. E. (1993). *Ordinary people and extraordinary evil: A report on the beguilings of evil.* Albany: State University of New York Press; Kekes, J. (2005). *The roots of evil.* Ithaca, NY: Cornell University Press; Peck, M. S. (1983). *People of the lie: The hope for healing human evil.* New York: Touchstone; Sanford, N., & Comstock, C. (Eds.). (1971). *Sanctions for evil.* San Francisco: Jossey-Bass; Vetelson, A. J. (2005). *Evil and human agency: Understanding collective evildoing.* Cambridge, England: Cambridge University Press. Of course, a host of other definitions are offered by major religions and philosophical systems.

2. Alford, C. F. (1997). *What evil means to us.* Ithaca, NY: Cornell University Press, p. 3.

3. Kekes.

4. Deutsch, M. (1990). Psychological roots of moral exclusion. *Journal of Social Issues, 46*(1), 21–25.

5. Opotow, S. (1990), Moral exclusion and injustice: An introduction. *Journal of Social Issues, 46*(1), 1–20.

6. Chang, I. (1997). *The rape of Nanking: The forgotten holocaust of World War II.* New York: Basic Books, p. 218.

7. Opotow, S. (2007). Moral exclusion and torture: The ticking bomb scenario and the slippery ethical slope. *Peace and Conflict: Journal of Peace Psychology, 13,* 457–461.

8. Opotow, S. (1990). Deterring moral exclusion. *Journal of Social Issues, 46*(1), 173–182.

9. Leets, L. (2001). Interrupting the cycle of moral exclusion: A communication contribution to social justice research. *Journal of Applied Social Psychology, 31,* 1859–1891, p. 1863.

10. Tileaga, C. (2006). Representing the "other": A discursive analysis of prejudice and moral exclusion in talk about Romanies. *Journal of Community & Applied Social Psychology, 16,* 19–41.

11. Bar-Tel, D. (1990). Causes and consequences of delegitimization: Models of conflict and ethnocentrism. *Journal of Social Issues, 46*(1), 65–81.

12. Peck.

13. Adams, G. B., & Balfour, D. L. (2009). *Unmasking administrative evil* (3rd ed.). Armonk, NY: M. E. Sharpe; Adams, G. B. (2011). The problem of administrative evil in a culture of technical rationality. *Public Integrity, 13,* 275–285.

14. Lewis, C. S. (1946). *The great divorce.* New York: Macmillan.

15. Fromm, E. (1964). *The heart of man: Its genius for good and evil.* New York: Harper & Row, p. 136.

16. Arendt, H. (1964). *Eichmann in Jerusalem: A report on the banality of evil.* New York: Viking.

17. Hatzfeld, J. (2005). *Machete season: The killers in Rwanda speak* (L. Coverdale, Trans.). New York: Farrar, Straus and Giroux.

18. Zimbardo, P. G. (2007). *The Lucifer effect: Understanding how good people turn evil.* New York: Random House; Zimbardo, P. G. (2005). A situationist perspective on the psychology of evil. In A. G. Miller (Ed.), *The social psychology of good and evil* (pp. 21–50). New York: Guilford. See also Waller, J. (2007). *Becoming evil: How ordinary people commit genocide and mass killing* (2nd ed.). Oxford, England: Oxford University Press.

19. Opotow, S., & Weiss, L. (2000). Denial and the process of moral exclusion in environmental conflict. *Journal of Social Issues, 56,* 475–490.

20. Opotow (1990), Deterring moral exclusion.

21. Morrow, L. (2003). *Evil: An investigation.* New York: Basic Books.

22. See Murphy, J. G. (2003). *Getting even: Forgiveness and its limits.* Oxford, England: Oxford University Press; Ransley, C., & Spy, T. (Eds.). (2004). *Forgiveness and the healing process: A central therapeutic concern.* New York: Brunner-Routledge; Janover, M. (2005). The limits of forgiveness and the ends of politics. *Journal of Intercultural Studies, 26,* 221–235.

23. Material on the definition and psychology of forgiveness is taken from the following: Enright, R. D., Freedman, S., & Rique, J. (1998). The psychology of interpersonal forgiveness. In R. D. Enright & J. North (Eds.), *Exploring forgiveness* (pp. 46–62). Madison: University of Wisconsin Press; Enright, R. D., & Gassin, E. A. (1992). Forgiveness: A developmental view. *Journal of Moral Education, 21,* 99–114; Freedman, S., Enright, R. D., & Knutson, J. (2005). A progress report on the process model of forgiveness. In E. L. Worthington, Jr. (Ed.), *Handbook of forgiveness* (pp. 393–406). New York: Routledge; Klatt, J. S., & Enright, R. D. (2011). Initial validation of the unfolding forgiveness process in a natural environment. *Counseling and Values, 56,* 25–42; McCullough, M. E., Pargament, K. I., & Thoresen, C. E. (2000). The psychology of forgiveness: History, conceptual issues, and overview. In M. E. McCullough, K. I. Pargament, & C. E. Thoresen (Eds.), *Forgiveness: Theory, research, and practice* (pp. 1–14). New York: Guilford; Musekura, C. (2010). *An assessment of contemporary models of forgiveness.* New York: Peter Lang; Thomas, G. (2000, January 10). The forgiveness factor. *Christianity Today,* pp. 38–43.

24. Enright et al., pp. 46–47.

25. For information on the by-products of forgiveness, see Casarjian, R. (1992). *Forgiveness: A bold choice for a peaceful heart.* New York: Bantam; Enright, R. D. (2012). *The forgiving life.* Washington, DC: American Psychological Association; Enright et al.; Freedman et al.; Klatt, J., & Enright, R. D. (2009). Investigating the place of forgiveness with the Positive Youth Development paradigm. *Journal of Moral Education, 38,* 35–52; McCullough, M. E., Sandage, S. J., & Worthington, E. L. (1997). *To forgive is human: How to put your past in the past.* Downers Grove, IL: InterVarsity Press; Thoresen, C. E., Harris, H. S., & Luskin, F. (2000). Forgiveness and health: An unanswered question. In M. E. McCullough, K. I. Pargament, & C. E. Thoresen (Eds.), *Forgiveness: Theory, research, and practice* (pp. 254–280). New York: Guilford; Worthington, E. L., Jr. (2005). Initial questions about the art and science of forgiving. In E. L. Worthington (Ed.), *Handbook of forgiveness* (pp. 1–13). New York: Routledge; Waltman, M. A., Russell, D. C., Coyle, C. T., Enright, R. D., Holter, A. C., & Swoboda, C. M. (2009). The effects of a forgiveness intervention on patients with coronary artery disease. *Psychology and Health, 24*(1), 11–27.

26. Shriver, D. W. (1995). *An ethic for enemies: Forgiveness in politics.* New York: Oxford University Press. See also Wilmot, W. W., & Hocker, J. L. (2001). *Interpersonal conflict*

(6th ed.). New York: McGraw-Hill Higher Education, Ch. 1.

27. Shriver, p. 8.

28. Forgiveness also extends to the self. Self-forgiveness acknowledges your dignity and equips you to move forward to restore relationships. See, for example, Holmgren, J. R. (1998). Self-forgiveness and responsible moral agency. *Journal of Value Inquiry, 32,* 75–91; Snow, N. E. (1993). Self-forgiveness. *Journal of Value Inquiry, 27,* 75–80.

29. For one list of prominent Americans who have been forced to apologize, see Hampton, R. (2013, January 18). Can you forgive Lance Armstrong? *USA Today,* p. A1.

30. Lazare, A. (2004). *On apology.* Oxford, England: Oxford University Press; Kador, J. (2009). *Effective apology: Mending fences, building bridges, and restoring trust.* San Francisco: Berrett-Koehler.

31. Lowenheim, N. (2009). A haunted past: Requesting forgiveness for wrongdoing in international relations. *Review of International Studies, 35,* 531–555; Shriver, D. W. (2001). Forgiveness: A bridge across abysses of revenge. In R. G. Helmick & R. L. Peterson (Eds.), *Forgiveness and reconciliation: Religion, public policy, and conflict transformation* (pp. 151–167). Philadelphia: Templeton Foundation Press; Griswold, C. L. (2007). *Forgiveness: A philosophical exploration.* Cambridge, England: Cambridge University Press; Nobles, M. (2008). *The politics of official apologies.* Cambridge, England: Cambridge University Press.

32. Lazare.

33. Kador, p. 11.

34. Oswick, C. (2009). Burgeoning workplace spirituality? A textual analysis of momentum and directions. *Journal of Management, Spirituality & Religion, 6,* 15–25.

35. King, S., Biberman, J., Robbins, L., & Nicol, D. M. (2007). Integrating spirituality into management education in academia and organizations: Origins, a conceptual framework, and current practices. In J. Biberman & M. D. Whitty (Eds.), *At work:*

Spirituality matters (pp. 243–256). Scranton, PA: University of Scranton Press.

36. Information on the benefits of workplace spirituality is taken from the following: Craigie, F. C. (1999). The spirit and work: Observations about spirituality and organizational life. *Journal of Psychology and Christianity, 18,* 43–53; Fairholm, G. W. (1996). Spiritual leadership: Fulfilling whole-self needs at work. *Leadership & Organization Development Journal, 17*(5), 11–17; Garcia-Zamor, J. C. (2003). Workplace spirituality and organizational performance. *Public Administration Review, 63,* 355–363; Giacalone, R. A., & Jurkiewicz, C. L. (2003). Right from wrong: The influence of spirituality on perceptions of unethical business activities. *Journal of Business Ethics, 46,* 85–97; Giacalone, R. A., & Jurkiewicz, C. L. (2003). Toward a science of workplace spirituality. In R. A. Giacalone & C. L. Jurkiewicz (Eds.), *Handbook of workplace spirituality and organizational performance* (pp. 3–28). Armonk, NY: M. E. Sharpe; Jurkiewicz, C. L., & Giacalone, R. A. (2004). A values framework for measuring the impact of workplace spirituality on organizational performance. *Journal of Business Ethics, 49,* 129–142; Karakas, F. (2010). Spirituality and performance in organizations: A literature review. *Journal of Business Ethics, 94,* 89–106; Mirvis, P. H. (1997). "Soul work" in organizations. *Organization Science, 8,* 193–206; Rego, A., & Pina e Cunha, M. (2008). Workplace spirituality and organizational commitment: An empirical study. *Journal of Organizational Change Management, 21,* 53–75.

37. Ashmos, D. P., & Duchon, D. (2000). Spirituality at work: A conceptualization and measure. *Journal of Management Inquiry, 9,* 134–145, p. 137; see also Duchon, D., & Plowman, D. A. (2005). Nurturing the spirit at work: Impact on work unit performance. *Leadership Quarterly, 16,* 807–833.

38. Pollard, C. W. (1996). *The soul of the firm.* Grand Rapids, MI: HarperBusiness, p. 25.

39. See Zinnbauer, B. J., & Pargament, K. I. (2005). Religiousness and spirituality. In

R. F. Paloutzian & C. L. Park (Eds.), *Handbook of the psychology of religion and spirituality* (pp. 21–42). New York: Guilford.

40. See Judge, W. Q. (1999). *The leader's shadow: Exploring and developing executive character.* Thousand Oaks, CA: Sage.

41. Reave, L. (2005). Spiritual values and practices related to leadership effectiveness. *Leadership Quarterly, 16,* 655–687.

42. One detailed list of personal and collective spiritual practices can be found in Foster, R. J. (1978). *Celebration of discipline: The path to spiritual growth.* New York: Harper & Row.

43. Fry, L. W. (2003). Toward a theory of spiritual leadership. *Leadership Quarterly, 14,* 693–727; Fry, L. W., Vitucci, S., & Cedillo, M. (2005). Spiritual leadership and army transformation: Theory, measurement, and establishing a baseline. *Leadership Quarterly, 16,* 835–862; Fry, L. W. (2005). Toward a theory of ethical and spiritual well-being, and corporate social responsibility through spiritual leadership. In

R. A. Giacalone, C. L. Jurkiewicz, & C. Dunn (Eds.), *Positive psychology in business ethics and corporate responsibility* (pp. 47–84). Greenwich, CT: Information Age; Fry, L. W. (2008). Spiritual leadership: State-of-the-art and future directions for theory, research, and practice. In J. Biberman & L. Tischler (Eds.), *Spirituality in business: Theory, practice, and future directions* (pp. 106–123). New York: Palgrave Macmillan.

44. Benefiel, M. (2005). *Soul at work: Spiritual leadership in organizations.* New York: Seabury Books; Benefiel, M. (2005). The second half of the journey: Spiritual leadership for organizational transformation. *Leadership Quarterly, 16,* 723–747.

45. Jurkiewicz & Giacalone.

46. Boje, D. (2008). Critical theory approaches to spirituality in business. In J. Biberman & L. Tischler (Eds.), *Spirituality in business: Theory, practice, and future directions* (pp. 160–187). New York: Palgrave Macmillan.

Ethical Standards and Strategies

5

Ethical Perspectives

Leaders are truly effective only when they are motivated by a concern for others.

—Business professors Rabindra Kanungo and
Manuel Mendonca

What's Ahead

This chapter surveys widely used ethical perspectives or systems that leaders can use when making ethical decisions. These approaches include utilitarianism, Kant's categorical imperative, Rawls's justice as fairness, pragmatism, and altruism. For each perspective, I provide a brief description and then offer some suggestions for applying the framework as well as some cautions about doing so.

In Chapter 2, I identified lack of expertise as one reason leaders unintentionally cast shadows. We may lack experience or we may not be aware of the ethical perspectives or frameworks we can apply to ethical dilemmas. The purpose of this chapter is to introduce some widely used systems that leaders can employ when making moral choices. These tools help us identify and clarify problems, force us to think systematically, encourage us to view issues from many different vantage points, and supply us with decision-making guidelines. They play a critical role in the decision-making formats described in the next chapter. I'll introduce each perspective and suggest how it can be applied to ethical decisions. I'll also offer some cautions about the limitations of each approach.

Resist the temptation to select one perspective for decision making while ignoring the others. That would be a mistake. Each offers unique insights. Applying several approaches to the same problem will give you a deeper understanding of the issue even if the different frameworks lead to different conclusions. You might also find that a particular perspective is more suited to some kinds of ethical dilemmas than to others. Case Study 5.3 ("Drone

Wars") is designed as a testing ground for the material in the chapter. After learning about each perspective, apply it to the case. Then come to a final conclusion based on your analysis that incorporates all five approaches.

Utilitarianism: Do the Greatest Good for the Greatest Number of People

Utilitarianism is based on the premise that ethical choices should be based on their consequences. People probably have always considered the likely outcomes of their decisions when determining what to do. However, this process wasn't formalized and given a name until the 18th and 19th centuries. English philosophers Jeremy Bentham (1748–1832) and John Stuart Mill (1806–1873) argued that the best decisions generate the most benefits, as compared with their disadvantages, and benefit the largest number of people.[1] In sum, utilitarianism is attempting to do the greatest good for the greatest number of people. Utility can be based on what is best in a specific case (act utilitarianism) or on what is generally best in most contexts (rule utilitarianism). For example, we can decide that telling a specific lie is justified in one situation (to protect someone's reputation) but, as a general rule, believe that lying is wrong because it causes more harm than good.

There are four steps to conducting a utilitarian analysis of an ethical problem.[2] First, clearly identify the action or issue under consideration. Second, specify all those who might be affected by the action (e.g., the organization, the local community, a professional group, society), not just those immediately involved in the situation. Third, determine the likely consequences, both good and bad, for those affected. Fourth, sum the good and the bad consequences. The action is morally right if the benefits outweigh the costs. (Turn to Case Study 5.1 for an example of a decision that involves choosing the less costly of two alternatives.)

Political leaders often take a utilitarian approach to ethical decision making. For instance, security screening procedures at American airports have been tightened based on utilitarian considerations. In response to the World Trade Center attacks of 2001, airport security personnel began X-raying baggage and carry-on items, patting down some passengers, and sending travelers through metal detectors. When a Nigerian airline passenger set off a packet of chemicals hidden in his underwear on Christmas Day in 2009, the Transportation Security Administration began to expand its use of body imaging devices. These screening technologies reveal metal and nonmetal objects hidden beneath clothing but can also produce graphic images of the human body. All these measures are costly. They are expensive, time-consuming, inconvenient, and intrusive. But so far federal officials and the majority of passengers believe that these costs are justified because the measures prevent attacks and save lives.

Applications and Cautions

Applications

- Build on your prior experience.

- Carefully examine the outcomes of your decisions.

- Set personal interests aside.

- Recognize when weighing likely consequences is critical.

The notion of weighing outcomes is easy to understand and to apply. Chances are you already use this technique, creating a series of mental balance sheets for all types of decisions, such as determining whether an item, a car, or a vacation package is worth the price; considering a job offer; or evaluating the merits of two political candidates. Take advantage of your experience when weighing the costs and benefits of ethical decisions. Keep your focus on outcomes, which will encourage you to think through your decisions. You'll also be less likely to make rash, unreasoned choices, which is particularly important when it comes to ethical dilemmas. The ultimate goal of evaluating consequences is admirable: to maximize benefits to as many people as possible (not just to yourself). As a result, your personal interests should not be the primary concern when making decisions. Remember, too, that utilitarianism is probably the most defensible approach in some situations. For example, in medical emergencies involving large numbers of injured victims, top priority should go to those who are most likely to survive. It does little good for medical personnel to spend time with terminal patients while other victims who would benefit from treatment die.

Cautions

- Probable consequences are difficult to identify, measure, and evaluate.

- There may be unanticipated outcomes.

- Decision makers may reach different conclusions.

Identifying possible consequences can be difficult, particularly for decision makers who represent a variety of constituencies or stakeholders. Take the case of a college president who must decide what academic programs to cut in a budget crisis. Many different groups have a stake in this decision, and each probably will reach a different conclusion about potential costs and benefits. Every department believes that it makes a valuable contribution to the university and serves the mission of the school. Powerful alumni may be alienated by the elimination of their majors. Members of the local community might suffer if the education department is terminated and no longer supplies teachers to area schools or if plays and concerts end because of cutbacks in the theater and music departments. Unanticipated consequences further complicate the choice. If student enrollments increase, the president may have to restore programs that she eliminated earlier. Yet failing to make cuts can put the future of the school in jeopardy.

Even when consequences are clear, you may find that evaluating their relative merits can be daunting. It is hard to compare different kinds of costs and benefits, for example. The construction of a housing development provides new homes but takes farmland out of production. How do we weigh the relative value of urban housing versus family farms? Also, utilitarianism says little about how benefits are to be distributed. "Doing the greatest good" may mean putting one group at a serious disadvantage so that everyone else will benefit. During World War II, for example, Japanese Americans were warehoused in camps based on the mistaken belief that this would make the nation as a whole safer. Conversely, utilitarian calculations may benefit the few at the expense of the majority. Many who donate funding to medical efforts in developing countries focus their contributions on one disease, such as malaria, hoping to have a major impact on that illness. Such an approach benefits those who suffer from the particular malady but ignores the needs of everyone else suffering from other medical problems, like HIV/AIDS, tuberculosis, cancer, kidney disease, dysentery, and cholera. We also tend to favor ourselves when making decisions. Thus, you are likely to put more weight on consequences that most directly affect you. It's all too easy to confuse the "greatest good" with your own selfish interests.

Given the difficulty of identifying and evaluating potential costs and benefits, utilitarian decision makers sometimes reach different conclusions when faced with the same dilemma. Americans are still debating the merits of heightened airport security measures. Many argue that the costs of stricter security are justified because no further attacks have succeeded in causing serious damage to planes or passengers. On the other hand, privacy groups and some in Congress oppose the use of body imaging devices, labeling them "digital strip searches."[3] A number of potential air travelers, turned off by the hassle of going through security checkpoints at airports, opt to drive to their destinations instead.

Kant's Categorical Imperative: Do What's Right No Matter the Cost

In sharp contrast to the utilitarians, European philosopher Immanuel Kant (1724–1804) argued that people should do what is morally right no matter the consequences.[4] (The term *categorical* means "without exception.") His approach to moral reasoning is the best-known example of deontological ethics. Deontological ethicists argue that we ought to make choices based on our duty (*deon* is the Greek word for duty). Fulfilling our obligations may run contrary to our personal interests. For example, revealing a product defect to a potential customer might cost us a sale but is nevertheless the ethical course of action.

According to Kant, what is right for one is right for all. We need to ask ourselves one question: Would I want everyone else to make the decision I did? If the answer is yes, the choice is justified. If the answer is no, the decision is wrong. Based on this reasoning, certain behaviors, such as truth telling and helping the poor, are always right. Other acts, such as lying, cheating, and murder, are always wrong. Testing and grading would be impossible if everyone cheated, for example, and cooperation would be impossible if no one could be trusted to tell the truth.

Kant lived well before the advent of the automobile, but violations of his decision-making rule could explain why law enforcement officials have to crack down on motorists who run red lights. So many Americans regularly disobey traffic signals (endangering pedestrians and other drivers) that some communities have installed cameras at intersections to catch violators. Drivers have failed to recognize one simple fact: They may save time by running lights, but they shouldn't do so because the system breaks down when large numbers of people ignore traffic signals.

Kant also emphasized the importance of respecting persons, which has become a key principle in Western moral philosophy.[5] According to Kant, "Act so that you treat humanity, whether in your own person or that of another, always as an end and never as a means only." Although others can help us reach our goals, they should never be considered solely as tools. Instead, we should respect and encourage the capacity of others to think and choose for themselves. Under this standard, it is wrong for companies to expose citizens living near manufacturing facilities to dangerous pollutants without their knowledge or consent. Coercion and violence are immoral because such tactics violate freedom of choice. Failing to assist a neighbor is unethical because ignoring this person's need limits his or her options.

Applications and Cautions

Applications

- Be duty-bound.

- Always ask yourself if you would want everyone to make the same choice.

- Demonstrate respect for others.

Duty should play a significant role in our ethical deliberations. In fact, the notion that we have a duty to take our ethical responsibilities seriously is a foundational principle of this text. Emphasis on duty encourages persistence and consistent behavior. If you are driven by the conviction that certain behaviors are either right or wrong no matter what the situation, you will be less likely to compromise your personal ethical standards. You are apt to "stay the course" despite group pressures and opposition and to follow through on your choices.

Kant offers two powerful decision-making tools. First, ask yourself if you would want everyone else to make the same decision. If not, reevaluate your choice before going forward. Second, always respect the dignity of others. Don't use them or violate their rights. Instead, respect the freedom of others to choose for themselves. Share information while avoiding deception, coercion, and violence.

Cautions

- Exceptions exist to nearly every "universal" law.

- Moral obligations may conflict with one another.

- Ethical guidelines are often demonstrated through unrealistic examples.

- This framework is hard to apply, particularly under stress.

Most attacks on Kant's system of reasoning center on his assertion that there are universal principles that should be followed in every situation. In almost every case, we can think of exceptions. For instance, many of us believe that lying is wrong yet would lie or withhold the truth to save the life of a friend. Countries regularly justify homicide during war. Then, too, moral obligations can conflict. It may be impossible for you to keep promises made to more than one group, for example. Raises promised to employees may have to be set aside so that promised dividends can be paid to stockholders. Or satisfying one duty may mean violating another, as in the case of a whistle-blower who puts truth telling above loyalty to the organization. (See Chapter 6 for more information on ethical dilemmas involving two right values.)

Some contemporary philosophers complain that ethical guidelines like those outlined by Bentham and Kant are applied to extreme situations, not to the types of decisions we typically make. Chances are you won't ever be faced with any of the extraordinary scenarios (e.g., stealing to save a life or lying to the secret police to protect a fugitive) that are often used to illustrate principled decision making.[6] Your dilemmas are likely to be less dramatic. You have to determine whether to confront a coworker about a sexist joke or tell someone the truth at the risk of hurting his or her feelings. You also face time pressures and uncertainty. In a crisis, you don't always have time to carefully weigh consequences or to determine which abstract principle to follow.

Justice as Fairness: Guaranteeing Equal Rights and Opportunities Behind the Veil of Ignorance

Many disputes in democratic societies center on questions of justice or fairness. Is it just to give more tax breaks to the rich than to the poor? What is equitable compensation for executives? Should a certain percentage of federal contracts be reserved for minority contractors? Is it fair that Native Americans are granted special fishing rights? Why should young workers have to contribute to the Social Security system when it may not be around when they retire?

In the last third of the 20th century, Harvard philosopher John Rawls addressed questions such as these in a series of books and articles.[7] He set out to identify principles that would foster cooperation in a society made up of free and equal citizens who, at the same time, must deal with inequalities (e.g., status and economic differences, varying levels of talent and abilities). Rawls rejected utilitarian principles because, as noted earlier, generating the greatest number of benefits for society as a whole can seriously disadvantage certain groups and individuals. Cutting corporate taxes is another case of how utilitarian reasoning can undermine the interests of some groups at the expense of others. This policy may spur a region's overall economic growth, but most of the benefits go to the owners of companies. Other citizens have to pay higher taxes to make up for the lost revenue. Those making minimum wage, who can barely pay for rent and food, are particularly hard-hit. They end up subsidizing wealthy corporate executives and stockholders.

Instead of basing decisions on cost–benefit analyses, Rawls argues, we should follow these principles of justice and build them into our social institutions:

> *Principle 1:* Each person has an equal right to the same basic liberties that are compatible with similar liberties for all.

> *Principle 2:* Social and economic inequalities are to satisfy two conditions:
> (a) They are to be attached to offices and positions open to all under conditions of fair equality of opportunity. (b) They are to provide the greatest benefit to the least advantaged members of society.

The first principle, the "principle of equal liberty," has priority. It states that certain rights, such as the right to vote, the right to hold property, and freedom of speech, are protected and must be held equal by all persons. Attempts to deny voting rights to minorities would be unethical according to this standard. Principle 2a asserts that everyone should have an equal opportunity to qualify for offices and jobs. Discrimination based on race, gender, or ethnic origin is forbidden. Furthermore, everyone in society ought to have access to the training and education needed to prepare for these roles. Principle 2b, "the difference principle," recognizes that inequalities exist but states that priority should be given to meeting the needs of the poor, immigrants, minorities, and other marginalized groups.

Rawls introduces the "veil of ignorance" to back up his claim that his principles provide a solid foundation for a democratic society such as the United States. Imagine, he says, a group of people who are asked to come up with a set of principles that will govern society. These group members are ignorant of their own characteristics or societal positions. Standing behind this veil of ignorance, these people would choose (a) equal liberty, because they would want the maximum amount of freedom to pursue their interests; (b) equal opportunity, because if they turned out to be the most talented members of society, they would probably land the best jobs and elected offices; and (c) the difference principle, because they would want to be sure they were cared for if they ended up disadvantaged.

Applications and Cautions

Applications

- Follow fairness guidelines.

- Weigh both individual freedom and the good of the community when making decisions.

- Step behind the veil of ignorance when making choices.

As noted in Chapter 1, leaders cast shadows by acting inconsistently. Inconsistent leaders violate commonly held standards of fairness, arbitrarily giving preferential treatment to some followers while denying the same benefits to others who are equally deserving (or more so). Rawls directly addresses the shadow of inconsistency by outlining a set of principles to help us act fairly: Guarantee basic rights to all followers; ensure that followers have equal access to promotion, training, and other benefits; and make special efforts to help followers who have unique needs. (Complete Self-Assessment 5.1 to determine how just your organization is.) Keep in mind the reality of inequalities but strive to balance both individual freedom and the common good. While you want to encourage more talented, skilled, or fortunate followers to pursue their goals, Rawls urges you to make sure the fruits of their labor also benefit their less fortunate neighbors or coworkers.

The veil of ignorance is an important guideline to follow when making moral choices. Whenever possible, try to set aside such considerations as wealth, education, gender, and race. The least advantaged usually benefit when social class differences are excluded from the decision-making process. Our judicial system is one example of an institution that should treat disputants fairly. Unfortunately, economic and racial considerations influence the selection of juries, the determination of guilt and innocence, the lengths of sentences (and where they are served), and nearly every other aspect of the judicial process.

Cautions

- Rawls's principles can only be applied to democratic societies.

- Groups disagree about the meanings of justice and fairness.

- There is lack of consensus about which rights are most important.

Rawls's theory of justice as fairness has come under sharp attack. Rawls himself acknowledges that his model applies only to liberal democratic societies. It cannot work in cultures governed by royal families or religious leaders who are given special powers and privileges denied to everyone else. In addition, the more diverse democratic nations become, the more difficult it is for groups to agree on common values and principles.[8]

Rawls's critics note that definitions of justice and fairness vary widely, a fact that undermines the usefulness of his principles. What seems fair to you often appears grossly unjust to others. Evidence of this fact is found in disputes over college admission criteria. Some assert that admission decisions should favor members of minority groups to redress past discrimination and to enable minorities to achieve equal footing with Whites. Others feel that admission standards that take minority status into account are unfair because they deny equal opportunity and ignore legitimate differences in abilities.

Some philosophers point out that there is no guarantee that parties who step behind the veil of ignorance would come up with the same set of principles as Rawls. Rather than emphasize fairness, these people might choose to make decisions based on utilitarian criteria or to emphasize certain rights. For example, libertarians hold that freedom from coercion is the most important human right. Every person should be able to produce and sell as he or she chooses regardless of impact on the poor. Capitalist theorists believe that benefits should be distributed based on the contributions each person makes to the group. They argue that helping out the less advantaged rewards laziness while discouraging productive people from doing their best. Because decision makers may reach different conclusions behind the veil, you may agree with skeptics who contend that Rawls's guidelines lack moral force. You may conclude that other approaches to managing society's inequities are just as valid as the notion of fairness.

Pragmatism: Ethics as Inquiry

The approaches discussed so far—utilitarianism, the categorical imperative, and justice as fairness—differ significantly, but all share one characteristic: They are rule-based approaches to resolving ethical dilemmas. Each outlines a set of principles or rules that can be applied to specific situations. In contrast, pragmatism focuses on the *process* of moral decision making. Those taking a pragmatic approach reject the use of abstract principles, believing instead that good ethical choices emerge through the use of inquiry.

Pragmatism was the dominant philosophical movement in the United States from the Civil War through World War II.[9] Charles Peirce (1839–1914) and William James (1842–1910) founded the movement, but it was John Dewey (1859–1952) who emerged as its most prominent spokesperson. Dewey wrote extensively on the topics of education, philosophy, science, and politics over his long career. In recent years, philosophers and ethicists have returned to the ideas of Dewey for insights into how to approach moral decision making.

Pragmatism gets its name from its focus on using philosophy to solve practical problems.[10] Dewey and other pragmatists believed that the scientific method can be applied to solving human dilemmas. In the scientific method, researchers develop hypotheses, which they then test through experiments. The hypotheses are then modified based on the experimental results. Conclusions are always subject to revision, depending on what the evidence reveals.

Dewey argued that ethical dilemmas should be approached scientifically as well. Ethical quandaries create a sense of unease or distress, which then prompts us to address the problem. Since we can't conduct an actual physical experiment (as we would when investigating a chemistry problem), we rely on our moral imaginations.[11] Exercising moral imagination involves mentally testing out various courses of action, considering likely outcomes, determining how others might respond, referring to how similar problems have been solved in the past, and so on. Humility and openness to other points of view are key to mental experimentation. We need to admit that our knowledge is limited and welcome new discoveries.[12] According to Dewey, democracy provides the best setting for encouraging this type of experimental thinking and action.

The term *dramatic rehearsal* describes mental imagination in action. In dramatic rehearsal, decision makers conduct a series of imaginary thought experiments to visualize how their decisions could turn out. According to philosopher John McVea, dramatic rehearsal differs in important ways from the calculative, deliberative approach typically used in ethical decision making.[13] Dramatic rehearsal takes into account the emotions of those involved rather than setting feelings aside. Creative solutions emerge through deliberation rather than through the application of rules. Dramatic rehearsal immerses the leader in the specifics of the situation instead of encouraging her or him to rely on abstract principles.

While Dewey focused on the process of ethical decision making, he also believed that every ethical decision must be made with an end or value in mind. Ethics needs to answer these questions: "What ends should I strive for?" and "What conduct should I engage in so that I attain these ends?"[14] Much like Aristotle, Dewey believed that every ethical decision or habit has an impact on the character of the person making the choice. Making wise choices fosters our character development.[15] The ultimate goal for Dewey was human happiness, happiness that takes the form of growth. Growth comes from solving problems, which opens up new possibilities for further growth and maturity. In Dewey's words:

> The process of growth, of improvement and progress, rather than the static outcome and result, becomes the significant thing. . . . The end is not longer a terminus or limit to be reached. It is the active process of transforming the existent situation. Not perfection as a final goal, but the ever-enduring process of perfecting, maturing, refining is the aim in living. . . . Growth itself is the only moral "end."[16]

Muhammad Yunus, founder of the Grameen Bank of Bangladesh, is an example of a leader who used dramatic rehearsal to address immediate ethical problems. In so doing, he developed his character.[17] In 1972 Yunus returned to his home country of Bangladesh to take up a teaching post after completing his doctorate in economics in the United States. However, the nation's suffering troubled Yunus, and he began to focus on alleviating poverty. He and his students then undertook a series of research projects in order to understand the causes of poverty. They discovered that inability to secure credit kept many from economic security. Rather than turn to charities or the government for help, Yunus developed a creative solution—he started a for-profit bank to lend small amounts to rural villagers. By immersing himself in the plight of the poor, he discovered that many village women had skills that they could use in small enterprises if they only had the capital to start their businesses. As a result, many of the bank's loans go to female entrepreneurs.

Later Yunus promoted the use of cell phones in remote villages. He envisioned that women could start businesses by renting out phones for calls and that the phones would give villagers access to market information. Cell phones would also reduce the isolation of women, which made them vulnerable to abuse.

Because he decided to work on eliminating poverty rather than teaching economics, Yunus ended up pursuing a different career and developing a new set of beliefs and values. Throughout his journey, he always kept the end in view when making decisions:

I was not trying to become a money lender. I had (originally) no intention of lending money to anyone; all I really wanted was to solve an immediate problem. Even to this day I still view myself, my work and that of my colleagues, as devoted to solving the same immediate problem: the problem of poverty which humiliates and denigrates everything that a human being stands for.[18]

Applications and Cautions

Applications

- Approach ethical problems as you would other dilemmas.

- Immerse yourself in the details of the situation.

- Engage your imagination.

- Acknowledge your limitations.

- Look for creative solutions.

- Embrace your emotions.

- Recognize that your ethical choices shape your character.

Solving ethical problems takes many of same strategies as solving other dilemmas, like determining how to lower costs or increase sales. You must identify options, consider possible outcomes, gather information, experiment, and adjust your conclusions in the light of new information (see Chapter 6). You need to immerse yourself in the details of the situation to gain a better understanding of the challenges you face.

Dramatic rehearsal is a useful tool when facing a moral dilemma. Imagination allows you to experiment with solutions and engage in perspective taking, both of which are essential to ethical problem solving. An experimental approach is particularly important when in a leadership role. You need to acknowledge your limitations—that means continually trying out ideas, recognizing when ideas need to be adjusted in the face of changing conditions, and respecting the input of followers. Whenever possible, seek novel solutions. These often emerge during the inquiry process. Rather than rejecting your emotions, embrace them. They can signal that an ethical problem exists and spur you to action.

Dewey also reminds us that ethical choices aren't isolated events. Ethical choices and the habits they develop have a cumulative impact. Taken together, they determine our character.

Cautions

- Pragmatism lacks a moral center.

- This approach can lead to undesirable decisions.

- The ultimate goal of ethical decision making is vague.

You may be troubled by the fact that pragmatism lacks a "normative core." It offers no guidelines, such as doing the greatest good for the greatest number, for determining right or wrong or for justifying a choice. Instead, you need to trust that a worthy solution will emerge through the process of inquiry. As some critics note, there is no guarantee that ethical inquiry and experimentation will produce ethical solutions. They point to the example of the Nazis, who engaged in a series of inhuman medical experiments. Doctors euthanized mentally challenged and disabled children, and Josef Mengele carried out gruesome medical experiments at Auschwitz.[19] Then, too, there is confusion about the ultimate goal of pragmatic ethical decision making. Dewey argues that we need to pursue human happiness and growth. You will have to define what these highly abstract goals mean for you.

FOCUS ON FOLLOWER ETHICS

The Growing Influence of Followers: Engaging With and Resisting Leaders

Harvard University political scientist Barbara Kellerman believes that followers are gaining power at the expense of leaders. "It's clear the gap between leaders and followers is closing," she asserts (p. 46). "Leaders need followers more than followers need leaders" (p. 242). Followers led the antiwar, civil rights, and women's movements in the United States, for example, and toppled Communism and the Berlin Wall. *Time* magazine named "the Protester" as its 2011 Person of the Year in recognition of the impact of the ordinary citizens who participated in the Arab Spring, which overthrew a number of Middle Eastern dictatorships, and the Occupy movement. Shareholders are becoming more active in corporate governance, and a number of autocratic CEOs and orchestra conductors have been replaced with friendlier, more approachable leaders. Kellerman attributes the growing influence of followers to the egalitarian spirit of the 1960s and the ongoing information revolution, which makes data accessible to everyone, not just leaders, and flattens organizational structures.

Professor Kellerman offers a follower typology based on the level of involvement that followers have with their leaders. *Isolate* followers are the least engaged, completely withdrawn and detached. *Bystander* followers observe and remain neutral. *Participant* followers are invested in helping or resisting their leaders. *Activist* followers are even more engaged in working on behalf of or against their leaders. *Die-hard* followers take great risks because they are strongly devoted to or strongly opposed to their leaders.

Kellerman argues that, at a minimum, ethical followers engage with their leaders. Isolates and bystanders therefore demonstrate bad followership. However, engagement alone is not enough to make followers "good." Participants, activists, and die-hards can support unethical leaders. Kellerman notes that the question then becomes "Willingness to engage to what end, for what purpose?" (p. 229). She concludes that good followers are not only involved; they are motivated to serve the public good, not selfish interests. To encourage followers to serve the greater good by resisting bad leaders, she offers a number of guidelines. Among them are the following:

- Be informed.
- Be engaged.
- Be independent.
- Be a watchdog.
- Be prepared to analyze and judge the situation, the leader, and the other followers.
- Be open to allies and to forming coalitions.
- Be prepared to be different.
- Be prepared to take a stand.
- Be loyal to the group, not to any single individual.
- Know the slippery slope—bad leaders who over time become more deeply embedded and more difficult to uproot.
- Know your options.
- Know the risk of doing something—and of doing nothing.
- Check your moral compass. (pp. 257–258)

SOURCE: Kellerman, B. (2008). *Followership: How followers are creating change and changing leaders.* Boston: Harvard Business School Press.

Altruism: Love Your Neighbor

Advocates of altruism argue that love of neighbor is the ultimate ethical standard. Our actions should be designed to help others, whatever the personal cost. The altruistic approach to moral reasoning shares much in common with virtue ethics. Many of the virtues that characterize people of high moral character, such as compassion, hospitality, empathy, and generosity, reflect concern for other people. Clearly, virtuous leaders are other-centered, not self-centered.

Altruism appears to be a universal value, one promoted in cultures in every region of the world. The Dalai Lama urges followers to practice an ethic of compassion, for instance, and Western thought has been greatly influenced by the altruistic emphasis of Judaism and Christianity. The command to love God and to love others as we love ourselves is our most important obligation in Judeo-Christian ethics. Because humans are made in the image of God and God is love, we have an obligation to love others no matter who they are and no matter their relationship to us. Jesus drove home this point in the parable of the Good Samaritan:

> A man was going down from Jerusalem to Jericho when he fell into the hands of robbers. They stripped him of his clothes, beat him, and went away, leaving him half dead. A priest happened to be going down the same road, and when he saw the man, he passed by on the other side. So too, a Levite, when he came to the place and saw him, passed by on the other side. But a Samaritan, as he traveled, came where the man was; and when he saw him, he took pity on him. He went to him and bandaged his wounds, pouring on oil and wine. Then he put the man on his own donkey, took him to an inn, and took care of him. The next day he took out two silver coins and gave them to the innkeeper. "Look after him," he said, "and when I return, I will reimburse you for any extra expense you may have." Which of these three do you think was a neighbor to the man who fell into the hands of robbers? The expert replied, "The one who had mercy on him." Jesus told him, "Go and do likewise." (Luke 1:3–35, New International Version)

Hospice volunteers provide a modern-day example of the unconditional love portrayed in the story of the Good Samaritan. They meet the needs of the dying regardless of their patients' social or religious backgrounds, providing help at significant personal cost without expecting anything in return. (An ethical approach specifically based on caring for others is described in Box 5.1.)

• • • BOX 5.1 THE ETHIC OF CARE • • •

The altruistic ethic of care developed as an alternative to what feminists label as the traditional male-oriented approach to ethics. The categorical imperative and justice-as-fairness approaches emphasize the importance of acting on abstract moral principles, being impartial, and treating others fairly. Carol Gilligan, Nel Noddings, and others initially argued that women take a different approach (have a "different voice") to moral decision making based on caring for others. Instead of expressing concern for people in abstract terms, women care for others through their relationships and tailor their responses to the particular needs of the other individual. Subsequent research revealed that the ethic of care is not exclusive to women. Men as well as women may prefer care to justice.

Philosopher Virginia Held identifies five key components of the care ethic:

1. *Focuses on the importance of noting and meeting the needs of those we are responsible for.* Most people are dependent for much of their existence, including during childhood, during illness, and near the end of life. Morality built on rights and autonomy overlooks this fact. The ethic of care makes concern for others central to human experience and puts the needs of specific individuals—a child, an elderly relative—first.

2. *Values emotions.* Sympathy, sensitivity, empathy, and responsiveness are moral emotions that need to be cultivated. This stands in sharp contrast to ethical approaches that urge decision makers to set aside their feelings in order to make rational, impartial determinations. However, emotions need to be carefully monitored and evaluated to make sure they are appropriate. For instance, caregivers caught up in empathy can deny their own needs or end up controlling the recipients of their care.

3. *Specific needs and relationships take priority above universal principles.* The ethic of care rejects the notion of impartiality and believes particular relationships are more important than universal moral principles like rights and freedom. For example, the needs of the immediate family take precedence over the needs of neighbors or of society as a whole. Persons in caring relationships aren't out to promote their personal interests or the interests of humanity; instead they want to foster ethical relationships

(Continued)

(Continued)

with each other. Family and friendships have great moral value in the ethic of care, and caregiving is a critical moral responsibility.

4. *Breaks down the barriers between the public and private spheres.* In the past, men were dominant in the public sphere while relegating women to the "private" sphere. Men largely made decisions about how to exercise political and economic power while women were marginalized and dependent. The ethic of care argues that the private domain is just as important as the public domain and that problems faced in the private sphere, such as inequality and dependence, also arise in the public sphere.

5. *Views persons as both relational and interdependent.* Each of us starts life depending on others, and we depend on our webs of interpersonal relationships throughout our time on Earth. In the ethic of care, individuals are seen as "embedded" in particular families, cultures, and historical periods. Being embedded means that we need to take responsibility for others, not merely leave them alone to exercise their individual rights.

Widespread adoption of the ethic of care would significantly change national priorities. Child rearing, education, elder care, and other caring activities would consume a greater proportion of governmental budgets. Societal leaders would ensure that caregivers receive more money, recognition, and status. More men would take on caregiving responsibilities. Organizational leaders would help employees strike a better balance between work and home responsibilities and provide more generous family leave policies. Corporations would devote more attention to addressing societal problems.

Sources

Gilligan, C. (1982). *In a different voice: Psychological theory and women's development.* Cambridge, MA: Harvard University Press.

Held, V. (2006). The ethics of care. In D. Copp (Ed.), *The Oxford handbook of ethical theory* (pp. 537–566). Oxford, England: Oxford University Press.

Larrabee, M. J. (Ed.). (1993). *An ethic of care: Feminist and interdisciplinary perspectives.* New York: Routledge.

Noddings, N. (2003). *Caring: A feminine approach to ethics and moral education.* Berkeley: University of California Press.

Tronto, J. C. (1993). *Moral boundaries: A political argument for an ethic of care.* New York: Routledge.

Concern for others promotes healthy social relationships. Society as a whole functions more effectively when people help one another in their daily interactions. Researchers in social psychology, economics, political science, and other fields have discovered that altruistic behavior is more often than not the norm, not the exception.[20] Every day we help others— by pitching in to help finish a project, shoveling the driveway of an elderly neighbor, listening to a roommate's problems, and so on. ("Leadership Ethics at the Movies: *Radio*" presents another example of compassion in action.) Altruism is the driving force behind all kinds of movements and organizations designed to help the less fortunate and to eliminate social problems. Name almost any nonprofit group, ranging from a hospital or medical relief team to a youth club or crisis hotline, and you'll find that it was launched by someone with an altruistic motive. In addition, when we compare good to evil, altruistic acts generally come to mind. Moral heroes and moral champions shine so brightly because they ignore personal risks to battle evil forces.

LEADERSHIP ETHICS AT THE MOVIES • • • • • • • • •

Radio

Key Cast Members: Ed Harris, Cuba Gooding, Jr., Debra Winger, S. Epatha Merkerson

Synopsis: Ed Harris plays Harold Jones, a high school football coach in the small town of Hanna, South Carolina, during the 1970s. Coach Jones takes an interest in James Robert Kennedy (Cuba Gooding, Jr.), a mentally challenged young man nicknamed "Radio," who wanders the town with a shopping cart. Radio becomes the football team's biggest booster and begins to attend classes at the high school. At first he barely talks, but he is soon announcing the daily lunch menu over the school's PA system. The coach's efforts to help his protégé meet with significant resistance from the school board, the town's biggest athletic booster, and some team members. However, Jones's persistence, coupled with the Radio's warm, forgiving nature, wins over the critics, and Radio becomes a "permanent 11th grader." The film is based on a true story, and the real Coach Jones and Radio, now middle-aged and still cheering the team on, appear during the credits.

Rating: PG for mild language and themes

Themes: altruism, the ethic of care, authentic leadership, trigger events, justice as fairness, forgiveness, courage

(Continued)

From this discussion, it's easy to see why altruism is a significant ethical consideration for all types of citizens. However, management professors Rabindra Kanungo and Manuel Mendonca believe that concern for others is even more important for leaders than it is for followers.[21] By definition, leaders exercise influence on behalf of others. They can't understand or articulate the needs of followers unless they focus on the concerns of constituents. To succeed, leaders may have to take risks and forgo personal gain. Leaders intent on benefiting followers will pursue organizational goals, rely on referent and expert power bases, and give power away. Leaders intent on benefiting themselves will focus on personal achievements; rely on legitimate, coercive, and reward power bases; and try to control followers. Kanungo and Mendonca identify four forms of leader altruistic behaviors. *Individual-focused* leader altruistic behaviors include providing training, technical assistance, and mentoring. *Group-focused* leader altruistic behaviors include team building, participative group decision making, and minority advancement programs. *Organizational-focused* leader altruistic attitudes and actions include demonstrating commitment and loyalty, protecting organizational resources, and whistle-blowing. *Societal-focused* leader altruistic behaviors include making contributions to promote social welfare, reducing pollution, ensuring product safety, and maintaining customer satisfaction.[22] (Self-Assessment 5.2, the Organizational Citizenship Behavior Scale, tests your willingness to engage in altruistic behavior on the job.)

Self-sacrifice is integral to altruistic leadership. In self-sacrifice, leaders postpone or give up personal benefits and share hardships with followers.[23] They may volunteer to do the most unpleasant or risky tasks, like leading a military squad into battle, put off their own salary increases and promotions, or live in poverty alongside those they serve. Self-sacrifice can occur at a specific point in time, as when the chair of Olivetti invested $17 million of his own money to rescue the firm when it was near bankruptcy. Or it can occur over time, as in the case of Ross Perot, president of Electronic Data Systems, who never claimed such privileges as an executive dining room, considering instead that "every employee was a full partner." (Turn to Case Study 5.2 for a vivid example of self-sacrifice in action.)

Self-sacrificial behavior has a powerful impact on followers.[24] Such behavior motivates subordinates to work together and to make sacrifices of their own. They feel a stronger sense of group identity and perform better on tasks. Self-sacrifice has the greatest influence when it is employed by democratic leaders who are confident in themselves and in the future of their groups and organizations.

Applications and Cautions

Applications

- Put the needs of followers before your own needs.

- Act as a role model.

- Use compassion as an important decision-making guideline.

Proponents of altruism make a compelling case for its importance. Compassion for others is critical to the health of society and to leadership. To be an effective leader, you need to be aware of the needs of your followers and be willing to sacrifice on their behalf. You can expect to give up personal benefits and to share hardships faced by your constituents. Put the goals of the group or organization first and empower followers. Practice the altruistic individual-, group-, organizational-, and societal-focused behaviors outlined earlier. By acting selflessly you inspire others to do the same. Compassion should also be an important consideration in every decision you make. Consider how your choices will affect others; seek solutions that will benefit them.

Cautions

- It is impossible to meet every need.

- Many who profess to love their neighbors fail to act as if they do.

- Altruism takes many different, sometimes conflicting, forms.

You've probably already discovered that love of neighbor is not an easy principle to put into practice. The world's needs far exceed our ability to meet them. How do you decide whom to help and whom to ignore? Then, too, far too many people who claim to follow the Christian ethic fail miserably. They come across as less, not more, caring than those who don't claim to follow this approach. Some of the bitterest wars are religious ones, fought by believers who seemingly ignore the altruistic values of their faiths. There is also disagreement about what constitutes loving behavior. For example, committed religious leaders disagree about the legitimacy of war. Some view military service as an act of love, one designed to defend their families and friends. Others oppose the military, believing that nonviolence is the only way to express compassion for others.

IMPLICATIONS AND APPLICATIONS

- Well-established ethical systems and values can help you make wise moral choices. Whenever possible, employ more than one perspective when faced with an ethical dilemma.

- Two well-meaning leaders can use the same ethical approach and reach different conclusions.

- Utilitarianism weighs the possible costs and benefits of moral choices. According to this approach, you should seek to do the greatest good for the greatest number of people.

- Kant's categorical imperative urges us to do what's right no matter the consequences. By this standard, some actions (truth telling, helping others) are always right, while others (lying, cheating, murder) are always wrong. Kant also urges us to treat followers with respect, never using them as tools for reaching our goals.

- The justice-as-fairness approach guarantees the same basic rights and opportunities to everyone in a democratic society. When these basic requirements are met, your responsibility as a leader is to give special consideration to the least advantaged.

- Pragmatism focuses on the process of ethical decision making. Use your imagination to test out options and courses of action. Immerse yourself in the details of the situation and embrace your emotions. Remember that every decision helps to make up your character.

- Altruism encourages you to put others first, no matter the personal cost. The ethic of care is an altruistic approach to ethics based on meeting the needs of specific individuals.

FOR FURTHER EXPLORATION, CHALLENGE, AND SELF-ASSESSMENT

1. In a group, generate a list of absolute moral laws or duties that must be obeyed without exception. To make the list, everyone in the group must agree on that item. Keep a separate list of the laws or duties that were nominated but failed to receive unanimous support. Present your lists to the rest of the class.

2. Reflect on one of your recent ethical decisions. What ethical system(s) did you follow? Were you satisfied with your choice?

3. Find a partner and generate additional applications and cautions for each of the ethical perspectives presented in this chapter.

4. Given that inequalities will always exist, what is the best way to allocate wealth, education, health care, and other benefits in a democratic society? In organizations? Write up your conclusions.

5. Debate one or more of the following propositions:

   • The scientific method is the best way to solve ethical problems.

   • To be effective, leaders must practice self-sacrifice.

   • When making ethical choices, compassion is more important than justice.

6. Create your own ethics case based on your personal experience or on current or historical events. Describe the key ethical issues raised in the case and evaluate the characters in the story according to each of the five ethical standards.

7. Apply each of the five perspectives to Case Study 5.3 to determine whether you support the use of drones against suspected terrorists. Write up your conclusions.

STUDENT STUDY SITE

Visit the student study site at **www.sagepub.com/johnsonmecl5e** to access full SAGE journal articles for further research and information on key chapter topics.

CASE STUDY 5.1

Deciding Between Two Evils: The Invasion of the Asian Carp

The Asian carp is one scary species of fish. Bighead, black, silver, and grass carp can consume nearly 40% of their body weight in food every day, growing to be 4 feet long and weighing 100 pounds. They can leap 4 feet out of the water when threatened (by a motor, for instance) and seriously injure boaters, fishermen, and Jet Skiers. However, the greatest danger they pose is to the environment. When introduced into a new habitat, Asian carp eat plankton and other foods that the native fish populations need to sustain themselves, and they reproduce rapidly with no natural predators. Soon they become the dominant species, and the ecosystem collapses.

Southern catfish farmers imported Asian carp into the United States during the 1970s to eat algae in their ponds. However, the fish escaped during flooding and began moving up the Mississippi River. Now they are poised to enter Lake Michigan via the Illinois River, which reportedly has the highest concentration of Asian carp in the world. Officials in states bordering the Great Lakes, as well as leaders in Canada, fear an environmental disaster if the carp enter Lake Michigan. Not only would they destroy "an American treasure," threatening a $7 billion fishing industry and tourism, but the invaders could then spread up tributaries and to the other Great Lakes.[1]

The U.S. Army Corps of Engineers installed an electric barrier to prevent the carp from moving from the Illinois River to Lake Michigan through the Chicago Sanitary and Ship Canal, which connects the lake with the Mississippi River system. Concerned that this would not be enough to deter the fish, Michigan, Wisconsin, Minnesota, Ohio, New York, Pennsylvania, and the province of Ontario sued to close the locks between the lake and the canal. But, the state of Illinois and barge owners, who use the canal to ship gravel, sewage, commercial goods, wastewater, petroleum, and other products, argued that the costs of shutting the locks outweighed the potential damage from keeping them open. They asserted that closing the locks would "have a devastating effect" on the regional economy, dramatically driving up shipping rates and costing thousands of jobs.[2]

The U.S. Supreme Court (which rules on cases involving competing states) sided with the shippers. Fisheries experts and regional governors weren't about to give up, though. They then sued the federal government in order to force permanent closure of the canal. The Obama administration ordered the Army Corps of Engineers to study the problem and come up with a recommendation. The number of shipments on Chicago waterways has been "flat or declining," but the expansion of the Panama Canal in 2014 may increase international shipping on the Mississippi River.

The fight over the Asian carp is typical of battles over invasive species. In these cases, leaders must select between unattractive alternatives. Letting unwelcome plant or animal species remain is costly (aquatic invasive species cost the Great Lakes region over $100 million a year), but so is removing the offenders. Officials in the Florida Everglades, for instance, must decide whether it is worth the financial cost and effort to remove the Burmese pythons that have moved into the area. The snakes can reach 17 feet in length and eat alligators, deer, endangered pumas, raccoons, birds, and family pets. They are blamed for eliminating many species of mammals from Everglades National Park. However, the pythons are difficult to find, and making a significant dent in their population would consume much of Florida's entire budget for fighting invasive species. In these cases, leaders use a form of utilitarian reasoning to decide which option is less costly than the other. In other words, they must choose between the lesser of two evils.

What is the lesser of two evils? Shutting down the canal locks to prevent the spread of the Asian carp or keeping the locks open? Why?

Notes

1. Guarino, M. (2009, December 29). Minnesota, Ohio join lawsuit against Illinois over Asian carp. *The Christian Science Monitor.* Retrieved from http://www.csmonitor.com/USA/2009/1229/Minnesota-Ohio-join-lawsuit-against-Illinois-over-Asian-carp

2. Eilperin, J. (2010, February 7). Fight over invasive species turns into fight over lesser of two evils. *The Oregonian*, p. A2.

Sources

Barry, D. (2008, September 15). On an infested river, battling invaders eye to eye. *The New York Times,* p. A13.

Bilger, B. (2009, April 20). Swamp things; Florida's uninvited predators. *The New Yorker,* p. 80.

Cauchon, D. (2009, December 1). Invasive carp threatens Great Lakes. *USA Today,* p. 17A.

Davey, M. (2009, December 13). Be careful what you fish for. *The New York Times,* p. WK3.

Hammer, K. (2009, October 14). Asian carp just one flop away from Great Lakes. *The Globe and Mail,* p. A3.

Jonsson, P. (2012, September 12). Asian carp policy: Is it keeping Obama and Romney up at night? *The Christian Science Monitor.*

Keen, J. (2012, July 9). Stopping "aquatic hitchhikers." *USA Today,* p. 3A.

Lydersen, K. (2012, January 1). Study of waterways stirs debate on roles in the region's future. *The New York Times,* p 25A.

Petry, C. (2010, January 22). Chicago locks will stay open, Supreme Court rules. *Metal Bulletin.*

Weise, E. (2012, January 12). Pythons strangling Everglades. *USA Today,* p. 3A.

CASE STUDY 5.2

The Fukushima 50

The massive earthquake that struck off the coast of Japan on March 11, 2011, sent a tidal wave over the seawalls protecting the Fukushima Daiichi Nuclear Power Plant. The tsunami knocked out power to the facility, shutting down the cooling systems and leading to explosions in three reactors. Some 90,000 people in the area had to be evacuated because of the dangers of radiation exposure. The facility was close to a total meltdown, which would have meant the release of a massive radioactive cloud, putting Tokyo at risk. As it was, the crisis at Fukushima was the worst nuclear disaster since Chernobyl.

Catastrophe was averted thanks to the heroic actions of the 'Fukushima 50." This group, made up of plant personnel, including middle-level managers, engineers, technicians, and lower-level workers (many of them temporary employees), stayed on the scene, removing rubble, cleaning up radiation, and restoring electricity. The Fukushima 50 cleared the way for fire crews to come in and spray water on the remaining reactors to cool them down. One observer describes the scene facing the 50 this way:

> What it must be like after a torrent of seawater has ravaged all around, lights are out, radiation is leaking in dangerous amounts, steam valves are pouring out scalding water, intermittent explosions are rending the fabric of the reactor buildings and earthquake aftershocks are convulsing the ground defies description. The hellish scenes painted by 15th-century painter Hieronymus Bosch come to mind.[1]

Engineers from the reactor manufacturer, members of the Japan Self-Defense Forces (charged with dropping water by helicopter on the reactors), and elite firefighters joined the initial 50. They worked around the clock, catching what little sleep they could in crowded conference rooms. The workers were exposed to more radiation in 20–30 minutes than most atomic workers are exposed to in their entire careers. They can expect to suffer from blood disorders and cancers as a result.

Some employees remained on the job out of fear (they worried they would never get another job in the nuclear industry); others were lured by promises of generous bonuses. Most, however, stayed out of a mix of duty, stoicism, and concern for others. The members of the Fukushima 50 shared the "dignified stoicism" that marked their country's overall response to the crisis. The Japanese term *gaman*, which translates roughly as "perseverance," describes the combination of endurance and self-denial demonstrated by the nation's citizens. Japanese caught in the disaster zone were determined to endure and were willing to sacrifice themselves for others and the community. The young took the elderly to shelters, for example, and neighbors cared for neighbors. Said one man who was delivering food to the poor, "I'm just doing what needs to be done. It's nothing special."[2] Employees at the power plant also demonstrated gaman. They recognized that abandoning the plant would cost the lives of their fellow citizens. One engineer volunteered to assist at the plant despite the concerns of his family, believing he had a responsibility to help because he knew how to operate nuclear reactors. He told a reporter, "I'm not leaving this until I'm done. Never."[3]

Sadly, the heroic efforts of the Fukushima 50 have been largely forgotten. The group's members remain anonymous and are afraid to describe what happened during the crisis for fear of being associated with the Tokyo Power Company (TEPCO), the plant operator. The Japanese public vilified TEPCO for failing to build higher seawalls despite warnings that the plant's defenses were inadequate and for hiding the true magnitude of the radiation danger during the crisis.

Discussion Probes

1. If similar explosions had occurred at a nuclear power plant in another country, do you think the workers there would have stayed on the job? Why or why not?

2. Can you think of other examples of where people risked their lives out of a sense of duty? What explains their actions?

3. In addition to duty, what other ethical principles appeared to motivate the Fukushima 50, those who joined their efforts, and other Japanese citizens?

4. How should Japan and the world honor those who stayed to save the plant?

5. What leadership and followership ethics lessons do you take from this case?

Notes

1. Rowley, A. (2011, March 24). Fukushima Fifty: Japan's new heroes. *The Business Times Singapore*.

2. Beech, H., Birmingham, L., Dirkse, T., & Mahr, K. (2011, March 28). How Japan will reawaken. *Time International*, pp. 32–37.

3. The twilight zone. (2011, November 15). *The Economist*, pp. 49–50.

Sources

Come back in 10 years' time. (2011, March 26). *The Economist*, pp. 47–48.

Kohler, N., Krolicki, K., Disavano, S., & Fuse, T. (2011, April 2). Wave predicted; engineers knew in 2007. *National Post*, p. A25.

Tabuchi, H. (2011, April 11). Less pay, fewer benefits, more radiation; disaster in Japan. *The International Herald Tribune*, p. 6.

Yokota, T., & Yamada, T. (2012, March 12). Disposable heroes. *Newsweek* (international ed.).

CASE STUDY 5.3

Drone Wars

Ever since the terrorist attacks on New York City and Washington, D.C., on September 11, 2001, drones have been an important weapon in America's War on Terror. Drones are robot-controlled aircraft armed with missiles. Using GPS trackers and cameras, drone operators thousands of miles away can direct strikes at very specific targets, like homes and cars.

The drone program, under the direction of the CIA, began under President George W. Bush but greatly expanded after Barack Obama took office in 2009. Bush ordered 42 drone strikes from 2004 to 2008; as of mid-2013, Obama had authorized more than 300, sometimes as many as 3 a week, resulting in as many as 4,000 deaths. The president must personally approve all drone attacks. Victims are chosen by what one writer has called "a sort of Grim Reaper debating society."[1] Nearly every week, 100 national security officials meet to review terrorist biographies and recommend who should die. CIA lawyers then write up a cable arguing that the individuals pose a grave danger to the United States. The president and his top security adviser then study the recommendations and approve the final kill list. An employee armed with a joystick, watching a live feed from a drone, pushes a button to launch a 5-foot-long Hellfire missile directed at the targeted individual.

Drones have been used to eliminate al-Qaeda and Taliban operatives in Pakistan, as well as in Afghanistan, Yemen, and Iraq. U.S. officials believe that drones have been key to weakening al-Qaeda. Captured letters from Osama Bin Laden, for instance, warned members of his organization to travel only on cloudy days.

Drone warfare offers a number of advantages over traditional military tactics. Strikes are narrowly targeted (proponents say with "surgical precision"), thus limiting collateral damage and civilian casualties. Drones are also relatively inexpensive, and using robotic planes keeps American personnel out of harm's way.

There are mounting concerns about drone warfare, however. The American Civil Liberties Union (ACLU), the Bureau of Investigative Journalism, and other groups have argued that despite the claims of Obama administration, many civilians have been killed in drone attacks, including as many as 176 children. Opponents are particularly critical of CIA "double taps." In a double tap, one attack is followed closely by another strike. Thus, when those nearby come to the aid of the victims of the first missile, they are then killed by a second missile. As a result, villagers now hesitate to come to their neighbors' assistance, and one humanitarian aid group waits six hours before responding to the site of any drone strike.

A group of scholars from Stanford University and New York University interviewed villagers in Pakistan and produced a report titled "Living Under the Drones." They found that residents live under continual stress as the drones circle constantly overhead, both day and night, a "looming specter of death from above."[2] Farmers are afraid to go out into their fields, parents hesitate to send their children to school, and mourners are leery about attending funerals. Villagers are reluctant to befriend others for fear of informants who might identify them as militants to the CIA in return for bounties. The authors of the report conclude that the drone program is counterproductive because it increases anti-American sentiment, making it easier for al-Qaeda, the Taliban, and other groups to recruit new terrorists. Another critic noted that while two-thirds of Americans approve of the drone war, "the rest of the world hates it."[3]

Controversy has also arisen over the legality of drone strikes. According to international human rights law, lethal force is permitted only when it is necessary to save human life. Targeted killing outside of war cannot be based on past unlawful activities but must respond to an imminent threat. There must be no other means, like arrest, for preventing the loss of life. CIA director John Brennan takes issue with complaints that the United States is acting illegally. He asserts that America is acting in self-defense and has the right to strike terrorists anywhere in the world because it is engaged in an ongoing conflict with al-Qaeda and related groups. The United Nations Charter forbids strikes against individuals in other countries without permission of the host government. The United States currently has the tacit approval of the Pakistani government for drone operations, but ongoing tensions between the two nations may end this support in the future. For example, Pakistani politician Imran Khan led a caravan into the tribal area near Pakistan's border with Afghanistan to protest the use of drones.

Further legal complications were raised by the death by drone of top al-Qaeda leader Anwar al-Awlaki. Al-Awlaki, an American citizen born in New Mexico, was believed to be involved in the plotting of attacks against the United Kingdom, the United States, and Australia. His death appears to violate the U.S. Bill of Rights, which states that no citizen can be deprived of life "without due process of law." Nevertheless, a memo written by the U.S. Department of Justice contended that the killing was justified because there was no "feasible" way to capture Al-Awlaki alive. Republican senator Rand Paul and a handful of Democratic senators joined forces to protest the killing of U.S. citizens overseas.

At the start of his second term, President Obama pledged to modify the drone program, admitting that making decisions on targeted killings troubled him. To start that process, his administration proposed putting the drone program under military control and setting more limits on when drones could be used. Members of Congress argue that clearer guidelines should be put into place for the program. Some representatives suggest setting up "drone courts." These panels would authorize killings, taking this power out of the hands of the president.

Experts predict that other nations will soon adopt drone technology. Russians may use drones to attack Chechen rebels, for instance, and the Chinese may target Uighur Muslims it identifies as terrorists. Future terrorists could send out their own drones armed with anthrax or radioactive waste. However, for now, debate over the morality of drone warfare is focused on the United States.

Should the United States continue to use drones in its fight against terrorism? If so, what changes, if any, should be made in the way the drone program operates?

Notes

1. Gibson, J. (2012, October 4). Living with death by drone. *Los Angeles Times*, p. A21.

2. Gibson.

3. Crowley, M. (2013, April 1). So, who can we kill? *Time*, pp. 20–23.

Sources

Beaumont, P. (2012, August 19). Are drones any more immoral than other weapons of war? *The Observer*, Comment, p. 30.

Hodge, A. (2012, October 8). Khan praises anti-drone protest. *The Australian*, World, p. 9.

Human Rights Watch (2011, December 19). Q&A: U.S. targeted killings and international laws. *Africa News*.

Macintyre, B. (2011, October 11). "Legalised" killing puts the world in danger. *The Times*.

Mazzetti, M., & Shane, S. (2013, March 22). As new drone policy is weighed, few practical effects are seen. *The New York Times*, p. A11.

Philip, C. (2011, November 19). Ethical conflicts of killing without risk. *The Times*, World News.

Savage, C., & Baker, P. (2013, May 22). Obama, in a shift, to limit targets of drone strikes. *The New York Times*, p. A1.

Shane, S. (2011, October 10). A world soon armed with drones. *The International Herald Tribune*, p. 8.

Shane, S. (2012, September 25). Report cites high civilian toll in Pakistan drone strikes. *The New York Times*, At War blog.

Shane, S. (2013, April 8). Targeted killing comes to define war on terror. *The New York Times*, p. A1.

Taylor, J. (2012, September 26). Outrage at CIA's deadly "double tap" drone attacks. *The Independent*.

SELF-ASSESSMENT 5.1

The Organizational Justice Scale

Instructions: Evaluate your employer or another organization of your choice on the following items. Respond to each of the statements on a scale of 1 (*strongly disagree*) to 5 (*strongly agree*).

1. In general, this company (organization) treats its employees (members) fairly.

   1   2   3   4   5

2. Generally employees (members) think of this company (organization) as fair.

   1   2   3   4   5

3. Rewards are allocated fairly in this firm (organization).

   1   2   3   4   5

4. Employees (members) in this firm (organization) are rewarded fairly.

1   2   3   4   5

5. In this firm (organization), people get the reward or punishment they deserve.

1   2   3   4   5

6. Supervisors (leaders) in this company (organization) treat employees (members) with dignity and respect.

1   2   3   4   5

7. Employees (members) can count on being treated with courtesy and respect in this firm (organization).

1   2   3   4   5

Scoring

Scores can range from 7 to 35. The higher the score, the more just you believe your organization to be. You may want to give this instrument to other organizational members to determine if their perceptions are similar to your own.

SOURCE: Adapted from Trevino, L. K., & Weaver, G. R. (2001). Organizational justice and ethics program "follow through": Influences on employees' harmful and helpful behavior. *Business Ethics Quarterly, 11,* 651–671. Used by permission.

SELF-ASSESSMENT 5.2

Organizational Citizenship Behavior Scale

Instructions: Take the following test to determine your willingness to engage in altruistic behavior in the work setting. Respond to each item on a 4-point scale ranging from 1 (*never engage in this behavior*) to 4 (*nearly always engage in this behavior*). Reverse the scale where indicated. Generate a total by adding up your scores. Maximum possible score: 80.

Response choices: 1 = not at all; 2 = somewhat; 3 = very much; 4 = exactly.

1. Help other employees with their work when they have been absent.   1 2 3 4

2. Exhibit punctuality in arriving at work on time in the morning and after lunch and breaks.   1 2 3 4

3. Volunteer to do things not formally required by the job.   1 2 3 4

4. Take undeserved work breaks. (Reverse)   1 2 3 4

5. Take the initiative to orient new employees to the department even though it is not part of the job description.   1 2 3 4

6. Exhibit attendance at work beyond the norm; for example, take fewer days off than most individuals or fewer than allowed.   1   2   3   4

7. Help others when their workload increases (assist others until they get over the hurdles).   1   2   3   4

8. Coast toward the end of the day. (Reverse)   1   2   3   4

9. Give advance notice if unable to come to work.   1   2   3   4

10. Spend a great deal of time in personal telephone conversations. (Reverse)   1   2   3   4

11. Do not take unnecessary time off work.   1   2   3   4

12. Assist others with their duties.   1   2   3   4

13. Make innovative suggestions to improve the overall quality of the department.   1   2   3   4

14. Do not take extra breaks.   1   2   3   4

15. Willingly attend functions not required by the organization but that help its overall image.   1   2   3   4

16. Do not spend a great deal of time in idle conversation.   1   2   3   4

NOTES

1. See the following: Barry, V. (1978). *Personal and social ethics: Moral problems with integrated theory*. Belmont, CA: Wadsworth; Bentham, J. (1948). *An introduction to the principles of morals and legislation*. New York: Hafner; Gorovitz, S. (Ed.). (1971). *Utilitarianism: Text and critical essays*. Indianapolis: Bobbs-Merrill; Timmons, M. (2002). *Moral theory: An introduction*. Lanham, MD: Rowman & Littlefield; Troyer, J. (2003). *The classical utilitarians: Bentham and Mill*. Indianapolis: Hackett; West, H. R. (2004). *An introduction to Mill's utilitarian ethics*. Cambridge, England: Cambridge University Press.

2. De George, R. T. (1995). *Business ethics* (4th ed.). Englewood Cliffs, NJ: Prentice Hall, Ch. 3.

3. Savage, D. G. (2010, January 13). Scanners put privacy against security. *Los Angeles Times*, p. A11.

4. Kant, I. (1964). *Groundwork of the metaphysics of morals* (H. J. Ryan, Trans.). New York: Harper & Row; Christians, C. G., Rotzell, K. B., & Fackler, M. (1999). *Media ethics* (3rd ed.). New York: Longman; Leslie, L. Z. (2000). *Mass communication ethics: Decision making in postmodern culture*. Boston: Houghton Mifflin; Velasquez, M. G. (1992). *Business ethics: Concepts and cases* (3rd ed.). Englewood Cliffs, NJ: Prentice Hall, Ch. 2; Sucher, S. J. (2008). *The moral leader: Challenges, tools, and insights*. London: Routledge; Timmons.

5. Graham, G. (2004). *Eight theories of ethics*. London: Routledge, Ch. 6.

6. Meilander, G. (1986). Virtue in contemporary religious thought. In R. J. Neuhaus (Ed.), *Virtue: Public and private* (pp. 7–30). Grand Rapids, MI: Eerdmans; Alderman, H. (1997). By virtue of a virtue. In D. Statman (Ed.),

Virtue ethics (pp. 145–164). Washington, DC: Georgetown University Press.

7. Material on Rawls's theory of justice, including criticism of his approach, is taken from Rawls, J. (1971). *A theory of justice.* Cambridge, MA: Belknap; Rawls, J. (1993). Distributive justice. In T. Donaldson & P. H. Werhane (Eds.), *Ethical issues in business: A philosophical approach* (4th ed., pp. 274–285). Englewood Cliffs, NJ: Prentice Hall; Rawls, J. (2001). *Justice as fairness: A restatement* (E. Kelly, Ed.). Cambridge, MA: Belknap; Velasquez; Warnke, G. (1993). *Justice and interpretation.* Cambridge: MIT Press, Ch. 3.

8. Rawls, J. (1993). *Political liberalism.* New York: Columbia University Press.

9. Margolis, J. (2006). Introduction: Pragmatism, retrospective and prospective. In J. R. Shook & J. Margolis (Eds.), *A companion to pragmatism* (pp. 1–9). Malden, MA: Blackwell.

10. Feinstein, M. (2008). John Dewey, inquiry ethics, and democracy. In C. Misak (Ed.), *The Oxford handbook of American philosophy* (pp. 87–109). Oxford, England: Oxford University Press.

11. Alexander, T. M. (1993). John Dewey and the moral imagination: Beyond Putnam and Rorty toward a postmodern ethics. *Transactions of the Charles S. Peirce Society, 29,* 369–400.

12. Weber, E. T. (2011). What experimentalism means in ethics. *Journal of Speculative Philosophy, 25*(1), 98–115.

13. McVea, J. (2008). Ethics and pragmatism: John Dewey's deliberative approach. In T. Donaldson & P. H. Werhane (Eds.), *Ethical issues in business: A philosophical approach* (8th ed., pp. 89–100). Upper Saddle River, NJ: Pearson Prentice Hall.

14. Moore, E. C. (1961). *American pragmatism: Peirce, James and Dewey.* Westport, CT: Greenwood Press.

15. Pagan, N. O. (2008). Configuring the moral self: Aristotle and Dewey. *Foundations of Science, 13,* 239–250; Carden, S. D. (2006). *Virtue ethics: Dewey and Macintyre.* London: Continuum.

16. Dewey, J. (1920). *Reconstruction in philosophy.* New York: Henry Holt, p. 177.

17. Example taken from McVea, J. F. (2007). Constructing good decisions in ethically charged situations: The role of dramatic rehearsal. *Journal of Business Ethics, 70,* 375–390.

18. Yunus, M. (1998, October 31). Banker to the poor. *The Guardian.*

19. Weber.

20. Piliavin, J. A., & Chang, H. W. (1990). Altruism: A review of recent theory and research. *American Sociological Review, 16,* 27–65; Batson, C. D., Van Lange, P. A. M., Ahmad, N., & Lishner, D. A. (2003). Altruism and helping behavior. In M. A. Hogg & J. Cooper (Eds.), *The Sage handbook of social psychology* (pp. 279–295). London: Sage; Flescher, A. M., & Worthen, D. L. (2007). *The altruistic species: Scientific, philosophical, and religious perspectives of human benevolence.* Philadelphia: Templeton Foundation Press.

21. Kanungo, R. N., & Mendonca, M. (1996). *Ethical dimensions of leadership.* Thousand Oaks, CA: Sage.

22. Kanungo, R. N., & Conger, J. A. (1990). The quest for altruism in organizations. In S. Srivastra & D. L. Cooperrider (Eds.), *Appreciative management and leadership* (pp. 228–256). San Francisco: Jossey-Bass.

23. Choi, Y., & Mai-Dalton, R. R. (1998). On the leadership function of self-sacrifice. *Leadership Quarterly, 9,* 475–501; Matteson, J. A., & Irving, J. A. (2006). Servant versus self-sacrificial leadership: A behavioral comparison of two follower-oriented leadership theories. *International Journal of Leadership Studies, 2,* 36–51.

24. Choi, Y. & Mai-Dalton, R. R. (1999). The model of followers' responses to self-sacrificial leadership: An empirical test. *Leadership Quarterly, 10,* 397–421; De Cremer, D. (2006). Affective and motivational consequences of leader self-sacrifice: The moderating effect of autocratic leadership. *Leadership Quarterly, 17,* 79–93; De Cremer, D., & van Knippenberg, D. (2004). Leader self-sacrifice and leadership effectiveness: The moderating role of leader self-confidence. *Organizational Behavior and Human Decision Processes, 95,* 140–155.

CHAPTER

6

Ethical Decision Making and Behavior

If it ain't got emotion, it ain't got moral swing.

—Neuroscientist Marc Hauser

As we practice resolving dilemmas we find ethics to be less a goal than a pathway, less a destination than a trip, less an inoculation than a process.

—Ethicist Rushworth Kidder

What's Ahead

This chapter begins with a look at the role of reason and emotion in ethical decision making. It then surveys the components of ethical behavior—moral sensitivity, moral judgment, moral motivation, and moral character—and introduces systematic approaches to ethical problem solving. We'll take a look at four decision-making formats: Kidder's ethical checkpoints, the SAD formula, Nash's 12 questions, and the case study method. After presenting each approach, I'll discuss its relative advantages and disadvantages.

Understanding how we make and follow through on ethical decisions is the first step to making better choices; taking a systematic approach is the second. We'll explore both of these steps in this chapter. After examining the ethical decision-making process, we'll see how guidelines or formats can guide our ethical deliberations.

Ethical Decision Making: A Dual-Process Approach

For decades, scholars viewed ethical decision making as a cognitive process. Moral psychologists, ethicists, and ethics educators focused on how individuals consciously use logic and reason to solve ethical problems. They assumed that leaders reach their conclusions after careful deliberation. Researchers ignored emotions or treated them with suspicion because feelings could undermine moral reasoning.

In recent years a growing number of scholars have challenged the cognitive approach to ethical decision making. One critic is University of Virginia psychologist Jonathan Haidt.[1] He argues that we quickly make ethical determinations and then use logic after the fact to justify our choices. Haidt points to *moral dumbfounding* as evidence that moral decision making is the product of intuition, not deliberation. In moral dumbfounding, leaders and followers have strong opinions about right and wrong but can't explain why they feel as they do. For example, when Haidt asked Americans if eating the family dog for dinner is morally wrong, most reported feeling disgusted, but they were at a loss to explain why they felt that way.

Haidt calls his approach to ethical decision making the *social intuitionist model* to highlight the role that intuition and social norms play in moral determinations. He argues that automatic processes are the elephant and logic is the rider. In most cases the elephant goes where it wants to go, though the rider can occasionally steer the pachyderm in a different direction. Our instantaneous intuitions about right and wrong are the products of social forces like our cultural backgrounds. For example, dogs are routinely eaten in some societies. In these cultures, which don't treat pets as family members, respondents would approve of eating a dog for dinner. (For more information on cultural differences in core values, see Chapter 11.) Haidt doesn't completely eliminate reason from his model. Other people may challenge our intuitions, introducing new information and arguments that lead us to change our initial positions. Or we may modify our attitudes based on self-reflection.

Researchers in cognitive neuroscience and neuroethics are also challenging the notion that ethical thinking is devoid of emotion.[2] One group of scientists employs the medical case study method. These researchers study individuals with brain damage who engage in antisocial and unethical behavior as a result of their injuries. One early case study involved Phineas Gage, an 18th-century railway worker who was injured when a railroad spike went through his skull. Gage retained his reasoning abilities (his IQ was left intact) but lost his emotional capacities. Following the accident he was unable to keep a job or to make wise decisions due to his emotional deficit. He also demonstrated disrespect for others and a lack of self-control. The same pattern has been found among contemporary patients who suffer damage to the regions of the brain that govern emotion.

Another group of neuroscientists uses neuroimaging to determine which areas of the brain are activated when we are faced with ethical choices. Study participants are placed in magnetic resonance imaging (MRI) machines and presented with ethical dilemmas. For instance, they may be asked whether it is okay for a pregnant teen to dump her newborn in a trash can or whether a mother, in order to save the lives of others, should smother her baby to stop its crying. Active brain cells require more oxygen than inactive ones, indicating which parts of the brain are functioning when volunteers are responding to moral problems. Neuroimaging studies reveal that ethical decision making is not localized in one portion of the brain but involves several different regions. Ethical thinking activates both cognitive and emotional areas of the brain.

Taking a dual-process approach is one way to sort through the relationship between logic and intuition.[3] The dual-process perspective is based on the premise that both logic and emotion are essential to making good ethical choices. When faced with a moral dilemma, we need our emotions and intuitions as well as our cognitive abilities. A "gut" feeling may prompt us to reexamine our initial conclusion, for instance, or reveal aspects of the situation our reason ignored. As neuroscientists have discovered, we can't make good ethical choices without employing our feelings. However, our intuitions and emotions can be wrong. They may be based on mistaken cultural beliefs, for example. Many Americans used to immediately condemn interracial couples. As time passed, however, society began to recognize that this reaction was biased, unfounded, and unjust. Then, too, logic is essential when wrestling with dilemmas that involve competing values or that pit one good option against another (as discussed later in this chapter).[4]

One way to draw on both reason and feeling is to record your initial reaction to an ethical dilemma. When confronted with an ethical scenario like those presented in Case Study 6.1, write down your initial reaction. Then use the decision-making formats and other cognitive tools discussed in this chapter to test your immediate response. When you're finished, compare your final decision to your initial reaction. Your ultimate conclusion after you've followed a series of steps may be the same as your first judgment. Or you might find that you've come to a significantly different decision. In any case, you should be comfortable with your solution because your deliberations were informed by your conscious reasoning as well as by your experiences, emotions, and intuitions. To assist you in dual processing, I'll be introducing research findings from both the cognitive and the intuitionist traditions in the next section of the chapter.

Components of Moral Action

There are a number of models of ethical decision making and action. For example, business ethics educators Charles Powers and David Vogel identify six factors or elements that underlie moral reasoning and behavior and that are particularly relevant in organizational settings.[5] The first is *moral imagination,* the recognition that even routine choices and relationships have an ethical dimension. The second is *moral identification and ordering,* which, as the name suggests, refers to the ability to identify important issues, determine priorities, and sort out competing values. The third factor is *moral evaluation,* or using analytical skills to evaluate options. The fourth element is *tolerating moral disagreement and ambiguity,* which arises when managers disagree about values and courses of action. The fifth is the ability to *integrate managerial competence with moral competence.* This integration involves anticipating possible ethical dilemmas, leading others in ethical decision making, and making sure any decision becomes part of the organization's systems and procedures. The sixth and final element is a sense of *moral obligation,* which serves as a motivating force to engage in moral judgment and to implement decisions.

James Rest of the University of Minnesota developed what may be the most widely used model of moral behavior. Rest built his four-component model by working backward. He started with the end product—moral action—and then determined the steps that produce such behavior. He concluded that ethical action is the result of four psychological subprocesses: (1) moral sensitivity (recognition), (2) moral judgment, (3) moral focus (motivation), and (4) moral character.[6]

Component 1: Moral Sensitivity (Recognition)

Moral sensitivity (recognizing the presence of an ethical issue) is the first step in ethical decision making because we can't solve a moral problem unless we first know that one exists. A great many moral failures stem from ethical insensitivity. The safety committee at Ford Motor Company decided not to fix the defective gas tank on the Pinto automobile (see Chapter 2) because members saw no problem with saving money rather than human lives. Wal-Mart was slow to respond to concerns raised by employees, labor groups, environmentalists, and others about wage violations, sexual discrimination, poor environmental practices, and other issues.[7] Many students, focused on finishing their degrees, see no problem with cheating. (You can test your ethical sensitivity by completing Self-Assessment 6.1, "Moral Attentiveness.")

According to Rest, problem recognition requires that we consider how our behavior affects others, identify possible courses of action, and determine the consequences of each potential strategy. Empathy and perspective skills are essential to this component of moral action. If we understand how others might feel or react, we are more sensitive to potential negative effects of our choices and can better predict the likely outcomes of each option.

A number of factors prevent us from recognizing ethical issues. We may not factor ethical considerations into our typical ways of thinking or mental models.[8] We may be reluctant to use moral terminology—*values, justice, right, wrong*—to describe our decisions because we want to avoid controversy or believe that keeping silent will make us appear strong and capable.[9] We may even deceive ourselves into thinking that we are acting morally when we are clearly not, a process called *ethical fading*. The moral aspects of a decision fade into the background if we use euphemisms to disguise unethical behavior, numb our consciences through repeated misbehavior, blame others, and claim that only we know the "truth."[10]

Fortunately, we can take steps to enhance our ethical sensitivity (and the sensitivity of our fellow leaders and followers) by doing the following:

- Active listening and role playing

- Imagining other perspectives

- Stepping back from a situation to determine whether it has moral implications

- Using moral terminology to discuss problems and issues

- Avoiding euphemisms

- Refusing to excuse misbehavior

- Accepting personal responsibility

- Practicing humility and openness to other points of view

In addition to these steps, we can also increase ethical sensitivity by making an issue more salient. The greater the moral intensity of an issue, the more likely it is that decision makers will take note of it and respond ethically.[11] We can build moral intensity by doing the following:

- Illustrating that the situation can cause significant harm or benefit to many people (magnitude of consequences)

- Establishing that there is social consensus or agreement that a behavior is moral or immoral (e.g., legal or illegal, approved or forbidden by a professional association)

- Demonstrating probability of effect, that the act will happen and will cause harm or benefit

- Showing that the consequences will happen soon (temporal immediacy)

- Emphasizing social, physical, or psychological closeness (proximity) with those affected by our actions

- Proving that one person or a group will suffer greatly as the result of a decision (concentration of effect)

Finally, paying attention to our emotions can provide an important clue that we are faced with an ethical dilemma. Moral emotions are part of our makeup as humans.[12] These feelings are triggered even when we do not have a personal stake in an event. For example, we may feel angry when we read about the mistreatment of migrant workers or sympathy when we see a photo of a refugee living in a squalid camp. Moral emotions also encourage us to take action that benefits other people and society as a whole. We might write a letter protesting the poor working conditions of migrant laborers, for instance, or send money to a humanitarian organization working with displaced persons.

Anger, disgust, and contempt are *other-condemning* emotions. They are elicited by unfairness, betrayal, immorality, cruelty, poor performance, and status differences. Anger can motivate us to redress injustices like racism, oppression, and poverty. Disgust encourages us to set up rewards and punishments to deter inappropriate behaviors. Contempt generally causes us to step back from others. Shame, embarrassment, and guilt are *self-conscious emotions* that encourage us to obey the rules and uphold the social order. These feelings are triggered when we violate norms and social conventions, present the wrong image to others, or fail to live up to moral guidelines. Shame and embarrassment can keep us from engaging in further damaging behavior and may drive us to withdraw from social contact. Guilt motivates us to help others and to treat them well.

Sympathy and compassion are *other-suffering emotions*. They are elicited when we perceive suffering or sorrow in our fellow human beings. Such feelings encourage us to comfort, help, and alleviate the pain of others. Gratitude, awe, and elevation are *other-praising (positive) emotions* that open us up to new opportunities and relationships. They are prompted when someone has done something on our behalf, when we run across moral beauty (acts of charity, loyalty, and self-sacrifice, for example), and when we read or hear about moral exemplars (see Chapter 3). Gratitude motivates us to repay others; awe and elevation encourage us to become better persons and to take steps to help others.

In sum, if we experience anger, disgust, guilt, sympathy, or other moral emotions, the chances are good that there is an ethical dimension to the situation that confronts us. We will need to look further to determine if this is indeed the case.

Component 2: Moral Judgment

Once an ethical problem is identified, decision makers select a course of action from the options generated in Component 1. In other words, they make judgments about what is the right or wrong thing to do in this situation.

Moral judgment has generated more research than the other components of Rest's model. Investigators have been particularly interested in (1) cognitive moral development, the process by which people develop their moral reasoning abilities over time; and (2) biases or errors that undermine the decision-making process.

Cognitive Moral Development

Harvard psychologist Lawrence Kohlberg argued that individuals progress through a series of moral stages just as they do physical ones.[13] Each stage is more advanced than the one before. Not only do people engage in more complex reasoning as they progress up the stages, but they also become less self-centered and develop broader definitions of morality.

Kohlberg identified three levels of moral development, each divided into two stages. Level I, *preconventional* thinking, is the most primitive and focuses on consequences. This form of moral reasoning is common among children who choose to obey to avoid punishment (Stage 1) or follow the rules in order to meet their interests (Stage 2). Stage 2 thinkers are interested in getting a fair deal: You help me, and I'll help you.

Conventional thinkers (Level II) look to others for guidance when deciding how to act. Stage 3 people want to live up to the expectations of those they respect, such as parents, siblings, and friends, and value concern for others and respect. Stage 4 individuals take a somewhat broader perspective, looking to society as a whole for direction. They believe in following rules at work, for example, and the law. Kohlberg found that most adults are Level II thinkers.

Level III, *postconventional* or *principled* reasoning, is the most advanced type of ethical thinking. Stage 5 people are guided by utilitarian principles. They are concerned for the needs of the entire group and want to make sure that rules and laws serve the greatest good for the greatest number. Stage 6 people operate according to internalized, universal principles such as justice, equality, and human dignity. These principles consistently guide their behavior and take precedence over the laws of any particular society. According to Kohlberg, fewer than 20% of American adults ever reach Stage 5, and almost no one reaches Stage 6.

Critics take issue with both the philosophical foundation of Kohlberg's model and its reliance on concrete stages of moral development.[14] They contend that Kohlberg based his postconventional stage on Rawls's justice-as-fairness theory and made deontological ethics superior to other ethical approaches. They note that the model applies more to societal issues than to individual ethical decisions. A great many psychologists challenge the notion that people go through a rigid or "hard" series of moral stages, leaving one stage completely behind before moving to the next. They argue instead that a person can engage in many ways of thinking about a problem, regardless of age.

Rest (who studied under Kohlberg), Darcia Narvaez, and their colleagues responded to the critics by replacing the hard stages with a staircase of developmental schemas.[15] Schemas are networks of knowledge organized around life events. We use schemas when we encounter new situations or information. You are able to master information in new classes, for instance, by using strategies you developed in previous courses. According to this "neo-Kohlbergian" approach, decision makers use increasingly sophisticated moral schemas as they develop. The least sophisticated schema is based on personal interest. People at this level are concerned only with what they may gain or lose in an ethical dilemma. They give no consideration to the needs of broader society. (See "Leadership Ethics at the Movies: *Margin Call*" for an example of a group of leaders who put their own interests first.)

LEADERSHIP ETHICS AT THE MOVIES • • • • • • • • • •

Margin Call

Key Cast Members: Kevin Spacey, Stanley Tucci, Zachary Quinto, Demi Moore, Paul Bettany, Jeremy Irons

Synopsis: As the financial crisis sets in on Wall Street in 2008, an investment bank risk analyst (Tucci) and his protégé (Quinto) discover that their firm is holding billions in toxic assets. The bank will collapse unless it clears these liabilities from its books. CEO John Tuld (played by Jeremy Irons) calls an emergency meeting to determine how to respond to the crisis. The executive committee decides to save the firm by holding a "fire sale" to unload the worthless products on unwitting clients during one trading day. If the scheme succeeds, most clients will refuse to do business with the bank again and most of the company's traders will lose their jobs. Head trader Sam Rogers (Spacey), who must orchestrate the fire sale, objects to the plan but faces heavy pressure from other executives to give in.

Rating: R for language

Themes: ethical decision making and behavior, ethical blind spots, conflict, greed, deception, abuse of power and privilege, corruption

Discussion Starters

1. What other options did the executive committee have aside from conducting the fire sale?

2. Was the bank justified in putting its survival ahead of the interests of clients, trading partners, and the financial community? Will the bank survive in the aftermath of the fire sale?

3. What made Rogers vulnerable to pressure from his superiors?

Those who reason at the next level, the maintaining norms schema, believe they have a moral obligation to maintain social order. They are concerned with following rules and laws and making sure that regulations apply to everyone. These thinkers believe that there is a clear hierarchy with carefully defined roles (e.g., bosses–subordinates, teachers–students, officers–enlisted personnel).

The postconventional schema is the most advanced level of moral reasoning. Thinking at this level is not limited to one ethical approach, as Kohlberg argued, but encompasses many different philosophical traditions. Postconventional individuals believe that moral obligations are to be based on shared ideals, should not favor some people at the expense of others, and are open to scrutiny (testing and examination). Such thinkers reason like moral philosophers, looking behind societal norms to determine whether those norms serve moral purposes. Rest developed the Defining Issues Test (DIT) to measure moral development. Subjects taking the DIT (and its successor, the DIT-2) respond to six ethical scenarios and then choose statements that best reflect the reasoning they used to come up with their choices. These statements, which correspond to the three levels of moral reasoning, are then scored. In the most widely known of these dilemmas, Heinz's wife is dying of cancer and needs a drug he cannot afford to buy. He must decide whether to steal the drug to save her life. (Turn to Self-Assessment 6.2 to test your level of moral judgment.)

Hundreds of studies using the DIT reveal that moral reasoning generally increases with age and education.[16] Undergraduate and graduate students benefit from their educational experiences in general and from ethical coursework in particular. When education stops, moral development stops. In addition, moral development is a universal concept, crossing cultural boundaries. Principled leaders can boost the moral judgment of a group by encouraging members to adopt more sophisticated ethical schemas.[17]

Models of cognitive development provide important insights into the process of ethical decision making. First, contextual variables play an important role in shaping ethical behavior. Most people look to others as well as to rules and regulations when making ethical determinations. They are more likely to make wise moral judgments if coworkers and supervisors encourage and model ethical behavior. As leaders, we need to build ethical environments. (We'll take a closer look at the formation of ethical groups and organizations in Chapters 8 and 9.) Second, education fosters moral reasoning. Pursuing a bachelor's, master's, or doctoral degree can promote your moral development. As part of your education, focus as much attention as you can on ethics (i.e., take ethics courses, discuss ethical issues in groups and classes, reflect on the ethical challenges you experience in internships). Third, a broader perspective is better. Consider the needs and viewpoints of others outside your immediate group or organization; determine what is good for the local area, the larger society, and the global community. Fourth, moral principles produce superior solutions. The best ethical thinkers base their choices on widely accepted ethical guidelines. Do the same by drawing on important ethical approaches such as utilitarianism, the categorical imperative, altruism, communitarianism, and justice-as-fairness theory.

Ethical Blind Spots

Harvard professor Max Bazerman and his colleagues believe that unethical choices often result from unconscious distortions. These ethical blind spots cause us to participate in or approve of behaviors we would normally condemn. Significant biases include the following:[18]

1. *Overestimating our ethicality.* Studies consistently demonstrate that, when it comes to ethics, we have an inflated opinion of ourselves. We boldly predict, for example, that we will do the right thing when faced with an ethical dilemma. Unfortunately, we often fall well short of our predictions. This is illustrated by the findings of a study in which female college students were asked how they would respond to inappropriate job interview questions like whether they had a boyfriend or whether they think it is appropriate for women to wear a bra to work. Of the participants, 60–70% said that they would refuse to answer these questions, challenge the interviewer, or tell him that such queries were inappropriate. However, when a male interviewer actually asked them the offensive questions, none refused to answer. At the end of the session only a few participants asked the interviewer why he had posed these queries.[19]

Our belief in our own inherent goodness may blind us to potential conflicts of interests that can undermine our objectivity and tempt us to make selfish choices. Take the case of professors at Harvard Medical School, for example. They received hundreds of thousands of dollars from the drug industry. A group of students worried that all this money was biasing material presented in the classroom, as in the case of the pharmacology professor who promoted the benefits of cholesterol drugs while serving as a paid consultant to cholesterol drug manufacturers. Based on student protests and the efforts of the Massachusetts legislature, Harvard Medical School changed it policy and now limits how much faculty can earn from outside sources.[20]

2. *Forgiving our own unethical behavior.* Driven by the desire to be moral and behave ethically, we feel a psychological tension called cognitive dissonance when we fall short of our ethical standards (e.g., lying when we believe that we are honest). Our "want self" (our desire for status and money) overcomes our "should self" (who we think we ought to be ethically). To relieve the distress generated when our actions and self-images don't match, we either change our behavior or excuse what we've done. We may convince ourselves that the objectionable behavior was really morally permissible (see the discussion of moral disengagement in Chapter 2). We blame the boss or claim that we were "just following orders " or that "everyone else is doing it." Professional baseball players and cyclists have employed the "everybody is doing it" excuse to justify their use of steroids and other performance-enhancing drugs. We may also become "revisionist historians." Using selective recall, we remember events in a way that supports our decisions. We recollect the times we stood up to an unjust boss or told the truth; we forget the times we caved in to pressure from a supervisor or lied to make a sale or to get a job.

3. *In-group favoritism.* Doing favors for people we know who share our nationality, neighborhood, religion, social class, or alma mater seems harmless. We may ask our neighbor to hire our son or daughter, for example, or recommend a sorority sister for an overseas program. Trouble comes because when those in power give resources to members of their in-groups, they discriminate against those who are different from them. Caucasian loan officers who relax lending standards for White applicants may end up refusing loans to better-qualified African American applicants, therefore hurting the bank's bottom line. In-group favoritism can also prompt us to excuse the unethical behavior of others. For example, when basketball players on our team knock opponents down, they are playing "hard." When players on the other team knock our team members to the floor, they are playing "dirty." We are particularly willing to forgive the shortcomings of others when we benefit from the choices they have made. Many bank and hedge fund managers funneled money into Bernie Madoff's fraudulent investment fund even though the returns Madoff promised were statistically impossible. They likely ignored the danger signs because they were receiving generous fees from Madoff. The financier cheated victims out of an estimated $65 billion in the biggest swindle in history.

4. *Implicit prejudice.* Implicit prejudice is different from visible or explicit forms of prejudice like racism and sexism. Individuals are not generally aware of their implicit biases, which are based on the human tendency to associate things that generally go together, like thunder and rain or wealthy people and luxury cars. However, these associations are not always accurate. Thunder doesn't always bring rain, and not all high-income individuals drive expensive vehicles. Unconscious biases can undermine ethical decision making. Take hiring decisions, for instance. Personnel managers are likely to exclude qualified applicants if they assume that persons with physical disabilities are

also mentally challenged or that women can't fill traditional "masculine" jobs. In one particularly tragic example of implicit prejudice, George Zimmerman, a Neighborhood Watch coordinator in Florida, apparently assumed that Trayvon Martin, a young African American male dressed in a hoodie, posed a serious threat. The resulting confrontation ended in the shooting death of the unarmed Black teenager.

5. *Judging based on outcomes, not the process.* Two leaders can follow the same process when making a decision, but we typically judge each differently, based on their results. When a decision turns out well, we consider the leader successful. If the outcome is poor, we believe the leader is a failure. Nevertheless, just because a poorly made decision had positive consequences in one case doesn't mean that following the same process will have positive results the next time. In fact, over the long term, poor decision-making procedures will produce bad (unethical) results. As we saw in Chapter 2, officials at the Peanut Corporation of America repeatedly shipped tainted peanut products. For a time, few if any people got sick. Eventually, however, a shipment of contaminated products caused eight deaths and sickened thousands.[21]

Bazerman and his colleagues argue that our good intentions and our determination to act ethically won't be enough to allow us to overcome these biases because we aren't aware of them. Instead, we need to acknowledge these blind spots. Admit that that you aren't as ethical and unbiased as you believe, for instance, and that you have a tendency to forgive your ethical misbehavior and that of other group members. Then take steps to combat these ethical distortions. Publicly commit yourself to an ethical course of action ahead of time so your "should self" doesn't get overwhelmed by your "want self" in the heat of the moment. Focus on the moral principles involved in a choice, not on the immediate benefit you might receive. Put yourself in environments that challenge your implicit stereotypes. Include a wider variety of people in the decision-making process; consider a wider variety of job applicants. Audit your organization to determine if it is trapped by in-group biases, and eliminate programs that perpetuate the hiring and promotion of those of similar backgrounds. Step behind the veil of ignorance (see Chapter 5) to make more equitable choices. Evaluate the quality of the decision-making process, not the outcome; don't condemn those who make good-quality decisions only to see them turn out badly.

Component 3: Moral Focus (Motivation)

After concluding what course of action is best, decision makers must be focused—motivated to follow through—on their choices. Moral values often conflict with other significant values. For instance, an accounting supervisor who wants to blow the whistle on illegal accounting practices at her firm must balance her desire to do the right thing against her desire to keep her job, provide income for her family, and maintain relationships with her fellow workers. She will report the accounting abuses to outside authorities only if moral considerations take precedence over these competing priorities.

Psychologists report that self-interest and hypocrisy undermine moral motivation.[22] Sometimes individuals genuinely want to do the right thing, but their integrity is "overpowered" when they discover that they will have to pay a personal cost for acting in an ethical manner. Others never intend to follow an ethical course of action but engage in *moral hypocrisy* instead. These decision makers "want to appear moral while, if possible, avoiding the cost of actually being moral."[23] In experimental settings, they say that assignments should be distributed fairly but then assign themselves the most desirable tasks while giving less desirable chores to others. Both self-interest and hypocrisy encourage leaders to set their moral principles aside. For example, corporate executives may declare that lower-level employees deserve higher wages. However, whether they really want to help workers or just want to appear as if they do, these executives are not likely to pay employees more if it means that the executives themselves will earn less as a result.

Rewards play an important role in ethical follow-through. People are more likely to give ethical values top priority when they are rewarded for doing so through raises, promotions, public recognition, and other means. Conversely, moral motivation drops when the reward system reinforces unethical behavior.[24] Unfortunately, misplaced rewards are all too common, as in the case of electronics retailers who reward employees for selling expensive extended warranties on new products. Such warranties are generally a bad deal for consumers.

Emotions also play a part in moral motivation.[25] As noted earlier, sympathy, disgust, guilt, and other moral emotions prompt us to take action. We can use their motivational force to help us punish wrongdoers, address injustice, provide assistance, and so on. Other researchers report that positive emotions such as joy and happiness make people more optimistic and more likely to live out their moral choices and to help others. Depression, on the other hand, lowers motivation, and jealousy, rage, and envy contribute to lying, revenge, stealing, and other antisocial behaviors.

To increase your moral motivation and the moral motivation of followers, seek out and create ethically rewarding environments. Make sure that your organization's reward system supports ethical behavior. Try to reduce the costs of behaving morally by instituting policies and procedures that make it easier for members to report unethical behavior, combat discrimination, and so on. Work to align rewards with desired behavior in your current organization. Be concerned about how goals are reached. If all else fails, reward yourself. Take pride in following through on your choices and on living up to your self-image as a person of integrity. Tap into moral emotions while making a conscious effort to control negative feelings and to put yourself in a positive frame of mind.

Component 4: Moral Character

Executing a plan of action takes character. Moral agents have to overcome opposition, resist distractions, cope with fatigue, and develop tactics and strategies for reaching their goals. This helps explain why there is only a moderate correlation between moral judgment and moral behavior. Deciding often does not lead to doing.

The positive virtues described in Chapter 3 contribute to ethical follow-through. Courage helps leaders implement their plans despite the risks and costs of doing so, while prudence helps them choose the best course of action. Integrity encourages leaders to be true to themselves and their choices. Humility forces leaders to address limitations that might prevent them from taking action. Reverence promotes self-sacrifice. Optimism equips leaders to persist in the face of obstacles and difficulties. Compassion and justice focus the attention of leaders on the needs of others rather than on personal priorities.

In addition to virtues, other personal characteristics contribute to moral action.[26] Those with a strong will as well as confidence in themselves and their abilities are more likely to persist. The same is true for those with an internal locus of control. Internally oriented people (internals) believe that they have control over their lives and can determine what happens to them. Externally oriented people (externals) believe that life events are beyond their control and are the products of fate or luck instead. Because they take personal responsibility for their actions, internals are more motivated to do what is right. Externals are more susceptible to situational pressures and therefore less likely to persist in ethical tasks.

Successful implementation of a plan also requires competence. For instance, modifying an organization's reward system may entail researching, organizing, arguing, networking, and relationship-building skills. These skills are put to maximum use when actors have an in-depth understanding of the organizational context: important policies, the group's history and culture, informal leaders, and so forth.

Following the character-building guidelines presented in Chapter 3 will go a long way to helping you build the virtues you need to put your moral choices into action. You may also want to look at your past performance to see why you succeeded or failed. Believe that you can have an impact. Otherwise, you are probably not going to carry through when obstacles surface. Develop your skills so that you can better put your moral choices into action and master the context in which you operate. (See Box 6.1 for more suggestions on how to follow through on your ethical choices.)

The Giving Voice to Values program, started by the Aspen Institute and Yale University and now housed at Babson College, is an international effort designed to help participants resist the pressure to set aside their personal standards. Mary Gentile, director of the Giving Voice to Values curriculum, argues that the first step toward acting on personal moral standards (developing "moral muscle") is to conduct a thought experiment. Ask, "What if you were going to act on your values—what would you say and do?"(p. xxxv). She then outlines seven pillars or foundational concepts that equip us to act on our ethical choices:

1. *Recognize that certain values are widely shared.* Identifying shared values like courage, compassion, integrity, and wisdom can provide the foundation for resolving values conflicts and for developing shared goals in a variety of cultural settings.

2. *Acknowledge the power of choice.* Most of us can think of a time when we acted on our ethical beliefs or, conversely, failed to do so. Telling the stories of such events reveals that we have the power to choose. These narratives help us identify the factors that contributed to success (enablers) or failure (disablers). Gentile reports that some common enablers include finding allies, gathering information, asking questions, taking incremental steps, and reframing (e.g., redefining ethical misbehavior as a risk, turning competition into a win–win negotiation).

3. *Treat values conflicts as normal.* Disagreements over ethical choices are common in organizations. If we acknowledge that fact, then we won't be surprised when such disputes arise and will remain calm. We'll also find it easier to appreciate the viewpoints of other parties instead of vilifying them.

4. *Consider your personal and professional purpose.* Before values conflicts arise, consider the impact you want to have in your job and career. Thinking about why you work and the mission of your organization can provide you with new arguments to use when voicing values. You'll feel more empowered to speak up, and others may be attracted to your purpose.

5. *Play to personal strengths.* We are more likely to speak up if we know who we are. Acting on values then arises out of our core identity. In addition to identifying your personal purpose, consider the degree of risk you are willing to take, your personal communication style, where your loyalties lie, and your image of yourself. Create a

(Continued)

(Continued)

personal narrative or self-story that builds on your strengths and encourages you to act on your convictions.

6. *Find your unique voice.* Expressing values is a learnable skill. There are many different ways to speak out about values in the work setting. Find and develop yours through reflection on your experience, practice (each time you speak up, you build moral muscle), and coaching from mentors and peers. When you voice your values as a leader, you encourage your followers to do the same.

7. *Anticipate rationalizations for unethical behavior.* Consider the most likely arguments that others may use to support immoral behavior. Common rationalizations include "Everyone does this; it's standard practice" and "This is not my responsibility; I'm just following orders." Then consider how you might best respond. For example, the "everybody is doing it" argument is an exaggeration, since (a) not everyone engages in the practice, and (b) if it were standard practice, then there wouldn't be a law against it. The "just following orders" argument reveals that the speaker is uncomfortable with her or his response to the situation and should be open to further discussion.

SOURCE: Gentile, M. C. (2010). *Giving voice to values: How to speak your mind when you know what's right.* New Haven, CT: Yale University Press. For additional information, visit http://www.givingvoicetovalues.com

Decision-Making Formats

Decision-making guidelines or formats can help us make better ethical choices. Taking a systematic approach encourages teams and individuals to define the problem carefully, gather information, apply ethical standards and values, identify and evaluate alternative courses of action, and follow through on their choices. They will also be better equipped to defend their decisions. Four ethical decision-making formats are described in the pages to come. I'll provide a balance sheet for each format, outlining its strengths and weaknesses (pros and cons). All four approaches are useful. You may want to use just one or a combination of all of them. The particular format you use is not important, as long as you take a systematic approach to moral reasoning. You can practice these guidelines by applying them to the scenarios described in Case Study 6.1.

Kidder's Ethical Checkpoints

Ethicist Rushworth Kidder suggested that the following nine steps or checkpoints can help bring order to otherwise confusing ethical issues:[27]

1. *Recognize that there is a problem.* This step is critically important because it forces us to acknowledge that there is an issue that deserves our attention and helps us separate moral questions from disagreements about manners and social conventions. For example, being late for a party may be bad manners and violate cultural expectations. However, this act does not translate into a moral problem involving right or wrong. On the other hand, deciding whether to accept a kickback from a supplier is an ethical dilemma.

2. *Determine the actor.* Once we've determined that there is an ethical issue, we need to decide who is responsible for addressing the problem. I may be concerned that the owner of a local business treats his employees poorly. Nonetheless, unless I work for the company or buy its products, there is little I can do to address this situation.

3. *Gather the relevant facts.* Adequate, accurate, and current information is important for making effective decisions of all kinds, including ethical ones. Details do make a difference. In deciding whether it is just to suspend a student for fighting, for instance, a school principal will want to hear from teachers, the student's classmates, and the offender to determine the seriousness of the offense, the student's reason for fighting, and the outcome of the altercation. The administrator will probably be more lenient if this is the offender's first offense and he was defending himself.

4. *Test for right-versus-wrong issues.* A choice is generally a poor one if it gives you a negative, gut-level reaction (the stench test), would make you uncomfortable if it appeared on the front page of tomorrow's newspaper (the front-page test), or would violate the moral code of someone you care a lot about (the mom test). If your decision violates any of these criteria, you had better reconsider.

5. *Test for right-versus-right values.* Many ethical dilemmas pit two core values against each other. Determine whether two good or right values are in conflict with one another in this situation. Right-versus-right value clashes include the following:

   - *Truth telling versus loyalty to others and institutions.* Telling the truth may threaten our allegiance to another person or to an organization, such as when leaders and followers are faced with the decision of whether to blow the whistle on organizational misbehavior. Kidder believes that truth versus loyalty is the most common type of conflict involving two deeply held values.

   - *Personal needs versus the needs of the community.* Our desire to serve our immediate group or ourselves can run counter to the needs of the larger group or community.

   - *Short-term benefits versus long-term negative consequences.* Sometimes satisfying the immediate needs of the group (giving a hefty pay raise to employees, for example) can lead to long-term negative consequences (endangering the future of the business).

- *Justice versus mercy.* Being fair and evenhanded may conflict with our desire to show love and compassion. (A clash between two other right values is at the heart of the case described in "Focus on Follower Ethics: The Case of Private Manning" later in this chapter.)

6. *Apply the ethical standards and perspectives.* Apply the ethical principle that is most relevant and useful to this specific issue. Is it justice as fairness? Utilitarianism? Kant's categorical imperative? Altruism? A combination of perspectives?

7. *Look for a third way.* Sometimes seemingly irreconcilable values can be resolved through compromise or the development of a creative solution. Negotiators often seek a third way to bring competing factions together. Such was the case in the deliberations that produced the Camp David Peace Accord. Egypt demanded that Israel return land on the West Bank seized in the 1967 War. Israel resisted because it wanted a buffer zone to protect its security. The dispute was settled when Egypt pledged that it would not attack Israel again. Assured of safety, the Israelis agreed to return the territory to Egypt.[28]

8. *Make the decision.* At some point we need to step up and make the decision. This seems a given (after all, the point of the whole process is to reach a conclusion). However, we may be mentally exhausted from wrestling with the problem, get caught up in the act of analysis, or lack the necessary courage to come to a decision. In Kidder's words:

> At this point in the process, there's little to do but decide. That requires moral courage—an attribute essential to leadership and one that, along with reason, distinguishes humanity most sharply from the animal world. Little wonder, then, that the exercise of ethical decision-making is often seen as the highest fulfillment of the human condition.[29]

9. *Revisit and reflect on the decision.* Learn from your choices. Once you've moved on to other issues, stop and reflect. What lessons emerged from this case that you can apply to future decisions? What ethical issues did it raise?

Balance Sheet

Advantages (Pros)

- Is thorough

- Considers problem ownership

- Emphasizes the importance of getting the facts straight

- Recognizes that dilemmas can involve right–right as well as right–wrong choices

- Encourages the search for creative solutions

- Sees ethical decision making as a learning process

Weaknesses (Cons)

- Determining who has the responsibility for solving a problem is not always easy

- The facts are not always available, or there may not be enough time to gather them

- Decisions don't always lead to action

There is a lot to be said for Kidder's approach to ethical decision making. For one thing, he seems to cover all the bases, beginning with defining the issue all the way through to learning from the situation after the dust has settled. He acknowledges that there are some problems that we can't do much about and that we need to pay particular attention to gathering as much information as possible. The ethicist recognizes that some decisions involve deciding between two "goods" and leaves the door open for creative solutions. Making a choice can be an act of courage, as Kidder points out, and we can apply lessons learned in one dilemma to future problems.

On the flip side, some of the strengths of Kidder's model can also be seen as weaknesses. As we'll see in Chapter 10, determining responsibility or ownership of a problem is getting harder in an increasingly interdependent world. Who is responsible for poor labor conditions in developing countries, for instance? The manufacturer? The subcontractor? The store that sells the products made in sweatshops? Those who buy the items? Kidder also seemed to assume that leaders will have the time to gather necessary information. Unfortunately, in some situations time is in short supply. Finally, the model seems to equate deciding with doing. As we saw in our earlier discussion of moral action, we can decide on a course of action but not follow through. Kidder is right to say that making ethical choices takes courage. However, it takes even more courage to put our choices into effect.

The SAD Formula

Media ethicist Louis Alvin Day of Louisiana State University developed the SAD formula in order to build important elements of critical thinking into moral reasoning. Critical thinking is a rational approach to decision making that emphasizes careful analysis and evaluation. It begins with an understanding of the subject to be evaluated, moves to identifying the issues, information, and assumptions surrounding the problem, and then concludes with evaluating alternatives and reaching a conclusion.[30]

Each stage of the SAD formula—situation definition, analysis of the situation, decision—addresses a component of critical thinking (see Box 6.2). To demonstrate this model, I'll use a conflict involving mandatory vaccinations of health care workers.

Situation Definition

Health care professionals are at risk for contracting infectious diseases and spreading them to their patients. Vaccination can reduce the likelihood of catching the flu by 70–80% and is one of the best ways to prevent a pandemic. However, fewer than half of U.S. and Australian health workers get flu shots every year, and only 55–65% of Canadian physicians are vaccinated. Medical personnel who fail to be inoculated often do so for the same reasons as other citizens: They don't like shots, it is not convenient to get them, they claim they seldom get sick, they don't think the injections are effective, or they believe the vaccine will make them ill (although scientists deny that this happens).[31]

Health officials have tried a variety of strategies to increase the percentage of doctors and nurses receiving vaccinations, including promotional campaigns and prize drawings. However, these voluntary efforts have fallen short. Concerned about low participation rates, Hospital Corporation of America, the province of British Columbia (Canada), MedStar Health (Maryland), Virginia Mason (Seattle, Washington), BJC HealthCare (St. Louis, Missouri), and the state of New York began mandatory vaccination programs. A number of clinics and doctors' offices followed suit. Employees were told they would lose their jobs if they did not get the vaccine. Exceptions were made for those likely to have an allergic reaction (eggs are used in the production of the shots) and those with religious objections. Some health care workers and their unions in Canada and the United States immediately protested the stricter vaccination policies, labeling such programs as intrusive violations of individual rights.

Day says that the ethical question to be addressed should be as narrow as possible. In our example, we will seek to answer the following query: *Are mandatory flu vaccination policies for health care workers ethically justified?*

Analysis

Evaluation of Values and Principles. Competing principles and values are clearly present in this situation. On one side, medical administrators and public health officials put a high value on the responsibility of medical personnel to patients and argue that mandatory vaccinations will save lives, particularly among vulnerable populations, like the sick, those with compromised immune systems, pregnant women, the very young, and the elderly. In requiring mandatory vaccinations in New York, the state's health commissioner asserted, "The rationale begins with health-care ethics, which is: The patient's well-being comes ahead of the personal preferences of health-care workers."[32] (The commissioner later rescinded his edict when there was a shortage of the vaccine.) The chief medical officer of MedStar Health said the decision to require vaccinations "is all about patient safety." On the other side of the debate are individuals, employee unions, and groups who place a high priority on individual rights. They believe that making flu shots a condition of employment takes away the employee's right to make personal medical decisions. According to the president of the nurses' union in British Columbia, "Anytime anything is put in a person's body, they should have sovereignty over their body and have the right to decide whether or not it's an appropriate thing to do."[33] An Ontario labor board ruled that mandatory flu shots violated the rights of health workers. Opponents also worried that mandatory programs would spread from the health care sector into other areas of society. Said a representative of an organization wanting to limit government expansion: "You start with health-care workers but then expand that umbrella to make it mandatory for everybody. It's all part of an encroachment on our liberties."[34]

External Factors. Some influenza strains, like H1N1 (swine flu), pose greater risks than other strains and spread more rapidly, making vaccinations even more important. Medical employees already have to be inoculated for other conditions, including mumps, measles, and tuberculosis, and there haven't been widespread protests about these requirements. In addition, medical personnel must follow such mandatory safety procedures as washing their hands before surgery. Vaccinations appear to be a safety measure like hand washing. However, past inoculation programs have made some medical professionals skeptical about current efforts. Earlier vaccines did make recipients sore and could cause mild flu-like symptoms. The swine flu vaccine seemed to be rushed into production, raising concerns that recipients were serving as "guinea pigs." Nurses, doctors, and home health caregivers, like other Americans, are increasingly worried about substances they put in their bodies.

Moral Duties or Loyalties. Day borrows from theologian Ralph Potter for this part of his model. Potter believes we need to take into account important duties or loyalties when making ethical choices.[35] In this case, the following duties have to be kept in mind:

- Loyalty to self (individual conscience)

- Loyalty to patients

- Loyalty to vulnerable populations

- Loyalty to fellow employees

- Loyalty to others in the same profession

- Loyalty to the public

Medical officials seem primarily concerned about patients, vulnerable populations, and the larger community. Low vaccination rates threaten patients and clients and help the virus spread. Health care workers who refuse flu shots also damage the credibility of the medical profession. Why should patients be vaccinated if their doctors and nurses don't think it is safe or necessary to do so? Vaccination objectors are more concerned about their individual rights and, in some cases, their personal safety. They seem to overlook their primary duty, which is to serve their patients. Yet not all appear to be acting out of selfish motives. Some resistors are concerned about setting a precedent that could reduce the rights of their fellow citizens in the years to come.

Moral Theories. From a utilitarian perspective, the benefit of protecting personal rights has to be weighed against the dangers of spreading the flu virus. However, the immediate benefits of slowing the virus also need to be weighed against the long-term costs—loss of individual rights and government intrusion. Based on Kant's categorical imperative, we could ask if we would want everyone to be vaccinated (probably) or if we would want everyone to refuse to be vaccinated (probably not). However, employees who resist the mandatory shots should carry through on their decision regardless of the consequences, such as losing their jobs. Rawls's theory could be applied to say that required vaccinations are justified because they protect the least advantaged members of society. Advocates of mandatory vaccinations have a stronger altruistic focus because such efforts are designed to reduce sickness and suffering. Opponents may argue, however, that they are demonstrating concern by protecting the rights of others.

Decision

Decisions often emerge out of careful definition and analysis of the problem. It may be clear which course of action is best after external constraints, principles, duties, and moral theories are identified and evaluated. In our example, mandatory flu vaccination programs for health care workers appear to be morally justified. Such programs put the needs of others first and reduce suffering and death. They seem consistent with other requirements placed on health care workers and support the patient-focused mission of the medical profession. Health care employees should prevent sickness, not spread it. This option also seems to be best supported by moral theory. Nonetheless, opponents of mandatory vaccination programs are right to point out that we should be cautious about requiring health treatments. Just because mandatory influenza vaccinations are justified for health care workers does not mean that we should require all citizens to be vaccinated (that's a different question for analysis) or force citizens into other medical treatments.

Balance Sheet

Advantages (Pros)

- Encourages orderly, systematic reasoning

- Incorporates situation definition, duties, and moral theories

Disadvantages (Cons)

- May fail to reach consensus

- Limits creativity by focusing on one question

- Ignores the implementation step

The SAD formula does encourage careful reasoning by building in key elements of the critical thinking process. Following the formula keeps decision makers from reaching hasty decisions. Instead of jumping immediately to solutions, they must carefully identify elements of the situation, examine and evaluate ethical alternatives, and then reach a conclusion.

Three elements of the SAD formula are particularly praiseworthy. First, the formula recognizes that the keys to solving a problem often lie in clearly identifying and describing it. Groups are far less likely to go astray when members clearly outline the question they are to answer. Second, Day's formula highlights duties or loyalties. In the case of vaccinations, prioritizing loyalties is key to supporting or opposing mandatory vaccination programs. Third, the formula incorporates moral theories directly into the decision-making process.

The strengths of the SAD model must be balanced against some troubling weaknesses. Day implies that a clear choice will emerge after the problem is defined and analyzed, but that may not always be the case. Even in our example, there is room for dispute. While it appears as if mandatory vaccinations are morally justified, those who put a high value on personal freedoms will likely remain unconvinced. They raise valid concerns about the long-term impacts of such programs as well. Focusing on a narrowly defined question may exclude creative options and make it hard to apply principles from one decision to other settings. Finally, the formula leaves out the important implementation stage.

Nash's 12 Questions

Ethics consultant Laura Nash offers 12 questions that can help businesses and other groups identify the responsibilities involved in making moral choices.[36] She argues that discussions based on these queries can be useful even if the group doesn't reach a conclusion. Managers who answer the questions surface ethical concerns that might otherwise remain hidden, identify common moral problems, clarify gaps between stated values and performance, and explore a variety of alternatives.

1. *Have you defined the problem accurately?* The ethical decision-making process begins with assembling the facts. Determine how many employees will be affected by layoffs, how much the cleanup of toxic materials will cost, or how many people have been injured by faulty products. Finding out the facts can help defuse the emotionalism of some issues (perhaps the damage is not as great as first feared).

2. *How would you define the problem if you stood on the other side of the fence?* Asking how others might feel forces self-examination. From a city government's point of view, constructing a bypass around the town to reduce congestion may make good sense. Farmers might have an entirely different perspective. Building the bypass means taking valuable cropland out of production.

3. *How did this situation occur in the first place?* This question separates the symptoms from the disease. Lying, cheating customers, and strained labor relations are generally symptoms of deeper problems. Firing an employee for unethical behavior is a

temporary solution. Probe to discover the underlying causes. For example, many dubious accounting practices are the result of pressure to produce high quarterly profits.

4. *To whom and to what do you give your loyalties as a person or group and as a member of the organization?* As we saw in Chapter 1, conflicts of loyalty are hard to sort through. However, wrestling with the problem of ultimate loyalty (work group? family? self? corporation?) can clarify the values operating in an ethical dilemma.

5. *What is your intention in making this decision?*

6. *How does this intention compare with the likely results?* These questions probe both the group's intentions and the likely products. Honorable motives don't guarantee positive results. Make sure that the outcomes reflect your motivations.

7. *Whom could your decision or action injure?* Too often groups consider possible injury only after they are sued. Try, in advance, to determine harmful consequences. What will happen if customers ignore label warnings and spread your pesticide indiscriminately, for example? Will the guns you manufacture end up in the hands of urban gang members? Based on these determinations, you may decide to abandon your plans to make these items or revise the way they are marketed.

8. *Can you engage the affected parties in a discussion of the problem before you make your decision?* Talking to affected parties is one way to make sure that you understand how your actions will influence them. Few of us would want other people to decide what's in our best interest. Yet we often push forward with projects that assume we know what's in the best interests of others.

9. *Are you confident that your position will be as valid over a long period of time as it seems now?* Make sure that your choice will stand the test of time. What seem like compelling reasons for a decision may not seem so important months or years later. Consider the U.S. decision to invade Iraq, for instance. American intelligence experts and political leaders tied Saddam Hussein to terrorist groups and claimed that he was hiding weapons of mass destruction. After the invasion, no solid links between Iraqis and international terrorists or weapons of mass destruction were discovered. Our decision to wage this war doesn't appear as justified now as it did in the months leading up to the conflict. Similarly, most Americans supported the ousting of Libyan dictator Muammar Qaddafi in 2011, but public opinion shifted after an attack on the American embassy in Benghazi killed the U.S. ambassador and several others in 2012.

10. *Could you disclose without qualm your decision or action to your boss, your CEO, the board of directors, your family, or society as a whole?* No ethical decision is too trivial to escape the disclosure test. If you or your group would not want to disclose this action, then you'd better reevaluate your choice.

11. *What is the symbolic potential of your action if understood? Misunderstood?* What you intend may not be what the public perceives (see Questions 5 and 6). If your company is a notorious polluter, its contributions to local arts groups may be seen as an attempt to divert attention from the firm's poor environmental record, not as a generous civic gesture.

12. *Under what conditions would you allow exceptions to your stand?* Moral consistency is critical, but is there any basis for making an exception? Dorm rules might require that visiting hours end at midnight on weekdays. Yet, as a resident assistant, is there any time you would be willing to overlook violations? During finals week? On the evening before classes start? When dorm residents and visitors are working on class projects?

Balance Sheet

Advantages (Pros)

- Highlights the importance of gathering facts

- Encourages perspective taking

- Forecasts results and consequences over time

Disadvantages (Cons)

- Can be extremely time-consuming

- Decision makers may not always reach a conclusion

- Ignores implementation step

Like Kidder's ethical checkpoints, Nash's 12 questions highlight the importance of problem identification and information gathering. They go a step further, however, by encouraging us to engage in perspective taking. We need to see the problem from the other party's point of view, consider the possible injury we might cause, invite others to give us feedback, and consider how our actions will be perceived. We also need to envision results and take a long-term perspective, imagining how our decisions will stand the test of time. Stepping back can keep us from making choices we might regret later. For example, the decision to test nuclear weapons on U.S. soil without warning citizens may have seemed justified to officials waging the Cold War. However, now even the federal government admits that conducting these tests was immoral.

I suspect that some groups will be frustrated by the amount of time it takes to answer the 12 questions. Discussing the problem with affected parties could require a series of meetings over a period of weeks or even months. Complex issues such as determining who should clean up river pollution involve a variety of constituencies with very different agendas—government agencies, company representatives, citizens' groups, conservation clubs. Some decision makers may also be put off by the model's ambiguity. Nash admits that experts may define problems differently, that there may be exceptions to the decision, and that groups may use the procedure and never reach a conclusion. Finally, none of the questions use the ethical standards we identified in Chapter 5 or address the problem of implementing the choice once it is made.

FOCUS ON FOLLOWER ETHICS

The Case of Private Manning

U.S. Army private Bradley Manning is at the center of an international controversy pitting those who want to protect government secrets against those who believe in the free flow of information. Manning, a military intelligence analyst once stationed in Iraq, is accused of disclosing massive amounts of classified material to WikiLeaks, a global website for whistle-blowers. This material included more than 250,000 diplomatic cables and over 90,000 intelligence reports on the war in Afghanistan, and a video of a military helicopter attack that killed two Reuters news reporters. Manning downloaded this information to a disc disguised as a Lady Gaga CD and then posted it in three separate data dumps. He was arrested after reaching out to a former computer hacker who turned him in because he feared that the leak could cost lives. Private First Class Manning pled guilty to 10 criminal counts related to misuse of classified information. He was later convicted of most of the charges against him but was found not guilty of the most serious charge—aiding the enemy. A military judge sentenced him to 35 years in prison.

Manning said he leaked the information because he wanted to "spark a debate about foreign policy," particularly in Iraq and Afghanistan. He believed that the military was so focused on killing or capturing insurgents that it didn't consider the damage it was doing to ordinary civilians. He was especially troubled by the "seemingly delightful blood lust" of the airmen in the helicopter attack video. After they killed the first group of men, the helicopter crew opened fire on a van that had stopped to help the victims.

Manning is a villain to some and a hero to others. State Department officials, the military, members of Congress, and the Obama administration were eager to punish him. They point out that the leaks damaged diplomatic relationships with allies, put the lives of soldiers in danger by releasing critical information to

(Continued)

(Continued)

insurgents, and could lead to the deaths of Afghan intelligence sources identified in the documents. Said the Defense Department: "We deplore WikiLeaks. . . . We know terrorist organizations have been mining the leaked Afghan documents for information to use against us."[1] For their part, antiwar activists and transparency advocates launched a "Free Bradley Manning" campaign, which helped to underwrite expenses for his legal defense. Julian Assange, founder of WikiLeaks, called Private Manning "the world's pre-eminent prisoner of conscience." Manning supporters deny that the release of the classified documents did any serious damage.

Should Private Manning be considered a villain or a hero for his actions? Why?

Note

1. Glenny, M. (2010, December 5). The gift of information. *The New York Times,* M2, p. 166.

Sources

Bumiller, E. (2010, June 8). Army leak suspect is turned in, by ex-hacker. *The New York Times,* p. A1.

Savage, C. (2011, March 3). Soldier faces 22 new WikiLeaks charges. *The New York Times,* p. A6.

Savage, C. (2013, March 1). Soldier admits providing files to WikiLeaks. *The New York Times,* p. A1.

Savage, C. (2013, July 31). Manning found not guilty of aiding the enemy. *The New York Times,* p. A1.

Shane, S. (2010, December 12). Keeping secrets WikiSafe. *The New York Times,* p. WK1.

Shane, S. (2011, January 14). Accused soldier stays in brig as WikiLeaks link is sought. *The New York Times,* p. A1.

Thompson, G. (2010, August 9). A soldier's path toward a leak investigation. *The New York Times,* p. A1.

Usborne, D. (2012, June 7). Thin and fragile, America's public enemy No. 1 Bradley Manning in court. *The Independent,* Americas.

The Case Study Method

The case study method is widely used for making medical diagnoses. At many hospitals, groups made up of doctors, nurses, and other staff members meet regularly to talk about particularly troublesome cases. They may be unable to determine the exact nature of an illness or how best to treat a patient. Many of these deliberations involve ethical issues, such as whether to keep a terminally ill person on life support or how to respond to patients who demand unnecessary tests and procedures. The group solicits a variety of viewpoints and gathers as much information as possible. Members engage in analogical reasoning, comparing the specifics of a particular case with similar cases by describing the patient, the illness, the patient's relationships with family members, and so on. Instead of focusing on how universal principles and standards can be applied in this situation, hospital personnel are more concerned with the details of the case itself. Participants balance competing perspectives and values, reach tentative conclusions, and look for similarities between the current case and earlier ones.

Medical ethicist and communication scholar David H. Smith argues that the case-based approach is a powerful technique because it is based on narrative or story.[37] When decision makers describe cases, they are telling stories. These narratives say as much about the storytellers as they do about the reality of the cases. "Facts" are not objective truth but rather are reflections of what the narrator thinks is true and important. Stories knit these perceptions into a coherent whole. When discussing the fate of a patient, it is not enough to know medical data. Hospital personnel need to learn about the patient's history, the costs and benefits of various treatment options, and other factors, such as the wishes of relatives and legal issues. Smith outlines the following steps for case-based decision making:

1. *Foster storytelling.* Alert participants to the fact that they will be sharing their stories about the problem. Framing the discussion as a storytelling session invokes a different set of evaluation criteria than is generally used in decision making. We judge evidence based on such factors as the quality of sources and logical consistency (see the discussion of argumentation in Chapter 8). We judge stories by how believable they seem to be, how well the elements fit together and mesh with what we know of the world, and the values reflected in the narratives.[38]

2. *Encourage elaboration of essential events and characters.* Details are essential to the case study method. Additional details make it easier to draw comparisons with other examples.

3. *Encourage the sharing of stories by everyone with an interest in the problem.* Bringing more perspectives to bear on the problem reveals more details. In the end, a better, shared story emerges. Consider the case of an elderly man refusing a heart operation that could extend his life. Finding out why he is rejecting the surgery is an important first step to solving this ethical dilemma. As nurses, social workers, and doctors share information, they may discover that the patient is suffering from depression or feels cut off from his family. Addressing these problems may encourage the patient to agree to the operation and thus resolve the moral issue.

4. *Offer alternative meanings.* Change the interpretation of a story by doing the following:

- Provide additional expert information and point out where the facts of the story do not fit with other facts. The first diagnosis may not be correct. Press on when necessary. In the case of our patient, claims that he is alienated from his family would be rejected if his children and grandchildren visit him daily.
- Focus attention on the characters in the story (the patient) rather than on some overarching ethical principle such as utilitarianism or the categorical imperative.
- Examine analogies critically to make sure they really hold. Don't assume that the reasons one patient turns down treatment are the same as those of other patients, for example.
- Offer alternative futures that might come to pass depending on decisions made by the group. In our case, what will be the likely outcome if treatment is delayed or never given? How much will the patient improve if he has the heart operation? Will attempts to persuade him backfire, locking him into his current position? What might happen if the hospital were to enlist his family to force him into compliance?

Balance Sheet

Advantages (Pros)

- Offers a unique approach to ethical decision making

- Harnesses the power of narrative and analogical reasoning

- Avoids ethical polarization and allows for ethical middle ground

Disadvantages (Cons)

- Downplays the importance of objective reality

- Details are not always available to decision makers

- Consensus on the right course of action is not always possible

The case study method is significantly different from the other approaches presented in this chapter. The other models outline linear, step-by-step processes for resolving ethical dilemmas that call for the application of universal ethical principles or standards. The case study approach is not linear but circular, calling on participants to share a variety of perspectives. Decision makers keep ethical principles in mind but don't try to invoke them to provide the resolution to a problem. They use them as general guides instead and focus on the case itself. Although unique, the case study method still requires decision makers to meet, systematically share information, analyze the problem, evaluate options, and reach a conclusion.

We often make choices based on stories. A good narrative is more persuasive than statistical evidence, for instance, and frequently uses the type of analogical reasoning reflected in the case study approach.[39] For example, when faced with an ethical decision about whether to tell your current employer about a job offer you've received from another firm, you probably would consider the following: (1) the details of the situation (your relationship with your immediate supervisor, how hard it will be to replace you, your loyalty to the organization), (2) similar situations or cases in your past (what happened when you revealed such information before leaving your last job), and (3) what your friends have done when facing similar circumstances. The case study method takes advantage of our natural tendency to reason through story and analogy.

As I noted in the discussion of character ethics in Chapter 3, universal principles can be difficult to apply to specific situations. There always seem to be exceptions to the rule ("In general, don't lie, but it may be okay to lie if it protects someone else from danger"). A strength of the case study approach is that it acknowledges that specific circumstances often shape how a general principle can be used to resolve a particular dilemma. This approach also avoids the polarization caused by invoking ethical absolutes. Take the abortion debate, for example. Proponents and opponents of abortion rights are locked into their positions by their interpretations of such values as freedom and the sanctity of life. The case study method suggests that some middle ground can be found by examining specific cases. After all, some pro-life advocates are willing to allow abortion in cases where the mother's life is in danger, and some in the pro-choice camp are uncomfortable with late-term abortions.

The case study approach has its downside. To begin, it minimizes objective reality. Although we always see ethical dilemmas through our perceptual filters, there do appear to be verifiable facts that ought to come into play in decision making. Crime scene evidence should be essential to determining a defendant's guilt or innocence, for instance. Some criticized the verdict of the O. J. Simpson murder trial in the mid-1990s because they thought that the jury overlooked factual DNA evidence and accepted the story of police misconduct instead. When the same evidence was offered in a later civil trial, jurors concluded that the football star was indeed guilty of murdering his ex-wife and her friend and forced him to pay damages to the families.

A practical problem with the case study method is its dependence on detail. In real life, leaders may not have the luxury of being able to solicit stories and probe for additional information. They must make decisions quickly, particularly in crises. Students face a similar problem when discussing cases in class. Short cases, such as the ones in this text, may leave out details you think are important. Yet you have to resolve them anyway.

Finally, consensus, although likely in this format, is not guaranteed. One overall story may emerge, but it may not. This is often the case in medical diagnoses. Two doctors may reach different conclusions about what is wrong with a patient. Differences in values, perspectives, and definitions of "facts" may keep ethical decision makers apart.

IMPLICATIONS AND APPLICATIONS _____

- Both logic and emotions are essential to ethical decision making. Draw on both processes when making moral choices. Your initial reaction to an ethical dilemma, based on your emotions, cultural influences, past experiences, and intuitions, can inform the conclusion you reach using a decision-making format.

- Ethical behavior is the product of moral sensitivity (recognition), moral judgment, moral focus (motivation), and moral character.

- Increase your sensitivity to potential ethical issues through perspective taking, using moral terminology, increasing the moral intensity of issues, and being sensitive to the presence of moral emotions like anger, disgust, guilt, and sympathy.

- Improve your ability to make moral judgments by creating an ethical environment that provides ethical role models and guidelines, continuing your education with a special focus on ethics, considering the needs and perspectives of broader audiences, and basing your decisions on widely accepted moral principles and guidelines.

- Ethical biases or blind spots can cause you to participate in or approve of behaviors you would normally condemn. These errors include overestimating your ethicality, forgiving your unethical behavior, in-group favoritism, implicit prejudice, and judging based on outcomes, not processes. Acknowledging that you could have these blind spots is the first step to overcoming them.

- Foster your moral motivation and that of followers by rewarding ethical choices, responding to moral emotions, and controlling negative feelings.

- Your chances of following through on ethical decisions (moral character) are higher if you demonstrate virtue, believe you have some control over events in your life, and develop the necessary skills to put your plan into action.

- Decision-making guidelines can help you make better ethical choices. Possible ethical decision-making formats include Kidder's ethical checkpoints, the SAD formula, Nash's 12 questions, and the case study method. The particular format you choose is not important, as long as you take a systematic approach to ethical decision making.

- Whatever format you follow, make every effort to gather in-depth, current, and accurate information.

- Creativity is as vital in making ethical decisions as it is in generating new products and programs. Sometimes you can come up with a "third way" to resolve an ethical conflict.

- Moral dilemmas often involve clashes between two core (good) values. Common right-versus-right dilemmas are truth versus loyalty, short-term versus long-term outcomes, individual versus community, and justice versus mercy.

- Think of ethical deliberation as an ongoing process. You may go through a sequence of steps and use them again. Return to your decision later to evaluate and learn from it. As soon as one ethical crisis passes, there's likely to be another on the horizon.

- Don't expect perfection. As a leader, make the best choice you can after thorough deliberation but recognize that sometimes you may have to choose between two flawed alternatives.

FOR FURTHER EXPLORATION, CHALLENGE, AND SELF-ASSESSMENT _____

1. Analyze your scores on the moral attentiveness test found in Self-Assessment 6.1. On which dimension did you score highest? Lowest? Why? What do you learn from this assessment? How can you improve your sensitivity to the presence of ethical issues?

2. Apply the four-component model to the process you went through when faced with a moral dilemma. How successfully did you complete each stage? What would you do differently next time? Write up your analysis.

3. Develop a plan for improving your moral reasoning as part of your education. How can you take advantage of your college experiences to become more of a postconventional thinker?

4. Create an original case study that demonstrates one or more of the ethical blind spots in action.

5. Which of the four decision-making formats do you find most useful? Why?

6. In a group, brainstorm a list of possible ethical dilemmas faced by a college student. How many of these problems involve a clash between two important values (right versus right)? Identify which values are in conflict in each situation.

7. Apply each of the formats to one of the scenarios in Case Study 6.1. First reach your own conclusion based on your initial reactions without using a format and then discuss the situation in a group using the models. See whether you can

reach a consensus. Make note of the important factors dividing or uniting group members. Do you reach different conclusions depending on the system you follow?

8. Use a format from this chapter to analyze an ethical decision facing society (e.g., gay marriage or gay ordination, universal health care, immigration). Write up your analysis and conclusions.

STUDENT STUDY SITE

Visit the student study site at **www.sagepub.com/johnsonmecl5e** to access full SAGE journal articles for further research and information on key chapter topics.

CASE STUDY 6.1

Ethical Scenarios for Analysis

Scenario A: Clothing the Camp Counselors

You are a first-year counselor at a camp for needy children, which is subsidized through contributions from individuals and local businesses. Yours is the only camp experience that these disadvantaged kids will ever have. One afternoon, a few hours before the next batch of children is due to arrive, a semitruck stops by with a donated shipment of new shoes, shirts, and shorts for your campers. Immediately the other counselors (all of whom have more experience than you do) begin selecting items for their personal use. They encourage you to do the same. When questioned, they argue that there is plenty to go around for both kids and counselors and that the clothes are a "fringe benefit" for underpaid camp staff.

Would you take any shoes or clothing to wear?

SOURCE: Kristina Findley.

Scenario B: Penalizing Timely Payments

You are the manager at a regional center that processes credit card payments. Company profits are down because of increased competition from other card issuers that charge lower interest rates. To boost income, your firm raised its penalties for late payments and reduced the length of the billing cycle. These changes were announced to cardholders. However, at the same time, company officials made an unofficial policy change. They instructed you and managers at the other processing centers to apply late penalties when checks arrive right before the due date. In these cases it will be difficult for cardholders to prove that their payments arrived on time. Some of your colleagues at other processing centers around the country have already begun this practice, knowing that failure to do so could cost them their jobs.

Will you institute this new policy at your processing center?

Scenario C: The Blowout

You are the coach of a high school girls' basketball team. This is your best season ever, and you are getting ready for the state play-offs. You teach an aggressive brand of basket-ball that involves playing full-court defense and fast breaking at every opportunity. As a result, your team scores lots of points. You tell the young women on your squad that they may not always win but that you want them to play hard and to always strive for excellence. Your last game of the regular sea-son is with the worst team in your league, one with many starters who had not played basketball before this year. Not only are they less experienced and less talented than your players, but they are much shorter as well. Within minutes the game turns into a rout. By halftime the score is 50 to 4. Some state high school athletic associations have "mercy rules" that shorten or end lopsided games. Your state does not. This is the last chance your team will have to "tune up" before mov-ing on to much stiffer competition.

In the second half will you deliberately try to keep the score down by changing how your team plays?

Sources

Brady, E., & Halley, J. (2009, February 24). The blowup over blowouts. *USA Today,* p. 1C.

Coutts, M. (2009, January 27). Would Jesus run up the score? Christian school under fire for winning 100–0. *National Post,* p. A1.

Halley, J. (2009, January 29). Lopsided games are often pointless. *USA Today,* p. 4C.

Scenario D: Would You Run These Ads?

You are the sales manager for a local radio station that has seen a dramatic downturn in ads and revenue as the local economy loses industries and small businesses. One of your biggest advertisers has been MighTY Mortgage. MighTY Mortgage spots feature the company president, Tom Tyler, promis-ing to "save our friends lots of cash." In these commercials Tyler claims that his company offers the lowest mortgage rates and will pay to have homes appraised.

Two weeks ago state regulators charged MighTY Mortgage with a variety of unethi-cal and illegal practices. The firm offers no proof that its loan rates are the lowest and charges enough in fees to more than cover the cost of the "free" appraisals. Investigators also found that, in most instances, MighTY failed to properly disclose loan terms to bor-rowers. The state wants to revoke the compa-ny's license, fine Tyler $250,000, and make sure the mortgage lender pays restitution to borrowers. However, final action has not been taken and won't be for several months.

After temporarily pulling his ads, Tom Tyler wants to go back on your station's airwaves with a new set of commercials. The new spots still promise to save listeners lots of money but no longer mention free appraisals. Instead of claiming to offer the lowest interest rate, MighTY Mortgage now says it offers a low interest rate.

Would you broadcast the new commer-cials for MighTY Mortgage?

SOURCE: Fictional case based on real-life events.

Scenario E: The Fertility Clinic Raffle

You are the business manager for a small fertility clinic that helps women conceive through the use of fertility drugs and other procedures. Other small clinics like yours have staged contests to build their mailing lists and to generate publicity, enabling them to compete against larger, better-known fertility centers. Sponsors claim that the contests are successful marketing tools that benefit women who can't afford the treatments, which cost $10,000–$15,000. In one type of contest, women compete for free treatments by submitting essays or videos explaining why they want to have a baby. In another type of contest, winners are selected randomly through raffles. You think that a contest could boost your marketing efforts as well. However, medical ethicists complain that fertility clinic contests take advantage of vulnerable couples and "trivialize" conception by raffling off the opportunity to have a baby. You realize that, if you hold a raffle, the winner might be a woman who could afford to pay for her treatment.

Would you hold a raffle or some other contest to market your fertility clinic?

SOURCE: Quenqua, D. (2012, October 21). Clinic raffles could make you a winner, and maybe a mother. *The New York Times*, p. A1.

SELF-ASSESSMENT 6.1

Moral Attentiveness

Instructions: Indicate the extent to which you agree with each of the following statements on a scale of 1 (*strongly disagree*) to 7 (*strongly agree*).

1. In a typical day, I face several ethical dilemmas.

2. I often have to choose between doing what's right and doing something that's wrong.

3. I regularly face decisions that have significant ethical implications.

4. My life has been filled with one moral predicament after another.

5. Many of the decisions that I make have ethical dimensions to them.

6. I regularly think about the ethical implications of my decisions.

7. I think about the morality of my actions almost every day.

8. I rarely face ethical dilemmas.

9. I frequently encounter ethical situations.

10. I often find myself pondering about ethical issues.

11. I often reflect on the moral aspects of my decisions.

12. I like to think about ethics.

Scoring

Reverse your score on item 8 and then add up your scores. Items 1–7 measure the extent to which you recognize moral aspects in your everyday experiences. Items 8–12 measure the extent to which you consider and reflect upon moral matters. Scores can range from 7 to 49 on items 1–7 and 5 to 35 on items 8–12. Total possible scores for the combined items range from 12 to 84. The higher your scores, the more attentive or sensitive you are to moral issues.

SOURCE: Reynolds, S. J. (2008). Moral attentiveness: Who pays attention to the moral aspects of life? *Journal of Applied Psychology, 93,* 1027–1041. Used by permission of the American Psychological Association.

SELF-ASSESSMENT 6.2

Moral Judgment Test

Instructions: Read the following story and reach a decision. After reaching your decision, try to justify and explain your statements as fully as possible. It is very important that you explain *why* you think it is right or why you think it should be done. Answer each question as best you can.

Evelyn

Evelyn worked for an automotive steel casting company. She was part of a small group asked to investigate the cause of an operating problem that had developed in the wheel castings of a new luxury automobile and to make recommendations for improvement. The problem did not directly create an unsafe condition, but it did lead to irritating sounds. The vice president of engineering told the group that he was certain that the problem was due to tensile stress in the castings. Evelyn and a lab technician conducted tests and found conclusive evidence that the problem was not tensile stress. As Evelyn began work on other possible explanations of the problem, she was told that the problem had been solved. A report prepared by Evelyn's boss strongly supported the tensile stress hypothesis. All of the data points from Evelyn's experiments had been changed to fit the curves, and some of the points that were far from where the theory would predict had been omitted. The report "proved" that tensile stress was responsible for the problem.

1. Should Evelyn contradict her boss's report? (Yes or No) Why or why not?

2. Should the potential conflict with Evelyn's boss have any impact on Evelyn's actions? Why, or why not?

3. If the lab technician working on the project issued the report supporting tensile stress hypothesis, should Evelyn contradict the report?

4. Is it important that people do everything they can to have the truth known? Explain.

5. Suppose the problem with the brake involved more than irritating sounds. Would it make a difference if the brake problem caused uneven brake applications and skids that could lead to possible human injury?

6. The data in the boss's report are false. Does that make it morally wrong if Evelyn fails to contradict the report?

7. Should people do everything they can to work within the corporate organization and support their superiors?

Scoring

Based on your answers to the questions above, determine your stage of moral reasoning using the form below, which is based on Kohlberg's stages of moral development (described in this chapter).

Stage Orientation	Moral Reasoning Explanation
1	Concern over the consequences of personal harm
2	Concern over the consequences of personal need
	Concern for personal satisfaction
	A sense of duty to oneself
3	Concern over the consequences to an immediate group
	Concern over personal relationships with others
	A sense of duty due to how others will perceive me, my actions
	Concern over personal integrity, how I will look to others
	A sense of duty to the consequences it may have for others
4	A sense of duty to a professional responsibility or group
	A sense of duty due to a commitment to a code, oath, principle
	A sense of duty to a larger, societal group
	Concern for social order, harmony
	Concern for society's laws
	Concern over the consequences to the larger societal group
5	Personally held values or beliefs of justice, fairness, rights
	Personally held belief in a moral law, above society's laws

Stage Orientation	Moral Reasoning Explanation
	A "social contract" to protect everyone's rights
	The greatest good for the greatest number of people affected
6	Universal principles of justice, fairness
	Universal laws governing behavior, superseding society's laws

SOURCE: Weber, J., & Wasieleski, D. (2001). Investigating influences on managers' moral reasoning: The impact of personal and organizational factors. *Business & Society, 40,* 105–107. Used by permission.

NOTES

1. Haidt, J. (2001). The emotional dog and its rational tail: A social intuitionist approach to moral judgment. *Psychological Review, 108,* 814–834; Haidt, J. (2012). *The righteous mind: Why good people are divided by politics and religion.* New York: Pantheon Books. Lapsley, D. K., & Hill, P. L. (2008). On dual processing and heuristic approaches to moral cognition. *Journal of Moral Education, 37,* 313–332.

2. Salvador, R., & Folger, R. G. (2009). Business ethics and the brain. *Business Ethics Quarterly, 19,* 1–31; Boksem, M. A. S., & De Cremer, D. (2009). The neural basis of morality. In D. De Cremer (Ed.), *Psychological perspectives on ethical behavior and decision-making* (pp. 153–166). Charlotte, NC: Information Age; Reynolds, S. J. (2006). A neurocognitive model of the ethical decision-making process: Implications for study and practice. *Journal of Applied Psychology, 91,* 737–748; Greene, J. (2005). Cognitive neuroscience and the structure of the moral mind (2005). In P. Carruthers, S. Laurence, & S. Stich (Eds.), *The innate mind: Structure and content* (pp. 338–352). Oxford, England: Oxford University Press; Casebeer, W. D. (2003). Moral cognition and its neural constituents. *Neuroscience, 4,* 841–846.

3. Salvador & Folger; Oum, R., & Lieberman, D. (2007). Emotion is cognition: An information-processing view of the mind. In K. D. Vohs, R. F. Baumeister, & G. Lowenstein (Eds.), *Do emotions help or hurt decision making? A hedgefoxian perspective* (pp. 133–154). New York: Russell Sage Foundation.

4. Monin, B., Pizarro, D. A., & Beer, J. S. (2007). Reason and emotion in moral judgment: Different prototypes lead to different theories. In K. D. Vohs, R. F. Baumeister, & G. Lowenstein (Eds.), *Do emotions help or hurt decision making? A hedgefoxian perspective* (pp. 219–244). New York: Russell Sage Foundation; Monin, B., Pizarro, D. A., & Beer, J. S. (2007). Deciding versus reacting: Conceptions of moral judgment and the reason–affect debate. *Review of General Psychology, 11,* 99–111.

5. Powers, C. W., & Vogel, D. (1980). *Ethics in the education of business managers.* Hastings-on-Hudson, NY: Institute of Society, Ethics and the Life Sciences.

6. Rest, J. R. (1986). *Moral development: Advances in research and theory.* New York: Praeger; Rest, J. R. (1993). Research on moral judgment in college students. In A. Garrod (Ed.), *Approaches to moral development*

(pp. 201–211). New York: Teachers College Press; Rest, J. R. (1994). Background: Theory and research. In J. R. Rest & D. Narvaez (Eds.), *Moral development in the professions: Psychology and applied ethics* (pp. 1–25). Hillsdale, NJ: Erlbaum.

7. Greenhouse, S., & Rosenbloom, S. (2008, December 24). Wal-Mart to settle suits over pay for $352 million. *The New York Times,* p. B1; Harris, J. (2009, October 16). Retail giant finds its green religion. *National Post,* p. FP12.

8. Werhane, P. (1999). *Moral imagination and management decision-making.* New York: Oxford University Press.

9. Bird, F. B. (1996). *The muted conscience: Moral silence and the practice of ethics in business.* Westport, CT: Quorum.

10. Tenbrunsel, A. E., & Messick, D. M. (2004). Ethical fading: The role of self-deception in unethical behavior. *Social Justice Research, 17,* 223–236.

11. Jones, T. M. (1991). Ethical decision making by individuals in organizations: An issue-contingent model. *Academy of Management Review, 15,* 366–395; Frey, B. F. (2000). The impact of moral intensity on decision making in a business context. *Journal of Business Ethics, 26,* 181–195; May, D. R., & Pauli, K. P. (2002). The role of moral intensity in ethical decision-making: A review and investigation of moral recognition, evaluation, and intention. *Business & Society, 41,* 84–117.

12. Haidt, J. (2003). The moral emotions. In R. J. Davidson, K. R. Scherer, & H. H. Goldsmith (Eds.), *Handbook of affective sciences* (pp. 852–870). Oxford, England: Oxford University Press; Moll, J., de Oliveira-Souza, R., Zahn, R., & Grafman, J. (2008). The cognitive neuroscience of moral emotions. In W. Sinnott-Armstrong (Ed.), *Moral psychology: Vol. 3. The neuroscience of morality: Emotion, brain disorders, and development* (pp. 1–17). Cambridge: MIT Press.

13. Kohlberg, L. A. (1984). *The psychology of moral development: The nature and validity of moral stages* (Vol. 2). San Francisco: Harper & Row; Kohlberg, L. A. (1986). A current statement on some theoretical issues. In S. Modgil & C. Modgil (Eds.), *Lawrence Kohlberg: Consensus and controversy* (pp. 485–546). Philadelphia: Palmer.

14. Rest, J., Narvaez, D., Bebeau, M. J., & Thoma, S. J. (1999). *Postconventional moral thinking: A neo-Kohlbergian approach.* Mahwah, NJ: Erlbaum; Trevino, L. K., & Weaver, G. R. (2003). *Managing ethics in business organizations: Social scientific perspectives.* Stanford, CA: Stanford University Press.

15. Rest et al.; Thoma, S. J. (2006). Research on the Defining Issues Test. In M. Killen & J. G. Smetana (Eds.), *Handbook of moral development* (pp. 67–91). Mahwah, NJ: Erlbaum.

16. See Rest, J., & Narvaez, D. (1991). The college experience and moral development. In W. M. Kurtines & J. L. Gewirtz (Eds.), *Handbook of moral behavior and development: Vol. 2. Research* (pp. 229–245). Hillsdale, NJ: Erlbaum; Rest (1993); Thoma.

17. Trevino & Weaver.

18. Bazerman, M. H., & Tenbrunsel, A. E. (2011). *Blind spots: Why we fail to do what's right and what to do about it.* Princeton, NJ: Princeton University Press; Why your negotiating behavior may be ethically challenged—and how to fix it. (2008, April). *Negotiation, 11*(4), 1–5; Epley, N., & Dunning, D. (2000). Feeling "'holier than thou": Are self-serving assessments produced by errors in self- or social prediction? *Journal of Personality and Social Psychology, 79,* 861–875; Tenbrunsel, A. E., Diekman, K. A., Wade-Benzoni, K. A., & Bazerman, M. H. (2009). *The ethical mirage: A temporal explanation as to why we aren't as ethical as we think we are.* Harvard Business School Working Paper No. 08-012. Retrieved from http://www.people.hbs.edu/mbazerman; Bandura, A. (1999). Moral disengagement in the perpetration of inhumanities. *Personality and Social Psychology Review, 3,* 193–209; Shu, L. L., Gino, F., & Bazerman, M. H. (2009). *Dishonest deed, clear conscience: Self-preservation through moral disengagement and motivated forgetting.* Harvard Business School Working Paper No. 09-078; Gino, F., Moore, D. A., & Bazerman, M. H. (2008, January). *See no evil: When we overlook other people's unethical behavior.* Harvard

Business School Working Paper No. 08-045. Retrieved from http://www.people.hbs.edu/mbazerman; Banaji, M. R., Bazerman, M. H., & Chugh, D. (2003, December). How (un)ethical are you? *Harvard Business Review,* pp. 56–64; Bazerman, M. H., Chugh, D., & Banaji, M. R. (2005, October). When good people (seem to) negotiate in bad faith. *Negotiation, 8,* 3–5; Gino, F., Moore, D. A., & Bazerman, M. H. (2009). *No harm, no foul: The outcome bias in ethical judgments.* Harvard Business School Working Paper 08-080. Retrieved from http://www.people.hbs.edu/mbazerman; Milkman, K. L., Chugh, D., & Bazerman, M. H. (2008). *How can decision-making be improved?* Harvard Business School Working Paper 08-102. Retrieved from http://www.people.hbs.edu/mbazerman

19. Woodzicka, J. A., & LaFrance, M. (2001). Real versus imagined gender harassment. *Journal of Social Issues 57,* 15–30.

20. Wilson, D. (2009, March 3). Patching a wound. *The New York Times,* p. B1; Wilson, D. (2010, July 22). A tougher conflict of interest policy at Harvard Medical School. *The New York Times,* p. B4.

21. Harris, G. (2009, February 12). Peanut foods shipped before testing came in. *The New York Times,* p. A24.

22. Batson, C. D., & Thompson, E. R. (2001). Why don't moral people act morally? Motivational considerations. *Current Directions in Psychological Science, 10,* 54–57; Batson, C. D., Thompson, E. R., & Chen, H. (2002). Moral hypocrisy: Addressing some alternatives. *Journal of Personality and Social Psychology, 83,* 330–339.

23. Batson & Thompson, p. 54.

24. James, H. S. (2000). Reinforcing ethical decision-making through organizational structure. *Journal of Business Ethics, 28,* 43–58; Werhane; O'Fallon, M. J., & Butterfield, K. D. (2005). A review of the empirical ethical decision-making literature: 1996–2003. *Journal of Business Ethics, 59,* 375–413.

25. See Connelly, S., Helton-Fauth, W., & Mumford, M. D. (2004). A managerial in-basket study of the impact of trait emotions on ethical choice. *Journal of Business Ethics,* 51, 245–267; Eisenberg, N. (2000). Emotion, regulation, and moral development. *Annual Review of Psychology, 51,* 665–697; Gaudine, A., & Thorne, L. (2001). Emotion and ethical decision-making in organizations. *Journal of Business Ethics, 31,* 175–187; Griffin, R. W., & O'Leary-Kelly, A. M. (Eds.). (2004). *The dark side of organizational behavior.* San Francisco: Jossey-Bass.

26. Trevino & Weaver; O'Fallon & Butterfield.

27. Kidder, R. M. (1995). *How good people make tough choices: Resolving the dilemmas of ethical living.* New York: Fireside.

28. Fisher, R., Ury, W., & Patton, B. (2011). *Getting to yes* (Rev. ed.). New York: Penguin.

29. Kidder, p. 186.

30. Day, L. A. (2006). *Ethics in media communications: Cases and controversies* (5th ed.). Belmont, CA: Wadsworth/Thomson, Ch. 3.

31. Park, A. (2009, October 19). It's a jab or your job. *Time,* p. 55; Miller, N. (2012, July 15). Compulsory jabs not just a shot in the dark. *Sunday Age* (Melbourne), Extra, p. 12; Hartocollis, A., & Chan, S. (2009, October 23). Flu vaccine requirement for health workers is lifted. *The New York Times,* p. A30; Geracimos, A. (2009, September 29). Health workers spurn flu shot; for some, jobs depend on it. *The Washington Times,* p. A1; Martin, R. (2009, September 17). Health care staff: Vaccinate thyself. *St. Petersburg Times,* p. 1A; McNeil, D. G., & Zrack, K. (2009, September 21). New York health care workers resist flu vaccine rule. *The New York Times,* p. A18; Blackwell, T. (2009, September 30). Mandatory flu shots rile health workers; "invasive procedure." *National Post,* p. A8; Hopper, T. (2012, October 23). Nurses fight for right to skip flu vaccination. *National Post,* p. A1.

32. Make flu shots mandatory for health-care workers. (2012, November 3). *The Gazette* (Montreal), p. B6.

33. Stein, R. (2009, September 26). Mandatory flu shots hit resistance. *The Washington Post,* p. A01.

34. Stein.

35. Potter, R. B. (1972). The logic of moral argument. In P. Deats (Ed.), *Toward a discipline*

of social ethics (pp. 93–114). Boston: Boston University Press.

36. Nash, L. L. (1989). Ethics without the sermon. In K. R. Andrews (Ed.), *Ethics in practice: Managing the moral corporation* (pp. 243–257). Boston: Harvard Business School Press.

37. Smith, D. H. (1993). Stories, values, and patient care decisions. In C. Conrad (Ed.), *The ethical nexus* (pp.123–148). Norwood, NJ: Ablex. For a history of the case study method, see Jonsen, A. R., & Toulmin, S. (1988). *The abuse of casuistry: A history of moral reasoning.* Berkeley: University of California Press.

38. Fisher, W. (1987). *Human communication as narration: Toward a philosophy of reason, value, and action.* Columbia: University of South Carolina Press.

39. Martin, J., & Powers, M. E. (1983). Truth or corporate propaganda: The value of a good story. In L. R. Pondy, P. J. Frost, G. Morgan, & T. C. Dandridge (Eds.), *Organizational symbolism* (pp. 93–107). Greenwich, CT: JAI Press.

CHAPTER 7

Normative Leadership Theories

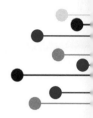

The whole point of studying leadership is to answer the question "What is good leadership?"

—Philosopher and ethicist Joanne Ciulla

There is nothing more practical than a good theory.

—Social psychologist Kurt Lewin

What's Ahead

In this chapter, we will look at leadership theories specifically designed to improve the ethical behavior of leaders and followers. These include transformational leadership, servant leadership, authentic leadership, aesthetic leadership, responsible leadership, and Taoism. As I did in discussing ethical perspectives in Chapter 5, I'll describe each theory and then make some suggestions for applying it as a leader. I'll also offer some cautions about the limitations of each approach.

Theories are key to the study of any discipline, including leadership. They organize knowledge in a field, explain the relationships between important concepts and variables, and help scholars and practitioners make predictions about what strategies will be effective. Theoretical approaches to leadership generally fall into one of two categories: descriptive or normative. Descriptive theories, as the name implies, describe *how* leaders act. Early researchers at the University of Michigan and Ohio State University, for instance, identified two underlying dimensions to leadership styles: task and relationship.[1] They found that some leaders are more focused on tasks while others are more focused on building relationships with followers. Normative leadership theories, in contrast, tell leaders how they *ought* to act. These theories (1) are explicitly built on moral principles or norms and

(2) provide guidelines for promoting ethical leader behavior. Proponents of each normative approach argue that adopting their perspective will enable leaders to function as both moral persons and moral managers. In this chapter I'll introduce several normative leadership theories that can help you cast more light than shadow.

Transformational Leadership: Raise the Ethical Bar

Interest in transformational leadership began in 1978 with the publication of the book *Leadership* by James MacGregor Burns, a political scientist, historian, and former presidential adviser.[2] Burns contrasts traditional forms of leadership, which he calls "transactional," with a more powerful form of leadership that he calls "transforming." Transactional leaders appeal to lower-level needs of followers—that is, the needs for food, shelter, and acceptance. They exchange money, benefits, recognition, and other rewards in return for the obedience and labor of followers; the underlying system remains unchanged. In contrast, transformational leaders speak to higher-level needs, such as esteem, competence, self-fulfillment, and self-actualization. In so doing, they change the very nature of the groups, organizations, or societies they guide. Burns points to Franklin Roosevelt and Mahatma Gandhi as examples of leaders who transformed the lives of followers and their cultures as a whole. In a more recent work, *Transforming Leadership,* Burns argues that the greatest task facing transformational leaders is defeating global poverty, which keeps the world's poorest people from meeting their basic needs for food, medicine, education, and shelter.[3]

Moral commitments are at the heart of Burns's definition of transforming leadership. "Such leadership," states Burns, "occurs when one or more persons *engage* with others in such a way that leaders and followers raise one another to higher levels of motivation and morality."[4] Transformational leaders focus on terminal values such as liberty, equality, and justice. These values mobilize and energize followers, create an agenda for action, and appeal to larger audiences.[5] Transforming leaders are driven by duty, the deontological ethical approach described in Chapter 5.[6] They are guided by universal ethical principles, feel a sense of obligation to the group, and treat followers with respect. They are also altruistic, making sacrifices for followers, empowering others, and focusing on shared goals and objectives. Transformational leaders engage in higher-level moral reasoning, demonstrate greater integrity, are more successful at leading organizational ethical turnarounds, encourage the development of positive ethical climates, institutionalize ethical practices, and foster corporate social responsibility.[7]

In contrast to transformational leaders, transactional leaders emphasize instrumental values such as responsibility, fairness, and honesty, which make routine interactions go smoothly. They take a utilitarian approach, judging the morality of actions based on their outcomes. They use their power and position to convince followers to comply so that both they and their subordinates will benefit. More focused on the self, transactional leaders are concerned with protecting their interests rather than with promoting the interests of the group. They are more likely to be controlling than empowering.

In a series of studies, leadership expert Bernard Bass and his colleagues identified the factors that characterize transactional and transformational forms of leadership and demonstrated that transformational leaders can be found in organizations.[8] They discovered that transactional leadership has both active and passive elements. Active transactional leaders engage in *contingent reward* and *management-by-exception.* They provide rewards and recognition contingent on followers' carrying out their roles and reaching their objectives. After specifying standards and the elements of acceptable performance, active transactional leaders then discipline followers when they fall short. *Passive–avoidant* or *laissez-faire* leaders wait for problems to arise before they take action, or they avoid taking any action at all. These leaders fail to provide goals and standards or to clarify expectations.

According to Bass and Avolio, transformational leadership is characterized by the following:

- *Idealized influence:* Transformational leaders become role models for followers who admire, respect, and trust them. They put followers' needs above their own, and their behavior is consistent with the values and principles of the group.

- *Inspirational motivation:* Transformational leaders motivate by providing meaning and challenge to the tasks of followers. They arouse team spirit, are enthusiastic and optimistic, and help followers develop desirable visions for the future.

- *Intellectual stimulation:* Transformational leaders stimulate innovation and creativity. They do so by encouraging followers to question assumptions, reframe situations, and approach old problems from new perspectives. Transforming leaders don't criticize mistakes but instead solicit solutions from followers.

- *Individualized consideration:* Transformational leaders act as coaches or mentors who foster personal development. They provide learning opportunities and a supportive climate for growth. Their coaching and mentoring are tailored to the individual needs and desires of each follower.

Burns believed that leaders display either transactional or transformational characteristics, but Bass found otherwise. Transforming leadership uses both transactional and transformational elements. Explains Bass: "Many of the great transformational leaders, including Abraham Lincoln, Franklin Delano Roosevelt, and John F. Kennedy, did not shy away from being transactional. They were able to move the nation as well as play petty politics."[9] The transformational leader uses the active elements of the transactional approach (contingent reward and management-by-exception) along with idealized influence, inspirational motivation, intellectual stimulation, and individualized consideration.[10]

The popularity of the transformational approach probably has more to do with practical considerations than with ethical ones. Evidence from more than 100 empirical studies establishes that transforming leaders are more successful than their transactional counterparts.[11] Their followers are more committed, form stronger bonds with colleagues, work harder, and persist in the face of obstacles. As a result, organizations led by transforming figures often achieve extraordinary results: higher quality, greater profits, improved service, military victories, and better win–loss records. James Kouzes, Barry Posner, Tom Peters, Warren Bennis, and Burt Nanus are just some of the popular scholars, consultants, and authors who promote the benefits of transformational leadership.[12]

Burns originally believed that the transforming leader is a moral leader because the ultimate products of transformational leadership are higher ethical standards and more ethical performance. However, his definition didn't account for the fact that some leaders can use transformational strategies to reach immoral ends. A leader can act as a role model, provide intellectual stimulation, and be passionate about a cause. Yet the end product of her or his efforts can be evil. Hitler had a clear vision for Germany but left a trail of unprecedented death and destruction.

Acknowledging the difference between ethical and unethical transformational leaders, Bass adopted the terms *authentic* and *pseudo-transformational* to distinguish between the two categories.[13] Authentic transformational leaders are motivated by altruism and marked by integrity. They don't impose ethical norms but allow followers free choice, hoping that constituents will voluntarily commit themselves to moral principles. Followers are viewed as ends in themselves, not as a means to some other end. Pseudo-transformational leaders are self-centered. They manipulate followers in order to reach their personal goals. Envy, greed, anger, and deception mark the groups they lead. Mahatma Gandhi and Martin Luther King, Jr., deserve to be classified as transformational because they promoted universal brotherhood. Iranian president Mahmoud Ahmadinejad appeared to be pseudo-transformational because he encouraged followers to reject those who hold different beliefs. A list of the products of transformational and pseudo-transformational leadership is found in Box 7.1. You can use this list to determine whether or not the leader described in Case Study 7.1 is transformational.

BOX 7.1 PRODUCTS OF TRANSFORMATIONAL AND PSEUDO-TRANSFORMATIONAL LEADERSHIP

Transformational Leaders

Raise awareness of moral standards

Highlight important priorities

Increase followers' need for achievement

Foster higher moral maturity in followers

Create an ethical climate (shared values, high ethical standards)

Encourage followers to look beyond self-interests to the common good

Promote cooperation and harmony

Use authentic, consistent means

Use persuasive appeals based on reason

Provide individual coaching and mentoring

Appeal to the ideals of followers

Allow followers freedom of choice

Pseudo-transformational Leaders

Promote special interests at the expense of the common good

Encourage the dependence of followers and may privately despise them

Foster competitiveness

Pursue personal goals

Foment greed, envy, hate, and deception

Engage in conflict rather than cooperation

Use inconsistent, irresponsible means

Use persuasive appeals based on emotion and false logic

Keep their distance from followers and expect blind obedience

Seek to become idols for followers

Manipulate followers

SOURCES: Bass, B. M. (1998). The ethics of transformational leadership. In J. B. Ciulla (Ed.), *Ethics, the heart of leadership* (pp. 169–192). Westport, CT: Praeger; Bass, B. M., & Steidlmeier, P. (1999). Ethics, character, and authentic transformational leadership behavior. *Leadership Quarterly, 10,* 181–217.

Applications and Cautions

Applications

- Start small.

- Employ the full range of leadership behaviors.

- Recognize the universal appeal of transformational leadership.

Transformational leadership can seem intimidating at first. Its proponents set a lofty standard—raising the level of morality in an organization or society while transforming its performance. However, you can act as a transformational leader no matter how modest your leadership role. Chances are you have benefited from the influence of lower-level transformational leaders. You can probably think of a coach, teacher, shift manager, counselor, pastor, or other figure who had a lasting impact on you and your team. You can exert similar positive influence by engaging in the behaviors that demonstrate idealized influence, inspirational motivation, intellectual stimulation, and individualized consideration. (Complete Self-Assessment 7.1 to determine how likely you are to use transformational strategies.) Keep in mind that transformational leaders also master active transactional tactics. Be prepared to penalize those who fall short of performance standards or break the rules, reward those who reach their objectives, and so on.

The good news is that you can use transformational behaviors in many contexts, ranging from small informal groups and military units to large complex organizations. Furthermore, transforming leadership appears to be effective in a variety of cultures. Researchers at the Global Leadership and Organizational Behavior Effectiveness (GLOBE) Research Project asked managers in 62 cultures to identify the characteristics of successful leaders. Nine transformational attributes were universally associated with outstanding leadership: motive arouser, foresight, encouraging, communicative, trustworthy, dynamic, positive, confidence builder, and motivational.[14]

Cautions

- Don't equate success with transformation.

- Transformational leadership has been criticized as leader-centric.

- This approach may foster dependence in followers.

Unfortunately, many writers and researchers appear more interested in what works than in what is right. To them, transformational leadership equates with successful or effective leadership; leaders are transforming because they achieve extraordinary, tangible results, such as rescuing failing corporations or winning battles. These theorists are less concerned with whether leaders foster higher moral standards or whether transforming tactics serve ethical ends.

It should be noted that transformational theorists have been labeled as "leader-centric" for paying too much attention to leaders while downplaying the contributions of followers. One critic describes the image presented by transformational theorists this way: "The picture is one in which extraordinary leaders exercise a unidirectional influence on more-or-less willing followers, who are presumably little more than empty vessels awaiting a transfusion of insight from their betters."[15] These skeptics have reason for concern. Burns, Bass, and other proponents of transformative leadership argue that leaders play the most important role in determining group morality and performance. Leaders craft the vision, challenge the status quo, and inspire. At times, they may decide to transform the organization in spite of, not because of, followers, as in the case of the CEO who overrules the recommendations of his staff in order to bring about change. Critics of transformational leadership argue that followers are just as important to the success of a group as leaders, if not more so. After all, followers do most of the work. Worse yet, transforming leaders can silence dissent and encourage subordinates to sacrifice their legitimate self-interests in order to meet the needs of the group.[16]

So much focus on the leader can create dependence and undermine such values as shared decision making and consensus. Followers won't act independently if they continually look to you for guidance. You may also get an inflated sense of your own importance, which can tempt you to cast shadows. Bass believes that the distinction between pseudo-transformational and authentic transformational leadership addresses these concerns. Authentic transforming leaders are much less prone to ethical abuses, he asserts, because they put the needs of others first, treat followers with respect, and seek worthy objectives. You'll need to decide for yourself whether transformational theorists have adequately responded to the dangers posed by their perspective.

Servant Leadership:
Put the Needs of Followers First

Servant leadership has roots in both Western and Eastern thought. Jesus told his disciples that "whoever wants to become great among you must be your servant, and whoever wants to be first must be slave of all" (Mark 1:43–44, New International Version). As we'll see in the final section of this chapter, Chinese philosophers encouraged leaders to be humble valleys. Robert Greenleaf sparked contemporary interest in leaders as servants. Greenleaf, who spent 40 years in research, development, and education at AT&T and 25 years as an organizational consultant, coined the term *servant leader* in the 1970s to describe a leadership model that puts the concerns of followers first.[17] Later he founded a center to promote servant leadership. A number of businesses (e.g., the Container Store, Aflac), nonprofit organizations, and community leadership programs have adopted his model.[18] Margaret Wheatley, Peter Block, Max DePree, and James Autry have joined Greenleaf in urging leaders to act like servants.

The basic premise of servant leadership is simple yet profound: Leaders should put the needs of followers before their own needs. In fact, what happens in the lives of followers should be the standard by which leaders are judged. According to Greenleaf, when evaluating a leader we ought to ask, "Do those served grow as persons? Do they, while being served, become healthier, wiser, freer, more autonomous, more likely themselves to become servants?"[19]

By continually reflecting on what would be best for their constituents, servant leaders are less likely to cast shadows by taking advantage of the trust of followers, acting inconsistently, or accumulating money and power. Theorists have identified a number of attributes that characterize servant leaders (see Box 7.2). While the lists of attributes vary, five related concepts appear central to servant leadership:

1. *Stewardship.* Being a servant leader means acting on behalf of others.[20] Leaders function as the agents of followers, who entrust them with special duties and opportunities for a limited time. Servant leaders are charged with protecting and nurturing their groups and organizations while making sure that these collectives serve the common good. Stewardship implies accountability for results. However, stewards reach their objectives through collaboration and persuasion rather than through coercion and control.

2. *Obligation.* Servant leaders take their obligations or responsibilities seriously. (Turn to Case Study 7.2 for a description of one group of leaders and followers who lost sight of their obligations.) Max DePree, former CEO of Herman Miller, a major office furniture manufacturer, offers one list of what leaders owe their followers and institutions.[21]

- *Assets:* Leaders need to ensure financial stability as well as the relationships and reputation that will ensure future prosperity. Leaders must also provide followers with adequate tools, equipment, and facilities.

- *A legacy:* When they depart, leaders ought to leave behind people who find more meaning, challenge, and joy in their work.

- *Clear institutional values:* Servant leaders articulate principles that shape both individual and organizational behavior.

- *Future leadership:* Current leaders are obligated to identify and then develop their successors.

- *Healthy institutional culture:* Servant leaders are responsible for fostering such organizational characteristics as quality, openness to change, and tolerance of diverse opinions.

- *Covenants:* Covenants are voluntary agreements that serve as reference points for organization members, providing them with direction. Leaders and followers who enter into a covenant are bound together in pursuit of a common goal.

- *Maturity:* Followers expect a certain level of maturity from their leaders. Mature leaders have a clear sense of self-worth, belonging, responsibility, accountability, and equality.

- *Rationality:* Leaders supply the reason and understanding that help followers make sense of organizational programs and relationships. A rational environment builds trust, allows followers to reach their full potential, and encourages ongoing organizational learning.

- *Space:* Space is a sense of freedom that allows followers and leaders to be and express themselves. Leaders who create adequate space allow for the giving and receiving of such gifts as new ideas, healing, dignity, and inclusion.

- *Momentum:* Servant leaders help create the feeling that the group is moving forward and achieving its goals. Momentum arises out of a clear vision and strategy supported by productive research, operations, financial, and marketing departments.

- *Effectiveness:* Effectiveness comes from enabling followers to reach their personal and institutional potential. Servant leaders allow followers to assume leadership roles when conditions warrant.

- *Civility and values:* A civilized institution is marked by good manners, respect for others, and service. Wise leaders can distinguish between what is healthy for the organization (dignity of work, hope, simplicity) and what is superficial and unhealthy (consumption, instant gratification, affluence).

3. *Partnership.* Servant leaders view followers as partners, not as subordinates. As a consequence, they strive for equity or justice in the distribution of power. Strategies for empowering followers include sharing information, delegating authority to carry out important tasks, and encouraging constituents to develop and exercise their talents. Concern for equity extends to the distribution of rewards as well. For example, both employees and executives receive bonuses when the company does well.

4. *Emotional healing.* Servant leaders help followers and organizations recover from disappointment, trauma, hardship, and broken relationships.[22] They are both empathetic and highly skilled as listeners. They create climates that facilitate the sharing of personal and work-related feelings and issues. Emotional healing restores a "sense of wholeness" to both individuals and organizations.

5. *Elevating purpose.* In addition to serving followers, servant leaders serve worthy missions, ideas, and causes. Seeking to fulfill a high moral purpose and understanding the role one plays in the process make work more meaningful to leaders and followers alike. Consider the example of three bricklayers at work in the English countryside. When asked by a traveler to describe what they were doing, the first replied, "I am laying bricks." The second said, "I am feeding my family by laying bricks." The third bricklayer, who had a clearer sense of the purpose for his labor, declared, "Through my work of laying bricks, I am constructing a cathedral, and thereby giving honor and praise to God."

• • • BOX 7.2 SERVANT LEADER ATTRIBUTES • • •

empathy agreeableness (Washington, Sutton, & Field, 2006)	competence	integrity/honesty
altruistic calling persuasive mapping (Babuton & Wheeler, 2006)	emotional healing wisdom	organizational stewardship
listening awareness foresight commitment to the growth of people (Spears, 2004)	empathy persuasion stewardship	healing conceptualization building community
vision trust pioneering communication visibility listening delegation (Russell & Stone)	honesty service empowerment credibility influence encouragement	integrity modeling appreciation of others competence persuasion teaching

Sources

Babuto, J. E., & Wheeler, D. W. (2006). Scale development and construct clarification of servant leadership. *Group & Organization Management, 31,* 300–326.

Reed, L. L., Vidaver-Cohen, D., & Colwell, S. R. (2011). A new scale to measure executive servant leadership: Development, analysis, and implications for research. *Journal of Business Ethics, 101,* 415–434.

Russell, R. F., & Stone, A. G. (2002). A review of servant leadership attributes: Developing a practical model. *Leadership & Organization Development Journal, 23,* 145–157.

Spears, L. C. (2004). The understanding and practice of servant leadership. In L. C. Spears & M. Lawrence (Eds.), *Practicing servant leadership: Succeeding through trust, bravery, and forgiveness* (pp. 9–24). San Francisco: Jossey-Bass.

Washington, R. R., Sutton, C. D., & Feild, H. S. (2006). Individual differences in servant leadership: The roles of values and personality. *Leadership & Organization Development Journal, 27,* 700–716.

For much of the theory's history, support for servant leadership was anecdotal, consisting largely of lists of servant characteristics and examples of servant leaders. More recently, scholars have begun to subject servant leadership to empirical testing. Servant leadership questionnaires like the one in Self-Assessment 7.2 have been developed, and researchers are exploring the impacts of servant leadership on followers and organizational performance. So far they have discovered that:

- Servant leaders help satisfy follower needs and boost followers' job satisfaction and job performance.

- Followers give servant leaders higher character ratings.

- Top-level servant leaders encourage lower-level leaders to act as servants.

- Servant leadership prompts employees to go beyond their job descriptions to help others.

- Employees led by servant leaders are less likely to quit their jobs.

- Servant leadership creates an ethical, trusting organizational climate.

- Servant leadership can increase profits.

- Servant leaders help team members believe in their group's ability to accomplish its tasks.

- Servant leadership is accepted across a variety of cultures, although the importance of the dimensions of servant leadership varies between societies.[23]

Applications and Cautions

Applications

- Focus on followers.

- Act as a steward.

- Cultivate self-awareness.

- Pursue elevating purposes.

Servant leadership is founded on altruism, which, as we saw in Chapter 5, is essential to ethical leadership. You can serve only if you commit yourself to the principle that others should come first. You are far less likely to cast shadows if you approach your leadership role with one goal in mind: the desire to serve. A great number of ethical abuses stem from leaders acting selfishly. Instead, act out of a sense of stewardship and obligation, promoting the growth of followers and the interests of the larger community. Remember what you "owe" followers. Share, rather than hoard, power, privilege, and information.

To function as a servant leader you need to cultivate self-awareness. Servant leaders listen to themselves as well as to others, take time for reflection, and recognize the importance of spiritual resources. They are also acutely aware of the importance of pursuing ethical purposes that bring meaning and fulfillment to work. Serving a transcendent goal means that every act of leadership has a moral dimension.

Cautions

- Servant leadership seems unrealistic.

- It may not work in every context.

- It poses the danger of serving the wrong cause or offering unwise service.

- The term *servant* carries a negative connotation.

Servant leadership has not met with universal approval. Cynicism is often the first response when this model is presented. "Sounds good in principle," listeners respond, "but it would never work at my company [in my family, at my condominium association meeting—fill in the blank]." Like other skeptics, you may have been "walked on" whenever you tried to be nice to poor performers at work, rebellious teenagers, or nasty neighbors. You may agree with others who equate a servant attitude with passivity.

Skepticism about servant leadership may stem in part from a misunderstanding that equates service with weakness. Servant leaders need to be tough. Sometimes the best way to serve someone is to reprimand or fire that person. Nevertheless, there may be situations in which servant leadership is extremely difficult, if not impossible, to implement, such as in prisons or military boot camps, or during emergencies.

Misplaced goals are problems for servant leaders and followers alike. The butler in the novel *The Remains of the Day,* by Kazuo Ishiguro, illustrates the danger of misspent service. He devotes his entire life to being the perfect servant who meets the needs of his English employer. Sadly, his sacrifice is wasted because the lord of the manor turns out to be a Nazi sympathizer. The desire to serve must be combined with careful reasoning and values clarification. You need to carefully examine who and what you serve, asking yourself questions such as the following: Is this group, individual, or organization worthy of my service? What values am I promoting? What is the product of my service: light or darkness?

You are also charged with giving wise service. Lots of well-intentioned efforts to help others are wasted when leaders fail to do their homework. After the earthquake in Central Asia in 2005, for example, outdoor equipment manufacturers donated high-tech mountaineering tents to victims. Unfortunately, such tents are highly flammable, and some caught fire from candles, kerosene lanterns, and cooking fires, burning and killing adults and children. After the Haiti earthquake, members of an Idaho church group who traveled to Haiti to provide aid were jailed when they tried to take orphans out of the country. It turned out that the children weren't orphans after all. Some critics go so far as to argue that not only are some humanitarian efforts wasted, but they can also make problems worse and foster dependence in recipients.[24]

Finally, members of some minority groups, particularly African Americans, associate the word *servant* with a history of slavery, oppression, and discrimination. If the negative connotations surrounding the word are keeping you from embracing the idea of servant leadership, you may want to abandon this term and focus instead on related concepts such as altruism and the virtues of concern and compassion.

Authentic Leadership: Know Yourself and to Your Own Self Be True

Ancient Greek and Roman philosophers prized authenticity. "Know thyself" was inscribed on the frieze above the oracle of Delphi and appears in the writings of Cicero and Ovid.[25] Greek thinkers also exhorted listeners "to thine own self be true." Modern scholars have rediscovered the importance of this quality. Proponents of authentic leadership theory (ALT) identify authenticity as the "root construct" or principle underlying all forms of positive leadership. The practice of authentic leadership leads to sustainable (long-term) and veritable (ethically sound) organizational performance.[26]

Authenticity has four components: self-awareness, balanced processing, internalized moral perspective, and relational transparency.[27] *Self-awareness* means being conscious of, and trusting in, our motives, desires, feelings, and self-concept. Self-aware people know their strengths and weaknesses, personal traits, and emotional patterns, and they are able to use this knowledge when interacting with others and their environments. *Balanced processing* describes remaining objective when receiving information. Inauthentic responses involve denying, distorting, or ignoring feedback we don't want to acknowledge. We may have to accept the fact that we aren't very good at certain activities—accounting, writing, playing basketball—or that we have problems managing our anger. *Internalized moral perspective* describes regulating our behavior according to our internal standards and values, not according to what others say. We act in harmony with what we believe and do not change our behavior to please others or to earn rewards or avoid punishment. *Relational transparency* refers to presenting the authentic self to others, openly expressing true thoughts and feelings appropriate for the situation.

According to Bruce Avolio, Fred Luthans, and their colleagues at the University of Washington, the Gallup Leadership Institute at the University of Nebraska at Lincoln, and elsewhere, authentic leadership has a strong moral component. These scholars make ethics a starting point for their theory, just as Burns does for transformational leadership. This moral element is reflected in their definition of authentic leaders as "those who are deeply aware of how they think and behave and are perceived by others as being aware of their own and others' values/moral perspectives, knowledge, and strengths; aware of the context in which they operate; and who are confident, hopeful, optimistic, resilient, and of high moral character."[28] Such leaders acknowledge the ethical responsibilities of their roles, can recognize and evaluate ethical issues, and take moral actions that are thoroughly grounded in their beliefs and values. In order to carry out these tasks, they draw on their courage and resilience—the ability to adapt when confronted with significant risk or adversity.[29]

Because authenticity is so critical to positive leadership performance, Avolio, Luthans, and others are interested in how leaders develop this quality. They report that critical incidents called *trigger events* play an important role in the development of the moral component of authentic leadership.[30] These events, like the crucible moments described in Chapter 3, can be positive or negative and promote introspection and reflection. Trigger experiences are often dramatic—facing racial hatred, visiting a village in a poor developing country—but can also be more mundane, such as reading a significant book. Sometimes a series of small events, like several minor successes or failures, can have a cumulative effect, triggering significant thought. Leaders develop a clearer sense of who they are, including their standards of right and wrong, through these experiences. They build a store of moral knowledge that they can draw on to make better choices when facing future ethical dilemmas.

Authenticity can also be fostered through training and education. For example, trainers and educators can help leaders develop their moral capacity by (1) encouraging them to think about the possible consequences of their leadership decisions, (2) enhancing their perspective taking through discussion and training, (3) exposing them to common moral dilemmas to help them recognize the ethical issues they will face in their jobs, (4) building their belief in their ability to follow through on choices, (5) helping them develop strategies for adapting and coping with new ethical challenges, and (6) pairing them with moral leaders so they can observe authentic behavior firsthand.[31]

Authentic leadership produces a number of positive ethical effects in followers.[32] Followers are likely to emulate the example of authentic leaders who set a high ethical standard. They feel empowered to make ethical choices on their own without the input of the leader and are more likely to act courageously. They align themselves with the values of the organization and become authentic moral agents themselves. Leader authenticity also fosters feelings of self-efficacy (competence), hope, optimism, and resilience in followers. Authentic followers, for their part, provide feedback that reinforces the authentic behavior of leaders and increases the leaders' self-knowledge. (See "Focus on Follower Ethics: Authentic Followership" for more information on the characteristics of authentic followers.) They also reward their leaders by giving them more latitude to make difficult, unpopular choices. Authentic leadership and followership are more likely to develop in organizational climates that provide the information and other resources that employees need to get their work done, encourage learning, treat members fairly, and set clear goals and performance standards.

FOCUS ON FOLLOWER ETHICS

Authentic Followership

Authenticity is the mark of ethical followership just as it is for ethical leadership. Authentic leaders and followers encourage transparency, self-awareness, and moral behavior in each other. Together they build open, healthy relationships and collaborate to achieve worthwhile objectives. Followers have the greatest impact on leaders when they develop psychological ownership, foster trust, and practice transparency.

Psychological ownership. Authentic followers feel as if they "own" the organizations where they work and volunteer. This sense of ownership is based on a sense of belonging ("This is *my* home"), a sense of identity ("I am a student at _____ University"), a sense of accountability ("*I* am responsible for this project"), and a sense of efficacy ("I *can* do this task"). Ownership encourages a variety of ethical behaviors, including (1) meeting the needs of customers when they first come in contact with the firm, (2) taking responsibility for making decisions at lower organizational levels, (3) going beyond what the job requires, and (4) doing whatever it takes to solve problems.

Trust. Authentic followers are vulnerable. They admit their mistakes and encourage their leaders to do the same. For example, when pharmacists admit to "near misses" (nearly filling prescriptions with the wrong medications), they prompt their supervisors to take further steps to reduce potential errors. Authentic followers don't take advantage of their leaders who admit their mistakes. They also build trust with their leaders by taking on challenges without being asked.

Transparency. Authentic followers say what they mean. By sharing their thoughts, values, and feelings, they help create transparent relationships with their leaders. These relationships are marked by honesty, feedback, and effective communication. Authentic followers also contribute to the creation of transparent organizational climates. In transparent climates, policies and procedures are visible to everyone. Members share important goals and values and put the needs of the group above their own concerns. Because they feel safe, employees reveal problems rather than creating the impression that everything is fine.

SOURCE: Avolio, B. J., & Reichard, R. J. (2008). The rise of authentic followership. In R. E. Riggio, I. Chaleff, & J. Lipman-Blumen (Eds.), *The art of followership: How great followers create great leaders and organizations* (pp. 325–337). San Francisco: Jossey-Bass.

Proponents of ALT argue that authenticity pays practical as well as ethical dividends. They cite evidence that authentic leadership is linked to higher follower performance, commitment, satisfaction, and effort.[33] Authentic leaders, particularly because they act with integrity, engender more trust, and trust, in turn, has been linked to higher organizational productivity and performance (see Chapter 9). The positive emotions fostered by leaders also enhance performance. Followers who believe in their abilities are more likely to take initiative and to achieve more, even in the face of difficult circumstances. Feelings of hope and optimism foster willpower. Resilience enables followers to recover more quickly from setbacks.[34]

ALT has moved into the next stage of development. Most of the initial articles and chapters on authentic leadership offered propositions about ALT that were not supported by empirical research, but now an ALT scale has been developed and tested.[35] Validation of the scale demonstrates that authentic leadership, while sharing features with transformational and servant leadership, is a distinct construct.

Applications and Cautions

Applications

- Recognize the significance of authenticity.

- Develop the four components of authenticity.

- Foster authenticity in others.

Advocates of ALT argue persuasively for the importance of authenticity—incorporating values, moral perspectives, virtues, and character in their definition of authentic leadership. Authentic leadership is effective as well as ethical. Authenticity multiplies the impact of leaders and lays the foundation for long-term organizational success. With this in mind, seek to be an authentic leader. Cultivate the four components of authenticity: Develop self-awareness, maintain objectivity when receiving information, rely on internal standards and values, and openly present yourself to others. Consider the trigger events in your life and what they reveal about who you are. Foster authenticity in others through your example and the training strategies described earlier.

Cautions

- ALT overstates the significance of authenticity.

- Theorists tend to equate authenticity with morality.

- Authenticity can be defined as a personal characteristic or as a perception.

- The theory needs to be tested in other cultures.

While authenticity is a critical component of ethical leadership, the underlying premise of ALT, that authenticity is the source of all positive forms of leadership, is subject to debate. There may be some other as yet undiscovered source instead. Or there may be multiple sources of ethical leadership. Proponents of ALT also seem to equate self-awareness with morality. The clearer you are about your self-concept, they claim, the more likely you are to act ethically. Yet the core values of some leaders promote self-seeking, destructive behavior. Then, too, expressing your "true" self can produce undesirable consequences. Take the case of the boss who fails to temper his criticism of a subordinate. By accurately reflecting what he feels at that moment, he may do lasting damage to the self-concept of his employee. The critical boss believes he is acting authentically; the unfortunate employee and observers probably will conclude that he is callous instead.

Investigations into the effects of authentic leadership have also identified a fundamental tension in the theory. On one hand, authenticity has been tied to the personal traits described earlier. On the other hand, for authenticity to have a positive influence on organizational behavior, observers must perceive that the leader's behavior is authentic.[36] Authenticity then becomes a product of perception, not of personal beliefs and behaviors. Leaders who hope to be successful must project an authentic image. In other words, *being* authentic is no longer enough—you must also *appear* authentic. This could tempt you to be untrue to yourself. You might fail to act on your values and self-understanding for fear that such behavior could be seen as inauthentic. In addition, an inauthentic (pseudo-authentic) leader could mislead followers by projecting an authentic image.[37] Further research and analysis are needed to resolve this apparent contradiction between the personal and perceptual dimensions of ALT. To date, ALT research has largely been conducted in the United States. Authenticity may not be an important element of ethical leadership in other cultures.

Aesthetic (Beautiful) Leadership

Aesthetic leadership, like authentic leadership, has its roots in classic Greek thought. The word *aesthetic* or *aisth* in ancient Greek means "feeling through physical perceptions."[38] Our sensory encounters with people, events, objects, and settings generate emotions. We then construct meanings based on those feelings. Take the case of an unsuccessful job interview, for example. Both individuals see, hear, listen to, smell, and touch one another during the meeting. Each then comes away from the encounter with feelings about the interview and the other party. The interviewer may be disappointed with the applicant and conclude that she or he was not prepared for the session. The frustrated interviewee may go home and complain about how the company representative was cold and distant.

The aesthetic perspective emphasizes the sensory and emotional dimension of organizational life.[39] From this vantage point, organizations serve as stages, and leadership is more of an art than a science. Leaders, like artists, make skillful use of dramatic elements (ritual, ceremony, gestures, oratory), design (they transform visions and programs into reality), and orchestration (they bring diverse individuals together to achieve worthy goals).[40] Followers serve as audiences who make aesthetic judgments about leaders and their performances. Successful leaders generate strong positive emotions and attributions. For example, President John F. Kennedy was youthful, energetic, and glamorous. In his speeches, such as the one in which he called upon the United States to put a man on the moon, he appealed to the aspirations of Americans and engaged their imaginations.[41] He is remembered as a highly effective leader even though he accomplished much less than other, less attractive presidents, like Lyndon Johnson and Richard Nixon. (Read the description in "Leadership Ethics at the Movies: *A Ripple of Hope*" to see how President Kennedy's brother Robert also functioned as an aesthetic, transformational leader.)

LEADERSHIP ETHICS AT THE MOVIES • • • • • • • • • •

A Ripple of Hope

Key Cast Members: Frank Mankiewicz, John Lewis, Adam Walinsky, Thurston Clarke

Synopsis: On April 4, 1968, civil rights leader Martin Luther King, Jr., was assassinated in Memphis, Tennessee, and riots broke out in cities across the nation. That evening, Senator Robert Kennedy, a presidential candidate, was scheduled to deliver a campaign speech to a largely African American audience in Indianapolis. Senator Kennedy ignored the warnings of police and addressed the angry crowd, some of whom were armed and ready to do violence. Standing on the back of a flatbed truck, the candidate spoke for the first time in public about the assassination of his brother John and quoted a Greek poet on the wisdom that can come through suffering. He appealed to both Blacks and Whites to put aside their hatred to work together to create a country that would meet the needs of all of its citizens. When the crowd dispersed, members of both races were hugging one another; the city remained calm. Tragically, Robert Kennedy was himself assassinated just a few months later in California.

Rating: Not rated

Themes: transformational leadership, authentic leadership, aesthetic leadership, leadership performance, compassion, courage

(Continued)

Discussion Starters

1. Why did Kennedy decide to give the speech despite the warnings of police? What might have happened had he canceled his scheduled appearance or given only a brief formal statement acknowledging King's death?

2. Why did Kennedy wait until this incident to talk publicly about the death of his brother?

3. What made his speech so powerful and beautiful?

Ethics is integral to aesthetic leadership. For the ancients, aesthetics meant pursuing goals that serve humankind. Aristotle (384–322 B.C.E.) believed that leaders should pursue "human flourishing" and the "good life." Plato (428–348 B.C.E.) argued that beauty must serve a good (moral) purpose. Aesthetic and moral judgments overlap. The most ethical course of action is also the most aesthetically pleasing or beautiful.

University of Exeter leadership professor Donna Ladkin identifies three components that contribute to a beautiful leadership performance.[42] The first is mastery. An ethical/beautiful leader is competent and possesses the necessary skills and abilities to perform in a given moment. He or she can improvise, applying the correct skills to a particular situation. The second component is coherence. The ethical/beautiful leader is authentic, acting in a way that is consistent with his or her message and purpose. The third component is purpose. The ethical/beautiful leader serves the best interests of the community and improves the human condition.

Captain Chesley "Sully" Sullenberger provides one example of a beautiful leadership performance.[43] On January 15, 2009, the commercial passenger aircraft that Sullenberger was piloting hit a flock of birds after taking off from New York's La Guardia Airport. Sullenberger immediately realized that he couldn't reach the nearest landing strip in New Jersey, so he decided to put the aircraft down on the Hudson River. He avoided bridges and nearby high-rise buildings while bringing the plane down with its nose up and its wings level. Once the plane was on the water, he walked through the cabin twice to make sure all passengers and crew members were safely off before he left. Not a single life was lost in the incident. Captain Sullenberger's behavior stands in sharp contrast to the ugly behavior of the captain of the *Costa Concordia* cruise ship in 2012. When his ocean liner crashed into the rocks off the Italian coast, Francesco Schettino abandoned ship and headed for shore, leaving many passengers still on board (32 died). Later the captain denied that he was in charge of the ship at the time of the crash—a claim contradicted by the ship's data recorder.[44]

Applications and Cautions

Applications

- Recognize the physical dimension of leadership.

- View leadership as a performing art.

- Make aesthetic judgments.

Leadership has a physical or sensory dimension. Followers will make attributions about your motives and effectiveness based on the interactions they have with you. Your behaviors will determine whether they think you are honest or dishonest, competent or incompetent, and so on. With this in mind, you should view leadership as a performing art. Make skillful use of the dramatic elements described above. Put on performances that reflect mastery, coherence, and purpose. To function as an artful leader, you will need to serve high moral purposes and demonstrate practical wisdom, courage, and other virtues.[45] Use beauty as a standard for judging the performances of other artist leaders.

Cautions

- Aesthetic leadership theory ignores the rational dimension of leadership.

- Definitions of beauty vary.

- Performances can be dishonest.

Resist the temptation to treat leadership as only an art. Leadership is best viewed as both an art and a science. Recognizing the aesthetic dimension of leadership doesn't mean that you should reject its rational aspects. To succeed, you will need to understand how organizations operate, make wise choices, engage in strategic planning, and so on. It is also not clear that followers share a given standard of beauty. They may not always agree on what is beautiful (ethical), demonstrating the truth of the old adage "Beauty is in the eye of the beholder." Viewing leadership as performance can also tempt you to engage in deceit. Leaders can hide their true intentions and manipulate audiences (see the discussion of authentic leadership above). In the early days of what is now Virgin Group, for example, company founder Richard Branson would use pay phones to call clients. He would start by ringing the operator and claiming that he'd lost his money in the phone. The operator was then required to connect his call and would say to the person answering, "I have Mr. Branson for you." This created the false impression that Branson was important enough to have someone to place his calls.[46]

Responsible Leadership: Promote Global Good Through Ethical Relationships

Responsible leadership is an offshoot of global corporate social responsibility (CSR). Socially responsible corporations operating in a global economy try to improve social conditions and the environment in addition to making a profit. (Social responsibility is described in more detail in Chapter 9.) These businesses pay a living wage to workers in developing countries, for example, and adopt environmentally friendly practices like recycling and reducing energy use and pollution. Responding to the claims of stakeholders is an important element of CSR. Stakeholders consist of any group affected by an organization's operations. For a multinational corporation, stakeholders include, for example, domestic and foreign governments, nongovernmental organizations (NGOs), suppliers, customers, and employees in locations around the world.

European researchers Nicola Pless and Thomas Maak believe that leaders can help their corporations become forces for global good by exercising responsible leadership.[47] Responsible leaders build ethical relationships with stakeholders. These relationships then create a sense of shared purpose as well as motivation to address social and environmental problems. Maak and Pless define responsible leadership as

> a values-based and principle-driven relationship between leaders and stakeholders who are connected through a shared sense of meaning and purpose through which they raise one another to higher ethical levels of motivation and commitment for achieving sustainable value creation and responsible change.[48]

Like transformational leadership, responsible leadership elevates the morality of the parties involved. However, responsible leadership incorporates all stakeholder groups affected by the leader and the organization, not just immediate followers. Responsible leaders establish a "web of inclusion" that connects with diverse constituencies. Relationship building can't be done from a position of authority. Instead, responsible leaders must function as equals who bring people together for a common purpose.

Character plays an important role in responsible leadership. Responsible leaders are authentic (see the section on authentic leadership above) and demonstrate such virtues as honesty, respect, service, and humility. They reflect moral maturity, practice reflection and critical thinking skills, and can generate creative ethical solutions. Drawing from this moral core, responsible leadership then manifests itself in the following roles:[49]

1. *The leader as steward.* Responsible leaders act as guardians of individual and organizational values, maintaining personal and collective integrity while helping the organization act responsibly. They are also custodians, protecting (and hopefully enriching) the values and resources they have been entrusted with. Stewardship incorporates a global perspective and considers the needs of the environment and future generations.

2. *The leader as servant.* Responsible leaders are focused on the needs of followers. They care for them through providing a safe and meaningful work environment, paying fair wages, listening to their concerns, and supporting their development. Responsible leaders also serve the needs of stakeholders through dialogue, by integrating the perspectives of many different groups, and by putting the good of the community above selfish concerns.

3. *The leader as coach.* Responsible leaders develop and support others, motivating diverse individuals and groups to work together to reach a common vision. This requires open communication, conflict management, managing cultural differences, and providing appropriate feedback. Moral development is an important element of coaching. Ethical leaders help others develop their moral reasoning and reflection skills.

4. *The leader as architect.* Responsible leaders focus on building integrity cultures, which are work environments that help diverse employees engage in meaningful labor; feel respected, included, and recognized; and reach their potential. Responsible leaders also engage in ongoing dialogue with external stakeholders.

5. *The leader as storyteller.* Responsible leaders communicate shared values and meaning through stories. Stories bring to life the organization's vision and values, help create meaning, and assist followers in making sense of the world. By sharing stories, leaders create a corporate identity, foster cooperation, and communicate their visions about their organization's social and environmental responsibilities.

6. *The leader as change agent.* Responsible leaders shape both the process and the product of change. They create a values-based vision, mobilize followers, keep change momentum going, and deal with the anxiety that always surrounds change efforts. In addition, they ensure that change helps create businesses that are founded on core values and sustainable over the long term.

7. *The leader as citizen.* Responsible leaders are just as concerned about the health of the community as they are about the health of their businesses. They recognize that private business and the public sphere are interdependent. Businesses need healthy communities in order to thrive, and healthy communities need the support of thriving businesses.

Maak and Pless outline an ambitious agenda for responsible leadership. They believe that corporate leaders have a duty to act as agents of social change and as "agents of world benefit."[50] Multinational corporations exert greater and greater economic power and enjoy more and more privileges. Therefore, they have a moral obligation to promote social justice by trying to solve political and social problems. Responsible leaders join government and nonprofit leaders in promoting human rights, alleviating poverty and hunger, and fighting HIV/AIDS, malaria, and other illnesses. Such collaboration creates *social capital*—a network of structures, resources, and lasting positive relationships—which can then be used to address other social problems.[51]

Applications and Cautions

Applications

- Encourage corporate social responsibility.

- Play the roles of the responsible leader.

- Broaden your focus to outside the organization.

Few of us are in a position to lead multinational corporations in the fight against global problems like poverty and substandard housing. Yet you can do your part to ensure that your organization is socially responsible. You can act as steward, servant, coach, architect, and storyteller no matter what your organizational status. Weave your own web of relationships founded on ethical principles and values. Act out of high character and demonstrate sound moral reasoning, building relationships grounded in trust and integrity. Be concerned about the needs and development of others, both inside and outside the organization. The creation of a more just global society is an ambitious goal, but it is one worth pursuing.

Of the theories discussed in this chapter, only responsible leadership incorporates globalization and stakeholder theory. It encourages leaders to work with others to solve difficult problems on every continent. This approach to leadership ethics highlights the fact that you must be concerned about all those who are affected by your actions, not just immediate followers.

Cautions

- Responsible leadership theory is in the early stages of development.

- Its principles overlap with those of other theories.

- Corporations are resistant to an expanded social role.

- Proponents reflect a liberal bias.

- The theorists focus exclusively on business leadership.

Responsible leadership theory is in the early stages of development, which accounts for many of its shortcomings.[52] To this point, only a small group of scholars have joined Maak and Pless in exploring the implications of responsible leadership, although the number is rapidly growing. Limited empirical evidence has been offered to support the theory's tenets. In fact, conducting research on the theory is a daunting task since investigators must examine values, decisions, and behaviors at many different levels—individual, organizational, societal, and global. The theorists incorporate elements of authentic leadership, transformational leadership, and servant leadership into their model. They are just beginning to clarify how their theory relates to these other approaches.

You may take issue with Pless and Maak's bold assertion that corporations and their leaders need to be agents of social justice and world benefit. They advocate that businesses take on responsibilities usually associated with governments to address global problems, such as world hunger. Like a great number of observers, you may be uneasy about multinational corporations acting as "quasi-states." Or you might take issue with liberal bias of the theory's advocates. Further, the traditional conception of social responsibility is much more limited than that advocated in responsible leadership. Corporate leaders typically tie their social efforts to their business goals, as in the case of a building supply company supporting a Habitat for Humanity construction project. Then, too, multinational businesses generally target problems related to their operations and locations. For instance, a socially conscious manufacturer will focus on improving living conditions in the communities surrounding its plants. Few corporate leaders appear ready to tackle global issues like the shortage of clean water and widespread poverty, as proponents of responsible leadership urge them to do. (See Case Study 7.3 for one example of a business leader taking on a major global concern.)

Additional theoretical development may address what is perhaps the greatest concern about responsible leadership, which is whether this perspective can serve as a general theory of leadership ethics. Maak and Pless developed their theory to foster greater social responsibility in multinational corporations. They specifically address business leaders. However, you may conclude that the components of responsible leadership would seem to apply to every type of organizational leader. Educators, agency heads, mayors, governors, and others also have to build values-based, principle-driven relationships with diverse stakeholder groups to achieve ethical objectives.

Taoism: Lead Nature's Way
• •

Taoism (pronounced "Dowism") is one of the world's oldest philosophies, dating back to ancient China (600–300 B.C.E.). The nation had enjoyed peace and prosperity under a series of imperial dynasties but had become a patchwork of warring city-states. Groups of philosophers traveled from one fiefdom to another offering leaders advice for restoring harmony. The Taoists were one of these "100 Schools of Thought."[53]

The *Tao Te Ching* (usually translated as *The Classic of the Way and Its Power and Virtue*) is Taoism's major text. According to popular tradition, a royal librarian named Lao-tzu authored this book as he departed China for self-imposed exile. However, most scholars believe that this short volume (5,000 words) is actually a collection of the teachings of several wise men or sages.

Taoism divided into religious and philosophical branches by 200 C.E. Religious Taoists sought to extend their lives through diet and exercise and developed a priesthood that presided over elaborate temple rituals. Today Taoist religious practices are popular in both the East and the West, but those interested in Taoist leadership principles generally draw from the movement's philosophical roots. These principles are described for Western audiences in such books as *The Tao of Leadership, The Tao of Personal Leadership,* and *Real Power: Business Lessons From the Tao Te Ching.*

Understanding the "Way," or Tao, is the key to understanding Taoist ethical principles. The Tao is the shapeless, nameless force or "nonbeing" that brings all things into existence, or being, and then sustains them. The Tao takes form in nature and reveals itself through natural principles. These principles then become the standards for ethical behavior. Ethical leaders and followers develop *te,* or character, by acting in harmony with the Tao, not by following rules and commandments. Laws reflect a distrust of human nature and create a new class of citizens—lawbreakers—instead of encouraging right behavior. Efforts to reduce crime, for example, seem to increase it instead:

Throw away holiness and wisdom,

And people will be a hundred times happier.

Throw away morality and justice,

And people will do the right thing.

Throw away industry and profit, and there won't be any thieves.[54]

"Leave well enough alone" seems to capture the essence of Taoist ethics. Consistent with their hands-off approach, Taoist sages argue that he or she governs best who governs least. Leading is like cooking a small fish: Don't overdo it. The ideal Taoist leader maintains a low profile, leading mostly by example and letting followers take ownership.

When the Master governs, the people

Are hardly aware that he exists.

Next best is a leader who is loved.

Next, one who is feared.

The worst is one who is despised.

If you don't trust the people,

You make them untrustworthy.

The Master doesn't talk, he acts.

When his work is done,

The people say, "Amazing:

We did it, all by ourselves!"[55]

Taoists rely on images or metaphors drawn from nature and daily life to illustrate the characteristics of model leaders. The first image is that of an uncarved block. An uncarved block of stone or wood is nameless and shapeless, like the Tao itself. Leaders should also be blocklike, avoiding wealth, status, and glory while they leave followers alone.

The second image is the child. Children serve as another reminder that wise leaders don't get caught up in the pursuit of power and privilege but remain humble. Mahatma Gandhi demonstrated childlike character. He dressed simply in clothes he made himself, owned almost nothing, and did not seek political office. Yet he emerged as one of history's most influential leaders.

The third image is water. Water provides an important insight into how leaders ought to influence others by illustrating that there is great strength in weakness. Water cuts through the hardest rock, given enough time. In the same way, the weak often overcome the powerful.[56] Authoritarian governments in Soviet Russia, Argentina, and the Philippines were overthrown not by military means but through the efforts of ordinary citizens. Leaders who use "soft" tactics (listening, empowering, and collaborating) rather than "hard" ones (threats and force) are more likely to overcome resistance to change. Flexibility or pliability is an important attribute of water as well. Water seeks new paths when it meets resistance; leaders should do the same.

The fourth image is the valley. To the Taoists, the universe is made up of two forces: the yin (negative, dark, cool, female, shadows) and the yang (positive, bright, warm, male, sun). Creation operates as it should when these forces are in balance. Although both the yin and the yang are important, Taoists highlight the importance of the yin, or feminine side, of leadership, which is represented by the valley metaphor. Leaders should seek to be valleys (which reflect the yin) rather than prominent peaks (which reflect the yang).

The fifth image is the clay pot, which celebrates emptiness by elevating nothing to higher status than something. The most useful part of a pot is the emptiness within. Similarly, the most useful part of a room is the empty space between the walls. Leaders ought to empty themselves, putting aside meaningless words, superficial thinking, technology, and selfishness. By being empty, leaders can use silence, contemplation, and observation to better understand the workings of the Tao and its ethical principles.

Applications and Cautions

Applications

- Use "soft" tactics.

- Focus on being, not doing.

- Temper your use of power and privilege.

- Follow nature's example.

Taoist thinkers encourage you to be flexible; use "soft" tactics that facilitate teamwork, such as listening and negotiation. Collaboration is becoming increasingly important in today's workplace as organizations become leaner and flatter. Taoists also emphasize being rather than doing. Act blocklike and childlike to develop your character. Embrace silence and contemplation, cultivate the inner self, reject ambition, and seek to serve rather than to be served.

Taoism cautions against the abuse of power and privilege. The authors of the *Tao Te Ching* reject the use of force except as a last resort. They criticize the feudal lords of their day for living in splendor while their people sank into poverty and starvation. It is difficult to imagine that Taoist sages would approve of the vast difference in pay between American executives and employees, for example, or give their blessing to politicians who enjoy extravagant lifestyles at taxpayer expense. In addition, Taoists encourage you to look to nature for insights about leadership. Contemporary authors have begun to follow their lead, identifying leadership lessons that can be drawn from the natural world.[57]

Cautions

- Taoism denies reason.

- Taoists reject codes and laws.

- The approach is ambiguous about many moral issues.

- Taoism does not adequately explain evil.

There are some serious disadvantages to Taoist ethics. In their attempt to follow nature, Taoists encourage leaders to empty themselves of, among other things, reason. Intuition has its place, but, as we saw in Chapter 6, we need to draw upon logic as well. Taoists are rightly skeptical about the effectiveness of moral codes and laws. Nevertheless, laws can change society for the better. For example, civil rights legislation played a significant role in reducing racial discrimination and changing cultural norms. In organizations, reasonable rules, professional guidelines, and codes of conduct can and do play a role in improving ethical climate (see Chapter 9).

Although Taoism has much to say about the shadow of power and our relationship to the world around us, you'll find it is silent on many common ethical dilemmas, such as the case of the manager asked to keep information about an upcoming merger to herself (see Chapter 1). What does it mean to follow nature's example when faced with this decision? Perhaps the manager should keep quiet to keep from intruding into the lives of followers. Nonetheless, withholding information would put her in the position of a mountain instead of a valley, giving her an advantage.

Basing moral decision making on conformity to principles manifested in the natural world promotes ethical relativism. The Taoists believe that the ethical action is the one that blends with natural rhythms to produce the desired outcome. In other words, what works is what is right. This approach seems to ignore the fact that what may "work" (generate profits, create pleasure, ensure job security, earn a raise) may be unethical (result in an unsafe product, destroy public trust, exploit workers). Like pragmatism, an ethical perspective introduced Chapter 5, Taoism seems to lack a moral center. Natural conditions are always changing: Seasons shift; plants and animals grow and die. The flexible leader adapts to shifting circumstances. However, this makes it impossible for the leader to come to any definite conclusion about right or wrong. What you determine to be the right moral choice in one context may be wrong in another.

One final concern should be noted: Taoism's firm conviction that humans, in their natural state, will act morally seems to deny the power of evil. My thesis has been that leaders and followers can and do act destructively, driven by their shadow sides.

IMPLICATIONS AND APPLICATIONS

- Seek to be a transforming leader who raises the level of morality in a group or an organization. Transformational leaders speak to higher-level needs and bring about profound changes. They are motivated by duty and altruism and marked by personal integrity. Dimensions of transformational leadership include idealized influence, inspirational motivation, intellectual stimulation, and individualized consideration.

- Putting the needs of followers first reduces the likelihood that you will cast ethical shadows. Servant leaders are stewards who have significant obligations to both their followers and their institutions, practice partnership, promote healing, and serve worthy purposes.

- Be careful who and what you serve. Make sure your efforts support worthy people and goals and are carefully thought out.

- Authentic leaders have an in-depth knowledge of themselves and act in ways that reflect their core values and beliefs. Authenticity multiplies the effectiveness of leaders and promotes ethical behavior in followers. To function as an authentic leader, you will have to demonstrate self-awareness, balanced processing, internalized moral perspective, and relational transparency.

- Aesthetic leadership emphasizes the sensory and emotional dimensions of organizational life. View leadership as an art and put on beautiful/ethical leadership performances that demonstrate mastery, coherence, and moral purpose.

- Responsible leaders build ethical relationships with stakeholders both inside and outside the organization in order to address global problems. In order to act as a responsible leader, you will need to act as a steward, a servant, a coach, an architect, a storyteller, a change agent, and a citizen.

- Taoists argue that nature and elements of everyday life serve as sources of ethical leadership lessons. You can learn from uncarved blocks, children, water, valleys, and clay pots.

FOR FURTHER EXPLORATION, CHALLENGE, AND SELF-ASSESSMENT

1. What additional applications and cautions can you add for each approach described in this chapter? Which perspective do you find most useful? Why?

2. Brainstorm a list of pseudo-transformational and transformational leaders. What factors distinguish between the two types of leaders? How do your characteristics compare with the ones presented in the chapter?

3. Discuss the following propositions in a group:

- Business leaders have an ethical duty to address global problems like poverty and hunger.
- Ethical leadership is beautiful leadership.

4. Make a diligent effort to serve your followers for a week. At the end of this period, reflect on your experience. Did focusing on the needs of followers change your behavior? What did you do differently? What would happen if you made this your leadership philosophy? Record your thoughts.

5. Write a case study. Option 1 is to base your case on someone you consider to be an authentic leader. How does this person demonstrate authenticity? What impact has this person had on followers and her or his organization? What can we learn from this leader's example? Option 2 is to base your case on someone you consider to be a responsible leader. How does this individual play the roles of responsible leadership? How has his or her business been an agent of global good? What can we learn from this leader's example?

6. Identify the trigger events in your life. How have they contributed to your moral development as a leader?

7. Analyze an instance in which you believe that a leader put on a beautiful performance. How did that individual demonstrate mastery, coherence, and purpose?

8. Which image from nature or daily life from Taoism do you find most interesting and helpful? Why? Can you think of additional natural metaphors that would be useful to leaders?

9. Read a popular book on transformational leadership or on a transformational leader. Write a review. Summarize the contents for those who have not read it. Next, evaluate the book. What are its strengths and weaknesses from an ethical point of view? Would you recommend it to others? Why or why not?

STUDENT STUDY SITE

Visit the student study site at **www.sagepub.com/johnsonmecl5e** to access full SAGE journal articles for further research and information on key chapter topics.

CASE STUDY 7.1

Transforming Clear Lake College

Clear Lake College was in serious trouble in 2000.[1] Enrollment at the midwestern school had dropped from 650 to 600 undergraduates. Because it had no emergency endowment fund, Clear Lake counted on tuition revenue to pay its bills. The loss of so many students threatened to close the 90-year-old institution. The college's president, who seemed unable to respond to the crisis, resigned.

The school's board of directors appointed Samuel (Sam) Thomas as the next president. Thomas had a PhD in higher education but came to Clear Lake directly out of a marketing position in business. Unlike his predecessor, Thomas didn't hesitate to make bold, sometimes risky decisions. He hired a new admissions staff, convinced faculty to agree to a salary and benefits freeze, and spent several hundred thousand dollars to launch the college's first graduate degree program.

The 2001 school year saw a surge in new students. The graduate program was a big success, and Sam used his marketing background to improve the college's visibility. An entrepreneur at heart, he encouraged faculty and staff to develop additional programs for new markets. In the next 10 years, enrollment grew to nearly 2,000 students. The college added more graduate degrees and several new undergraduate majors. Clear Lake College earned a national listing as "one of America's hidden educational gems."

Thomas had many admirable leadership qualities. To begin, he was a "people person" who enjoyed mixing with donors, students, faculty, and administrators at other schools. No one would think of calling him "Dr. Thomas." He was "Sam" to everyone. Second, he was more than willing to tackle tough problems and fire those who weren't performing up to standards. Third, he kept his word to faculty and staff. When the financial picture of the school improved, he raised faculty salaries dramatically. Fourth, he had an uncanny ability to sense new educational markets. He never made a major miscalculation when it came to proposing additional programs.

Yet all was not well under Sam's leadership. His friendly exterior masked an explosive temper. He dressed down faculty and other employees in public meetings and made personnel decisions on his own, based on his instincts rather than on hard data. A number of employees were let go without warning, and many of his hires lasted less than a year. In several instances, the college had to offer generous severance packages to dismissed employees in order to avoid costly lawsuits. Sam's autocratic style wasn't limited strictly to personnel decisions. He would change the school's governance structure without consulting faculty, who expected to participate in these choices. In addition, he engaged in micromanagement. He read minutes from every department meeting held on campus, for example, and didn't hesitate to send scathing memos if he disagreed with a group's conclusions.

Sam received many accolades for his success at Clear Lake College. He was credited with the school's turnaround and was named as the area's outstanding citizen one year. He was popular with other university presidents, serving on national collegiate boards and commissions. Clear Lake's board was eager to renew his contract despite the concerns of the faculty. Unfortunately, Sam's successes made him less, not more, flexible. Frustrated by faculty criticism, he made even fewer efforts to consult them when making decisions. He began to call students who had offended him into his office to berate them.

By the end of the first decade of the new century, it looked as if the college had "outgrown" Sam's leadership style. After all, the school was much bigger and more complex than it had been when he took over. Thomas had no intention of stepping down, however. He referred to Clear Lake as "my college" and continued to be involved in every detail of college life. In fact, he had to be forced to resign when he was diagnosed with Parkinson's disease in 2010. The college has continued to grow under the leadership of a new president who, while maintaining a good deal of decision-making power, relies heavily on his vice presidents and has very little input in the day-to-day operations of most departments.

Discussion Probes

1. What elements of transactional and transforming leadership did Thomas exhibit?

2. Was Sam a transformational or a pseudo-transformational leader?

3. How would you evaluate the actions of the college's board of directors?

4. Have you ever had to confront a leader about her or his behavior? If so, what did you say or do? What was the outcome of the encounter? Would you do anything differently next time?

5. How do you determine when to remove a leader, particularly one who has a proven track record of success?

Note

1. This is a fictional case inspired by actual events.

CASE STUDY 7.2

From the Secret Service to the Secret Circus

The life of a Secret Service agent is a life of sacrifice. Agents assigned to protect the president and other dignitaries must put their jobs first. They set aside vacations and family obligations in order to travel with the president. Unlike other law enforcement employees, they do not always get to go home at the end of the day. At any moment they may be called upon to risk their lives to save their charges. When President John F. Kennedy was shot, agent Rufus Youngblood pushed Vice President Lyndon Johnson, who had been riding two cars behind Kennedy in the same motorcade, to the floor of the vehicle and threw himself over the seat to cover his body, shouting, "Get down! Get down!" Agents also stepped between President Ronald Reagan and shooter John Hinckley. No wonder, then, that the Secret Service has been the most revered agency in the federal government.

Recent scandals have threatened the sterling image of the Secret Service, however. The most serious took place in Cartagena, Colombia, in 2012. An advance team of Secret Service agents and military personnel assigned to make arrangements for a presidential visit invited 20 prostitutes to their hotel. A dispute then broke out when an agent refused to pay one of the women. Twelve Secret Service employees (including three supervisors) were investigated. Eight were fired, three were cleared, and one lost his security clearance. Seven soldiers and two marines were also disciplined. Bringing any outsiders into a safe zone compromises the agency's mission. As Senator Susan Collins of Maine, ranking Republican on the Senate Homeland Security Committee, pointed out (tongue in cheek): "Thank goodness it was just prostitutes. They could have been spies planting equipment. They could have blackmailed or drugged agents. This is Colombia, for heaven's sake."[1]

The Cartagena scandal wasn't the first involving agents traveling while on duty. In 2002, agents were sent home from the Olympic Games in Salt Lake City, Utah, for abusing alcohol and having underage girls in their hotel rooms. In 2011, Secret Service employees may have hired prostitutes and strippers before President Obama's visit to El Salvador. The behavior of some employees while traveling prompted others in the agency to nickname road trips the "Secret Circus." There have also been a number of incidents involving off-duty agents, including cases of domestic violence, solicitation of prostitution, burglary, and driving under the influence of alcohol.

The culture of the Secret Service is part of the problem. Women are significantly underrepresented in protection teams, making up only 10% of agents and uniformed officers. In this macho climate, heavy drinking and sexual activities are tolerated, making the women who do serve uncomfortable. Male agents put loyalty to other men first, which may account for the results of a survey of Secret Service personnel that found that only 58% would report ethical problems.

The Secret Service has taken steps to improve personnel behavior both on and off the road, including assigning chaperones, banning foreign nationals from hotel rooms, limiting the consumption of alcohol while off duty, and prohibiting drinking within 10 hours of going on duty. These measures, and the appointment of the agency's first female director, Julia Person, may not be enough to curb misbehavior, however, if agents once again lose sight of their mission, which requires sacrifice in order to serve and protect the nation's leaders.

Discussion Probes

1. Should Secret Service agents be held to a higher ethical standard than other government employees both on and off the job?

2. Will the new rules and the appointment of a female director prevent future scandals in the Secret Service?

3. What additional steps can the agency take to change its culture?

4. How can the Secret Service encourage more women to join its protection teams?

5. How can the agency reinforce the importance of its mission?

Note

1. Dowd, M. (2012, May 27). The party animals at the Secret Service. *The New York Times*, p. SR11.

Sources

At least 20 women involved in Secret Service scandal. (2012, April 17). *The Telegraph*.

Baldor, L. C. (2012, August 4). New details in Colombian scandal revealed. *The Washington Post*, p. A03.

Leonnig, C. D., & Nakamura, D. (2012, June 16). Third supervisor involved in Secret Service prostitution scandal. *The Washington Post,* p. A05.

McElhatton, J. (2012, June 19). Alcohol plays role in reports involving the Secret Service. *The Washington Times,* p. A1.

Mudhani, A. (2013, March 23). Obama: New Secret Service director breaking the mold. *USA Today.*

Ninan, R. (2012, April 28). Secret Service scandal. *World News Saturday* (ABC), p. 1.

Tucker, E. (2012, May 7). Scandal highlights lack of women in US Secret Service. *The Nation.*

CASE STUDY 7.3

Yvon Chouinard: Putting the Environment First at Patagonia

Few business leaders take their social responsibilities as seriously as Yvon Chouinard. Chouinard started his career in the 1950s as an elite rock climber, scaling walls at Yosemite and elsewhere. Dissatisfied with available climbing gear, Chouinard began manufacturing pitons—metal stakes that climbers hammer into rocks to secure ropes—and selling them out of the trunk of his car. In 1973 he formed the Patagonia Company to sell shirts, climbing shorts, and other outdoor clothing items.

Chouinard's love of climbing and the outdoors is reflected in Patagonia's extraordinarily strong environmental commitment. Early on, Chouinard declared that his company was an "environmental villain" for making pitons that damaged rock. He then discontinued making pitons (his core business) and began offering aluminum chocks instead. In a few months the sales of the chocks were soaring. The company donates 1% of its proceeds from sales (pretax) to environmental causes. Patagonia was the first major company to sell fleeces made out of recycled plastic bottles. When it realized the environmental harm done by traditional cotton farming methods, the firm switched to making items out of organic fibers.

Recently, Patagonia representatives have taken to telling prospective customers to buy only what they need. According to the company's vice president of global marketing: "We want our customers to do some research and make an educated decision about whether they really need the product, and how to use it. So it's a case of 'Buy less, buy smart.'"[1] Patagonia also offers a free repair service to discourage buyers from tossing their damaged or worn garments and asks customers to sign a pledge to return items they no longer need to company outlets to be recycled. The firm claims that it is able to recycle 100% of its polyester goods, pulling off the buttons and zippers and sending the garments to Asia for remanufacturing. Patagonia's Footprint Chronicles initiative enables consumers to track all the steps of a product's life cycle online, from raw materials through design and manufacture to disposal or remanufacturing.

Chouinard's environmental vision extends well beyond his company. Patagonia cofounded the Sustainable Apparel Coalition with other clothing manufacturers and retailers, including Wal-Mart, Target, and Levi Strauss, with the goal of reducing the environmental impact of their businesses. Patagonia's founder seeks "to create a company others companies want to emulate" and reports that leaders of other businesses have turned to him for advice on how to preserve the environment. Patagonia and other companies are helping to create a national park in Chile, which will be two-thirds the size of Yellowstone.

To ensure that Patagonia's green commitment continues after he is gone, Chouinard was the first company leader to file "benefit corporation" papers in California. The California legislature created this new corporate category for firms that "create material positive impact on society and the environment." This law protects companies that want to donate proceeds to social causes from lawsuits brought by shareholders claiming that these policies dilute their stock value. (Similar programs can be found in other states.) Businesses registered as benefit corporations have to file annual reports outlining the public benefits they provide and have to be evaluated by third parties that determine if they have met the required standards. Patagonia can now continue to contribute to environmental causes even if the company goes public following the death of Chouinard and his wife. After registering his company as a benefit corporation, the 72-year-old Chouinard said: "My work is over. I feel that we've done what we set out to do. This benefit corporation allows us a way to ensure the values of my company continue."[2]

Patagonia's environmental focus has not hurt its bottom line. The company had to lay off employees only once in its history (a moment Chouinard recalls as extremely painful). During the recent sluggish economy, sales rose more than 30% in a 12-month period, to $540 million. Financial analysts suggest that the increase may be due in part to the fact that many Americans, instead of traveling abroad, elected to stay home and participate in outdoor activities. But there can be no doubt that Chouinard and Patagonia have created relationships with stakeholders who share their commitment to a greener world.

Discussion Probes

1. How does Yvon Chouinard function as a responsible leader?

2. Can you think of other business executives who also meet the criteria for responsible leadership?

3. Could leaders of publicly held corporations follow Chouinard's example? Should they try to do so?

4. Does Patagonia put too much emphasis on the environment? Who might be hurt by this commitment?

5. Should all U.S. states adopt benefit corporation laws? What are the potential benefits and costs of doing so?

Notes

1. Wright, M. (2011, November 7). Success means telling people to buy less. *The Guardian*.

2. Herdt, T. (2012, January 4). Patagonia first in line to register as a "benefit corporation." *Ventura County Star*.

Sources

Archer, M. (2005, October 31). Founder of Patagonia became a businessman accidentally. *USA Today*, Money, p. 5.

Mara, J. (2008, January 17). Patagonia CEO turns retailers green. *Contra Costa Times*.

Martin, J. (2012, May 25). Clothier's products all come in green. *Los Angeles Times*, p. B1.

SELF-ASSESSMENT 7.1

Transformational Leadership scale

Instructions: Think about a situation in which you either assumed or were given a leadership role. Think about your own behaviors within this context. To what extent does each of the following statements characterize your leadership orientation?

Very Little			A Moderate Amount			Very Much
1	2	3	4	5	6	7

1. Have a clear understanding of where we are going.

2. Paint an interesting picture of the future for my group.

3. Am always seeking new opportunities for the organization/group.

4. Inspire others with my plans for the future.

5. Am able to get others to be committed to my dreams.

6. Lead by "doing," rather than simply by "telling."

7. Provide a good model for others to follow.

8. Lead by example.

9. Foster collaboration among group members.

10. Encourage employees to be "team players."

11. Get the group to work together for the same goal.

12. Develop a team attitude and spirit among employees.

13. Show that I expect a lot from others

14. Insist on only the best performance.

15. Will not settle for second best.

16. Act without considering the feelings of others.

17. Show respect for the personal feelings of others.

18. Behave in a manner thoughtful of the personal needs of others.

19. Treat others without considering their personal feelings.

20. Challenge others to think about old problems in new ways.

21. Ask questions that prompt others to think.

22. Stimulate others to rethink the way they do things.

23. Have ideas that challenge others to reexamine some of their basic assumptions about work.

24. Always give positive feedback when others perform well.

25. Give special recognition when others' work is very good.

26. Commend others when they do a better-than-average job.

27. Personally compliment others when they do outstanding work.

28. Frequently do not acknowledge the good performance of others.

Scoring

Reverse your scores on questions 16, 19, and 28. There are seven dimension scores to be computed. *Articulate vision:* Sum your responses to questions 1–5 and divide by 5. *Provide appropriate model:* Sum your responses to questions 6–8 and divide by 3. *Foster acceptance of goals:* Sum your responses to questions 9–12 and divide by 4. *High performance expectations:* Sum your responses to questions 13–15 and divide by 3. *Individual support:* Sum your responses to questions 16–19 and divide by 4. *Intellectual stimulation:* Sum your responses to questions 20–23 and divide by 4. *Transactional leader behaviors:* Sum your responses to questions 24–28 and divide by 5.

My scores are

Articulate vision_____

Role model _____

Foster goal acceptance _____

Performance expectations _____

Individual support _____

Intellectual stimulation _____

Transactional leader behavior _____

A high score of 6 and greater reflects a strong orientation to engage in each of these behaviors. A low score of 2 or less reflects that you are unlikely to engage in each of these behaviors.

SOURCES: Podsakoff, P. M., MacKenzie, S. B., Moorman, R. H., & Fetter, R. (1990). Transformational leader behaviors and their effects on followers' trust in leader, satisfaction, and organizational citizenship behavior. *Leadership Quarterly, 1,* 107–142. Scale reprinted from Pierce, J. L., & Newstrom, J. W. (2011). *Leaders and the leadership process: Readings, self-assessments and applications* (6th ed.). New York: McGraw-Hill, pp. 369–370. Used by permission.

SELF-ASSESSMENT 7.2

Servant Leadership Questionnaire

Instructions: You can use this questionnaire to rate the servant leadership behaviors of one of your leaders or ask someone else to rate you. Respond to each question on the following scale: 1 = *strongly disagree,* 2 = *somewhat disagree,* 3 = *somewhat agree,* 4 = *strongly agree.* The scale rates five dimensions of servant leadership, which are described below. Add up the item ratings to come up with the total score for each component. Add the component scores to come up with a total servant leadership rating (range 24–96).

1. This person puts my best interests ahead of his/her own.   1 2 3 4

2. This person does everything he/she can do to serve me.   1 2 3 4

3. This person is one I would turn to if I had a personal trauma.   1 2 3 4

4. This person seems alert to what's happening.   1 2 3 4

5. This person offers compelling reasons to get me to do things.   1 2 3 4

6. This person encourages me to dream "big dreams" about the organization. 1 2 3 4

7. This person is good at anticipating the consequences of decisions.   1 2 3 4

8. This person is good at helping me with my emotional issues.   1 2 3 4

9. This person has great awareness of what is going on.   1 2 3 4

10. This person is very persuasive.   1 2 3 4

11. This person believes that the organization needs to
    play a moral role in society.   1 2 3 4

12. This person is talented at helping me to heal emotionally.   1   2   3   4

13. This person seems in touch with what's happening.   1   2   3   4

14. This person is good at convincing me to do things.   1   2   3   4

15. This person believes that our organization needs to
function as a community.   1   2   3   4

16. This person sacrifices his/her own interests to meet my needs.   1   2   3   4

17. This person is one who could help me mend my hard feelings.   1   2   3   4

18. This person is gifted when it comes to persuading me.   1   2   3   4

19. This person is talented at helping me to heal emotionally.   1   2   3   4

20. This person sees the organization for its potential to contribute to society.   1   2   3   4

21. This person encourages me to have a community spirit in the workplace.   1   2   3   4

22. This person goes above and beyond the call of duty to meet my needs.   1   2   3   4

23. This person seems to know what is going to happen.   1   2   3   4

24. This person is preparing the organization to make a positive
difference in the future.   1   2   3   4

Scoring

Altruistic Calling (deep-rooted desire to make a positive difference)

Item 1 _____

Item 2 _____

Item 21 _____

Item 22 _____

Total _____ out of 16

Emotional Healing (fostering spiritual recovery from hardship or trauma)

Item 3 _____

Item 8 _____

Item 12 _____

Item 17 _____

Item 19 _____

Total _____ out of 20

Wisdom (awareness of surroundings and anticipation of consequences)

Item 4 _____

Item 7 _____

Item 9 _____

Item 13 _____

Item 23 _____

Total _____ out of 20

Persuasive Mapping (use of sound reasoning and mental frameworks)

Item 5 _____

Item 6 _____

Item 10 _____

Item 14 _____

Item 18 _____

Total _____ out of 20

Organizational Development (making a collective positive contribution to society)

Item 11 _____

Item 15 _____

Item 20 _____

Item 21 _____

Item 24 _____

Total _____ out of 20

Overall score _____ out of 96

SOURCE: Adapted from Barbuto, J. E., & Wheeler, D. W. (2006). Scale development and construct clarification of servant leadership. *Group & Organization Management, 31,* 300–326. Used by permission. Published by SAGE Publications.

NOTES _____

1. See, for example, Katz, D., Maccoby, N., Gurin, G., & Floor, L. (1951). *Productivity, supervision, and morale among railroad workers.* Ann Arbor: University of Michigan, Institute for Social Research; Stogdill, R. M., & Coons, A. E. (1957). *Leader behavior: Its description and measurement.* Columbus: Ohio State University, Bureau of Business Research.

2. Burns J. M. (1978). *Leadership.* New York: Harper & Row.

3. Burns, J. M. (2003). *Transforming leadership: A new pursuit of happiness.* New York: Atlantic Monthly Press.

4. Burns (1978), p. 2.

5. Burns (2003), Ch. 12.

6. Kanungo, R. N. (2001). Ethical values of transactional and transformational leaders. *Canadian Journal of Administrative Sciences, 18,* 257–265.

7. Turner, N., Barling, J., Epitropaki, O., Butcher, V., & Milner, C. (2002, April). Transformational leadership and moral reasoning. *Journal of Applied Psychology, 87,* 304–311; Toor, S. R., & Ofori, G. (2009). Ethical leadership: Examining the relationships with full range leadership model, employee outcomes, and organizational culture. *Journal of Business Ethics, 90,* 533–547; Hood, J. N. (2003). The relationship of leadership style and CEO values to ethical practices in organizations. *Journal of Business Ethics, 43,* 263–273; Carlson, D. S., & Perrewe, P. L. (1995). Institutionalization of organizational ethics through transformational leadership. *Journal of Business Ethics, 14,* 829–838; Puffer, S. M., & McCarthy, D. J. (2008). Ethical turnarounds and transformational leadership: A global imperative for corporate social responsibility. *Thunderbird International Business Review, 50,* 304–314.

8. See Bass, B. M. (1996). *A new paradigm of leadership: An inquiry into transformational leadership.* Alexandria, VA: U.S. Army Research Institute for the Behavioral and Social Sciences; Bass, B. M., Avolio, B. J., Jung, D. I., & Berson, Y. (2003). Predicting unit performance by assessing transformational and transactional leadership. *Journal of Applied Psychology, 88,* 207–218.

9. Bass, B. M. (1990). *Bass and Stogdill's handbook of leadership* (3rd ed.). New York: Free Press, p. 53.

10. See Bass, B. M., & Avolio, B. J. (1993). Transformational leadership: A response to critiques. In M. M. Chemers & R. Ayman (Eds.), *Leadership theory and research: Perspectives and directions* (pp. 49–80). San Diego: Academic Press; Waldman, D. A., Bass, B. M., & Yammarino, F. J. (1990). Adding to contingent-reward behavior: The augmenting effect of charismatic leadership. *Group and Organizational Studies, 15,* 381–394.

11. For evidence of the effectiveness of transformational leadership, see Bass et al. (2003) and the following: DeGroot, T., Kiker, D. S., & Cross, T. C. (2000). A meta-analysis to review organizational outcomes related to charismatic leadership. *Canadian Journal of Administrative Sciences, 17,* 356–371; Fiol, C. M., Harris, D., & House, R. J. (1999). Charismatic leadership: Strategies for effecting social change. *Leadership Quarterly, 10,* 449–482; Lowe, K. B., & Kroeck, K. G. (1996). Effectiveness correlates of transformational and transactional leadership: A meta-analytic review. *Leadership Quarterly, 7,* 385–425.

12. A few examples of popular leadership sources based on a transformational approach include Bennis, W., & Nanus, B. (2003). *Leaders: Strategies for taking charge.* New York: Harper Business Essentials; Kotter, J. P. (1990). *A force for change: How leadership differs from management.* New York: Free Press; Kouzes, J. M., & Posner, B. Z. (2012). *The leadership challenge* (5th ed.). San Francisco: Jossey-Bass; Nanus, B. (1992). *Visionary leadership.* San Francisco: Jossey-Bass; Peters, T. (1992). *Liberation management.* New York: Ballantine.

13. Bass, B. M. (1998). The ethics of transformational leadership. In J. B. Ciulla (Ed.), *Ethics, the heart of leadership* (pp. 169–192). Westport, CT: Praeger.

14. Den Hartog, D. N., House, R. J., Hanges, P. U., Ruiz-Quintanilla, S. A., & Dorfman, P. W.

(1999). Culture-specific and cross-culturally generalizable implicit leadership theories: Are attributes of charismatic/transformational leadership universally endorsed? *Leadership Quarterly, 10,* 219–257.

15. Tourish, D. (2008). Challenging the transformational agenda: Leadership theory in transition? *Management Communication Quarterly, 21,* 522–528, p. 523.

16. Criticisms of transformational leadership can be found in the following: Kelley, R. (1992). *The power of followership.* New York: Doubleday/Currency; Tourish, D., & Pinnington, A. (2002). Transformational leadership, corporate cultism, and the spirituality paradigm: An unholy trinity in the workplace? *Human Relations, 55,* 147–172; Tourish, D. (2013). *The dark side of transformational leadership: A critical perspective.* New York: Routledge.

17. Greenleaf, R. K. (1977). *Servant leadership.* New York: Paulist Press.

18. Spears, L. (1998). Introduction: Tracing the growing impact of servant-leadership. In L. C. Spears (Ed.), *Insights on leadership* (pp. 1–12). New York: John Wiley; Ruschman, N. L. (2002). Servant-leadership and the best companies to work for in America. In L. C. Spears & M. Lawrence (Eds.), *Focus on leadership: Servant-leadership for the twenty-first century* (pp. 123–139). New York: John Wiley; Sendjaya, S., & Sarros, J. C. (2002). Servant leadership: Its origin, development, and application in organizations. *Journal of Leadership & Organizational Studies, 9*(2), 57–64.

19. Greenleaf, pp. 13–14.

20. Block, P. (1996). *Stewardship: Choosing service over self-interest.* San Francisco: Berrett-Koehler; DePree, M. (2003). Servant-leadership: Three things necessary. In L. C. Spears & M. Lawrence (Eds.), *Focus on leadership: Servant-leadership for the 21st century* (pp. 89–97). New York: John Wiley.

21. DePree, M. (1989). *Leadership is an art.* New York: Doubleday.

22. Barbuto, J. E., & Wheeler, D. W. (2006). Scale development and construct clarification of servant leadership. *Group & Organization Management, 31,* 300–326; Spears, L. C. (2004). The understanding and practice of servant leadership. In L. C. Spears & M. Lawrence (Eds.), *Practicing servant leadership: Succeeding through trust, bravery, and forgiveness* (pp. 9–24). San Francisco: Jossey-Bass.

23. Barbuto & Wheeler; Russell, R. F., & Stone, A. G. (2002). A review of servant leadership attributes: Developing a practical model. *Leadership & Organization Development Journal, 23,* 145–157; Washington, R. R., Sutton, C. D., & Feild, H. S. (2006). Individual differences in servant leadership: The roles of values and personality. *Leadership & Organization Development Journal, 27,* 700–716; Mayers, D., Bardes, M., & Piccolo, R. F. (2008). Do servant-leaders help satisfy follower needs? An organizational justice perspective. *European Journal of Work and Organizational Psychology, 17,* 180–197; Jaramillo, F., Grisaffe, D. B., Chonko, L. B., & Roberts, J. A. (2009). Examining the impact of servant leadership on sales force performance. *Journal of Personal Selling & Sales Management, 29,* 257–275; Jaramillo, F., Grisaffe, D. B., Chonko, L. B., & Roberts, J. A. (2009). Examining the impact of servant leadership on salesperson's turnover intention. *Journal of Personal Selling & Sales Management, 29,* 351–365; Jones, D. (2012). Does servant leadership lead to greater customer focus and employee satisfaction? *Business Studies Journal, 4,* 21–35; Melchar, D. E., & Bosco, S. M. (2010). Achieving high organization performance through servant leadership. *Journal of Business Inquiry, 9,* 74–88; Walumbwa, F. O., Hartnell, C. A., & Oke, A. (2010). Servant leadership, procedural justice climate, service climate, employee attitudes, and organizational citizenship behavior: A cross-level investigation. *Journal of Applied Psychology, 95,* 517–529; Ehrhart, M. G. (2004). Leadership and procedural justice climate as antecedents of unit-level organizational citizenship behavior. *Personnel Psychology, 57,* 61–94; Hale, J. R., & Fields, D. (2007). Exploring servant leadership across cultures: A study of followers in Ghana and the USA. *Leadership,*

3, 397–417; Mehta, S., & Pillay, R. (2011). Revisiting servant leadership: An empirical study in Indian context. *Journal of Contemporary Management Research, 5*(2), 24–41.

24. Kennedy, D. (2004). *The dark sides of virtue: Reassessing international humanitarianism.* Princeton, NJ: Princeton University Press.

25. Klenke, K. (2005). The internal theater of the authentic leader: Integrating cognitive, affective, conative and spiritual facets of authentic leadership. In W. L. Gardner, B. J. Avolio, & F. O. Walumbwa (Eds.), *Authentic leadership theory and practice: Origins, effects and development* (pp. 43–81). Amsterdam: Elsevier.

26. Avolio, B. J., & Gardner, W. L. (2005). Authentic leadership development: Getting to the root of positive forms of leadership. *Leadership Quarterly, 16,* 315–340; Chan, A., Hannah, S. T., & Gardner, W. L. (2005). Veritable authentic leadership: Emergence, functioning, and impacts. In W. L. Gardner, B. J. Avolio, & F. O. Walumbwa (Eds.), *Authentic leadership theory and practice: Origins, effects and development* (pp. 3–41). Amsterdam: Elsevier.

27. Walumbwa, F. O., Avolio, B. J., Gardner, W. L., Wernsing, T. S., & Peterson, S. J. (2008). Authentic leadership: Development and validation of a theory-based measure. *Journal of Management, 34,* 89–126; Kernis, M. H. (2003). Toward a conceptualization of optimal self-esteem. *Psychological Inquiry, 14,* 1–26.

28. Avolio & Gardner, p. 321.

29. May, D. R., Chan, A. Y. L., Hodges, T. D., & Avolio, B. J. (2003). Developing the moral component of authentic leadership. *Organizational Dynamics, 32,* 247–260; Hanna, S. T., Lester, P. B., & Vogelgesang, G. R. (2005). Moral leadership: Explicating the moral component of authentic leadership. In W. L. Gardner, B. J. Avolio, & F. O. Walumbwa (Eds.), *Authentic leadership theory and practice: Origins, effects and development* (pp. 43–81). Amsterdam: Elsevier.

30. Gardner, W. L., Avolio, B. J., Luthans, F., May, D. R., & Walumbwa, F. O. (2005). "Can you see the real me?" A self-based model of authentic leader and follower development. *Leadership Quarterly, 16,* 343–372.

31. May et al.; Ilies, R., Morgeson, F. P., & Nahrgang, J. D. (2005). Authentic leadership and eudemonic well-being: Understanding leader–follower outcomes. *Leadership Quarterly, 16,* 373–394.

32. Gardner et al.; Harvey, P., Martinko, M. J., & Gardner, W. L. (2006). Promoting authentic behavior in organizations: An attributional perspective. *Journal of Leadership & Organizational Studies, 12*(3), 1–11; Zhu, W., May, D. R., & Avolio, B. J. (2004). The impact of ethical leadership behavior on employee outcomes: The roles of psychological empowerment and authenticity. *Journal of Leadership & Organizational Studies, 11*(1), 16–26; Avolio, B. J., Gardner, W. L., Walumbwa, F. O., Luthans, F., & May, D. R. (2004). Unlocking the mask: A look at the process by which authentic leaders impact follower attitudes and behaviors. *Leadership Quarterly, 15,* 801–823; Clapp-Smith, R., Vogelgesang, G. R., & Avey, J. B. (2009). Authentic leadership and positive psychological capital: The mediating role of trust at the group level of analysis. *Journal of Leadership & Organizational Studies, 15,* 227–240.

33. See, for example, Leroy, H., Palanski, M. E., & Simons, T. (2012). Authentic leadership and behavioral integrity as drivers of follower commitment and performance. *Journal of Business Ethics, 107,* 255–264; Peus, C., Wesche, J. S., Streicher, B., Braun, S., & Frey, D. (2012). Authentic leadership: An empirical test of its antecedents, consequences, and mediating mechanisms. *Journal of Business Ethics, 107,* 331–348; Walumbwa, F. O., Luthans, F., Avey, J. B., & Oke, A. (2011). Authentically leading groups: The mediating role of collective psychological capital and trust. *Journal of Organizational Behavior, 32,* 4–24.

34. Clapp-Smith et al.

35. Walumbwa et al. (2008).

36. Clapp-Smith et al.

37. Chan et al.

38. Ladkin, D. (2006). The enchantment of the charismatic leader: Charisma reconsidered as aesthetic encounter. *Leadership, 2,* 165–179.

39. Hansen, H., Ropo, A., & Sauer, E. (2007). Aesthetic leadership. *Leadership Quarterly, 18,* 544–560.

40. Duke, D. L. (1986). The aesthetics of leadership. *Educational Administration Quarterly, 22*(1), 7–27.

41. Ladkin (2006); Ladkin, D. (2010). *Rethinking leadership: A new look at old leadership questions.* Cheltenham, England: Edward Elgar.

42. Ladkin, D. (2008). Leading beautifully: How mastery congruence and purpose create the aesthetic of embodied leadership practice. *Leadership Quarterly, 19,* 31–41.

43. Haberman, C. (2009, November 29). The story of a landing. *The New York Times,* p. BR15.

44. Squires, N. (2012, July 11). *Costa Concordia* captain: "I ****** up." *The Telegraph.*

45. Dobson, J. (1999). *The art of management and the aesthetic manager.* Westport, CT: Quorum Books.

46. Ladkin (2008).

47. Maak, T., & Pless, N. M. (2006). Responsible leadership in a stakeholder society: A relational perspective. *Journal of Business Ethics, 66,* 99–115; Maak, T., & Pless, N. M. (2006). Responsible leadership: A relational approach. In T. Maak & N. M. Pless (Eds.), *Responsible leadership* (pp. 33–53). London: Routledge; Pless, N. M. (2007). Understanding responsible leadership: Role identity and motivational drivers. *Journal of Business Ethics, 74,* 437–456.

48. Maak, T., & Pless, N. M. (2009). Business leaders as citizens of the world: Advancing humanism on a global scale. *Journal of Business Ethics, 88,* 537–550, p. 539.

49. Maak & Pless, Responsible leadership: A relational approach (2006); Pless.

50. Pless, N. M., & Maak, T. (2009). Responsible leaders as agents of world benefit: Learnings from "Project Ulysses." *Journal of Business Ethics, 85,* 59–71: Maak & Pless (2009).

51. Maak, T. (2007). Responsible leadership, stakeholder engagement, and the emergence of social capital. *Journal of Business Ethics, 74,* 329–343.

52. For more information on the limitations of responsible leadership and its ongoing development, see Pless, N. M., & Maak, T. (2011). Responsible leadership: Pathways to the future. *Journal of Business Ethics, 98,* 3–13; Waldman, D. A. (2011). Moving forward with the concept of responsible leadership: Three caveats to guide theory and research. *Journal of Business Ethics, 98,* 75–83.

53. Material on key components of Taoist thought is adopted from Johnson, C. E. (1997). A leadership journey to the East. *Journal of Leadership Studies, 4*(2), 82–88; Johnson, C. E. (2000). Emerging perspectives in leadership ethics. *Proceedings of the International Leadership Association,* pp. 48–54; Johnson, C. E. (2000). Taoist leadership ethics. *Journal of Leadership & Organizational Studies, 7*(1), 82–91. For an alternative perspective on the origins of Taoism, see Kirkland, R. (2002). Self-fulfillment through selflessness: The moral teachings of the Daode Jing. In M. Barnhart (Ed.), *Varieties of ethical reflection: New directions for ethics in a global context* (pp. 21–48). Lanham, MD: Lexington Books.

54. Mitchell, S. (Trans.). (1988). *Tao te ching: A new English version.* New York: HarperPerennial, p. 19.

55. Mitchell, p. 17.

56. Chan, W. (Trans.). (1963). *The way of Lao Tzu.* Indianapolis: Bobbs-Merrill, p. 236.

57. See Kiuchi, T., & Shireman, B. (2002). *What we learned in the rainforest: Business lessons from nature.* San Francisco: Berrett-Koehler; White, B. J., & Prywes, Y. (2007). *The nature of leadership: Reptiles, mammals, and the challenge of becoming a great leader.* New York: AMACOM.

Shaping Ethical Contexts

CHAPTER 8

Building an Ethical Small Group

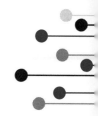

Cooperation is the thorough conviction that nobody can get there unless everybody gets there.

—Author Virginia Burden Tower

Never underestimate a minority.

—British prime minister Winston Churchill

What's Ahead

This chapter examines ethical leadership in the small-group context. Groups are often charged with making ethical decisions because they have the potential to make better choices than individuals. To make the most of the small-group advantage, however, leaders must foster individual ethical accountability among group members, ensure ethical group interaction, avoid moral pitfalls, and establish ethical relationships with other teams.

In his metaphor of the leader's light or shadow, Parker Palmer emphasizes that leaders shape the settings or contexts around them. According to Palmer, leaders are people who have "an unusual degree of power to create the conditions under which other people must live and move and have their being, conditions that can either be as illuminating as heaven or as shadowy as hell."[1] In this final section of the text, I'll describe some of the ways we can create conditions that illuminate the lives of followers in small-group, organizational, diverse, and crisis settings. Shedding light means both resisting and exerting influence. We must fend off pressures to engage in unethical behavior while actively seeking to create healthier moral environments.

The Leader and the Small Group

Leaders spend a great deal of their time in small groups, either chairing or participating in meetings. You can expect to devote more of your workday to meetings with every step up the organizational hierarchy. Top-level executives spend a third of their time working in committees, task forces, and other small-group settings.[2] Meeting expert John Tropman points out that high-quality management is the product of high-quality meetings that render high-quality decisions. Meetings aren't distractions from our work, he argues; they *are* the work. Successful meetings are "absolutely central to the achievement of organizational goals."[3]

Groups meet for many different purposes: to coordinate activities, to pass along important information, to clarify misunderstandings, and to build relationships. In this chapter, however, I'll focus on the role of groups in making ethical decisions. Examples of ethical group dilemmas include the following:

- A congressional panel debating how to avoid sending the country over a "fiscal cliff"

- Court justices determining the legal rights of terrorist suspects

- The board of the local United Way responding to a funding request from an abortion clinic or a Boy Scout troop considering whether to allow gay men to be leaders

- State Department officials deciding whether to impose sanctions on a famine-stricken nation that is developing a nuclear weapons program

- Student officers disciplining a campus organization that has violated university and student government policies

- Corporate executives devising a plan to reduce the company's carbon footprint

Groups have significant advantages over lone decision makers when it comes to solving ethical problems such as those described above as well as the dilemmas presented in Case Studies 8.1 and 8.2. In a group, members can pool their information, divide up assignments, draw from a variety of perspectives, and challenge questionable assumptions. They are more likely to render carefully reasoned, defensible decisions as a result.[4] Of course, groups don't always make good moral choices, as in the case of executives who decide to hide product defects from the public or city officials who bypass regulations and award construction contracts to friends. Our task as leaders is to create the conditions that ensure that teams make the most of the small-group advantage. In particular, we must encourage members to take their ethical responsibilities seriously, promote ethical interaction, prevent the group from falling victim to moral pitfalls, and establish ethical relationships with other teams.

Fostering Individual Ethical Accountability

A group's success or failure is highly dependent on the behaviors of its individual members. Destructive behavior by just one person can be enough to derail the group process. Every team member has an ethical responsibility to take her or his duties seriously. The job of the leader, then, is to foster ethical accountability, to encourage followers to live up to their moral responsibilities to the rest of the group.

A critical moral duty of group members is to pursue shared goals—to cooperate. Although this might seem like a basic requirement for joining a team, far too many people act selfishly or competitively when working with others. Those pursuing individual goals ignore the needs of teammates. For example, some athletes care more about their own individual statistics, such as points and goals, than about team victories. Competitive individuals seek to advance at the expense of others. For instance, the ambitious salesperson hopes to beat out the rest of the sales group to earn the largest bonus. (For a tragic example of a failed attempt at cooperation, see Case Study 8.3.)

Cooperative groups are more productive than those with an individualistic or competitive focus. Cooperative groups[5]

- are more willing to take on difficult tasks and to persist in the face of difficulties;

- retain more information;

- engage in higher-level reasoning and more critical thinking;

- generate more creative ideas, tactics, and solutions;

- transfer more learning from the group to individual members;

- are more positive about the task; and

- spend more time working on tasks.

In addition to being more effective, cooperative groups foster more positive relationships and cohesion between members. This cohesion reduces absenteeism and turnover while producing higher commitment and satisfaction. Members of cooperative groups also enjoy better psychological health (i.e., emotional maturity, autonomy, self-confidence) and learn important social and communication skills.[6] (I'll have more to say about group communication skills later in the chapter.)

As a leader, you can focus attention on shared goals by (1) emphasizing the moral responsibility members have to cooperate with one another, (2) structuring the task so that no one person succeeds unless the group as a whole succeeds, (3) ensuring that all group members are fairly rewarded (don't reward one person for a group achievement, for example), (4) providing feedback on how well the group and individuals are meeting performance standards, (5) encouraging individuals to help each other complete tasks, and (6) setting aside time for process sessions where the group reflects on how well it is working together and how it might improve.[7]

Creating a cooperative climate is also difficult when group members fail to do their fair share of the work. Social psychologists use the term *social loafing* to describe the fact that individuals often reduce their efforts when placed in groups.[8] Social loafing has been found in teams charged with all kinds of tasks, ranging from shouting and rope pulling to generating ideas, rating poems, writing songs, and evaluating job candidates. Gender, nationality, and age don't seem to have much impact on the rate of social loafing, although women and people from Eastern cultures are less likely to reduce their efforts. (Determine the level of social loafing in your team by completing Self-Assessment 8.1.)

A number of explanations have been offered for social loafing. When people work in a group, they may feel that their efforts will have little impact on the final result. Responsibility for the collective product is shared or diffused throughout the team. It is difficult to identify and evaluate the input of individual participants. The collective effort model, developed by Steven Karau and Kipling Williams, is an attempt to integrate the various explanations for social loafing into one framework. Karau and Williams believe that "individuals will be willing to exert effort on a collective task only to the degree that they expect their efforts to be instrumental in obtaining outcomes that they value personally."[9] According to this definition, the motivation of group members depends on three factors: *expectancy,* or how much a person expects that her or his effort will lead to high group performance; *instrumentality,* the belief that one's personal contribution and the group's collective effort will bring about the desired result; and *valence,* how desirable the outcome is for individual group members.[10] Motivation drops if any of these factors are low. Consider the typical class project group, for example. Team members often slack off because they believe that the group will succeed in completing the project and getting a passing grade even if they do little (low expectancy). Participants may also be convinced that the group won't get an A no matter how hard they and others try (low instrumentality). Or some on the team may have other priorities and don't think that doing well on the project is all that important (low valence).

Social loafers take advantage of others in the group and violate norms for fairness or justice. Those being victimized are less likely to cooperate and may slack off for fear of being seen as "suckers." The small-group advantage can be lost because members aren't giving their best effort. Leaders need to take steps to minimize social loafing. According to the collective effort model, they can do so by taking the following steps:

- Evaluating the inputs of individual members

- Keeping the size of work groups small

- Making sure that each person makes a unique and important contribution to the task

- Providing meaningful tasks that are intrinsically interesting and personally involving

- Emphasizing the collective group identity

- Offering performance incentives

- Fostering a sense of belonging

Promoting Ethical Group Interaction

Fostering individual accountability is an important first step toward improving a group's ethical performance. However, team members can be cooperative and hardworking but still make poor moral choices as a group. Leaders, then, must also pay close attention to how group members interact during their deliberations. In particular, they need to encourage productive communication patterns that enable members to establish positive bonds and make wise ethical choices. Important communication skills and tactics include comprehensive, critical listening; supportive communication; emotional intelligence; productive conflict management; effective argumentation; and expression of minority opinion.

Comprehensive, Critical Listening

We spend much more time listening than speaking in small groups. If you belong to a team with 10 members, you can expect to devote approximately 10% of your time to talking and 90% to listening to what others have to say. All listening involves receiving, paying attention to, interpreting, and then remembering messages. However, our motives for listening vary.[11] *Discriminative listening* processes the verbal and nonverbal components of a message. It serves as the foundation for the other forms of listening because we can't accurately process or interpret messages unless we first understand what is being said and how the message is being delivered. Tom and Ray Magliozzi of National Public Radio's *Car Talk* demonstrate the importance of discriminative listening on their weekly call-in program. They frequently ask callers to repeat the sounds made by their vehicles. A "clunk" sound can signal one type of engine problem; a "chunk" noise might indicate that something else is wrong.

Comprehensive listening is motivated by the need to understand and retain messages. We engage in this type of listening when we attend lectures, receive job instructions, attend oral briefings, or watch the evening weather report. *Therapeutic* or *empathetic listening* is aimed at helping the speaker resolve an issue by encouraging him or her to talk about the problem. Those in helping professions such as social work and psychiatry routinely engage in this listening process. All of us act as empathetic listeners, however, when friends and family come to us for help. *Critical listening* leads to evaluation. Critical listeners pay careful attention to message content, logic, language, and other elements of persuasive attempts so that they can identify strengths and weaknesses and render a judgment. *Appreciative listening* is prompted by the desire for relaxation and entertainment. We act as appreciative listeners when we enjoy a CD, live concert, or play.

Group members engage in all five types of listening during meetings, but comprehensive and critical listening are essential to ethical problem solving. Coming up with a high-quality decision is nearly impossible unless group members first understand and remember what others have said. Participants also have to analyze the arguments of other group members critically in order to identify errors (see the discussion of conflict and argumentation that follows).

There are several barriers to comprehensive, critical listening in the group context. In one-to-one conversations, we know that we must respond to the speaker, so we tend to pay closer attention. In a group, we don't have to carry as much of the conversational load, so we're tempted to lose focus or to talk to the person sitting next to us. The content of the discussion can also make listening difficult. Ethical issues can generate strong emotional reactions because they involve deeply held values and beliefs. The natural tendency is to reject the speaker ("What does he know?" "He's got it all wrong!") and become absorbed in our counterarguments instead of concentrating on the message.[12] Reaching an agreement then becomes more difficult because we don't understand the other person's position but are more committed than ever to our point of view.

Listening experts Larry Barker, Patrice Johnson, and Kittie Watson make the following suggestions for improving listening performance in a group setting. Our responsibility as leaders is to model these behaviors and encourage other participants to follow our example.[13]

- *Avoid interruptions.* Give the speaker a chance to finish before you respond or ask questions. The speaker may address your concerns before he or she finishes, and you can't properly evaluate a message until you've first understood it.

- *Seek areas of agreement.* Take a positive approach by searching for common ground. What do you and the speaker have in common? Commitment to solving the problem? Similar values and background?

- *Search for meanings and avoid arguing about specific words.* Discussions of terms can keep the group from addressing the real issue. Stay focused on what speakers mean; don't be distracted if they use different terms than you do.

- *Ask questions and request clarification.* When you don't understand, don't be afraid to ask for clarification. Chances are others in the group are also confused and will appreciate more information. However, asking too many questions can give the impression that you're trying to control the speaker.

- *Be patient.* We can process information faster than speakers can deliver it. Use the extra time to reflect on the message instead of focusing on your own reactions or daydreaming.

- *Compensate for attitudinal biases.* All of us have biases based on such factors as personal appearance, age differences, and irritating mannerisms. Among my pet peeves? Men with Elvis hairdos, grown women with little-girl voices, and nearly anyone who clutters his or her speech with "ums" and "uhs." I have to suppress my urge to dismiss these kinds of speakers and concentrate on listening carefully. (Sadly, I don't always succeed.)

- *Listen for principles, concepts, and feelings.* Try to understand how individual facts fit into the bigger picture. Don't overlook nonverbal cues, such as tone of voice and posture, that reveal emotions and, at times, can contradict verbal statements. If a speaker's words and nonverbal behaviors don't seem to match (as in an expression of support uttered with a sigh of resignation), probe further to make sure you clearly understand the person's position.

- *Compensate for emotion-arousing words and ideas.* Certain words and concepts, such as *fundamentalist, gay pride, terrorist,* and *fascist,* spark strong emotional responses. We need to overcome our knee-jerk reactions to these labels and strive instead to remain objective.

- *Be flexible.* Acknowledge that others' views may have merit, even though you may not completely agree with them.

- *Listen, even if the message is boring or tough to follow.* Not all messages are exciting and simple to digest, but we need to try to understand them anyway. A boring comment made early in a group discussion may later turn out to be critical to the team's success.

Defensive Versus Supportive Communication

Defensiveness is a major threat to accurate listening. When group members feel threatened, they divert their attention from the task to defending themselves. As their anxiety levels increase, they think less about how to solve the problem and more about how they are coming across to others, about winning, and about protecting themselves. Listening suffers because participants distort the messages they receive, misinterpreting the motives, values, and emotions of senders. On the other hand, supportive messages increase accuracy because group members devote more energy to interpreting the content and emotional states of sources. Psychologist Jack Gibb identified six pairs of behaviors, described below, that promote either a defensive or a supportive group atmosphere.[14] Our job as group leader is to engage in supportive communication, which contributes to a positive emotional climate and accurate understanding. At the same time, we need to challenge comments that spark defensive reactions and lead to poor ethical choices.

Evaluation Versus Description. Evaluative messages are judgmental. They can be sent through statements ("What a lousy idea!") or through such nonverbal cues as a sarcastic tone of voice or a raised eyebrow. Those being evaluated are likely to respond by placing blame and making judgments of their own ("Your proposal is no better than mine"). Supportive messages ("I think I see where you're coming from," attentive posture, eye contact) create a more positive environment.

Control Versus Problem Orientation. Controlling messages imply that the recipient is inadequate (i.e., uninformed, immature, stubborn, overly emotional) and needs to change. Control, like evaluation, can be communicated both verbally (issuing orders, threats) and nonverbally (stares, threatening body posture). Problem-centered messages reflect a willingness to collaborate, to work together to resolve the issue. Examples of problem-oriented statements include "What do you think we ought to do?" and "I believe we can work this out if we sit down and identify the issues."

Strategy Versus Spontaneity. Strategic communicators are seen as manipulators who try to hide their true motivations. They say they want to work with others yet withhold information and appear to be listening when they're not. This "false spontaneity" angers the rest of the group. On the other hand, behavior that is truly spontaneous and honest reduces defensiveness.

Neutrality Versus Empathy. Neutral messages such as "You'll get over it" and "Don't take it so seriously" imply that the listener doesn't care. Empathetic statements, such as "I can see why you would be depressed" and "I'll be thinking about you when you have that appointment with your boss," communicate reassurance and acceptance. Those who receive them enjoy a boost in self-esteem.

Superiority Versus Equality. Attempts at one-upmanship generally provoke immediate defensive responses. The comment "I got an A in my ethics class" is likely to be met with this kind of reply: "Well, you may have a lot of book learning, but I had to deal with a lot of real-world ethical problems when I worked at the advertising agency." Superiority can be based on a number of factors, including wealth, social class, organizational position, and power. All groups contain members who differ in their social standing and abilities. However, these differences are less disruptive if participants indicate that they want to work with others on an equal basis.

Certainty Versus Provisionalism. Dogmatic group members—those who are inflexible and claim to have all the answers—are unwilling to change or consider other points of view. As a consequence, they appear more interested in being right than in solving the problem. Listeners often perceive certainty as a mask for feelings of inferiority. In contrast to dogmatic individuals, provisional discussants signal that they are willing to work with the rest of the team in order to investigate issues and come up with a sound ethical decision.

Emotional Intelligence

Recognizing and managing emotions is essential to maintaining productive, healthy relationships in a group. Consider the negative impact of envy, for instance. Envy arises when people compare themselves to others and fall short. They then experience resentment, hostility, frustration, inferiority, longing, and ill will toward the envied individuals. Envy is common in organizations, which distribute assignments, raises, office space, and other resources unequally among members. However, this feeling may be even more frequent in teams because members know each other well and have more opportunity to engage in comparisons. Those who envy others in the group tend to reduce their efforts (see the earlier discussion of social loafing), are more likely to miss meetings, and are less satisfied with their group experience. The team as a whole is less cohesive and less successful.[15]

Experts assert that groups, like individuals, can learn how to cope with envy and other destructive feelings, as well as foster positive moods, through developing emotional intelligence. They also report that emotionally intelligent groups are more effective and productive.[16] Emotional intelligence consists of (1) being aware of and managing personal emotions and (2) recognizing and exerting influence on the emotions of others. Teams with high emotional intelligence (EI) effectively address three levels of emotions: individual, within the team, and between the team and outside groups.[17] At the individual level, they recognize when a member is distracted or defensive. They point out when someone's behavior (e.g., moodiness, tardiness) is disrupting the group and provide extra support for those who need it. At the group level, high-EI teams engage in continual self-evaluation to determine their emotional states. Members speak out when the team is discouraged, for instance, and build an affirmative climate. They develop resources like a common vocabulary and rituals to deal with unhealthy moods. For example, one executive team set 10 minutes aside for a "wailing wall." During these 10 minutes members could vent their frustrations. They then were ready to tackle the problems they faced.

Raising team EI is an important leadership responsibility, which is accomplished largely through role modeling and establishing norms. As leaders, we must demonstrate our personal emotional intelligence before we can hope to improve the emotional climate of the group. Effective leaders display emotions that are appropriate to the situation, refrain from hostility, are sensitive to group moods, and take the lead in confronting emotional issues. Confrontation can mean reminding a group member not to criticize new ideas; phoning a member between meetings to talk about his or her rude, dismissive behavior; removing insensitive individuals from the team; calling on quiet members to hear their opinions; or bringing the group together to discuss members' feelings of frustration or discouragement. Modeling such behaviors is critical to establishing healthy emotional norms or habits in the team, like speaking up when the group is discouraged or unproductive and celebrating collective victories. One list of group emotional norms can be found in Box 8.1.

● ● ● BOX 8.1 GROUP EMOTIONAL NORMS ● ● ●

Norms That Create Awareness of Emotions

Interpersonal Understanding

1. Take time away from group tasks to get to know one another.
2. Have a "check-in" at the beginning of the meeting—that is, ask how everyone is doing.
3. Assume that undesirable behavior takes place for a reason. Find out what that reason is. Ask questions and listen. Avoid negative attributions.
4. Tell your teammates what you're thinking and how you're feeling.

Team Self-Evaluation

1. Schedule time to examine team effectiveness.
2. Create measurable task and process objectives and then measure them.
3. Acknowledge and discuss group moods.
4. Communicate your sense of what is transpiring in the team.
5. Allow members to call a "process check." (For instance, a team member might say, "Process check: Is this the most effective use of our time right now?")

Organizational Understanding

1. Find out the concerns and needs of others in the organization.

2. Consider who can influence the team's ability to accomplish its goals.

3. Discuss the culture and politics in the organization.

4. Ask whether proposed team actions are congruent with the organization's culture and politics.

Norms That Help Regulate Emotions

Confronting

1. Set ground rules and use them to point out errant behavior.

2. Call members out on errant behavior.

3. Create playful devices for pointing out such behavior. These often emerge from the group spontaneously. Reinforce them.

Caring

1. Support members: Volunteer to help them if they need it, be flexible, and provide emotional support.

2. Validate members' contributions. Let members know they are valued.

3. Protect members from attack.

4. Respect individuality and differences in perspectives. Listen.

5. Never be derogatory or demeaning.

Creating Resources for Working With Emotions

1. Make time to discuss difficult issues and address the emotions that surround them.

2. Find creative, shorthand ways to acknowledge and express the emotion in the group.

3. Create fun ways to acknowledge and relieve stress and tension.

4. Express acceptance of members' emotions.

(Continued)

(Continued)

Creating an Affirmative Environment

1. Reinforce that the team can meet a challenge. For example, say things like "We can get through this" or "Nothing will stop us."

2. Focus on what you can control.

3. Remind members of the group's important and positive mission.

4. Remind members how the group solved a similar problem before.

5. Focus on problem solving, not blaming.

Building External Relationships

1. Create opportunities for networking and interaction.

2. Ask about the needs of other teams.

3. Provide support for other teams.

4. Invite others to team meetings if they might have a stake in what you are doing.

SOURCE: Condensed from Durskat, V. U., & Wolff, S. B. (2001, March). Building the emotional intelligence of groups. *Harvard Business Review*, pp. 80–90. Used by permission of the publisher.

Productive Conflict

In healthy groups, members examine and debate the merits of the proposal before the group, a task-related process that experts call *substantive (constructive) conflict.*[18] Substantive conflicts produce a number of positive outcomes, including these:

- Accurate understanding of the arguments and positions of others in the group

- Higher-level moral reasoning

- Thorough problem analysis

- Improved self-understanding and self-improvement

- Stronger, deeper relationships

- Creativity and change

- Greater motivation to solve the problem

- Improved mastery and retention of information

- Deeper commitment to the outcome of the discussion

- Increased group cohesion and cooperation

- Improved ability to deal with future conflicts

- High-quality solutions that integrate the perspectives of all members

It is important to differentiate between substantive conflict and *affective (destructive) conflict,* which is centered on the personal relationships between group members. Those caught in personality-based conflicts find themselves either trying to avoid the problem or, when the conflict can't be ignored, escalating hostilities through name-calling, sarcasm, threats, and other unethical means. (Complete Self-Assessment 8.2 to determine whether your group engages in substantive or affective conflict.) In this poisoned environment, members aren't as committed to the group process, sacrifice in-depth discussion of the problem in order to get done as soon as possible, and distance themselves from the decision. The end result? A decline in moral reasoning that produces an unpopular, low-quality solution.

Sometimes constructive conflict degenerates into affective conflict.[19] This occurs when disagreement about ideas is seen as an insult or a threat and members display anger because they feel their self-concepts are threatened. Others respond in kind. Members can also become frustrated when task-oriented conflicts seem to drag on and on without resolution. There are a number of ways that you as a leader can encourage substantive conflict while preventing it from being "corrupted" into affective conflict. Begin by paying attention to the membership of the group. Form teams made up of people with significantly different backgrounds. Groups concerned with medical ethics, for example, generally include members from both inside the medical profession (nurses, surgeons, hospital administrators) and outside (theologians, ethicists, government officials).

Next, lay down some procedural ground rules—a conflict covenant—before discussion begins. Come up with a list of conflict guideposts as a group: "Absolutely no name-calling or threats." "No idea is a dumb idea." "Direct all critical comments toward the problem, not the person." "You must repeat the message of the previous speaker—to that person's satisfaction—before you can add your comments." Highlight the fact that conflict about ideas is an integral part of group discussion and caution against hasty decisions. Encourage individuals to stand firm instead of capitulating. This is also a good time to remind members of the importance of cooperation and emotional intelligence. Groups that emphasize shared goals view conflict as a mutual problem that needs everyone's attention. As a result, team members feel more confident dealing with conflict, and collective performance improves.[20] Teams that demonstrate high levels of EI are also more equipped to manage conflict and therefore perform better. In particular, if members can collectively control their emotions, they listen more closely to opposing ideas and seek the best solution without being upset when their proposals are rejected.[21]

During the discussion, make sure that members follow their conflict covenant and don't engage in conflict avoidance or escalation. Stop to revisit the ground rules when necessary. Be prepared to support your position. Challenge and analyze the arguments of others as you encourage them to do the same. If members get stuck in a battle of wills, reframe the discussion by asking such questions as "What kind of information would help you change your mind?" "Why shouldn't we pursue other options?" or "What would you do if you were in my position?"[22] You can also ask participants to develop new ways to describe their ideas (in graphs, as numbers, as bulleted lists) and ask them to step back and revisit their initial assumptions in order to find common ground.

After the decision is made, ensure that the team and its members will continue to develop their conflict management skills. Debrief the decision-making process to determine whether the group achieved its goals, work on repairing relationships that might have been bruised during the discussion, and celebrate or remember stories of outstanding conflict management.[23]

LEADERSHIP ETHICS AT THE MOVIES • • • • • • • • •

The Avengers

Key Cast Members: Robert Downey, Jr., Chris Evans, Mark Ruffalo, Scarlett Johansson, Chris Hemsworth, Samuel L. Jackson

Synopsis: In this science fiction blockbuster based on Marvel Comics characters, a group of superheroes known as the Avengers stands between Earth and hostile forces from another planet. However, before they can battle the extraterrestrials out to subjugate humankind, Iron Man (Downey), Captain America (Evans), the Hulk (Ruffalo), and other team members must first stop fighting among themselves. They finally manage to unite, successfully combining their unique powers to repel the invaders.

Engaging in Effective Argument

Making arguments is the best way to influence others when the group is faced with a controversial decision. That's why argumentative people are more likely to emerge as leaders.[24] An argument is an assertion or a claim that is supported by evidence and reasons. In the argumentation process, group members interact with each other using claims, evidence, and reasoning in hopes of reaching the best decision. They avoid the personal attacks that characterize affective conflicts.

Argumentation in a small group is not as formal and sophisticated as a legal brief or a debate at a college forensics tournament. In more formal settings, there are strict limits on such things as how long arguers can speak, what evidence they can introduce, how they should address the audience, and how the argument should be constructed. Argumentation in a group is much less structured. No one enforces time limits for individual speakers, and members may interrupt each other and get off track. Nonetheless, when leading a group, you'll have to make sure the group carries out the same basic tasks as the members of a university debate team.[25]

The first task is to identify just what the controversy is about. All too often teams waste their time debating the wrong issues and end up solving the wrong problem. In Case Study 8.1, the controversy surrounds boosting benefits for college athletes. The commission must determine its response to the following assertion: "The NCAA should provide college athletes with more benefits." The decision is *not* a referendum on the role of sports in American society or on whether the NCAA should be abolished (although some critics argue that it should be).

Once the controversy is clearly identified, you need to assemble and present your arguments. As I noted earlier, an argument consists of a claim supported by evidence and reasons. Back up your claim with examples, personal experience, testimonials from others, and statistics. Also, supply reasons or logic for your position. The most common patterns of logic include *analogical* (drawing similarities between one case and another, as we saw in Chapter 6), *causal* (one event leads to another), *inductive* (generalizing from one or a few cases to many), and *deductive* (moving from a larger category or grouping to a smaller one).

You could use all four types of reasoning if you believe that college athletes ought to be paid. You might note that college athletes are employees of the university and deserve the same benefits as other workers (analogical reasoning). You could argue that the current system drives up coaches' salaries while taking advantage of players (causal reasoning). You could illustrate the likely advantages of paying players by pointing to how this practice has helped Olympic athletes. They, too, used to be treated as amateurs but now can earn money from their sports (inductive reasoning). You might note that the push for more benefits for athletes is a natural outcome of the growth of college sports (deductive reasoning).

While you formulate your position, you need to identify and attack the weaknesses in the positions of other participants. This process is often neglected during group discussions. Group communication experts Dennis Gouran and Randy Hirokawa found that undetected errors are the primary cause of poor-quality decisions.[26] These errors include incomplete data, accepting bad information as fact, selecting only the information that supports a flawed choice, rejecting valid evidence, poor reasoning, and making unreasonable inferences from the facts. Be on the lookout for the common errors in evidence and reasoning listed in Box 8.2. According to Gouran and Hirokawa, all groups make mistakes, but members of successful groups catch their errors and get their groups back on track through corrective communication called *counteractive influence*.

• • • BOX 8.2 COMMON FALLACIES • • •

Faulty Evidence

Unreliable and biased sources

Sources lacking proper knowledge and background

Inconsistency (disagrees with other sources, source contradicts him- or herself)

Outdated evidence

Evidence that appears to support a claim but does not

Information gathered from secondhand observers

Uncritical acceptance of statistical data

Inaccurate or incomplete citation of sources and quotations

Plagiarism (using the ideas or words of others without proper attribution)

Faulty Reasoning

Comparing two things that are not alike (false analogy)

Drawing conclusions based on too few examples or examples that aren't typical of the population as a whole (hasty generalization)

Believing that the event that happens first always causes the event that happens second (false cause)

Arguing that complicated problems have only one cause (single cause)

Assuming without evidence that one event will inevitably lead to a bad result (slippery slope)

Using the argument to support the argument (begging the question)

Failing to offer evidence that supports the position (non sequitur)

Attacking the person instead of the argument (ad hominem)

Appealing to the crowd or popular opinion (ad populum)

Resisting change based on past practices (appeal to tradition)

Attacking a weakened version of an opponent's argument (straw argument)

SOURCE: Inch, E. S., Warnick, B., & Endres, D. (2006). *Critical thinking and communication: The use of reason in argument* (5th ed.). Boston: Pearson.

Minority Opinion

As we'll see in the next section of the chapter, hearing from members who take issue with the prevailing group opinion is essential if the team is to avoid moral failure. Further, minority dissent can significantly improve group performance.[27] A team with minority members generally comes up with a superior solution even if the group doesn't change its collective mind. If there is no minority opinion, members focus on one solution. They have little reason to explore the problem in depth, so they disregard novel solutions and quickly converge on one position. Minorities cast doubt on group consensus, stimulating more thought about the dilemma. Members exert more effort because they must resolve the conflict between the majority and minority solutions. They pay closer attention to all aspects of the issue, consider more viewpoints, are more willing to share information, and employ a wider variety of problem-solving strategies. Such divergent thinking produces more creative, higher-quality solutions. When minority dissent is present across a range of groups, the organization as a whole is more innovative. Minorities also block groups from making harmful changes or adopting extreme positions. Responding to the dissenting views of minorities encourages team members to resist conformity in other settings.[28]

Minorities can have an immediate, powerful impact on group opinion under certain conditions. Minorities are most likely to influence the rest of the group when the members are still formulating their positions on an issue, when dissenters can clearly demonstrate the superiority of their stance, and when minorities can frame their positions to fit into the values and beliefs of the group. Well-respected dissenters who consistently advocate for their positions are generally more persuasive. However, more often than not, minority influence is slow and indirect.[29] Majorities initially reject the dissenters' ideas but, over time, forget the source of the arguments and focus instead on the merits of their proposals. This can gradually convert them to the minority viewpoint. At other times, minorities aren't successful at convincing members to go along with them on one issue but shape their opinions on related issues. For example, in one experiment, a minority advocating for homosexuals to serve openly in the military did not change opinions on that topic but did influence attitudes toward gun control, a related subject.[30]

Being in the minority is tough because it runs contrary to our strong desire to be liked and accepted by others. Those who take a minority position are frequently the targets of dislike or disdain. Leaders, then, need to both foster minority opinion and protect dissenters. You can do so by taking these steps:[31]

1. Form groups made up of members who have significantly different backgrounds and perspectives.

2. Encourage participation from all group members.

3. Appoint individuals to argue for an alternative point of view.

4. Develop two options for group members to evaluate based on two different sets of assumptions.

5. Remind members of the importance of minority views.

6. Create a group learning orientation that is more focused on finding better solutions than on defending one position or another.

7. Offer dissenters your support.

Avoiding Moral Pitfalls

Even with positive interaction, moral traps or pitfalls can arise during the course of the group's discussion that will derail the decision-making process. As team members communicate, leaders need to help the group steer clear of the following dangers: groupthink, mismanaged or false agreement, and escalating commitment.

Groupthink

Social psychologist Irving Janis believed that cohesion is the greatest obstacle faced by groups charged with making effective, ethical decisions. He developed the label *groupthink* to describe groups that put unanimous agreement ahead of reasoned problem solving. Groups suffering from this symptom are both ineffective and unethical.[32] They fail to (a) consider all the alternatives, (b) gather additional information, (c) reexamine a course of action when it's not working, (d) carefully weigh risks, (e) work out contingency plans, or (f) discuss important moral issues. Janis first noted faulty thinking in small groups of ordinary citizens—such as an antismoking support group that decided that quitting was impossible. He captured the attention of fellow scholars and the public through his analysis of major U.S. policy disasters such as the failure to anticipate the attack on Pearl Harbor, the invasion of North Korea, the Bay of Pigs fiasco, and the escalation of the Vietnam War. In each of these incidents, some of the brightest (and presumably most ethically minded) political and military leaders in our nation's history made terrible choices.

Janis identified the following as symptoms of groupthink. The greater the number of these characteristics displayed by a group, the greater the likelihood that members have made cohesiveness their top priority.

Signs of Overconfidence

- *Illusion of invulnerability.* Members are overly optimistic and prone to take extraordinary risks.

- *Belief in the inherent morality of the group.* Participants ignore the ethical consequences of their actions and decisions.

Signs of Closed-Mindedness

- *Collective rationalization.* Group members invent rationalizations to protect themselves from any feedback that would challenge their operating assumptions.

- *Stereotypes of outside groups.* Group members underestimate the capabilities of other groups (armies, citizens, teams), thinking that people in these groups are weak or stupid.

Signs of Group Pressure

- *Pressure on dissenters.* Dissenters are coerced to go along with the prevailing opinion in the group.

- *Self-censorship.* Individuals keep their doubts about group decisions to themselves.

- *Illusion of unanimity.* Because members keep quiet, the group mistakenly assumes that everyone agrees on a course of action.

- *Self-appointed mind guards.* Certain members take it on themselves to protect the leader and others from dissenting opinions that might disrupt the group's consensus.

The risk of groupthink increases when teams made up of members from similar backgrounds are isolated from contact with other groups. The risks increase still further when group members are under stress (due to recent failure, for instance) and follow a leader who pushes one particular solution. Self-directed work teams (SDWTs), described in more detail in "Focus on Follower Ethics: Self-Leadership in Self-Managed Teams," are particularly vulnerable to groupthink. Members, working under strict time limits, are often isolated and undertrained. They may fail at first, and the need to function as a cohesive unit may blind them to ethical dilemmas.[33]

FOCUS ON FOLLOWER ETHICS

Self-Leadership in Self-Managed Teams

An estimated 90% of all U.S. firms employ self-directed work teams (SDWTs) or another form of self-managed groups.[1] An SDWT is made up of 6 to 10 employees from a variety of departments who manage themselves and their tasks. SDWTs operate much like small businesses within the larger organization, overseeing the development of a service or product from start to finish. SDWTs have been credited with improving everything from workplace attendance and morale to productivity and product quality. In self-directed work teams, individual members have more responsibilities than they do in traditional groups where leaders make the decisions. Those in SDWTs are involved in additional tasks (e.g., staffing, evaluation, scheduling), and they have to develop new knowledge and skills to carry out these duties. Further, the ultimate success of the team now rests with followers, not leaders. In self-directed groups it is more important than ever that followers meet their ethical obligation to complete their work.

Business experts Christopher Neck and Charles Manz believe that self-leadership is key to living up to our duties as followers. Self-leadership is the process of exercising influence over our thoughts, attitudes, and behaviors and is key not just to our individual success as followers but to team success as well. According to Neck and Manz, "Self-leadership is just as important when you are working in a team as when you are working alone. . . . In fact, only by effectively leading yourself as a team member can you help the team lead itself, reach its potential, and thus achieve synergy" (p. 82).

There are three key components to self-leadership. First, we need to lead ourselves to do unattractive but necessary tasks. Altering our immediate worlds and exercising direct control over the self can accomplish this objective. World-altering strategies include (1) using physical reminders and cues (notes, lists, objects) to focus our attention on important tasks; (2) removing negative cues, such as those that are distracting; (3) identifying and increasing positive cues (pleasant settings, music) that encourage us to undertake the work; and (4) associating with other people who reinforce our desirable behavior. Self-control strategies include observing, recording, and analyzing our use of desirable and undesirable behaviors; setting short- and long-term goals; determining our ultimate purpose; rewarding our achievements; and engaging in physical and mental practice to improve performance.

The second component of self-leadership is taking advantage of naturally rewarding activities. Some activities make us feel competent and in control and supply us with a sense of purpose. We don't need external motivation to get us to read a novel, for example, or to play a game of pickup basketball, knit, or paint, if we find these hobbies enjoyable. When we build natural rewards into our endeavors, we are more likely to complete them. For instance, if we enjoy interacting with others, we can make sure that we leave time for informal talk during team meetings. We can also focus on the naturally rewarding aspects of our tasks instead

(Continued)

Irving Janis made several suggestions for reducing groupthink. If you're appointed as the group's leader, avoid expressing a preference for a particular solution. Divide regularly into subgroups and then bring the entire group back together to negotiate differences. Bring in outsiders—experts or colleagues—to challenge the group's ideas. Avoid isolation, keeping in contact with other groups. Role-play the reactions of other groups and organizations to reduce the effects of stereotyping and rationalization. Once the decision has been made, give group members one last chance to express any remaining doubts about the decision. Janis points to the ancient Persians as an example of how to revisit decisions. The Persians made every major decision twice—once while sober and again while under the influence of wine!

A number of investigators have explored the causes and prevention of groupthink.[34] They have discovered that a group is in greatest danger when the leader actively promotes his or her agenda and when it doesn't have any procedures in place (like those described in Chapter 6) for solving problems. With this in mind, don't offer your opinions as a leader but solicit ideas from group members instead. Make sure that the group adopts a decision-making format before discussing an ethical problem.

There are two structured approaches specifically designed to build disagreement or conflict into the decision-making process to reduce the likelihood of groupthink.[35] In the devil's advocate technique, an individual or a subgroup is assigned to criticize the group's decision. The individual's or subgroup's goal is to highlight potential problems with the group's assumptions, logic, evidence, and recommendations. Following the critique, the team gathers additional information and adopts, modifies, or discontinues the proposed course of action. In the dialectic inquiry method, a subgroup or the team as a whole develops a solution. After the group identifies the underlying assumptions of the proposal, selected group members develop a counterproposal based on a different set of assumptions. Advocates of each position present and debate the merits of their proposals. The team or outside decision makers determine whether to adopt one position or the other, integrate the plans, or opt for a different solution altogether. Both approaches can take more than one round to complete. For example, a team may decide to submit a second plan for critique or present several counterproposals before reaching a conclusion.

Charles Manz and his colleagues believe that self-managing work teams should replace groupthink with "teamthink."[36] In teamthink, groups encourage divergent views, combining the open expression of concerns and doubts with a healthy respect for their limitations. The teamthink process is an extension of *thought self-leadership,* introduced earlier. Like individuals, groups can improve their performance (lead themselves) by adopting constructive thought patterns: visualizing successful performances, eliminating critical and destructive self-talk, and challenging unrealistic assumptions.

Teamthink, like thought self-leadership, is a combination of mental imagery, self-dialogue, and realistic thinking. Members of successful groups use mental imagery to visualize how they will complete a project and jointly establish a common vision ("to provide better housing to the homeless," "to develop the best new software package for the company"). When talking with each other (self-dialogue), leaders and followers are particularly careful not to put pressure on deviant members, and, at the same time, they encourage divergent views.

Teamthink members challenge three forms of faulty reasoning that are common to small groups. The first is all-or-nothing thinking. If a risk doesn't seem threatening, too many groups dismiss it and proceed without a backup plan. In contrast, teamthink groups realistically assess the dangers and anticipate possible setbacks. The second common form of faulty group thinking, described earlier, is the assumption that the team is inherently moral. Groups in the grip of this misconception think that anything they do (including lying and sabotaging the work of other groups) is justified. Ethically insensitive, they don't stop to consider the moral implications of their decisions. Teamthink groups avoid this trap, questioning their motivations and raising ethical issues. The third faulty group assumption is the conviction that the task is too difficult, that the obstacles are too great to overcome. Effective, ethical groups instead view obstacles as opportunities and focus their efforts on reaching and implementing decisions.

False Agreement

George Washington University management professor Jerry Harvey offers an alternative to groupthink based on *false agreement*.[37] Harvey believes that blaming group pressure is just an excuse for our individual shortcomings. He calls this the *Gunsmoke* myth. In this myth, the lone Western sheriff (Matt Dillon in the radio and television series) stands down a mob of armed townsfolk out to lynch his prisoner. If group tyranny is really at work, Harvey argues, Dillon stands no chance. After all, he is outnumbered 100 to 1 and could be felled with a single bullet from one rioter. The mob disbands because its members really didn't want to lynch the prisoner in the first place. Harvey contends that falling prey to the *Gunsmoke* myth is immoral because as long as we can blame our peers, we don't have to accept personal responsibility as group members. In reality, we always have a choice as to how to respond.

Professor Harvey introduces the Abilene paradox as an alternative to the *Gunsmoke* myth. He describes a time when his family decided to drive (without air conditioning) 100 miles across the desert from their home in Coleman, Texas, to Abilene to eat dinner. After returning home, family members discovered that no one had really wanted to make the trip. Each agreed to go to Abilene based on the assumption that everyone else in the group was enthusiastic about eating out. Harvey believes that organizations and small groups, like his family, also take needless "trips." An example of the Abilene paradox would be teams who carry out illegal activities that everyone in the group is uneasy about. Five psychological factors account for the paradox:

1. *Action anxiety.* Group members know what should be done but are too anxious to speak up.

2. *Negative fantasies.* Action anxiety is driven in part by the negative fantasies members have about what will happen if they voice their opinions. These fantasies ("I'll be fired or branded as disloyal") serve as an excuse for not attacking the problem.

3. *Real risk.* There are risks to expressing dissent: getting fired, losing income, damaging relationships. However, most of the time the danger is not as great as we think.

4. *Fear of separation.* Alienation and loneliness constitute the most powerful force behind the paradox. Group members fear being cut off or separated from others. To escape this fate, they cheat, lie, break the law, and so forth.

5. *Psychological reversal of risk and certainty.* Being trapped in the Abilene paradox means confusing fantasy with real risk. This confusion produces a self-fulfilling prophecy. Caught up in the fantasy that something bad may happen, decision makers act in a way that fulfills the fantasy. For instance, group members may support a project with no chances of success because they are afraid they will be fired or demoted if they don't. Ironically, they are likely to be fired or demoted anyway when the flawed project fails.

Breaking out of the paradox begins with diagnosing its symptoms in your group or organization. If the group is headed in the wrong direction, call a meeting where you own up to your true feelings and invite feedback and encourage others to do the same. (Of course, you must confront your fear of being separated from the rest of the group to take this step.) The team may immediately come up with a better approach or engage in extended conflict that generates a more creative solution. You might suffer for your honesty, but you could be rewarded for saying what everyone else was thinking. In any case, you'll feel better about yourself for speaking up.

Escalation of Commitment

One of the consequences of mismanaged agreement is continuing to pursue a failed course of action. Social psychologists refer to this tendency as *escalation of commitment.* Instead of cutting their losses, individuals and groups continue to "throw good money after bad," pouring in more resources. Costs multiply until the moment that the team admits defeat or an outside agency intervenes.[38] Escalation of commitment is a moral trap because it wastes time, money, and effort; threatens the health of the group and the organization; fails to meet important needs; and can even result in significant loss of life. Escalating commitment helps explain why state agencies continue to implement defective software programs, promoters put more money into advertising unpopular music acts, and investors buy additional shares of declining stocks. History is replete with well-publicized examples of this phenomenon, including the automated baggage system at the Denver International Airport (which delayed the opening of the facility and never worked) and the Taurus automated London Stock Exchange system that had to be scrapped. Escalation played a key role in the K2 incident described in Case Study 8.3. Climbers continued to summit even when they should have turned back because they were so close to reaching the top. Many also had corporate sponsors and felt additional pressure to succeed.

Escalation of commitment is driven by a number of factors.[39] The first is *self-enhancement,* or the need to look good. Decision makers are compelled to justify their prior investments, so they reinvest in the original project in order to demonstrate that their initial choice was correct. They deny negative feedback and concentrate on defending past choices instead of focusing on future outcomes as they ought to. Group members find it hard to admit failure publicly because doing so threatens their identity or suggests that they are incompetent. Occasionally groups escalate in order to show off, as in the case of a company that buys another firm just to demonstrate that it is an important player in the industry.

Sunk costs also drive escalation. It's hard emotionally for group members to give up on previous investments even though such costs cannot influence future outcomes. Imagine, for example, you have two frozen dinners in your freezer, both of which have reached their "use by" date. The dinners are the same except for their price tags. If one cost $3 and the other $5, you will likely choose the more expensive meal for dinner because it seems less wasteful. However, it should make no difference which meal you choose since the dinners are already purchased and your money is spent. Sunk costs help explain why those near the end of a project are more likely to spend additional funds to finish it. In addition, sunk costs can encourage teams to become overoptimistic. The presence of the previous investment tempts decision makers to inflate their estimates of future success. Then, too, decision makers often labor under the illusion of control. They believe that they can control events—business trends, employee behavior, the weather—that are outside their influence.[40]

Risk seeking is a third factor driving escalation. When faced with decisions between two losses, individuals tend to take bigger risks than warranted. They stay the course because they believe that continuing in business or putting more money into the software project will enable them to recoup their losses. They are like the gambler who goes to the horse track and loses $95 of the $100 he intended to bet. When the last race of the day is run, he bets on a long shot, hoping to win back his entire $95.00. He would be much better off making a safer bet and winning back some of his losses instead. Group interaction can magnify the tendency to take risks because responsibility for the choice is dispersed among group members.

Management professors Mark Keil and Ramiro Montealegre offer insights to leaders who want to help their teams de-escalate from a failed course of action. De-escalation begins with recognizing that there is a problem, followed by reexamining the prior course of action, then searching for alternative courses of action, and finally planning an exit strategy. Keil and Montealegre offer seven steps to help leaders and groups navigate this process:[41]

1. *Don't ignore negative feedback or external pressure.* These are signs that something is amiss. Recognizing these signs early on can greatly reduce escalation costs.

2. *Hire an external auditor.* Bringing in an outside expert or fresh "set of eyes" can help the group recognize the extent of the problem. A consultant can also recommend action that would be difficult for insiders to suggest.

3. *Don't be afraid to withhold further funding.* Don't provide additional money until more information can be gathered. Withholding funding is a sign to others that something is wrong and also reasserts the leader's control over the project.

4. *Look for opportunities to redefine the problem.* Seek creative solutions and identify additional alternatives. Encourage team members to express their concerns.

5. *Manage impressions.* Help group members to save face by putting the blame on others (if appropriate), by relying on the recommendations of consultants, and by the taking blame yourself.

6. *Prepare your stakeholders.* Warn important stakeholders in the project that you may be shutting it down. Consult with them to get their input.

7. *Deinstitutionalize the project.* Move the project from the "core" of the firm to the periphery. That might mean, for example, physically relocating the project or de-emphasizing the importance of the project to the group or organization. In the case of the Denver airport baggage system, city officials and the airlines agreed to open the complex without the new system, thus making baggage handling less important to the airport as a whole.

Establishing Ethical Relationships With Other Groups

So far our focus has been on how leaders can encourage ethical behavior within their groups. Yet groups rarely operate in isolation. The typical organization is made of subgroups, not individuals, for example. If the organization is to succeed, these teams must coordinate their actions. Leaders must foster ethical interaction between, as well as within, teams. *Intergroup leadership* is the process of bringing diverse groups together to achieve common goals. Intergroup leadership is becoming increasingly important as organizations decentralize and rely more on teams.[42] In the past, coordinating group activities was the duty of top executives. Now lower-level leaders must redesign work processes, share information, coordinate patient care and curriculum decisions, develop fund-raising campaigns, and so on.

Competition and conflict are significant barriers to intergroup leadership. Often the organizational units being asked to work together have been competing for staff, money, office space, and other organizational resources. These groups may also differ in status. Take the case of a business acquisition, for instance. Members of the company being acquired are at a significant disadvantage when compared to their colleagues at the parent firm. They may feel alienated, believing that the dominant group is imposing its policies and values on them.

However, group identity is the major obstacle to intergroup leadership. Individuals who define themselves as students, business majors, teachers, accountants, managers, executives, or engineers find it hard to collaborate with those of other identities.

Intergroup leadership expert Todd Pittinsky offers five strategies or pathways to collaboration.[43] Pathway 1 is encouraging intergroup contact. Groups in conflict rarely come into contact with each other, so leaders must bring diverse teams together. Such contact can break down stereotypes and foster liking. Nonetheless, interacting with outsiders does not guarantee that group members will develop positive feelings about their counterparts in other groups. Negative interaction, such as when members of the parent company act in a condescending manner toward members of the acquired firm, can reinforce stereotypes and generate further hostility. Try to lay the groundwork for positive contacts by emphasizing that the teams need to work together to achieve a superordinate or shared objective like instituting a change initiative.

Pathway 2 is managing conflicts over resources by fostering trust. Act in a trustworthy fashion and elicit cooperative behaviors from both groups.

Pathway 3 is creating a superordinate identity. Encourage team members to see themselves as part of a larger organization, which helps break down the "us versus them" mentality. Outline a shared vision and continually emphasize the importance of coordination. Politicians in the United States use this tactic when they emphasize that, while we have our differences, we are all Americans.

Pathway 4 is promoting dual identities. At the same time you highlight shared overarching goals and memberships, encourage subgroups to maintain their distinctive identities. To put it another way, help create *intergroup relational identity*.[44] Effective intergroup leaders help team members recognize that they are part of a larger organization but, at the same time, retain their identities as members of subgroups. Encourage followers to see themselves as members of teams that operate in relationship with other teams. Back up your rhetoric by acting as a boundary spanner.[45] Bridge or span groups by having frequent contact with each team and developing positive relationships with individuals from every group. Be careful not to favor one group over another. Ultimately your goal is to embody intergroup relational identity because you are seen as leading both teams, not one group or another. Serve as a role model for cooperation.

Pathway 5 is attacking negative attitudes while promoting positive attitudes.[46] At the same time you promote liking through intergroup contact and other means, address negative attitudes. Help followers overcome their dislike of other groups by challenging stereotypes and encouraging them to live up to such values as equality and justice. Pearl Fryar of Bishopville, South Carolina, provides one example of someone who combated a negative stereotype and reduced disliking between racial groups. Whites objected when Fryar, an

African American, wanted to move into their neighborhood because they believed Black people didn't take care of their yards. Fryar proved them wrong by making his property into a topiary garden filled with plant sculptures. He became the first African American to win the town's Garden of the Month award, and his artistic creations became the centerpiece of a major revitalization effort for his small southern town.

IMPLICATIONS AND APPLICATIONS

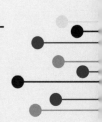

- As a leader, you will do much of your work in committees, boards, task forces, and other small groups. Making ethical choices is one of a team's most important responsibilities. Your task is to foster the conditions that promote effective, ethical decisions.

- Because destructive behavior on the part of just one member can derail the group process, encourage participants to take their ethical responsibilities seriously. Promote commitment to shared goals and take steps to minimize social loafing.

- Expect to spend most of your time in a group listening rather than speaking. Model effective comprehensive, critical listening behaviors that overcome distractions, biases, and other listening barriers.

- Build a positive group climate through supportive messages that are descriptive, problem oriented, spontaneous, empathetic, focused on equality, and provisional.

- Model emotional regulation and encourage the development of positive norms that address the needs of individuals, the team, and outside groups.

- To improve problem solving, foster substantive or task-oriented conflict about ideas and opinions. Set ground rules to help the group avoid affective (relational) conflict involving personalities.

- Encourage effective argument based on clearly identifying the controversy, assembling and presenting arguments, and addressing the weaknesses of opposing arguments.

- Foster minority opinion in order to promote creative, higher-quality solutions.

- An overemphasis on group cohesion is a significant threat to ethical decision making. Be alert for the symptoms of groupthink. These include signs of overconfidence (illusion of invulnerability, belief in the inherent morality of the group), signs of closed-mindedness (collective rationalization, stereotypes of outside groups), and signs of group pressure (pressure on dissenters, self-censorship, illusion of unanimity, and self-appointed mind guards).

- The devil's advocate and dialectic inquiry methods are two ways to build in disagreement and reduce the likelihood of groupthink.

- Avoid false agreement or consensus by speaking out if you are concerned about the group's direction.

- Continuing in a failed course of action wastes time and resources. Help your team de-escalate by paying close attention to negative feedback, bringing in outsiders, withholding further funding, redefining the problem, and moving the project to the periphery of the organization.

- As a leader, you will need to help your team establish ethical relationships with other groups. Act as an intergroup leader in order to bring diverse groups together to achieve common goals. Help team members see themselves as part of a larger organization or community while retaining their identities as members of subgroups. Become a boundary spanner; model cooperation.

FOR FURTHER EXPLORATION, CHALLENGE, AND SELF-ASSESSMENT

1. Interview a leader at your school or in another organization to develop a "meeting profile" for this person. Find out how much time this individual spends in meetings during an average week and whether this is typical of other leaders in the same organization. Identify the types of meetings she or he attends and her or his role. Determine whether ethical issues are part of these discussions. As part of your profile, record your reactions. Are you surprised by your findings? Has this assignment changed your understanding of what leaders do?

2. Brainstorm strategies for encouraging commitment to shared goals in a group that you lead or belong to. What steps can you take to implement these strategies?

3. Evaluate the level of social loafing in your group using Self-Assessment 8.1. What factors encourage members to reduce their efforts? What can you as a leader do to raise the motivation level of participants?

4. Evaluate a recent ethical decision made by one of your groups. Was it a high-quality decision? Why or why not? What factors contributed to the group's success or failure? How did the leader (you or someone else) shape the outcome, for better or worse? How would you evaluate your performance as a leader or team member? Write up your analysis.

5. Develop a plan for becoming a better listener in a group. Implement your plan and then evaluate your progress.

6. Use the self-leadership strategies in "Focus on Follower Ethics: Self-Leadership in Self-Managed Teams" to develop a strategy for carrying out your team responsibilities.

7. Have you ever been part of a group that was victimized by groupthink? If so, which symptoms were present? How did they affect the group's ethical decisions and actions? Does the Abilene paradox (false agreement) offer a better explanation for what happened?

8. Draw from current events to create an escalation of commitment case study. Describe what happened, why the group continued in a failed course of action, and the de-escalation process (if any). Identify what lessons can be learned from this case.

9. Identify forms of faulty evidence and reasoning in a public argument about an ethical issue. Draw from talk shows, newspaper editorials, speeches, interviews, debates, congressional hearings, and other sources. Possible topics might include national health care, stem cell research, illegal immigration, gun control, and reducing the national debt.

10. With other team members, develop a conflict covenant. Determine how you will enforce this code. Or, as an alternative, complete Self-Assessment 8.2, the Task/Relationship Conflict Scale, as a group and develop strategies for engaging in more substantive conflict.

11. Fishbowl discussion: In a fishbowl discussion, one group discusses a problem while the rest of the class looks on and then provides feedback. Assign a group to Case Study 8.1 or 8.2. Make sure that each discussant has one or more observers who specifically note his or her behavior. When the discussion is over, observers should meet with their "fish." Then the class as a whole should give its impressions of the overall performance of the team. Draw on the concepts discussed in this chapter when evaluating the work of individual participants and the group.

12. Evaluate your team's relationship with outside groups based on the last section of the chapter.

STUDENT STUDY SITE

Visit the student study site at **www.sagepub.com/johnsonmecl5e** to access full SAGE journal articles for further research and information on key chapter topics.

CASE STUDY 8.1

Pay for Play?

College athletics is very big business and getting bigger. The Division I public institutions of the National Collegiate Athletic Association (NCAA) spend $6.7 billion a year on their athletic programs. CBS and Turner Broadcasting signed a $10.8 billion deal with the NCAA to cover its Division I basketball tournament. ESPN reportedly will pay $608 million annually to broadcast the new NCAA football championship play-offs starting in 2014. At the same time, athletic conferences are expanding and establishing their own television networks. Schools also generate an estimated $4 billion each year through the sale of licensed merchandise associated with their sports teams.

Lucrative television contracts and other income streams have boosted coaches' salaries. The average salary package for NCAA Division I head football coaches is

$1.64 million, up 70% since 2006. This figure does not include such additional benefits as broadcast deals, shoe contracts, family travel expenses, game tickets, luxury suites, and cuts of stadium revenue, as well as free cars and country club memberships. Alabama's Nick Saban is the highest-paid college football coach, making $5.62 million a year. Pay for assistant football coaches has also skyrocketed in recent years.

While college athletics may be big business, college athletes are still treated as amateurs by the NCAA, which is chartered as a nonprofit organization. As a result, player benefits are restricted. Athletic scholarships—which are offered on a renewable, yearly basis— do not cover all the expenses of attending school, leaving athletes with a gap of between $200 and $6,000 per school year to cover out of their own pockets. Often the demands of their sports make it impossible for them to supplement their incomes with part-time work. (Limited funds are available to athletes for special educational needs and emergencies, although it took a lawsuit to increase access to these moneys.) More than 80% of college players on full scholarships live below the poverty line. Health care for athletes is also an issue. Many players have to provide their own health coverage or fall under university plans that don't cover the cost of injuries caused by athletic participation, leaving some former athletes thousands of dollars in debt. Unlike coaches, players can't change schools at will. They must forfeit a year of eligibility if they transfer.

The National College Players Association (NCPA), founded by former UCLA linebacker Ramogi Huma with the assistance of the United Steelworkers labor union, hopes to improve the financial standing (and safety) of college athletes. The organization claims to have pressured the NCAA into establishing a $10 million fund to assist former players, improving catastrophic health care coverage, and eliminating limits on the amount that players can earn from part-time jobs. It hopes to convince the NCAA to raise scholarship amounts, allow multiple-year scholarships, permit athletes to transfer one time without punishment, and provide better sports-related medical coverage. Some critics urge direct payment to players based on their sports and positions. Others, like the NCPA, argue that players should be able to sign endorsement deals and receive a portion of the royalties generated by jersey sales and the use of their images in video games. In an ongoing court case, former players are suing the NCAA in order to receive payment for appearing in rebroadcasts of past contests.

Proponents of paying athletes argue that it isn't fair that players receive so little when colleges, coaches, merchandisers, the NCAA, and others benefit so much from their labor. They use such terms as *sweatshop* and *indentured servitude* to describe playing conditions and the plight of college athletes. In the current system players often suffer genuine financial and physical hardship. Right now it is the athletes who "pay to play." Pay-for-play advocates also take issue with what they see as the NCAA's hypocrisy. The organization says it wants to promote student-athletes but operates like a corporation instead. According to Ramogi Huma, "The NCAA says one of its principles is to protect the athlete from commercial exploitation, then they turn around and exploit players for their commercial gain."[1] Current limits on scholarship amounts also make players more susceptible to illegal gifts from boosters and gamblers. Between 2001 and 2010 nearly half of all large college athletic programs were caught in NCAA rules violations. Said one former sports agent, "As long as you have a prohibition, you're going to have bootleggers."[2]

Those who support the current system hold fast to the ideal of amateur athletics. Said former NCAA president Myles Brand: "The NCAA historically has been against pay for play. I couldn't agree more with that position. If you start paying student-athletes (other than assisting them through financial aid), you essentially ruin the integrity of the college game."[3] Others argue that current scholarships are generous compared to what other students receive, and some players go on to highly lucrative pro careers. They note that most athletic programs lose money. Only a few sports generate surplus moneys, but athletes in all sports would have to be compensated, which would be prohibitively expensive. Additional costs would mean that some minor sports would have to be cut from university athletic programs. Under pay for play, the "rich would get richer," because the top football programs would be able to pay more for players than other schools.

Imagine that you are a member of a special commission convened to determine if the NCAA should provide college athletes with additional benefits (e.g., larger scholarships, salaries, profits from merchandise). You should come out of your discussion with a decision (including which, if any, additional benefits you would propose) and a list of reasons for your decision.

Notes

1. Kriegel, M. (2009, July 25). NCAA video game stance is pure hypocrisy. Fox Sports. Retrieved from http://msn.foxsports.com/collegefootball/story/NCAA-video-game-stance-is-pure-hypocrisy?r_src=ramp

2. Huma, R., & Staurowsky, E. J. (2012). The price of poverty in big time college sport. National College Players Association. Retrieved from http://assets.usw.org/ncpa/The-Price-of-Poverty-in-Big-Time-College-Sport.pdf

3. Whiteside, K. (2004, September 1). College athletes want cut of action. *USA Today*, p. 3C.

Sources

Berkowitz, S. (2012, November 21). Contract perks big deal for some football coaches. *USA Today*, p. 8C.

Brady, E., Berkowitz, S., & Upton, J. (2012, November 20). "Average" salary: $1.64 million. *USA Today*, p. 1A.

Carey, J., & Gardiner, A. (2008, January 30). Settlement gives aid to athletes. *USA Today*, p. 6C.

Ferguson, R. (2002, January 18). NCAA a "sweatshop," Steelworkers chief says. *Toronto Star*, p. E11.

Hiestand, M. (2012, November 16). ESPN opens checkbook for college bowl rights. *USA Today*, p. 3C.

Huma, R., Waters, T., & Staurowsky, E. J. (2009, March 26). Scholarship shortfall study reveals college athletes pay to play. National College Players Association, news release. Retrieved from http://www.ncpanow.org/releases_advisories?id=0009

Nocera, J. (2011, December 30). Let's start paying college athletes. *The New York Times.* Retrieved from http://www.nytimes.com

Peterson, K. (2009, July 16). After injuries, college athletes are often left to pay the bills. *The New York Times,* p. A1.

Raissman, B. (2008, March 21). Brackets of millions, players net nothing. *Daily News,* p. 93.

Sack, A. (2008, March 7). Should college athletes be paid? *The Christian Science Monitor,* Opinion, p. 9.

Upton, J., & Berkowitz, S. (2012, May 15). Budget disparity growing among NCAA Division I schools. *USA Today.* Retrieved from http://www.usatoday.com

Upton, J., & Wieberg, S. (2006, November 16). Million-dollar coaches move into mainstream. *USA Today,* p. 1A.

CASE STUDY 8.2

Weed and the Workplace

In 2012, voters in Colorado and Washington State voted to legalize the recreational use of marijuana. Residents of Colorado can possess up to an ounce of pot (although they can't smoke it in public) and grow up to six marijuana plants. Citizens of Washington can buy up to an ounce, and the state plans to tax pot sales and oversee a system of licensed growers, processors, and stores.

Passage of the recreational pot measures added to the legal confusion generated by earlier initiatives that decriminalized the medical use of marijuana. Eighteen states now permit patients to use pot prescribed by doctors for pain, nausea, muscle spasms, and other conditions. Such state statutes conflict with federal law, which classifies marijuana as a banned substance. Employers are caught in the middle. There are no federal guidelines for them to follow since the national government doesn't recognize that marijuana has any legitimate medical use. Firms with federal contracts must have zero-tolerance drug policies in place (this includes all colleges and universities receiving federal grants). Many other employers also have drug-free policies. For example, a Home Depot employee in Hawaii was told by his doctor to smoke a small amount of marijuana at night to relieve muscle stiffness and shooting pains in his arms caused by a congenital condition. He was fired when his drug test came back positive, even though he informed the human resources manager about his prescription. A software employee in California lost his job even though his physician prescribed pot to alleviate his back pain.

The fact that THC, the active chemical in marijuana, can stay in a person's system for weeks further complicates matters. Recreational users can test positive for pot they smoked legally. Current tests cannot distinguish between marijuana used hours or weeks ago and cannot establish if an employee's performance is impaired.

So far courts in Washington, Oregon, and California have ruled in favor of employers who decide to fire workers who test positive for THC. The U.S. Supreme Court determined that state pot statutes don't exempt users from federal drug laws. Nonetheless, changing attitudes toward pot are likely to further heat up the debate between employers who enforce drug-free policies and employees and others who argue that workers shouldn't be fired for engaging in a legal activity. According to a spokesperson for the California Chamber of Commerce: "It really boils down to this: An employer's right to maintain a drug-free workplace is critical. It protects the safety of all workers and limits exposure to potentially costly litigation."[1] A Seattle attorney representing terminated pot users makes the opposite argument: "Once it's legal, there's just not a legitimate interest for an employer to say, 'You tested positive, you're fired.'"[2]

Discussion Probes

1. Would you have voted for the marijuana initiatives in Colorado and Washington? Why or why not?

2. Do you think that marijuana has any legitimate medical uses?

3. What values are in conflict in this case?

4. What ethical principles can employers apply when deciding whether or not to fire workers who test positive for THC because of legal marijuana use?

5. Is it ethical for employers to fire employees who use marijuana legally? Why or why not?

Notes

1. Schwartz, S. K. (2010, April 20). Medical pot use can conflict with job rules. *USA Today*, p. 7A.

2. Martin, J. (2012, November 17). The battle is on: I-502 vs. drug-free policies at work. *Seattle Times*.

Sources

Gogek, E. (2012, November 8). A bad trip for democrats. *The New York Times*, p. A23.

Guarino, M. (2012, November 12). How will feds deal with marijuana legalization in Colorado and Washington? *The Christian Science Monitor*.

Horwitz, S. (2012, November 10). Marijuana legality elicits confusion. *The Washington Post*, p. A03.

Johnson, K. (2012, November 18). Counting the days till marijuana's legal. *The New York Times*, p. A20.

Martin, J. (2011, February 7). Can legal use of medical marijuana get you fired? State supreme court to decide. *Seattle Times*.

Mascia, J. (2010, August 29). Medical use of marijuana costs some a paycheck. *The New York Times*, p. A14.

Pearce, M. (2012, November 11). Unlikely allies, arguments lead voters to legalize pot. *Los Angeles Times*, p. A22.

CASE STUDY 8.3

Chaos on K2

K2 has been called the most dangerous mountain in the world. At 28,251 feet, K2 is only slightly shorter than nearby Mt. Everest but is much more difficult to climb. While more than 3,000 have summited Everest, approximately 300 have made it to the top of K2. Among those climbing Everest, 10% die trying, while the death rate on K2 is at

26%. There are several reasons K2 has been nicknamed the "Savage Mountain." Further north than Everest, it is subject to colder and harsher weather conditions. It is also steeper and harder to climb.

During the summer of 2008, climbers jammed into the highest base camp on K2 and prepared to summit. The group was a "virtual UN of expeditions," including teams from the Netherlands, Korea, the United States, Serbia, Australia, and Singapore, along with independent alpinists. Language differences hindered communication. Personality differences and different approaches to climbing generated friction between groups. In one case, for example, a Dutch expedition member shunned an American independent climber because the American didn't bring the right equipment. Tensions increased as weather conditions kept the teams in base camp.

Despite the tensions, team leaders realized that they would need to coordinate their efforts if such a large group were to have any chance at reaching the top. They agreed to send a trail-breaking team out first to pack down snow and set safety lines for those who would come later.

When the weather cleared, 22 climbers launched their ascent in the early morning hours of August 1. Trouble began almost immediately. Some tasked with laying down rope didn't show up, and the leader of the trail-breaking team—the only person who had previously summited—fell ill. Members of the first group didn't bring enough line and laid out the rope too soon. As a result, they ran out of line before reaching the most dangerous section of the climb, called the Bottleneck. Rope then had to be passed from the bottom to be anchored farther up the slope, delaying the climb. (Later, those who successfully descended failed to mark the way back to camp with flags as they had promised.) A Serbian fell to his death as he started his ascent, and a Pakistani porter died trying to retrieve the body. Soon climbers were clustered at the bottom of the Bottleneck.

Eighteen climbers managed to make it to the living room–sized summit, which tied the previous single-day K2 record. However, the last climber didn't reach the top until 7:30 p.m. Those who continued ascending past early afternoon put themselves in grave danger. The delay meant they would have to descend in darkness or camp out on the side of the mountain (nicknamed the Death Zone) in temperatures reaching 40 degrees below zero. One climber who summited tried to tell others that it was too late to continue on, but he soon gave up. "As I descended," he said, "everyone stopped to ask me how far it was to the summit. Did I tell people to turn around? No, you can't. There are a lot of people and they are all going up together. It's the majority against you."[1]

As the teams descended, tragedy struck again as a huge ice sheet broke off, sweeping climbers to their deaths. The falling piece of glacier also carried away the ropes that those above the Bottleneck were depending on to lead them to the safety of base camp. Smaller icefalls and avalanches during the night and the next day buried other climbers. Eleven died, making this one of the worst climbing disasters of all time.

Responses to the deadly chaos unfolding on K2 ranged from selfish to heroic. Many focused on their own survival, ignoring the plight of others. Said the head of Dutch team: "They were thinking of using my gas, my rope. Everybody was fighting for himself, and I still do not understand why everybody were leaving each other."[2] The Sherpa climbers, on the other hand, did their best to help. They returned up the mountain from base camp to rescue disoriented climbers. Two Sherpas died while trying to rescue three Koreans tangled in rope. In an amazing feat of mountaineering, one Sherpa tied himself to a colleague who had lost his ice ax. They managed to descend using only one ax between them.

Much of the 2008 K2 disaster can be blamed on natural forces. Icefalls and avalanches claimed the majority of victims. However, human factors played a major role as well. The teams were not able to coordinate their efforts, team members didn't follow through on their responsibilities, and too many climbers fell victim to "summit fever," deciding to continue upward when they should have turned back. Self-centeredness was also a contributing factor. In the past, mountaineering teams viewed their climbs as mutual endeavors and took responsibility for one another. Not so in recent years. As one mountaineering historian noted, modern climbing now is marked by "an ethos stressing individualism and self-preservation."[3]

Ironically, one of the greatest examples of mountaineering selflessness came in a 1954 American summit attempt on K2. When a fellow climber fell ill, his colleagues abandoned their summit attempt and carried him thousands of feet down the mountain, only to see him swept away as they neared safety. A memorial to this climber and others who have died on the mountain still stands. The names of the 11 who died in 2008 were added to this monument.

Discussion Probes

1. Did divisions among the teams doom any attempt to cooperate?

2. Would the teams have been better off climbing on their own?

3. What steps, if any, could the team leaders have taken to foster intergroup identity?

4. Why do you think climbers continued to the top even after they should have turned back?

5. Why are modern climbers apparently more selfish than climbers of the past? What can be done to change the culture of climbing?

6. What leadership and followership ethics lessons do you take from this case?

Notes

1. Viesturs, E., & Roberts, D. (2009). *K2: Life and death on the world's most dangerous mountain.* New York: Broadway, p. 18.

2. Isserman, M. (2008, August 11). The descent of men; a different K2 drama. *The International Herald Tribune,* Opinion, p. 4.

3. Isserman.

Sources

Bowley, G., & Kannapell, A. (2008, August 6). Chaos on the "mountain that invites death." *The New York Times,* p. A1.

Haider, K. (2008, August 5). "Death zone" tragedy. *National Post,* p. A3.

Peterson, S. (2008, August 6). In K2 aftermath, lessons learned. *The Christian Science Monitor.*

Power, M. (2008, November). K2: The killing peak. *Men's Journal.*

Ramesh, R. (2008, August 5). K2 tragedy: Death toll on world's most treacherous mountain reaches 11. *The Guardian,* Home Pages, p. 2.

Taylor, J. (2008, August 5). What makes K2 the most perilous challenge a mountaineer can face? *The Independent,* Comment, p. 30.

Zuckerman, P., & Padoan, A. (2012*). Buried in the sky: The extraordinary story of the Sherpa climbers on K2's deadliest day.* New York: Norton, p. 11.

SELF-ASSESSMENT 8.1

The Social Loafing Scale

Instructions: This scale is written for the retail sales setting but can easily be adapted to other work contexts. Indicate how characteristic each of the items is of the person you are rating: 1 = not at all characteristic; 2 = slightly characteristic; 3 = somewhat characteristic; 4 = characteristic; 5 = very characteristic.

Sum the responses to the 10 items to come up with a social loafing score for each person (range: 10–50). To come up with an overall score for the group, rate all the members (including yourself), add up the scores, and divide by the number of group members.

1. Defers responsibilities he or she should assume to other salespeople.

2. Puts forth less effort on the job when other salespeople are around to do the work.

3. Does not do his or her share of the work.

4. Spends less time helping customers if other salespeople are present to serve customers.

5. Puts forth less effort than other members of his or her work group.

6. Avoids performing housekeeping tasks as much as possible.

7. Leaves work for the next shift that he or she should really complete.

8. Is less likely to approach a customer if another salesperson is available to do this.

9. Takes it easy if other salespeople are around to do the work.

10. Defers customer service activities to other salespeople if they are present.

SOURCE: From George, J. M. (1995). Asymmetrical effects of rewards and punishments: The case of social loafing. *Journal of Occupational and Organizational Psychology, 68*, 327–338. Reprinted with permission from the *Journal of Occupational and Organizational Psychology,* © The British Psychological Society.

SELF-ASSESSMENT 8.2

Task/Relationship Conflict Scale

Instructions: The following scale will help you determine if your team is engaged in affective or substantive conflict. Choose a problem-solving group from work or school and answer each of the following questions.

Very Little						A Great Deal
1	2	3	4	5	6	7

1. How much friction is there among members in your group? _____

2. How much are personality conflicts evident in your group? _____

3. How much tension is there among members in your group? _____

4. How much emotional conflict is there among members in your group? _____

5. How often do people in your group disagree about opinions? _____

6. How frequently are there conflicts about ideas in your group? _____

7. How much conflict about the work you do is there in your group? _____

8. To what extent are there differences of opinion in your group? _____

Scoring

Add up your scores from Questions 1–4 and record the total below. The higher the score, the greater the level of affective conflict in your group. Add up your scores from Questions 5–8 and record the total below. The higher the score, the greater the level of substantive or task conflict in your team.

Affective conflict _____ out of 28   Substantive/task conflict _____ out of 28

SOURCE: Reprinted from "A multi-method examination of the benefits and detriments of intragroup conflict" by Karen A. Jehn. Published in *Administrative Science Quarterly* vol. 40, pp. 256–282, June 1995. © Johnson Graduate School of Management, Cornell University.

NOTES

1. Palmer, P. (1996). Leading from within. In L. C. Spears (Ed.), *Insights on leadership: Service, stewardship, spirit, and servant-leadership* (pp. 197–208). New York: John Wiley, p. 200.
2. Silverman, R. E. (2012, February 4). Where's the boss? Trapped in a meeting. *The Wall Street Journal*.
3. Tropman, J. (2003). *Making meetings work: Achieving high quality group decisions* (2nd ed.). Thousand Oaks, CA: Sage, p. 196.
4. Dukerich, J. M., Nichols, M. L., Elm, D. R., & Voltrath, D. A. (1990). Moral reasoning in groups: Leaders make a difference. *Human Relations, 43*, 473–493; Nichols, M. L., & Day, V. E. (1982). A comparison of moral reasoning of groups and individuals on the "Defining Issues Test." *Academy of Management Journal, 24*, 21–28.
5. Johnson, D. W., Maruyama, G., Johnson, R., Nelson, D., & Skon, L. (1981). Effects of cooperative, competitive, and individualistic goal structures on achievement: A meta-analysis. *Psychological Bulletin, 82*, 47–62; Johnson, D. W., & Johnson, R. T. (1989). *Cooperation and competition: Theory and research*. Edina, MN: Interaction; Johnson, D. W., & Johnson, F. P. (2000). *Joining together: Group theory and group skills* (7th ed.). Boston: Allyn & Bacon.
6. Johnson, D. W., & Johnson, R. T. (2005). Training for cooperative group work. In M. A. West, D. Tjosvold, & K. G. Smith (Eds.), *The essentials of teamworking: International perspectives* (pp. 131–147). West Sussex, England: John Wiley.
7. Johnson & Johnson (2000); Johnson & Johnson (2005).
8. Amichai-Hamburger, Y. (2003). Understanding social loafing. In A. Sagie, S. Stashevsky, & M. Koslowsky (Eds.), *Misbehaviour and dysfunctional attitudes in organizations* (pp. 79–102). Basingstoke, England: Palgrave Macmillan.
9. Karau, S. J., & Williams, K. D. (2001). Understanding individual motivation in groups: The collective effort model. In M. E. Turner (Ed.), *Groups at work: Theory and research* (pp. 113–141). Mahwah, NJ: Erlbaum, p. 119.

10. Karau, S. J., & Williams, K. D. (1995). Social loafing: Research findings, implications, and future directions. *Current Directions in Psychological Science, 4,* 134–140; Williams, K. D., Harkins, S. G., & Karau, S. J. (2003). Social performance. In M. A. Hogg & J. Cooper (Eds.), *The Sage handbook of social psychology* (pp. 327–346). London: Sage.

11. Wolvin, A. D., & Coakley, G. C. (1993). A listening taxonomy. In A. D. Wolvin & C. G. Coakley (Eds.), *Perspectives in listening* (pp. 15–22). Norwood, NJ: Ablex.

12. Johnson, J. (1993). Functions and processes of inner speech in listening. In D. Wolvin & C. G. Coakley (Eds.), *Perspectives in listening* (pp. 170–184). Norwood, NJ: Ablex.

13. Barker, L., Johnson, P., & Watson, K. (1991). The role of listening in managing interpersonal and group conflict. In D. Borisoff & M. Purdy (Eds.), *Listening in everyday life: A personal and professional approach* (pp. 139–157). Lanham, MD: University Press of America.

14. Gibb, J. R. (1961). Defensive communication. *Journal of Communication, 11–12,* 141–148. See also Borisoff, D., & Victor, D. A. (1998). *Conflict management: A communication skills approach* (2nd ed.). Boston: Allyn & Bacon, Ch. 2.

15. Duffy, M. K., & & Shaw, J. D. (2000). The Salieri syndrome: Consequences of envy in groups. *Small Group Research, 31,* 3–23.

16. Goleman, D., Boyatzis, R., & McKee, A. (2002). The emotional reality of teams. *Journal of Organizational Excellence, 21*(2), 55–65; Rapisarda, B. A. (2002). The impact of emotional intelligence on work team cohesiveness and performance. *International Journal of Organizational Analysis, 10,* 363–370; Prati, L. M., Douglas, C., Ferris, G. R., Ammeter, A. P., & Buckley, M. R. (2003). Emotional intelligence, leadership effectiveness, and team outcomes. *International Journal of Organizational Analysis, 11,* 21–40. Some examples in this section are taken from these sources.

17. Durskat, V. U., & Wolff, S. B. (2001, March). Building the emotional intelligence of groups. *Harvard Business Review,* pp. 80–90.

18. See Amason, A. C., Thompson, K. R., Hochwarter, W. A., & Harrison, A. W. (1995). Conflict: An important dimension in successful management teams. *Organizational Dynamics, 23,* 20–35; Amason, A. C. (1996). Distinguishing the effects of functional and dysfunctional conflict on strategic decision making: Resolving a paradox for top management teams. *Academy of Management Journal, 39,* 123–148; Bell, M. A. (1974). The effects of substantive and affective conflict in problem-solving groups. *Speech Monographs, 41,* 19–23; Bell, M. A. (1979). The effects of substantive and affective verbal conflict on the quality of decisions of small problem-solving groups. *Central States Speech Journal, 3,* 75–82; Johnson, D. W., & Tjosvold, D. (1983). *Productive conflict management.* New York: Irvington.

19. Kotlyar, I., & Karakowsky, L. (2006). Leading conflict? Linkages between leader behaviors and group conflict. *Small Group Research, 37,* 377–403.

20. Alper, S., Tjosvold, D., & Law, K. S. (2000). Conflict management, efficacy, and performance in organizational teams. *Personnel Psychology, 53,* 625–642.

21. Jordan, P. J., & Troth, A. C. (2004). Managing emotions during team problem solving: Emotional intelligence and conflict resolution. *Human Performance, 17,* 195–218.

22. Roberto, M. A. (2005). *Why great leaders don't take yes for an answer.* Upper Saddle River, NJ: Wharton School Publishing

23. Roberto.

24. Schultz, B. (1982). Argumentativeness: Its effect in group decision-making and its role in leadership perception. *Communication Quarterly, 3,* 368–375.

25. Infante, D., & Rancer, A. (1996). Argumentativeness and verbal aggressiveness: A review of recent theory and research. In B. Burleson (Ed.), *Communication yearbook 19* (pp. 319–351). Thousand Oaks, CA: Sage;

Infante, D. (1988). *Arguing constructively.* Prospect Heights, IL: Waveland; Rancer, A. S., & Avtgis, T. A. (2006). *Argumentative and aggressive communication: Theory, research, and application.* Thousand Oaks, CA: Sage.

26. Gouran, D. S., Hirokawa, R. Y., Julian, K. M., & Leatham, G. B. (1993). The evolution and current status of the functional perspective on communication in decision-making and problem-solving groups. In S. A. Deetz (Ed.), *Communication yearbook 16* (pp. 573–576). Newbury Park, CA: Sage; Gouran, D. S., & Hirokawa, R. Y. (1986). Counteractive functions of communication in effective group decision making. In R. Y. Hirokawa & M. S. Poole (Eds.), *Communication and group decision making* (pp. 81–89). Beverly Hills, CA: Sage.

27. For summaries of research on minority influence processes, see Martin, R., & Hewstone, M (Eds.), *Minority influence and innovations: Antecedents, processes and consequences* (pp. 365–394). Hoboken, NJ: Psychology Press; Crano, W. D., & Seyranian, V. (2009). How minorities prevail: The context/comparison-leniency contract model. *Journal of Social Issues, 65,* 335–363; Moscovici, S., Mucchi-Faina, A., & Maass, A. (Eds.). (1994). *Minority influence.* Chicago: Nelson-Hall; Moscovici, S., Mugny, G., & Van Avermaet, E. (Eds.). (1985). *Perspectives on minority influence.* Cambridge, England: Cambridge University Press; Maas, A., & Clark, R. D. (1984). Hidden impact of minorities: Fifteen years of minority influence research. *Psychological Bulletin, 95,* 428–445; Nemeth, C., & Chiles, C. (1986). Modeling courage: The role of dissent in fostering independence. *European Journal of Social Psychology, 18,* 275–280; Nemeth, C. (1994). The value of minority dissent. In S. Moscovici, A. Mucchi-Faina, & A. Maass (Eds.), *Minority influence* (pp. 3–15). Chicago: Nelson-Hall; De Dreu, C. K. W., & Beersma, B. (2001). Minority influence in organizations: Its origins and implications for learning and group performance. In C. K. W. De Dreu & N. K. De Vries (Eds.), *Group consensus and minority influence: Implications for innovation* (pp. 258–283). Malden, MA: Blackwell.

28. Nemeth, C. (1995). Dissent, group process and creativity: The contribution of minority influence research. In E. Lawler (Ed.), *Advances in group processes* (Vol. 2, pp. 57–75). Greenwich, CT: JAI Press; Nemeth & Chiles.

29. Smith, C. M., & Tindale, R. S. (2009). Direct and indirect minority influence in groups. In R. Martin & M. Hewstone (Eds.), *Minority influence and innovations: Antecedents, processes and consequences* (pp. 263–284). Hoboken, NJ: Psychology Press.

30. Alvaro, E. M., & Crano, W. D. (1997). Indirect minority influence: Evidence for leniency in source evaluation and counterargumentation. *Journal of Personality and Social Psychology, 72,* 949–964.

31. See, for example, Park, G., & DeShon, R. P. (2010). A multilevel model of minority opinion expression and team decision-making effectiveness. *Journal of Applied Psychology, 95,* 824–853; De Dreu, C. K. W., & West, M. A. (2001). Minority dissent and team innovation: The importance of participation in decision making. *Journal of Applied Psychology, 86,* 1191–1201; Valacich, J. S., & Schewenk, C. (1995). Devil's advocacy and dialectical inquiry effects on face-to-face and computer-mediated group decision making. *Organizational Behavior and Human Decision Processes, 63,* 158–173; La Pine, J. A. (2005). Adaptation of teams in response to unforeseen change: Effects of goal difficulty and team composition in terms of cognitive ability and goal orientation. *Journal of Applied Psychology, 90,* 1153–1167.

32. Janis, I. (1971, November). Groupthink: The problems of conformity. *Psychology Today,* 271–279; Janis, I. (1982). *Groupthink* (2nd ed.). Boston: Houghton Mifflin; Janis, I. (1989). *Crucial decisions: Leadership in policymaking and crisis management.* New York: Free Press.

33. Moorhead, G., Neck, C. P., & West, M. S. (1998). The tendency toward defective decision making within self-managing teams: The relevance of groupthink for the

21st century. *Organizational Behavior and Human Decision Processes, 73,* 327–351.

34. See Chen, A., Lawson, R. B., Gordon, L. R., & McIntosh, B. (1996). Groupthink: Deciding with the leader and the devil. *Psychological Record, 46,* 581–590; Esser, J. K. (1998). Alive and well after 25 years: A review of groupthink research. *Organizational Behavior and Human Decision Processes, 73,* 116–141; Flippen, A. R. (1999). Understanding groupthink from a self-regulatory perspective. *Small Group Research, 3,* 139–165; Jones, P. E., & Roelofsma, P. H. M. P. (2000). The potential for social contextual and group biases in team decision-making: Biases, conditions and psychological mechanisms. *Ergonomics, 43,* 1129–1152; Street, M. D. (1997). Groupthink: An examination of theoretical issues, implications, and future research suggestions. *Small Group Research, 28,* 72–93.

35. Cosier, R. A., & Schwenk, C. R. (1990). Agreement and thinking alike: Ingredients for poor decision. *Academy of Management Executive, 4,* 69–74; Schweiger, D. M., Sandberg, W. R., & Rechner, P. (1989). Experiential effects of dialectical inquiry, devil's advocacy, and consensus approaches to strategic decision making. *Academy of Management Journal, 32,* 745–772.

36. Manz, C. C., & Neck, C. P. (1995). Teamthink: Beyond the groupthink syndrome in self-managing work teams. *Journal of Managerial Psychology, 10*(1), 7–15; Manz, C. C., & Sims, H. P. (1989). *Superleadership: Leading others to lead themselves.* Upper Saddle River, NJ: Prentice Hall.

37. Harvey, J. B. (1988). *The Abilene paradox and other meditations on management.* New York: Simon & Schuster. See also Harvey, J. B. (1999). *How come every time I get stabbed in the back my fingerprints are on the knife?* San Francisco: Jossey-Bass.

38. See, for example, Edwards, J. C. (2001). Self-fulfilling prophecy and escalating commitment: Fuel for the Waco fire. *Journal of Applied Behavioral Science, 37,* 343–360; Staw, B. M. (1981). The escalation of commitment to a course of action. *Academy of Management*

Review, 6, 577–587; Ross, J., & Staw, B. M. (1993). Organizational escalation and exit: Lessons from the Shoreham Nuclear Plant. *Academy of Management Journal, 36,* 701–732; Bobocel, D. R., & Meyer, J. P. (1994). Escalating commitment to a failing course of action: Separating the roles of choice and justification. *Journal of Applied Psychology, 79,* 360–363; McNamara, G., Moon, H., & Bromiley, P. (2002). Banking on commitment: Intended and unintended consequences of an organization's attempt to attenuate escalation of commitment. *Academy of Management Journal, 45,* 443–452.

39. Drummond, H., & Hodgson, J. (2011). *Escalation in decision-making: Behavioral economics in business.* Burlington, VT: Gower; Sleesman, D. J., Conlon, D. E., McNamara, G., & Miles, J. E. (2012). Cleaning up the big muddy: A meta-analytic review of the determinants of escalation of commitment. *Academy of Management Journal, 3,* 541–562.

40. McKenna, F. P. (1993). It won't happen to me: Unrealistic optimism or illusion of control? *British Journal of Psychology, 84,* 39–50.

41. Keil, M., & Montealegre, R. (2000). Cutting your losses: Extricating your organization when a big project goes awry. *Sloan Management Review, 41,* 55–68. See also Simonson, I., & Staw, B M. (1992). Deescalation strategies: A comparison of techniques for reducing commitment to losing courses of action. *Journal of Applied Psychology, 77,* 419–426; Drummond & Hodgson.

42. Pittinsky, T. L., & Simon, S. (2007). Intergroup leadership. *Leadership Quarterly, 18,* 586–605; Ernst, C., & Yip., J. (2009). Boundary-spanning leadership: Tactics to bridge social identity groups in organizations. In T. L. Pittinsky, (Ed.), *Crossing the divide: Intergroup leadership in a world of difference* (pp. 87–99). Boston: Harvard Business Press.

43. Pittinsky & Simon; Ernst & Yip.

44. Hogg, M. A., Knippenberg, D., & Rast, D. E. (2012). Intergroup leadership in organizations: Leading across group and organizational boundaries. *Academy of Management Review, 37,* 232–255.

45. Marrone, J. A. (2010). Team boundary spanning: A multilevel review of past research and proposals for the future. *Journal of Management, 36,* 911–940; Duck, J. M., & Fielding, K. S. (2003). Leaders and their treatment of subgroups: Implications for evaluations of the leader and the superordinate group. *European Journal of Social Psychology, 33,* 387–401; Richter, A. W., West, M. A., Van Dick, R., & Dawson, J. F. (2006). Boundary spanners' identification, intergroup contact, and effective intergroup relations. *Academy of Management Journal, 49,* 1252–1269.

46. Pittinsky, T. L. (2010). A two-dimensional model of intergroup leadership: The case of national diversity. *American Psychologist, 65,* 194–200.

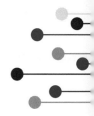

CHAPTER 9

Creating an Ethical Organizational Climate

Corruption is a durable and adaptable virus.

—Management professor Yadong Luo

Bad ethics is bad business.

—Anonymous

What's Ahead

Leaders act as ethics officers for their organizations by exercising influence through the process of social learning and by building positive ethical climates. Healthy ethical climates are marked by humility, zero tolerance for individual and collective destructive behaviors, justice, integrity (ethical soundness, wholeness, and consistency), trust, concern for process as well as product, structural reinforcement, and social responsibility. Important tools for building an ethical organizational climate include core ideology, codes of ethics, and ethics training.

The Leader as Ethics Officer

In the introduction to this text, I argued that ethics is at the heart of leadership. When we become leaders, we assume the ethical responsibilities that come with that role. Nowhere is this more apparent than in the organizational context. Examine nearly any corporate scandal—News Corporation, Massey Energy, Enron, New England Compounding Center, Peanut Corporation of America—and you'll find leaders who engaged in immoral behavior and encouraged their followers to do the same. The same pattern can be found in the nonprofit and governmental sectors (e.g., ACORN, the Vatican, Detroit city hall). On a more positive note, leaders are largely responsible for creating the organizations we admire for their ethical behavior.

Leaders are the ethics officers of their organizations, casting light or shadow in large part through the example they set.[1] Michael Brown and Linda Trevino draw on social learning theory to explain why and how ethical organizational leaders influence followers.[2] Social learning theory is based on the premise that people learn by observing and then emulating the values, attitudes, and behaviors of people they find legitimate, attractive, and credible. When it comes to ethics, followers look to their leaders as role models and act accordingly. Leaders are generally seen as legitimate, credible, and attractive because they occupy positions of authority with power and status. Ethical leaders build on this foundation. They increase their legitimacy by treating employees fairly and boost their attractiveness by expressing care and concern for followers. They enhance their credibility—particularly perceptions of their trustworthiness—by living up to the values they espouse. Such leaders are open and honest and set clear, high standards that they follow themselves.

Moral leaders make sure that ethics messages aren't drowned out by other messages about tasks and profits. They focus attention on ethics through frequent communication about values, mission, corporate standards, and the importance of ethical behavior. They reinforce follower learning by using rewards and punishments to regulate behavior, which makes it clear which actions are acceptable and which are not.

Trevino, Brown, and their colleagues distinguish between ethical leaders and those who are unethical, hypocritical, or ethically neutral.[3] The *unethical leader* falls short as both a moral person and a moral influence agent. This person casts one or more of the shadows described in Chapter 1 by bullying others, deceiving investors, acting irresponsibly, and so on. At the same time, the unethical leader clearly communicates that ethics don't matter; only results do. "Chainsaw" Al Dunlap was one such leader. As CEO of Sunbeam he drove up the company's stock price by eliminating thousands of jobs while inflating sales figures. The *hypocritical leader* talks a lot about ethical values but doesn't live up to the rhetoric. Prominent pastor Ted Haggard is an example of a hypocritical leader. As leader of the National Association of Evangelicals, he led public efforts to condemn homosexuality while he was carrying on an affair with a male prostitute.

The *ethically neutral leader* is not clearly seen as either ethical or unethical. This person doesn't send out strong messages about ethics and leaves followers unsure about where he or she stands on moral issues. Ethically neutral leaders appear to be self-centered and focus exclusively on the bottom line. Sandy Weill, former Citigroup CEO, typifies the ethically neutral leader. Weill stayed on the sidelines when it came to ethics, rewarding his managers according to their results. It was during his tenure that star analyst Jack Grubman continued to promote WorldCom and other telecom companies even as they were heading for bankruptcy. Hewlett-Packard's past CEO, Carly Fiorina, is another a leader who appeared to focus more on financial performance than on ethics.[4] During her tenure at HP the company lost its outstanding ethical reputation. Salespeople adopted questionable tactics to make their numbers, and financial analysts began to doubt the company's quarterly reports. Conflict over HP's merger with Compaq set the stage for a scandal involving board members after Fiorina departed. Under the direction of the board chair, private investigators spied on company directors and obtained information about journalists under false pretenses.

From their analysis of the three categories of ethical leadership, Trevino and her colleagues conclude that acting ethically is not enough. Executives must also ensure that employees know that they care (aren't just neutral) about ethics. Otherwise, followers will continue to focus on financial results without concern for ethics. Ethical leaders make ethical considerations a top organizational priority. They create positive ethical climates that promote moral behavior by leaders and followers alike. Identifying the characteristics of healthy ethical climates is the subject of the next section.

Ethical Climates

Ethical climate is best understood as part of an organization's culture. From the cultural vantage point, an organization is a tribe. As tribal members gather, they develop their own language, stories, beliefs, assumptions, ceremonies, and power structures. These elements combine to form a unique perspective on the world called the organization's culture.[5] How an organization responds to ethical issues is a part of this culture. Every organization faces a special set of ethical challenges, creates its own set of values and norms, develops guidelines for enforcing its ethical standards, honors particular ethical heroes, and so on. Ethical climate, in turn, determines what members believe is right or wrong and shapes their ethical decision making and behavior.

Management professors Bart Victor and John Cullen argue that ethical climates can be classified according to the criteria members use to make moral choices and the groups that members refer to when making ethical determinations.[6] Victor and Cullen identify five primary climate types. *Instrumental* climates follow the principle of ethical egotism. Ethical egotists make decisions based on selfish interests that serve the individual and his or her immediate group and organization. *Caring* climates emphasize concern or care for others. *Law and order* climates are driven by external criteria such as professional codes of conduct. *Rules* climates are governed by the policies, rules, and procedures developed in the organization. *Independence* climates give members wide latitude to make their own decisions. (To determine the ethical climate of your company or organization, complete Self-Assessment 9.1.)

Leaders would do well to know the particular ethical orientation of their organizations. To begin, each of the five climate types poses unique ethical challenges. Members of instrumental organizations often ignore the needs of others, whereas those driven by a care ethic are tempted to overlook the rules to help out friends and colleagues. Leaders and followers in law and order cultures may be blind to the needs of coworkers because they rely on outside standards for guidance. On the other hand, those who play by organizational rules may be blinded to societal norms. Independence produces the best results when members have the knowledge and skills they need to make good decisions.

Studies using the Victor and Cullen climate types suggest that self-interest poses the greatest threat to ethical performance.[7] Rates of immoral behavior are highest in work units and organizations with instrumental climates. Members of these groups are also less committed to their organizations and less satisfied with their jobs. Caring (benevolent) climates promote employee loyalty and contentment with their jobs. Rules climates discourage ethical misbehavior but don't encourage attachment to the organization. External laws and codes that are internalized into an organization's climate are positively linked with such outcomes as job satisfaction and psychological well-being.

Signs of Healthy Ethical Climates

There is no one-size-fits-all approach to creating an ethical climate. Rather, we need to identify principles and practices that characterize positive ethical climates. Then we have to adapt these elements to our particular organizational setting. Key markers of highly ethical organizations include humility, zero tolerance for individual and collective destructive behaviors, justice, integrity, trust, a focus on process, structural reinforcement, and social responsibility.

Humility

Any attempt to foster a positive ethical climate must begin by acknowledging the reality that organizations, like individuals, have their "dark sides." (See "Leadership Ethics at the Movies: *Inside Job*" for a description of an entire industry that casts significant shadows.) In particular, organizations are likely to fall victim to success and self-centeredness. High-performance businesses are always in danger of accepting unethical behavior as the normal way of operating. Like Icarus of ancient Greek mythology, who fell to earth after soaring too close to the heat of the sun, modern-day highfliers are also likely to crash. In the Icarus syndrome, the same factors that contribute to the success of high-performing corporations like Salomon Brothers, WorldCom, Enron, and Tyco often lead to their downfall.[8] First, a culture of competition encourages members to break the rules to get a competitive advantage and to excuse their moral failings. Second, high-performance organizations are so focused on results (generally financial) that they tolerate wrongdoing if it achieves their objectives. Third, an exaggerated focus on mission encourages members to ignore the rules. Fourth, members tell stories that justify their poor behavior by, for example, demonizing their opponents. Fifth, the culture becomes isolated. As a consequence, group members accept behaviors like bribery, cheating, and deception that would be seen as unethical by society.

LEADERSHIP ETHICS AT THE MOVIES • • • • • • • • •

Inside Job

Key Cast Members: George Soros, Ben Bernanke, Barney Frank, Larry Summers, Frederic Mishkin, Christine Lagarde, Eliot Spitzer

Synopsis: Narrated by Matt Damon, this Oscar-winning documentary examines the excesses of the U.S. financial services industry that led to the economic crisis of 2008. It includes interviews with many of those who played a part in the events leading up to and following the crash. The filmmakers highlight the role that politicians, rating services, and academics played in enabling greedy bankers and financial investors to enrich themselves while putting the world's economy at risk. Many Wall Street executives continued to receive lavish bonuses even after they had caused the financial disaster; none have been charged with crimes.

Rating: PG-13 for language and adult themes

Themes: greed, ethical danger signs, fraud, deception, abuse of power and privilege, leadership shadows

Discussion Starters

1. How was the financial crisis an "inside job"?

2. What ethical danger signs were present in the financial services industry before the crash? After the crash?

3. What steps, if any, should be taken to reform Wall Street?

Organizations can also be ensnared by narcissism. In organization narcissism, members believe that the group has special, unique qualities. They develop a great deal of pride (hubris), believing they have the power to control events. Leaders of narcissistic organizations are quick to dismiss other groups and to treat them with contempt. Long-Term Capital Management (LTCM) is a case in point.[9] The staff of this 1990s hedge fund included two Nobel Prize winners and a former vice chair of the American Federal Bank, as well as top Wall Street traders. The fund was highly profitable at first. However, its managers made increasingly large investments in markets where they had no experience. Worse yet, as the global economy soured in 1998, fund managers continued to take large risks even as other banks and investment funds were becoming more cautious. LTCM officials apparently hoped to demonstrate their superiority by making money when their competitors could not. Instead, LTCM had to be bailed out by the federal government and closed shortly thereafter.

Ethical leaders play a critical role in alerting followers and other leaders to the dangers of success and self-centeredness. They promote humility as a collective virtue as they nurture this character trait in themselves (see the discussion of humility in Chapter 3). They encourage the group to be aware of its strengths and limitations, to be open to new ideas and knowledge, and to acknowledge the importance of serving a higher power. Humility prevents hubris and the disdainful treatment of outsiders. Humble organizations are also sensitive to the signs of ethical trouble described in Box 9.1.

• • • BOX 9.1 SIGNS OF ETHICAL COLLAPSE • • •

Arizona State University professor Marianne Jennings identifies seven signs that a company may be at risk for moral failure. Recognizing and responding to these symptoms can help you and your organization avoid disaster.

Sign 1: Pressure to Maintain Numbers

The first sign of ethical trouble is obsession with meeting quantifiable goals. Driven by numbers, companies overstate sales, hide expenses, make bad loans, and ship defective products. Nonprofits also feel the pressure to reach their goal numbers. Universities want to be ranked highly by *U.S. News & World Report* and other publications, so they may lie about graduation and placement rates. Atlanta public school administrators are charged with altering standardized test scores in order to earn performance bonuses. Charities, driven to achieve their fund-raising objectives, may make false claims about how many people they serve.

Sign 2: Fear and Silence

In every moral meltdown, there are indications that something is seriously amiss. For example, employees at Enron circulated a list titled "Top Ten Reasons Enron Restructures So Frequently." Item 7 on the list said, "To keep the outside investment analysts so confused that they will not be able to figure out that we don't know what we're doing." However, few challenge the status quo because those who do so are publicly shamed, demoted, or dismissed. Others don't want to believe that the organization is in trouble; still others are bribed into silence through generous salaries and loan packages.

Sign 3: Young 'Uns and a Bigger-Than-Life CEO

Some CEOs become icons who are adored by the community and the media (although often not by employees). Outsiders are loath to criticize the legendary CEO when everyone else is singing his or her praises. The iconic CEO also surrounds him- or herself with loyal supporters who are often young and inexperienced. For example, CEOs brought in their sons and daughters to help them run AIG, Archer Daniels Midland, and Adelphia, all companies that ran afoul of the law.

Sign 4: Weak Board

The boards of companies on the verge of moral collapse are weak for a variety of reasons. They may have inexperienced members, be made up of friends of the CEO, or be reluctant to reign in a legendary CEO. Members may fail to attend meetings or devote the necessary time to their board roles. The board of HealthSouth is a case in point. HealthSouth— which engaged in Medicare and accounting fraud—was made up of company officers and outsiders who had contracts and other financial relationships with CEO Richard Scrushy and the firm. The HealthSouth board ignored lawsuits and federal investigations that indicated that the company was in trouble.

Sign 5: Conflicts of Interest

Conflicts of interest arise when an individual plays two roles and the interests of one role are at odds with those of the other role. Officers of the company are then tempted to profit at the expense of stockholders, employees, and others. That was the case with CFO Andrew Fastow of Enron, who made millions from the entities he designed to hide company debt.

(Continued)

(Continued)

Sign 6: Innovation Like No Other

Highly successful companies often believe that they can defy economic and business reality. They might have been the first in a new industry or be headed by an entrepreneurial leader who succeeded against all odds. Their arrogance convinces them that they can continually innovate themselves out of any tight spot. Instead, these groups and their leaders innovate themselves into moral trouble by inventing illegal accounting practices, tax evasion schemes, and faulty business models. Finova Group grew rapidly by making loans to small businesses and time-share properties turned down by other financial institutions. The firm could charge higher interest, generating greater margins. However, Finova soon had a portfolio full of bad loans. Rather than write these loans off, the company used creative accounting to hide these losses. In some cases, company officers even counted the poor loans as assets.

Sign 7: Goodness in Some Areas Atones for Evil in Others

A good many fallen organizations and leaders try to atone for their sins in one area by doing good in others. Tyco and Dennis Kozlowski, WorldCom and Bernie Ebbers, and Adelphia and John Rigas were all known for their charitable acts, giving to universities and local communities, contributing to disaster relief, encouraging employees to volunteer for service projects, and so on. In the case of endangered organizations, the motive for philanthropy is not serving the common good but soothing the consciences of those involved in fraud, insider trading, accounting tricks, and other misdeeds.

SOURCE: Jennings, M. M. (2006). *The seven signs of ethical collapse: How to spot moral meltdowns in companies . . . before it's too late.* New York: St. Martin's Press.

Zero Tolerance for Individual and Collective Destructive Behaviors

Dark-side behaviors are destructive or antisocial actions that deliberately attempt to harm others or the organization.[10] Those who engage in such unethical behaviors are driven to meet their own needs at the expense of coworkers and the group as a whole. Common categories of misbehaviors include incivility, aggression, sexual harassment, and discrimination.

Incivility consists of rude or discourteous actions that disregard others and violate norms for respect.[11] Such actions can be intentional or unintentional. They include leaving a mess for the maintenance staff to pick up, sending a "flaming" e-mail, claiming credit for someone else's work, making fun of a peer, and inadvertently ignoring a team member on the way into the office. Incivility reduces employee job satisfaction, task performance, motivation, loyalty, performance, creativity, and willingness to cooperate.

Aggression refers to consciously trying to hurt others or the organization itself.[12] Aggressive behaviors can take a variety of forms, ranging from refusing to answer e-mails to swearing at coworkers to murder. Such behaviors can be categorized along three dimensions. They can be physical–verbal (destructive words or deeds), active–passive (doing harm by acting or failing to act), or direct–indirect (doing harm directly to the other person or indirectly through an intermediary and attacking something that the target values). Aggression does extensive damage to individuals and organizations. Victims may be hurt; experience more stress, which leads to poor health; become fearful, depressed, or angry; lose the ability to concentrate; and feel less committed to their jobs. Observers of aggressive incidents also experience more anxiety and have a lower sense of well-being and commitment. Performance at the organizational level drops as a product of the aggressive actions of employees. Workplace aggression reduces productivity while increasing absenteeism and turnover. Organizations become the targets of lawsuits and negative publicity.

Sexual harassment is a form of aggression directed largely at women.[13] Quid pro quo harassment occurs when targets are coerced into providing sexual favors in return for keeping their jobs or getting promoted. Hostile work environment harassment exists when job conditions interfere with job performance. Components of hostile working conditions include demeaning comments, suggestive gestures, threats, propositions, bribes, and sexual assault. The work performance of victims drops, and they may quit their jobs. Targets also suffer physically (headaches, sleep loss, nausea, eating disorders) and psychologically (depression, fear, a sense of helplessness).

Discrimination is putting members of selected groups, such as women, minorities, disabled employees, older workers, and homeless people, at a disadvantage. Such negative treatment is generally based on stereotypes and prejudice (e.g., older workers can't learn new skills, Hispanics are lazy). Because of the passage of antidiscrimination laws and changes in societal values, employment discrimination is generally expressed subtly through such behaviors as dismissing the achievements of people of color and women, avoiding members of low-status groups, and hiring and promoting those of similar backgrounds.[14]

Destructive behaviors are all too common in modern organizations. In one study, 20% of the sample reported being the targets of uncivil messages in a given week. There were 15,000 incidents of violence resulting in time away from work in one 12-month period in the United States; assaults and suicides account for 13% of all deaths on the job; and an average of 564 work-related homicides occurred each year over a recent five-year span. Among female students and employees, 50–60% report being the targets of harassing actions. Unemployment rates are significantly higher for minorities, and people of color have accumulated only a fraction of the wealth of Whites.[15]

Fortunately, leaders can significantly reduce the rate of destructive behaviors by actively seeking to prevent and control them. Moral leaders do the following:

1. *Create zero-tolerance policies that prohibit antisocial actions.* (We'll take a closer look at codes of ethics later in the chapter.) They insist on employee-to-employee civility, forbid aggression and sexual harassment, and prohibit discrimination. These policies also outlaw other unethical practices like lying to customers or paying kickbacks.

2. *Obey guidelines.* As noted earlier, leaders are powerful role models. Zero-tolerance policies will have little effect if leaders do not follow the rules they set. Ironically, leaders are most likely to violate standards because they believe that they are exceptions to the rules (see the discussion of unhealthy motivations in Chapter 2). Furthermore, because they are in positions of power, leaders are freer to act uncivilly, to bully others, or to offer favors in return for sex.

3. *Constantly monitor for possible violations.* Destructive behavior may be hidden from the view of top leaders. Some managers are good at "kissing up and kicking down," for example. They act respectfully toward superiors while bullying employees and treating them with disrespect. Ethical leaders actively seek feedback from employees further down the organizational hierarchy. They conduct 360-degree reviews that allow employees to rate their supervisors and provide channels—human relations departments, open-door policies—for reporting misbehaviors. Those who come forward with complaints are protected from retribution.

4. *Move quickly when standards are violated.* Ethical leaders recognize that failing to act sends the wrong message, undermining ethical climate. If left unchecked, incivility escalates into aggression. A culture of aggression forms when abusive members are allowed to act as role models. Victims of sexual harassment won't come forward if they think that their leaders won't respond. Patterns of discrimination perpetuate themselves unless leaders intervene. The U.S. military has been accused of moving slowly to address sexual assaults of both women and men. Officers often discourage victims from reporting sex crimes. Even if the defendant is convicted, the unit's commanding officer can throw out the verdict.[16]

5. *Address the underlying factors that trigger destructive actions.* Moral leaders try to screen out potential employees who have a history of destructive behavior. They also try to eliminate situational elements that produce antisocial action. Important contextual

triggers include unpleasant working conditions, job stress, oppressive supervision, perceived injustice (see the discussion below), and extreme competitiveness.[17]

Moral leaders also move quickly to address the destructive actions of groups of employees. In *collective corruption* two or more individuals cooperate in unethical behavior.[18] They abuse their organizational positions and authority to benefit themselves, their work units, or their organizations. Examples of collective corruption include accounting fraud, price-fixing and bribery, covering up criminal behavior, graft, and nepotism. (A more complete list of corrupt activities is found in Box 9.2.) Observers note that corruption is a "slippery slope" where the corrupt behaviors of a few individuals can rapidly become part of the organization's culture and ethical climate. First, an individual or group—often encouraged by a leader—decides to engage in an unethical behavior, like bribing a local official to secure a construction contract. If the corrupt decision or act is successful (the bribe leads to a significant profits), then this information is stored in organizational memory and the destructive behavior (bribery) is more likely to be used again in the future. Corruption then becomes the normal routine. Those participating in corrupt activities use a variety of rationalizations to defend their behavior. For instance, they deny that anyone was harmed, claim that they were forced to go along, and appeal to group loyalty to defend their choices. As new members join the group, they are socialized into the corrupt culture. (See "Focus on Follower Ethics: The Journey to Corruption" for a closer look at how the corrupt socialization process unfolds.)

● ● ● BOX 9.2 CATEGORIES OF FRAUD AND MISCONDUCT ASSESSED IN KPMG FORENSIC SURVEY (2006) ● ● ●

KPMG, an accounting and consulting firm, periodically surveys top executives to determine their perceptions of fraud and misconduct in their organizations. KPMG categorizes misbehaviors according to how they affect important groups. The survey assesses the following categories of fraud and misconduct:

Compromising customer or marketplace trust by

- Engaging in false or deceptive sales practices
- Submitting false or misleading invoices to customers

(Continued)

(Continued)

- Engaging in anticompetitive practices (e.g., market rigging)
- Improperly gathering competitors' confidential information
- Fabricating product quality or safety test results
- Breaching customer or consumer privacy
- Entering into customer contract relationships without proper terms, contracts, or approvals
- Violating contract terms with customers

Compromising shareholder or organizational trust by

- Falsifying or manipulating financial reporting information
- Stealing or misappropriating assets
- Falsifying time and expense reports
- Breaching computer, network, or database controls
- Mishandling confidential or proprietary information
- Violating document retention rules
- Providing inappropriate information to analysts or investors
- Trading securities based on "inside" information
- Engaging in activities that pose a conflict of interest
- Wasting, mismanaging, or abusing the organization's resources

Compromising employee trust by

- Discriminating against employees
- Engaging in sexual harassment or creating a hostile work environment
- Violating workplace health and safety rules
- Violating employee wage, overtime, or benefit rules

- Breaching employee privacy

- Abusing substances (drugs, alcohol) at work

Compromising supplier trust by

- Violating or circumventing supplier selection rules

- Accepting inappropriate gifts or kickbacks from suppliers

- Paying suppliers without accurate invoices or records

- Entering into supplier contracts that lack proper terms, conditions, or approvals

- Violating the intellectual property rights or confidential information of suppliers

- Violating contract or payment terms with suppliers

- Doing business with disreputable suppliers

Compromising public or community trust by

- Violating environmental standards

- Exposing the public to safety risk

- Making false or misleading claims to the media

- Providing regulators with false or misleading information

- Making improper political contributions to domestic officials

- Making improper payments or bribes to foreign officials

- Doing business with third parties that may be involved in money laundering

- Doing business with third parties prohibited under international trade restrictions and embargoes

- Violating international or human rights

General

- Violating company values and principles

SOURCE: KPMG Forensic. Fraud survey 2006. Retrieved from http://www.global/compliance.com. Used by permission.

Leaders need to set forth clear ethical expectations and punish offenders before their isolated misbehaviors become part of the organization's memory and operations. If corruption does become part of the group's normal way of doing business, more drastic steps, like those described in Case Study 9.1, are required.

Justice

Treating people fairly or justly is another hallmark of an ethical organizational climate.[19] Justice in the workplace takes three forms: distributive, procedural, and interactional. Ethical organizations strive to distribute outcomes like pay, office space, time off, and other organizational resources as fairly as possible. They use fair procedures or policies to make these determinations. Further, moral leaders treat people with dignity and respect and share information about how decisions are made.[20]

Perceptions of justice or injustice have been found to have powerful effects on the attitudes and behaviors of organizational members.[21] Those who believe that their organizations are just are generally more satisfied, committed, trusting, and accepting of authority. They are also more likely to engage in such moral behaviors as helping out other employees and reporting ethical violations to management. In contrast, perceptions of unfair treatment increase such withdrawal behaviors as neglecting job responsibilities, absenteeism, and quitting. Those who believe they have experienced injustice are also more likely to engage in dark-side behaviors like sexual harassment, incivility, and exacting revenge on coworkers or the organization as a whole. In addition, they are less likely to report ethical problems to management.

Strategies for promoting fairness or justice include the following:

- Distribute pay and other benefits according to a well-structured system; explain how pay raises are granted.

- Provide other benefits (training, time off) to employees when they are asked to do more but the budget doesn't allow for raises.

- Offer clear explanations for how resources like budgets and space are distributed; tie decisions to organizational values and purpose.

- Base performance appraisal on job-related criteria; clarify standards and expectations in advance and allow for feedback.

- Involve followers in decision-making processes (grant them a significant voice).

- Allow employees to challenge or appeal job decisions.

- Deal truthfully with organizational members.

- Supply rationales for layoffs and firings; express sincerity, kindness, and remorse.

- Follow through on reports of ethical violations; punish wrongdoers.

- Offer public apologies for injustices and offer compensation to victims of injustice.

FOCUS ON FOLLOWER ETHICS

The Journey to Corruption

Most people believe that they have high moral standards. If that's the case, then how do so many employees become actively involved in collective corruption? Ethical theorists Blake Ashforth and Vikas Anand argue that organizational newcomers are socialized into corrupt activities. They accept unethical and illegal behavior as part of becoming a group member. They can be corrupted through three different avenues: co-optation, incrementalism, and compromise. In co-optation, leaders offer rewards that reduce newcomers' discomfort with unethical behavior. Followers may not realize that these incentives are skewing their judgment, making it easier to rationalize destructive behavior. For example, health maintenance organization (HMO) doctors earning cost-reduction bonuses may convince themselves that they are justified in not ordering needed medical tests for patients.

Incrementalism gradually introduces newcomers to unethical practices, leading them up the "ladder of corruption." New members are first persuaded to engage in a practice that is only mildly unethical, such as using private customer information to make additional sales. They then turn to rationalizations offered by peers ("Everybody does it"; "Nobody was really hurt"; "They got what they deserved") to relieve the cognitive dissonance produced by this act. After the initial practice becomes typical, acceptable behavior, individuals are then encouraged to move to increasingly corrupt activities. Eventually they find themselves engaging in behaviors (e.g., secretly selling private customer information to other companies) they would have rejected when they first joined the organization.

(Continued)

(Continued)

Compromise "backs" individuals into corruption as they try to solve difficult problems and resolve conflicts. Politicians, for example, make lots of compromises as they try to keep and expand their power. Cutting deals and forming alliances makes it harder for them to maintain their ethical principles. Police detectives also find themselves making compromises. To gather the information they need to solve crimes, they may compromise with informants. First they overlook minor crimes committed by their sources. Later they may excuse their informants when they engage in much more serious crimes.

The danger of dysfunctional socialization is greatest when followers join *social cocoons*. A social cocoon is a strong culture that holds values and norms very different from those held by the rest of the organization or society as a whole. New employees who strongly identify with the group tend to compartmentalize their lives, holding one set of values while at work and another outside the job.

Ashforth and Anand believe that recognizing the routes to corruption can equip followers to resist their influence, as can considering the perspective of suppliers, community members, and others outside the group. These investigators encourage organizations to have periodic "introspection days" when organizational members take a careful look at all of their activities and determine the ethical implications of their actions. External facilitators can help employees determine if they are using rationalizations to excuse corrupt behavior.

SOURCES: Anand, V., Ashforth, B. E., & Joshi, M. (2004). Business as usual: The acceptance and perpetuation of corruption in organizations. *Academy of Management Executive, 18,* 39–53; Ashforth, B. E., & Anand, V. (2003). The normalization of corruption in organizations. *Research in Organizational Behavior, 25,* 1–52.

Integrity

Integrity is ethical soundness, wholeness, and consistency.[22] All units and organizational levels share a commitment to high moral standards, backing up their ethical talk with their ethical walk. Consistency increases the level of trust, encouraging members and units to be vulnerable to one another.

According to business ethicist Lynn Paine, managers who act with integrity see ethics as a driving force of an enterprise. These leaders recognize that ethical values largely define what an organization is and what it hopes to accomplish. They keep these values in mind when making routine decisions. Their goal? To help constituents learn to govern their own behavior by following these same principles. Paine believes that any effort to improve organizational integrity must include the following elements.[23]

There are sensible, clearly communicated values and commitments. These values and commitments spell out the organization's obligations to external stakeholders (customers, suppliers, neighbors) while appealing to insiders. In highly ethical organizations, members take shared values seriously and don't hesitate to talk about them.

Company leaders are committed to and act on the values. Leaders consistently back the values, use them when making choices, and determine priorities when ethical obligations conflict with one another. For example, former Southwest Airlines president Herb Kelleher put a high value both on the needs of his employees and on customer service. However, it's clear that his workers came first. He didn't hesitate to take their side when customers unfairly criticized them. Such principled leadership was missing at Arthur Andersen, which used to be one of the largest accounting firms in the country. Andersen accountants certified the financial statements of Qwest, Waste Management, Boston Chicken, Global Crossing, WorldCom, and the Baptist Foundation of Arizona, which were all found guilty of accounting fraud. They were reluctant to challenge the accounting practices of clients because they didn't want to lose lucrative consulting contracts with these organizations. Andersen's managing partners dissolved the firm after executives were convicted for obstruction of justice for shredding Enron documents.[24]

The values are part of the routine decision-making process and are factored into every important organizational activity. Ethical considerations shape such activities as planning and goal setting, spending, gathering and sharing information, evaluation, and promotion.

Systems and structures support and reinforce organizational commitments. Systems and structures, such as the organizational chart, how work is processed, budgeting procedures, and product development, serve the organization's values. (I'll have more to say about the relationship between ethics and structure later in the chapter.)

Leaders throughout the organization have the knowledge and skills they need to make ethical decisions. Organizational leaders make ethical choices every day. To demonstrate integrity, they must have the necessary skills, knowledge, and experience. Ethics education and training must be part of their professional development.

Paine and other observers warn us not to confuse integrity with compliance. Ethical compliance strategies are generally responses to outside pressures such as media scrutiny, the U.S. Sentencing Commission guidelines, or the Sarbanes–Oxley Act. Under these federal guidelines, corporate executives can be fined and jailed not only for their ethical misdeeds but also for failing to take reasonable steps to prevent the illegal behavior of employees. Although compliance tactics look good to outsiders, they frequently don't have a lasting impact on ethical climate.[25] Large firms typically have formal ethics strategies in place, including ethics codes and policies, ethics officers, and systems for registering and dealing with ethical concerns and complaints. However, all too often these programs have minimal influence on company operations. Policies may not be enforced; some complaint hotlines are rarely used; compliance efforts might be underfunded; CEOs may fail to communicate to employees about ethics.[26]

Trust

Ethical organizations are marked by a high degree of trust. Not only do members trust one another, but also, together, they develop a shared or aggregate level of trust that becomes part of the group's culture. *Organizational trust* describes the collective set of positive expectations members hold about the intentions and behaviors of other stakeholders (coworkers, superiors, followers, other departments), which are based on their experiences and interactions as organizational members.[27] These expectations shape how vulnerable individuals and groups are when interacting with one another and with the organization as a whole. For example, a follower who trusts her supervisor is more likely to take the risk of admitting that a project isn't going well. Two team leaders who trust each other are more likely to cooperate to carry out a new change initiative. On the other hand, employees who don't believe that the organization carries through on its commitments aren't likely to put forth their best efforts.

Over the past 30 years trust has moved from the periphery to the center of organizational studies, primarily because it has been linked to so many positive outcomes.[28] Trust binds group members together, fostering collaboration and communication; lowering costs; reducing turnover; encouraging organizational learning, innovation, and work effort; and generating employee satisfaction and commitment. High-trust organizations make higher-quality decisions, operate more efficiently, and are more productive and profitable. They also behave in a more ethical manner. That's because trust involves vulnerability and obligation or duty. Those who trust believe that the other party—individual, group, or organization—will carry through on promises and commitments. They put themselves in a vulnerable position because they are depending on others and will suffer if these parties break their commitments. High-trust organizations fulfill their moral obligation or duty by protecting the rights and interests of members and outsiders.

Collective trust is made up of several factors or dimensions. According to one classification system, members judge an organization to be trustworthy if (1) the group makes good-faith efforts to keep its commitments, (2) is honest when negotiating such commitments, and (3) does not take unfair advantage of members even when provided with the opportunity to do so.[29] (To determine your work group's degree of trust in another department, complete Self-Assessment 9.2, the Organizational Trust Inventory.) Other researchers identify five dimensions of organizational trust: competence, openness, concern, reliability, and identification.[30] *Competence* is the collective perception that leadership—both supervisory and top management—is effective and that the organization can survive. Organizational survival depends on such factors as the ability to create new products rapidly, meet competitive pressures, and find new markets. *Openness* or honesty is the belief that management shares information and is sincere. *Concern* reflects caring and empathy. Concerned leaders (and followers) don't take advantage of the vulnerability of others. *Reliability* describes perceptions of consistent and dependable behavior. Those organizations that match their words and actions generate trust; those that fail to "walk the talk" undermine trust. *Identification* is the feeling of affiliation and association with the organization.

Leaders are key to the development of organizational trust. Moral leaders lay the foundation for collective trust by acting in a trustworthy manner. They demonstrate the character traits described in Chapter 3 (e.g., compassion, honesty, courage). They also communicate a clear sense of mission and vision, foster an atmosphere that encourages openness and sharing, are consistent in their behavior, demonstrate caring, follow through on promises and commitments, and so forth. (See Case Study 9.2 for an example of a CEO who may have lowered the trust level of her firm.)

Process Focus (Concern for Means and Ends)

Concern for how an organization achieves its goals is another important indicator of a healthy ethical climate. In far too many organizations, leaders set demanding performance goals but intentionally or unintentionally ignore how these objectives are to be reached. Instead, they pressure employees to produce sales and profits by whatever means possible. Followers then feel powerless and alienated, becoming estranged from the rest of the group. Sociologists use the term *anomie* to refer to this sense of normlessness and unease that results when rules lose their force.[31] Anomie increases the likelihood that group members will engage in illegal activities and reduces their resistance to demands from authority figures who want them to break the law. Loss of confidence in the organization may also encourage alienated employees to retaliate against coworkers and the group as a whole.

Leaders can address the problem of anomie by making sure that goals are achieved through ethical means. False promises cannot be used to land accounts, all debts must be fully disclosed to investors, kickbacks are prohibited, and so on. They can also make a stronger link between means and ends through ethics programs that address all aspects of organizational ethical performance.

Structural Reinforcement

An organization's structure and policies shouldn't undermine the ethical standards of its members. Instead, as I noted in our discussion of integrity, structure should encourage higher ethical performance on the part of both leaders and followers. Three elements of an organization's structure have a particularly strong impact on moral behavior:

1. *Monetary and nonmonetary reward systems.* Organizations often encourage unethical behavior by rewarding it.[32] Consider the case of the software company that paid programmers $20 for each software bug they found and corrected. Soon programmers were deliberately creating bugs to fix! Another software firm headquartered in Korea gave large incentives to salespeople for making lofty sales targets. This encouraged employees to misrepresent sales by reporting that customers had paid when they had not and by having fellow workers pose as clients. In one 9-month period, 70% of reported sales were fictitious.[33] A visit to the local 10-minute oil change shop provides another case of the impact of misplaced rewards. Some lube and oil franchises pay managers and employees based in part on how many additional services and parts they sell beyond the basic oil change. As a consequence, unscrupulous mechanics persuade car owners to buy unneeded air filters, transmission flushes, and wiper blades. It is not

always easy to determine all the consequences of a particular reward system. However, ethical leaders make every effort to ensure that desired moral behaviors are rewarded, not discouraged.

2. *Performance and evaluation processes.* Performance and evaluation processes must reflect the balance between means and ends described earlier, monitoring both *how* and *whether* goals are achieved. Ethically insensitive monitoring processes fail to detect illegal and immoral behavior and may actually make such practices more likely. As noted earlier, when poor behavior goes unpunished, followers may assume that leaders condone and expect such actions. Former giant brokerage house Salomon Brothers is a case in point. In the early 1990s, a government securities trader at the firm violated U.S. Treasury Department regulations and confessed to then-CEO John Gutfreund. Gutfreund took no action against the rogue trader, in part because he was a star performer. Failure to swiftly punish this star employee enabled him to continue his criminal behavior and cost Salomon millions in fines and much of its stock and bond business.[34]

3. *Decision-making rights and responsibilities.* Ethical conduct is more likely when workers are responsible for ethical decisions and have the authority to choose how to respond. Leaders at ethical organizations do all they can to ensure that those closest to the process or problem can communicate their concerns about ethical issues. These managers also empower followers to make and implement their choices. Unfortunately, employees with the most knowledge are often excluded from the decision-making process or lack the power to follow through on their choices. Such was the case in the *Columbia* space shuttle disaster. Lower-level managers were concerned that a piece of foam had damaged the shuttle's protective shield during liftoff. However, higher-ranking NASA officials dismissed their worries. During reentry, superheated gas entered a 6- to 10-inch hole, triggering an explosion that killed seven astronauts.[35] Case Study 9.3 provides another example of a situation in which frontline employees were not empowered to make ethical decisions.

Social Responsibility

Concern for those outside the organization is another sign of a healthy ethical climate. For example, ethical businesses recognize that they have several sets of responsibilities: (1) economic (produce needed goods to sell at fair prices, make profits, reward investors), (2) legal (obey laws and regulations), (3) ethical (avoid questionable activities and do what is "right, fair, and just"), and (4) philanthropic (be a good corporate citizen by giving back to the community).[36] As a result, responsible corporations engage in "triple bottom line" accounting.[37] They evaluate their success based not just on financial results but also on their social and environmental performance. Good corporate citizens send volunteers to work on Habitat for Humanity building projects, sponsor food drives, set up philanthropic organizations to give money to needy causes, and so forth.[38] At the same time, they address environmental problems by taking such steps as capping plant emissions, using recycled components, creating less toxic products, reducing oil consumption, and buying from environmentally friendly suppliers. For example, Starbucks incorporates social responsibility into its corporate values. Every April the company sponsors a global month of service, and it hopes to encourage employees and customers to donate a million volunteer hours by 2015. The coffee seller funds youth leadership programs, clean water initiatives, and education programs in China. In order to support its coffee, tea, and cocoa producers, Starbucks sponsors community projects in developing nations. Individual stores are free to promote local charities through volunteer hours, store products, and cash contributions. To measure its progress, the firm commissions an annual social responsibility report that indicates whether the company is reaching its social goals.[39] (More examples of socially responsible corporations can be found in the discussion of corporate values to follow.)

Recognizing the legitimate claims of stakeholders is key to social responsibility. Stakeholders are any group affected by or having a stake in the organization's policies and operations. Organizational stakeholders might include shareholders, suppliers, competitors, customers, creditors, unions, social activists, governments, local communities, and the general public.[40] Stakeholder theorists argue that organizational leaders have an ethical obligation to consider such groups because they have intrinsic value and ought to be treated justly. Reaching out to these parties contributes to the common good of society.[41] Socially responsible organizations try to identify all stakeholders and their interests (stakes). They seek to be accountable to, and to engage with, these groups, cooperating with them whenever possible and minimizing the negative impact of organizational activities. When needed, these organizations engage in dialogue with their critics, as Nike did after years of ignoring public outcry about conditions at the factories of its overseas suppliers. The firm invited human rights, labor, and environmental officials to company headquarters to discuss international worker issues.[42]

Climate-Building Tools

To build or create ethical organizational climates, leaders rely heavily on three tools: core ideology, codes of ethics, and ethics training.

Discovering Core Ideology

Management experts James Collins and Jerry Porras use the term *core ideology* to refer to the central identity or character of an organization. The character of outstanding companies remains constant even as these firms continually learn and adapt. According to Collins and Porras, "Truly great companies understand the difference between what should never change and what should be open for change, between what is genuinely sacred and what is not."[43]

Core values are the first component of core ideology. (See Box 9.3 for some examples.) One way to determine whether a value is sacred to your organization is to ask, "What would happen if we were penalized for holding this standard?" If you can't honestly say that you would keep this value if it cost your group market share or profits, then it shouldn't show up on your final list. To determine core values, Collins and Porras recommend the Mars Group technique. In this approach, participants imagine they have been asked to re-create the very best attributes of their organization (school, business, nonprofit) on another planet. Groups are limited to five to seven people since space on the rocket ship is scarce. Group members work from personal to organizational values by considering these questions:

- What core values (values that you would hold regardless of whether they were rewarded) do you personally bring to your work?

- What values would you tell your children that you hold at work and that you hope they will hold as working adults?

- If you woke up tomorrow morning with enough money to retire, would you continue to live with those core values? Can you envision them being as valid for you 100 years from now as they are today?

- Would you want to hold these core values even if one or more of them became a competitive disadvantage?

- If you were to start a new organization in a different line of work, what core values would you build into the new organization regardless of industry?

Groups summarize their conclusions and present them to others in the organization, comparing their values with those of other groups traveling on other spaceships.

BOX 9.3 CORE VALUES

Eaton Corporation

- Make our customers the focus of everything we do

- Recognize our people as our greatest asset

- Treat each other with respect

- Be fair, honest, and open

- Be considerate of the environment and our communities

- Keep our commitments

- Strive for excellence

Levi Strauss

- Empathy—Walking in other people's shoes

- Originality—Being authentic and innovative

- Integrity—Doing the right thing

- Courage—Standing up for what we believe

Amgen Inc.

- Be science-based

- Compete intensely and win

- Create value for patients, staff, and stockholders

- Be ethical

- Trust and respect each other

- Ensure quality

- Work in teams

- Collaborate, communicate, and be accountable

Denny's

- Giving our best

- Appreciating others

- A can-do attitude

First Horizon National Corporation

- Exceptional teamwork

- Individual accountability

- Absolute determination

- Knowing our customers

- Doing the right thing

Charles Stewart Mott Foundation

- Act honestly, truthfully, and with integrity

- Treat every individual with dignity and respect

- Be responsible, transparent, and accountable

- Benefit communities

SOURCES: Abrahams, J. (2007). *101 mission statements from top companies*. Berkeley, CA: Ten Speed Press; Kidder, R. M. (2004). Foundation codes of ethics: Why do they matter, what are they, and how are they relevant to philanthropy? *New Decisions for Philanthropic Fundraising, 45*, 75–83.

Core purpose is the second part of an organization's ideology. *Purpose* is the group's reason for being that reflects the ideals of its members. Here are some examples of corporate purpose/mission statements from some of the largest corporations in four English-speaking nations:[44]

United States

To provide comprehensive pharmacy solutions that improve productivity, profitability and result in superior patient care and satisfaction. (McKesson)

We are a global family with a proud heritage passionately committed to providing personal mobility for people around the world. (Ford Motor)

Use our pioneering spirit to responsibly deliver energy to the world. (ConocoPhillips)

Australia

To help our customers fulfill their aspirations. (National Australia Bank)

To deliver to customers the right shopping experience each and every time. (Woolworths)

To be the leading international property company. (Lend Lease)

Canada

To be the best at helping customers become financially better off. (Bank of Nova Scotia)

To be the world's best gold mining company by finding, acquiring, developing, and producing quality reserves in a safe, profitable, and socially responsible manner. (Barrick Gold)

To be the world's leading manufacturer of planes and trains. (Bombardier)

Britain

To create value for customers to earn their lifetime loyalty. (Tesco)

Deliver an ever-improving quality shopping experience for our customers with great products at fair prices. (J. Sainsbury)

To be the Leading Systems Company, Innovating for a Safer World. (BAE Systems)

Asking the "Five Whys" is one way to identify organizational purpose. Start with a description of what your organization does and then ask why that activity is important five separate times. Each "Why?" will get you closer to the fundamental mission of your group.

Your organization's purpose statement should inspire members. (Don't make high profits or stock dividends your goal, because these don't motivate people at every level of the organization.) Your purpose should also serve as an organizational anchor. Every other element of your organization—business plans, expansion efforts, buildings, products—will come and go, but your purpose and values will remain.

Appreciative inquiry (AI) is another effective tool for developing a shared understanding of ethical values. Participants in the AI process set out to discover the organization's "positive core" and use the group's strengths to guide individual and collective action.[45] Appreciative inquiry has been used in a variety of organizational settings to, for example, promote creativity and innovation, facilitate strategic planning, boost quality, and reduce employee turnover, as well as to improve ethical performance.

AI begins by choosing an affirmative topic, based on the assumption that what organizational members study will determine the kind of organizations they create. Asking positive questions ("What are our values?" "What does ethics mean to us?") elicits positive examples and achievements. Once the affirmative topic is selected, appreciative inquiry moves through four stages: discovery, dream, design, and destiny.

The discovery phase identifies "the best of what has been and what is." Interviews and brainstorming sessions highlight organizational achievements and important traditions. These could include stories of organizational heroes and how the organization lived up to its commitments during tough times or descriptions of the group's tradition of social responsibility. In the dream phase participants look to the future to ask, "What might be?" They develop a vision of the organization's ethical future, focusing on the group's ultimate purpose ("What is the world calling us to become?"). The design stage incorporates both the discovery and dream phases by describing exactly how the organization will look and act if it lives up to its values. This ideal organization integrates the positive core elements of the group into the dream created by participants. For example, a place where everyone can voice his or her concerns about unethical behavior without fear of punishment, or a place where commitment to the community takes precedence over short-term profits. In the last stage—destiny—participants collectively commit themselves to building the desired organization. They might design tactics for encouraging dissent, for instance, or develop new community outreach programs.

South African industrial/organizational psychologists Leon van Vuuren and Freddie Crous describe how one university department used appreciative inquiry to develop "an ethical way forward."[46] After identifying core ethical values and experiences during the discovery phase, department members identified key themes during the dream stage. They then put these values in the form of propositions during the design phase. Their important propositions included "We are committed to personal growth and meaningful work," "We respect the uniqueness and contributions of others," and "We act with integrity supported by visible ethical leadership." Departmental members committed themselves to supporting these values, which were formalized in a code of ethics, during the destiny stage.

Codes of Ethics

Codes of ethics are among the most common ethics tools. Companies listed on the New York Stock Exchange and the NASDAQ are required to have them, and under the Sarbanes–Oxley Act public firms must disclose whether they have such codes for their senior executives.[47] Many government departments, professional associations, social service agencies, and schools have developed codes as well. Nevertheless, formal ethics statements are as controversial as they are popular. Skeptics make these criticisms:[48]

- Codes are too vague to be useful.

- Codes may not be widely distributed or read.

- Most codes are developed as public relations documents designed solely to improve an organization's image.

- Codes don't improve the ethical climate of organizations or produce more ethical behavior.

- Codes often become the final word on the subject of ethics.

- Codes are hard to apply across cultures and in different situations.

- Codes often lack adequate enforcement provisions.

- Codes often fail to spell out which ethical obligations should take priority, or they put the needs of the organization ahead of those of society as a whole.

- Adherence to codes often goes unrewarded.

The experience of Enron highlights the shortcomings of formal ethical statements. Company officials had a "beautifully written" code of ethics that specifically prohibited the off-the-books financial deals that led to its bankruptcy.[49] Unfortunately, these same executives convinced the board of directors to waive this prohibition.

Defenders of ethical codes point to their potential benefits. First, a code describes an organization's ethical stance both to members and to the outside world. Newcomers, in particular, look to the code for guidance about an organization's ethical standards and values. They learn about potential ethical problems they may face in carrying out their duties. Second, a formal ethics statement can improve the group's image while protecting it from lawsuits and further regulation. In the case of wrongdoing, an organization can point to the code as evidence that the unethical behavior is limited to a few individuals and not the policy of the company as a whole. Third, referring to a code can encourage followers and leaders to resist unethical group and organizational pressures. Fourth, a written document can have a direct, positive influence on ethical behavior. Students who sign honor codes, for example, are significantly less likely to plagiarize and cheat on tests.[50] Employees in companies with formal codes of ethics judge themselves, their coworkers, and their leaders to be more ethical than do workers in companies that don't have codes. Members of code organizations believe that their organizations are more supportive of ethical behavior and express a higher level of organizational commitment.[51]

There's no doubt that a code of ethics can be a vague document that has little impact on how members act. A number of organizations use these statements for purposes of image, not integrity. They want to appear concerned about ethical issues while protecting themselves from litigation. Just having a code on file, as in the case of Enron, doesn't mean that it will be read or used. Nonetheless, creating an ethical statement can be an important first step on the road to organizational integrity. Although a code doesn't guarantee moral improvement, it is hard to imagine an ethical organization without one. Codes can focus attention on important ethical standards, outline expectations, and help people act more appropriately. They have the most impact when senior executives make them a priority and follow their provisions while rewarding followers who do the same.

Communication ethicists Richard Johannesen, Kathleen Valde, and Karen Whedbee believe that many of the objections to formal codes could be overcome if organizations followed these guidelines:[52]

- Distinguish between ideals and minimum conditions. Identify which parts of the statement are goals to strive for and which are minimal or basic ethical standards.

- Design the code for ordinary circumstances. Members shouldn't have to demonstrate extraordinary courage or make unusual sacrifices in order to follow the code. Ensure that average employees can follow its guidelines.

- Use clear, specific language. Important abstract terms such as *reasonable, distort,* and *falsify* should be explained and illustrated.

- Be logically coherent. Prioritize obligations. Which commitments are most important: The client? The public? The employer? The profession?

- Protect the larger community. Don't protect the interests of the organization at the expense of the public. Speak to the needs of outside groups.

- Focus on issues of particular importance to group members. Every organization and profession will face particular ethical dilemmas and temptations. For instance, lawyers must balance duties to clients with their responsibilities as officers of the court. Doctors try to provide the best care while HMOs pressure them to keep costs down. The code should address the group's unique moral issues.

- Stimulate further discussion and modification. Don't file the code away or treat it as the final word on the subject of collective ethics. Use it to spark ethical discussion and modify its provisions when needed.

- Provide guidance for the entire organization and the profession to which it belongs. Spell out the consequences when the business or nonprofit as a whole acts unethically. Who should respond, and how? What role should outside groups (professional associations, accrediting bodies, regulatory agencies) play in responding to the organization's ethical transgressions?

- Outline the moral principles behind the code. Explain *why* an action is right based on ethical standards (deontology, utilitarianism, altruism) like those described in Chapter 5.

- Encourage widespread input. Draw on all constituencies, including management, union members, and professionals, when developing the provisions of the code.

- Back the code with enforcement. Create procedures for interpreting the code and applying sanctions. Ethics offices and officers should set up systems for reporting problems, investigating charges, and reaching conclusions. Possible punishments for ethical transgressions include informal warnings, formal reprimands that are entered into employment files, suspensions without pay, and terminations.

Most codes of ethics address the following:[53]

- *Conflicts of interest.* Conflicts of interest arise when an employee benefits at the expense of the organization or can't exercise independent judgment because of an investment, activity, or association. Even the appearance of a conflict of interest is problematic.

- *Records, funds, and assets.* Organizations must keep accurate records and protect funds and other assets. Such records (including financial statements) must meet state and federal regulations.

- *Information.* In for-profit organizations, employees can be liable if they or even their families reveal confidential information that undermines performance or competitive advantage. In the public sector, codes of ethics encourage employees to share information rather than to withhold it from the public.

- *Outside relationships.* This category addresses contact with customers, suppliers, competitors, contractors, and other outside individuals and organizations, and includes prohibitions against bad-mouthing the competition, price-fixing, and the sharing of sensitive information.

- *Employment practices.* This category covers discrimination, sexual harassment, drug use, voluntary activities, and related human resource issues.

- *Other practices.* This category sets policies related to a variety of other topics, including health and safety, the use of technology, the environment, political activities, and the use of organizational assets for personal benefit.

If you're interested in developing or refining a code of ethics, you can use the examples in Box 9.4 as a model.

• • • BOX 9.4 ETHICS CODES • • •

A Sampler

Conflicts of Interest (Cummins Inc.)

All of Cummins's employees are expected to use nondiscriminatory practices throughout the supplier selection process. Every employee is expected to avoid any situation in which his or her interests (or those of his or her family) may conflict with the interests of the company. Every employee with a financial interest in any actual or potential supplier or customer must disclose that interest to his or her supervisor immediately and, if applicable, in his or her annual Ethics Certification Statement.

Records, Funds, and Assets (PPG Industries)

Every individual involved in creating, transmitting or entering information into PPG's financial records is responsible for doing so accurately, completely and with appropriate supporting documentation. Compliance with established accounting procedures and controls is necessary at all times. PPG's records, books and documents must accurately reflect the Company's transactions and provide a full account of the organization's assets, liabilities, revenues and expenses.

(Continued)

(Continued)

Protecting Information (Citigroup)

You must safeguard all personal and confidential information about our clients by ensuring that client information is used only for authorized purposes relating to your job, only shared with authorized persons and organizations, and is properly and securely maintained.

Outside Relationships (Hewlett-Packard)

We honor human rights.

- Support and respect the protection of human rights and ensure that our business partners and suppliers do the same.

- Ensure that child labor, prison or forced labor, and physical punishment are never permitted in any operation of HP or our business partners or suppliers.

Employment Practices (Cummins Inc.)

Treatment of Each Other at Work

Each employee will treat every other employee, every customer, every vendor, and all others met in the course of work with dignity and respect. Harassment of any type in the workplace will not be tolerated.

Other Practices (Coca-Cola)

Personal Political Activity

The Coca-Cola Company encourages personal participation in the political process in a manner consistent with all relevant laws and Company guidelines.

- The Company will not reimburse employees for personal political activity.

- Do not use the Company's reputation or assets, including your time at work, to further your own political activities or interests.

SOURCES: Center for the Study of Ethics in the Professions at Illinois Institute of Technology. (2013). *Index of codes.* Retrieved from http://ethics.iit.edu/codes; Citigroup, Coca-Cola, Cummins, Eaton, Hewlett-Packard, and PPG corporate websites.

Ethics Training

Formal ethics training can play an important role in creating and maintaining ethical climates. When part of the socialization process, ethics instruction can help prevent newcomers from joining in corrupt activities. Training sessions for experienced employees can heighten sensitivity to moral danger signs, reduce destructive behaviors, foster trust, promote organizational integrity, reinforce shared purpose and values, and clarify ethical standards and expectations. Ethics training plays a critical role in helping large organizations meet compliance guidelines set by the U.S. Sentencing Commission. Of course, training efforts do not guarantee that participants will make better moral choices or behave ethically. Nevertheless, effective ethics training can make a positive difference. Effective training does the following:[54]

1. *Focuses on the organization's unique ethical problems.* Every organization faces a unique set of ethical problems and issues. Issues that accountants face (audits, tax advice, financial statements, earnings projections, quarterly earnings statements) are different from those faced by sales professionals (product safety, pricing, product placement, advertising claims), for instance. Introduce examples drawn directly from the organization, industry, and profession. Then equip trainees with the tools they need to address these dilemmas.

2. *Taps into the experiences of participants.* Encourage trainees to reflect on their own values and decision-making strategies as well as important moral moments or episodes in their lives. Solicit their input when selecting issues and cases to discuss. Ask participants to provide dilemmas and insights from their own experiences. They then become instructors, "teaching" one another. They also receive valuable feedback that enables them to better manage their dilemmas.

3. *Actively engages participants.* Key concepts can be presented in lectures and handouts, but spend most class time in dyadic, small-group, and large-group discussion, acting as a facilitator. Introduce case studies that raise significant issues and engage the emotions of participants (see the discussion of dual processing in Chapter 6). Ask questions and debate issues. Make sure the training space can be adapted to a variety of teaching strategies. Use online tools to augment, not replace, classroom interaction. Even though Web-based ethics training is becoming increasingly popular because it is cheap and convenient, online-only programs don't appear to be as effective as classroom training. That's because online instruction doesn't facilitate in-depth consideration of complex ethical cases and issues.

4. *Reinforces the organization's ideology and standards.* Training sessions should reinforce other components of the group's ethical climate. Trainers, supervisors, and executives should highlight the group's purpose and core values, tell stories about the organization's ethical heroes, discuss the code of ethics, provide information about reporting systems, and so on.

5. *Is integrated into the entire curriculum.* Ethics instruction shouldn't be limited only to stand-alone sessions but should be integrated throughout the organization's training program. For example, discussion of bribery and price-fixing can be integrated into sales instruction. Incorporating ethics in a variety of workshops increases the likelihood that moral concerns will become part of the organization's fabric, helping it to act with integrity.

IMPLICATIONS AND APPLICATIONS

- As a leader, you will serve as an ethics officer of your organization, exercising influence by the example you set for followers and by making sure that ethical messages aren't drowned out by messages about tasks and profits.

- Recognize the dangers posed by organizational success and narcissism. Foster humility as a collective virtue and be alert to signs that the organization may be headed for moral failure.

- Organizations have varying ethical orientations or ethical climates that affect their ethical decision making and behavior. Climates marked by self-interest are most likely to encourage unethical behavior.

- Combat the shadow side of organizational life by creating zero-tolerance policies for individual (incivility, aggression, sexual harassment, discrimination) and collective (fraud, bribery, price-fixing) destructive actions.

- Create perceptions of organizational justice by distributing resources fairly, following equitable processes, and treating others with dignity and respect.

- Build organizational trust—collective perceptions of competence, openness, concern, reliability, and identification—by acting in a trustworthy manner and encouraging others to do the same.

- Integrity develops through clearly communicated values and commitments, leaders who are committed to these values, application of the values to routine decisions, systems and structures that support organizational commitments, and members who are equipped to make wise ethical choices.

- Don't confuse compliance with integrity. Compliance protects an organization from regulation and public criticism but often has little impact on day-to-day operations. Integrity is at the center of an organization's activities, influencing every type of decision and activity.

- Pay close attention to how your organization achieves its goals. Failure to do so will create anomie and undermine ethical performance.

- Reinforce ethical commitments in your organization through the design of monetary and nonmonetary reward systems, performance and evaluation processes, and allocation of decision-making authority.

- Ethical organizations recognize their obligations to their communities, demonstrating concern for social and environmental performance. Help your organization act in a socially responsible manner by honoring its ethical duty to stakeholder groups.

- Core ideology is essential to any healthy ethical climate. Encourage your organization to identify and communicate its values and purpose.

- Useful codes of ethics can play an important role in shaping ethical climate. Make sure they define and illustrate important terms and address the problems faced by the members of your particular organization. View ethics statements as discussion starters, not as the final word on the topic of organizational morality.

- Effective ethics training can promote positive ethical climate if it is adapted to the ethical problems of the organization, taps into the experiences of participants, and actively engages them. Instruction should reinforce other elements of the organization's ethics strategy and be integrated into the entire training program.

FOR FURTHER EXPLORATION, CHALLENGE, AND SELF-ASSESSMENT

1. Select a well-known senior executive and determine whether this person should be classified as ethical, hypocritical, ethically neutral, or unethical. Provide evidence to support your conclusion.

2. Analyze the ethical climate of your organization. In your paper, consider the following questions: How would you classify the organization's ethical orientation based on Self-Assessment 9.1, the Ethical Climate Questionnaire? Overall, would you characterize the climate as positive or negative? Why? What factors shape the moral atmosphere? What role have leaders played in its formation and maintenance?

What steps does the organization take to deal with misbehaviors? Does the organization consider both means and ends? How does the group's structure reinforce (or fail to reinforce) espoused values and ethical behavior? What inconsistencies do you note?

3. Discuss each of the following statements in a group or, as an alternative, argue for and against each proposition in a formal debate. Your instructor will set the rules and time limits. Refer to the discussion of argumentation and Box 8.2 ("Common Fallacies") in the previous chapter for

more information on constructing effective arguments.

- Pro or con: Organizations are less ethical now than they were 10 years ago.

- Pro or con: Formal codes of ethics do more harm than good.

- Pro or con: Ethical businesses are more profitable over the long term.

- Pro or con: Organizational values can't be developed; they must be uncovered or discovered instead.

- Pro or con: An organization's purpose has to be inspirational.

- Pro or con: An organization can change everything except its core values and purpose.

4. Write a research paper on one form of individual or collective destructive behavior in the workplace. Conclude with suggestions to help leaders curb this type of behavior.

5. Compare and contrast an organization that has a climate of integrity with one that pursues ethical compliance.

6. Describe a time when you experienced anomie in an organization. What factors led to your feelings of powerlessness and alienation? How did anomie influence your behavior? As an alternative, reflect on a time when you felt you were treated unjustly in an organization. What factors led you to believe you were being treated unfairly? How did experiencing injustice influence your behavior?

7. Develop a shared set of values for your class using strategies presented in this chapter.

8. Conduct an analysis of the mission statements of 10 different companies or organizations. Which are most effective? Why?

9. Evaluate an ethical code based on the guidelines presented in this chapter. What are its strengths and weaknesses? How useful would it be to members of the organization? How could the code be improved? What can we learn from this statement?

10. Design an ethics training program for your organization using the guidelines presented in this chapter.

STUDENT STUDY SITE _____

Visit the student study site at **www.sagepub.com/johnsonmecl5e** to access full SAGE journal articles for further research and information on key chapter topics.

CASE STUDY 9.1

Rooting Out Corruption at Siemens Global

For many years offering bribes was business as usual at Siemens Global, the giant German engineering firm. Siemens employees channeled payments to government officials, primarily in developing countries, in order to secure contracts. For example, Siemens paid as much as $60 million in bribes to win the right to produce Argentina's national identity cards, $20 million to build power plants in Israel, $14 million to supply medical equipment in China, $14 million to construct rail lines in Venezuela, and $5 million to supply phone equipment in Bangladesh. The company also made secret payments to Saddam Hussein's Iraqi government to participate in the United Nations–sponsored oil-for-food program. Bribes typically ranged from 5% to 6% of a contract's value, although they could go as high 40% in highly corrupt nations. Money that could have gone to roads, schools, and hospitals in needy areas went to dishonest government officials instead. Residents of poor countries paid more than they should have for power plants, highways, railways, and phone equipment.

Siemens executives covered up illegal payments by transferring money to foreign accounts in countries with lax banking regulations. They also funneled money to phony companies in nations where they were bidding for contracts. Local "consultants" then delivered the payoffs to officials, often using suitcases or bags stuffed with cash. Between 2001 and 2006, one midlevel executive supervised the payoff program—with an annual budget of $40 million to $60 million—to make sure that the payments were disguised and that employees didn't siphon off funds designated for foreign officials. Noted a spokesperson for German federal prosecutors: "Bribery was Siemens' business model. Siemens had institutionalized corruption."[1]

The illegal payment scheme was unearthed in 2006. Siemens, with more than 400,000 employees and annual sales in excess of 72 billion euros, paid $1.6 billion in fines in Germany and the United States (where it is listed on the New York Stock Exchange) and must spend another $1 billion to monitor its compliance to antibribery statutes. (The penalties would have been much higher, but the firm cooperated with U.S. investigators.) Siemens also had to pay $100 million to the World Bank to support anticorruption work and was banned from bidding on World Bank contracts for two years. Several German employees of the firm, including a former board member, have been convicted of fraud and other crimes. Six former executives are charged with providing payments to former Argentine presidents.

CEO Peter Loescher, appointed as the firm's first non-German chief executive in 2007, spearheaded the task of rooting out corruption at Siemens and restoring the company's reputation. The first step he took was to announce a zero-tolerance policy: "The approach was very simple—zero tolerance. From Day One, what I have clearly communicated to everyone is that we have a Zero-Tolerance policy that there is absolutely no grey zone and that Siemens stands for clean business everywhere, and at all times."[2] To implement this policy, Loescher hired a chief ethics officer and

- removed half of the management board,

- selected the company's general counsel to be chief compliance officer and made him a member of the board,

- fired offenders even if they didn't violate local laws,

- centralized business functions to make it harder for individuals and divisions to operate illegally,

- established an amnesty program so that employees could come forward with information without fear of punishment,

- adopted new antibribery rules,

- hired outside legal and financial investigators to identify suspicious payments,

- hired the cofounder of Transparency International to develop an anticorruption training program for employees,

- increased the compliance staff from 86 to 500, and

- created a Web portal that employees can use to ethically evaluate their interactions with customers and consultants.

The anticorruption campaign apparently succeeded. Siemens received the highest possible rating on the Dow Jones Sustainability World Index. U.S. regulators praised the firm for its anticorruption initiatives, holding it up as a model for other companies charged with corruption. And good models are needed. Prosecutions under the U.S. Foreign Corrupt Practices Act (FCPA) have surged. Foreign firms are subject to the provisions of the FCPA (which prohibits bribes) if they are listed on a U.S. stock exchange. Mercedes-Benz maker Daimler, French telecommunications company Alcatel-Lucent, Japanese consulting company UGC, U.S. contractor KBR, and other firms have paid more than $3.2 billion in settlements. At last count, 78 companies, including Alcoa, Avon, Goldman Sachs, Pfizer, and Wal-Mart, were under investigation.

Discussion Probes

1. Given the company's massive size and the scale of its corrupt activities, did Siemens get off too easy? Should it have faced additional financial penalties?

2. What should be the elements of a zero-tolerance ethics policy? Are any of these elements missing at Siemens Global?

3. What lessons do you take away from Siemens's efforts to eliminate corruption?

4. Should the United States prosecute companies headquartered in other countries for violating its Foreign Corrupt Practices Act?

5. What steps can multinational firms take to prevent their employees from offering bribes, particularly to government officials in poor nations?

Notes

1. Schubert, S., & Miller, T. C. (2008, December 21). Where bribery was just a line item. *The New York Times,* p. BU1.

2. James, K. (2008, May 24). Siemens' straight shooter. *The Business Times Singapore.*

Sources

Big victory against global bribery. (2008, December 17). *The Christian Science Monitor,* p. 8.

CEO's moral compass steers Siemens. (2010, February 15). *USA Today,* p. 3B.

Dennis, B. (2011, December 14). 6 former Siemens officials indicted. *The Washington Post,* p. A18.

Dougherty, C. (2008, October 7). The sheriff at Siemens, at work under Justice Dept's watchful eye. *The New York Times,* p. B11.

Gow, D. (2008, January 25). Siemens prepares to pay $2bn fine to clear up slush fund scandal. *The Guardian,* p. 34.

O'Reilly, C., & Matussek, K. (2008, December 16). Siemens settles bribery cases. *The Washington Post,* p. D2.

Siemens settles World Bank with $100 million for anti-fight corruption. (2009, July 6). *Africa News.*

Wayne, L. (2012, March 11). Hits, and misses, in a war on bribery. *The New York Times,* p. BU1.

Wayne, L. (2012, September 4). Foreign firms most affected by a U.S. law barring bribes. *The New York Times,* p. B1.

CASE STUDY 9.2

Trust and Telecommuting

Yahoo! CEO Marissa Mayer surprised observers when she told workers that they could no longer work from home. She issued a memo to employees stating: "To become the absolute best place to work, communication and collaboration will be important, so we need to be working side-by-side. Speed and quality are often sacrificed when we work from home."[1] Not only is Yahoo! a high-tech company, but Mayer is also a working mother who broke the glass ceiling in a male-dominated industry. Immediately after being hired at Yahoo!, she had her first child. Mayer went back to work after only two weeks of maternity leave but had a nursery built next to her office so she could work longer hours. Her return-to-the-office decree seemed to be a setback for work–life balance, particularly for working women who telework, or telecommute, to stay close to their children. Mayer appeared to be trying to reverse a national trend in which 10% of workers report that they work from home at least one day a week. To make the office more enticing for employees, however, Mayer added perks like free lunches and Android devices.

Reaction to Mayer's memo was sharply divided. Supporters praised her for taking a bold step to help save the company, which had lost much of its stock value. According to a Stanford researcher:

> Yahoo is one messed-up company right now. The culture is in awful shape—values, loyalty, you name it. Marissa inherited a complete mess. By bringing everyone in-house, she'll be able to reprogram the company's work culture while also easily jettisoning a lot of deadwood.[2]

Some hoped that Yahoo's move would prompt reconsideration of the work-from-home movement, complaining that telecommuting has been "romanticized" and can be a "career killer." Researchers report that the typical telecommuter is a 49-year-old male, not a young mother.

Critics of Mayer's move pointed to surveys that demonstrate that work-at-home employees are more productive and more satisfied. Many companies encourage teleworking to cut the need for office space, reduce traffic, and give employees more flexibility. A growing number of younger workers will likely expect to work from home. Of *Fortune*'s "Best Companies to Work For," 80% allow telecommuting. More than one commentator noted that Mayer's decision seemed to be signaling that she doesn't trust her employees. Said one work–life balance expert: "She's effectively taking a huge chunk of autonomy away from these people and she's actually saying to them 'I think you're not smart enough to figure out when you should come in and collaborate with your colleagues versus when you can work more effectively at home.'"[3] Even a fellow CEO expressed his opposition to Mayer's decision to force workers back to the office. Virgin Group founder Richard Branson pointed out that successful leadership rests on "trusting people to get their work done wherever they are, without supervision."[4]

Discussion Probes

1. Do you think requiring employees to return to the office increases employee productivity?

2. What limits, if any, should be placed on teleworking?

3. Was it fair for Mayer to require that working mothers return to the office when she could afford to build a nursery for her own child?

4. What does Mayer's work-at-the-office memo say about her values and the values that she wants to instill at Yahoo!?

5. Will the return-to-the-office decree significantly lower the level of organizational trust at Yahoo!? Why or why not?

6. Should other leaders follow the example of Mayer and require that their employees work at the office?

Notes

1. Boesveld, S. (2013, March 2). A CEO first: Yahoo's Marissa Mayer meets criticism for telling employees to come into the office or quit. *National Post*, p. A3.

2. Weise, E. (2013, February 26). Telecommuters to Yahoo: Boo. *USA Today*, p. 1A.

3. Boesveld.

4. Mendoza, D. (2013, February 27). Yahoo work-from-home policy riles workers everywhere. CNN Tech. Retrieved from http://www.cnn.com/TECH

Sources

Collamer, N. (2013, March 1). The problem with Yahoo's work-at-home ban. *Forbes.* Retrieved from Forbes.com.

Hampson, R. (2013, March 12). Boss vs. you: The work-from-home tug of war. *USA Today*, pp. 1A, 2A.

Onstad, K. (2013, March 1). Yahoo for you, boss. What about progress? *The Globe and Mail*, p. L2.

CASE STUDY 9.3

Just Say No to CPR

What could be more heartless than refusing to give CPR to a dying person? That's what millions of American wondered when they heard the recording of a 911 call between an emergency operator and a staff member at an assisted living facility in Bakersfield, California. On the tape the dispatcher pleads with Colleen (identified as a nurse) to begin efforts to revive resident Lorraine Bayless. The 87-year-old had collapsed in the dining room at Glenwood Gardens, an assisted living center. Colleen refuses, citing company policy. The increasingly frantic 911 operator then asks Colleen to find someone else who would begin the procedure. "I understand if your boss is telling you you can't do it. But . . . as a human being . . . you know . . . is there anybody that's willing to help this lady and not let her die?" Colleen answers, "Not at this time."[1] Mrs. Bayless later died in a local hospital.

CPR probably would not have been effective on Mrs. Bayless since she suffered a stroke, not a heart attack, and survival rates following CPR are low after age 80. Mrs. Bayless's family members said they were satisfied with the response of Glenwood Gardens and promised not to sue. In a statement they noted that their mother and grandmother wanted to die "without any kind of life-prolonging intervention"[2] and hoped that the circumstances surrounding her death would provide "a lesson we can all learn from."[3]

Company officials at Brookdale Senior Living of Tennessee, the operators of Glenwood Gardens, claimed that Colleen (who was not acting as a nurse but as an activities director) misunderstood corporate guidelines. They promised to review the firm's emergency medical care procedures. If the company follows guidelines provided by the Assisted Living Federation of America, it will instruct employees to comply with the orders of emergency responders. Many other independent living facilities, which are similar to apartment complexes and are not licensed to provide medical care, perform CPR unless the resident has a "do not resuscitate" directive on file. (Mrs. Bayless did not have such an order.)

As more facts came out, outrage over Glenwood Gardens' refusal to provide CPR died down. Nevertheless, this incident highlights the fact that organizational policies can conflict with our basic moral obligations as humans. According to Dale Jamieson, director of the Center for Bioethics at New York University: "All of us have a duty to respond to people in life-threatening situations. This is a general ethical commitment we have to each other as part of living in society."[4]

Discussion Probes

1. If you were the Glenwood Gardens employee on the 911 call, would you have violated company policy and performed CPR?

2. Since the family was satisfied with the response of Glenwood Gardens, does this justify the decision not to offer CPR?

3. Should Colleen be punished if she acted in good faith but misinterpreted the policy?

4. What emergency care policies should elderly independent living facilities have in place? What steps should leaders take to make sure that all employees and residents understand these guidelines?

5. Is responding to life-threatening situations a "general ethical commitment we have to each other as part of living in society"? Why or why not?

6. How do you determine when your moral duties to others outweigh your obligations to your organization?

Notes

1. Fantz, A. (2013, March 13). To perform CPR or not? Woman's death raises questions. CNN. Retrieved from http://www.CNN.com

2. Graham, J. (2013, March 6). Amid CPR controversy, many unanswered questions. *The New York Times.* Retrieved from http://www.nytimes.com

3. DeVine, J. (2013, March 20). Death at CA facility after no CPR has some reviewing policies. WSMV-TV (Nashville, TN). Retrieved from http://www.wsmv.com

4. Graham.

SELF-ASSESSMENT 9.1

Ethical Climate Questionnaire

Instructions: Indicate whether you agree with each of the following statements about your company or organization. Use the scale below and write the number that best represents your answer in the space next to the item.

Completely False	Mostly False	Somewhat False	Somewhat True	Mostly True	Completely True
0	1	2	3	4	5

1. In this company (organization), people are mostly out for themselves. _____

2. The major responsibility for people in this company (organization) is to control costs. _____

3. In this company (organization), people are expected to follow their own personal and moral beliefs. _____

4. People are expected to do anything to further the company's (organization's) interests, regardless of the consequences. _____

5. In this company (organization), people look out for each other's good. _____

6. There is no room for one's personal morals or ethics in this company (organization). _____

7. It is very important to follow strictly the company's (organization's) rules and procedures here. _____

8. Work is considered substandard only when it hurts the company's (organization's) interests. _____

9. Each person in this company (organization) decides for him- or herself what is right and wrong. _____

10. In this company (organization), people protect their own interests above other considerations. _____

11. The most important consideration in this company (organization) is each person's sense of right and wrong. _____

12. The most important concern is the good of all the people in the company (organization). _____

13. The first consideration is whether a decision violates any law. _____

14. People are expected to comply with the law and professional standards over and above other considerations. _____

15. Everyone is expected to stick by company (organization) rules and procedures. _____

16. In the company (organization), our major concern is always what is best for the other person. _____

17. People are concerned with the company's (organization's) interests—to the exclusion of all else. _____

18. Successful people in this company (organization) go by the book. _____

19. The most efficient way is always the right way in this company (organization). _____

20. In this company (organization), people are expected to strictly follow legal or professional standards. _____

21. Our major consideration is what is best for everyone in the company (organization). _____

22. In this company (organization), people are guided by their own personal ethics. _____

23. Successful people in this company (organization) strictly obey the company (organization) policies. _____

24. In this company (organization), the law or ethical code of one's profession is the major consideration. _____

25. In this company (organization), each person is expected, above all, to work efficiently. _____

26. It is expected that you will always do what is right for the customer and public. _____

Scoring

Caring Climate Score
Add up scores on items 5, 12, 16, 19, 21, 25, 26 =   (Range 0–35) ____

Law and Code Climate Score
Add up scores on items 13, 14, 20, 24 =   (Range 0–20) ____

Rules Climate Score
Add up scores on items 7, 15, 18, 23 =   (Range 0–20) ____

Instrumental Climate Score
Add up scores on items 1, 2, 4, 6, 8, 10, 17 =   (Range 0–35) ____

Independence Climate Score
Add up scores on items 3, 9, 11, 22 =   (Range 0–20) ____

SOURCES: Cullen, J. B., Victor, B., & Bronson, J. W. (1993). The Ethical Climate Questionnaire: An assessment of its development and validity. *Psychological Reports, 73,* 667–674; used by permission. See also Victor, B., & Cullen, J. B. (1988). The organizational bases of ethical work climates. *Administrative Science Quarterly, 33,* 101–125.

SELF-ASSESSMENT 9.2

Organizational Trust Inventory

Instructions: Please choose the unit or department about which you can most knowledgeably report the opinions of members of your department or unit.

1. Your department or unit is _____ (enter name of department/unit).

2. The other department or unit about which you are responding is _____ (enter name of department/unit).

Please circle the number to the right of each statement that most closely describes the opinion of members of your department toward the other department. Interpret the blank spaces as referring to the other department about which you are commenting.

1	2	3	4	5	6	7
Strongly Disagree	Disagree	Slightly Disagree	Neither Agree nor Disagree	Slightly Agree	Agree	Strongly Agree

1. We think the people in _____ tell the truth in negotiations.

2. We think that _____ meets its negotiated obligations to our department.

3. In our opinion, _____ is reliable.

4. We think that the people in _____ succeed by stepping on other people. (Reverse)

5. We feel that _____ tries to get the upper hand. (Reverse)

6. We think that _____ takes advantage of our problems. (Reverse)

7. We feel that _____ negotiates with us honestly.

8. We feel that _____ will keep its word.

9. We think _____ does not mislead us.

10. We feel that _____ tries to get out of its commitments. (Reverse)

11. We feel that _____ negotiates joint expectations fairly.

12. We feel that _____ takes advantage of people who are vulnerable. (Reverse)

Scoring

Reverse item scores where indicated and then add your scores. Total scores can range from 12 to 84. The higher the score, the greater your unit's trust in the members of the other department.

SOURCE: Cummings, L. L., & Bromiley, P. (1996). The Organizational Trust Inventory (OTI): Development and validation. In *Trust in organizations: Frontiers of theory and research* (pp. 302–330). Thousand Oaks, CA: Sage. Used by permission of the authors.

NOTES _____

1. See, for example, Grojean, M. W., Resick, C. J., Dickson, M. W., & Smith, D. B. (2004). Leaders, values, and organizational climate: Examining leadership strategies for establishing an organizational climate regarding ethics. *Journal of Business Ethics, 55,* 223–241; Gottlieb, J. Z., & Sabzgiri, J. (1996). Towards an ethical dimension of decision making in organizations. *Journal of Business Ethics, 15,* 1275–1285.

2. Trevino, L. K., Hartman, L. P., & Brown, M. (2000). Moral person and moral manager: How executives develop a reputation for ethical leadership. *California Management Review, 42*(4), 128–133; Trevino, L. K., Brown, M., & Pincus, L. (2003). A qualitative investigation of perceived executive ethical leadership: Perceptions from inside and outside the executive suite. *Human Relations, 56,* 5–37; Brown, M. E., Trevino, L. K., & Harrison, D. (2005). Ethical leadership: A social learning perspective for construct development and testing. *Organizational Behavior and Human Decision Processes, 97,* 117–134; Trevino, L. K., & Brown, M. E. (2005). The role of leaders in influencing unethical behavior in the workplace. In R. E. Kidwell & C. L. Martin (Eds.), *Managing organizational deviance* (pp. 69–87). Thousand Oaks, CA: Sage; Brown, M. E., & Trevino L. K. (2006). Ethical leadership: A review and future directions. *Leadership Quarterly, 17,* 595–616.

3. Trevino et al. (2000); Trevino, L. K., & Nelson, K. A. (2004). *Managing business ethics: Straight talk about how to do it right* (3rd ed.). Hoboken, NJ: John Wiley, Ch. 9.

4. Johnson, C. E. (2008). The rise and fall of Carly Fiorina: An ethical case study. *Journal of Leadership & Organizational Studies, 15,* 188–196.

5. Pacanowsky, M. E., & O'Donnell-Trujillo, N. (1983). Organizational communication as cultural performance. *Communication Monographs, 5,* 126–147.

6. Victor, B., & Cullen, J. B. (1988). The organizational bases of ethical work climates. *Administrative Science Quarterly, 33,* 101–125; Victor, B., & Cullen, J. B. (1990). A theory and measure of ethical climate in organizations. In W. C. Frederick & L. E. Preston (Eds.), *Business ethics: Research issues and empirical studies* (pp. 77–97). Greenwich, CT: JAI Press; Cullen, J. B., Victor, B., & Bronson, J. W. (1993). The Ethical Climate Questionnaire: An assessment of its development and validity. *Psychological Reports, 73,* 667–674.

7. Fritzsche, D. J. (2000). Ethical climates and the ethical dimension of decision making. *Journal of Business Ethics, 24,* 125–140; Peterson, D. K. (2002). The relationship between unethical behavior and the dimensions of the Ethical Climate Questionnaire. *Journal of Business Ethics, 41,* 313–326; Cullen, J. B., Parboteeah, K. P., & Victor, B. (2003). The effects of ethical climates on organizational commitment: A two-study analysis. *Journal of Business Ethics, 46,* 127–141; Sims, R. L., & Keon, T. L. (1997). Ethical work climate as a factor in the development of person–organization fit. *Journal of Business Ethics, 16,* 1095–1105; Trevino, L. K., Butterfield, K. D., & McCabe, D. L. (1998). The ethical context in organizations: Influences on employee attitudes and behaviors. *Business Ethics Quarterly, 8,* 447–476; Martin, K. D., & Cullen, J. B. (2006). Continuities and extensions of ethical climate theory: A meta-analytic review. *Journal of Business Ethics, 69,* 175–194; Wang, Y.-D, & Hseih, J.-H. (2012). Toward a better understanding of the link between ethical climate and job satisfaction: A multilevel analysis. *Journal of Business Ethics, 15,* 535–545.

8. Balch, D. R., & Armstrong, R. W. (2010). The Icarus syndrome and banality of wrongdoing. *Journal of Business Ethics, 92,* 291–303.

9. Stein, M. (2003). Unbounded irrationality: Risk and organization narcissism at Long Term Capital Management. *Human Relations, 56,* 523–540. See also Brown, A. D. (1997). Narcissism, identity, and legitimacy. *Academy of Management Review, 22,* 643–686.

10. Griffin, R. W., & O'Leary-Kelly, A. M. (Eds.). (2004). *The dark side of organizational behavior.* San Francisco: Jossey-Bass; Mumford, M. D., Gessner, T. L., Connelly, M. S., O'Conner, J. A., & Clifton, T. (1993). Leadership and destructive acts: Individual and situational influences. *Leadership Quarterly, 4,* 115–147.

11. Pearson, C. M., & Porath, C. L. (2004). On incivility, its impact and directions for future research. In R. W. Griffin & A. M. O'Leary-Kelly (Eds.), *The dark side of organizational behavior* (pp. 131–158). San Francisco: Jossey-Bass; Porath, C. L., & Erez, A. (2007). Does rudeness really matter? The effects of rudeness on task performance and helpfulness. *Academy of Management Journal, 50,* 1181–1197; Pearson, C. M., & Porath, C. I. (2005). On the nature, consequences and remedies of workplace incivility: No time for "nice"? Think again. *Academy of Management Executive, 19,* 7–18.

12. Buss, A. H. (1961). *The psychology of aggression.* New York: John Wiley.

13. Levy, A. C., & Paludi, M. A. (2002). *Workplace sexual harassment* (2nd ed.). Upper Saddle River, NJ: Prentice Hall.

14. Diboye, R. L., & Halverson, S. K. (2004). Subtle (and not so subtle) discrimination in organizations. In R. W. Griffin & A. M. O'Leary-Kelly (Eds.), *The dark side of organizational behavior* (pp. 404–425). San Francisco: Jossey-Bass.

15. U.S. Department of Labor. (2010, July). Frequently asked questions (FAQs). Retrieved from http://www.dol.gov/dolfaq/dolfaq. asp; Ilies, R., Hauserman, N., Schwochau, S., & Stibal, J. (2003). Reported incidence rates of work-related sexual harassment in the United States: Using meta-analysis to explain reported rate disparities. *Personnel Psychology, 56,* 607–651; Diboye & Halverson; Department of Numbers. (2013). Unemployment demographics. Retrieved from http://deptofnumbers.com/unemployment/demographics; Yen, H. (2011, July 26). Wealth gap between whites, minorities widens to greatest level in a quarter century. Huffington Post.

16. Alexander, D. (2013, March 13). Lawmakers angered at U.S. military's handling of sex assault problem. Yahoo! News. Retrieved from http://news.yahoo.com; Military injustice on sexual assault. (2013, March 14). *Newsday.*

17. Baron, R. A. (2004). Workplace aggression and violence: Insights from basic research. In R. W. Griffin & A. M. O'Leary-Kelly (Eds.), *The dark side of organizational behavior* (pp. 23–61). San Francisco: Jossey-Bass.

18. Ashforth, B. E., & Anand, V. (2003). The normalization of corruption in organizations. *Research in Organizational Behavior, 25,* 1–52; Anand, V., Ashforth, B. E., & Joshi, M. (2004). Business as usual: The acceptance and perpetuation of corruption in organizations. *Academy of Management Executive, 18,* 39–53; Darley, J. M. (1996). How organizations socialize individuals into evildoing. In D. M. Messick & A. E. Tenbrunsel (Eds.), *Codes of conduct: Behavioral research into business ethics* (pp. 12–43). New York: Russell Sage Foundation; Luo, Y. (2004). An organizational perspective of corruption. *Management and Organization Review, 1,* 119–154.

19. Cropanzano, R., & Stein, J. H. (2009). Organizational justice and behavioral ethics: Promises and prospects. *Business Ethics Quarterly, 19,* 193–233.

20. Colquitt, J. A., Conlon, D. E., Wesson, M. J., Porter, C. O. L. H., & Yee, N. K. (2001). Justice at the millennium: A meta-analytic review of 25 years of organizational justice research. *Journal of Applied Psychology, 86,* 425–445; Fortin, M. (2008). Perspectives on organizational justice: Concept clarification, social context integration, time and links with morality. *International Journal of Management Reviews, 10,* 93–126; Trevino, L. K., & Weaver, G. R. (2001). Organizational justice and ethics program "follow-through": Influences on employee's harmful and helpful behavior. *Business Ethics Quarterly, 11,* 651–671.

21. Greenberg, J., & Wiethoff, C. (2001). Organization justice as proaction and reaction: Implications for research and application. In R. Cropanzano (Ed.), *Justice in the workplace* (Vol. 2, pp. 271–302). Mahwah, NJ: Erlbaum; Folger, R., & Baron, R. A. (1996). Violence

and hostility at work: A model of reactions to perceived injustice. In G. R. VandenBos & E. Q. Bulato (Eds.), *Violence on the job: Identifying risks and developing solutions* (pp. 51–85). Washington, DC: American Psychological Association; Reb, J., Goldman, B. M., Kray, L. J., & Cropanzano, R. (2006). Different wrongs, different remedies? Reactions to organizational remedies after procedural and interactional injustice. *Personnel Psychology, 59,* 31–64; Kickul, J. (2001). When organizations break their promises: Employee reactions to unfair processes and treatment. *Journal of Business Ethics, 29,* 289–307; Trevino & Weaver.

22. A number of authors use the term *integrity* to describe ideal managers and organizations. See Brown, M. T. (2005). *Corporate integrity: Rethinking organizational ethics and leadership.* Cambridge, England: Cambridge University Press; Pearson, G. (1995). *Integrity in organizations: An alternative business ethic.* London: McGraw-Hill; Petrick, J. A. (1998). Building organizational integrity and quality with the four Ps: Perspectives, paradigms, processes, and principles. In M. Schminke (Ed.), *Managerial ethics: Moral management of people and processes* (pp. 115–131). Mahwah, NJ: Erlbaum; Solomon, R. C. (1992). *Ethics and excellence: Cooperation and integrity in business.* New York: Oxford University Press; Srivastva, S. (Ed.). (1988). *Executive integrity.* San Francisco: Jossey-Bass.

23. Paine, L. S. (1996, March–April). Managing for organizational integrity. *Harvard Business Review,* pp. 106–117.

24. Toffler, B. L., & Reingold, J. (2003). *Final accounting: Ambition, greed, and the fall of Arthur Andersen.* New York: Broadway.

25. McKendall, M., DeMarr, B., & Jones-Rikkers, C. (2002). Ethical compliance programs and corporate illegality: Testing the assumptions of the corporate sentencing guidelines. *Journal of Business Ethics, 37,* 367–383; Rockness, H., & Rockness, J. (2005). Legislated ethics: From Enron to Sarbanes–Oxley, the impact on corporate America. *Journal of Business Ethics, 57,* 31–54; Andreoli, N., & Lefkowitz, J. (2008). Individual and organizational antecedents of misconduct in organizations. *Journal of Business Ethics, 85,* 309–332.

26. Weber, J., & Wasieleski, D. M. (2013). Corporate ethics and compliance programs: A report, analysis and critiques. *Journal of Business Ethics, 112,* 609–626; Weaver, G. R., Trevino, L. K., & Cochran, P. L. (1999). Integrated and decoupled corporate social performance: Management commitments, external pressures, and corporate ethics practices. *Academy of Management Journal, 42,* 539–552.

27. Shockley-Zalabak, P., Ellis, K., & Winograd, G. (2000). Organizational trust: What it means, why it matters. *Organization Development Journal, 18*(4), 35–47; Shockley-Zalabak, P., Ellis, K., & Cesaria, R. (2000). *Measuring organizational trust: A diagnostic survey and international indicator.* San Francisco: International Association of Business Communicators; Kramer, F. M. (2010). Collective trust within organizations: Conceptual foundations and empirical insights. *Corporate Reputation Review, 13,* 82–97.

28. See, for example, Bruhn, J. G. (2001). *Trust and the health of organizations.* New York: Kluwer/Plenum; Shockley-Zalabak, P., Morreale, S. P., & Hackman, M. Z. (2010). *Building the high-trust organization: Strategies for supporting five key dimensions of trust.* San Francisco: Jossey-Bass; Dirks, K. T. (1999). The effects of interpersonal trust on work group performance. *Journal of Applied Psychology, 84,* 445–455.

29. Cummings, L. L., & Bromiley, P. (1996). The Organizational Trust Inventory (OTI): Development and validation. In R. M. Kramer & T. R. Tyler (Eds.), *Trust in organizations: Frontiers of theory and research* (pp. 302–329). Thousand Oaks, CA: Sage.

30. Shockley-Zalabak et al. (2010).

31. Cohen, D. V. (1993). Creating and maintaining ethical work climates: Anomie in the workplace and implications for managing change. *Business Ethics Quarterly, 3,* 343–358.

32. James, H. S. (2002). Reinforcing ethical decision-making through organizational structure. *Journal of Business Ethics, 28,* 43–58.

33. Dunn, J., & Schweitzer, M. E. (2005). Why good employees make unethical decisions. In E. W. Kidwell & C. L. Martin (Eds.), *Managing organizational deviance* (pp. 39–60). Thousand Oaks, CA: Sage.

34. Useem, M. (1998). *The leadership moment: Nine stories of triumph and disaster and their lessons for us all.* New York: Times Books, Ch. 7.

35. Sawyer, K. (2003, August 24). Shuttle's "smoking gun" took time to register. *The Washington Post,* p. A1; Glanz, W. (2003, August 27). NASA ignored dangers to shuttle, panel says. *The Washington Times,* p. A1.

36. Carroll, A. B., & Buchholtz, A. K. (2012). *Business and society: Ethics, sustainability, and stakeholder management* (8th ed.). Mason, OH; South-Western Cengage Learning. See also Schwartz, M. S. (2011). *Corporate social responsibility: An ethical approach.* Peterborough, Ontario: Broadview.

37. Panchak, P. (2002). Time for a triple bottom line. *Industry Week,* p. 7; Robins, F. (2006). The challenge of TBL: A responsibility to whom? *Business and Society Review, 111,* 1–14.

38. Kotler, P., & Lee, N. (2005). *Corporate social responsibility: Doing the most good for your company and your cause.* Hoboken, NJ: John Wiley.

39. Information on the Global Responsibility Report can be found on the Starbucks website (see http://www.starbucks.com/responsibility).

40. Buchholz, R. A., & Rosenthal, S. B. (2005). Toward a conceptual framework for stakeholder theory. *Journal of Business Ethics, 58,* 137–148; Sims, R. R. (2003). *Ethics and corporate social responsibility: Why giants fall.* Westport, CT: Praeger.

41. Buchholtz & Carroll; Donaldson, T., & Preston, L. E. (1995). The stakeholder theory of the corporation: Concepts, evidence, and implications. *Academy of Management Review, 20,* 65–91; Cooper, S. (2004). *Corporate social performance: A stakeholder approach.* Burlington, VT: Ashgate; Goodpaster, K. E. (1991). Business ethics and stakeholder analysis. *Business Ethics Quarterly, 1,* 53–27; Philips, R. (2003). *Stakeholder theory and organizational ethics.* San Francisco: Berrett-Koehler; Freeman, R. E., Harrison, J. S., & Wicks, A. C. (2007). *Managing for stakeholders: Survival, reputation, and success.* New Haven, CT: Yale University Press.

42. Zadek, S. (2004, December). The path to corporate responsibility. *Harvard Business Review,* pp. 125–132.

43. Collins, J. C., & Porras, J. I. (1996, September–October). Building your company's vision. *Harvard Business Review,* p. 66. See also Collins, J. (2001). *Vision framework.* Retrieved from http://www.jimcollins.com/tools/vision-framework.pdf

44. King, D., Case, C. J., & Premo, K. M. (2011). A mission statement analysis comparing the United States and three other English speaking countries. *Academy of Strategic Management Journal, 10,* Special Issue, 21–45.

45. See, for example, Cooperrider, D. L., & Whitney, D. (2005). *Appreciative inquiry: A positive revolution in change.* San Francisco: Berrett-Koehler; Lewis, D., Medland, J., Malone, S., Murphy, M., Reno, K., & Vaccaro, G. (2006). Appreciative leadership: Defining effective leadership methods. *Organization Development Journal, 24*(1), 87–100; Whitney, D., & Trosten-Bloom, A. (2003). *The power of appreciative inquiry: A practical guide to positive change.* San Francisco: Berrett-Koehler.

46. Van Vuuren, L. J., & Crous, F. (2005). Utilising appreciative inquiry (AI) in creating a shared meaning of ethics in organizations. *Journal of Business Ethics, 57,* 399–412.

47. Paine, L., Deshpandé, R., Margolis, J. D., & Bettcher, K. E. (2005, December). Up to code: Does your company meet world-class standards? *Harvard Business Review,* pp. 122–133.

48. For more information on the pros and cons of codes of conduct, see Darley, J. M. (2001). The dynamics of authority influence in organizations and the unintended action consequences. In J. M. Darley, D. M. Messick, & T. R. Tyler (Eds.), *Social influences on ethical behavior in organizations* (pp. 37–52). Mahwah, NJ: Erlbaum; Hatcher, T. (2002). *Ethics and HRD: A new approach to leading*

responsible organizations. Cambridge, MA: Perseus; Mathews, M. C. (1990). Codes of ethics: Organizational behavior and misbehavior. In W. C. Frederick & L. E. Preston (Eds.), *Business ethics: Research issues and empirical studies* (pp. 99–122). Greenwich, CT: JAI Press; Metzger, M., Dalton, D. R., & Hill, J. W. (1993). The organization of ethics and the ethics of organizations: The case for expanded organizational ethics audits. *Business Ethics Quarterly, 3,* 27–43; Trevino et al. (1998); Wright, D. K. (1993). Enforcement dilemma: Voluntary nature of public relations codes. *Public Relations Review, 19,* 13–20.

49. Countryman, A. (2001, December 7). Leadership key ingredient in ethics recipe, experts say. *Chicago Tribune,* pp. B1, B6.

50. McCabe, D., & Trevino, L. K. (1993). Academic dishonesty: Honor codes and other contextual influences. *Journal of Higher Education, 64,* 522–569.

51. Adams, J. S., Taschian, A., & Shore, T. H. (2001). Codes of ethics as signals for ethical behavior. *Journal of Business Ethics, 29,* 199–211; Valentine, S., & Barnett, T. (2003). Ethics code awareness, perceived ethical values, and organizational commitment. *Journal of Personal Selling & Sales Management, 23,* 359–367.

52. Johannesen, R. L., Valde, K. S., & Whedbee, K. E. (2008). *Ethics in human communication* (6th ed.). Long Grove, IL: Waveland Press, Ch. 10.

53. Hopen, D. (2002). Guiding corporate behavior: A leadership obligation, not a choice. *Journal for Quality & Participation, 25,* 15–19.

54. See, for example, Sauser, W. I. (2011). Beyond the classroom: Business ethics training for professionals. In R. R. Sims & W. I. Sauser (Eds.), *Experiences in teaching business ethics* (pp. 247–261). Charlotte, NC: Information Age; Knapp, J. C. (2011). Rethinking ethics training: New approaches to enhance effectiveness. In R. R. Sims & W. I. Sauser (Eds.), *Experiences in teaching business ethics* (pp. 217–230). Charlotte, NC: Information Age; Petrick, J. A. (2008). Using the business integrity capacity model to advance ethics education. In D. L. Swanson & D. G. Fisher (Eds.), *Advancing business ethics education* (pp. 103–124). Charlotte, NC: Information Age; Waples, E. P., Antes, A., Murphy, S. T., Connelly, S., & Mumford, M. D. (2009). A meta-analytic investigation of business ethics instruction. *Journal of Business Ethics, 87,* 133–151; Weber, J. A. (2007). Business ethics training: Insights from learning theory. *Journal of Business Ethics, 70,* 61–85.

CHAPTER

10

Meeting the Ethical Challenges of Diversity

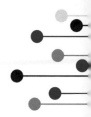

One may also observe in one's travels to distant countries the feelings of recognition and affiliation that link every human being to every other human being.

—Ancient Greek philosopher Aristotle

Human beings draw close to one another by their common nature, but habits and customs keep them apart.

—Confucian saying

What's Ahead

In this chapter, we examine the problems and opportunities posed by cultural and other differences. Leaders have an ethical obligation to foster diversity in their organizations. At the same time, they must master the ethical challenges of leadership in a global society. Ethical global leaders acknowledge the dark side of globalization and recognize the impacts of ethical diversity. They understand the relationship between cultural values and ethical choices, seek ethical common ground, and develop strategies for making choices in cross-cultural settings.

Promoting Diversity in the Organization: An Ethical Imperative

Globalization may be the most important trend of the 21st century. We now live in a global economy shaped by multinational corporations, international travel, the Internet, immigration, and satellite communication systems. Greater cultural diversity is one product of globalization. Non-Whites account for most of the population growth in the United States, and 22 of the nation's 100 largest cities have majority minority populations. In other industrialized nations, most new workers are immigrants or members of groups currently underrepresented in the workplace. Italy and Germany will need hundreds of thousands of new immigrants each year to maintain their working-age populations to 2050, for example. However, cultural diversity isn't the only reason that the workforce is becoming more heterogeneous. Women are participating in the labor force at historically high rates, no longer dropping out after marriage. Among women with children under age 18 in the United States, 71% work outside the home; women account for 51% of those employed in management and professional occupations. Governments around the world have instituted laws that prohibit discrimination against racial minorities, women, gays and lesbians, individuals with disabilities, older workers, and others.[1]

In light of these trends, diversity expert Taylor Cox concludes that managing diversity is the core of modern organizational leadership. Cox and others define managing diversity or diversity management as taking advantage of the benefits of a diverse workforce while coping with the problems that can arise when people from different backgrounds work together. The goal is to enable all employees, regardless of ethnicity, age, gender, sexual orientation, or physical ability, to achieve their full potential and to contribute to organizational goals and performance.[2]

Researchers and organizational leaders have discovered that there are many benefits to a diverse workforce. Diverse organizations are more innovative, make better decisions (see the discussion of minority influence in Chapter 8), have lower absentee and turnover rates, attract higher-quality employees, improve their public image, and gain market share.[3] These benefits make the "business case" for encouraging diversity. However, the best reason for promoting diversity is that it is the right thing to do based on the ethical perspectives described in Chapter 5. In addition to doing more good than harm (utilitarianism), honoring differences recognizes the dignity of individuals (Kant) and promotes justice (Rawls). Helping followers of all kinds reach their full potential also reflects love of neighbor (altruism).

Although fostering diversity is an ethical imperative, there are significant barriers to carrying out this task. Consider, for example, disputes over religious clothing in public schools.[4] France, the Netherlands, Kosovo, and several German states ban female Muslim students from wearing headscarves, but districts in the United States generally allow the practice. Bans on religious clothing and jewelry can also include Sikh turbans, Jewish yarmulkes, and Christian crosses. Opponents of religious attire are concerned that such clothing violates religious neutrality and, in the case of veils, symbolizes sexual discrimination. Proponents of religious clothing in public schools base their support on principles of human rights and freedom of religion.

Prejudice, stereotypes, and ethnocentrism are important attitudinal obstacles. *Prejudice* is the prejudgment of out-group members based on prior experiences and beliefs. Prejudice is universal, but the degree of prejudice varies from person to person, ranging from slight bias to extreme prejudice such as that displayed by racist skinheads. Negative prejudgments can be dangerous because they produce discriminatory behavior. For instance, police in many urban areas of the United States believe that African Americans are more likely than members of other groups to commit crimes. As a consequence, officers are more likely to stop and question Black citizens, particularly young men, and to use force if they show the slightest sign of resistance.[5]

Stereotyping is the process of classifying group members according to their perceived similarities while overlooking their individual differences. For example, one persistent stereotype is that Asian Americans have strong technical skills but little managerial aptitude. As a result, some organizations are eager to hire Asian Americans as engineers but are reluctant to put them in managerial roles. Because of perceptual biases, stereotypes are particularly devastating to marginalized groups. The natural tendency is to blame our failures on outside factors and to attribute our success to internal factors. The opposite is true when we evaluate the behavior of low-status groups. When we fall short, we blame other people, bad luck, bad weather, and other external forces. When we succeed, we point to our knowledge, character, skills, motivation, and training. Conversely, when members of marginalized groups fail, it is their laziness, low intelligence, or poor character that is to blame. When they succeed, however, we give the credit to the help they get from others rather than to their individual skills and effort.[6]

Ethnocentrism is the tendency to see the world from our cultural group's point of view. From this vantage point, our customs and values become the standard by which the rest of the world is judged. Our cultural ways seem natural; those of other groups fall short. A certain degree of ethnocentrism is probably inevitable.[7] Ethnocentrism can help a group band together and survive in the face of outside threats. However, ethnocentrism is a significant barrier to cross-cultural communication and problem solving. High levels of ethnocentrism can lead to the following problems:

- Inaccurate attributions about the behavior of those who differ from us (we interpret their behavior from our point of view, not theirs)

- Expressions of disparagement or animosity (ethnic slurs, belittling nicknames)

- Reduced contact with outsiders

- Indifference and insensitivity to the perspectives of members of marginalized groups

- Pressure on other groups to conform to our cultural standards

- Justification for war and violence as a means of expressing cultural dominance

Examples of ethnocentrism abound. For many years, the Bureau of Indian Affairs made assimilation its official policy, forcing Native Americans to send their children to reservation schools, where they were punished for speaking their tribal languages. In other instances, well-meaning people assume that their values and practices are the only "right" ones. Many early missionaries equated Christianity with Western lifestyles and required converts to dress, live, think, and worship like Europeans or North Americans.

Organizations (often unconsciously) erect barriers to diversity through routine practices. These can include (1) inaccessible facilities that make it hard for people with disabilities to enter workplaces, movie theaters, churches, and other buildings; (2) long workweeks and evening and weekend hours, which increase stress for working mothers; (3) an emphasis on self-promotion, which makes people from cultures that value modesty (such as Japan) uncomfortable; and (4) informal networks that exclude minorities, women, individuals with disabilities, and others from information and contacts for promotion.[8]

Overcoming the barriers described here begins with addressing our attitudes. We can reduce our levels of negative prejudice, stereotyping, and ethnocentrism by committing ourselves to the following.

Mindfulness. In most routine encounters, we tend to operate on "autopilot" and perform our roles mechanically, without much reflection. When we're engaged in such mindless interaction, we're not likely to challenge the ethnocentric assumption that ours is the only way to solve problems. Mindfulness is the opposite of mindlessness. When we're mindful, we pay close attention to our attitudes and behaviors. Three psychological processes take place.[9]

The first is *openness to new categories.* Being mindful makes us more sensitive to differences. Instead of lumping people into broad categories based on age, race, gender, or role, we make finer distinctions within these classifications. We discover that not all student government officers, retirees, engineers, Japanese exchange students, and professors are alike.

The second psychological process involves *openness to new information.* Mindless communication closes us off to new data, and we fail to note the kinds of cultural differences described earlier. We assume that others hold the same ethical values. In mindful communication, we pick up new information as we closely monitor our behavior along with the behavior of others.

The third psychological process is *recognizing the existence of more than one perspective.* Mindlessness results in tunnel vision that ignores potential solutions. Mindfulness, on the other hand, opens our eyes to other possibilities. For example, there can be more than one way to make and implement ethical choices.

Dignity and Integrity. Dignity and integrity ought to characterize all of our interactions with people of other cultures. We maintain our own dignity by confronting others who engage in prejudicial comments or actions; we maintain the dignity of others by respecting their views. Respect doesn't mean that we have to agree with another's moral stance. But when we disagree, we need to respond in a civil, sensitive manner.

Cosmopolitanism. The term *cosmopolitan* describes an attitude or a perspective that incorporates mindfulness, human dignity, and moral inclusion.[10] Cosmopolitans view themselves as citizens of the world with global obligations. If we adopt this perspective, we will honor the intrinsic value of all people, not just members of our immediate group, and will seek to establish a just global society. While maintaining our identification with a particular region or culture, we will not be bound by all of its values and customs. Instead, we will acknowledge our group's shortcomings while, at the same time, appreciating the value of other cultural approaches and recognizing that everyone shares an "essential humanity."[11] (See "Leadership Ethics at the Movies: *The Motorcycle Diaries*" for an example of cosmopolitanism in action.)

LEADERSHIP ETHICS AT THE MOVIES • • • • • • • • •

The Motorcycle Diaries

Key Cast Members: Gael García Bernal, Rodrigo de la Serna, Mía Maestro, Gustavo Bueno, Jorge Chiarella

Synopsis: In 1952 two young friends, one a medical student, the other a biochemist, set off from Buenos Aires for a road trip around South America on an old motorcycle. Their adventure soon becomes a journey of discovery that will change them forever. As they travel through Argentina, Chile, and Peru, they encounter injustice and the suffering of the poor, displaced indigenous peoples, and lepers. Ernesto (played by Bernal) will later become famous as the revolutionary Che Guevara. Alberto (played by de la Serna) will establish a medical clinic in Communist Cuba. The film is based largely on Guevara's journal recorded during the trip.

Rating: R for language and sexuality

Themes: cosmopolitanism, mindfulness, global shadow of power and privilege, character, cultural differences, universal ethical principles

Discussion Starters

1. What character traits and attitudes equip Ernesto and Alberto to deal with a variety of cultures and people?

2. What are key moments or turning points that mark the friends' growing recognition of injustice and suffering?

3. Can you think of other leaders who were shaped by their travel experiences and encounters with different cultures?

By committing ourselves as leaders to mindful communication, the dignity of others, moral inclusion, and cosmopolitanism, we can reduce ethnocentrism and prejudice in the group as a whole. Using morally inclusive language and disputing prejudiced statements, for instance, improves ethical climate because followers will be less likely to attack other groups in our presence. However, if we don't speak out when followers disparage members of out-groups, the practice will continue. We'll share some of the responsibility for creating a hostile atmosphere.

In addition to addressing attitudes about diversity, we can initiate diversity programs. Diversity initiatives address the organizational obstacles to diversity described earlier, highlight the importance of diversity, prevent discrimination, and build diversity practices into routine processes and operations. Effective diversity initiatives include the following:[12]

- Involvement of senior management (taking the lead in diversity projects, hiring consultants, participating in diversity training and programs)

- Integration of diversity into the organization's strategic plan

- Formation of diversity committees and task forces and the hiring of diversity managers and personnel

- Education and training featuring seminars and workshops that help employees understand the value of a diverse workforce, overcome prejudice and discrimination, and develop the skills they need to lead multicultural teams

- Creation of diversity action plans for business units and the entire organization

- Emphasis on holding managers' accountable for diversity results

- Flexible work arrangements—telecommuting, job sharing, working at home, part-time employment—offered to accommodate the needs of diverse employees

- Provision of career development opportunities for members of marginalized groups that increase the likelihood of promotion and entry into management

Complete Self-Assessment 10.1, the Diversity Perceptions Scale, to determine your perceptions of the diversity climate of your organization and your level of comfort with diversity issues.

Mastering the Ethical Challenges of Leadership in a Global Society

So far we've focused on our ethical obligation to foster diversity within our organizations. However, globalization means that we also have to master the ethical challenges of leading across national and cultural boundaries. Meeting these challenges begins with acknowledging the dark side of the globalization process and recognizing the impact of ethical diversity.

The Dark Side of Globalization

Supporters of globalization point to its benefits. Free trade produces new wealth by opening up international markets, they argue. At the same time, the costs of goods and services drop. Cheaper, faster means of communication and travel encourage unprecedented cross-cultural contact.[13] The greater flow of information and people puts pressure on repressive governments to reform.

Critics of globalization paint a much bleaker picture. They note that global capitalism encourages greed rather than concern for others. Ethical and spiritual values have been overshadowed by the profit motive. Local cultural traditions and the environment are being destroyed in the name of economic growth. The gap between the rich and the poor keeps growing.[14]

Debate over whether the benefits of globalization outweigh its costs is not likely to end anytime soon. This much is clear, however: As leaders, we need to give serious consideration to the dark side of the global society in order to help prevent ethical abuse. With that in mind, let's take a closer look at how leaders cast the shadows outlined in Chapter 1 in a global environment.

The Global Shadow of Power

In the modern world, a leader's power is no longer limited by national boundaries. Increasing interdependence brought about by the integration of markets, communication systems, computers, and financial institutions means that the actions of one leader or nation can have a dramatic impact on the rest of the world. Take the Greek financial crisis, for instance. Not only did the country appear likely to default on its debt, but it also threatened to abandon the euro as its national currency. The entire European Union was shaken as a result. This led to significant declines in stock markets, not only in Europe but also in the United States. Global economic recovery slowed.[15]

Ethical leadership in the multinational context must take into account the potential far-ranging consequences of every choice. Shadows fall when leaders forget this fact. For example, the U.S. government refused for decades to increase mileage requirements for trucks and automobiles, which contributed to global warming. Saudi Arabia's unwillingness to ban terrorist groups contributed to the World Trade Center and Bali bombings. Apple,

Intel, Research in Motion (the makers of BlackBerry), and other electronics manufacturers were accused of funding mass rape, murder, and slave labor in the Congo through their purchase of "conflict minerals" mined in the region. Now they must disclose whether they use Congolese titanium, tantalum, tungsten, and gold in their products.[16]

Concentration of power is a by-product of globalization that increases the likelihood of abuse. The United States is a case in point. Critics accuse the world's only superpower of throwing its political and military weight around. Corporations also wield great influence in the global marketplace. Multinational companies have more economic clout than many nations. According to one estimate, 44 of the world's 100 largest economies are corporations.[17] Wal-Mart, which has revenues exceeding the gross national products of 174 countries, has been accused of using its economic power to bribe officials to get rapid approval of new store locations in Mexico.[18]

The Global Shadow of Privilege

As noted earlier, globalization appears to be increasing, not decreasing, the gap between the haves and the have-nots both within and between nations. The United Nations reports that the richest 1% of the world's population owns 40% of the world's wealth; the poorest half owns barely 1%.[19] So far, leaders of wealthy nations have been more interested in promoting the sale of their goods than in opening up their markets to poorer countries. Privileged nations also consume more, which leads to environmental damage in the form of logging, oil drilling, and mineral extraction. This damage has a disproportionate impact on the disadvantaged. Whereas the wealthy can move to cleaner areas, the poor cannot. Instead, poor citizens must deal with the loss of hunting and fishing grounds, clean air, and safe water.

The book *First World Problems* humorously highlights the differences between the haves and the have-nots by describing some of the issues faced by those living in the developed world. While those in so-called Third World nations have to worry about malnutrition, poverty, disease, and lack of medical care, "First Worlders" are concerned about "problems" such as these:[20]

- Paying for an all-you-can-eat buffet and getting full after consuming only one plate of salad

- Discovering there is no 3G coverage in the office bathroom

- Finding foam in a "no foam pumpkin-caramel latte"

- Being forced to run outdoors after the treadmill breaks

- Discovering there are no cup holders in the car

Leaders will continue to cast shadows unless they take steps to make globalization more equitable. To do so, they must (a) put the common (international) good above private gain or self- or national interest, (b) create a global economy that recognizes the interconnectedness of all peoples and the importance of sustaining the environment, (c) practice restraint and moderation in the consumption of goods, and (d) seek justice and compassion by helping marginalized groups.[21]

The Global Shadow of Mismanaged Information

Deceit is all too common on the international stage. Nations routinely spy on each other for economic and military purposes and do their best to deceive their enemies. Businesses from industrialized countries frequently take advantage of consumers in economically depressed regions. Take the marketing of infant formula, for instance. Save the Children estimates that the lives of 3,800 babies could be saved every day if they were adequately breast-fed rather than bottle-fed.[22] Breast-fed babies are more resistant to disease and are less likely to sicken and die in impoverished countries where infant formula is frequently diluted or mixed with polluted water. As an added benefit, poor households could then spend their money on other pressing needs. Despite the adoption of the International Code of Marketing of Breast-Milk Substitutes in 1981, formula manufacturers continue to engage in a variety of deceptive sales practices, which have drawn the ire of health officials at the World Health Organization and in Bangladesh, Nigeria, the Philippines, and other developing nations. These practices include (a) claiming that baby formula is equal to or better than breast-feeding; (b) playing on women's fears that they won't produce enough milk; (c) representing healthy, thriving babies in television ads and on packaging, leaflets, and posters (many women in impoverished nations are particularly vulnerable to these images because they can't read); (d) disguising salespeople as health workers; and (e) gaining medical endorsement by providing free samples to hospitals and gifts to doctors.

In addition to casting shadows through deception, global leaders cast shadows by withholding information. They don't feel as much obligation to share data about safety problems and environmental hazards with foreign nationals as they do with their own citizens. They are guilty of extracting information from poor countries and giving little in return. For example, clinical drug trials in developing countries produce data that go back to company headquarters in Europe or the United States. Weaker countries are given little support in their efforts to develop their own research facilities.[23] (See Scenario B, "Clinical Trials Outsourcing," in Case Study 10.1 for more information on the ethical challenges of conducting medical research in developing nations.)

The Global Shadow of Inconsistency

Economic and social disparities make it hard for leaders of multinational firms and nonprofits to act consistently. For instance, what are "fair" wages and working conditions in developing nations? Do workers in these countries deserve to be protected by the same safety standards as employees in industrialized countries? Should drugs that are banned in the United States for their undesirable side effects be sold in countries where their potential health benefits outweigh their risks? Should a multinational corporation follow the stringent pollution regulations of its home country or the lower standards of a host nation? All too often global leaders answer these questions in ways that cast shadows on disadvantaged world citizens. They pay the bare minimum to workers in developing countries, pay less attention to safety and environmental problems in overseas locations, dump dangerous products they can't sell in their homelands, and so forth.

The shadow of inconsistency grows deeper and longer when leaders ignore human rights abuses and cooperate with repressive regimes in order to benefit from the status quo. That appears to be the case with Unocal (a division of Chevron) and Total, a French petroleum company. They operate Myanmar's (Burma's) Yadana oil field, which produces approximately 630 million cubic feet of natural gas annually.[24] The two companies pay the Burmese military government hundreds of millions in taxes and revenues each year. Despite recent signs that the junta is weakening its grip, this regime is one of the most repressive in the world. Very little of the country's oil money helps the average citizen. At least 40% of the Burmese national budget goes to the military; only 2–3% is devoted to health and welfare. As a result, the nation suffers from widespread poverty, inadequate medical care, and substandard education (fewer than half of all children attend primary school). A group of Myanmar citizens successfully brought suit against Unocal in a U.S. court for human rights violations. The court found that the Burmese military used murder and rape to clear the way for the Yadana pipeline and forced citizens to construct it. While Unocal did not endorse the brutality, the firm benefited from the military's actions.

The Global Shadow of Misplaced and Broken Loyalties

Traditional loyalties are eroding in an integrated world. In the past, national leaders were expected to meet the needs of their citizens. Now, because their actions affect the lives of residents of other nations, they must consider their duties to people they may never meet. Failure to do so produces shadow in the form of environmental damage, poverty, hunger, and the widening income gap.

Broken loyalties cast shadows in a global society just as they do in individual leader–follower relationships. Many poorer world citizens feel betrayed by the shattered promises of globalization. Trade barriers remain in place, and special interests in wealthy nations continue to receive favored treatment. Economic exploitation adds to this sense of betrayal. Low labor costs drive the investments of many multinational companies. Executives at these firms are continually on the lookout for cheaper labor, so they transfer production to even more economically depressed regions.

The Global Shadow of Irresponsibility

Globalization increases the breadth of leaders' responsibilities because they are accountable for the actions of followers in many different geographic locations. Like local leaders, they can't be blamed for all the misdeeds of their followers. Yet they should be held to the same set of responsibility standards outlined in our discussion of the shadow side of leadership in Chapter 1. In order to cast light instead of shadow, global leaders must do the following:

1. *Make reasonable efforts to prevent followers' misdeeds.* Fostering a consistent, ethical organizational climate in every location can prevent many moral abuses. Integrity and a clear set of guiding values should be as characteristic of branch offices as they are of headquarters. Leaders can establish such climates by (a) clearly stating organizational values, (b) communicating these values to all branches through print and electronic media and training programs, (c) letting business partners know about standards, and (d) translating ethical behavior into performance standards and then evaluating followers based on those criteria.[25]

2. *Acknowledge and address ethical problems wherever they occur.* Geographic and cultural distance makes it easy for global leaders to deny responsibility for the misbehavior of followers. Subcontractors often get the blame for low wages and poor working conditions at foreign manufacturing facilities. More responsible firms acknowledge their duty to adequately supervise the activities of their contractors.

3. *Shoulder responsibility for the consequences of their directives.* Wise global leaders recognize that in trying to do the right thing, they might end up producing some unintended negative consequences. Take well-intentioned efforts to eliminate child labor, for instance. Removing children from the factory floor in developing countries can do significant harm. Poor children are an important source of income for their families. When fired from their manufacturing jobs, they often are forced into prostitution or begging. Levi Strauss realized that eliminating child laborers from its Bangladesh plants could do damage to both the children and their families. After identifying workers under age 14 (the international standard for child labor), company officials asked their contractors to remove these children from the production line while continuing to pay their wages. Levi Strauss covered the kids' school costs—tuition, uniforms, books—and agreed to rehire them when they reached working age.[26]

4. *Admit their duties to followers.* Multinational leaders have obligations to all their followers, regardless of citizenship or ethnic and cultural background, and to the communities where they operate. Total, the French petroleum firm, claims that its purpose is to locate oil and it is not responsible for the actions of the Burmese government. Nevertheless, the company helps to underwrite an oppressive government that abuses its citizens.

5. *Hold themselves to the same standards as followers.* Leaders are not above the values, rules, and codes of conduct they impose on their global organizations. While they hold diverse followers to consistent standards, ethical leaders also live up to the same guidelines.

Leadership and Ethical Diversity

Along with taking stock of the potential moral pitfalls of globalization, leaders need to recognize that cultural diversity makes the always difficult process of ethical decision making even harder. Every ethnic group, nation, and religion approaches moral dilemmas from a different perspective. What is perfectly acceptable to members of one group may raise serious ethical concerns for another. Consider the differing responses to these common ethical problems.[27]

Bribery

Spurred by reports that ExxonMobil had paid $59 million to Italian politicians in order to do business in that country, Congress passed the Foreign Corrupt Practices Act of 1977, which forbids U.S. corporations from exchanging money or goods for something in return. Those guilty of bribery can be fined and sent to prison. Malaysia has even stricter bribery statutes, executing corporate officers who offer and accept bribes. On the other hand, bribery is a common, accepted practice in many countries in Africa, Asia, and the Middle East. In recognition of this fact, small payments to facilitate travel and business in less developed nations are permitted under the FCPA.

False Information

Mexico and the United States might be geographic neighbors, but citizens of these countries react differently to deception. In one encounter, American businesspeople were offended when their Mexican counterparts promised to complete a project by an impossible deadline. The Mexicans, on the other hand, viewed their deception as a way to smooth relations between the two sides while protecting their interests.

Intellectual Property Rights

Copyright laws are rigorously enforced in many Western nations but are less binding in many Asian countries. In fact, piracy is legal in Thailand, Indonesia, and Malaysia.

Gender Equality

Treatment of women varies widely. Denmark and Sweden have done the most to promote gender equality, whereas Japan and Saudi Arabia offer some of the stiffest resistance to women's rights. In Japan, women are expected to care for the home and are excluded from leadership positions in government and business. In Saudi Arabia, women (who must wear traditional garb) aren't allowed to drive or form relationships with non-Muslim men.

The challenges posed by cultural variables can discourage leaders from making reasoned moral choices. They may decide to cling to their old ways of thinking or blindly follow local customs. Cultural relativism ("When in Rome do as the Romans do") is an attractive option for many. Nevertheless, being in a new culture or working with a diverse group of followers doesn't excuse leaders from engaging in careful ethical deliberation. Just because a culture has adopted a practice doesn't make it right. Female circumcision may still be carried out in parts of Africa, but the vast majority of those in the West are appalled by this custom. Fortunately, we can expand our capacity to act ethically in a global society and brighten the lives of diverse groups of followers. To do so, we have to deepen our understanding of the relationship between cultural differences and ethical values. Then we need to search for moral common ground and identify strategies for making decisions in cross-cultural settings.

Cultural Differences and Ethical Values

Defining Culture

The same factors that make up an organization's culture—language, rituals, stories, buildings, beliefs, assumptions, power structures—also form the cultures of communities, ethnic groups, and nations. Cultures are comprehensive, incorporating both the visible (architecture, physical objects, nonverbal behavior) and the invisible (thoughts, attitudes, values). In sum, a culture is "the total way of life of a people, composed of their learned and shared behavior patterns, values, norms, and material objects."[28]

Several features of cultures are worth noting in more detail. These elements include the following:

- *Created.* Ethnocentrism would have us believe that ours is the only way to solve problems. In fact, there are countless ways to deal with the environment, manage interpersonal relationships, produce food, and cope with death. Each cultural group devises its own way of responding to circumstances.

- *Learned.* Elements of culture are passed on from generation to generation and from person to person. Cultural conditioning is both a formal and an informal process that takes place in every context—homes, schools, playgrounds, camps, games. The most crucial aspects of a culture, such as loyalty to country, are constantly reinforced. Patriotism in the United States is promoted through high school civics classes, the singing of the national anthem at sporting events, flags flying on everything from pickup trucks to skyscrapers and giant construction cranes, and Fourth of July and Memorial Day programs.

- *Shared.* The shared nature of culture becomes apparent when we break the rules that are set and enforced by the group. There are negative consequences for violating cultural norms of all types. Punishments vary depending on the severity of the offense. For example, you might receive a cold stare from your professor when your cell phone goes off in class. However, you may face jail time if you break drug laws.

- *Dynamic.* Cultures aren't static but evolve. Over time, the changes can be dramatic. Compare the cultural values of the *Leave It to Beaver* television show with those found in modern situation comedies. The world of the Cleavers (a suburban, heterosexual, two-parent family with a well-dressed, stay-at-home mom) has been replaced by portrayals of unmarried friends, single parents, blended families, and gay partners and spouses.

Ethical decisions and practices are shaped by widely held cultural values. Although each culture has its own set of ethical priorities, researchers have discovered that ethnic groups and nations hold values in common. As a result, cultures can be grouped according to their value orientations. These orientations help explain ethical differences and enable leaders to predict how members of other cultural groups will respond to moral dilemmas. In this section of the chapter, I'll describe two widely used cultural classification systems. I will also introduce a third approach specifically developed to explain moral similarities and differences across cultures. Before we examine the cultural classification systems, however, there are four cautions to keep in mind. First, all categories are gross overgeneralizations. They describe what most people in that culture value. Not all U.S. residents are individualistic, for example, and not all Japanese citizens are collectivists. However, *in general,* more Americans put the individual first, whereas more Japanese emphasize group relations. Second, scholars may categorize the same nation differently and have not studied some regions of the world (such as Africa) as intensively as others (Europe, Asia, and the United States). Third, political and cultural boundaries aren't always identical. For instance, the Basque people live in both France and Spain. Fourth, as noted earlier, cultures are dynamic, so values change. A society may change its ethical priorities over time.

Programmed Value Patterns

Geert Hofstede of the Netherlands conducted an extensive investigation of cultural value patterns.[29] According to Hofstede, important values are "programmed" into members of every culture. He surveyed more than 100,000 IBM employees in 50 countries and three multicountry regions to uncover these value dimensions. He then checked his findings against those of other researchers who studied the same countries. The following four value orientations emerged.

Power Distance

The first category describes the relative importance of power differences. Status differences are universal, but cultures treat them differently. In high–power distance cultures

(Philippines, Mexico), inequality is accepted as part of the natural order. Leaders enjoy special privileges and make no attempt to reduce power differentials; however, they are expected to care for the less fortunate. Low–power distance cultures (Ireland, New Zealand), in contrast, are uneasy with large gaps in wealth, power, privilege, and status. Superiors tend to downplay these differences and strive for a greater degree of equality.

Individualism Versus Collectivism

Hofstede's second value category divides cultures according to their preference for either the individual or the group. Individualistic cultures put the needs and goals of the person and her or his immediate family first. Members of these cultures see themselves as independent actors. In contrast, collectivistic cultures give top priority to the desires of the larger group—extended family, tribe, community. Members of these societies stress connection instead of separateness, putting a high value on their place in the collective. Think back to your decision to attend your current college or university. As a resident of Canada or the United States, you probably asked friends, high school counselors, and family members for advice, but in the end, you made the choice. In a collectivistic society such as Peru or Pakistan, your family or village might well have made this decision for you. There's no guarantee that you would have even gone to college. Families with limited resources can afford to send only one child to school. You might have been expected to go to work to help pay for the education of a brother or sister. (You can determine your individualistic or collectivistic tendencies by completing Self-Assessment 10.2.)

Masculinity Versus Femininity

The third dimension reflects attitudes toward the roles of men and women. Highly masculine cultures such as Venezuela and Italy maintain clearly defined sex roles. Men are expected to be decisive, assertive, dominant, ambitious, and materialistic; women are encouraged to serve. Females are to care for the family, interpersonal relationships, and the weaker members of society. In feminine cultures such as Finland, Denmark, and the Netherlands, the differences between the sexes are blurred. Both men and women can be competitive and caring, assertive and nurturing. These cultures are more likely to stress interdependence, intuition, and concern for others.

Uncertainty Avoidance

This dimension describes the way in which cultures respond to uncertainty. Three indicators measure this orientation: anxiety level, widely held attitudes about rules, and employment stability. Members of high–uncertainty avoidance societies (Greece, Portugal) feel anxious about uncertainty and view it as a threat. They believe in written rules and regulations, engage in more rituals, and accept directives from those in authority. In addition, they are less likely to change jobs and view long-term employment as a right. People who live in low–uncertainty avoidance cultures (Ireland, Sweden) are more comfortable with uncertainty, viewing ambiguity as a fact of life. They experience lower stress and are more likely to take risks such as starting a new company or accepting a new job in another part of the country. These people are less reliant on written regulations and rituals and are more likely to trust their own judgments instead of obeying authority figures.

Hofstede argues that value patterns have a significant impact on ethical behavior.[30] For example, masculine European countries give little to international development programs but invest heavily in weapons. Feminine European nations do just the opposite. High–uncertainty avoidance cultures are prone to ethnocentrism and prejudice because they follow the credo "What is different is dangerous." Low–uncertainty avoidance cultures follow the credo "What is different is curious" and are more tolerant of strangers and new ideas.

Other researchers have joined Hofstede in linking value patterns to ethical attitudes and behavior.[31] They have discovered that members of feminine cultures are more sensitive to the presence of moral issues. Masculine/high–power distance/high–uncertainty avoidance countries are generally more corrupt, and their citizens are more likely to look to formal codes and policies for ethical guidance. Firms operating in these cultures are generally less sensitive to the concerns of stakeholders. Consumers from short-term orientation/low–power distance/low–uncertainty avoidance societies generally punish socially irresponsible firms. National accounting organizations in high-individualism/high–uncertainty avoidance societies are less likely to adopt ethical standards set by international accounting groups.

Of the four value dimensions, individualism versus collectivism has attracted the most attention. Scholars have used this dimension to explain a variety of cultural differences, including variations in ethical behavior. Management professors Stephen Carroll and Martin Gannon report that individualistic countries prefer universal ethical standards such as Kant's categorical imperative.[32] Collectivistic societies take a more utilitarian approach, seeking to generate the greatest good for in-group members. Citizens of these nations are more sensitive to elements of the situation. To see how these orientations affect ethical decisions, let's return to the four dilemmas I introduced earlier in the chapter.

- *Bribery.* Payoffs tend to be more common in collectivistic nations and may be a way to meet obligations to the community. In some cases, there are laws against the practice, but they take a backseat to history and custom. Individualistic nations view bribery as a form of corruption; payoffs destroy trust and benefit some companies and people at the expense of others.

- *False information.* Individualists are more likely to lie in order to protect their privacy; collectivists are more likely to lie in order to protect the group or family. This accounts for the conflict between the Mexican and U.S. businesspeople described earlier. Mexicans, who tend to have a collectivistic orientation, promise what they can't deliver in order to reduce tensions between their in-group and outsiders. Americans—among the world's most individualistic peoples—condemn this practice as deceptive and therefore unethical. Individualists and collectivists also express disagreement differently. For instance, Germans and Americans don't hesitate to say no directly to another party. Japanese may answer by saying "That will be difficult" rather than by offering an out-and-out refusal. This indirect strategy is designed to save the face or image of the receiver.

- *Intellectual property rights.* Whereas individuals own the rights to their creative ideas in individualistic societies, they are expected to share their knowledge in collectivistic nations. Copyright laws are a Western invention based on the belief that individuals should be rewarded for their efforts.

- *Gender equality.* Resistance to gender equality is strongest in collectivistic nations such as Saudi Arabia and Japan. Women are seen as an out-group in these societies. Many men fear that granting women more status—better jobs, leadership positions—would threaten group stability. Individualistic nations are more likely to have laws that promote equal opportunity, although in many of these countries, such as the United States, women hold fewer leadership positions than men and continue to earn less.

In addition to shaping our moral choices, both individualism and collectivism create ethical blind spots. Being self- or group-focused can make us particularly susceptible to certain types of ethical abuses. Individualism is linked to high crime rates, narcissism, violence, materialism, suicide, and drug abuse. Collectivism is tied to suppression of individual thought, blind obedience, harsh treatment of outside groups, human rights violations, and wife beating and killing.[33]

Project GLOBE

Project GLOBE (Global Leadership and Organizational Behavior Effectiveness) is an international effort involving 170 researchers who have gathered data from more than 17,000 managers in 62 countries. The researchers hope to better equip global managers by identifying the relationship between cultural values and effective leadership behaviors. Like Hofstede, the GLOBE researchers identify power distance, uncertainty avoidance, gender differentiation (masculinity and femininity), and individualism versus collectivism as important cultural dimensions. However, they extend Hofstede's list by including the following.[34]

In-Group Collectivism

This dimension describes the degree to which societal members take pride in their small groups, families, and organizations. In-group collectivism differs from Hofstede's collectivism dimension, which describes maintaining harmony and cooperation throughout society as a whole. Being a member of a family, a close group, or an employing organization is very important to members of in-group collectivist societies (Iran, India, China), and they have high expectations of other group members. People living in countries that score low on this dimension, such as Denmark, Sweden, and New Zealand, don't have similar expectations of friends and family.

Assertiveness

Assertiveness is the extent to which a culture encourages individuals to be tough, confrontational, and competitive, as opposed to modest and tender. Spain and the United States rate high on this dimension; Sweden and New Zealand rate low. Those in highly assertive societies have a take-charge attitude and value competition. They are not particularly sympathetic to the weak and less fortunate. Members of less assertive cultures place more value on empathy, loyalty, and solidarity.

Future Orientation

This is the extent to which a society fosters and reinforces such future-oriented activities as planning and investing (Singapore, Switzerland, the Netherlands) rather than immediate gratification (Russia, Argentina, Poland).

Performance Orientation

This is the degree to which a society encourages and rewards group members for improving performance and demonstrating excellence. In places such as Hong Kong, Singapore, and the United States, training and development are valued, and people take initiative. Citizens prefer a direct communication style and feel a sense of urgency. In countries such as Russia, Italy, and Argentina, people put loyalty and belonging ahead of performance. They are uncomfortable with feedback and competition and place more weight on someone's family and background than on performance.

Humane Orientation

Humane orientation is the extent to which a culture encourages and honors people for being altruistic, caring, kind, fair, and generous. Support for the weak and vulnerable is particularly high in countries such as Malaysia, Ireland, and the Philippines. People are usually friendly and tolerant and may develop patronage and paternalistic relationships with their leaders. In contrast, power and material possessions motivate people in the former West Germany, Spain, and France. Self-enhancement takes precedence. Individuals are to solve their own problems; children are expected to be independent.

It is clear that differences on these values dimensions can cause some serious ethical conflicts. Those scoring high on in-group collectivism see no problem with hiring friends and family members even when more qualified candidates are available, a fact that will trouble those who believe that members of their in-groups should not expect preferential treatment. (See Scenario A, "The *Raccomandazione*," in Case Study 10.1.) People oriented toward the future will save and invest. They will condemn those who live in the moment and spend all they earn. Competition, direct communication, power, and personal advancement are applauded in assertive, performance-oriented, less humane groups. These elements are undesirable to people who put more value on harmony, cooperation, family, and concern for others. Those living in assertive, performance-oriented cultures are tempted to engage in unethical activities in order to succeed. The businesses they create are more likely to be focused on shareholders, profits, and results instead of on stakeholders and social responsibility.[35]

Although there is plenty of evidence of ethical diversity in the GLOBE study, there are also signs of common ethical ground. As I noted in Chapter 7, the GLOBE researchers discovered that many of the characteristics associated with transformational leadership—motive arouser, foresight, encouraging, dynamic, motivational, trustworthy, positive, confidence builder, communicative—are admired across cultures (although to varying degrees).[36] In another study, researchers from Florida Atlantic University, the University of Maryland, and Wayne State University analyzed the GLOBE data to determine whether there are aspects of ethical leadership that are important for effective leadership across cultures. Four attributes emerged, although the extent to which each is endorsed and how each is implemented differs across cultures. (See "Focus on Follower Ethics: Ethical Expectations Across Cultures" for a closer look at how the ethical expectations of leaders vary between the United States and two other countries.) Character and integrity (consistency, virtue) were rated as important. So were altruism, collective motivation (putting the interests of the group ahead of personal interests), and encouraging and empowering (helping followers feel competent).[37] Taken together, these dimensions describe positive, people-oriented leadership that respects the rights and dignity of others. The fact that observers from many different cultural backgrounds agree on the attributes of ethical leadership suggests that there are common ethical standards shared by all cultures. We'll take a closer look at those standards later in the chapter.

Ethical Expectations Across Cultures

While followers from different cultures look for similar attributes in their ethical leaders, cultural differences remain. The relative importance of particular ethical leadership qualities varies by country. In one study, Christian Resick and his colleagues asked middle managers in Ireland and the United States to rate the importance of ethical leadership traits. Respondents in both countries gave equal ratings to (1) altruism (being compassionate and generous), (2) collective (team-oriented) motivation that inspires subordinates to work toward shared goals and to put the needs of the team first, and (3) encouragement that empowers followers to develop self-confidence and self-sufficiency. However, managers in the United States were significantly more likely than their Irish counterparts to rate character/integrity as important. This may be due to in part to differences in collectivism/individualism. In Ireland, which is more collectivist and does business through informal relationships, character and integrity are tied to social networks. In the United States, which is highly individualistic, the character of the leader, who acts largely on his or her own, is more important.

In a second study, Resick and his fellow researchers compared German and U.S. perspectives on ethical leadership. They found that character/integrity, collective motivation, and encouragement were strongly endorsed by managers in each nation, while altruism was rated as less important. As in the Ireland project, U.S. managers placed higher emphasis on character. German subordinates judge integrity based on how the leader treats others, including organizational members and stakeholders; U.S. employees judge the leader based on her or his consistency, honesty, and sincerity. Germans and Americans also differ in how they regulate ethical behavior. Germans prefer self-regulation while Americans rely on codes of ethics and outside regulations like the Sarbanes–Oxley Act. International leaders need to be aware of these subtle differences as they address ethical issues across cultures. For example, the American manager who tries to institute detailed ethical policies in a German subsidiary may communicate that she or he doesn't trust employees.

Sources

Keating, M., Martin, G. S., Resick, C. J., & Dickson, M. W. (2007). A comparative study of the endorsement of ethical leadership in Ireland and the United States. *Irish Journal of Management, 28,* 5–30.

Martin, G. S., Resick, C. J., Keating, M. A., & Dickson, M. W. (2009). Ethical leadership across cultures: A comparative analysis of German and US perspectives. *Business Ethics: A European Review, 18,* 127–144.

Resick, C. J., Hanges, P. J., Dickson, M. W., & Mitchelson, J. K. (2006). A cross-cultural examination of the endorsement of ethical leadership. *Journal of Business Ethics, 63,* 345–359.

Psychological Systems

University of Virginia moral psychologist Jonathan Haidt and others believe that to understand ethical diversity we first need to understand the psychological systems or foundations of morality. These mental foundations, which are part of our genetic makeup, enable humans to live together successfully in groups. Cultures shape how these systems are used, emphasizing one or more values over the others. Haidt compares these moral intuitions to taste buds. Nearly everyone is born with the same set of taste receptors. But each culture develops its own cuisine, which emphasizes different tastes.

Haidt identifies five foundations for our moral intuitions:[38]

1. *Harm/care.* All species are sensitive to suffering in their own offspring, but humans are also sensitive to suffering beyond the family and can feel sympathy for outsiders. Because groups are attuned to cruelty and harm, they generally approve of those who prevent or alleviate suffering and make virtues out of kindness and compassion. However, the other four moral foundations temper the amount of compassion that individuals in different cultures display.

2. *Fairness/reciprocity.* Reciprocity—paying back others—is essential for the formation of alliances between individuals who are not related to each other. All cultures have virtues related to justice and fairness. Yet while some societies value individual rights and equality, a great many more groups do not.

3. *In-group/loyalty.* Trusting fellow in-group members and distrusting those who belong to other groups have been essential for human survival. As a result, most cultures create virtues out of patriotism, loyalty, and heroism, and some societies (Japan, for instance) put a high value on in-group cohesion. Even when the society as a whole doesn't emphasize loyalty, there are usually subgroups that do (e.g., the police and the military).

4. *Authority/respect.* Hierarchy is a fact of life in primate as well as human groups. While primates rely on brute strength to assert their dominance, people use such factors as prestige and deference. In many cultures followers feel respect, awe, and admiration for leaders and expect good leaders to act like wise parents.

5. *Purity/sanctity.* Only humans appear to feel disgust, which helps to protect the body against the transmission of disease through contact with corpses, feces, vomit, and other possible contaminants. Purity has a social dimension as well. For instance, disgust can be felt for those with deformities or for those of lower social class, such as the untouchables in India. Members of most cultural groups disapprove of those individuals who are contaminated by lust, gluttony, greed, and uncontrolled anger.

The United States and many other Western nations largely focus on reducing harm and promoting autonomy. That is not the case in much of the rest of the world, however. In Brazil, morality is based on loyalty, family, respect, and purity, in addition to care. Confucian and Hindu values systems emphasize authority and stability. Muslim societies place a high priority on purity, which is reflected in the segregation of men and women and separation from infidels. Haidt urges leaders to keep all five moral systems in mind when dealing with diverse groups. We need to realize that although purity and authority may not be important to us, they are to a great proportion of the world's population. We must acknowledge and address these concerns. Unless we are dealing with a highly liberal Western audience, our ethical appeals will be most effective if they speak to loyalty, authority, and purity in addition to care and fairness.

Standing on Moral Common Ground

Confronted with a wide range of ethical values and standards, a number of philosophers, business leaders, anthropologists, and others opt for ethical relativism. In ethical relativism, there are no universal moral codes or standards. Each group or society is unique. Therefore, members of one culture can't pass moral judgment on members of another group.

I'll admit that, at first glance, ethical relativism is appealing. It avoids the problem of ethnocentrism while simplifying the decision-making process. We can concentrate on fitting in with the prevailing culture and never have to pass judgment. On closer examination, however, the difficulties of ethical relativism become all too apparent.[39] Without shared standards, there's little hope that the peoples of the world can work together to address global problems. There may be no basis on which to condemn the evil of notorious leaders who are popular in their own countries. Furthermore, the standard of cultural relativism obligates us to follow (or at least not to protest against) abhorrent local practices such as the killing of brides by their in-laws in the rural villages of Pakistan. (See Case Study 10.2 for a recent case where local standards generated international outrage.) Without universal rights and wrongs, we have no basis on which to contest such practices.

Cross-cultural research suggests that there might be moral commonalities when making ethical decisions. To determine if there are universal moral principles or a "moral grammar" built into the mental capacities of all humans, investigators use variations of the "trolley problem." In the trolley problem, an out-of-control trolley threatens to kill five people unless immediate action is taken. In one case, the trolley operator is incapacitated, and a passenger has to decide whether or not to throw a switch, diverting the vehicle to safety on a sidetrack (and saving the five passengers) but killing a pedestrian who happens to be standing on the rails. In the other case, someone standing by the tracks must decide whether or not to intervene directly by throwing another bystander into the path of the trolley to slow it down and save the five passengers.

One group of researchers collected responses to the trolley problem from 30,000 subjects in 120 countries.[40] There was widespread agreement across all national, religious, and education groups. By a significant margin, participants said they would throw the switch to save the trolley passengers but not throw someone onto the tracks to accomplish the same goal. Respondents reported that throwing a switch is an impersonal act, and they saw the death of the pedestrian as an unfortunate consequence. On the other hand, throwing a bystander onto the track is a deliberate, highly personal act that makes the victim a means to an end.

The trolley problem may be hypothetical, but it has parallels in real life. The American Medical Association believes that hastening death by withholding treatment is more acceptable than hastening death through a drug overdose. The medical group permits passive euthanasia for terminally ill patients (which is similar to throwing the trolley switch). However, the AMA opposes active euthanasia (which raises the same concerns as throwing a bystander onto the trolley track).

Research into the neurological basis of moral judgments is in the initial stages (see the discussion of dual processing in Chapter 6) but suggests that, when it comes to ethics, there might some cultural unity to go along with cultural diversity. Additional evidence of ethical common ground comes from universal standards, which have enabled members of the world community to punish crimes against humanity and to create international regulatory bodies. Responsible multinational corporations such as The Body Shop, Nike, and Starbucks adhere to widely held moral principles as they conduct business in a variety of cultural settings. In this section, I'll describe four different approaches to universal ethics: the Universal Declaration of Human Rights, a global ethic, the Global Business Standards Codex, and the Caux Principles. Any one of these approaches could serve as a worldwide standard. As you read each description, look for commonalities. Then decide for yourself which approach or combination of approaches best captures the foundational values of humankind.

The United Nations Universal Declaration of Human Rights

Following World War II, a conflict fought in large part to protect human freedoms, the United Nations adopted the Universal Declaration of Human Rights. According to this document, human rights are granted to individuals based solely on their status as persons, or, to put it another way, "We are all entitled to human rights simply on the basis that we are human beings."[41] These rights protect the inherent dignity of every person regardless of race, ethnic background, place of residence, age, income, physical ability, or social status. Some of the key rights spelled out in the Universal Declaration are:[42]

Article 4. No one shall be held in slavery or servitude; slavery and the slave trade shall be prohibited in all their forms.

Article 5. No one shall be subjected to torture or to cruel, inhuman, or degrading treatment or punishment.

Article 9. No one shall be subjected to arbitrary arrest, detention, or exile.

Article 13. Everyone has the right to freedom of movement and residence.

Article 19. Everyone has the right to freedom of thought, conscience, and religion.

Article 25. Everyone has the right to a standard of living adequate for the health and well-being of himself [or herself] and of his [or her] family.

Article 26. Everyone has a right to an education.

More recently, the United Nations launched the Global Compact to encourage multinational corporations to honor human rights, labor rights, and the environment while at the same time fighting corruption. The Compact has more than 8,600 business and nonbusiness members from more than 130 countries. Business participants undergo an annual certification process to measure how well they are adhering to 10 universal principles (e.g., avoiding human rights abuse, eliminating child labor, working against extortion and bribery). They work with nongovernmental organizations (NGOs) and other groups to tackle societal and environmental problems.[43]

A Global Ethic

Many of the world's conflicts center on religious differences: Hindu versus Muslim, Protestant versus Catholic, Muslim versus Jew. However, these hostilities didn't prevent 6,500 representatives from a wide range of religious faiths from reaching agreement on a global ethic.[44] A council of former heads of state and prime ministers then ratified this statement. Delegates of both groups agreed on two universal principles. First, every person must be treated humanely regardless of language, skin color, mental ability, political beliefs, or national or social origin. Every person and group, no matter how powerful, must respect the dignity of others. Second, "what you wish done to yourself, do to others" (or the Golden Rule). These two foundational principles, in turn, lead to the following ethical directives or imperatives:

- Commitment to a culture of nonviolence and respect for all life

- Commitment to a culture of solidarity and a just economic order (do not steal; deal fairly and honestly with others)

- Commitment to a culture of tolerance and truthfulness

- Commitment to a culture of equal rights and partnership between men and women (avoid immorality; respect and love members of both genders)

The Global Business Standards Codex

Harvard business professor Lynn Paine and her colleagues argue that world-class corporations base their codes of ethics on a set of eight universal, overarching ethical principles.[45] Paine's group compiled these guidelines after surveying a variety of global and corporate codes of conduct and government regulations. The researchers offer their Global Business Standards Codex as a benchmark for those who want to conform to universal standards of corporate conduct.

I. *Fiduciary principle.* Act on behalf of the company and its investors. Be diligent and loyal in carrying out the firm's business. As a trustee, be candid (open and honest).

II. *Property principle.* Respect and protect property and the rights of its owners. Don't steal or misuse company assets, including information, funds, and equipment. Avoid waste and take care of property entrusted to you.

III. *Reliability principle.* Honor all commitments. Keep promises and follow through on agreements even when they are not in the form of legally binding contracts.

IV. *Transparency principle.* Do business in a truthful manner. Avoid deceptive acts and practices and keep accurate records. Release information that should be shared in a timely fashion but maintain confidentiality and privacy as necessary.

V. *Dignity principle.* Respect the dignity of all who come in contact with the corporation, including employees, suppliers, customers, and the public. Protect their health, privacy, and rights. Avoid coercion. Promote human development instead by providing learning and development opportunities.

VI. *Fairness principle.* Deal fairly with everyone. Engage in fair competition, provide just compensation to employees, and be evenhanded in dealings with suppliers and corporate partners. Practice nondiscrimination in both employment and contracting.

VII. *Citizenship principle.* Act as a responsible member of the community by (a) obeying the law, (b) protecting the public good (not engaging in corruption, protecting the environment), (c) cooperating with public authorities, (d) avoiding improper involvement in politics, and (e) contributing to the community (e.g., economic and social development, giving to charitable causes).

VIII. *Responsiveness principle.* Engage with outsiders (neighborhood groups, activists, customers) that may have concerns about the company's activities. Work with other groups to better society while not usurping the government's role in protecting the public interest.

The Caux Principles

The Caux Round Table is made up of business executives from the United States, Japan, and Europe who meet periodically in Caux, Switzerland. Round Table members hope to set a world standard by which to judge business behavior. Their principles are based on twin ethical ideals. The first is the Japanese concept of *kyosei,* which refers to living and working together for the common good. The second is the Western notion of human dignity, the sacredness and value of each person as an end rather than as a means to someone else's end.[46]

Principle 1. The responsibilities of corporations: Beyond shareholders toward stakeholders. Corporations have a responsibility to improve the lives of everyone they come in contact with, starting with employees, shareholders, and suppliers, and then extending out to local, national, regional, and global communities.

Principle 2. The economic and social impact of corporations: Toward innovation, justice, and world community. Companies in foreign countries should not only create jobs and wealth but also foster better social conditions—education, welfare, and human rights. Corporations have an obligation to enrich the world community through innovation, the wise use of resources, and fair competition.

Principle 3. Corporate behavior: Beyond the letter of law toward a spirit of trust. Businesses ought to promote honesty, transparency, integrity, and keeping promises. These behaviors make it easier to conduct international business and to support a global economy.

Principle 4. Respect for rules: Beyond trade friction toward cooperation. Leaders of international firms must respect both international and local laws in order to reduce trade wars and to promote the free flow of goods and services.

Principle 5. Support for multilateral trade: Beyond isolation toward world community. Firms should support international trading systems and agreements and eliminate domestic measures that undermine free trade.

Principle 6. Respect for the environment: Beyond protection toward enhancement. A corporation ought to protect and, if possible, improve the physical environment through sustainable development and cutting back on the wasteful use of natural resources.

Principle 7. Avoidance of illicit operations: Beyond profit toward peace. Global business leaders must ensure that their organizations aren't involved in such forbidden activities as bribery, money laundering, support of terrorism, drug trafficking, and organized crime.

After spelling out general principles, the Caux accord applies them to important stakeholder groups. Leaders following these standards hope to (a) treat customers and employees with dignity, (b) honor the trust of investors, (c) create relationships with suppliers based on mutual trust, (d) engage in just behavior with competitors, and (e) work for reform and human rights in host communities. The Caux Round Table has also developed principles to guide NGOs. Integrity—remaining faithful to the group's mission to serve the common good—should be the fundamental operating principle for NGOs. Starting from this foundation of integrity, these organizations should serve the public benefit, operate transparently, practice open governance, remain independent, respect the law, demonstrate care, and be accountable.[47]

Making Ethical Choices in Culturally Diverse Settings

The universal principles described in the last section play an important role when we are faced with making ethical decisions involving more than one culture. According to business ethicists Thomas Donaldson and Thomas Dunfee, we need to hold fast to global principles while we take local values into account.[48] Their integrative social contracts theory (ISCT) provides one set of guidelines for balancing respect for ethical diversity with adherence to universal ethical standards.

ISCT is based on the idea of social contracts—agreements that spell out the duties of institutions, communities, and societies. The theory is integrative because it incorporates two kinds of contracts: macrosocial and microsocial. *Macrosocial* contracts are broader and lay the foundation for how people interact with one another. The requirement that the government protect its citizens and the belief that employers should respect the rights of workers are examples of ideal contracts. *Microsocial* contracts govern the relationships between the members of specific groups (local towns, regions, nations, companies, professions). These contracts are revealed by the norms of the group. For example, those who participate in auctions must adhere to the norms of the auction community, which include revealing whether participants have the means to back up their bids and not interfering with others who are making bids. Community contracts are considered authentic or binding if members of the group have a voice in the creation of the norms, members can exit the group if they disagree with prevailing norms, and the norms are widely recognized and practiced by group members. Under these standards, prohibitions against free speech in countries ruled by repressive regimes would not be authentic because citizens had no say in creating these rules and can't leave the community if they want to.

Local communities have a great deal of latitude or *moral free space* to create their own rules, and these norms should be respected whenever possible. An Indonesian manager participating in an Australian real estate auction should obey Australian auction norms, for instance. However, universal principles such as those described in the previous section (what Donaldson and Dunfee call *hypernorms*) take priority when global principles clash with community standards. Exploitation of workers through excessive hours, low pay, imprisonment, and sexual abuse might be the norm in some developing countries. But such practices should be rejected because they violate hypernorms that urge us to respect the dignity of other human beings, treat them fairly and humanely, and follow the Golden Rule.

To make decisions following ISCT guidelines, follow these steps:

1. Identify all relevant stakeholders or communities.
2. Determine whether these communities are legitimate (do they allow voice and exit by members?).
3. Identify authentic norms (those that are widely known and shared).
4. Determine whether the norms are legitimate (do not conflict with hypernorms).
5. Resolve any conflicts between legitimate norms. (If both sets of norms do not conflict with universal standards, go with the option that is dominant—the one accepted by the larger community.)

University of Louisiana professors J. Brooke Hamilton, Stephen Knouse, and Vanessa Hill (HKH) offer another set of guidelines for making choices in ethically diverse contexts. They provide six questions specifically designed to help managers at multinational enterprises (MNEs) make moral choices when corporate values conflict with business practices in the host country.[49] The questions described below, which make up the HKH model, are designed to serve as a discussion/decision guide, not as a rigid set of steps. Managers don't have to come to a definite answer to one question before moving to another. They may return to earlier questions later and answer them differently.

1. *What is the Questionable Practice (QP) in this situation?*
   - In the initial stage of the HKH decision-making format, managers determine that the norms of the MNE clash with the norms of the local culture. At this point the disparity

is labeled as "questionable" because it may involve cultural differences rather than ethical issues. The key is to come to a clear understanding of the nature of the conflict.

2. *Does the QP violate any laws that are enforced?*
    - If the QP violates laws of the home country (the U.S. Foreign Corrupt Practices Act, for example, or European Union prohibitions against bribery) or the host country, it should be discontinued.

3. *Is the QP simply a cultural difference, or is it also a potential ethics problem?*
    - A QP reflects a cultural difference if it "does not cause harm and appears to be that culture's legitimate way of achieving some worthwhile business or social outcome."[50] It rises to the level of a potential ethical issue if it creates harm or violates a universal global principle like treating people with respect and practicing the Golden Rule.

4. *Does the QP violate the firm's core values or code of conduct, an industry-wide or international code to which the firm subscribes, or a firmly established hypernorm?*
    - How managers answer this question will be determined by whether they believe that their companies are driven solely by the desire to comply with the law or whether they believe their firms are committed to ethical integrity instead (see Chapter 9). Compliance-driven firms are more likely to conform to local rules because they are primarily interested in following the law; survival is the core value. Integrity-driven firms have a higher standard. Managers at these firms judge local practices based on whether they conform to important corporate values (customer service, treating employees fairly) and such international guidelines as the Caux Principles and the Global Business Standards Codex.

5. *Does the firm have leverage (something of value to offer) in the host country that allows the firm to follow its own practices rather than the QP?*
    - Only managers at integrity-driven companies will ask this question, as managers at compliance-oriented firms will go along with local practices. If the firm can offer significant benefits like jobs, cash, training, and new technology, it can better resist the pressure to engage in unethical activity and can negotiate a way to adapt to local customs without violating its core values. For instance, a large Western oil firm that values equal treatment of both genders may be able to leverage its power in a traditionalist Middle Eastern country to promote women to positions of organizational authority.

6. *Will market practices in the host country improve if the firm follows its own practices rather than the QP in the host country marketplace?*
    - A company without leverage will have to conform to customs of the home country or exit the market. However, if the firm has such leverage, it has an obligation to try to improve conditions in the countries in which it operates. Modeling respect for

individuals, honest business practices, and concern for the environment can encourage local firms and other MNEs to do the same and result in better living and working conditions and a healthier economy.

You can practice your ability to make cross-cultural ethical choices by applying the steps of the ISCT and HKH models to Case Study 10.3. This case highlights the difficult ethical choices facing Google and other American technology companies operating under China's Communist regime.

IMPLICATIONS AND APPLICATIONS

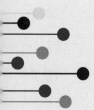

- Fostering diversity is not just good business strategy; it is an ethical imperative for leaders.

- Prejudice, stereotypes, and ethnocentrism are barriers to diversity and lead to moral abuses. You can avoid casting shadows if you commit yourself to mindfulness, human dignity, moral inclusiveness, and cosmopolitanism.

- Acknowledging the dark side of globalization reduces the likelihood of ethical abuse on the world stage. As a leader in a global environment, you must take additional care to avoid casting shadows of power, privilege, mismanaged information, inconsistency, misplaced and broken loyalties, and irresponsibility.

- Cultural differences make ethical decisions more difficult. Nevertheless, resist the temptation to revert to your old ways of thinking or to blindly follow local customs. Try instead to expand your capacity to act ethically in multicultural situations.

- Understanding the relationship between cultural differences and ethical values can help you predict how members of another group will respond to moral questions.

- Two popular cultural value classification systems are Hofstede's programmed values (power distance, individualism versus collectivism, masculinity versus femininity, uncertainty avoidance) and the GLOBE cultural dimensions, which include Hofstede's categories along with in-group collectivism, assertiveness, future orientation, performance orientation, and humane orientation.

- All humans seem concerned about care, fairness, loyalty, respect for authority, and purity. But cultures differ in the relative importance they put on each of these moral foundations, which leads to ethical conflicts. Keep all five psychological or moral systems in mind when dealing with diverse groups.

- Universal standards can help you establish common ground with diverse followers. These shared standards can take the form of human rights, religious commitments, or world business standards.

- To make ethical decisions in cross-cultural settings, take both local values and global principles into account. Follow community norms except when they conflict with universal moral standards. As a business leader, make the most of your company's leverage in another country to improve local conditions.

FOR FURTHER EXPLORATION, CHALLENGE, AND SELF-ASSESSMENT

1. Distribute Self-Assessment 10.1, the Diversity Perceptions Scale, to other members of your organization and discuss your responses. What factors contributed to your organizational and personal perceptions? What can you do to boost your individual and collective scores?

2. Complete Self-Assessment 10.2, the Individualism/Collectivism Scale. How do your individualistic and collectivistic tendencies influence your perspective on ethical issues? (Supply examples.) What might be your ethical blind spots? How can you address these blind spots? Write up your reflections.

3. Form groups and debate the following proposition: Overall, globalization does more harm than good.

4. Pair off and brainstorm a list of the advantages and disadvantages of ethical diversity. What conclusions do you draw from your list?

5. Using the Internet, compare press coverage of an international ethical issue from a variety of countries. How does the coverage differ and why? Write up your findings.

6. Rate yourself on one or both of the cultural classification systems described in this chapter. Create a value profile of your community, organization, or university. How well do you fit in?

7. In a research paper, analyze the cultural values that likely influenced the ethical decision of a prominent leader.

8. Use the five psychological moral systems or foundations to explain an ethical conflict. Share your analysis with the rest of the class.

9. Write a response to the following: Is there a common morality that peoples of all nations can share? Which of the global codes described in the chapter best reflects these shared standards and values? If you were to create your own declaration of global ethics, what would you put on it?

STUDENT STUDY SITE

Visit the student study site at **www.sagepub.com/johnsonmecl5e** to access full SAGE journal articles for further research and information on key chapter topics.

CASE STUDY 10.1

Ethical Diversity Scenarios

Scenario A: The *Raccomandazione*

In Italy, it's not what you know but whom you know that is key to getting a job. A recommendation from the right person (a *raccomandazione*) often gets someone hired, even if the applicant is not the most qualified for the position. The emphasis on connections is blamed for Italy's brain drain, as many outstanding graduates are forced to seek work abroad. You have recently arrived in Italy to manage a small branch office of an international consulting firm. Your best employee asks you to write a letter of recommendation for his daughter who wants a position with one of your major clients. You don't want to offend him, and you recognize the importance that Italians place on their families. At the same time, you don't believe his daughter is any more than an average candidate for this position.

Would you provide the raccomandazione *for the employee's daughter?*

SOURCE: Associated Press. (2012, September 25). In crisis-hit Europe, nepotism and connection culture stifle youth. *The Daily Star* (Lebanon).

Scenario B: Clinical Trials Outsourcing

You are the newly hired research director for a large pharmaceutical company. Like your competitors, your firm is outsourcing clinical drug trials to contract research organizations (CROs) in such emerging markets as Brazil, Mexico, India, China, and South Africa. Clinical trials involve the use of human subjects to test the effectiveness of new medications. Outsourcing drug tests is becoming increasingly popular. Not only are drug companies having a difficult time finding patients in Western countries, but outsourcing can significantly reduce expenses (clinical trials can account for up to 60% of drug development costs) and the time it takes to get a new drug to market, which can take 9–12 years on average.

While lower costs and development times boost profitability and stock prices while speeding treatment to patients, relying on CROs greatly increases the chances of ethical abuses. Your company adheres to the World Medical Association's Declaration of Helsinki, which lays out ethical guidelines for medical testing. According to the declaration, subjects must be fully informed of the risks they face when participating in clinical trials. Trial protocols are to be overseen by ethics committees. Every patient who participates in a research project should have access to the most effective treatment identified in the study after it is over. Participants should never be given an ineffective placebo if it leaves them without adequate treatment.

There is evidence that CROs often ignore the Helsinki guidelines. Local review boards, like those in Mexico, are often ineffective, and government regulation is lax. Clinical researchers out to reduce their costs may conduct trials without review, test illegal drugs, and misrepresent the nature of the trials to patients. Some subjects in developing nations don't understand the risks even when the dangers are explained to them. Or they are so desperate for money that they ignore the risks. The best medications may not be given to subjects. Then, too, distance makes it difficult for drug manufacturers to supervise overseas contractors.

You recognize that while your firm may not be held legally liable for any CRO violations, it will be held morally responsible in the court of international opinion.

Will you continue to outsource clinical drug trials to developing nations? If so, what steps might you take to ensure that your CROs will adhere to the Helsinki guidelines?

SOURCE: Abodor, H. (2012). Ethical issues in outsourcing: The case of contract medical research and the global pharmaceutical industry. *Journal of Business Ethics, 105,* 239–255.

Scenario C: International Adoption Restrictions

For over half a century, Americans have adopted more foreign children than any other country in the world. In 2010, for example, U.S. parents adopted more than 11,000 children from overseas, followed by the Italians (4,130) and the French (3,504). However, the number of foreign children adopted by American parents declined by 60% between 2004 (the peak year for international adoptions) and 2011. Fewer children have been available for adoption due in large part to the Hague Adoption Convention. This international agreement, which requires signatories to set up a central authority for processing adoptions, is designed to clean up corruption in the adoption process. Take the case of Guatemala. Investigators discovered that adoption paperwork in that nation was frequently forged and that babies were kidnapped from hospitals or stolen from their parents. A number of nations have stopped adoptions as they work to comply with the Adoption Convention. Attitudes toward foreign adoption are also shifting. Improving economic conditions, such as in China, encourage parents to keep their babies. Residents in some provider nations resent international adoption because it signals that they can't take care of their own children. They are supported by UNICEF, the United Nations children's rights organization, which argues that foreign adoptions should be allowed only in cases where children cannot be properly cared for in their home countries.

As the director of a U.S. adoption agency, you applaud efforts to curb corruption in international adoptions and to promote children's rights. However, you recognize that restrictions are sad news for American parents who believe they can provide education, medical care, and stable homes for needy kids who would otherwise go without. When Kyrgyzstan halted international adoptions, for example, 2 of 65 children scheduled to come to the United States died in orphanages before their prospective American parents could claim them. Of course, greater restrictions mean that your agency will likely process fewer adoptions.

Would you support efforts to lessen restrictions on international adoptions?

SOURCE: Webley, K. (2013, January 21). The baby deficit. *Time,* pp. 30–39.

Scenario D: Medical Treatment Policies

Your Europe-based clothing manufacturing company has plants in several sub-Saharan African countries. Your firm pays higher-than-average wages for the region and offers superior working conditions. However, the local media have been critical of your policy toward on-the-job injuries. If a European or other expatriate employee working at a plant gets hurt, he or she is taken to the local private hospital, which provides superior care. If a local worker sustains the same injury, he or she sees the company nurse or is taken to the local public hospital, which is poorly staffed and provides minimal care.

Your company's treatment of local employees is better than the practice of other manufacturers in the region, many of which do not have nurses on staff. Your medical policy has not kept locals from applying to work at your plants (you have a long list of applicants on file). Further, you can't attract expatriates to work at your facilities unless you offer high-quality medical care.

As human resources director, would you recommend that the company change its medical policies to provide the same care for local workers as it provides for expatriate employees?

SOURCE: Mitchell, C. (2003). *International business ethics: Combining ethics and profits in global business.* Novato, CA: World Trade Press. Used by permission.

Scenario E: The Exiled President

You are a diplomat in a small Central American country. For years your home government has pushed for the development of stable democracies in Central America, hoping to end the military coups that once were common in the region. The latest democratically elected president in your host state came to office with a commitment to the poor. Within weeks of assuming the presidency, he threatened to nationalize the local holdings of several of your home nation's multinational corporations. He condemned your government, and those of several other Western countries, for engaging in "capitalist imperialism." The president's leftist policies angered local business interests, and they soon drove him into exile with the help of the army. Military officers installed a new president who promised to be friendlier toward your nation. However, the new president has yet to set a timeline for holding elections. In the meantime, the exiled president, who still enjoys widespread support among the poor and working classes, wants to return to office. He has asked for help from the international community.

Would you recommend that your government support the deposed president's efforts to return to office? If so, what steps should it take?

SOURCE: Fictional case based on actual international events.

CASE STUDY 10.2

A Hundred Million "Missing Women"

The brutal gang rape of a medical student focused international attention on the plight of women in India. The young woman and her boyfriend were trying to catch a ride home after seeing a movie in New Delhi when they were lured onto a private bus containing six young men out for a "joy ride." First the men berated the woman for being out after dark with a male who was not her husband. Then they took turns raping her and beating both of them with an iron rod. After about an hour the attackers dumped the naked, unconscious couple on the road, leaving them for dead, and sped away. The student, who had just qualified to practice as a physiotherapist, suffered massive internal injuries and died after having 90% of her intestines removed. Her companion is now confined to a wheelchair. Six men were later charged with the crime. Four were sentenced to death.

Reports of the rape and murder triggered protests throughout India aimed at the failure of the police and government leaders to protect women. Few men are ever convicted of rape, and cases can drag on for years. Estimates are that victims report only 1 in every 50 rapes because they fear that police officers will blame them for what happened. National officials appear to be indifferent to the problem. Some prominent religious and political officials go so far as to offer excuses for rape. Politicians, lawyers, and police officers blame sexual assaults on everything from women wearing skirts and using cell phones to talk to others outside their families, to females eating chow mein and hanging out with men who are not their relatives. Asaram Bapu, a Hindu guru, said the victim in the Delhi case should have begged for forgiveness, stopping the rape by taking the hand of one of the alleged rapists and saying, "I consider you my brother."[1] Said a lawyer for three of the accused of the New Delhi rape and murder, "Until today I have not seen a single incident or example of rape with a respected lady."[2]

Rape is only one of the dangers faced by Indian women. Women now receive the same schooling as men, are entering the workforce in greater numbers, and serve as political leaders. Nevertheless, they are still the targets of discrimination and violence. Researchers estimate that 25,000–100,000 women are killed every year in disputes over dowries. Female fetuses are far more likely to be aborted than male ones. Male infants are breast-fed longer and receive more solid food when they get older. In addition, families provide boys with better medical care by, for example, buying them mosquito netting to protect them from malaria. As a consequence, death rates from infectious and respiratory diseases among girls under 4 years old are higher than in other nations. Each year 130,000 women die during childbirth, and older Indian women are more likely than their male counterparts to perish of heart attacks, which indicates that they receive a lower quality of care throughout their lives. Researchers estimate that these factors contribute to the ranks of 100 million "missing women." These missing women would still be alive today if the death rate of Indian women relative to the death rate of Indian men was the same as in more developed nations.

The Delhi rape case had an immediate impact on India's judicial system. Indian president Pranab Mukherjee signed a new antirape law setting higher minimum sentences. Authorities now plan to fast-track rape cases. Nevertheless, the ranks of the missing women will continue to grow by an estimated 2 million a year unless there is a fundamental change in Indian attitudes. Said one Delhi rape protester: "It's a much bigger problem with our society. We have not gone beyond the traditions of thousands of years in which women were inferior to men and we have to change that."[3]

Discussion Probes

1. What cultural values contribute to discrimination against women in India?

2. What steps should Indian political leaders take to reduce the number of "missing women"?

3. Should NGOs and the governments of other nations intervene to try to improve India's treatment of women? If so, what steps should they take?

4. Do multinational companies operating in India have an ethical responsibility to improve the status of Indian women?

5. How could applying the U.N. Universal Declaration of Human Rights or the global ethic improve the standing of women in India?

Notes

1. Indian officials make excuses for rape. (2013, January 12). *The Toronto Star*, p. A4.

2. Indian officials make excuses for rape.

3. Death of Delhi gang rape victim horrifies India. (2012, December 30). *The Telegraph*. Retrieved from http://www.telegraph.co.uk

Sources

Associated Press. (2013, January 24). Trial in India gang rape case begins in New Delhi. *USA Today*. Retrieved from http://www.usatoday.com/story/news/world

Delhi rape case; defendants face first witness evidence. (2013, February 5). BBCNews India.

Harris, G. (2013, January 14). For women in India, peril in many guises. *The International Herald Tribune*, p. 1.

Timmons, H., Trivedi, A., & Gottipati, S. (2012, December 31). Six charged with murder in India as rape victim dies. *The New York Times*.

CASE STUDY 10.3

Google Bounces Off the Great Firewall of China

The Chinese Internet market is massive, with as many as 600 million potential users. To enter this lucrative marketplace, American technology firms must participate in the Communist government's censorship program, which has been dubbed the "Great Firewall of China." The Chinese Communist government uses a variety of strategies to police websites and Internet traffic to determine whether users are breaking the law by defaming the government, divulging state secrets, or promoting separatist movements. Chinese officials ban such "subversive" material as government criticism, pornography, and information about Tibet, Taiwanese independence, and the Falun Gong religious sect. Thousands of human censors monitor Internet traffic and set up fake sites to catch offenders. Student volunteers steer university chat room discussions, and cartoon icons remind users of the Internet rules. Automatic censoring systems remove offensive chat room and bulletin board postings within minutes by detecting and then eliminating messages containing such words as dictatorship, corruption, freedom, or truth. Access to a number of websites is blocked, and users can access only portions of other sites. For example, a Chinese citizen may be able to visit an American university website but not be able to access material on a Chinese prodemocracy speaker sponsored by the university.

American firms have done their part to shore up the Great Firewall. Cisco Systems and Juniper Networks sell China's government networking hardware that enables officials to filter out content, allowing access to the World Wide Web but only to information favorable to the Chinese government. Yahoo! screens content and de-lists websites like The New York Times and Human Rights Watch from its search engine and, until its merger with a Chinese provider, did so without notifying users. Yahoo! also gave Chinese authorities the e-mail address of a journalist who is now serving a 10-year prison term for sending material to a democracy website. MSN (Microsoft) censors words and removes blogs at the government's request.

Google initially supported China's censorship efforts, blocking content that Beijing deems controversial. For instance, Westerners using the search term Tiananmen might get images of protesters being overrun by tanks in 1989. In China, the same search would generate an image of a U.S. official posing for a snapshot in Tiananmen Square. The company's decision to censor appeared to contradict its motto "Don't be evil" and undermined its efforts to provide unlimited access to information. Google justified its action by arguing that censorship is the lesser of two evils. "Filtering our search

results clearly compromises our mission," the firm admitted. "Failing to offer Google search at all to a fifth of the world's population, however, does so far more severely."[1]

Critics, such as Reporters Without Borders, Amnesty International, and some members of Congress, took issue with Google's assertions. Human rights advocates pointed out that censorship violates the United Nations Universal Declaration of Human Rights by denying freedom of speech and information. Iowa Republican congressman Jim Leach argued that Google's actions turned it into a "functionary of the Chinese government."[2] California representative Tom Lantos (a Holocaust survivor) told Google, Yahoo!, and other Internet firms doing business in China, "While technologically you are giants, morally you are pygmies."[3]

In early 2010, after an attack on its computer systems allegedly originating in China, Google closed its Internet search service in mainland China and directed users to an uncensored search engine in Hong Kong. The Chinese government responded by accusing Google of violating its pledge to follow censorship laws and of collaborating with U.S. spy agencies. Chinese business partners began to cut off their relationships with Google.

Since 2010, China's Great Firewall has grown even higher. Officials shut down virtual private networks (VPNs) that had enabled expatriates, entrepreneurs, researchers, and others to bypass computerized censorship to access Twitter, Facebook, The New York Times, and other overseas sites. They also greatly expanded the list of banned websites and search terms. Internet users now must register their real identities before they can access online services, which will significantly reduce the number of bloggers who criticize government officials for corruption. The Chinese military's Cybercommand is accused of launching Internet attacks on foreign companies aimed at stealing commercial trade secrets.

In late 2012 Google apparently conceded defeat in its battle against censorship after the Chinese government temporarily blocked access to all the firm's services, including Maps, Docs, and Gmail. The company had been notifying users when it believed their accounts were being hacked by state-sponsored groups. It also notified searchers when a term was censored by the government and told them how they might work around the block. Google quietly dropped these warnings, concluding that it was "counterproductive" to continue the censorship fight.

Discussion Probes

1. Google initially argued that filtering Internet content is less damaging than not making its search engine available in the Chinese market. Do you agree?

2. Why do you think Google has gotten more criticism for operating in China than other U.S. high-tech firms?

3. Use the steps of integrative social contracts theory or the HKH decision-making process to determine whether Google and other American high-tech firms should participate in the Great Firewall of China. What do you conclude?

4. Should the U.S. government prevent American technology companies from working with repressive regimes in China and elsewhere?

5. Is Internet access to information a human right or a privilege?

6. Is Internet censorship ever justified? What topics, if any, should be filtered?

Notes

1. Grossman, L., & Beech, H. (2006, February 13). Google under the gun. *Time.*

2. Silla, B., Knight, D., & Fang, B. (2006, February 27). Learning to live with big brother. *U.S. News & World Report.*

3. Hamilton, J. B., Knouse, S. B., & Hill, V. (2009). Google in China: A manager-friendly heuristic model for resolving cross-cultural ethical conflicts. *Journal of Business Ethics, 86,* 143–157.

Sources

Benkert, G. G. (2008). Google, human rights, and moral compromise. *Journal of Business Ethics, 85,* 453–478.

Bort, J. (2013, January 6). Google quietly gives up its fight to combat censorship in China. Business Insider. Retrieved from http://www.businessinsider.com

Dann, G. E., & Haddow, N. (2007). Just doing business or doing just business: Google, Microsoft, Yahoo! and the business of censoring China's Internet. *Journal of Business Ethics, 79,* 219–234.

Einhorn, B. (2006, August 9). Search engines censured for censorship. *Bloomberg Businessweek.* Retrieved from http://www.businessweek.com/stories/2006-08-09/search-engines-censured-for-censorship

Farrell, K. (2008). Corporate complicity in the Chinese censorship regime: When freedom of expression and profitability collide. *Internet Law, 11*(1), 11–21.

LaFraniere, S., & Barboza, D. (2011). China, mindful of Arab revolts, tightens grip on communications. *The International Herald Tribune,* News, p. 5.

Levy, S. (2006, February 13). Google and the China syndrome. *Newsweek,* p. 14.

The party, the people and the power of cyber-talk. (2006, April 29). *The Economist,* pp. 27–30.

Pierson, D. (2012, December 28). China closing loophole in nation's Great Firewall. *Los Angeles Times,* p. B2.

Ramstack, T. (2008, May 21). U.S. web services misused by oppressors. *The Washington Times,* p. C08.

Sanger, D. (2013, February 26). Washington treads warily on Chinese cyberattacks. *The International Herald Tribune,* News, p. 3.

Wiseman, P. (2008, April 23). In China, a battle over Web censorship. *USA Today,* p. 1A.

Wright, M. (2013, January 7). Google shows China the white flag of surrender. *The Telegraph.* Retrieved from http://www.telegraph.co.uk

SELF-ASSESSMENT 10.1

Diversity Perceptions Scale

Instructions: Respond to each item by circling the appropriate number (1 = *strongly disagree,* 6 = *strongly agree*).

1. I feel that I have been treated differently here because of my race, gender, sexual orientation, religion, or age. (Reverse)

   1   2   3   4   5   6

2. Managers here have a track record of hiring and promoting employees objectively, regardless of their race, gender, sexual orientation, religion, or age.

   1   2   3   4   5   6

3. Managers here give feedback and evaluate employees fairly, regardless of employees' race, gender, sexual orientation, religion, age, or social background.

   1   2   3   4   5   6

4. Managers here make layoff decisions fairly, regardless of factors such as employees' race, gender, age, or social background.

   1   2   3   4   5   6

5. Managers interpret human resource policies (such as sick leave) fairly for all employees.

   1   2   3   4   5   6

6. Managers give assignments based on the skills and abilities of employees.

   1   2   3   4   5   6

7. Management here encourages the formation of employee network support groups.

   1   2   3   4   5   6

8. There is a mentoring program in use here that identifies and prepares all minority and female employees for promotion.

   1   2   3   4   5   6

9. The "old boys' network" is alive and well here. (Reverse)

   1   2   3   4   5   6

10. The company spends enough money and time on diversity awareness and related training.

    1   2   3   4   5   6

11. Knowing more about cultural norms of diverse groups would help me be more effective in my job.

    1   2   3   4   5   6

12. I think that diverse viewpoints add value.

    1   2   3   4   5   6

13. I believe diversity is a strategic business issue.

    1   2   3   4   5   6

14. I feel at ease with people from backgrounds different from my own.

    1   2   3   4   5   6

15. I am afraid to disagree with members of other groups for fear of being called prejudiced. (Reverse)

    1   2   3   4   5   6

16. Diversity issues keep some work teams here from performing to their maximum effectiveness. (Reverse)

1	2	3	4	5	6

Scoring

This scale measures two dimensions—the organizational and the personal—each of which contains two factors as follows:

I. Organizational dimension

   a. Organizational fairness factor (Items 1–6)

   b. Organizational inclusion factor (Items 7–10)

II. Personal dimension

   c. Personal diversity value factor (Items 11–13)

   d. Personal comfort with diversity (Items 14–16)

Reverse scores on Items 1, 9, 15, and 16. Then add up your responses to all 16 items (maximum score 96). The higher your total score, the more positive your view of the diversity climate. Similarly, the higher your score on each of the item subsets described above, the more positive your perceptions on that factor.

SOURCE: Adapted from Mor Barak, M. E. (2011). *Managing diversity: Toward a globally inclusive workplace* (2nd ed.). Thousand Oaks, CA: Sage, pp. 328–332. Used by permission.

SELF-ASSESSMENT 10.2

Individualism/Collectivism Scale

Instructions: This questionnaire will help you assess your individualistic and collectivistic tendencies. Respond by indicating the degree to which the values reflected in each phrase are important to you: "opposed to my values" (answer 1), "not important to me" (answer 2), "somewhat important to me" (answer 3), "important to me" (answer 4), or "very important to me" (answer 5).

_____ 1. Obtaining pleasure or sensuous gratification

_____ 2. Preserving the welfare of others

_____ 3. Being successful by demonstrating my individual competency

_____ 4. Restraining my behavior if it is going to harm others

_____ 5. Being independent in thought and action

_____ 6. Having safety and stability of people with whom I identify

_____ 7. Obtaining status and prestige

_____ 8. Having harmony in my relations with others

_____ 9. Having an exciting and challenging life

_____ 10. Accepting cultural and religious traditions

_____ 11. Being recognized for my individual work

_____ 12. Avoiding the violation of social norms

_____ 13. Leading a comfortable life

_____ 14. Living in a stable society

_____ 15. Being logical in my approach to work

_____ 16. Being polite to others

_____ 17. Being ambitious

_____ 18. Being self-controlled

_____ 19. Being able to choose what I do

_____ 20. Enhancing the welfare of others

Scoring

To find your individualism score, add your responses to the _odd-numbered_ items. To find your collectivism score, add your responses to the _even-numbered_ items. Both scores will range from 10 to 50. The higher your scores, the more individualistic and/or collectivistic you are.

SOURCE: Gudykunst, W. B. (2004). _Bridging differences: Effective intergroup communication_ (4th ed.). Thousand Oaks, CA: Sage. Used by permission.

NOTES

1. Mor Barak, M. E. (2011). *Managing diversity: Toward a globally inclusive workplace* (2nd ed.). Thousand Oaks, CA: Sage; Kahn, A. E., & Maxwell, D. J. (2008). Ethics in diversity management leadership. In S. A. Quatro & R. R. Sims (Eds.), *Executive ethics: Ethical dilemmas and challenges for the C-suite* (pp. 247–262). Charlotte, NC: Information Age; Konrad, A. M. (2006). Leveraging workplace diversity in organizations. *Organization Management Journal, 3,* 164–189; Frey, W. H. (2011). *The new metro minority map: Regional shifts in Hispanics, Asians, and Blacks from Census 2010.* Brookings Institution. Retrieved from http://www.brookings.edu/ research/ papers/2011/08/31-census-race-frey; U.S. Bureau of Labor Statistics. (2013). *Women in the labor force: A databook.* Retrieved from http://www.bls.gov

2. Cox, T. (1993). *Cultural diversity in organizations: Theory, research and practice.* San Francisco: Berrett-Koehler; Cox, T. (2001). *Creating the multicultural organization: A strategy for capturing the power of diversity.* San Francisco: Jossey-Bass.

3. See Hays-Thomas, R. (2004). Why now? The contemporary focus on managing diversity. In M. S. Stockdale & F. J. Crosby (Eds.), *The psychology and management of workplace diversity* (pp. 3–30). Malden, MA: Blackwell; Konrad; Koonce, R. (2001, December). Redefining diversity. *Training & Development,* pp. 22–28; Kossek, E. E., Lobel, S. A., & Brown, J. (2006). Human resource strategies to manage workplace diversity: Examining the "business case." In A. M. Konrad, P. Prasad, & J. K. Pringle (Eds.), *Handbook of workplace diversity* (pp. 53–74). London: Sage; Mor Barak.

4. Chrisafis, A. (2009, January 27). Veiled threats: Row over Islamic dress opens bitter divisions in France. *The Guardian,* International, p. 24; Ahmetaji, A. (2013, February 11). Kosovo high school bans girl in headscarf from attending classes. BBC Monitoring Europe-Political; Coyne, I. (2008, January 15). Turbans make targets, some Sikhs find. *The New York Times,* p. NJ1; Wu, A. (2008, January 3). Balancing rights and burqas. *The Washington Times,* p. A17.

5. Drummond, T. (2000, April 3). Coping with cops. *Time,* pp. 72–73.

6. Brown, R. (1995). *Prejudice: Its social psychology.* Oxford, England: Blackwell; Fiske, S. T. (1998). Stereotyping, prejudice, and discrimination. In D. T. Gilbert, S. T. Fiske, & G. Lindzey (Eds.), *The handbook of social psychology* (Vol. 2, pp. 357–411). Boston: McGraw-Hill.

7. Gudykunst, W. B., & Kim, Y. Y. (1997). *Communicating with strangers: An approach to intercultural communication* (3rd ed.). New York: McGraw-Hill; Gudykunst, W. B. (2004). *Bridging differences: Effective intergroup communication* (4th ed.). Thousand Oaks, CA: Sage; Cox (1993), Ch. 13.

8. Cox (1993), Ch. 13.

9. Langer, E. J. (1989). *Mindfulness.* Reading, MA: Addison-Wesley; Langer, E. J. (1997). *The power of mindful learning.* Reading, MA: Addison-Wesley.

10. Smith, W. (2007). Cosmopolitan citizenship: Virtue, irony and worldliness. *European Journal of Social Theory, 10,* 37–52; Maak, T., & Pless, N. M. (2009). Business leaders as citizens of the world: Advancing humanism on a global scale. *Journal of Business Ethics, 88,* 537–550; Appiah, K. A. (2006). *Cosmopolitanism: Ethics in a world of strangers.* New York: Norton; Delanty, G. (2012). Introduction: The emerging field of cosmopolitanism studies. In G. Delanty (Ed.), *International handbook of cosmopolitan studies* (pp. 1–8). Hoboken, NJ: Routledge.

11. Fine, R., & Boon, V. (2007). Introduction: Cosmopolitanism: Between past and future. *European Journal of Social Theory, 10,* 5–16.

12. Wentling, R. M. (2004). Factors that assist and barriers that hinder the success of diversity initiatives in multinational corporations. *Human Resource Development International,*

7, 165–180; Kalev, A., Dobbin, F., & Kelly, E. (2006). Best practices or best guesses? Assessing the efficacy of corporate affirmative action and diversity policies. *American Sociological Review, 71,* 589–617; Mor Barak; Cox (2001); Morrison, A. M. (1996). *The new leaders: Guidelines on leadership diversity in America.* San Francisco: Jossey-Bass; Konrad.

13. Tavis, T. (2000). The globalization phenomenon and multinational corporate developmental responsibility. In O. F. Williams (Ed.), *Global codes of conduct: An idea whose time has come* (pp. 13–36). Notre Dame, IN: University of Notre Dame Press; Dunning, J. H. (2003). Overview. In J. H. Dunning (Ed.), *Making globalization good: The moral challenges of global capitalism* (pp. 11–40). Oxford, England: Oxford University Press.

14. Muzaffar, C. (2002). Conclusion. In P. F. Knitter & C. Muzaffar (Eds.), *Subverting greed: Religious perspectives on the global economy* (pp. 154–172). Maryknoll, NY: Orbis; Ritzer, G. (2004). *The globalization of nothing.* Thousand Oaks, CA: Pine Forge; Dunning, J. H. (2000). Whither global capitalism? *Global Focus, 12,* 117–136; Stott, B. R. (2001, January–February). The great divide in the global village. *Foreign Affairs,* pp. 160–177.

15. Kulish, N., & Donadio, R. (2012, May 15). Risk of Greek euro exit rattles markets, but hints of more talks emerge. *The New York Times,* p. A4.

16. Kristof, N. D. (2010, June 27). Death by gadget. *The New York Times,* p. WK11; Wyatt, E. (2012, March 20). Behind the blood money. *The New York Times,* p. B1.

17. Keys, T., & Malnight, T. *Corporate clout: The influence of the world's largest 100 economic entities.* Global Trends. Retrieved from http://www.globaltrends.com

18. Barstow, D. (2012, April 22). Vast Mexico bribery case hushed up by Wal-Mart after top-level struggle. *The New York Times,* p. A1.

19. Randerson, J. (2006, December 6). World's richest 1% own 40% of all wealth. *The Guardian.*

20. Bear, M. (2012). *First World problems.* San Francisco: Weldon Owen.

21. Muzaffar.

22. Brady, J. P. (2012). Marketing breast milk substitutes: Problems and perils throughout the world. *Archives of Disease in Children Online.* Retrieved from http://adc.bmj.com; Richter, J. (2001). *Holding corporations accountable: Corporate conduct, international codes and citizen action.* London: Zed; Perez, J. (2006, December 4). Yellow pad: What the milk companies don't want you to know. *BusinessWorld,* pp. 1–5; Moorhead, J. (2007, May 15). Milking it. *The Guardian,* p. 8; NAFDAC warns violators of BMS international code. (2007, August 7). *Africa News.*

23. Karim, A. (2000, June 23). Globalization, ethics, and AIDS vaccines. *Science,* pp. 21–29.

24. The mess that the army has made—Myanmar. (2005, July 23). *The Economist,* Special Report; Armitage, J., & Conde, B. (2007, October 19). Why the French are so keen to stay in Burma despite unrest. *The Evening Standard,* p. B34; Campbell, D. (2004, December 14). Energy giant agrees settlement with Burmese villagers. *The Guardian,* Foreign Affairs, p. 17.

25. Solomon, C. M. (2001). Put your ethics to a global test. In M. H. Albrecht (Ed.), *International HRM: Managing diversity in the workplace* (pp. 329–335). Oxford, England: Blackwell.

26. Donaldson, T. (1996, September–October). Values in tension: Ethics away from home. *Harvard Business Review,* pp. 48–57.

27. Carroll, S. J., & Gannon, M. J. (1997). *Ethical dimensions of management.* Thousand Oaks, CA: Sage.

28. Rogers, E. M., & Steinfatt, T. M. (1999). *Intercultural communication.* Prospect Heights, IL: Waveland, p. 79.

29. Hofstede, G. (1984). *Culture's consequences.* Beverly Hills, CA: Sage; Hofstede, G., & Hofstede, G. J. (2005). *Cultures and organizations: Software of the mind.* London: McGraw-Hill. For a recent review of Hofstede's cultural dimensions, see Taras, V., Kirkman, B. L., & Steel, P. (2010). Examining the impact of *Culture's consequences*: A three-decade, multilevel, meta-analytic review of Hofstede's cultural value dimensions. *Journal of Applied Psychology, 95,* 405–439.

30. Hofstede, G. (2001). Difference and danger: Cultural profiles of nations and limits to tolerance. In M. H. Albrecht (Ed.), *International HRM: Managing diversity in the workplace* (pp. 9–23). Oxford, England: Blackwell.

31. Husted, B. W. (1999). Wealth, culture and corruption. *Journal of International Business Studies, 30,* 339–359; Vitell, S. J., Nwachukwu, S. L., & Barnes, J. H. (1993). The effects of culture on ethical decision-making: An application of Hofstede's typology. *Journal of Business Ethics, 12,* 753–760; Davis, J. H., & Ruhe, J. A. (2003). Perceptions of country corruption: Antecedents and outcomes. *Journal of Business Ethics, 43,* 275–288; Franke, G. R., & Nadler, S. S. (2008). Culture, economic development, and national ethical attitudes. *Journal of Business Research, 61,* 254–264; Williams, G., & Zinkin, J. (2008). The effect of culture on consumers' willingness to punish irresponsible corporate behaviour: Applying Hofstede's typology to the punishment aspect of corporate social responsibility. *Business Ethics: A European Review, 17,* 210–226; Clements, C. E., Neill, J. D., & Stovall, O. S. (2009). The impact of cultural differences on the convergence of international accounting codes of ethics. *Journal of Business Ethics, 90,* 383–391; Chan, A. W. H., & Cheung, H. Y. (2012). Cultural dimensions, ethical sensitivity, and corporate governance. *Journal of Business Ethics, 110,* 45–59.

32. Carroll & Gannon.

33. Triandis, H. C. (1995). *Individualism and collectivism.* Boulder, CO: Westview Press.

34. Javidan, M., & House, R. J. (2001). Cultural acumen for the global manager: Lessons from Project GLOBE. *Organizational Dynamics, 29,* 289–305; House, R. J., Hanges, P. J., Javidan, M., Dorfman, P. W., & Gupta, V. (Eds.). (2004). *Culture, leadership, and organizations: The GLOBE study of 62 societies.* Thousand Oaks, CA: Sage; Chhokar, J. S., Brodbeck, F. C., & House, R. J. (Eds.). (2007). *Culture and leadership across the world: The GLOBE book of in-depth studies of 25 societies.* Mahwah, NJ: Erlbaum; Bertsch, A. M. (2012). Validating GLOBE's societal values scales: A test in the U.S.A. *International Journal of Business and Social Science, 3,* 10–23.

35. Quigley, N. R., Sully de Luque, M., & House, R. J. (2005). Responsible leadership and governance in a global context: Insights from the GLOBE study. In J. P. Doh & S. A. Sumpf (Eds.), *Handbook on responsible leadership and governance in global business* (pp. 352–379). Cheltenham, England: Edward Elgar.

36. Den Hartog, D. N., House, R. J., Hanges, P. U., Ruiz-Quintanilla, S. A., & Dorfman, P. W. (1999). Culture-specific and cross-culturally generalizable implicit leadership theories: Are attributes of charismatic/transformational leadership universally endorsed? *Leadership Quarterly, 10,* 219–257.

37. Resick, C. J., Hanges, P. J., Dickson, M. W., & Mitchelson, J. K. (2006). A cross-cultural examination of the endorsement of ethical leadership. *Journal of Business Ethics, 63,* 345–359.

38. Haidt, J. (2012). *The righteous mind: Why good people are divided by politics and religion.* New York: Pantheon Books; Haidt, J., & Bjorklund, F. (2008). Social intuitionists answer six questions about moral psychology. In W. Sinnott-Armstrong (Ed.), *Moral psychology: Vol. 2. The cognitive science of morality: Intuition and diversity* (pp. 182–217). Cambridge: MIT Press; Haidt, J., & Graham, J. (2007). When morality opposes justice: Conservatives have moral intuitions that liberals may not recognize. *Social Justice Research, 20,* 98–116; Jacobs, T. (2009, May). Morals authority. *Miller-McCune,* pp. 47–55.

39. Talbot, M. (1999). Against relativism. In J. M. Halstead & T. H. McLaughlin (Eds.), *Education in morality* (pp. 206–217). London: Routledge.

40. Hauser, M. D., Young, L., & Cushman, F. (2008). Reviving Rawls's linguistic analogy: Operative principles and the causal structure of moral actions. In W. Sinnott-Armstrong (Ed.), *Moral psychology: Vol. 2. The cognitive science of morality: Intuition and diversity* (pp. 107–144). Cambridge: MIT Press.

41. James, S. A. (2007). *Universal human rights: Origins and development.* New York: LFB Scholarly Publications, p. 2.

42. United Nations. (1948). The Universal Declaration of Human Rights. Retrieved from http://www.un.org/en/documents/udhr/index.shtmlUN Declaration of Human Rights

43. Rasche, A., & Gilbert, D. U. (2012). Institutionalizing global governance: The role of the United Nations Global Compact. *Business Ethics: A European Review, 21,* 100–114.

44. Kung, H. (1998). *A global ethic for global politics and economics.* New York: Oxford University Press; Kung, H. (1999). A global ethic in an age of globalization. In G. Enderle (Ed.), *International business ethics: Challenges and approaches* (pp. 19–127). Notre Dame, IN: University of Notre Dame Press; Kung, H. (2003). An ethical framework for the global market economy. In J. H. Dunning (Ed.), *Making globalization good: The moral challenges of global capitalism* (pp. 146–158). Oxford, England: Oxford University Press.

45. Paine, L., Deshpandé, R., Margolis, J. D., & Bettcher, K. E. (2005, December). Up to code: Does your company meet world-class standards? *Harvard Business Review,* pp. 122–133.

46. Caux Round Table. (2000). Appendix 26: The Caux Principles. In O. F. Williams (Ed.), *Global codes of conduct: An idea whose time has come* (pp. 384–388). Notre Dame, IN: University of Notre Dame Press.

47. Caux Round Table. (2006). Principles for non-governmental organizations. Retrieved from http://www.cauxroundtable.org/index.cfm?&menuid=101

48. Donaldson, T., & Dunfee, T. W. (1994). Toward a unified conception of business ethics: Integrative social contracts theory. *Academy of Management Review, 19,* 252–284; Donaldson, T., & Dunfee T. W. (1999). *Ties that bind: A social contracts approach to business ethics.* Boston: Harvard Business School Press; Donaldson, T. (2009). Compass and dead reckoning: The dynamic implications of ISCT. *Journal of Business Ethics, 88,* 659–664.

49. Hamilton, J. B., Knouse, S. B., & Hill, V. (2009). Google in China: A manager-friendly heuristic model for resolving cross-cultural ethical conflicts. *Journal of Business Ethics, 86,* 143–157. See also Hamilton, J. B., & Knouse, S. B. (2001). Multinational enterprise decision principles for dealing with cross cultural ethical conflicts. *Journal of Business Ethics, 31,* 77–94.

50. Hamilton et al., p. 149.

CHAPTER 11

Ethical Crisis Leadership

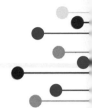

One of the extraordinary things about human events is that the unthinkable becomes thinkable.

—Author Salman Rushdie

Never waste the opportunities offered by a good crisis.

—Philosopher Niccolò Machiavelli

What's Ahead

This chapter examines ethical leadership in crisis situations. Crises are major unexpected events that pose significant threats to groups and organizations. They pass through three stages: precrisis, crisis event, and postcrisis. Ethical leaders have a series of tasks to carry out during each phase. Five ethical principles and strategies are essential to fulfilling these moral duties: assume broad responsibility, practice transparency, demonstrate care and concern, engage the head as well as the heart, and improvise from a strong moral foundation.

Managing a crisis is the ultimate test of ethical leadership. Bankruptcies, hurricanes, tornados, political scandals, industrial accidents, school shootings, food-borne illnesses, oil spills, fraud, computer data theft, terrorist attacks, and other crisis events bring out the worst or the best in leaders. Decisions must be made quickly under the glare of media scrutiny. Manufacturing plants, office buildings, planes, homes, jobs, and lives may be lost. Entire organizations, groups, societies, and economic and political systems might be at risk. As we've seen throughout this text, leaders often fail to meet the ethical challenges posed by crises. At the News Corporation, the New England Compounding Center, and the Secret Service, leaders sparked crises through their unethical behavior. For their part, leaders on K2 and at the Jefferson County, Colorado, sheriff's office ignored widely held moral standards and values in response to crisis events. On the other hand, we have also seen how other leaders, like Captain Sullenberger and executives at Siemens Global, coped effectively with crisis events. Their values become clearer; their moral commitments become greater.

This chapter introduces the ethical challenges posed by leadership in crisis, building on the foundation laid in earlier chapters. To ethically manage crisis events, you will need to draw upon concepts we have discussed previously—values, moral reasoning, ethical decision-making formats, group decision making, and ethical perspectives, to name a few. However, you will also need to understand the characteristics of crisis as well as the elements of ethical crisis management. The first section of this chapter provides an overview of the nature and stages of crises. It identifies important leadership tasks that must be carried out in each crisis phase. The second section identifies principles and strategies that equip leaders to ethically carry out these responsibilities.

Crisis: An Overview

A crisis is any major unanticipated event that poses a significant threat. Such events are rare (making them difficult to prepare for), they generate a good deal of uncertainty (their causes and effects are unclear), and they are hard to resolve (there is no set formula for determining how to act). Further, decisions about how to deal with a particular crisis must be made rapidly, and those outside the immediate group—customers, clients, suppliers, and neighbors—are also affected.[1]

The stress and anxiety generated by crises makes them particularly hard to manage in an ethical manner. Stress interferes with cognitive abilities. Individuals tend to narrow their focus to just a few perspectives and alternatives. They often perceive the world less accurately and ignore important information. At the organizational level, stress prompts groups to delegate decision-making authority to a small team of top officials, limiting access to diverse viewpoints. Time limits also prevent talking to a variety of stakeholders. All of these factors subvert ethical reasoning and creative problem solving while increasing the likelihood that the needs of some stakeholders will be overlooked.[2]

Investigators divide crises into different types. These types can help leaders better prepare for, and respond to, crisis events. Groups and organizations will be more vulnerable to some types of crises than others. Manufacturers have to be highly concerned about product safety; coastal communities have to be ready for ocean storms. When disaster strikes, the nature of the crisis will also help to determine the course of action. Responding to the disruption of a work stoppage requires one set of strategies, while responding to a computer security breach demands another.

Crisis management experts Matthew Seeger, Timothy Sellnow, and Robert Ulmer identify ten types of crises:[3]

1. *Public perception:* negative stories about the organization's products, personnel, or services; negative rumors; blogs and websites

2. *Natural disasters:* tornadoes, hurricanes, mudslides, wildfires, blizzards, earthquakes, volcano eruptions

3. *Product or service:* product recalls, food-borne illnesses, concern about products and services generated by the media

4. *Terrorist attacks:* bombings, hijackings, abductions, poisonings

5. *Economic:* cash shortages, bankruptcies, hostile takeovers, accounting scandals

6. *Human resource:* workplace violence, strikes, labor unrest, discrimination, sexual harassment, school and workplace shootings, theft, fraud

7. *Industrial:* mine collapses, nuclear accidents, fires, explosions

8. *Oil and chemical spills:* tanker and railway spills, pipeline and well leaks

9. *Transportation:* train derailments, plane crashes, truck accidents, multivehicle pileups

10. *Outside environment:* collapse of financial systems, rising fuel prices, deregulation, nationalization of private companies, mortgage crisis

Ian Mitroff, former director of the Center for Crisis Management at the University of Southern California, offers an alternative typology based on the intentions of those involved in the crisis event.[4] He notes that there has been a sharp rise in what he labels *abnormal accidents*—deliberate acts that are intentionally designed to disrupt or destroy systems. He contrasts abnormal accidents with *normal accidents,* those unintentional events that cause systems to break down. The Oklahoma City bombing, kidnappings, the release of nerve gas in a Tokyo subway, Enron's collapse, and cyberattacks on large corporations and the military would be examples of abnormal accidents. The *Deepwater Horizon* oil spill, plane crashes, and mining disasters are normal accidents that reflect problems with routine operating procedures. Abnormal accidents are harder to prepare for, but modern organizations have no choice but to plan for them. For example, since most terrorist acts are aimed at private businesses, not the government, Mitroff argues business has to do its part to respond to terrorist threats. (See Case Study 11.1 for a closer look at one of the ethical issues raised by terrorism.) He also points out that even routine crises are becoming harder to deal with in an increasingly complex, interconnected society. When power went out on the East Coast in 2003, for instance, every organization in the region was affected, and airline traffic throughout the whole country was disrupted.[5]

The Three Stages of a Crisis

Whatever the type, every crisis passes through three stages: precrisis, crisis event, and postcrisis.[6] In each stage leaders have a moral obligation to carry out particular tasks or functions. I'll describe these tasks and offer some steps for carrying them out.

Stage 1. Precrisis

Precrisis is the period of normalcy between crisis events. During this, the longest phase, the group or organization typically believes that it understands the risks it faces and can handle any contingency that arises. The temptation to become overconfident grows as the time between crises increases. Funding for backup data sites, disaster drills, training, and other types of crisis preparation may be cut, which increases the likelihood of another crisis.

Complacency isn't the only barrier to crisis prevention. Human biases (decision-making and judgment errors), institutional failures (organizational breakdowns in processing information), and special-interest groups (resistance from groups looking out for the interests of their own members) can derail crisis preparedness as well.[7] These factors are summarized in Box 11.1.

● ● ● BOX 11.1 BARRIERS TO CRISIS PREVENTION ● ● ●

Human Biases

- Positive illusions that falsely convince decision makers that a problem doesn't exist or isn't severe enough to require action

- Interpreting events in an egocentric manner that favors the leader and the organization while blaming outsiders

- Discounting the future by ignoring possible long-term costs; refusing to invest resources now to prevent future crises

- Maintaining the dysfunctional status quo by refusing to inflict any harm (such as higher Social Security taxes) that would address a mounting problem (the danger that the Social Security system will become insolvent)

- Failure to recognize problems because they aren't vivid (they are not personally experienced as direct threats)

Institutional Failures

- Failure to collect adequate data due to (a) ignoring certain problems and discounting evidence, (b) the presence of conflicting information, and (c) information overload

- Information is not integrated into the organization as a whole because departments operate independently and managers maintain secrecy

- Members lack incentive to take action because they are rewarded for acting selfishly or believe that everyone agrees with current procedures

- Leaders fail to learn from experience or to disseminate lessons learned because information is not recorded or shared or because key organizational members are lost

Special-Interest Groups

- Impose social burdens—higher taxes, water pollution, high drug prices—in order to benefit themselves

- Blame complex problems on individuals rather than on systems that are at fault

- Oppose reform efforts

SOURCE: Bazerman, M. H., & Watkins, M. D. (2004). *Predictable surprises: The disasters you should have seen coming, and how to prevent them*. Boston: Harvard Business School Press. Reprinted by permission of Waveland Press, Inc. from Hackman, M. Z., & Johnson, C. E. *Leadership: A communication perspective*, p. 413. Long Grove, IL: Waveland Press, Inc. 2013. All rights reserved.

Terry Pauchant and Ian Mitroff argue that, in addition to the factors outlined above, misguided ethical assumptions or myths can undermine crisis management. They identify and debunk five unethical beliefs about crisis management:[8]

> *Myth 1: "Crises are inevitable."* Some but not all crises are inevitable. But even if some crises (storms and earthquakes) can't be prevented, leaders have an ethical responsibility to do everything they can to prepare for them.

> *Myth 2: "We lack the basic knowledge to prevent or understand crises."* Researchers don't know everything about crisis management. However, they have identified a number of steps leaders can take to prevent crises and to manage them when they occur. When leaders fail to act, the problem is not a lack of knowledge but a lack of will.

Myth 3: "Better technology will prevent future crises." Resolving crises calls for more than technical solutions. Leaders must also communicate effectively, demonstrate flexibility, and think creatively, for example.

A variation of this third myth is the belief that an organization is too large to experience a major crisis. A business clinging to this misconception is really making an unethical statement. In essence, it is saying, "Whenever an organization is so big and powerful that its size will protect it from a major disaster or crisis, then it has no responsibility toward its employees and the surrounding environment and is justified in expressing no concern toward the environment."[9] These same corporations may use formulas to estimate the likelihood and cost of possible disasters. If the formula shows that the risk is low or that the costs of prevention outweigh the costs of disaster, they decide they shouldn't take any action at all, which is unethical. Such was the case with the Love Canal environmental crisis of the late 1970s.[10] Hooker Chemical dumped 21,000 tons of hazardous waste into a canal and conducted a cost-benefit analysis. Officials estimated that cleanup would cost $20 million and treated future residents as potential benefits. Individuals working outside the home were valued based on their modest working-class salaries and on the assumption that their children would earn the same wages. Since the costs of the cleanup apparently outweighed the financial value of neighborhood residents, the company sold the property to the town of Niagara Falls instead of removing the toxic chemicals. An elementary school and homes were built on the site, and residents soon developed blood disorders, kidney and respiratory problems, and other serious health issues. Eventually the residents were evacuated, and the chemical company and the state of New York were forced to clean up the site at an estimated cost of $137 million. People were sickened and died because, as one resident pointed out, "they decided that we weren't worthy of doing anything."[11]

Myth 4: "Crisis management is inherently detrimental to progress." Risk can never be totally eliminated. Yet some crisis-prone organizations and leaders shouldn't be allowed to engage in dangerous activities without some oversight. Following the financial crisis that began in 2008, for instance, many observers argued that greater restrictions should be placed on the financial industry to prevent future recessions.

Myth 5: "Emotions have no place in crisis management." Emotions have a key role to play in crisis management, as they do in other kinds of ethical decision making (see Chapter 5). Leaders need to see ethics as a conversation, connecting with stakeholders before, during, and after the crisis. They also need to acknowledge the pain and suffering generated by the crisis, which may have been caused by their decisions and actions.

Ethical leaders in the precrisis stage help their groups detect possible trouble and develop strategies for managing crises should they strike. Crisis expert Stephen Fink uses the Greek word *prodromes* (which means "running before") to describe the warning signs that precede a crisis. Ignoring or downplaying these signs generally results in disaster.[12] Parents, school officials, and law enforcement officers had plenty of warning that Eric Harris and Dylan Klebold were threats, for example (Chapter 4), and TEPCO had been warned that there was a significant chance that a tsunami would overrun the seawalls at the Fukushima power plant (Chapter 5). Prodromes were ignored in both the Boston Marathon bombings and the West, Texas, fertilizer plant explosion, events that occurred during the same week in April 2013. Before the bombings in Boston, Russian officials suspected that one of the alleged bombers had ties to extremist groups and asked the FBI to investigate (they discovered no such links). The West fertilizer plant had been fined months earlier for safety violations. Few people in the small town paid much attention to the fact that the plant was located only a few hundred yards from three public schools, an apartment complex, and a nursing home.

Crisis management experts offer a variety of strategies for recognizing danger signs. To pick up on prodromes, organizations must continually scan the environment, looking outward and inward.[13] In external scanning, organizational leaders survey the broadcast media, websites, YouTube, Twitter, trade journals, and other sources to identify potential dangers. Internal scanning means identifying danger signs coming from those who have an ongoing relationship with the organization, like customers, suppliers, and donors. Surges in product returns and complaints, as well as public criticism and protests, can signal something is amiss.

In addition to environmental scanning, organizations can go looking for trouble. Looking for trouble means actively seeking weaknesses that could prove harmful or fatal to the organization. One commonly used troubleshooting tactic is to brainstorm a list of possible crises. There are host of possible crises that could strike your college or university, for instance, ranging from floods to campus shootings to student protests to faculty strikes. In a variation on this strategy, develop a "wheel of crises" with the types of crises your company or nonprofit can face.[14] Spin the wheel and wherever it stops, brainstorm all the kinds of possible crises that might occur in that category. Another troubleshooting strategy is to ask members of your organization to play the role of villains and imagine ways to destroy products and processes. (You might also hire outsiders to "spy" on your organization to expose weaknesses.) Yet another tactic is to look to other industries to determine if the dangers they face could pose a threat to your type of organization. One large electronics manufacturer took this approach, imagining itself as part of the food industry. Leaders at this firm thought about how "microbes" and "bugs" might "infect" their products. They even hired an infectious disease specialist to help prevent such infections. Based on this analysis, executives determined that disgruntled workers could introduce pathogens (computer viruses or faulty parts, for example) into company products. They decided to quarantine suspect shipments until the items were inoculated (repaired). You can determine your crisis readiness and that of your work organization by completing Self-Assessment 11.1, the Crisis and/or Disaster Preparedness Scale.

Once weaknesses have been identified, develop a crisis management plan (CMP) to cope with each type of emergency. Key components of a CMP include the following:[15]

1. Cover page (identify the document and when it was written and revised)
2. Introduction (generally written by the CEO to emphasize the importance of the plan)
3. Acknowledgments (an official signed record that key crisis managers and executives have read the plan)
4. Rehearsal dates (record when the plan has been practiced)
5. Purpose and objectives (specify the goal of the plan, the desire to be accurate and truthful with publics)
6. List of key publics (identify the stakeholders or publics to receive communication during the crisis)
7. Notifying publics (detail how each stakeholder group will be contacted)
8. Crisis management team (identify team members as well as their backups)
9. Crisis directory (phone numbers and contact information for crisis team members)
10. Media spokesperson (usually the CEO)
11. List of emergency personnel and local officials
12. List of key media and contact information
13. Spokespersons for related organizations (those who might be contacted to comment on your organization)
14. Crisis communications control center (specify several alternative locations)
15. Equipment and supplies needed by employees and visitors
16. Pregathered information (e.g., safety and company reports, company fact sheets)
17. Key messages to be delivered during the crisis (can include sample press releases)
18. Website information
19. Trick questions that might be asked by the media
20. List of URLs from organizations that might have important information needed during the crisis
21. Evaluation form for distributing to internal groups to critique the crisis response

Crisis preparation pays off. Crisis-ready organizations are less likely to experience unexpected threats, suffer significantly less damage if such events do strike, and recover much more quickly.[16] In one study, Oxford University researchers compared the stock price of major corporations faced with significant crises.[17] Those firms mishandling crises saw a 7% decline in their stock price after a year. Companies effectively managing crises saw their year-end stock price close an average of 7% higher than before disaster struck. The researchers concluded that it wasn't the amount of damage that made the difference in how the stocks performed. Rather, the key was how management responded when in the media spotlight. Effective response boosted confidence in leadership; ineffective response lowered investor confidence.

SOURCE: Dilbert: @Scott Adams/United Features Syndicate, Inc.

Stage 2: Crisis Event

The second stage commences with a "trigger event," like an explosion, a shooting, or bankruptcy, and the recognition that a crisis has occurred. It ends when the crisis is resolved. Realization that a crisis has erupted sparks strong emotions, including surprise, anger, fear, and disbelief. Confusion reigns as group members try to understand what is happening and worry about what will happen to the group and to themselves. At the same time, significant harm is done to people, property, and the larger environment, and the incident garners significant press coverage.

Ethical leaders play a critical role during this stage. They first recognize that a crisis has occurred and persuade others that the group is in grave danger. This is not always an easy task. When tsunamis struck Thailand's beaches in 2004, some 30,000 Swedes were vacationing in the area. A low-ranking official on duty in the Swedish Foreign Ministry recognized the danger to Swedish citizens and alerted her bosses. They, however, did not find the situation alarming. When she persisted in her efforts to warn them, she was reprimanded and called hysterical.[18] (Following the crisis she was commended for her courage in speaking up.)

Once the crisis is recognized, leaders then implement the crisis management plan, mobilize the crisis management team, and focus on damage control. Immediate threats to individuals, property, and the environment take priority. Leaders may need to redeploy staff and such resources as equipment, phone lines, and office space while cooperating with emergency personnel, government officials, neighborhood associations, the media, and other outside groups.

Because the crisis management team is so critical to coping with an active crisis, leaders should pay particular attention to the group's membership. While the exact composition of the team may vary depending on the particular crisis, the typical crisis management team for a large organization consists of the following members:[19]

- Attorney to review messages, reduce legal risk, and specify legal requirements

- Public relations director or coordinator to manage internal and external communication tactics as well as media relations

- Operational managers to coordinate recovery

- Controller or another financial manager with knowledge of financial assets and insurance coverage

- Institutional technology manager to ensure that communication channels are open and to maintain databases

- Regulatory expert to handle coordination with government agencies and to represent the interests of the public

- The CEO or a representative from her or his office

One person—typically the chief executive officer—should take primary responsibility as spokesperson in the case of an emergency. This prevents conflicting messages and the spread of misinformation. An effective spokesperson goes to the scene of the crisis, cooperates with the media, and provides accurate information. Those directly affected by the crisis have particularly important information needs and should take top priority. They not only need to know what happened but also need to learn how to protect themselves. Potential victims of a flu epidemic need to be vaccinated, for example. City residents in the path of a tornado need to be warned to take shelter. Consumers need to learn of contaminated food products. (Turn to Box 11.2 for an example of an effective crisis spokesperson in action.)

• • • BOX 11.2 MOURNER-IN-CHIEF • • •

When disasters like terrorist attacks, storms, and shootings occur, Americans look to their president to express the sorrow of the nation. In these cases, the president becomes the nation's "mourner-in-chief." In 1983, for example, Ronald Reagan expressed the shock of the nation and the world at the downing of a South Korean passenger airliner by a Russian fighter plane. After the shooting of 20 first graders and 6 adults in Newtown, Connecticut, President Barack Obama offered the following statement at a White House press conference. What made the address particularly powerful was the fact that the president, who normally appears "cool" and collected, had to stop during his remarks to wipe away tears.

This afternoon, I spoke with Governor Malloy and FBI Director Mueller. I offered Governor Malloy my condolences on behalf of the nation and made it clear he will have every single resource that he needs to investigate this heinous crime, care for the victims, counsel their families.

We've endured too many of these tragedies in the past few years. And each time I learn the news, I react not as a president, but as anybody else would as a parent. And that was especially true today. I know there's not a parent in America who doesn't feel the same overwhelming grief that I do.

The majority of those who died today were children—beautiful, little kids between the ages of 5 and 10 years old. They had their entire lives ahead of them—birthdays, graduations, weddings, kids of their own. Among the fallen were also teachers, men and women who devoted their lives to helping our children fulfill their dreams.

So our hearts are broken today for the parents and grandparents, sisters and brothers of these little children, and for the families of the adults who were lost.

Our hearts are broken for the parents of the survivors, as well, for as blessed as they are to have their children home tonight, they know that their children's innocence has been torn away from them too early and there are no words that will ease their pain.

As a country, we have been through this too many times. Whether it is an elementary school in Newtown, or a shopping mall in Oregon, or a temple in Wisconsin, or a

(Continued)

(Continued)

movie theater in Aurora, or a street corner in Chicago, these neighborhoods are our neighborhoods and these children are our children. And we're going to have to come together and take meaningful action to prevent more tragedies like this, regardless of the politics.

This evening, Michelle and I will do what I know every parent in America will do, which is hug our children a little tighter, and we'll tell them that we love them, and we'll remind each other how deeply we love one another. But there are families in Connecticut who cannot do that tonight, and they need all of us right now. In the hard days to come, that community needs us to be at our best as Americans, and I will do everything in my power as president to help, because while nothing can fill the space of a lost child or loved one, all of us can extend a hand to those in need, to remind them that we are there for them, that we are praying for them, that the love they felt for those they lost endures not just in their memories, but also in ours.

May God bless the memory of the victims and, in the words of Scripture, heal the brokenhearted and bind up their wounds.

SOURCE: Copyright National Public Radio. Used by permission.

Stage 3: Postcrisis

Investigation and analysis take place during the third and final stage. Group members try to determine what went wrong, who was to blame, how to prevent a recurrence of the problem, and so on. This is also a period of recovery during which ethical leaders try to salvage the legitimacy of the group or organization, help group members learn from the crisis experience, and promote healing.

The image of an organization generally suffers during a crisis as outsiders blame it for failing to prevent the disaster, causing harm, and not moving quickly enough to help victims. As a consequence, an effective leader must convince the public that the organization has a legitimate reason to exist and can be trusted. The best way to rebuild an organization's image depends a great deal on the particular crisis and the past history of the group. If the organization is not at fault and has a good reputation, simple denial ("We are not at fault") may be sufficient. However, if the organization is to blame, it should admit responsibility, offer compensation to victims, and take corrective action by improving safety procedures, recalling products, and so forth. Not only is this the moral course of action, but attempts to deny truthful accusations typically backfire, further damaging the group's reputation.[20] (One organization facing a major challenge to its reputation is described in Case Study 11.2.)

The second leadership task in the postcrisis stage is to encourage the group to learn from the experience lest it be repeated again. Organizational crisis learning takes three forms.[21] *Retrospective sense making* looks for causation, determining what members overlooked and identifying faulty assumptions and rationalizations that contributed to the disaster. Such processing broadens the group's base of knowledge and gives it more options for responding in the future. *Reconsidering structure* refers to making major changes in leadership, mission, organizational structure, and policies as a result of the disruption caused by the crisis event. Disaster commissions are sometimes formed to capture learning from crises and to suggest reforms. Following the Twin Towers attack, for example, the 9/11 Commission report led to a major overhaul of the U.S. intelligence system.[22] *Vicarious learning* draws from the experiences of other groups and organizations, both good and bad. Some organizations illustrate what *not* to do, while others serve as exemplary role models. Government response to Hurricane Katrina has emerged as a classic example of crisis *mis*management. Local and state officials were slow to order a mandatory evacuation and stranded poorer residents who didn't have cars. The Federal Emergency Management Agency (led by an unqualified manager) waited too long to implement emergency plans, and the president didn't get involved until days had passed. A House congressional committee investigating the disaster concluded that the government's response to Katrina was a "litany of mistakes, misjudgments, lapses, and absurdities."[23] There is also much to learn from how BP and the federal government mismanaged the oil spill off the coast of Louisiana. Fortunately, the state and federal response to Hurricane Sandy was much more effective, with a majority of residents expressing approval for the way that government officials intervened.[24]

The third leadership task in the postcrisis stage is to promote healing, which helps members move beyond the crisis. Healing begins with explaining what happened. A cause needs to be identified and corrective action taken. Corrective steps might include, for instance, strengthening levees after a hurricane and tightening computer security measures after data have been stolen. Forgetting, which is replacing feelings of stress, anxiety, and loss with positive emotions like optimism and confidence, is easier when such preventive measures have been put in place. Ethical leaders also shape the memories of what happened by honoring crisis heroes and by marking important anniversaries.

Fostering a sense of renewal that sets aside blame and looks ahead is part of the healing process. The *discourse of renewal* is spontaneous, not carefully planned, and comes directly out of the character and reputation of the leader.[25] Renewal focuses on the future rather than on the past. Optimistic leaders may even talk about rebuilding before the immediate crisis is over. The discourse of renewal also highlights the opportunities created by the crisis.

Milt Cole of Cole Hardwoods and Aaron Feuerstein of Malden Mills engaged in renewal after their plants burned down. Both men could have taken the insurance settlements and retired. Instead, they immediately decided to rebuild because of their commitment to their employees and communities. The new plants they built were far better than the ones lost in the fires. (Box 11.3 summarizes critical competencies for leading in crisis situations.)

● ● ● BOX 11.3 CRISIS LEADERSHIP COMPETENCIES ● ● ●

To determine the specific skills leaders need to successfully manage crisis situations, Lynn Perry Wooten and Erika Hayes James sampled 20 business crises occurring from 2000 to 2006. Their data set included an Alaska Airlines crash, financial fraud at Tyco, a hepatitis outbreak at Chi-Chi's restaurants, Wal-Mart's response to a gender discrimination lawsuit, and Hurricane Katrina. The researchers found that firms often mishandle one phase of a crisis while responding more effectively to another. They also identified key competencies, described below, that are essential to navigating each crisis phase.

Precrisis

- *Sense making.* Sense making answers these questions: How does something become an event? What does the event mean? What should I do relative to the event? The crisis leader then puts the answers to these queries together to develop a plan of action. Making sense of what appear to be unrelated events is also critical to identifying and responding to such warning signs as accident reports, quality problems, and customer complaints.

- *Perspective taking.* Empathy is critical to anticipating and responding to crises. Leaders need to be particularly sensitive to the needs of those who might be hurt by a crisis (victims and victims families), not just those who are most vocal, like activists and shareholders. This broader perspective can alert leaders to potential dangers and prepare them to act on behalf of stakeholders.

- *Issue selling.* Middle managers, in particular, must be able to convince top management that the organization needs to engage in crisis planning, which is difficult given the fact that crisis planning is "rarely seen as a pressing concern among key decision makers."

- *Organizational agility.* Since crises threaten the organization as a whole, leaders have to bring a variety of departments and units together to prepare for disaster.

- *Creativity.* It takes creativity to design a crisis management plan that identifies a variety of weaknesses, possible scenarios, and effective responses.

Crisis Event

- *Decision making under pressure.* Competent crisis leaders must be able to overcome negative emotions like fear and anxiety, as well as time pressures and public scrutiny, to make wise choices.

- *Communicating effectively.* During the height of the crisis leaders are responsible for connecting to a variety of audiences—employees, customers, investors, community leaders, neighbors. They need to provide information, instruction, and assurance while gathering data. They must also express empathy and shape public opinion.

- *Risk taking.* The pressure of a crisis can prompt leaders to fall back on their habits or traditional ways of responding. A crisis, however, often calls for a unique response. For example, the board of Martha Stewart Living Omnimedia was able to shift to a new way of thinking when the company's namesake was jailed for insider trading. The CEO took Martha Stewart off of magazine covers and de-emphasized her connection to other products. Top management also reorganized into executive teams to supervise business units.

Postcrisis

- *Promoting organizational resilience.* This competency takes the organization beyond where it was before the crisis struck. When this ability is exercised, individuals and the organization as a whole are able to bounce back from the stress and perform at a higher level.

- *Acting with integrity.* Effective crisis leaders demonstrate personal integrity and make ethical decisions. They act consistently, matching their words and actions. They don't deny responsibility for an industrial accident, for instance, and later admit guilt to settle a lawsuit. They are able to rebuild public trust by following through on their statements and commitments.

- *Learning orientation.* Any opportunity offered by a crisis is lost unless leaders engage in learning and reflection. Competent crisis leaders learn from their experiences and change the way their organizations operate.

SOURCE: Wooten, L. P., & James, E. H. (2008). Linking crisis management and leadership competencies: The role of human resource development. *Advances in Developing Human Resources, 10,* 352–379.

Components of Ethical Crisis Management

As we saw in the previous section, ethical leaders have important tasks to carry out in each stage of crisis development. Theorists and researchers have identified five principles and/or strategies that equip them to fulfill these duties. Moral leaders assume broad responsibility, practice transparency, demonstrate care and concern, use their heads as well as their hearts, and improvise from a strong moral foundation.

Assume Broad Responsibility

Responsibility is the foundation of ethical crisis leadership.[26] Preventing, managing, and recovering from crises all depend on the willingness of leaders and followers to accept their moral responsibilities. Society grants individuals and organizations significant freedom to make and carry out decisions. Such freedom means that people and groups are accountable for their actions. They have an ethical duty to prevent crises because such events do significant harm. The first step in preventing crises is to behave as a moral person. Since a great many crises (fraud, accounting scandals, embezzlement, sexual harassment) are the direct result of the immoral actions of leaders, eliminating these behaviors greatly reduces the group's exposure to scandal. Moral leaders also create healthy ethical organizational climates that have a low risk of moral failure and crisis (see Chapter 9).

In addition to engaging in, and fostering, ethical behavior, the responsible crisis leader fights against complacency, human biases, institutional weaknesses, special-interest groups, and other obstacles to crisis prevention. He or she commits the money and resources needed to identify, prevent, and manage trouble spots. This includes assigning groups to brainstorm potential weaknesses, investing in computer security, holding disaster drills, and creating crisis management plans. Leaders aren't the only ones who are responsible for crisis prevention, however. This duty extends to everyone who has a role, no matter how small, in anticipating such events. According to crisis prevention expert Robert Allinson, "Anyone who is in any way connected with a potential or actual disaster is responsible for its occurrence."[27]

Sadly, a significant number of organizations still fail to take their crisis prevention responsibilities seriously. A corporate survey revealed that, while the vast majority had crisis management plans, a significant portion (approximately one-fifth) did not.[28] Case Study 11.3 describes one example of an organization that is a model of disaster *unpreparedness*.

If a crisis does erupt, leaders are obligated to mitigate the harm they and/or their followers cause to others through, for instance, deceptive advertising, fraud, or industrial accidents. A rapid response is key to fulfilling this ethical duty. Exxon continues to be used as an example of poor crisis management in large part because of its slow response to the grounding of the *Exxon Valdez,* which caused the largest oil spill up to that point in U.S. history. Then CEO Lawrence Rawl didn't get to the scene of the accident until 10 days after the spill, initial containment efforts were ineffective, and the firm denied at first that it had any responsibility for what happened.[29] More recently, executives at Toyota were slow to respond to sudden acceleration problems in their vehicles.[30]

When the immediate danger is past, leaders have an obligation to ensure that a similar crisis doesn't happen again and to assure the public of that fact. Their ethical duties include carrying out the postcrisis tasks noted earlier: rebuilding the group's image, helping members learn from the crisis, and promoting healing.

Crises broaden both the scope and the depth of a leader's ethical obligations. In a crisis, the breadth of a leader's responsibility greatly expands. New stakeholder groups are formed, including those who had no previous interest in the organization but are currently threatened as well as members of the general public who learn about the crisis event. Leaders may also need to go to extraordinary lengths (depth) to meet the needs of victims. Take the case of Marsh & McLennan Companies, for example. When the terrorist planes hit the World Trade Center in 2001, 295 of its employees were killed. Company officials at the professional services firm responded by creating a set of benefits and services for the families of those who died, which included assigning "relationship managers" to help each family get the help it needed, providing counseling services, enhancing salary and insurance benefits, setting up a victims' relief fund, and creating memorials for the victims.[31]

Practice Transparency

Like responsibility, transparency is another requirement placed on groups and organizations operating freely in society. We want governments to reveal the ways they spend our tax dollars, for instance, and require audited financial statements and annual reports from publicly held corporations. Failure to disclose information spawns abuses of power and privilege and makes it impossible for individuals to act as informed members of the community.[32] Transparency is key to exercising personal freedom and establishing healthy relationships between people, between people and organizations, and between organizations.[33] When crisis strikes, transparency takes on added significance.

Transparency begins with openness. When faced with the challenge of mismanaged information, the transparent leader tells the truth and avoids hiding or distorting information. A transparent group is open about its policies, compensation packages, safety measures, values, spending, positions on political issues, and so on. Leaders regularly share this information through websites, presentations, publications, press releases, and other means. Openness, in turn, is marked by candor and integrity. Ethical leaders are willing to share bad as well as good news, such as when earnings are down and construction plans have to be shelved. Johnson & Johnson's response to the Tylenol poisoning has become a "textbook" case of crisis management in part because of the firm's honesty. During the product tampering crisis, corporate officials initially denied that there was any potassium cyanide used in the manufacture of Tylenol.[34] Later, when leaders discovered that minute amounts of the chemical were used during testing at some facilities, it immediately released this information to the public. Such candor helped the company recover quickly from this abnormal accident.

Transparency also involves symmetry.[35] Symmetry refers to maintaining balanced relationships with outside groups based on two-way communication. Instead of imposing their will on others, organizations engaged in symmetrical relationships seek to understand and to respond to the concerns of stakeholders. They regularly interact with, and gather information from, customers, vendors, neighbors, activist groups, and others. Even more important, they act on these data, changing their plans as needed. For example, if neighbors strenuously object to the construction of a new product distribution facility, executives may find another location or modify the design of the building to meet the concerns of those living nearby. A study of excellent public relations programs found that the best public relations efforts—those that increase organizational effectiveness and benefit society—are based on symmetrical relationships with stakeholder groups.[36]

Crisis preparedness and trust are two positive by-products of transparency. Openness makes it less likely that leaders will engage in unethical behavior. As ethicist Jeremy Bentham noted, "The more strictly we are watched, the better we behave." Symmetry also serves as an early warning system. Partnerships foster two-way communication that will reveal if customers are having problems with products or services, if activist groups are offended by the organization's environmental practices, and so forth.

Stakeholders and the general public are more prone to trust organizations they perceive as open and give them the benefit of the doubt in crisis situations. As a consequence, these groups suffer less damage to their image and regain their legitimacy more rapidly. For example, Pepsi was the victim of a hoax that started in Seattle. Consumers placed syringes in cans of Diet Pepsi and then complained to the media. The corporation's reputation for safety and quality, as well as its Seattle bottler's work in the community, helped Pepsi weather the crisis and recover quickly.[37]

Maintaining transparency is particularly difficult when a crisis is triggered. First, there are privacy concerns. Victims' families may need to be notified before information can be released to the press. Second, admitting fault can put the organization at a disadvantage in case of a lawsuit. Third, there may be proprietary information about, say, manufacturing processes and recipes, which should not be released to competitors. (Even the leading proponents of corporate transparency agree that businesses have a right to privacy, to security, and to control of certain types of information.)[38] Fourth, uncertainty makes it difficult for an organization to determine what its course of action should be, and, as a result, to communicate concrete details to the public. Fifth, being specific may offend some stakeholders who feel that they have been treated unfairly. Sixth, making a commitment to a single course of action too soon may limit the group's ability to deal with the crisis.[39]

Some observers suggest that leaders in a crisis situation use *strategic ambiguity* as an alternative to transparency. In strategic ambiguity, communicators are deliberately vague, which allows them to appeal to multiple audiences.[40] For example, the promise to respond "forcefully" to a crisis is an abstract statement, which can be interpreted many different ways by stakeholders. It also leaves the door open for the group to choose a variety of possible strategies for managing the crisis event. If challenged, the leader can claim that she or he never made a specific commitment to particular stakeholder groups. Then, too, ambiguous messages are appropriate in early stages of a crisis, when information is scarce and conditions are rapidly changing.[41]

More often than not, however, strategic ambiguity is unethical, used to shift the blame and to confuse stakeholders while providing them with biased and/or incomplete information. This appears to be the case with Jack in the Box.[42] In 1993, children in Washington State were sickened with *E. coli* poisoning after eating hamburgers at the firm's restaurants. Throughout the crisis Jack in the Box president Robert Nugent made use of ambiguous communication. He emphasized that there was a "potential" link between the illnesses and company food. He pointed to other possible contributors—including a food supplier—to the outbreak and claimed that the firm intended to follow state and federal regulations. (Later it was revealed that Jack in the Box had failed to adopt Washington's stricter cooking times, which likely would have prevented the outbreak.) The restaurant chain's response was unethical because it (a) favored the needs of internal stakeholders (employees, managers, shareholders) over those of external stakeholders (consumers, regulators) and (b) provided outsiders with incomplete and inaccurate information.

While the amount and type of information to be shared will vary with each crisis, the goal should always be to be as open as possible. Cooperate with the media and government officials, respond quickly to inquiries, provide detailed background information on the crisis, be honest about what happened, release information as soon as it is available, and be more concerned about meeting the needs of victims than about protecting organizational assets (see the discussion of compassion in the next section).

Rhetorician Keith Hearit illustrates how an organization can practice transparency when communicating to stakeholders during a crisis. Hearit believes that, in order to be ethical, the group's explanation of events and response to public criticism must have the right manner and content.[43] *Manner* refers to the form of the communication, which needs to (1) be truthful (disclose relevant information that matches up with the reality of what happened), (2) be sincere (express true regret, reflect the seriousness of the event and its impact, demonstrate commitment to taking corrective action and reconciling with stakeholders), (3) be timely (immediately after the event, in time to help victims deal with the damage), (4) be voluntary (not coerced but driven by moral considerations, seek reconciliation, humble), (5) address all stakeholders (speak to all who were wronged, not just a few groups), and (6) be in the proper context (available to all victims).

The *content* of the message is just as important as the form it takes. The ethical story of events

- clearly acknowledges wrongdoing;

- accepts full responsibility for what happened;

- expresses regret for the offense, the harm done, and failure to carry out responsibilities;

- identifies with the injured parties (both with their suffering and with the damage done to relationships);

- asks for forgiveness;

- seeks reconciliation with injured parties;

- fully discloses information related to the offense;

- offers to carry out appropriate corrective action; and

- offers appropriate compensation.

Demonstrate Care

Demonstrating concern has practical as well as ethical benefits. Nothing draws more public condemnation than a group that refuses to take responsibility for harming others, as in the case of the *Exxon Valdez,* or appears callous, as when NASA declared that there had been "an apparent malfunction" as millions watched the explosion of the *Challenger* shuttle on television. (More recently, BP's CEO was criticized after saying that he was anxious for the Gulf oil spill crisis to end because he would "like his life back." This remark appeared callous to the families of the 11 BP employees who were killed when a drilling rig exploded, triggering the massive leak.) Victims who have received adequate assistance are less likely to sue the organization later.

When harm occurs, people hold organizations and their leaders responsible even if they didn't mean to hurt others, which is called the *intention effect*.[44] Observers blame leaders when things go wrong but don't give leaders credit when things go right. Apparently the mere existence of harm triggers the impression that the individual or group involved was deliberately out to damage others. (You can see how the intention effect operates by responding to the vignettes in Self-Assessment 11.2.) Observers also expect corporations to anticipate potential harm—the *foresight effect*. This effect is illustrated by the stiff punishments administered to corporate defendants in civil court cases. Jurors believe that corporations have greater responsibility for harm because they should have greater ability to foresee the consequences of their actions. Jurors also expect a higher level of care from companies based on their greater power, the sense that they have more obligations because they have more resources, and the fact that corporate misdeeds have greater consequences than do those of individuals operating on their own.

While it is in the interest of leaders and organizations to act in a compassionate manner for image and financial reasons, as well as to meet the expectations of observers, it is even more important that they do so for ethical reasons. Altruism is an important ethical principle, as we saw in Chapter 5, and is particularly relevant to crisis situations. Love of neighbor urges us to meet the needs of those threatened by crisis, no matter who they are. Victims deserve our help because of their status as human beings. Showing concern during a crisis goes well beyond addressing the physical and financial needs of victims. Those harmed by a crisis have significant emotional and spiritual needs too.[45] They may be overwhelmed with feelings of loss and grief as well as guilt for surviving when others did not. Their sense of security, meaning, and purpose is threatened. Posttraumatic stress disorder, where individuals periodically relive the terror, is common. Of course, victims aren't the only ones to experience many of these reactions. The triggering event, as noted earlier, generates surprise, anger, fear, and disbelief for crisis managers, other group members, and outside observers as well. For instance, a series of shootings in Arizona, Colorado, Wisconsin, Connecticut, and Oregon in 2012 were traumatic events, not only for local residents but also for the country as a whole.

The emotional and spiritual demands of crises mean that ethical leaders need to address the whole person during the crisis and postcrisis stages. They stay in constant communication with group members, calming their fears. They help followers regain their focus and emphasize the importance of community. They arrange for emotional and spiritual counseling and recognize that the whole organization may need to pass through a grieving process. Ethical leaders also recognize that, if the group is to heal, they must foster hope while honoring the past.

The ethic of care, introduced in Chapter 5, has been specifically applied to crisis management. The care ethic fosters crisis preparation because those concerned about others are more likely to take their complaints seriously and are therefore more alert to possible signs of trouble. Once they have identified prodromes, they are more likely to give voice to their concerns instead of exiting the organization.[46]

Concern for others can also prompt a group or an organization to go well beyond what the law or fairness requires when responding to a crisis. Consider the case of the San Ysidro, California, McDonald's shooting, for example.[47] On July 18, 1984, a lone gunman out to "hunt humans" shot 40 people at the restaurant (21 died). McDonald's was not at fault and was, in fact, a victim of the attack. But rather than declaring its innocence or decrying the unfairness of headlines blaming it for the carnage, McDonald's followed the "Horwitz Rule." Executive VP and General Counsel Don Horwitz told management: "I don't want you people to worry or care about the legal implications of what you might say. We are going to do what's right for the survivors and families of the victims, and we'll worry about lawsuits later."[48] (It could have been argued that providing help was evidence that McDonald's was in some way responsible for what happened.) The company then suspended its national advertising campaign out of respect for victims and their families, sent personnel to help with funeral arrangements, paid hospital bills, and flew in relatives to be with their families. Corporate executives sought the counsel of an important local religious leader, attended funerals, demolished the restaurant, and then donated the land to the city.

The steps taken by McDonald's in this instance weren't "fair" and devalued the rights of the firm. After all, the restaurant chain wasn't to blame, and yet its leaders spent millions suspending advertising, creating a fund for families of victims, demolishing the restaurant, donating the land, and so on. Driven by care, corporate officials kept their focus on responsibility to victims and the importance of acknowledging their pain. They listened to the community and worked hard at maintaining connections with local political, community, and religious groups.

LEADERSHIP ETHICS AT THE MOVIES • • • • • • • • • •

Argo

Key Cast Members: Ben Affleck, John Goodman, Alan Arkin, Bryan Cranston, Victor Garber

Synopsis: When angry Iranians occupy the American embassy in 1979, taking 50 Americans hostage, 6 staffers manage to escape to the Canadian embassy compound. CIA operative Tony Mendez (played by Affleck) must come up with a way to "extract" the group. Mendez hatches a plot to free the fugitives by pretending to film a science fiction movie called *Argo*. He enlists the help of a makeup guru (Goodman) and a Hollywood producer (Arkin) to create a fake movie studio, hire actors, and create stories about the film in movie trade papers. Mendez then flies to Iran posing as an associate producer looking for desert film locations. He provides false Canadian identities to the six Americans and then flies them out. However, he has to disobey orders to succeed in his mission. As unlikely as the plot of the film seems, it is based on true events.

Rating: R for language and limited violence

Themes: ethical crisis management, moral decision making, crisis management competencies, courage, compassion, conflict, argumentation, collaboration, creativity

Discussion Starters

1. How would you evaluate the crisis preparedness of the embassy staff?

2. What risks did the Canadian ambassador, his staff, and the Canadian government face in harboring the fugitives?

3. What components of ethical crisis management and what crisis leadership skills do you see in the story of the rescue of the six Americans?

Engage the Head as Well as the Heart

Rational thought, problem solving, and other cognitive skills and strategies are important complements to care and compassion in ethical crisis management. Moral leaders respond with their heads as well as their hearts.[49] In particular, they are highly mindful and engage in strategic and ethical rational thinking. (Followers must also engage their heads as well as their hearts—see "Focus on Follower Ethics: Blowing the Whistle: Ethical Tension Points.")

FOCUS ON FOLLOWER ETHICS

Blowing the Whistle: Ethical Tension Points

Deciding to go public with information about organizational misbehavior can cause a crisis. Not only do whistle-blowers put their careers, health, and relationships at

(Continued)

(Continued)

risk (see Chapter 2), they also put their leaders, their coworkers, and the group as a whole in danger. Everyone suffers when the whistle blows. Employees lose their jobs, donations dry up, contracts are canceled, stock prices decline, and so on. Followers must determine whether the benefits of going public (e.g., improving patient safety, protecting the public, eliminating waste and fraud) justify such wide-scale disruption. To make this determination, ethics professor J. Vernon Jensen argues that potential whistle-blowers must respond to a series of questions or issues that he calls "ethical tension points." We can use these questions as a guide if we are faced with the choice of going public or keeping silent. Jensen identifies the following as key ethical tension points in whistle-blowing:

- *What is our obligation to the organization?* Do conditions warrant breaking contractual agreements, confidentiality, and loyalty to the group?

- *What are our moral obligations to colleagues in the organization?* How will their lives be affected? How will they respond?

- *What are our ethical obligations to our profession?* Does loyalty to the organization take precedence, or do professional standards?

- *Will the act of whistle-blowing adversely affect our families and others close to us?* Is it fair to make them suffer? How much will they be hurt by our actions?

- *What moral obligation do we have to ourselves?* Do the costs of going public outweigh the benefits of integrity and feelings of self-worth that come from doing so?

- *What is our ethical obligation toward the general public?* How will outsiders respond to our message? Do the long-term benefits of speaking out outweigh any short-term costs (fear, anger, uneasiness)?

- *How will my action affect important values such as freedom of expression, truthfulness, courage, justice, cooperativeness, and loyalty?* Will my coming forward strengthen these values or weaken them? What values (friendship, security) will have to take lower priority?

SOURCE: Jensen, J. V. (1996). Ethical tension points in whistleblowing. In J. A. Jaksa & M. S. Pritchard (Eds.), *Responsible communication: Ethical issues in business, industry, and the professions* (pp. 41–51). Cresskill, NJ: Hampton.

Ethical crisis leaders, in addition to paying heedful attention themselves (see Chapter 10), create *mindful* cultures. University of Michigan business professors Karl Weick and Kathleen Sutcliffe argue that collective mindfulness is the key to creating "high-reliability organizations" (HROs).[50] HROs (emergency rooms, air traffic control systems, power plants) rarely fail even though they face lots of unexpected events. Attention to minor problems sets HROs apart from their less reliable counterparts. Unlike crisis-prone organizations that ignore minor deviations until they magnify into a crisis, HROs respond forcefully to the weakest signal that something is wrong.

Weick and Sutcliffe use the deck of an aircraft carrier to illustrate the characteristics of mindful cultures that prevent harmful crises from occurring. One naval crew member described an aircraft carrier this way:

> Imagine that it's a busy day, and you shrink San Francisco Airport to only one short runway and one ramp and one gate. Make planes take off and land at the same time, at half the present time interval, rock the runway from side to side, and require that everyone who leaves in the morning returns that same day. Make sure the equipment is so close to the edge of the envelope that it's fragile. Then turn off the radar to avoid detection, impose strict controls on radios, fuel the aircraft in place with their engines running, put an enemy in the air, and scatter live bombs and rockets around. Now, wet the whole thing down with salt water and oil, and man it with 20-year-olds, half of whom have never seen an airplane close up. Oh, and by the way, try not to kill anyone.[51]

Despite the dangers, very few carrier accidents occur because navy leaders encourage five mindful practices. First, carrier crews are *preoccupied with failure.* Every landing is graded, and small problems like a plane in the wrong position are treated as signs that there may be larger issues like poor communication or training. Second, those who work on carriers are *reluctant to simplify.* Each plane is inspected multiple times, and pilots and deck crew communicate responsibilities through hand and voice signals and different-colored uniforms. Third, carrier crews sustain continuous *sensitivity to operations.* Everyone on board is focused on launching and landing aircraft. Officers observe all activities and communicate with each other constantly. Fourth, people on carriers share a *commitment to resilience.* Their knowledge equips them to come up with creative solutions when unexpected events like equipment failures or severe weather occur. Fifth, carrier personnel demonstrate *deference to expertise.* Lower-ranking individuals can overrule their superiors if they have more expertise in, for example, landing damaged planes.

Leaders responding to crises also need to employ *ethical rationality.* Ethical rationality ties together research on business ethics, strategy, and crisis management. Rationality is defined as "a firm's ability to make decisions based on comprehensive information and analysis."[52] Rational firms and leaders (which are generally more successful) do a thorough job of scanning the environment and analyzing the information they gather. They are also able to quickly generate lots of alternative solutions and ideas.[53] At the same time, ethics is at the core of their corporate strategy.[54] Such organizations keep the needs of stakeholders in mind and are concerned about building a "good society." They make routine choices based on moral principles like utilitarianism and the categorical imperative.

Ethical rationality serves firms well in crisis management. They are less likely to experience crisis events because they continually scan the environment and analyze the data they collect. Leaders are not prone to act selfishly (e.g., lie, ignore stakeholder groups, hurt the environment) because they recognize that all stakeholders have intrinsic value and they are committed to the greater good. When a crisis is triggered, they have more information on hand and can rapidly generate and evaluate alternative courses of action under time pressures. Such firms have a clearer understanding of their stakeholder groups and how they might be affected by crisis events. Further, ethically rational companies (and nonprofits) are more likely to make sound moral choices during a crisis because leaders are in the practice of incorporating ethical principles into routine decision making.

Improvise From a Strong Moral Foundation

Dartmouth professor Paul Argenti interviewed corporate executives whose firms successfully weathered the World Trade Center terrorist attacks. One of the lessons of 9/11, according to Argenti, is that, during a disaster, managers must make quick decisions without guidance.[55] They are more likely to make wise choices if they are prepared. Preparation includes not only training and planning but also instilling corporate values. Employees of several undamaged Starbucks stores near Ground Zero kept their locations open even as the rest of the company's outlets in the United States were closed for the day. They provided free coffee and pastries to hospital staff and rescue workers. Several people were saved when Starbucks workers pulled them inside, rescuing them from collapsing buildings. Leaders and followers at these stores were acting in accordance with one of the eight principles of the Starbucks mission statement, which is "Contribute positively to our communities and our environment." Employees at *The New York Times* and Oppenheimer Funds also drew from their organizations' core ideology to continue to serve readers, customers, and clients.

The ability to ethically improvise is critical in a crisis because no amount of planning and practice can totally equip individuals for the specific challenges they will face during the crisis event. Unethical decisions, such as refusing to take action or responsibility, can cause significant harm and undermine the future of the group or organization. In addition, the crisis forces changes in priorities. Concern for profit must be set aside in favor of damage control and helping victims. The stakeholders who are normally most important (e.g., corporate stockholders and owners) take a backseat to those most directly affected by events.

Successful improvisation requires that employees be empowered to act on their own initiative. They must not only know the moral course of action but also be able to act on their choices, like the Starbucks employees on September 11, 2001. Their decision to distribute free food and drinks cost Starbucks money, but corporate headquarters supported their actions.

A number of observers have noted that organizations, like individuals, have moral character.[56] They argue that virtuous organizations as well as virtuous people are more likely to make the right ethical choices under pressure. When crises strike, organizations must act quickly, and their responses will reflect (or fail to reflect) their character. Those groups that ethically manage crises demonstrate such virtues as courage, compassion, optimism, humility, and integrity.

Richard Nielsen of Boston College and Ronald Dufresne of St. Joseph's University believe that crises can spur both individual and organizational character development.[57] The key is to engage in dialogue or conversation that is grounded in the ethical tradition of the group. The group then adapts to the crisis while protecting its essential values. Nielsen and Dufresne offer a four-step method—drawn from the work of Danish philosopher Søren Kierkegaard—for promoting collective character growth. They illustrate this "uplifting method" using a crisis caused by the death of a cancer patient at the Dana-Farber Cancer Institute in Boston. The patient died after receiving four times the prescribed amount of an experimental chemotherapy drug.

Step 1 of the uplifting method is to approach others in a friendly, open, and respectful manner. Dana-Farber Cancer Institute leaders were open and respectful with both the public and the press and candid about shortcomings that might have led to the drug overdose. Step 2 is to frame the problem or crisis as a conflict between "a potentially destructive environment and our internal tradition." Institute officials noted that the drive to generate grants through aggressive research had overshadowed the group's mission to treat patients. Step 3 is to consider alternatives based on ethical tradition while, at the same time, adapting tradition in light of possible solutions. Leaders at Dana-Farber implemented changes, like suspending some research, increasing treatment protocol training, and requiring more oversight of chemotherapy dosages. However, the organization did not suspend all cancer research. Step 4 is to adopt solutions that are informed by the group's ethical tradition but adjust them as needed. Dana-Farber administrators not only implemented the steps described above but also increased focus on the "total care" of cancer patients. All staff members (including researchers) work together to treat patients. At the same time, the institute also continues to look for cancer cures.

IMPLICATIONS AND APPLICATIONS _____

- A crisis, which is any major unanticipated event that poses a significant threat, will be the ultimate test of your ability to provide ethical leadership.

- Crises can be divided into 10 types: public perception, natural disasters, product or service, terrorist attacks, economic, human resource, industrial, oil and chemical spills, transportation, and outside environment.

- Deliberate attempts to disrupt or destroy systems (abnormal accidents) are on the rise, and you must help your group or organization prepare for them.

- All crises follow a three-stage pattern of development: precrisis, crisis event, and postcrisis.

- Precrisis is the period of normalcy between crisis events. Ethical, effective leaders use this time to identify potential trouble spots and to prepare crisis management plans.

- The crisis event starts with a "trigger event" and the recognition that a crisis has occurred. This stage ends when the immediate crisis is resolved. During this phase ethical leaders identify the crisis, activate crisis management plans and teams, appoint a spokesperson, and try to limit the damage.

- Postcrisis is a period of investigation and recovery. Moral leaders try to determine what went wrong and institute corrective measures. They also help the group salvage its reputation, engage in crisis learning, and begin the healing process by honoring victims and looking to future opportunities.

- Responsibility is the foundation for ethical crisis leadership. As a leader, you have a duty to try to prevent the harm caused by a crisis, to mitigate the damage caused by your group, to address the needs of all affected stakeholder groups, to take steps to prevent a similar event from happening again, to help the organization learn from the experience, and to foster renewal.

- In an emergency, make transparency your goal. As much as possible, be open with stakeholders and strive to maintain symmetrical relationships with these groups based on two-way communication.

- Altruism (care) should be the driving ethical principle during crisis events. Address the emotional and spiritual concerns of those affected, not just their financial and physical needs. Go beyond what the law and justice require.

- As a leader, you will need to engage the head as well as the heart when responding to crises. Create a mindful culture that closely monitors and corrects even minor problems and deviations. Base decisions on information and analysis, as well as on moral values, in order to better anticipate and manage crisis events.

- No amount of preparation can prepare you and the rest of your group for every contingency, so you will need to ethically improvise. Successful improvisation draws on the core mission and values of your group or organization.

- Crises reveal the moral character of groups as well as individuals. Conversation grounded in the ethical tradition of the organization, which also adapts to the demands of the crisis, can spur collective character development.

FOR FURTHER EXPLORATION, CHALLENGE, AND SELF-ASSESSMENT

1. Use Self-Assessment 11.1, the Crisis and/or Disaster Preparedness Scale, to determine your readiness level and that of your organization. If possible, distribute the instrument to others in your organization and compare scores.

2. Form teams and argue for or against the use of extreme measures in supreme emergencies (see Case Study 11.1).

3. Form a team at your organization and create a crisis management plan. Or evaluate the organization's current crisis management plan.

4. In a group, brainstorm a list of possible crises that could strike your college or university or a work organization. Then select one of these events and outline a crisis management strategy for dealing with this situation. If time permits, assume the role of organizational leaders and conduct a mock press conference, using other members of the class as media representatives.

5. In a research paper, evaluate the crisis response of an organization using the ethical standards/strategies described in this chapter. Describe the events and provide an analysis. Include suggestions that would help the organization do a better job of ethical crisis management in the future.

6. React to the following statement: Crises reveal the true character of an organization.

7. Create a case study that demonstrates how an organization was able to ethically improvise during a crisis event. Or, as an alternative, create a case study that demonstrates how an organization was able to learn from a crisis event.

8. In a group, come up with a list of guidelines for determining what to reveal and what to keep secret in a crisis.

STUDENT STUDY SITE

Visit the student study site at **www.sagepub.com/johnsonmecl5e** to access full SAGE journal articles for further research and information on key chapter topics.

CASE STUDY 11.1

The Terrorist and the Ticking Bomb: Ethical Leadership in Supreme Emergencies

Philosophers and ethicists use the term *supreme emergencies* to refer to situations where, many argue, normal rules should be set aside for extreme measures. For example, during World War II Winston Churchill ordered the bombing of German cities in order to defeat Hitler, which resulted in the deaths of 300,000 civilians and serious injury to an additional 780,000. The British prime minister determined that the threat justified killing noncombatants.

The War on Terror has renewed debate over whether there are ever times when extreme measures are morally justified. The "ticking bomb" scenario is often used to illustrate this dilemma. In the scenario, security forces have captured a suspect they believe has planted a bomb that will kill hundreds or thousands of people. Time is short, and the captive refuses to cooperate. Authorities must determine if they should use torture to get the suspected terrorist to reveal the location of the explosive device.

Opposition to torture is generally based on deontological grounds. Such interrogational techniques demean the value of human beings and treat people as a means to an end. Torture can do irreversible physical and psychological damage and violates basic human rights and international law. However, when faced with the ticking bomb scenario, many of those who oppose torture in principle agree that torture is justified in this particular set of circumstances.

They adopt a utilitarian approach, arguing that the likely positive consequences (saving many lives) justify the damage caused to one person. This logic has been used by the U.S. government to support the "enhanced interrogation" (torture) of prisoners in Iraq and Afghanistan as well as the "outsourcing" of suspects to countries like Egypt that place few restrictions on interrogation techniques.

Do supreme emergencies justify setting aside normal moral standards? Perhaps not. Many who died in Germany during World War II (including children) had little or no connection to the war effort. Utilitarian reasoning alone does not justify killing a greater number of people in Germany to save a smaller number of people in Great Britain. Then, too, there are other costs associated with killing innocent civilians. Some British officers felt that bombing non-military targets violated their professional honor and failed to differentiate the Allies from Hitler. (The Nazis also engaged in the killing of civilians, on a much larger scale.)

British philosopher Bob Brecher takes issue with those who use the ticking bomb scenario to justify interrogational torture. He begins by pointing out the logical weaknesses of the hypothetical case. In reality, there likely wouldn't be enough time between the planting of the bomb and its detonation to detain and question a suspect. The prisoner may not know where the device is planted or be innocent. (Of 5,000 terrorist suspects detained without access to legal counsel in the two and a half years after 9/11, only 3 were charged with terrorist acts, and 2 of the 3 were later acquitted.) Eliciting the location of the explosive would take a skilled interrogator, and information gained through torture is notoriously unreliable. Many suspects are likely to say anything to get the torturer to stop. Those trained to resist torture would likely give false answers at first, further delaying discovery of the bomb.

Brecher also points out the long-term damage caused by interrogational torture. Such activity encourages the creation of a new profession—torturer—and of a society that tolerates such activity. He argues that who we are as civilized nations means that we cannot engage in torture of any kind. Further, there is no such thing as "torture lite." Those who have undergone even limited or focused torture aimed at eliciting information often never recover. Even innocent subjects of torture are humiliated, their wills broken.

Despite the concerns of Brecher and other critics, support for extreme measures in supreme emergencies appears to be widespread. Taxpayers continue to fund nuclear missile systems that would incinerate hundreds of thousands of civilians, for instance. Polls report that approximately one-half of all Americans support the use of torture to gather information that protects the nation from further attacks.

Do you believe that extreme measures like killing civilians and interrogational torture are ever justified? Why or why not?

Sources

Alexander, L. (2000, Fall). Deontology at the threshold. *San Diego Law Review, 37,* 893–912.

Brecher, B. (2007). *Torture and the ticking bomb.* Malden, MA: Blackwell.

Statman, D. (2006). Supreme emergencies revisited. *Ethics, 117,* 58–79.

United Press International. (2009, April 24). Poll: U.S. split on torture. Retrieved from http://www.upi.com/Top_News/2009/04/24/Poll-US-split-on-torture/UPI-55341240631033

Walzer, M. (1977). *Just and unjust wars: A moral argument with historical illustrations.* New York: Basic Books.

CASE STUDY 11.2

The Deadly Prank Call

Two Australian radio hosts thought they had scored a colossal publicity coup with a prank call to the London hospital treating the pregnant Duchess of Cambridge. Catherine, wife of Prince William, was at King Edward VII's Hospital receiving treatment for severe morning sickness when Sydney 2Day FM radio personalities Mel Greig and Michael Christian called, impersonating Queen Elizabeth and Prince Charles. Nurse Jacintha Saldana picked up the phone because the receptionist was not on duty. Believing that she was talking to the royals, she then forwarded the call to the ward where the duchess was being treated. The nurse on duty then held a conversation with Greig and Christian about Kate's condition.

The tape of the call was aired on 2Day FM and picked up online and by media outlets around the world. Station owner Southern Cross

Austereo publicized the call on its website and showed the two presenters laughing and joking about the hoax. Greig and Christian also bragged about the prank on their Twitter accounts. However, reaction to the prank call changed dramatically when, within 72 hours of the hoax, Jacintha Saldana, described as "an excellent nurse" who was "well respected by co-workers," committed suicide, reportedly out of a sense of shame for being taken in by the hoax. The DJs began getting death threats, closed their Twitter accounts, and went into hiding. Major sponsors pulled their ads from the station. Southern Cross Austereo CEO Rhys Holleran first put the DJs on leave, saying this was "mutually decided," and then fired them soon after. In a press conference, Holleran stated, "This is a tragic event that could not have been reasonably foreseen and we are deeply saddened by it." He went on to say that he was "very confident that we haven't done anything illegal."[1] Holleran apologized to the Saldana family and pledged $500,000 to an account set up for the nurse's husband and two children.

When a tearful Christian and Greig came out of seclusion, they expressed their sorrow and regret. They declared that their intent was harmless and that because of their "terrible accents" they never expected to actually make it past the hospital switchboard. The pair claimed that the final decision to air the piece, which was prerecorded, was station management's. It was up to company lawyers and managers to vet the call, although Christian and Greig were not clear as to how the process worked. Station executives said they made five attempts to contact the hospital to get permission to air the call. The hospital, for its part, denied that any of its officials spoke with 2Day FM representatives. The hospital CEO had harsh words for Southern Cross Austereo executives. He called the decision to air the tape "truly appalling." He went on to say, "The immediate consequence of these premeditated and ill-considered actions was the humiliation of two dedicated and caring nurses who were simply doing their job tending to their patients."[2]

This was not the first time 2Day FM had gotten into trouble for on-air stunts. In 2009, a 14-year-old girl revealed that she had been raped while hooked up to a lie detector while live on the air.

Discussion Probes

1. What warning signs were ignored in this crisis?

2. Was it ethical for the DJs to make a prank call to a hospital? Should all prank calls be banned?

3. Would you evaluate the prank call differently if it hadn't resulted in the death of a nurse? Why or why not?

4. How much blame should be assigned to the DJs, to the station, and to the hospital for what happened?

5. How would you evaluate the crisis response of Southern Cross Austereo? What did it do right? Wrong?

6. What steps should Southern Cross Austereo take to restore the firm's reputation and that of station 2Day FM?

Notes

1. Smith-Spark, L. (2012, December 8). Hospital nurse found dead after taking prank call on Catherine. CNN. Retrieved from http://www.cnn.com

2. Santora, M. (2012, December 8). After radio prank, hospital chairman condemns Australian network. *The New York Times,* The Lede blog.

Sources

Duell, M., Andrews, E., Greenhill, S., & Shears, R. (2012, December 10). Now hospital which treated Kate denies hoax call radio station contacted managers or press officers. *The Daily Mail.* Retrieved from http://www.dailymail.co.uk

Gregory, A. (2012, December 8). We'll kill you both. *Daily Mirror,* News, pp. 4–5.

London, B. (2012, December 12). Radio personalities apologize for prank call to duchess's hospital. CNN. Retrieved from http://www.cnn.com

McLaughlin, M. (2012, December 8). Kate hospital prank call nurse found dead. *The Scotsman,* p. 1.

Smith-Spark, L., & Brocchetto, M. (2012, December 11). Prank call radio station to donate funds to nurse's family. CNN. Retrieved from http://www.cnn.com

CASE STUDY 11.3

Disaster Unpreparedness at Long Island Power Authority

If there were an award given to the organization *least* prepared for a crisis, the Long Island Power Authority would likely be the winner. The Long Island Power Authority (LIPA) is a state agency that serves customers near New York City. LIPA was formed after the local utility failed to respond quickly to Hurricane Gloria and wasted millions trying to build the Shoreham nuclear plant, which never opened. State authorities stepped in, hoping to improve communication with customers, keep rates down, and respond more effectively to future disasters.

LIPA's goals have not been achieved. There have been ongoing complaints about the agency's customer service, and residents continue to pay some of the highest electricity rates in the country. If anything, LIPA's disaster response is worse than ever. During tropical storm Irene in 2011, 534,000 customers were stranded without electricity for nine days. Utility managers relied on paper charts and documents to guide their efforts to restore power. An outdated record system made it hard for workers to tell customers where the power was out and when it would be restored. Following the storm, experts recommended that LIPA prepare for future storms by investing in a state-of-the-art monitoring and information system and trimming tree limbs over power lines.

Officials at LIPA ignored the expert advice they received following Irene and therefore were ill prepared for Hurricane Sandy, which caused even more damage and shut off power to 900,000 users. Untrimmed limbs fell on power lines, phone lines went answered, service maps were inaccurate, and repair crews failed to show up when promised. One local town official described what happened in his community. At first he couldn't get any crews to come. When two crews finally came, they weren't much help:

> The upper management couldn't communicate with middle management. The middle management couldn't

communicate with the crews. And finally, when we had sufficient crews coming in—resources that should have been arranged before—they came in and had very little direction and they were flabbergasted at the condition of the infrastructure. The wiring, the entire system.[1]

LIPA customers were the last in the New York/New Jersey region to see their power restored but continued to be billed for electricity they never received. Worse yet, the agency threatened customers with late fees if they didn't make their payments.

LIPA's crisis unpreparedness can largely be traced back to its leadership and structure. Agency leaders are generally political appointees who know little or nothing about running a utility. In fact, the authority doesn't actually operate the power grid but contracts with an outside company. One board member said the group considers itself "an oversight board of citizens." Prior to Sandy, 5 of the 15 seats on the authority's board remained unfilled. LIPA's CEO stayed on two years longer than planned because he had no replacement. During its last meeting as Sandy approached, LIPA's governing board only spent 39 seconds talking about the impending disaster, believing that a "plan was in place." Instead, board members discussed other issues, including a proposal to hire a brand consultant.

Following Superstorm Sandy, New York governor Andrew Cuomo formed a special commission to investigate the utility's response to Irene and Sandy, and a State Senate committee vowed to do the same. Said Cuomo: "I believe something like this is going to happen again. I think we need to be better prepared. We need to learn from it."[2] The governor didn't rule out abolishing the agency and privatizing the authority. An attorney filed a class-action lawsuit on behalf of the customers who lost power, blaming the utility for "a lack of appropriate preparation, misinformation, delays and disorganization that slowed restoration."[3]

Discussion Probes

1. Why do you think officials at LIPA ignored the advice of experts?

2. Can you think of other organizations that are unprepared for crisis? What characteristics do they share with LIPA?

3. What steps do leaders need to take to better prepare LIPA for future disasters? What obstacles could they face as they take these actions?

4. Should the utility be held legally liable for damages suffered by those who lost power?

5. Can LIPA be saved, or should it be converted into a private utility?

Notes

1. Hakim, D., McGeehan, P., & Moss, M. (2012, November 14). Suffering on L.I. as power agency shows its flaws. *The New York Times,* p. A1.

2. Lovett, K., & Blain, G. (2012, November 14). Dolts jolted LIPA big bolts as gov. sets up probe. *Daily News,* p. 10.

3. Solnik, C. (2012, November 13). Class action lawsuit filed against Long Island Power Authority, national grid. *Long Island Business.*

Sources

Billing misstep is typical LIPA. (2012, November 28). *Newsday,* p. A34.

Harrington, M. (2012, November 27). LIPA bill changes. *Newsday,* p. A05.

Crisis and/or Disaster Preparedness Scale

This instrument measures how prepared you think you and your organization are for a natural disaster, a terrorist attack, an industrial accident, or another form of crisis. The higher your score (possible scores range from 21 to 84), the higher your level of perceived preparedness.

Instructions: Score each of the following as 1 = *strongly disagree*, 2 = *disagree*, 3 = *agree*, 4 = *strongly agree*. Reverse scores where indicated.

1. I am very familiar with our building's evacuation plan. 1 2 3 4

2. It would be easy for a potentially threatening nonemployee to gain access to my workplace. (Reverse) 1 2 3 4

3. If my organization suffered a serious crisis, I might lose my job. (Reverse) 1 2 3 4

4. If my organization suffered a serious crisis, I would still get paid until we could reopen. 1 2 3 4

5. My organization has provided each employee with a basic emergency preparedness kit (e.g., flashlight, smoke mask). 1 2 3 4

6. The security at my workplace is adequate. 1 2 3 4

7. If a crisis occurred at my organization, I am familiar with the plan for how family members can get information on the status (e.g., safety) of their relatives. 1 2 3 4

8. In the event of an emergency or a disaster, I am familiar with my organization's plan to continue operations from another location. 1 2 3 4

9. All organization members are required to rehearse portions of our crisis plan (e.g., evacuation). 1 2 3 4

10. If my organization suffered a serous crisis, I would still have my job. 1 2 3 4

11. If my organization suffered a crisis, I would still be covered by my organization's employee benefits (e.g., health insurance). 1 2 3 4

12. Security at my workplace has been significantly increased since September 11, 2001. 1 2 3 4

13. I know where the nearest fire extinguisher is to my desk/workstation.　　1　2　3　4

14. If a crisis and evacuation occurred at my organization, I am familiar with our plan on how to communicate with my fellow employees from scattered or emergency locations (e.g., cell phone numbers, websites, e-mail lists).　　1　2　3　4

15. Most of our employees are familiar with my organization's crisis/disaster plan.　　1　2　3　4

16. As part of our emergency plan, customers and suppliers would be able to contact us for information.　　1　2　3　4

17. If my organization suffered a crisis/disaster, I would have the data I need to do my job backed up at a remote site.　　1　2　3　4

18. My organization offers to pay to have volunteer employees trained in basic life support techniques (e.g., CPR, first aid).　　1　2　3　4

19. My organization has contingency plans in place so our customers would be covered if we suffered a disaster.　　1　2　3　4

20. I know where the nearest emergency exits are to my desk/workstation.　　1　2　3　4

21. My organization's emergency plan has been coordinated with local agencies (e.g., the fire department, hospitals).　　1　2　3　4

SOURCE: Fowler, K. L., Kling, N. D., & Larson, M. D. (2007). Organizational preparedness for coping with a major crisis or disaster. *Business & Society, 46,* 100–101. Published by SAGE Publications, Inc.

SELF-ASSESSMENT 11.2

Intentionality Vignettes

Instructions: Read each of the following stories. After you read each one, answer the question that follows.

Vignette 1

The vice president of a company went to the chairman of the board and said: "We are thinking of starting a new program. It will help us increase profits, but it will also harm the environment." The chairman of the board answered: "I don't care at all about harming the environment. I just want to make as much profit as I can. Let's start the new program."

They started the new program. Sure enough, the environment was harmed.

Did the chairman of the board intentionally harm the environment?

Vignette 2

The vice president of a company went to the chairman of the board and said: "We are thinking of starting a new program. It will help us increase profits, and it will also help the environment." The chairman of the board answered: "I don't care at all about helping the environment. I just want to make as much profit as I can. Let's start the new program."

They started the new program. Sure enough, the environment was helped.

Did the chairman of the board intentionally help the environment?

Scoring

If you are like the vast majority of people responding to these vignettes, you answered yes to the question after the first vignette and no to the question after the second story. Researchers point to this pattern of response as evidence for the intention effect. In the harm scenario, the leader is seen to intentionally cause damage. In the help scenario, the leader generally gets little credit for improving the environment.

SOURCE: Knobe, J., & Burra, A. (2006). The folk concepts of intention and intentional action: A cross-cultural study. *Journal of Cognition and Culture, 6,* 113–132. Used by permission of the publisher.

NOTES

1. Pearson, C. M., & Judith, A. C. (1998). Reframing crisis management. *Academy of Management Review, 23,* 59–71; Fearn-Banks, K. (2007). *Crisis communications: A casebook approach* (3rd ed.). Mahwah, NJ: Erlbaum.
2. Christensen, S. L., & Kohls, J. (2003). Ethical decision making in times of organizational crises: A framework for analysis. *Business & Society, 42,* 328–358.
3. Coombs, W. T. (1999). *Ongoing crisis communication: Planning, managing, and responding.* Thousand Oaks, CA: Sage; Seeger, M. W., Sellnow, T. L., & Ulmer, R. R. (2003). *Communication and organizational crisis.* Westport, CT: Praeger.
4. Mitroff, I. I. (2005). *Why some companies emerge stronger and better from a crisis.* New York: AMACOM.
5. For more information on the relationship between complexity and crises, see Perrow, C. (1999). *Normal accidents: Living with high-risk technologies.* Princeton, NJ: Princeton University Press.
6. Seeger et al.
7. Bazerman, M. H., & Watkins, M. D. (2004). *Predictable surprises: The disasters you should have seen coming and how to prevent them.* Boston: Harvard Business School Press.
8. Pauchant, T. C., & Mitroff, I. I. (1992). *Transforming the crisis-prone organization: Preventing individual, organizational, and environmental tragedies.* San Francisco: Jossey-Bass.
9. Pauchant & Mitroff, p. 186.
10. Simola, S. (2010). Anti-corporate anger as a form of care-based moral agency. *Journal of Business Ethics, 94,* 255–269.

11. Livesey, S. M. (2003). Organizing and leading the grassroots: An interview with Lois Gibbs, Love Canal Homeowners Association activist. *Organization, 16,* 448–503.

12. Fink, S. (2002). *Crisis management: Planning for the inevitable.* Lincoln, NE: Backinprint.com.

13. See, for example, Mitroff, I. I., Pearson, C. M., & Harrington, L. K. (1996). *The essential guide to managing corporate crises: A step-by-step handbook for surviving major catastrophes.* New York: Oxford University Press; Mitroff, I. I., & Anagnos, G. (2001). *Managing crises before they happen: What every executive and manager needs to know about crisis management.* New York: American Management Association.

14. Mitroff, I. I., & Alpsaian, M. C. (2003, April). Preparing for evil. *Harvard Business Review,* pp. 109–115.

15. Fearn-Banks.

16. Lee, J., Woeste, J. H., & Heath, R. L. (2007). Getting ready for crises: Strategic excellence. *Public Relations Review, 33,* 334–336.

17. Knight, R. F., & Pretty, D. J. (1996). *The impact of catastrophes on shareholder value.* Oxford, England: Templeton College, University of Oxford.

18. Daleus, P., & Hansen, D. (2011). Inherent ethical challenges in bureaucratic crisis management: The Swedish experience with the 2004 tsunami disaster. In L. Svedin (Ed.), *Ethics and crisis management* (pp. 21–36). Charlotte, NC: Information Age.

19. Barton, L. (2001). *Crisis in organizations II.* Cincinnati: South-Western.

20. Coombs, W. T., & Holladay, S. J. (2004). Reasoned action in crisis communication: An attribution theory–based approach to crisis management. In D. P. Millar & R. L. Heath (Eds.), *Responding to crisis: A rhetorical approach to crisis communication* (pp. 95–115). Mahwah, NJ: Erlbaum; Benoit, W. L. (2004). Image restoration discourse and crisis communication. In D. P. Millar & R. L. Heath (Eds.), *Responding to crisis: A rhetorical approach to crisis communication* (pp. 263–280). Mahwah, NJ: Erlbaum.

21. Weick, K. E., & Sutcliffe, K. M. (2001). *Managing the unexpected: Assuring high performance in an age of complexity.* San Francisco: Jossey-Bass.

22. Parker, C. F. (2011). The purpose, functions, and ethical dimensions of postcrisis investigations: The case of the 9/11 Commission. In L. Svedin (Ed.), *Ethics and crisis management* (pp. 183–198). Charlotte NC: Information Age.

23. Harris, S., Smallen, J., & Mitchell, C. (2006, February 18). Katrina report spreads blame. *National Journal,* p. 38; Marek, A. C. (2006, February 27). A post-Katrina public flaying. *U.S. News & World Report,* pp. 62–64.

24. 55% rate government response to Hurricane Sandy positively. (2012, November 12). Rasmussen Reports. Retrieved from http://www.rasmussenreports.com

25. Ulmer, R. R., Seeger, M. W., & Sellnow, T. L. (2007). Post-crisis communication and renewal: Expanding the parameters of post-crisis discourse. *Public Relations Review, 33,* 130–134; Ulmer, R. R., Sellnow, T. L., & Seeger, M. W. (2008). Post-crisis communication and renewal: Understanding the potential for positive outcomes in crisis communication. In R. L. Heath & D. H. O'Hair (Eds.), *Handbook of risk and crisis communication* (pp. 302–322). Hoboken, NJ: Routledge.

26. Seeger et al.

27. Allinson, R. E. (1993). *Global disasters: Inquiries into management ethics.* New York: Prentice Hall, p. 16.

28. Lee et al.

29. Fearn-Banks.

30. Whoriskey, P. (2010, March 19). Toyota resisted government safety findings; automaker followed "game plan," escaped a broad early recall. *The Washington Post,* p. A01.

31. Greenberg, J. W. (2002, October). September 11, 2001: A CEO's story. *Harvard Business Review,* pp. 58–64.

32. Birkinshaw, P. (2006). Transparency as a human right. In C. Hood & D. Heald (Eds.), *Transparency: The key to better governance?* (pp. 47–57). Oxford, England: Oxford University Press.

33. Lazarus, H., & McManus, T. (2006). Transparency guru: An interview with Tom McManus. *Journal of Management Development, 25,* 923–936.

34. Fearn-Banks.

35. Christensen, L. T., & Langer, R. (2009). Public relations and the strategic use of transparency: Consistency, hypocrisy, and corporate change.

In R. L. Heath, E. L. Toth, & D. Waymer (Eds.), *Rhetorical and critical approaches to public relations II* (pp. 129–153). New York: Routledge.

36. Grunig, L. A., Grunig, J. E., & Dozier, D. M. (2002). *Excellent public relations and effective organizations: A study of communication management in three countries.* Mahwah, NJ: Erlbaum; Grunig, J. E. (2001). Two-way symmetrical public relations: Past, present, and future. In R. L. Heath (Ed.), *Handbook of public relations* (pp. 11–30). Thousand Oaks, CA: Sage.

37. Fearn-Banks.

38. Lazarus & McManus.

39. Ulmer, R. R., & Sellnow, T. L. (2000). Consistent questions of ambiguity in organizational crisis communication: Jack in the Box as a case study. *Journal of Business Ethics, 25,* 143–155.

40. Eisenberg, E. M. (1984). Ambiguity as strategy in organizational communication. *Communication Monographs, 51,* 227–242; Paul, J., & Strbiak, C. A. (1997). The ethics of strategic ambiguity. *Journal of Business Communication, 34,* 149–159.

41. Kline, S. L., Simunich, B., & Weber, H. (2009). The use of equivocal messages in responding to corporate challenges. *Journal of Applied Communication Research, 37,* 40–58.

42. Ulmer & Sellnow.

43. Hearit, K. M. (2006). *Crisis management by apology: Corporate response to allegations of wrongdoing.* Mahwah, NJ: Erlbaum, Ch. 4.

44. Bauman, D. C. (2011). Evaluating ethical approaches to crisis leadership: Insights from unintentional harm research. *Journal of Business Ethics, 98,* 281–295; Knobe, J. (2006). The concept of intentional action: A case study in the uses of folk psychology. *Philosophical Studies, 130,* 203–231; Knobe, J., & Burra, A. (2006). The folk concepts of intention and intentional action: A cross-cultural study. *Journal of Cognition and Culture, 6,* 113–132.

45. See, for example, Hodgkinson, P. E., & Stewart, M. (1991). *Coping with catastrophe: A handbook of disaster management.* London: Routledge; Mitroff.

46. Simola, S. (2005). Concepts of care in organizational crisis prevention. *Journal of Business Ethics, 62,* 341–353.

47. Simola, S. (2003). Ethics of justice and care in corporate crisis management. *Journal of Business Ethics, 46,* 351–361.

48. Starmann, R. G. (1993). Tragedy at McDonald's. In J. A. Gottschalk (Ed.), *Crisis response: Inside stories on managing image under siege* (pp. 309–322). Detroit, MI: Gale Group.

49. Witt, J. L., & Morgan, J. (2002). *Stronger in the broken places: Nine lessons for turning crisis into triumph.* New York: Times Books/Henry Holt.

50. Weick & Sutcliffe. See also Roberts, K. H. (2006). Some characteristics of one type of high reliability organization. In D. Smith & D. Elliott (Eds.), *Key readings in crisis management: Systems and structures for prevention and recovery* (pp. 159–179). London: Routledge; Weick, K. E., & Roberts, K. H. (2006). Collective minds in organizations: Heedful interrelating on flight decks. In D. Smith & D. Elliott (Eds.), *Key readings in crisis management: Systems and structures for prevention and recovery* (pp. 343–368). London: Routledge.

51. Rochlin, G. I., LaPorte, T. R., & Roberts, K. H. (1987). The self-designing high-reliability organization: Aircraft carrier flight operations at sea. *Naval War College Review, 40*(4), 76–90.

52. Snyder, P., Hall, M., Robertson, J., Jasinski, T., & Miller, J. S. (2006). Ethical rationality: A strategic approach to organizational crisis. *Journal of Business Ethics, 63,* 371–383.

53. Eisenhardt, K. M. (1989). Making fast strategic decisions in high-velocity environments. *Academy of Management Journal, 32,* 543–576.

54. Hosmer, L. T. (1994). Strategic planning as if ethics mattered. *Strategic Management Journal, 15,* 17–34.

55. Argenti, P. (2002, December). Crisis communication: Lessons from 9/11. *Harvard Business Review,* pp. 103–109.

56. Sandin, P. (2009). Approaches to ethics for corporate crisis management. *Journal of Business Ethics, 87,* 109–116; Seeger, M. W., & Ulmer, R. R. (2001). Virtuous responses to organizational crisis: Aaron Feuerstein and Milt Cole. *Journal of Business Ethics, 31,* 369–376.

57. Nielsen, R. P., & Dufresne, R. (2005). Can ethical organizational character be stimulated and enabled? "Upbuilding" dialog as crisis management method. *Journal of Business Ethics, 57,* 311–326.

Epilogue

It's only fair to tell you fellows now that we're not likely to come out of this.

—Captain Joshua James, speaking to his crew during the hurricane of 1888

Captain Joshua James (1826–1902) is the "patron saint" of the search and rescue unit of the U.S. Coast Guard. James led rescue efforts to save sailors who crashed off the shores of Massachusetts. When word came of a shipwreck, James and his volunteer crew would launch a large rowboat into heavy seas. James would keep an eye out for the stricken vessel as his men rowed, steering with a large wooden rudder. During his career, he never lost a crewman or a shipwrecked person who had been alive when picked up. The captain's finest hour came during a tremendous storm in late November 1888. Over a 24-hour period, James (62 years old at the time) and his men rescued 29 sailors from five ships.

Philip Hallie, who writes about James in his book *Tales of Good and Evil, Help and Harm,* argues that we can understand James's courageous leadership only as an extension of his larger community. James lived in Hull, a tiny, impoverished town on the Massachusetts coast. Most coastal villages of the time profited from shipwrecks. Beachcombers would scavenge everything from the cargo to the sunken ships' timbers and anchors. Unscrupulous people called "mooncussers" would lure boats aground. On dark, moonless nights, they would hang a lantern from a donkey and trick sea captains into sailing onto the rocks.

Unlike their neighbors up and down the coast, the people of Hull tried to stop the carnage. They built shelters for those who washed ashore, cared for the sick and injured, protested against shipping companies and insurers who sent inexperienced captains and crews into danger, and had their lifeboat always at the ready. During the storm of 1888, citizens burned their fences to light the way for Captain James, his crew, and victims alike. According to Hallie:

> Many of the other people of Hull tore up some picket fences near the crest of the hill and built a big fire that lit up the wreck and helped the lifesavers to avoid the flopping, slashing debris around the boat. The loose and broken spars of a ruined ship were one of the main dangers lifesavers had to face. But the sailors on the wrecked ship needed the firelight too. It showed them what the lifesavers were doing, and what they could do to help them. And it gave them hope: It showed them that they were not alone.[1]

The story of Captain James and his fellow villagers is a fitting end to this text. In their actions, they embodied many of the themes introduced earlier: character; values; good versus evil; moral action; altruism; cooperation; transformational, authentic, aesthetic, and servant leadership; social responsibility; ethical crisis leadership; and purpose. The captain, who lost his mother and baby sister in a shipwreck, had one mission in life: saving lives at sea. Following his lead, residents took on nearly insurmountable challenges at great personal cost. They recognized that helpers often need help. By burning their fences, these followers—living in extremely modest conditions—cast a light that literally made the difference between life and death. But like other groups of leaders and followers, they were far from perfect. In the winter hurricane season, the villagers did their best to save lives. In the summer, pickpockets (helped by a corrupt police force) preyed on those who visited the town's resorts. The dark side of Hull shouldn't diminish the astonishing feats of Captain James and his neighbors, however. Hallie calls what James did during the storm of 1888 an example of "moral beauty."

> And moral beauty happens when someone carves out a place for compassion in a largely ruthless universe. It happened in the French village of Le Chambon during the war, and it happened in and near the American village of Hull during the long lifetime of Joshua James.

> It happens, and it fails to happen, in almost every event of people's lives together—in streets, in kitchens, in bedrooms, in workplaces, in wars. But sometimes it happens in a way that engrosses the mind and captivates memory. Sometimes it happens in such a way that the people who make it happen seem to unify the universe around themselves like powerful magnets. Somehow they seem to redeem us all from deathlike indifference. They carve a place for caring in the very middle of the quiet and loud storms of uncaring that surround—and eventually kill—us all.[2]

Notes

1. Hallie, P. (1997). *Tales of good and evil, help and harm*. New York: HarperCollins, p. 146.
2. Hallie, p. 173.

References

Aasland, M. S., Skogstad, A., Notelaers, G., Nielson, M. B., & Einarsen, S. (2010). The prevalence of destructive leadership behavior. *British Journal of Management, 21,* 438–452.

Abodor, H. (2012). Ethical issues in outsourcing: The case of contract medical research and the global pharmaceutical industry. *Journal of Business Ethics, 105,* 239–255.

Abrahams, J. (2007). *101 mission statements from top companies.* Berkeley, CA: Ten Speed Press.

Adams, G. B. (2011). The problem of administrative evil in a culture of technical rationality. *Public Integrity, 13,* 275–285.

Adams, G. B., & Balfour, D. L. (2009). *Unmasking administrative evil* (3rd ed.). Armonk, NY: M. E. Sharpe.

Adams, J. S., Taschian, A., & Shore, T. H. (2001). Codes of ethics as signals for ethical behavior. *Journal of Business Ethics, 29,* 199–211.

Ahmetaji, A. (2013, February 11). Kosovo high school bans girl in headscarf from attending classes. BBC Monitoring Europe-Political.

Alderman, H. (1997). By virtue of a virtue. In D. Statman (Ed.), *Virtue ethics* (pp. 145–164). Washington, DC: Georgetown University Press.

Alexander, D. (2013, March 13). Lawmakers angered at U.S. military's handling of sex assault problem. Yahoo News. Retrieved from http://news.yahoo.com

Alexander, L. (2000). Deontology at the threshold. *San Diego Law Review, 37,* 893–912.

Alexander, T. M. (1993). John Dewey and the moral imagination: Beyond Putnam and Rorty toward a postmodern ethics. *Transactions of the Charles S. Peirce Society, 29,* 369–400.

Alford, C. F. (1997). *What evil means to us.* Ithaca, NY: Cornell University Press.

Allinson, R. E. (1993). *Global disasters: Inquiries into management ethics.* New York: Prentice Hall.

Allport, G. (1961). *Pattern and growth in personality.* New York: Holt, Rinehart & Winston.

Alper, S., Tjosvold, D., & Law, K. S. (2000). Conflict management, efficacy, and performance in organizational teams. *Personnel Psychology, 53,* 625–642.

Alvaro, E. M., & Crano, W. D. (1997). Indirect minority influence: Evidence for leniency in source evaluation and counterargumentation. *Journal of Personality and Social Psychology, 72,* 949–964.

Amason, A. C. (1996). Distinguishing the effects of functional and dysfunctional conflict on strategic decision making: Resolving a paradox for top management teams. *Academy of Management Journal, 39,* 123–148.

Amason, A. C., Thompson, K. R., Hochwarter, W. A., & Harrison, A. W. (1995). Conflict: An important dimension in successful management teams. *Organizational Dynamics, 23,* 20–35.

Amichai-Hamburger, Y. (2003). Understanding social loafing. In A. Sagie, S. Stashevsky, & M. Koslowsky (Eds.), *Misbehaviour and dysfunctional attitudes in organizations* (pp. 79–102). Basingstoke, England: Palgrave Macmillan.

Anand, V., Ashforth, B. E., & Joshi, M. (2004). Business as usual: The acceptance and perpetuation of corruption in organizations. *Academy of Management Executive, 18,* 39–53.

Andreoli, N., & Lefkowitz, J. (2008). Individual and organizational antecedents of misconduct in organizations. *Journal of Business Ethics, 85,* 309–332.

Annas, J. (2006). Virtue ethics. In D. Copp (Ed.), *The Oxford handbook of ethical theory* (pp. 515–536). Oxford, England: Oxford University Press.

Appelbaum, S. H., Bethune, M., & Tanenbaum, R. (1999).

Downsizing and the emergence of self-managed teams. *Participation and Empowerment: An International Journal, 7,* 109–130.

Appiah, K. A. (2006). *Cosmopolitanism: Ethics in a world of strangers.* New York: Norton.

Archer, M. (2005, October 31). Founder of Patagonia became a businessman accidentally. *USA Today,* Money, p. 5.

Arendt, H. (1964). *Eichmann in Jerusalem: A report on the banality of evil.* New York: Viking.

Argenti, P. (2002, December). Crisis communication: Lessons from 9/11. *Harvard Business Review,* pp. 103–109.

Aristotle. (1962). *Nichomachean ethics* (M. Ostwald, Trans.). Indianapolis: Bobbs-Merrill.

Armitage, J., & Conde, B. (2007, October 19). Why the French are so keen to stay in Burma despite unrest. *The Evening Standard,* p. B34.

Armour, S. (2006. November 8). Employers look closely at what workers do on job. *USA Today,* pp. B1–B2.

Ashforth, B. E. (1997). Petty tyranny in organizations: A preliminary examination of antecedents and consequences. *Canadian Journal of Administrative Sciences, 14,* 126–140.

Ashforth, B. E., & Anand, V. (2003). The normalization of corruption in organizations. *Research in Organizational Behavior, 25,* 1–52.

Ashmos, D. P., & Duchon, D. (2000). Spirituality at work: A conceptualization and measure. *Journal of Management Inquiry, 9,* 134–145.

Aspinwall, L. G., & Staudinger, U. M. (Eds.). (2002). *A psychology of human strengths: Fundamental questions about future directions for a positive psychology.* Washington, DC: American Psychological Association.

Associated Press. (2012, September 25). In crisis-hit Europe, nepotism and connection culture stifle youth. *The Daily Star* (Lebanon).

Associated Press. (2013, January 24). Trial in India gang rape case begins in New Delhi. *USA Today.* Retrieved from http://www.usatoday.com/story/news/world

At least 20 women involved in Secret Service scandal. (2012, April 17). *The Telegraph.*

Avolio, B. J., & Gardner, W. L. (2005). Authentic leadership development: Getting to the root of positive forms of leadership. *Leadership Quarterly, 16,* 315–340.

Avolio, B. J., Gardner, W. L., Walumbwa, F. O., Luthans, F., & May, D. R. (2004). Unlocking the mask: A look at the process by which authentic leaders impact follower attitudes and behaviors. *Leadership Quarterly, 15,* 801–823.

Avolio, B. J., & Reichard, R. J. (2008). The rise of authentic followership. In R. E. Riggio, I. Chaleff, & J. Lipman-Blumen (Eds.), *The art of followership: How great followers create great leaders and organizations* (pp. 325–337). San Francisco: Jossey-Bass.

Bad bosses drain productivity. (2005, November). *Training & Development,* p. 15.

Bailon, R. R., Moya, M., & Yzerbyt, V. (2000). Why do superiors attend to negative stereotypic information about their subordinates? Effects of power legitimacy on social perception. *European Journal of Social Psychology, 30,* 651–671.

Balch, D. R., & Armstrong, R. W. (2010). The Icarus syndrome and banality of wrongdoing. *Journal of Business Ethics, 92,* 291–303.

Baldor, L. C. (2012, August 4). New details in Colombian scandal revealed. *The Washington Post,* p. A03.

Banaji, M. R., Bazerman, M. H., & Chugh, D. (2003, December). How (un)ethical are you? *Harvard Business Review,* pp. 56–64.

Bandura, A. (1999). Moral disengagement in the perpetration of inhumanities. *Personality and Social Psychology Review, 3,* 193–209.

Bandura, A. (2002). Selective moral disengagement in the

exercise of moral agency. *Journal of Moral Education, 31,* 101–119.

Bandura, A., Barbaranelli, C., Caprara, G. V., & Pastoreli, C. (1996). Mechanisms of moral disengagement in the exercise of moral agency. *Journal of Personality and Social Psychology, 71,* 364–374.

Barbuto, J. E. (2000). Influence triggers: A framework for understanding follower compliance. *Leadership Quarterly, 11,* 365–387.

Barbuto, J. E., & Wheeler, D. W. (2006). Scale development and construct clarification of servant leadership. *Group & Organization Management, 31,* 300–326.

Barker, L., Johnson, P., & Watson, K. (1991). The role of listening in managing interpersonal and group conflict. In D. Borisoff & M. Purdy (Eds.), *Listening in everyday life: A personal and professional approach* (pp. 139–157). Lanham, MD: University Press of America.

Baron, R. A. (2004). Workplace aggression and violence: Insights from basic research. In R. W. Griffin & A. M. O'Leary-Kelly (Eds.), *The dark side of organizational behavior* (pp. 23–61). San Francisco: Jossey-Bass.

Barry, D. (2008, September 15). On an infested river, battling invaders eye to eye. *The New York Times,* p. A13.

Barry, V. (1978). *Personal and social ethics: Moral problems with integrated theory.* Belmont, CA: Wadsworth.

Barsky, A. (2011). Investigating the effects of moral disengagement and participation on unethical work behavior. *Journal of Business Ethics, 104,* 59–75.

Barstow, D. (2012, April 22). Vast Mexico bribery case hushed up by Wal-Mart after top-level struggle. *The New York Times,* p. A1.

Bar-Tel, D. (1990). Causes and consequences of delegitimization: Models of conflict and ethnocentrism. *Journal of Social Issues, 46*(1), 65–81.

Bartholomew, C. S., & Gustafson, S. B. (1998). Perceived leader integrity scale: An instrument for assessing employee perceptions of leader integrity. *Leadership Quarterly, 9,* 143–144.

Barton, L. (2001). *Crisis in organizations II.* Cincinnati: South-Western.

Bass, B. M. (1990). *Bass and Stogdill's handbook of leadership* (3rd ed.). New York: Free Press.

Bass, B. M. (1996). *A new paradigm of leadership: An inquiry into transformational leadership.* Alexandria, VA: U.S. Army Research Institute for the Behavioral and Social Sciences.

Bass, B. M. (1998). The ethics of transformational leadership.

In J. B. Ciulla (Ed.), *Ethics, the heart of leadership* (pp. 169–192). Westport, CT: Praeger.

Bass, B. M., & Avolio, B. J. (1993). Transformational leadership: A response to critiques. In M. M. Chemers & R. Ayman (Eds.), *Leadership theory and research: Perspectives and directions* (pp. 49–80). San Diego: Academic Press.

Bass, B. M., Avolio, B. J., Jung, D. I., & Berson, Y. (2003). Predicting unit performance by assessing transformational and transactional leadership. *Journal of Applied Psychology, 88,* 207–218.

Bass, B. M., & Steidlmeier, P. (1999). Ethics, character, and authentic transformational leadership behavior. *Leadership Quarterly, 10,* 181–217.

Batson, C. D., & Thompson, E. R. (2001). Why don't moral people act morally? Motivational considerations. *Current Directions in Psychological Science, 10,* 54–57.

Batson, C. D., Thompson, E. R., & Chen, H. (2002). Moral hypocrisy: Addressing some alternatives. *Journal of Personality and Social Psychology, 83,* 330–339.

Batson, C. D., Van Lange, P. A. M., Ahmad, N., & Lishner, D. A. (2003). Altruism and helping behavior. In M. A. Hogg & J. Cooper (Eds.), *The Sage handbook of social psychology* (pp. 279–295). London: Sage.

Bauby, J.-D. (1997). *The diving bell and the butterfly: A memoir of life in death.* New York: Vintage Books.

Bauman, D. C. (2011). Evaluating ethical approaches to crisis leadership: Insights from unintentional harm research. *Journal of Business Ethics, 98,* 281–295.

Bazerman, M. H. (1986). *Management in managerial decision making.* New York: John Wiley.

Bazerman, M. H., Chugh, D., & Banaji, M. R. (2005, October). When good people (seem to) negotiate in bad faith. *Negotiation, 8,* 3–5.

Bazerman, M. H., & Tenbrunsel, A. E. (2011). *Blind spots: Why we fail to do what's right and what to do about it.* Princeton, NJ: Princeton University Press.

Bazerman, M. H., & Watkins, M. D. (2004). *Predictable surprises: The disasters you should have seen coming and how to prevent them.* Boston: Harvard Business School Press.

Bear, M. (2012). *First World problems.* San Francisco: Weldon Owen.

Beaumont, P. (2012, August 19). Are drones any more immoral than other weapons of war? *The Observer,* Comment, p. 30.

Becker, J. A. H., & O'Hair, H. D. (2007). Machiavellians' motives in organizational citizenship behavior. *Journal of Applied Communication Research, 35,* 246–267.

Bedian, A. G. (2007). Even if the tower is "ivory," it isn't "white": Understanding the consequences of faculty cynicism. *Academy of Management Learning and Education, 6,* 9–32.

Beech, H., Birmingham, L., Dirkse, T., & Mahr, K. (2011, March 28). How Japan will reawaken. *Time International,* pp. 32–37.

Bell, M. A. (1974). The effects of substantive and affective conflict in problem-solving groups. *Speech Monographs, 41,* 19–23.

Bell, M. A. (1979). The effects of substantive and affective verbal conflict on the quality of decisions of small problem-solving groups. *Central States Speech Journal, 3,* 75–82.

Belson, K., & Pilon, M. (2012, October 18). Armstrong is dropped by Nike and steps down as foundation chairman. *The New York Times,* p. B17.

Benefiel, M. (2005). The second half of the journey: Spiritual leadership for organizational transformation. *Leadership Quarterly, 16,* 723–747.

Benefiel, M. (2005). *Soul at work: Spiritual leadership in organizations.* New York: Seabury Books.

Benjamin, M., & Calabresi, M. (2012, August 13). News Corp's U. S. hacking problem. *Time,* pp. 43–45.

Benkert, G. G. (2008). Google, human rights, and moral compromise. *Journal of Business Ethics, 85,* 453–478.

Bennis, W., & Nanus, B. (2003). *Leaders: Strategies for taking charge.* New York: Harper Business Essentials.

Bennis, W. G., & Thomas, R. J. (2002). *Geeks and geezers: How era, values, and defining moments shape leaders.* Boston: Harvard Business School Press.

Benoit, W. L. (2004). Image restoration discourse and crisis communication. In D. P. Millar & R. L. Heath (Eds.), *Responding to crisis: A rhetorical approach to crisis communication* (pp. 263–280). Mahwah, NJ: Erlbaum.

Bentham, J. (1948). *An introduction to the principles of morals and legislation.* New York: Hafner.

Berkowitz, S. (2012, November 21). Contract perks big deal for some football coaches. *USA Today,* p. 8C.

Berman, D. K. (2008, October 28). The game: Post-Enron crackdown comes up woefully short. *The Wall Street Journal,* p. C2.

Bertsch, A. M. (2012). Validating GLOBE's societal values scales: A test in the U.S.A. *International Journal of Business and Social Science, 3,* 10–23.

Bestselling author owes charity $1M. *The Toronto Star,* p. A12.

Bies, R. J., & Tripp, T. M. (1998). Two faces of the powerless: Coping with tyranny in organizations. In R. M. Kramer & M. A Neale (Eds.), *Power and influence in organizations* (pp. 203–219). Thousand Oaks, CA: Sage.

Big victory against global bribery. (2008, December 17). *The Christian Science Monitor,* p. 8.

Bilger, B. (2009, April 20). Swamp things; Florida's uninvited predators. *The New Yorker,* p. 80.

Billing misstep is typical LIPA. (2012, November 28). *Newsday,* p. A34.

Bing, S. (2000). *What would Machiavelli do? The ends justify the meanness.* New York: HarperBusiness.

Bird, F. B. (1996). *The muted conscience: Moral silence and the practice of ethics in business.* Westport, CT: Quorum.

Birkinshaw, P. (2006). Transparency as a human right. In C. Hood & D. Heald (Eds.), *Transparency: The key to better governance?* (pp. 47–57). Oxford, England: Oxford University Press.

Blackwell, T. (2009, September 30). Mandatory flu shots rile health workers; "invasive procedure." *National Post,* p. A8.

Blasi, A. (1984). Moral identity: Its role in moral functioning. In

W. M. Kurtines & J. L. Gewirtz (Eds.), *Morality, moral behavior, and moral development* (pp. 128–139). New York: John Wiley.

Block, P. (1996). *Stewardship: Choosing service over self-interest.* San Francisco: Berrett-Koehler.

Boardley, I. D., & Kavussanu, M. (2007). Development and validation of the Moral Disengagement in Sport Scale. *Journal of Sport & Exercise Psychology, 29,* 608–628.

Boardley, I. D., & Kavussanu, M. (2008). The Moral Disengagement in Sport Scale—Short. *Journal of Sports Sciences, 26,* 1507–1517.

Bobocel, D. R., & Meyer, J. P. (1994). Escalating commitment to a failing course of action: Separating the roles of choice and justification. *Journal of Applied Psychology, 79,* 360–363.

Boesveld, S. (2013, March 2). A CEO first: Yahoo's Marissa Mayer meets criticism for telling employees to come into the office or quit. *National Post,* p. A3.

Boje, D. (2008). Critical theory approaches to spirituality in business. In J. Biberman & L. Tischler (Eds.), *Spirituality in business: Theory, practice, and future directions* (pp. 160–187). New York: Palgrave Macmillan.

Boksem, M. A. S., & De Cremer, D. (2009). The neural basis of morality. In D. De Cremer (Ed.), *Psychological*

perspectives on ethical behavior and decision-making (pp. 153–166). Charlotte, NC: Information Age.

Bordas, J. (1995). Becoming a servant-leader: The personal development path. In L. Spears (Ed.), *Reflections on leadership* (pp. 149–160). New York: John Wiley.

Borisoff, D., & Victor, D. A. (1998). *Conflict management: A communication skills approach* (2nd ed.). Boston: Allyn & Bacon.

Bort, J. (2013, January 6). Google quietly gives up its fight to combat censorship in China. Business Insider. Retrieved from http://www .businessinsider.com

Bowie, N. E., & Werhane, P. H. (2005). *Management ethics.* Malden, MA: Blackwell.

Bowley, G., & Kannapell, A. (2008, August 6). Chaos on the "mountain that invites death." *The New York Times,* p. A1.

Boyle, E. H., Jr., Forsyth, D. R., Banks, G. C., & McDaniel, M. A. (2012). A meta-analysis of the dark triad and work behavior: A social exchange perspective. *Journal of Applied Psychology, 97,* 557–579.

Brady, E., Berkowitz, S., & Upton, J. (2012, November 20). "Average" salary: $1.64 million. *USA Today,* p. 1A.

Brady, E., & Halley, J. (2009, February 24). The blowup over blowouts. *USA Today,* p. 1C.

Brady, J. P. (2012). Marketing breast milk substitutes: Problems and perils throughout the world. *Archives of Disease in Children Online.* Retrieved from http://adc.bmj.com

Bratton, V. K., & Kacmar, K. M. (2004). Extreme careerism: The dark side of impression management. In W. Griffin & K. O'Reilly (Eds.), *The dark side of organizational behavior* (pp. 291–308). San Francisco: Jossey-Bass.

Brecher, B. (2007). *Torture and the ticking bomb.* Malden, MA: Blackwell.

Brissett, D., & Edgley, C. (1990). The dramaturgical perspective. In D. Brissett & C. Edgley (Eds.), *Life as theater: A dramaturgical sourcebook* (2nd ed., pp. 1–46). New York: Aldine de Gruyter.

Brown, A. D. (1997). Narcissism, identity, and legitimacy. *Academy of Management Review, 22,* 643–686.

Brown, D. J., Scott, K. A., & Lewis, H. (2004). Information processing and leadership. In J. Antonakis, A. T. Cianciolo, & R. J. Sternberg (Eds.), *The nature of leadership* (pp. 125–147). Thousand Oaks, CA: Sage.

Brown, M. E., & Trevino, L. K. (2006). Ethical leadership: A review and future directions. *Leadership Quarterly, 17,* 595–616.

Brown, M. E., & Trevino, L. K. (2006). Socialized charismatic leadership, values congruence, and deviance in work groups. *Journal of Applied Psychology, 91,* 954–962.

Brown, M. E., Trevino, L. K., & Harrison, D. A. (2005). Ethical leadership: A social learning perspective for construct development and testing. *Organizational Behavior and Human Decision Processes, 97,* 117–134.

Brown, M. T. (2005). *Corporate integrity: Rethinking organizational ethics and leadership.* Cambridge, England: Cambridge University Press.

Brown, R. (1995). *Prejudice: Its social psychology.* Oxford, England: Blackwell.

Brown, R. P. (2003). Measuring individual differences in the tendency to forgive: Construct validity and links with depression. *Personality and Social Psychology Bulletin, 29,* 759–771.

Bruhn, J. G. (2001). *Trust and the health of organizations.* New York: Kluwer/Plenum.

Buchholz, R. A., & Rosenthal, S. B. (2005). Toward a conceptual framework for stakeholder theory. *Journal of Business Ethics, 58,* 137–148.

Bumiller, E. (2010, June 8). Army leak suspect is turned in, by ex-hacker. *The New York Times,* p. A1.

Burns, J. F. (2012, May 2). Cameron stands to lose much as scandal wears on. *The New York Times.* Retrieved from http://www.nytimes.com

Burns J. F., & Cowell, A. (2012, April 12). Murdoch case shifts to a minister. *The New York Times,* p. A1.

Burns, J. F., & Cowell, A. (2012, November 30). Hacking report says new regulatory system needed for British newspapers. *The New York Times,* p. A8.

Burns, J. M. (1978). *Leadership.* New York: Harper & Row.

Burns, J. M. (2003). *Transforming leadership: A new pursuit of happiness.* New York: Atlantic Monthly Press.

Burton, J. P., & Hoobler, J. M. (2006). Subordinate self-esteem and abusive supervision. *Journal of Managerial Science, 3,* 340–355.

Buss, A. H. (1961). *The psychology of aggression.* New York: John Wiley.

Campbell, D. (2004, December 14). Energy giant agrees settlement with Burmese villagers. *The Guardian,* Foreign Affairs, p. 17.

Carden, S. D. (2006). *Virtue ethics: Dewey and Macintyre.* London: Continuum.

Carey, J., & Gardiner, A. (2008, January 30). Settlement gives aid to athletes. *USA Today,* p. 6C.

Carlson, D. S., & Perrewe, P. L. (1995). Institutionalization of organizational ethics through transformational leadership. *Journal of Business Ethics, 14,* 829–838.

Carr, D. (2012, May 7). News Corp. board's cozy compliance. *The New York Times,* p. B1.

Carroll, A. B., & Buchholtz, A. K. (2012). *Business and society: Ethics, sustainability, and stakeholder management* (8th ed.). Mason, OH; South-Western Cengage Learning.

Carroll, S. J., & Gannon, M. J. (1997). *Ethical dimensions of management.* Thousand Oaks, CA: Sage.

Carvajal, D., & de Blume, M. (2012). Strauss-Kahn says sex parties went too far, but lust is not crime. *The New York Times,* p. A1.

Carver, C. S., & Scheier, M. F. (2005). Optimism. In C. R. Snyder & S. J. Lopez (Eds.), *Handbook of positive psychology* (pp. 231–243). Oxford, England: Oxford University Press.

Casarjian, R. (1992). *Forgiveness: A bold choice for a peaceful heart.* New York: Bantam.

Casebeer, W. D. (2003). Moral cognition and its neural constituents. *Neuroscience, 4,* 841–846.

Cauchon, D. (2009, December 1). Invasive carp threatens Great Lakes. *USA Today,* p. 17A.

Caudron, S. (1995, September 4). The boss from hell. *Industry Week,* pp. 12–16.

Caux Round Table. (2000). Appendix 26: The Caux principles. In O. F. Williams (Ed.), *Global codes of conduct: An idea whose time has come* (pp. 384–388). Notre Dame, IN: University of Notre Dame Press.

Caux Round Table. (2006). Principles for non-governmental organizations. Retrieved from http://www.cauxroundtable.org/index.cfm?&menuid=101

Cavanagh, G. F., & Moberg, D. J. (1999). The virtue of courage within the organization. In M. L. Pava & P. Primeaux (Eds.), *Research in ethical issues in organizations* (Vol. 1, pp. 1–25). Stamford, CT: JAI Press.

Center for the Study of Ethics in the Professions at Illinois Institute of Technology. (2013). *Index of codes.* Retrieved from http://ethics.iit.edu/codes

CEO's moral compass steers Siemens. (2010, February 15). *USA Today,* p. 3B.

Chadbrand, I. (2013, January 25). Wiggins: I know Lance lied about comeback. *The Daily Telegraph,* Sport, p. 13.

Chaleff, I. (2003). *The courageous follower: Standing up to and for our leaders* (2nd ed.). San Francisco: Berrett-Koehler.

Chan, A., Hannah, S. T., & Gardner, W. L. (2005). Veritable authentic leadership: Emergence, functioning, and impacts. In W. L. Gardner, B. J. Avolio, & F. O. Walumbwa (Eds.), *Authentic leadership theory and practice: Origins, effects and development* (pp. 3–41). Amsterdam: Elsevier.

Chan, A. W. H., & Cheung, H. Y. (2012). Cultural dimensions, ethical sensitivity, and corporate governance. *Journal of Business Ethics, 110,* 45–59.

Chan, W. (Trans.). (1963). *The way of Lao Tzu.* Indianapolis: Bobbs-Merrill.

Chang, I. (1997). *The rape of Nanking: The forgotten holocaust of World War II.* New York: Basic Books.

Charges possible in outbreak. (2009, February 15). *Newsday,* p. A50.

The cheat sheet. (2009, July 9). *The Boston Globe,* p. G23.

Chen, A., Lawson, R. B., Gordon, L. R., & McIntosh, B. (1996). Groupthink: Deciding with the leader and the devil. *Psychological Record, 46,* 581–590.

Cheng, B. L., Wu, T., Huang, M., & Farh, J. (2004). Paternalistic leadership and subordinate responses: Establishing a leadership model in Chinese organizations. *Asian Journal of Social Psychology, 7,* 89–117.

Chhokar, J. S., Brodbeck, F. C., & House, R. J. (Eds.). (2007). *Culture and leadership across the world: The GLOBE book of in-depth studies of 25 societies.* Mahwah, NJ: Erlbaum.

Choi, Y., & Mai-Dalton, R. R. (1998). On the leadership

function of self-sacrifice. *Leadership Quarterly, 9,* 475–501.

Choi, Y., & Mai-Dalton, R. R. (1999). The model of followers' responses to self-sacrificial leadership: An empirical test. *Leadership Quarterly, 10,* 397–421.

Chrisafis, A. (2009, January 27). Veiled threats: Row over Islamic dress opens bitter divisions in France. *The Guardian,* International, p. 24.

Christensen, L. T., & Langer, R. (2009). Public relations and the strategic use of transparency: Consistency, hypocrisy, and corporate change. In R. L. Heath, E. L. Toth, & D. Waymer (Eds.), *Rhetorical and critical approaches to public relations II* (pp. 129–153). New York: Routledge.

Christensen, S. L., & Kohls, J. (2003). Ethical decision making in times of organizational crises: A framework for analysis. *Business & Society, 42,* 328–358.

Christians, C. G., Rotzell, K. B., & Fackler, M. (1999). *Media ethics* (3rd ed.). New York: Longman.

Christie, R., & Geis, F. L. (1970). *Studies in Machiavellianism.* New York: Academic Press.

Ciulla, J. B. (2004). Leadership ethics: Mapping the territory. In J. B. Ciulla (Ed.), *Ethics, the heart of leadership* (2nd ed., pp. 3–24). Westport, CT: Praeger.

Clapp-Smith, R., Vogelgesang, G. R., & Avey, J. B. (2009). Authentic leadership and positive psychological capital: The mediating role of trust at the group level of analysis. *Journal of Leadership & Organizational Studies, 15,* 227–240.

Clements, C. E., Neill, J. D., & Stovall, O. S. (2009). The impact of cultural differences on the convergence of international accounting codes of ethics. *Journal of Business Ethics, 90,* 383–391.

Cohen, D. V. (1993). Creating and maintaining ethical work climates: Anomie in the workplace and implications for managing change. *Business Ethics Quarterly, 3,* 343–358.

Cohen-Charash, Y., & Spector, P. E. (2001). The role of justice in organizations: A meta-analysis. *Organizational Behavior and Human Decision Processes, 86,* 278–321.

Colby, A., & Damon, W. (1992). *Some do care: Contemporary lives of moral commitment.* New York: Free Press.

Colby, A., & Damon, W. (1995). The development of extraordinary moral commitment. In M. Killen & D. Hart (Eds.), *Morality in everyday life: Developmental perspectives* (pp. 342–369). Cambridge, England: Cambridge University Press.

Collamer, N. (2013, March 1). The problem with Yahoo's work-at-home ban. *Forbes.* Retrieved from Forbes.com.

Collins, J. (2001). *Vision framework.* Retrieved from http://www.jimcollins.com/tools/vision-framework.pdf

Collins, J. C., & Porras, J. I. (1996, September–October). Building your company's vision. *Harvard Business Review,* pp. 65–77.

Colquitt, J. A., Conlon, D. E., Wesson, M. J., Porter, C. O., & Yee, N. K. (2001). Justice at the millennium: A meta-analytic review of 25 years of organizational justice research. *Journal of Applied Psychology, 86,* 425–445.

Come back in 10 years' time. (2011, March 26). *Economist,* pp. 47–48.

Comte-Sponville, A. (2001). *A small treatise on the great virtues: The uses of philosophy in everyday life.* New York: Metropolitan.

Connelly, S., Helton-Fauth, W., & Mumford, M. D. (2004). A managerial in-basket study of the impact of trait emotions on ethical choice. *Journal of Business Ethics, 51,* 245–267.

Coombs, W. T. (1999). *Ongoing crisis communication: Planning, managing, and responding.* Thousand Oaks, CA: Sage.

Coombs, W. T., & Holladay, S. J. (2004). Reasoned action in crisis communication: An attribution theory–based approach to crisis

management. In D. P. Millar &
R. L. Heath (Eds.), *Responding
to crisis: A rhetorical approach to
crisis communication* (pp. 95–
115). Mahwah, NJ: Erlbaum.

Cooper, S. (2004). *Corporate
social performance: A stakeholder
approach.* Burlington, VT:
Ashgate.

Cooperrider, D. L., &
Whitney, D. (2005).
*Appreciative inquiry: A positive
revolution in change.* San
Francisco: Berrett-Koehler.

Cosier, R. A., & Schwenk,
C. R. (1990). Agreement and
thinking alike: Ingredients
for poor decision. *Academy
of Management Executive, 4,*
69–74.

Countryman, A. (2001,
December 7). Leadership key
ingredient in ethics recipe,
experts say. *Chicago Tribune,*
pp. B1, B6.

Courchane, C. (2011, June 27).
Three Cups of Tea's bitter taste.
The Washington Times, p. C10.

Coutts, M. (2009, January 27).
Would Jesus run up the score?
Christian school under fire for
winning 100–0. *National Post,*
p. A1.

Covey, S. R. (1989). *The seven
habits of highly effective people.*
New York: Simon & Schuster.

Cowell, A., & Burns, J. F.
(2012, November 21).
Ex-leaders at News Corp. face
new round of charges. *The
International Herald Tribune,*
News, p. 3.

Cowley, S. (2012, July 11).
Google to pay $22.5 million
fine for Safari privacy evasion.
CNNMoney. Retrieved from
http://money.cnn.com

Cox, T. (1993). *Cultural
diversity in organizations: Theory,
research and practice.* San
Francisco: Berrett-Koehler.

Cox, T. (2001). *Creating the
multicultural organization: A
strategy for capturing the power
of diversity.* San Francisco:
Jossey-Bass.

Coyne, I. (2008, January 15).
Turbans make targets, some
Sikhs find. *The New York Times,*
p. NJ1.

Craigie, F. C. (1999). The spirit
and work: Observations about
spirituality and organizational
life. *Journal of Psychology and
Christianity, 18,* 43–53.

Crano, W. D., & Seyranian,
V. (2009). How minorities
prevail: The context/
comparison-leniency contract
model. *Journal of Social Issues,
65,* 335–363.

Cropanzano, R., & Stein,
J. H. (2009). Organizational
justice and behavioral ethics:
Promises and prospects.
Business Ethics Quarterly, 19,
193–233.

Crosariol, B. (2005, November
21). The diminishing allure of
rock-star executives. *The Globe
and Mail,* p. B12.

Crowley, M. (2013, April 1).
So, who can we kill? *Time,* pp.
20–23.

Cullen, D. (2009). *Columbine.*
New York: Twelve.

Cullen, J. B., Parboteeah,
K. P., & Victor, B. (2003). The
effects of ethical climates on
organizational commitment: A
two-study analysis. *Journal of
Business Ethics, 46,* 127–141.

Cullen, J. B., Victor, B., &
Bronson, J. W. (1993). The
Ethical Climate Questionnaire:
An assessment of its
development and validity.
Psychological Reports, 73,
667–674.

Cummings, L. L., & Bromiley,
P. (1996). The Organizational
Trust Inventory (OTI):
Development and validation.
In R. M. Kramer & T. R. Tyler
(Eds.), *Trust in organizations:
Frontiers of theory and research*
(pp. 302–329). Thousand
Oaks, CA: Sage.

Daleus, P., & Hansen, D.
(2011). Inherent ethical
challenges in bureaucratic
crisis management: The
Swedish experience with the
2004 tsunami disaster. In
L. Svedin (Ed.), *Ethics and
crisis management* (pp.
21–36). Charlotte, NC:
Information Age.

Dann, G. E., & Haddow, N.
(2007). Just doing business or
doing just business: Google,
Microsoft, Yahoo! and the
business of censoring China's
Internet. *Journal of Business
Ethics, 79,* 219–234.

Darley, J. M. (1996). How
organizations socialize
individuals into evildoing.

In D. M. Messick & A. E. Tenbrunsel (Eds.), *Codes of conduct: Behavioral research into business ethics* (pp. 12–43). New York: Russell Sage Foundation.

Darley, J. M. (2001). The dynamics of authority influence in organizations and the unintended action consequences. In J. M. Darley, D. M. Messick, & T. R. Tyler (Eds.), *Social influences on ethical behavior in organizations* (pp. 37–52). Mahwah, NJ: Erlbaum.

Davey, M. (2009, December 13). Be careful what you fish for. *The New York Times*, p. WK3.

Davis, A. L., & Rothstein, H. R. (2006). The effects of the perceived behavioral integrity of managers on employee attitudes: A meta-analysis. *Journal of Business Ethics, 67,* 407–419.

Davis, B., & Gauthier-Villars, D. (2008, October 22). IMF chief facing fresh claim of abusing power. *The Australian,* World, p. 12.

Davis, J. H., & Ruhe, J. A. (2003). Perceptions of country corruption: Antecedents and outcomes. *Journal of Business Ethics, 43,* 275–288.

Day, L. A. (2006). *Ethics in media communications: Cases and controversies* (5th ed.). Belmont, CA: Wadsworth/Thomson.

Dean, J. W., Brandes, P., & Dharwadkar, R. (1998).

Organizational cynicism. *Academy of Management Review, 23,* 341–352.

Death of Delhi gang rape victim horrifies India. (2012, December 30). *The Telegraph.* Retrieved from http://www.telegraph.co.uk

De Cremer, D. (2006). Affective and motivational consequences of leader self-sacrifice: The moderating effect of autocratic leadership. *Leadership Quarterly, 17,* 79–93.

De Cremer, D., & Van Dijk, E. (2005). When and why leaders put themselves first: Leader behaviour in resource allocations as a function of feeling entitled. *European Journal of Social Psychology, 35,* 553–563.

De Cremer, D., & van Knippenberg, D. (2004). Leader self-sacrifice and leadership effectiveness: The moderating role of leader self-confidence. *Organizational Behavior and Human Decision Processes, 95,* 140–155.

De Dreu, C. K. W., & Beersma, B. (2001). Minority influence in organizations: Its origins and implications for learning and group performance. In C. K. W. De Dreu & N. K. De Vries (Eds.), *Group consensus and minority influence: Implications for innovation* (pp. 258–283). Malden, MA: Blackwell.

De Dreu, C. K. W., & West, M. A. (2001). Minority dissent and team innovation: The

importance of participation in decision making. *Journal of Applied Psychology, 86,* 1191–1201.

De George, R. T. (1995). *Business ethics* (4th ed.). Englewood Cliffs, NJ: Prentice Hall.

DeGroot, T., Kiker, D. S., & Cross, T. C. (2000). A meta-analysis to review organizational outcomes related to charismatic leadership. *Canadian Journal of Administrative Sciences, 17,* 356–371.

Delanty, G. (2012). Introduction: The emerging field of cosmopolitanism studies. In G. Delanty (Ed.), *International handbook of cosmopolitan studies* (pp. 1–8). Hoboken, NJ: Routledge.

Delhi rape case; defendants face first witness evidence. (2013, February 5). BBCNews India.

Den Hartog, D. N., House, R. J., Hanges, P. U., Ruiz-Quintanilla, S. A., & Dorfman, P. W. (1999). Culture-specific and cross-culturally generalizable implicit leadership theories: Are attributes of charismatic/transformational leadership universally endorsed? *Leadership Quarterly, 10,* 219–257.

Dennis, B. (2011, December 14). 6 former Siemens officials indicted. *The Washington Post,* p. A18.

Department of Numbers. (2013). Unemployment

demographics. Retrieved from http://deptofnumbers.com/unemployment/demographics

DePree, M. (1989). *Leadership is an art.* New York: Doubleday.

DePree, M. (2003). Servant-leadership: Three things necessary. In L. C. Spears & M. Lawrence (Eds.), *Focus on leadership: Servant-leadership for the 21st century* (pp. 89–97). New York: John Wiley.

Deutsch, M. (1990). Psychological roots of moral exclusion. *Journal of Social Issues, 46*(1), 21–25.

DeVine, J. (2013, March 20). Death at CA facility after no CPR has some reviewing policies. WSMV-TV (Nashville, TN). Retrieved from http://www.wsmv.com

Devine, T., Seuk, J. H., & Wilson, A. (2001). *Cultivating heart and character: Educating for life's most essential goals.* Chapel Hill, NC: Character Development.

Dewey, J. (1920). *Reconstruction in philosophy.* New York: Henry Holt.

Diboye, R. L., & Halverson, S. K. (2004). Subtle (and not so subtle) discrimination in organizations. In R. W. Griffin & A. M. O'Leary-Kelly (Eds.), *The dark side of organizational behavior* (pp. 404–425). San Francisco: Jossey-Bass.

Dickson, D. M. (2009, July 31). Doing well—regardless; billions in bonuses paid

employees despite losses. *The Washington Times,* p. A10.

Dirks, K. T. (1999). The effects of interpersonal trust on work group performance. *Journal of Applied Psychology, 84,* 445–455.

Dobson, J. (1999). *The art of management and the aesthetic manager.* Westport, CT: Quorum Books.

Donaldson, T. (1996, September–October). Values in tension: Ethics away from home. *Harvard Business Review,* pp. 48–57.

Donaldson, T. (2009). Compass and dead reckoning: The dynamic implications of ISCT. *Journal of Business Ethics, 88,* 659–664.

Donaldson, T., & Dunfee, T. W. (1994). Toward a unified conception of business ethics: Integrative social contracts theory. *Academy of Management Review, 19,* 252–284.

Donaldson, T., & Dunfee, T. W. (1999). *Ties that bind: A social contracts approach to business ethics.* Boston: Harvard Business School Press.

Donaldson, T., & Preston, L. E. (1995). The stakeholder theory of the corporation: Concepts, evidence, and implications. *Academy of Management Review, 20,* 65–91.

Dotlich, D. L., Noel, J. L., & Walker, N. (2008). Learning for leadership: Failure as a second chance. In J. V. Gallos

(Ed.), *Business leadership* (2nd ed., pp.478–485). San Francisco: Jossey-Bass.

Dougherty, C. (2008, October 7). The sheriff at Siemens, at work under Justice Dept's watchful eye. *The New York Times,* p. B11.

Dowd, M. (2012, May 27). The party animals at the Secret Service. *The New York Times,* p. SR11.

Drummond, H., & Hodgson, J. (2011). *Escalation in decision-making: Behavioral economics in business.* Burlington, VT: Gower.

Drummond, T. (2000, April 3). Coping with cops. *Time,* pp. 72–73.

Duchon, D., & Plowman, D. A. (2005). Nurturing the spirit at work: Impact on work unit performance. *Leadership Quarterly, 16,* 807–833.

Duck, J. M., & Fielding, K. S. (2003). Leaders and their treatment of subgroups: Implications for evaluations of the leader and the superordinate group. *European Journal of Social Psychology, 33,* 387–401.

Duell, M., Andrews, E., Greenhill, S., & Shears, R. (2012, December 10). Now hospital which treated Kate denies hoax call radio station contacted managers or press officers. *The Daily Mail.* Retrieved from http://www.dailymail.co.uk

Duffy, M. K., & & Shaw, J. D. (2000). The Salieri syndrome:

Consequences of envy in groups. *Small Group Research, 31,* 3–23.

Duke, D. L. (1986). The aesthetics of leadership. *Educational Administration Quarterly, 22*(1), 7–27.

Dukerich, J. M., Nichols, M. L., Elm, D. R., & Voltrath, D. A. (1990). Moral reasoning in groups: Leaders make a difference. *Human Relations, 43,* 473–493.

Dunn, J., & Schweitzer, M. E. (2005). Why good employees make unethical decisions. In E. W. Kidwell & C. L. Martin (Eds.), *Managing organizational deviance* (pp. 39–60). Thousand Oaks, CA: Sage.

Dunning, J. H. (2000). Whither global capitalism? *Global Focus, 12,* 117–136.

Dunning, J. H. (2003). Overview. In J. H. Dunning (Ed.), *Making globalization good: The moral challenges of global capitalism* (pp. 11–40). Oxford, England: Oxford University Press.

Durskat, V. U., & Wolff, S. B. (2001, March). Building the emotional intelligence of groups. *Harvard Business Review,* pp. 80–90.

Dyer, E. (2012, May 2). North Korea continues to brutalize its people and yet we do nothing. *The Telegraph.*

Edwards, J. C. (2001). Self-fulfilling prophecy and escalating commitment: Fuel for the Waco fire. *Journal of Applied Behavioral Science, 37,* 343–360.

Ehrhart, M. G. (2004). Leadership and procedural justice climate as antecedents of unit-level organizational citizenship behavior. *Personnel Psychology, 57,* 61–94.

Eilperin, J. (2010, February 7). Fight over invasive species turns into fight over lesser of two evils. *The Oregonian,* p. A2.

Einarsen, S., Aasland, M. S., & Skogstad, A. (2007). Destructive leadership behaviour: A definition and conceptual model. *Leadership Quarterly, 18,* 207–216.

Einhorn, B. (2006, August 9). Search engines censured for censorship. *Bloomberg Businessweek.* Retrieved from http://www.businessweek.com/stories/2006-08-09/search-engines-censured-for-censorship

Eisenberg, E. M. (1984). Ambiguity as strategy in organizational communication. *Communication Monographs, 51,* 227–242.

Eisenberg, N. (2000). Emotion, regulation, and moral development. *Annual Review of Psychology, 51,* 665–697.

Eisenhardt, K. M. (1989). Making fast strategic decisions in high-velocity environments. *Academy of Management Journal, 32,* 543–576.

Elangovan, A. R., & Shapiro, D. L. (1998). Betrayal of trust in organizations. *Academy of Management Review, 23,* 547–566.

Ellenwood, S. (2006). Revisiting character education: From McGuffey to narratives. *Journal of Education, 187,* 21–43.

Enright, R. D. (2012). *The forgiving life.* Washington, DC: American Psychological Association.

Enright, R. D., Freedman, S., & Rique, J. (1998). The psychology of interpersonal forgiveness. In R. D. Enright & J. North (Eds.), *Exploring forgiveness* (pp. 46–62). Madison: University of Wisconsin Press.

Enright, R. D., & Gassin, E. A. (1992). Forgiveness: A developmental view. *Journal of Moral Education, 21,* 99–114.

Epley, N., & Dunning, D. (2000). Feeling '"holier than thou": Are self-serving assessments produced by errors in self- or social prediction? *Journal of Personality and Social Psychology, 79,* 861–875.

Erbin, G. S., & Guneser, A. B. (2007). The relationship between paternalistic leadership and organizational commitment: Investigating the role of climate regarding ethics. *Journal of Business Ethics, 82,* 955–968.

Erickson, A., Shaw, J. B., & Agabe, Z. (2007). An empirical investigation of the antecedents, behaviors, and outcomes of bad leadership. *Journal of Leadership Studies, 1*(3), 26–43.

Ernst, C., & Yip, J. (2009). Boundary-spanning leadership: Tactics to bridge social identity groups in organizations. In T. L. Pittinsky (Ed.), *Crossing the divide: Intergroup leadership in a world of difference* (pp. 87–99). Boston: Harvard Business Press.

Esser, J. K. (1998). Alive and well after 25 years: A review of groupthink research. *Organizational Behavior and Human Decision Processes, 73,* 116–141.

Fairholm, G. W. (1996). Spiritual leadership: Fulfilling whole-self needs at work. *Leadership & Organization Development Journal, 17*(5), 11–17.

Fantz, A. (2013, March 13). To perform CPR or not? Woman's death raises questions. CNN. Retrieved from http://www.cnn.com

Farrell, K. (2008). Corporate complicity in the Chinese censorship regime: When freedom of expression and profitability collide. *Internet Law, 11*(1), 11–21.

Fearn-Banks, K. (2007). *Crisis communications: A casebook approach* (3rd ed.). Mahwah, NJ: Erlbaum.

Feinstein, M. (2008). John Dewey, inquiry ethics, and democracy. In C. Misak (Ed.), *The Oxford handbook of American philosophy* (pp. 87–109). Oxford, England: Oxford University Press.

Ferguson, R. (2002, January 18). NCAA a "sweatshop," Steelworkers chief says. *Toronto Star,* p. E11.

55% rate government response to Hurricane Sandy positively. (2012, November 12). Rasmussen Reports. Retrieved from http://www.rasmussenreports.com

Fine, R., & Boon, V. (2007). Introduction: Cosmopolitanism: Between past and future. *European Journal of Social Theory 10,* 5–16.

Fink, S. (2002). *Crisis management: Planning for the inevitable.* Lincoln, NE: Backinprint.com.

Fiol, C. M., Harris, D., & House, R. J. (1999). Charismatic leadership: Strategies for effecting social change. *Leadership Quarterly, 10,* 449–482.

Fisher, R., Ury, W., & Patton, B. (2011). *Getting to yes* (rev. ed.). New York: Penguin

Fisher, W. (1987). *Human communication as narration: Toward a philosophy of reason, value, and action.* Columbia: University of South Carolina Press.

Fiske, S. T. (1993). Controlling other people: The impact of power on stereotyping. *American Psychologist, 48,* 621–628.

Fiske S. T. (1998). Stereotyping, prejudice, and discrimination. In D. T. Gilbert, S. T. Fiske, & G. Lindzey (Eds.), *The handbook of social psychology* (Vol. 2, pp. 357–411). Boston: McGraw-Hill.

Flescher, A. M., & Worthen, D. L. (2007). *The altruistic species: Scientific, philosophical, and religious perspectives of human benevolence.* Philadelphia: Templeton Foundation Press.

Fletcher, G. (1993). *Loyalty: An essay on the morality of relationships.* New York: Oxford University Press.

Flippen, A. R. (1999). Understanding groupthink from a self-regulatory perspective. *Small Group Research, 3,* 139–165.

Folger, R., & Baron, R. A. (1996). Violence and hostility at work: A model of reactions to perceived injustice. In G. R. VandenBos & E. Q. Bulato (Eds.), *Violence on the job: Identifying risks and developing solutions* (pp. 51–85). Washington, DC: American Psychological Association.

Fortin, M. (2008). Perspectives on organizational justice: Concept clarification, social context integration, time and links with morality. *International Journal of Management Reviews, 10,* 93–126.

Foster, R. J. (1978). *Celebration of discipline: The path to spiritual growth.* New York: Harper & Row.

Fowler, K. L., Kling, N. D., & Larson, M. D. (2007). Organizational preparedness for coping with a major crisis or disaster. *Business & Society, 46*, 100–101.

Franke, G. R., & Nadler, S. S. (2008). Culture, economic development, and national ethical attitudes. *Journal of Business Research, 61*, 254–264.

Freedman, S., Enright, R. D., & Knutson, J. (2005). A progress report on the process model of forgiveness. In E. L. Worthington, Jr. (Ed.), *Handbook of forgiveness* (pp. 393–406). New York: Routledge.

Freeman, R. E., Harrison, J. S., & Wicks, A. C. (2007). *Managing for stakeholders: Survival, reputation, and success.* New Haven, CT: Yale University Press.

French, R. P., & Raven, B. (1959). The bases of social power. In D. Cartwright (Ed.), *Studies in social power* (pp. 150–167). Ann Arbor: University of Michigan, Institute for Social Research.

Frey, B. F. (2000). The impact of moral intensity on decision making in a business context. *Journal of Business Ethics, 26*, 181–195.

Frey, W. H. (2011). *The new metro minority map: Regional shifts in Hispanics, Asians, and Blacks from Census 2010.* Brookings Institution. Retrieved from http://www.brookings.edu/research/papers/2011/08/31-census-race-frey

Fritzsche, D. J. (2000). Ethical climates and the ethical dimension of decision making. *Journal of Business Ethics, 24*, 125–140.

Fromm, E. (1964). *The heart of man: Its genius for good and evil.* New York: Harper & Row.

Fry, L. W. (2003). Toward a theory of spiritual leadership. *Leadership Quarterly, 14*, 693–727.

Fry, L. W. (2005). Toward a theory of ethical and spiritual well-being, and corporate social responsibility through spiritual leadership. In R. A. Giacalone, C. L. Jurkiewicz, & C. Dunn (Eds.), *Positive psychology in business ethics and corporate responsibility* (pp. 47–84). Greenwich, CT: Information Age.

Fry, L. W. (2008). Spiritual leadership: State-of-the-art and future directions for theory, research, and practice. In J. Biberman & L. Tischler (Eds.), *Spirituality in business: Theory, practice, and future directions* (pp. 106–123). New York: Palgrave Macmillan.

Fry, L. W., Vitucci, S., & Cedillo, M. (2005). Spiritual leadership and army transformation: Theory, measurement, and establishing a baseline. *Leadership Quarterly, 16*, 835–862.

Garcia-Zamor, J. C. (2003). Workplace spirituality and organizational performance. *Public Administration Review, 63*, 355–363.

Gardner, W. L., Avolio, B. J., Luthans, F., May, D. R., & Walumbwa, F. O. (2005). "Can you see the real me?" A self-based model of authentic leader and follower development. *Leadership Quarterly, 16*, 343–372.

Garvin, D. A. (1993, July–August). Building a learning organization. *Harvard Business Review*, pp. 78–91.

Gaudine, A., & Thorne, L. (2001). Emotion and ethical decision-making in organizations. *Journal of Business Ethics, 31*, 175–187.

Gentile, M. C. (2010). *Giving voice to values: How to speak your mind when you know what's right.* New Haven, CT: Yale University Press.

George, J. M. (1995). Asymmetrical effects of rewards and punishments: The case of social loafing. *Journal of Occupational and Organizational Psychology, 68*, 327–338.

Geracimos, A. (2009, September 29). Health workers spurn flu shot; for some, jobs depend on it. *The Washington Times*, p. A1.

Ghosh, B. (2010, March 29). Sins of the fathers. *Time*, pp. 34–37.

Giacalone, R. A., & Jurkiewicz, C. L. (2003). Right from wrong: The influence of spirituality on perceptions of unethical business activities. *Journal of Business Ethics, 46,* 85–97.

Giacalone, R. A., & Jurkiewicz, C. L. (2003). Toward a science of workplace spirituality. In R. A. Giacalone & C. L. Jurkiewicz (Eds.), *Handbook of workplace spirituality and organizational performance* (pp. 3–28). Armonk, NY: M. E. Sharpe.

Gibb, J. R. (1961). Defensive communication. *Journal of Communication, 11–12,* 141–148.

Gibbs, N. (2011, May 11). Men behaving badly: What is it about power that makes men crazy? *Time,* pp. 16–30.

Gibson, J. (2012, October 4). Living with death by drone. *Los Angeles Times,* p. A21.

Gilligan, C. (1982). *In a different voice: Psychological theory and women's development.* Cambridge, MA: Harvard University Press.

Gino, F., Moore, D. A., & Bazerman, M. H. (2008, January). *See no evil: When we overlook other people's unethical behavior.* Harvard Business School Working Paper No. 08-045.

Gino, F., Moore, D. A., & Bazerman, M. H. (2009). *No harm, no foul: The outcome bias in ethical judgments.* Harvard Business School Working Paper 08-080.

Gioia, D. A. (1992). Pinto fires and personal ethics: A script analysis of missed opportunities. *Journal of Business Ethics, 11,* 379–389.

Gladwell, M. (2009, July 27). Cocksure. *The New Yorker,* pp. 24ff.

Glanton, D. (2009, February 8). Peanut recall puts town "in hot water." *Los Angeles Times,* p. A28.

Glanton, D. (2009, February 9). Ex-peanut plant workers tell of rats, filth, mold. *The Oregonian,* pp. A1, A4.

Glanz, W. (2003, August 27). NASA ignored dangers to shuttle, panel says. *The Washington Times,* p. A1.

Glenny, M. (2010, December 5). The gift of information. *The New York Times,* M2, p. 166.

Gogek, E. (2012, November 8). A bad trip for democrats. *The New York Times,* p. A23.

Goldberg, M. (1997). Doesn't anybody read the Bible anymo'? In O. F. Williams (Ed.), *The moral imagination: How literature and films can stimulate ethical reflection in the business world* (pp. 19–32). Notre Dame, IN: University of Notre Dame Press.

Goleman, D., Boyatzis, R., & McKee, A. (2002). The emotional reality of teams. *Journal of Organizational Excellence, 21*(2), 55–65.

Goldfarb, A. Z. (2012, June 12). JPMorgan CEO Jamie Dimon apologizes for trading losses in Hill testimony. *The Washington Post.*

Gomez, R., & Fisher, J. W. (2003). Domains of spiritual well-being and development and validation of the Spiritual Well-Being Questionnaire. *Personality and Individual Differences, 35,* 1975–1991.

Goodnough, A., Tavernise, S., & Pollack, A. (2012, October 25). Spotlight put on founders of drug firm in outbreak. *The New York Times,* p. A18.

Goodpaster, K. E. (1991). Business ethics and stakeholder analysis. *Business Ethics Quarterly, 1,* 53–27.

Gorovitz, S. (Ed.). (1971). *Utilitarianism: Text and critical essays.* Indianapolis: Bobbs-Merrill.

Gottlieb, J. Z., & Sabzgiri, J. (1996). Towards an ethical dimension of decision making in organizations. *Journal of Business Ethics 15,* 1275–1285.

Gouran, D. S., & Hirokawa, R. Y. (1986). Counteractive functions of communication in effective group decision making. In R. Y. Hirokawa & M. S. Poole (Eds.), *Communication and group decision making* (pp. 81–89). Beverly Hills, CA: Sage.

Gouran, D. S., Hirokawa, R. Y., Julian, K. M., & Leatham, G. B. (1993). The evolution and current status of the functional perspective on communication in decision-making and problem-solving groups. In S. A. Deetz (Ed.), *Communication yearbook 16* (pp. 573–576). Newbury Park, CA: Sage.

Gose, B. (2012, April 15). $1-million settlement in "Three cups" scandal offers warning to boards. *Chronicle of Philanthropy*.

Gow, D. (2008, January 25). Siemens prepares to pay $2bn fine to clear up slush fund scandal. *The Guardian*, p. 34.

Grady, D. (2012, November 20). Deaths stir a dispute on powers of the F.D.A. *The New York Times*, p. D5.

Grady, D. (2012, December 22). Dangerous abscesses add to tainted drug's threat. *The New York Times*, p. A3.

Grady, D., & Tavernise, S. (2012, November 13). F.D.A. finds safety problems at company supplying drugs. *The New York Times*, p. A13.

Graen, G. B., & Graen, J. A. (Eds.). (2007). *New multinational network sharing*. Charlotte, NC: Information Age.

Graen, G. B., & Uhl-Bien, M. (1998). Relationship-based approach to leadership. Development of leader–member exchange (LMX) theory of leadership over 25 years: Applying a multi-level multi-domain perspective. In F. Dansereau & F. J. Yammarino (Eds.), *Leadership: The multiple-level approaches* (pp. 103–158). Stamford, CT: JAI Press.

Graham, G. (2004). *Eight theories of ethics*. London: Routledge.

Graham, J. (2013, March 6). Amid CPR controversy, many unanswered questions. *The New York Times*. Retrieved from http://www.nytimes.com

Greenberg, J., & Wiethoff, C. (2001). Organization justice as proaction and reaction: Implications for research and application. In R. Cropanzano (Ed.), *Justice in the workplace* (Vol. 2, pp. 271–302). Mahwah, NJ: Erlbaum.

Greenberg, J. W. (2002, October). September 11, 2001: A CEO's story. *Harvard Business Review*, pp. 58–64.

Greene, J. (2005). Cognitive neuroscience and the structure of the moral mind (2005). In P. Carruthers, S. Laurence, & S. Stich (Eds.), *The innate mind: Structure and content* (pp. 338–352). Oxford, England: Oxford University Press.

Greenhouse, S., & Rosenbloom, S. (2008, December 24). Wal-Mart to settle suits over pay for $352 million. *The New York Times*, p. B1.

Greenleaf, R. K. (1977). *Servant leadership*. New York: Paulist Press.

Greenstone, M., & Looney, A. (2012, October 12). The uncomfortable truth about American wages. *The New York Times*, Economix blog.

Gregory, A. (2012, December 8). We'll kill you both. *Daily Mirror*, News, pp. 4–5.

Griffin, R. W., & O'Leary-Kelly, A. M. (Eds.). (2004). *The dark side of organizational behavior*. San Francisco: Jossey-Bass.

Griswold, C. L. (2007). *Forgiveness: A philosophical exploration*. Cambridge, England: Cambridge University Press.

Grojean, M. W., Resick, C. J., Dickson, M. W., & Smith, D. B. (2004). Leaders, values, and organizational climate: Examining leadership strategies for establishing an organizational climate regarding ethics. *Journal of Business Ethics, 55*, 223–241.

Grossman, C. L. (2012, December 27). N.Y. gun-owner database draws ire. *USA Today*, p. 3A.

Grossman, L., & Beech, H. (2006, February 13). Google under the gun. *Time*.

Grunig, J. E. (2001). Two-way symmetrical public relations: Past, present, and future. In R. L. Heath (Ed.), *Handbook of public relations* (pp. 11–30). Thousand Oaks, CA: Sage.

Grunig, L. A., Grunig, J. E., Dozier, D. M. (2002). *Excellent public relations and effective organizations: A study of communication management in three countries*. Mahwah, NJ: Erlbaum.

Guarino, M. (2009, December 29). Minnesota, Ohio join

lawsuit against Illinois over Asian carp. *The Christian Science Monitor.* Retrieved from http://www.csmonitor.com/USA/2009/1229/Minnesota-Ohio-join-lawsuit-against-Illinois-over-Asian-carp

Guarino, M. (2012, November 12). How will feds deal with marijuana legalization in Colorado and Washington? *The Christian Science Monitor.*

Gudykunst, W. B. (2004). *Bridging differences: Effective intergroup communication* (4th ed.). Thousand Oaks, CA: Sage.

Gudykunst, W. B., & Kim, Y. Y. (1997). *Communicating with strangers: An approach to intercultural communication* (3rd ed.). New York: McGraw-Hill.

Guroian, V. (1996). Awakening the moral imagination. *Intercollegiate Review, 32,* 3–13.

Guth, W. D., & Tagiuri, R. (1965, September–October). Personal values and corporate strategy. *Harvard Business Review,* pp. 123–132.

Haberman, C. (2009, November 29). The story of a landing. *The New York Times,* p. BR15.

Hackman, M. Z., & Johnson, C. E. (2013). *Leadership: A communication perspective* (6th ed.). Prospect Heights, IL: Waveland.

Haider, K. (2008, August 5). "Death zone" tragedy. *National Post,* p. A3.

Haidt, J. (2001). The emotional dog and its rational tail: A social intuitionist approach to moral judgment. *Psychological Review, 108,* 814–834.

Haidt, J. (2003). The moral emotions. In R. J. Davidson, K. R. Scherer, & H. H. Goldsmith (Eds.), *Handbook of affective sciences* (pp. 852–870). Oxford, England: Oxford University Press.

Haidt, J. (2012). *The righteous mind: Why good people are divided by politics and religion.* New York: Pantheon Books.

Haidt, J., & Bjorklund, F. (2008). Social intuitionists answer six questions about moral psychology. In W. Sinnott-Armstrong (Ed.), *Moral psychology:Vol. 2. The cognitive science of morality: Intuition and diversity* (pp. 182–217). Cambridge: MIT Press.

Haidt, J., & Graham, J. (2007). When morality opposes justice: Conservatives have moral intuitions that liberals may not recognize. *Social Justice Research, 20,* 98–116.

Hajdin, M. (2005). Employee loyalty: An examination. *Journal of Business Ethics, 59,* 259–280.

Hakim, D., McGeehan, P., & Moss, M. (2012, November 14). Suffering on L.I. as power agency shows its flaws. *The New York Times,* p. A1.

Hale, J. R., & Fields, D. (2007). Exploring servant leadership across cultures: A

study of followers in Ghana and the USA. *Leadership, 3,* 397–417.

Halley, J. (2009, January 29). Lopsided games are often pointless. *USA Today,* p. 4C.

Hallie, P. (1979). *Lest innocent blood be shed: The story of the village of Le Chambon and how goodness happened there.* New York: Harper & Row.

Hallie, P. (1997). *Tales of good and evil, help and harm.* New York: HarperCollins.

Hamilton, J. B., & Knouse, S. B. (2001). Multinational enterprise decision principles for dealing with cross cultural ethical conflicts. *Journal of Business Ethics, 31,* 77–94.

Hamilton, J. B., Knouse, S. B., & Hill, V. (2009). Google in China: A manager-friendly heuristic model for resolving cross-cultural ethical conflicts. *Journal of Business Ethics, 86,* 143–157.

Hamilton, W. (2009, July 31). Payouts lavish despite bailout. *Los Angeles Times,* p. A1.

Hammer, K. (2009, October 14). Asian carp just one flop away from Great Lakes. *The Globe and Mail,* p. A3.

Hampson, R. (2013, March 12). Boss vs. you: The work-from-home tug of war. *USA Today,* pp. 1A, 2A.

Hampton, R. (2013, January 18). Can you forgive Lance Armstrong? *USA Today,* p. A1.

Hanna, S. T., Lester, P. B., & Vogelgesang, G. R. (2005). Moral leadership: Explicating the moral component of authentic leadership. In W. L. Gardner, B. J. Avolio, & F. O. Walumbwa (Eds.), *Authentic leadership theory and practice: Origins, effects and development* (pp. 43–81). Amsterdam: Elsevier.

Hansen, H., Ropo, A., & Sauer, E. (2007). Aesthetic leadership. *Leadership Quarterly, 18,* 544–560.

Harper, B., & Harper, A. (1992). *Succeeding as a self-directed work team.* Mohegan Lake, NY: MW Corporation.

Harrington, M. (2012, November 27). LIPA bill changes. *Newsday,* p. A05.

Harris, G. (2009, January 31). Peanut plant recall leads to criminal investigation. *The New York Times,* p. A17.

Harris, G. (2009, February 12). Peanut foods shipped before testing came in. *The New York Times,* p. A24.

Harris, G. (2013, January 14). For women in India, peril in many guises. *The International Herald Tribune,* p. 1.

Harris, J. (2009, October 16). Retail giant finds its green religion. *National Post,* p. FP12.

Harris, S., Smallen, J., & Mitchell, C. (2006, February 18). Katrina report spreads blame. *National Journal,* p. 38.

Hart, D. K. (1992). The moral exemplar in an organizational society. In T. L. Cooper & N. D. Wright (Eds.), *Exemplary public administrators: Character and leadership in government* (pp. 9–29). San Francisco: Jossey-Bass.

Hartocollis, A., & Chan, S. (2009, October 23). Flu vaccine requirement for health workers is lifted. *The New York Times,* p. A30.

Harvey, J. B. (1988). *The Abilene paradox and other meditations on management.* New York: Simon & Schuster.

Harvey, J. B. (1999). *How come every time I get stabbed in the back my fingerprints are on the knife?* San Francisco: Jossey-Bass.

Harvey, P., Martinko, M. J., & Gardner, W. L. (2006). Promoting authentic behavior in organizations: An attributional perspective. *Journal of Leadership & Organizational Studies, 12*(3), 1–11.

Hatcher, T. (2002). *Ethics and HRD: A new approach to leading responsible organizations.* Cambridge, MA: Perseus.

Hatzfeld, J. (2005). *Machete season: The killers in Rwanda speak* (L. Coverdale, Trans.). New York: Farrar, Straus and Giroux.

Hauerwas, S. (1981). *A community of character.* Notre Dame, IN: University of Notre Dame Press.

Hauser, M. D., Young, L., & Cushman, F. (2008). Reviving Rawls's linguistic analogy: Operative principles and the causal structure of moral actions. In W. Sinnott-Armstrong (Ed.), *Moral psychology: Vol. 2. The cognitive science of morality: Intuition and diversity* (pp. 107–144). Cambridge: MIT Press.

Hays-Thomas, R. (2004). Why now? The contemporary focus on managing diversity. In M. S. Stockdale & F. J. Crosby (Eds.), *The psychology and management of workplace diversity* (pp. 3–30). Malden, MA: Blackwell.

Hearit, K. M. (2006). *Crisis management by apology: Corporate response to allegations of wrongdoing.* Mahwah, NJ: Erlbaum.

Held, V. (2006). The ethics of care. In D. Copp (Ed.), *The Oxford handbook of ethical theory* (pp. 537–566). Oxford, England: Oxford University Press.

Herdt, T. (2012, January 4). Patagonia first in line to register as a "benefit corporation." *Ventura County Star.*

Hiestand, M. (2012, November 16). ESPN opens checkbook for college bowl rights. *USA Today,* p. 3C.

Higgs, M. (2009). The good, the bad and the ugly: Leadership and narcissism. *Journal of Change Management, 9,* 165–178.

Hinken, T. R., & Schriesheim, C. A. (1989). Development and

application of new scales to measure the French and Raven (1959) bases of social power. *Journal of Applied Psychology, 74,* 561–567.

Hodge, A. (2012, October 8). Khan praises anti-drone protest. *The Australian,* World, p. 9.

Hodgkinson, P. E., & Stewart, M. (1991). *Coping with catastrophe: A handbook of disaster management.* London: Routledge.

Hodgson, G. (2009, August 12). Eunice Kennedy Shriver; mental health campaigner who founded the Special Olympics. *The Independent,* Obituaries, p. 26.

Hofstede, G. (1984). *Culture's consequences.* Beverly Hills, CA: Sage.

Hofstede, G. (2001). Difference and danger: Cultural profiles of nations and limits to tolerance. In M. H. Albrecht (Ed.), *International HRM: Managing diversity in the workplace* (pp. 9–23). Oxford, England: Blackwell.

Hofstede, G., & Hofstede, G. J. (2005). *Cultures and organizations: Software of the mind.* London: McGraw-Hill.

Hogg, M. A., Knippenberg, D., & Rast, D. E. (2012). Intergroup leadership in organizations: Leading across group and organizational boundaries. *Academy of Management Review, 37,* 232–255.

Hollander, E. P. (1992). The essential interdependence of leadership and followership. *Current Directions in Psychological Science, 1,* 71–75.

Holmgren, J. R. (1998). Self-forgiveness and responsible moral agency. *Journal of Value Inquiry, 32,* 75–91.

Hood, J. N. (2003). The relationship of leadership style and CEO values to ethical practices in organizations. *Journal of Business Ethics, 43,* 263–273.

Hopen, D. (2002). Guiding corporate behavior: A leadership obligation, not a choice. *Journal for Quality & Participation, 25,* 15–19.

Hopper, T. (2012, October 23). Nurses fight for right to skip flu vaccination. *National Post,* p. A1.

Hornstein, H. A. (1996). *Brutal bosses and their prey.* New York: Riverhead.

Horwitz, S. (2012, November 10). Marijuana legality elicits confusion. *The Washington Post,* p. A03.

Hosmer, L. T. (1994). Strategic planning as if ethics mattered. *Strategic Management Journal, 15,* 17–34.

House, R. J., Hanges, P. J., Javidan, M., Dorfman, P. W., & Gupta, V. (Eds.). (2004). *Culture, leadership, and organizations: The GLOBE study of 62 societies.* Thousand Oaks, CA: Sage.

Howell, J., & Avolio, B. J. (1992). The ethics of charismatic leadership: Submission or liberation? *Academy of Management Executive, 6,* 43–54.

Howerton, J. (2012, December 27). NY paper broke no laws with gun owner map—but is it ever ethical to publish personal info to push an agenda? The Blaze. Retrieved from http://www.theblaze.com

Hubbartt, W. S. (1998). *The new battle over workplace privacy.* New York: AMACOM.

Huma, R., & Staurowsky, E. J. (2012). The price of poverty in big time college sport. National College Players Association. Retrieved from http://assets.usw.org/ncpa/The-Price-of-Poverty-in-Big-Time-College-Sport.pdf

Huma, R., Walters, T., & Staurowsky, E. J. (2009, March 26). Scholarship shortfall study reveals college athletes pay to play. National College Players Association, news release. Retrieved from http://www.ncpa.ow.org/releases-advisories?id=0009

Human Rights Watch. (2011, December 19). Q&A: U.S. targeted killings and international laws. *Africa News.*

Husted, B. W. (1999). Wealth, culture and corruption. *Journal of International Business Studies, 30,* 339–359.

Ilies, R., Hauserman, N., Schwochau, S., & Stibal, J.

(2003). Reported incidence rates of work-related sexual harassment in the United States: Using meta-analysis to explain reported rate disparities. *Personnel Psychology, 56,* 607–651.

Ilies, R., Morgeson, F. P., & Nahrgang, J. D. (2005). Authentic leadership and eudemonic well-being: Understanding leader–follower outcomes. *Leadership Quarterly, 16,* 373–394.

Inch, E. S., Warnick, B., & Endres, D. (2006). *Critical thinking and communication: The use of reason in argument* (5th ed.). Boston: Pearson.

Indian officials make excuses for rape. (2013, January 12). *The Toronto Star,* p. A4.

Infante, D. (1988). *Arguing constructively.* Prospect Heights, IL: Waveland.

Infante, D., & Rancer, A. (1996). Argumentativeness and verbal aggressiveness: A review of recent theory and research. In B. Burleson (Ed.), *Communication yearbook 19* (pp. 319–351). Thousand Oaks, CA: Sage.

Isserman, M. (2008, August 11). The descent of men; a different K2 drama. *The International Herald Tribune,* Opinion, p. 4.

Iversen, K. (2012). *Full body burden: Growing up in the nuclear shadow of Rocky Flats.* New York: Crown.

Jacobs, T. (2009, May). Morals authority. *Miller-McCune,* pp. 47–55.

James, H. S. (2000). Reinforcing ethical decision-making through organizational structure. *Journal of Business Ethics, 28,* 43–58.

James, K. (2008, May 24). Siemens' straight shooter. *The Business Times Singapore.*

James, S. A. (2007). *Universal human rights: Origins and development.* New York: LFB Scholarly Publications.

Janis, I. (1971, November). Groupthink: The problems of conformity. *Psychology Today,* pp. 271–279.

Janis, I. (1982). *Groupthink* (2nd ed.). Boston: Houghton Mifflin.

Janis, I. (1989). *Crucial decisions: Leadership in policymaking and crisis management.* New York: Free Press.

Janis, I., & Mann, L. (1977). *Decision making.* New York: Free Press.

Janover, M. (2005). The limits of forgiveness and the ends of politics. *Journal of Intercultural Studies, 26,* 221–235.

Jaramillo, F., Grisaffe, D. B., Chonko, L. B., & Roberts, J. A. (2009). Examining the impact of servant leadership on sales force performance. *Journal of Personal Selling & Sales Management, 29,* 257–275.

Jaramillo, F., Grisaffe, D. B., Chonko, L. B., & Roberts, J. A. (2009). Examining the impact of servant leadership on salesperson's turnover intention. *Journal of Personal Selling & Sales Management, 29,* 351–365

Javidan, M., & House, R. J. (2001). Cultural acumen for the global manager: Lessons from Project GLOBE. *Organizational Dynamics, 29,* 289–305.

Jehn, K. A. (1995). A multi-method examination of the benefits and detriments of intragroup conflict. *Administrative Science Quarterly, 40,* 256–282.

Jennings, M. M. (2006). *The seven signs of ethical collapse: How to spot moral meltdowns in companies . . . before it's too late.* New York: St. Martin's Press.

Jensen, J. V. (1996). Ethical tension points in whistleblowing. In J. A. Jaksa & M. S. Pritchard (Eds.), *Responsible communication: Ethical issues in business, industry, and the professions* (pp. 41–51). Cresskill, NJ: Hampton.

Johannesen, R. L. (1991). Virtue ethics, character, and political communication. In R. E. Denton (Ed.), *Ethical dimensions of political communication* (pp. 69–90). New York: Praeger.

Johannesen, R. L. (2002). *Ethics in human communication* (5th ed.). Prospect Heights, IL: Waveland.

Johannesen, R. L., Valde, K. S., & Whedbee, K. E. (2008). *Ethics in human communication* (6th ed.). Long Grove, IL: Waveland Press.

Johnson, C. E. (1997). A leadership journey to the East. *Journal of Leadership Studies, 4*(2), 82–88.

Johnson, C. E. (2000). Emerging perspectives in leadership ethics. *Proceedings of the International Leadership Association*, pp. 48–54.

Johnson, C. E. (2000). Taoist leadership ethics. *Journal of Leadership & Organizational Studies, 7*(1), 82–91.

Johnson, C. E. (2007). Best practices in ethical leadership. In J. A. Conger & R. E. Riggio (Eds.), *The practice of leadership: Developing the next generation of leaders* (pp. 150–171). San Francisco: Jossey-Bass.

Johnson, C. E. (2008). The rise and fall of Carly Fiorina: An ethical case study. *Journal of Leadership & Organizational Studies, 15,* 188–196.

Johnson, C. E. (2012). *Organizational ethics: A practical approach* (2nd ed.). Thousand Oaks, CA: Sage.

Johnson, C. E., & Hackman, M. Z. (1997). *Rediscovering the power of followership in the leadership communication text.* Paper presented at the annual convention of the National Communication Association, Chicago.

Johnson, C. E., Shelton, P. M., & Yates, L. (2012). Nice guys (and gals) finish first: Ethical leadership and organizational trust, satisfaction, and effectiveness. *International Leadership Journal, 4*(1), 3–19.

Johnson, D. W., & Johnson, F. P. (2000). *Joining together: Group theory and group skills* (7th ed.). Boston: Allyn & Bacon.

Johnson, D. W., & Johnson, R. T. (1989). *Cooperation and competition: Theory and research.* Edina, MN: Interaction.

Johnson, D. W., & Johnson, R. T. (2005). Training for cooperative group work. In M. A. West, D. Tjosvold, & K. G. Smith (Eds.), *The essentials of teamworking: International perspectives* (pp. 131–147). West Sussex, England: John Wiley.

Johnson, D. W., Maruyama, G., Johnson, R., Nelson, D., & Skon, L. (1981). Effects of cooperative, competitive, and individualistic goal structures on achievement: A meta-analysis. *Psychological Bulletin, 82,* 47–62.

Johnson, D. W., & Tjosvold, D. (1983). *Productive conflict management.* New York: Irvington.

Johnson, J. (1993). Functions and processes of inner speech in listening. In D. Wolvin & C. G. Coakley (Eds.), *Perspectives in listening* (pp. 170–184). Norwood, NJ: Ablex.

Johnson, J., & Orange, M. (2003). *The man who tried to buy the world: Jean-Marie Messier and Vivendi Universal.* New York: Portfolio.

Johnson, K. (2012, November 18). Counting the days till marijuana's legal. *The New York Times,* p. A20.

Johnson, M. (1993). *Moral imagination: Implications of cognitive science for ethics.* Chicago: University of Chicago Press.

Joint United Nations Programme on HIV/AIDS. (2012). *2012 UNAIDS report on the AIDS global epidemic.* Retrieved from http://www.unaids.org

Jones, D. (2012). Does servant leadership lead to greater customer focus and employee satisfaction? *Business Studies Journal, 4,* 21–35.

Jones, L. B. (1996). *The path: Creating your mission statement for work and for life.* New York: Hyperion.

Jones, P. E., & Roelofsma, P. H. M. P. (2000). The potential for social contextual and group biases in team decision-making: Biases, conditions and psychological mechanisms. *Ergonomics, 43,* 1129–1152.

Jones, T. M. (1991). Ethical decision making by individuals in organizations: An issue-contingent model. *Academy of Management Review, 15,* 366–395.

Jonsen, A. R., & Toulmin, S. (1988). *The abuse of casuistry:*

A history of moral reasoning. Berkeley: University of California Press.

Jonsson, P. (2011, December 23). Concord pandemonium: "Sneakerheads" flock to grab Air Jordans. *The Christian Science Monitor.*

Jonsson, P. (2012, September 12). Asian carp policy: Is it keeping Obama and Romney up at night? *The Christian Science Monitor.*

Jordan, P. J., & Troth, A. C. (2004). Managing emotions during team problem solving: Emotional intelligence and conflict resolution. *Human Performance, 17,* 195–218.

Jourdan, G. (1998). Indirect causes and effects in policy change: The Brent Spar case. *Public Administration, 76,* 713–770.

Judge, W. Q. (1999). *The leader's shadow: Exploring and developing executive character.* Thousand Oaks, CA: Sage.

Jurkiewicz, C. L., & Giacalone, R. A. (2004). A values framework for measuring the impact of workplace spirituality on organizational performance. *Journal of Business Ethics, 49,* 129–142.

Kahn, A. E., & Maxwell, D. J. (2008). Ethics in diversity management leadership. In S. A. Quatro & R. R. Sims (Eds.), *Executive ethics: Ethical dilemmas and challenges for the C-suite* (pp. 247–262). Charlotte, NC: Information Age.

Kalev, A., Dobbin, F., & Kelly, E. (2006). Best practices or best guesses? Assessing the efficacy of corporate affirmative action and diversity policies. *American Sociological Review, 71,* 589–617.

Kant, I. (1964). *Groundwork of the metaphysics of morals* (H. J. Ryan, Trans.). New York: Harper & Row.

Kanter, R. M. (1979, July–August). Power failure in management circuits. *Harvard Business Review,* pp. 65–75.

Kanungo, R. N. (2001). Ethical values of transactional and transformational leaders. *Canadian Journal of Administrative Sciences, 18,* 257–265.

Kanungo, R. N., & Conger, J. A. (1990). The quest for altruism in organizations. In S. Srivastra & D. L. Cooperrider (Eds.), *Appreciative management and leadership* (pp. 228–256). San Francisco: Jossey-Bass.

Kanungo, R. N., & Mendonca, M. (1996). *Ethical dimensions of leadership.* Thousand Oaks, CA: Sage.

Kaplan, B. (2012, August 29). Footloose and fanciful. *National Post,* p. AL8.

Karakas, F. (2010). Spirituality and performance in organizations: A literature review. *Journal of Business Ethics, 94,* 89–106.

Karau, S. J., & Williams, K. D. (1995). Social loafing: Research findings, implications, and future directions. *Current Directions in Psychological Science, 4,* 134–140.

Karau, S. J., & Williams, K. D. (2001). Understanding individual motivation in groups: The collective effort model. In M. E. Turner (Ed.), *Groups at work: Theory and research* (pp. 113–141). Mahwah, NJ: Erlbaum.

Karim, A. (2000, June 23). Globalization, ethics, and AIDS vaccines. *Science,* pp. 21–29.

Katz, D., Maccoby, N., Gurin, G., & Floor, L. (1951). *Productivity, supervision, and morale among railroad workers.* Ann Arbor: University of Michigan, Institute for Social Research.

Katz, F. E. (1993). *Ordinary people and extraordinary evil: A report on the beguilings of evil.* Albany: State University of New York Press.

Keating, M., Martin, G. S., Resick, C. J., & Dickson, M. W. (2007). A comparative study of the endorsement of ethical leadership in Ireland and the United States. *Irish Journal of Management, 28,* 5–30.

Keen, J. (2012, July 9). Stopping "aquatic hitchhikers." *USA Today,* p. 3A.

Keil, M., & Montealegre, R. (2000). Cutting your losses: Extricating your organization when a big project goes awry. *Sloan Management Review, 41,* 55–68.

Kekes, J. (1991). Moral imagination, freedom, and the humanities. *American Philosophical Quarterly, 28,* 101–111.

Kekes, J. (2005). *The roots of evil.* Ithaca, NY: Cornell University Press.

Kellerman, B. (2004). *Bad leadership: What it is, how it happens, why it matters.* Boston: Harvard Business School Press.

Kellerman, B. (2008). Bad leadership—and ways to avoid it. In J. V. Gallos (Ed.), *Business leadership* (2nd ed., pp. 423–432). San Francisco: Jossey-Bass.

Kellerman, B. (2008). *Followership: How followers are creating change and changing leaders.* Boston: Harvard Business School Press.

Kelley, R. (1992). *The power of followership.* New York: Doubleday/Currency.

Keltner, D., Langner, C. A., & Allison, M. L. (2006). Power and moral leadership. In D. L. Rhode (Ed.), *Moral leadership: The theory and practice of power, judgment, and policy* (pp. 177–194). San Francisco: Jossey-Bass.

Kennedy, D. (2004). *The dark side of virtue: Reassessing international humanitarianism.* Princeton, NJ: Princeton University Press.

Kernis, M. H. (2003). Toward a conceptualization of optimal self-esteem. *Psychological Inquiry, 14,* 1–26.

Kessler, E. H., & Bailey, J. R. (2007). Introduction: Understanding, applying, and developing organizational and managerial wisdom. In E. H. Kessler & J. R. Bailey (Eds.), *Handbook of organizational and managerial wisdom* (pp. xv–lxxiv). Thousand Oaks, CA: Sage.

Keys, T., & Malnight, T. (2013). *Corporate clout: The influence of the world's largest 100 economic entities.* Global Trends. Retrieved from http://www.globaltrends.com

Khuntia, R., & Suar, D. (2004). A scale to assess ethical leadership of Indian and public sector managers. *Journal of Business Ethics, 49,* 13–26.

Kickul, J. (2001). When organizations break their promises: Employee reactions to unfair processes and treatment. *Journal of Business Ethics, 29,* 289–307.

Kidder, R. M. (1995). *How good people make tough choices: Resolving the dilemmas of ethical living.* New York: Fireside.

Kidder, R. M. (2004). Foundation codes of ethics: Why do they matter, what are they, and how are they relevant to philanthropy? *New Decisions for Philanthropic Fundraising, 45,* 75–83.

Kidder, R. M. (2005). *Moral courage.* New York: William Morrow.

Kim, H.-W. (2011, December 19). Genocide and politicide alert: North Korea. *Genocide Watch.*

King, D., Case, C. J., & Premo, K. M. (2011). A mission statement analysis comparing the United States and three other English speaking countries. *Academy of Strategic Management Journal, 10,* Special Issue, 21–45.

King, S., Biberman, J., Robbins, L., & Nicol, D. M. (2007). Integrating spirituality into management education in academia and organizations: Origins, a conceptual framework, and current practices. In J. Biberman & M. D. Whitty (Eds.), *At work: Spirituality matters* (pp. 243–256). Scranton, PA: University of Scranton Press.

Kipnis, D. (1972). Does power corrupt? *Journal of Personality and Social Psychology, 24,* 33–41.

Kirkland, R. (2002). Self-fulfillment through selflessness: The moral teachings of the Daode Jing. In M. Barnhart (Ed.), *Varieties of ethical reflection: New directions for ethics in a global context* (pp. 21–48). Lanham, MD: Lexington Books.

Kiuchi, T., & Shireman, B. (2002). *What we learned in the rainforest: Business lessons from nature.* San Francisco: Berrett-Koehler.

Klatt, J., & Enright, R. D. (2009). Investigating the place of forgiveness with the Positive Youth Development paradigm.

Journal of Moral Education, 38, 35–52.

Klatt, J. S., & Enright, R. D. (2011). Initial validation of the unfolding forgiveness process in a natural environment. *Counseling and Values, 56,* 25–42.

Klenke, K. (2005). The internal theater of the authentic leader: Integrating cognitive, affective, conative and spiritual facets of authentic leadership. In W. L. Gardner, B. J. Avolio, & F. O. Walumbwa (Eds.), *Authentic leadership theory and practice: Origins, effects and development* (pp. 43–81). Amsterdam: Elsevier.

Kline, S. L., Simunich, B., & Weber, H. (2009). The use of equivocal messages in responding to corporate challenges. *Journal of Applied Communication Research, 37,* 40–58.

Knight, R. F., & Pretty, D. J. (1996). *The impact of catastrophes on shareholder value.* Oxford, England: Templeton College, University of Oxford.

Knapp, J. C. (2011). Rethinking ethics training: New approaches to enhance effectiveness. In R.R. Sims & W. I. Sauser (Eds.), *Experiences in teaching business ethics* (pp. 217–230). Charlotte, NC: Information Age.

Knobe, J. (2006). The concept of intentional action: A case study in the uses of folk psychology. *Philosophical Studies, 130,* 203–231.

Knobe, J., & Burra, A. (2006). The folk concepts of intention and intentional action: A cross-cultural study. *Journal of Cognition and Culture, 6,* 113–132.

Kohlberg, L. A. (1984). *The psychology of moral development: The nature and validity of moral stages* (Vol. 2). San Francisco: Harper & Row.

Kohlberg, L. A. (1986). A current statement on some theoretical issues. In S. Modgil & C. Modgil (Eds.), *Lawrence Kohlberg: Consensus and controversy* (pp. 485–546). Philadelphia: Palmer.

Kohler, N., Krolicki, K., Disavano, S., & Fuse, T. (2011, April 2). Wave predicted. *National Post,* p. A25.

Kolditz, T. A. (2005, Fall). The in extremis leader. *Leader to Leader,* pp. 6–18.

Kolditz, T. A. (2007). *In extremis leadership: Leading as if your life depended on it.* San Francisco: Jossey-Bass.

Kolditz, T. A., & Brazil, D. M. (2005). Authentic leadership in *in extremis* settings: A concept for extraordinary leaders in exceptional situations. In W. L. Gardner, B. J. Avolio, & F. O. Walumbwa (Eds.), *Authentic leadership theory and practice: Origins, effects and development* (pp. 345–356). Amsterdam: Elsevier.

Kolp, A., & Rea, P. (2006). *Leading with integrity: Character-based leadership.* Cincinnati, OH: AtomicDog.

Konrad, A. M. (2006). Leveraging workplace diversity in organizations. *Organization Management Journal, 3,* 164–189.

Koonce, R. (2001, December). Redefining diversity. *Training & Development,* pp. 22–28.

Kossek, E. E., Lobel, S. A., & Brown, J. (2006). Human resource strategies to manage workplace diversity: Examining the "business case." In A. M. Konrad, P. Prasad, & J. K. Pringle (Eds.), *Handbook of workplace diversity* (pp. 53–74). London: Sage.

Kotler, P., & Lee, N. (2005). *Corporate social responsibility: Doing the most good for your company and your cause.* Hoboken, NJ: John Wiley.

Kotlyar, I., & Karakowsky, L. (2006). Leading conflict? Linkages between leader behaviors and group conflict. *Small Group Research, 37,* 377–403.

Kotter, J. P. (1990). *A force for change: How leadership differs from management.* New York: Free Press.

Kouzes, J. M., & Posner, B. Z. (2003). *Credibility: How leaders gain and lose it, why people demand it.* San Francisco: Jossey-Bass.

Kouzes, J. M., & Posner, B. Z. (2012). *The leadership challenge*

(5th ed.). San Francisco: Jossey-Bass.

Krado, J. (2009). *Effective apology: Mending fences, building bridges, and restoring trust.* San Francisco: Berrett-Koehler.

Krakauer, J. (2009). *Where men win glory: The odyssey of Pat Tillman.* New York: Doubleday.

Kramer, R. M. (2010). Collective trust within organizations: Conceptual foundations and empirical insights. *Corporate Reputation Review, 13,* 82–97.

Kramer, R. M., & Tyler, T. R. (Eds.). (1996). *Trust in organizations: Frontiers of theory and research.* Thousand Oaks, CA: Sage.

Kriegel, M. (2009, July 25). NCAA video game stance is pure hypocrisy. Fox Sports. Retrieved from http://msn.foxsports.com/collegefootball/story/NCAA-video-game-stance-is-pure-hypocrisy?r_src=ramp

Kristof, N. D. (2010, June 27). Death by gadget. *The New York Times,* p. WK11.

Kulish, N., & Donadio, R. (2012, May 15). Risk of Greek euro exit rattles markets, but hints of more talks emerge. *The New York Times,* p. A4.

Kung, H. (1998). *A global ethic for global politics and economics.* New York: Oxford University Press.

Kung, H. (1999). A global ethic in an age of globalization. In

G. Enderle (Ed.), *International business ethics: Challenges and approaches* (pp. 19–127). Notre Dame, IN: University of Notre Dame Press.

Kung, H. (2003). An ethical framework for the global market economy. In J. H. Dunning (Ed.), *Making globalization good: The moral challenges of global capitalism* (pp. 146–158). Oxford, England: Oxford University Press.

Ladkin, D. (2006). The enchantment of the charismatic leader: Charisma reconsidered as aesthetic encounter. *Leadership, 2,* 165–179.

Ladkin, D. (2008). Leading beautifully: How mastery congruence and purpose create the aesthetic of embodied leadership practice. *Leadership Quarterly, 19,* 31–41.

Ladkin, D. (2010). *Rethinking leadership: A new look at old leadership questions.* Cheltenham, England: Edward Elgar.

LaFasto, F., & Larson, C. (2012). *The humanitarian leader in each of us: Seven choices that shape a socially responsible life.* Thousand Oaks, CA: Sage.

LaFraniere, S., & Barboza, D. (2011). China, mindful of Arab revolts, tightens grip on communications. *The International Herald Tribune,* News, p. 5.

Lamb, C. (2011, April 24). Beautiful fantasy of a fallen

hero. *The Sunday Times,* Features, pp. 2–3.

Lammers, J., Stoker, J. I., Pollman, M., & Stapel, D. A. (2011). Power increases infidelity among men and women. *Psychological Science, 22,* 1191–1197.

Lance Armstrong & Oprah Winfrey: Part two interview transcript. BBC. Retrieved from http://www.bbc.co.uk

Lance Armstrong's interview with Oprah Winfrey: The transcript. (2013, January 18). *The Telegraph.* Retrieved from http://www.telegraph.co.uk.

Langer, E. J. (1989). *Mindfulness.* Reading, MA: Addison-Wesley.

Langer, E. J. (1997). *The power of mindful learning.* Reading, MA: Addison-Wesley.

La Pine, J. A. (2005). Adaptation of teams in response to unforeseen change: Effects of goal difficulty and team composition in terms of cognitive ability and goal orientation. *Journal of Applied Psychology, 90,* 1153–1167.

Lapsley, D. K., & Hill, P. L. (2008). On dual processing and heuristic approaches to moral cognition. *Journal of Moral Education, 37,* 313–332.

Larrabee, M. J. (Ed.). (1993). *An ethic of care: Feminist and interdisciplinary perspectives.* New York: Routledge.

Layton, L. (2009, January 29). Every peanut product from Ga. Plant recalled. *The Washington Post,* p. A01.

Layton, L. (2009, April 3). FDA hasn't intensified inspections at peanut facilities, despite illness. *The Washington Post,* p. A04.

Layton, L. (2009, May 28). House calls for closer watch on food supply. *The Washington Post,* p. A17.

Lazare, A. (2004). *On apology.* Oxford, England: Oxford University Press.

Lazarus, H., & McManus, T. (2006). Transparency guru: An interview with Tom McManus. *Journal of Management Development, 25,* 923–936.

Lee, J., Woeste, J. H., & Heath, R. L. (2007). Getting ready for crises: Strategic excellence. *Public Relations Review, 33,* 334–336.

Leets, L. (2001). Interrupting the cycle of moral exclusion: A communication contribution to social justice research. *Journal of Applied Social Psychology, 31,* 1859–1891.

Leonnig, C. D., & Nakamura, D. (2012, June 16). Third supervisor involved in Secret Service prostitution scandal. *The Washington Post,* p. A05.

Leroy, H., Palanski, M. E., & Simons, T. (2012). Authentic leadership and behavioral integrity as drivers of follower commitment and performance.

Journal of Business Ethics, 107, 255–264.

Leslie, L. Z. (2000). *Mass communication ethics: Decision making in postmodern culture.* Boston: Houghton Mifflin.

Levy, A. C., & Paludi, M. A. (2002). *Workplace sexual harassment* (2nd ed.). Upper Saddle River, NJ: Prentice Hall.

Levy, S. (2006, February 13). Google and the China syndrome. *Newsweek,* p. 14.

Lewis, C. S. (1946). *The great divorce.* New York: Macmillan.

Lewis, D., Medland, J., Malone, S., Murphy, M., Reno, K., & Vaccaro, G. (2006). Appreciative leadership: Defining effective leadership methods. *Organization Development Journal, 24*(1), 87–100.

Lipman-Blumen, J. (2005). *The allure of toxic leaders: Why we follow destructive bosses and corrupt politicians—and how we can survive them.* Oxford, England: Oxford University Press.

Lisman, C. D. (1996). *The curricular integration of ethics: Theory and practice.* Westport, CT: Praeger.

Livesey, S. M. (2003). Organizing and leading the grassroots: An interview with Lois Gibbs, Love Canal Homeowners Association activist. *Organization, 16,* 448–503.

London, B. (2012, December 12). Radio personalities apologize for prank call to duchess's hospital. CNN. Retrieved from http://www .cnn.com

Lopez, S. J., Rasmussen, H. N, Skorupski, W. P., Koetting, K., Petersen, S. E., & Yang, Y. (2010). Folk conceptualizations of courage. In C. L. S. Pury & S. J. Lopez (Eds.), *The psychology of courage: Modern research on an ancient virtue* (pp. 23–45). Washington, DC: American Psychological Association.

Lovett, K., & Blain, G. (2012, November 14). Dolts jolted LIPA big bolts as gov. sets up probe. *Daily News,* p. 10.

Lowe, K. B., & Kroeck, K. G. (1996). Effectiveness correlates of transformational and transactional leadership: A meta-analytic review. *Leadership Quarterly, 7,* 385–425.

Lowenheim N. (2009). A haunted past: Requesting forgiveness for wrongdoing in international relations. *Review of International Studies, 35,* 531–555.

Lubit, R. (2002). The long-term organizational impact of destructively narcissistic managers. *Academy of Management Executive, 18,* 127–183.

Ludwig, D. C., & Longnecker, C. O. (1993). The Bathsheba syndrome: The ethical failure of successful leaders. *Journal of Business Ethics, 12,* 265–273.

Luo, Y. (2004). An organizational perspective of corruption. *Management and Organization Review, 1,* 119–154.

Lydersen, K. (2012, January 1). Study of waterways stirs debate on roles in the region's future. *The New York Times,* p. 25A.

Maak, T. (2007). Responsible leadership, stakeholder engagement, and the emergence of social capital. *Journal of Business Ethics, 74,* 329–343.

Maak, T., & Pless, N. M. (2006). Responsible leadership: A relational approach. In T. Maak & N. M. Press (Eds.), *Responsible leadership* (pp. 33–53). London: Routledge.

Maak, T., & Pless, N. M. (2006). Responsible leadership in a stakeholder society: A relational perspective. *Journal of Business Ethics, 66,* 99–115.

Maak, T., & Pless, N. M. (2009). Business leaders as citizens of the world: Advancing humanism on a global scale. *Journal of Business Ethics, 88,* 537–550.

Maas, A., & Clark, R. D. (1984). Hidden impact of minorities: Fifteen years of minority influence research. *Psychological Bulletin, 95,* 428–445.

Maas, K. C., & Levs, J. (2012, December 27). Newspaper sparks outrage for publishing names, addresses of gun permit holders. CNN. Retrieved from http://www.cnn.com

Maathai, W. (2004). *The Green Belt Movement: Sharing the approach and the experience.* New York: Lantern Books.

Maathai, W. (2007). *Unbowed.* New York: Anchor Books.

MacIntyre, A. (1984). *After virtue: A study in moral theory* (2nd ed.). Notre Dame, IN: University of Notre Dame Press.

Macintyre, B. (2011, October 11). "Legalised" killing puts the world in danger. *The Times.*

Macur, J. (2012, August 24). Armstrong ends fight against doping charges. *The New York Times,* p. A1.

Macur, J. (2012, August 24). Questions and answers on the Armstrong doping case. *The New York Times,* p. A1.

Macur, J. (2013, January 17). What to ask after years of denials. *The New York Times,* p. B15.

Macur, J. (2013, January 18). Confessing, but continuing to fight. *The New York Times,* p. B11.

Macur, J., & Austen, I. (2013, January 19). After the tears, some questions remain unanswered. *The New York Times,* p. D2.

Magnay, J. (2013, January 13). Lance Armstrong gave "weasel answers" in interview with Oprah Winfrey. *The Telegraph.* Retrieved from http://www.telegraph.co.uk

Make flu shots mandatory for health-care workers. (2012, November 3). *The Gazette* (Montreal), p. B6.

Making the food supply safer. (2009, August 10). *The Oregonian,* p. A10.

Mallon, T. (1997, June 15). In the blink of an eye [review of *The diving bell and the butterfly,* by J.-D. Bauby]. *The New York Times.* Retrieved from http://www.nytimes.com/books/97/06/15/reviews/970615.mallon.html

Manz, C. C., & Neck, C. P. (1995). Teamthink: Beyond the groupthink syndrome in self-managing work teams. *Journal of Managerial Psychology, 10*(1), 7–15.

Manz, C. C., & Sims, H. P. (1989). *Superleadership: Leading others to lead themselves.* Upper Saddle River, NJ: Prentice Hall.

Mara, J. (2008, January 17). Patagonia CEO turns retailers green. *Contra Costa Times.*

Marek, A. C. (2006, February 27). A post-Katrina public flaying. *U.S. News & World Report,* pp. 62–64.

Margolis, J. (2006). Introduction: Pragmatism, retrospective and prospective. In J. R. Shook & J. Margolis (Eds.), *A companion to pragmatism* (pp. 1–9). Malden, MA: Blackwell.

Marquand, R. (2011, July 22). The metamorphosis of "Murdochgate." *The Christian Science Monitor.*

Marquand, R. (2012, February 13). Murdoch media crisis deepens with five new arrests. *The Christian Science Monitor.*

Marquand, R. (2012, July 24). Phone hacking scandal: Two UK media leaders charged with conspiracy. *The Christian Science Monitor.*

Marrone, J. A. (2010). Team boundary spanning: A multilevel review of past research and proposals for the future. *Journal of Management, 36,* 911–940.

Martin, C. E., & Cary, J. (2011, April 24). Greg Mortenson and our false ideas about social change. *The Christian Science Monitor.*

Martin, G. S., Resick, C. J., Keating, M. A., & Dickson, M. W. (2009). Ethical leadership across cultures: A comparative analysis of German and US perspectives. *Business Ethics: A European Review, 18,* 127–144.

Martin, J. (2011, February 7). Can legal use of medical marijuana get you fired? State supreme court to decide. *Seattle Times.*

Martin, J. (2012, May 25). Clothier's products all come in green. *Los Angeles Times,* p. B1.

Martin, J. (2012, August 22). $300 sneaker rankles some. *USA Today,* p. 1C.

Martin, J. (2012, November 17). The battle is on: I-502 vs. drug-free policies at work. *Seattle Times.*

Martin, J., & Powers, M. E. (1983). Truth or corporate propaganda: The value of a good story. In L. R. Pondy, P. J. Frost, G. Morgan, & T. C. Dandridge (Eds.), *Organizational symbolism* (pp. 93–107). Greenwich, CT: JAI Press.

Martin, K. D., & Cullen, J. B. (2006). Continuities and extensions of ethical climate theory: A meta-analytic review. *Journal of Business Ethics, 69,* 175–194.

Martin, R. (2009, September 17). Health care staff: Vaccinate thyself. *St. Petersburg Times,* p. 1A.

Martin, R., & Hewstone, M. (Eds.). (2010). *Minority influence and innovations: Antecedents, processes and consequences* (pp. 365–394). Hoboken, NJ: Psychology Press.

Mascia, J. (2010, August 29). Medical use of marijuana costs some a paycheck. *The New York Times,* p. A14.

Mathews, M. C. (1990). Codes of ethics: Organizational behavior and misbehavior. In W. C. Frederick & L. E. Preston (Eds.), *Business ethics: Research issues and*

empirical studies (pp. 99–122). Greenwich, CT: JAI Press.

Matteson, J. A., & Irving, J. A. (2006). Servant versus self-sacrificial leadership: A behavioral comparison of two follower-oriented leadership theories. *International Journal of Leadership Studies, 2,* 36–51.

Maugh, T. H., & Engel, M. (2009, February 7). FDA says firm lied about peanut butter. *Los Angeles Times,* p. A1.

May, D. R., Chan, A. Y. L., Hodges, T. D., & Avolio, B. J. (2003). Developing the moral component of authentic leadership. *Organizational Dynamics, 32,* 247–260.

May, D. R., & Pauli, K. P. (2002). The role of moral intensity in ethical decision-making: A review and investigation of moral recognition, evaluation, and intention. *Business & Society, 41,* 84–117.

Mayers, D., Bardes, M., & Piccolo, R. F. (2008). Do servant-leaders help satisfy follower needs? An organizational justice perspective. *European Journal of Work and Organizational Psychology, 17,* 180–197.

Mazzetti, M., & Shane, S. (2013, March 22). As new drone policy is weighed, few practical effects are seen. *The New York Times,* p. A11.

McCabe, D., & Trevino, L. K. (1993). Academic dishonesty: Honor codes and other contextual influences. *Journal of Higher Education, 64,* 522–569.

McCauley, C. D., & Van Velsor, E. (Eds.). (2004). *The Center for Creative Leadership handbook of leadership development* (2nd ed.). San Francisco: Jossey-Bass.

McCullough, M. E., Pargament, K. I., & Thoresen, C. E. (2000). The psychology of forgiveness: History, conceptual issues, and overview. In M. E. McCullough, K. I. Pargament, & C. E. Thoresen (Eds.), *Forgiveness: Theory, research, and practice* (pp. 1–14). New York: Guilford.

McCullough, M. E., Sandage, S. J., & Worthington, E. L. (1997). *To forgive is human: How to put your past in the past.* Downers Grove, IL: InterVarsity Press.

McElhatton, J. (2012, June 19). Alcohol plays role in reports involving the Secret Service. *The Washington Times,* p. A1.

McFarlin, D. B., & Sweeney, P. D. (2010). The corporate reflecting pool: Antecedents and consequences of narcissism in executives. In B. Schyns & T. Hansbrough (Eds.), *When leadership goes wrong: Destructive leadership, mistakes, and ethical failures* (pp. 247–284). Charlotte, NC: Information Age.

McGeough, P. (2012, July 22). When charity bites the hand that feeds it. *The Sun Herald.*

McKendall, M., DeMarr, B., & Jones-Rikkers, C. (2002). Ethical compliance programs and corporate illegality: Testing the assumptions of the corporate sentencing guidelines. *Journal of Business Ethics, 37,* 367–383.

McKenna, F. P. (1993). It won't happen to me: Unrealistic optimism or illusion of control? *British Journal of Psychology, 84,* 39–50.

McLaughlin, M. (2012, December 8). Kate hospital prank call nurse found dead. *The Scotsman,* p. 1.

McNamara, G., Moon, H., & Bromiley, P. (2002). Banking on commitment: Intended and unintended consequences of an organization's attempt to attenuate escalation of commitment. *Academy of Management Journal, 45,* 443–452.

McNeil, D. G., & Zrack, K. (2009, September 21). New York health care workers resist flu vaccine rule. *The New York Times,* p. A18.

McVea, J. F. (2007). Constructing good decisions in ethically charged situations: The role of dramatic rehearsal. *Journal of Business Ethics, 70,* 375–390.

McVea, J. F. (2008). Ethics and pragmatism: John Dewey's deliberative approach. In T. Donaldson & P. H. Werhane (Eds.), *Ethical issues in business: A philosophical approach* (8th ed., pp. 89–100). Upper

Saddle River, NJ: Pearson Prentice Hall.

McVeigh, K. (2012, November 13). Meningitis outbreak: Pharmacy flagged by FDA as early as 2003. *The Guardian.*

Mehta, S., & Pillay, R. (2011). Revisiting servant leadership: An empirical study in Indian context. *Journal of Contemporary Management Research, 5*(2), 24–41.

Meilander, G. (1986). Virtue in contemporary religious thought. In R. J. Neuhaus (Ed.), *Virtue: Public and private* (pp. 7–30). Grand Rapids, MI: Eerdmans.

Melchar, D. E., & Bosco, S. M. (2010). Achieving high organization performance through servant leadership. *Journal of Business Inquiry, 9,* 74–88.

Mendoza, D. (2013, February 27). Yahoo work-from-home policy riles workers everywhere. CNN Tech. Retrieved from http://www.cnn.com/TECH

The mess that the army has made—Myanmar. (2005, July 23). *The Economist,* Special Report.

Messick, D. M., & Bazerman, M. H. (1996, Winter). Ethical leadership and the psychology of decision making. *Sloan Management Review, 37*(2), 9–23.

Metzger, M., Dalton, D. R., & Hill, J. W. (1993). The

organization of ethics and the ethics of organizations: The case for expanded organizational ethics audits. *Business Ethics Quarterly, 3,* 27–43.

Michaelson, A. (2009). *The foreclosure of America: The inside story of the rise and fall of Countrywide Home Loans, the mortgage crisis, and the default of the American dream.* New York: Berkley Books.

Milgram, S. (1965). Some conditions of obedience and disobedience to authority. *Human Relations, 18,* 57–76.

Milgram redux. (2008, September). *Psychologist,* p. 478.

Military injustice on sexual assault. (2013, March 14). *Newsday.*

Milkman, K. L., Chugh, D., & Bazerman, M. H. (2008). *How can decision-making be improved?* Harvard Business School Working Paper 08-102.

Miller, N. (2012, July 15). Compulsory jabs not just a shot in the dark. *Sunday Age* (Melbourne), Extra, p. 12.

Mirvis, P. H. (1997). "Soul work" in organizations. *Organization Science, 8,* 193–206.

Mitchell, C. (2003). *International business ethics: Combining ethics and profits in global business.* Novato, CA: World Trade Press.

Mitchell, S. (Trans.). (1988). *Tao te ching: A new English version.* New York: Harper Perennial.

Mitroff, I. I. (2005). *Why some companies emerge stronger and better from a crisis.* New York: AMACOM.

Mitroff, I. I., & Alpsaian, M. C. (2003, April). Preparing for evil. *Harvard Business Review,* pp. 109–115.

Mitroff, I. I., & Anagnos, G. (2001). *Managing crises before they happen: What every executive and manager needs to know about crisis management.* New York: American Management Association.

Mitroff, I. I., Pearson, C. M., & Harrington, L. K. (1996). *The essential guide to managing corporate crises: A step-by-step handbook for surviving major catastrophes.* New York: Oxford University Press.

Moll, J., de Oliveira-Souza, R., Zahn, R., & Grafman, J. (2008). The cognitive neuroscience of moral emotions. In W. Sinnott-Armstrong (Ed.), *Moral psychology: Vol. 3. The neuroscience of morality: Emotion, brain disorders, and development* (pp. 1–17). Cambridge: MIT Press.

Monin, B., Pizarro, D. A., & Beer, J. S. (2007). Deciding versus reacting: Conceptions of moral judgment and the reason–affect debate. *Review of General Psychology, 11,* 99–111.

Monin, B., Pizarro, D. A., & Beer, J. S. (2007). Reason and emotion in moral judgment: Different prototypes lead to different theories. In K. D. Vohs, R. F. Baumeister, & G. Lowenstein (Eds.), *Do emotions help or hurt decision making? A hedgefoxian perspective* (pp. 219–244). New York: Russell Sage Foundation.

Moore, C., Detert, J. R., Trevino, L. K., Baker, V. L., & Mayer, D. M. (2012). Why employees do bad things: Moral disengagement and unethical organizational behavior. *Personnel Psychology, 65,* 1–48.

Moore, E. C. (1961). *American pragmatism: Peirce, James and Dewey.* Westport CT: Greenwood Press.

Moorhead, G., Neck, C. P., & West, M. S. (1998). The tendency toward defective decision making within self-managing teams: The relevance of groupthink for the 21st century. *Organizational Behavior and Human Decision Processes, 73,* 327–351.

Moorhead, J. (2007, May 15). Milking it. *The Guardian,* p. 8.

Mor Barak, M. E. (2011). *Managing diversity: Toward a globally inclusive workplace* (2nd ed.). Thousand Oaks, CA: Sage.

Morgan, D. (2009, August 16). Democratic dissenters. *The Oregonian,* p. D5.

Morris, J. A., Brotheridge, C. M., & Urbanski, J. C.

(2005). Bringing humility to leadership: Antecedents and consequences of leader humility. *Human Relations, 58,* 1323–1350.

Morrison, A. M. (1996). *The new leaders: Guidelines on leadership diversity in America.* San Francisco: Jossey-Bass.

Morrow, L. (2003). *Evil: An investigation.* New York: Basic Books.

Mortenson, G. (2009). *Stones into schools: Promoting peace with books, not bombs, in Afghanistan and Pakistan.*

Mortenson, G., & Relin, D. O. (2006). *Three cups of tea: One man's mission to promote peace . . . one school at a time.* New York: Penguin Group.

Moscovici, S., Mucchi-Faina, A., & Maass, A. (Eds.). (1994). *Minority influence.* Chicago: Nelson-Hall.

Moscovici, S., Mugny, G., & Van Avermaet, E. (Eds.). (1985). *Perspectives on minority influence.* Cambridge, England: Cambridge University Press.

Moses, A. (2012, December 23). Privacy concern as apps share data from kids left to their own devices. *Sunday Age* (Melbourne, Australia), News, p. 3.

Moss, M. (2009, February 9). Peanut case shows holes in food safety net. *The New York Times,* p. A1.

Moss, M., & Martin, A. (2009, March 6). Food safety

problems elude private inspectors. *The New York Times,* p. A1.

Moutet, A. (2011, May 7). "I love women, et alors?" *The Daily Telegraph,* p. A3.

Moxley, R. S., & Pulley, M. L. (2004). Hardships. In C. D. McCauley & E. Van Velsor (Eds.), *The Center for Creative Leadership handbook of leadership development* (2nd ed., pp. 183–203). San Francisco: Jossey-Bass.

Mudhani, A. (2013, March 23). Obama: New Secret Service director breaking the mold. *USA Today.*

Mumford, M. D., Gessner, T. L., Connelly, M. S., O'Conner, J. A., & Clifton, T. (1993). Leadership and destructive acts: Individual and situational influences. *Leadership Quarterly, 4,* 115–147.

Murphy, J. G. (2003). *Getting even: Forgiveness and its limits.* Oxford, England: Oxford University Press.

Musekura, C. (2010). *An assessment of contemporary models of forgiveness.* New York: Peter Lang.

Muzaffar, C. (2002). Conclusion. In P. F. Knitter & C. Muzaffar (Eds.), *Subverting greed: Religious perspectives on the global economy* (pp. 154–172). Maryknoll, NY: Orbis.

NAFDAC warns violators of BMS international code (2007, August 7). *Africa News.*

Nanus, B. (1992). *Visionary leadership.* San Francisco: Jossey-Bass.

Narvaez, D. (2006). Integrative ethical education. In M. Killen & J. Smetana (Eds.), *Handbook of moral development* (pp. 717–728). Mahwah, NJ: Erlbaum.

Narvaez, D., & Lapsley, D. K. (2005). The psychological foundations of everyday morality and moral expertise. In D. K. Lapsley & F. C. Power (Eds.), *Character psychology and character education* (pp. 140–165). Notre Dame, IN: University of Notre Dame Press.

Nash, L. L. (1989). Ethics without the sermon. In K. R. Andrews (Ed.), *Ethics in practice: Managing the moral corporation* (pp. 243–257). Boston: Harvard Business School Press.

Nash, L. L. (1990). *Good intentions aside: A manager's guide to resolving ethical problems.* Boston: Harvard Business School Press.

Navarick, D. J. (2009). Reviving the Milgram obedience paradigm in the era of informed consent. *Psychological Record, 59,* 155–170.

Neck, C. P., & Manz, C. C. (2010). *Mastering self-leadership: Empowering yourself for personal excellence* (5th ed.). Upper Saddle River, NJ: Prentice Hall.

Nemeth, C. (1994). The value of minority dissent. In

S. Moscovici, A. Mucchi-Faina, & A. Maass (Eds.), *Minority influence* (pp. 3–15). Chicago: Nelson-Hall.

Nemeth, C. (1995). Dissent, group process and creativity: The contribution of minority influence research. In E. Lawler (Ed.), *Advances in group processes* (Vol. 2, pp. 57–75). Greenwich, CT: JAI Press.

Nemeth, C., & Chiles, C. (1986). Modeling courage: The role of dissent in fostering independence. *European Journal of Social Psychology, 18,* 275–280.

Neubert, M. J., Carlson, D. S., Kacmar, K. M., Roberts, J. A., & Chonko, L. B. (2009). The virtuous influence of ethical leadership behavior: Evidence from the field. *Journal of Business Ethics, 90,* 157–170.

Neuman, W. (2011, September 28). Deaths rise in outbreak of listeria. *The New York Times,* p. B1.

Nichols, M. L., & Day, V. E. (1982). A comparison of moral reasoning of groups and individuals on the "Defining Issues Test." *Academy of Management Journal, 24,* 21–28.

Nielsen, R. P., & Dufresne, R. (2005). Can ethical organizational character be stimulated and enabled? "Upbuilding" dialog as crisis management method. *Journal of Business Ethics, 57,* 311–326.

Ninan, R. (2012, April 28). Secret Service scandal. *World News Saturday* (ABC), p. 1.

Nobles, M. (2008). *The politics of official apologies.* Cambridge, England: Cambridge University Press.

Nocera, J. (2011, December 30). Let's start paying college athletes. *The New York Times.* Retrieved from http://www.nytimes.com

Noddings, N. (2003). *Caring: A feminine approach to ethics and moral education.* Berkeley: University of California Press.

Nye, J. S. (2008). *The powers to lead.* Oxford, England: Oxford University Press.

O'Brien, K. J. (2012, December 8). Dismayed at Google's privacy policy, European group is weighing censure. *The New York Times,* p. B3.

O'Fallon, M. J., & Butterfield, K. D. (2005). A review of the empirical ethical decision-making literature: 1996–2003. *Journal of Business Ethics, 59,* 375–413.

Olmsted, K. S. (2009). *Real enemies: Conspiracy theories and American democracy, World War I to 9/11.* Oxford, England: Oxford University Press.

150,000 N. Koreans incarcerated in Soviet-style gulag: Report. (2012, April 11). *Korea Times.*

Onstad, K. (2013, March 1). Yahoo for you, boss. What about progress? *The Globe and Mail,* p. L2.

Opotow, S. (1990). Deterring moral exclusion. *Journal of Social Issues, 46*(1), 173–182.

Opotow, S. (1990). Moral exclusion and injustice: An introduction. *Journal of Social Issues, 46*(1), 1–20.

Opotow, S. (2007). Moral exclusion and torture: The ticking bomb scenario and the slippery ethical slope. *Peace and Conflict: Journal of Peace Psychology, 13,* 457–461.

Opotow, S., Gerson, J., & Woodside, S. (2005). From moral exclusion to moral inclusion: Theory for teaching peace. *Theory Into Practice 44,* 303–318.

Opotow, S., & Weiss, L. (2000). Denial and the process of moral exclusion in environmental conflict. *Journal of Social Issues, 56,* 475–490.

O'Reilly, C., & Matussek, K. (2008, December 16). Siemens settles bribery cases. *The Washington Post,* p. D2.

Organ, D. W. (1988). *Organizational citizenship behavior: The good soldier syndrome.* Lexington, MA: Lexington Books.

Osswald, S., Greitemeyer, T., Fischer, P., & Frey, D. (2010). What is moral courage? Definition, explication, and classification of a complex construct. In C. L. S. Pury & S. J. Lopez (Eds.), *The psychology of courage: Modern* research on an ancient virtue (pp. 149–164). Washington, DC: American Psychological Association

Oswick, C. (2009). Burgeoning workplace spirituality? A textual analysis of momentum and directions. *Journal of Management, Spirituality & Religion, 6,* 15–25.

Otken, A., & Cenkci, T. (2012). The impact of paternalistic leadership on ethical climate: The moderating role of trust in leader. *Journal of Business Ethics, 108,* 525–536.

Oum, R., & Lieberman, D. (2007). Emotion is cognition: An information-processing view of the mind. In K. D. Vohs, R. F. Baumeister, & G. Lowenstein (Eds.), *Do emotions help or hurt decision making? A hedgefoxian perspective* (pp. 133–154). New York: Russell Sage Foundation.

Owner won't talk. (2009, February 12). *Newsday,* p. A08.

Pacanowsky, M. E., & O'Donnell-Trujillo, N. (1983). Organizational communication as cultural performance. *Communication Monographs, 5,* 126–147.

Padilla, A., Hogan, R., & Kaiser, R. B. (2007). The toxic triangle: Destructive leaders, susceptible followers, and conducive environments. *Leadership Quarterly, 18,* 176–194.

Pagan, N. O. (2008). Configuring the moral

self: Aristotle and Dewey. *Foundations of Science, 13,* 239–250.

Paine, L. S. (1996, March–April). Managing for organizational integrity. *Harvard Business Review,* pp. 106–117.

Paine, L. S., Deshpandé, R., Margolis, J. D., & Bettcher, K. E. (2005, December). Up to code: Does your company meet world-class standards? *Harvard Business Review,* pp. 122–133.

Palanski, M. E., & Yammarino, F. J. (2007). Integrity and leadership: A multi-level conceptual framework. *Leadership Quarterly, 20,* 405–420.

Palmer, P. (1996). Leading from within. In L. C. Spears (Ed.), *Insights on leadership: Service, stewardship, spirit, and servant-leadership* (pp. 197–208). New York: John Wiley.

Panchak, P. (2002). Time for a triple bottom line. *Industry Week,* p. 7.

Park, A. (2009, October 19). It's a jab or your job. *Time,* p. 55.

Park, G., & DeShon, R. P. (2010). A multilevel model of minority opinion expression and team decision-making effectiveness. *Journal of Applied Psychology, 95,* 824–853.

Park, R. (2012, November 24). Genocide and crimes of humanity ongoing in North Korea. *Forbes.*

Parker, C. F. (2011). The purpose, functions, and ethical dimensions of postcrisis investigations: The case of the 9/11 Commission. In L. Svedin (Ed.), *Ethics and crisis management* (pp. 183–198). Charlotte NC: Information Age.

The party, the people and the power of cyber-talk. (2006, April 29). *The Economist,* pp. 27–30.

Patel-Predd, P. (2009, January). The all-seeing employer. *IEEE Spectrum,* p. 23.

Pauchant, T. C., & Mitroff, I. I. (1992). *Transforming the crisis-prone organization: Preventing individual, organizational, and environmental tragedies.* San Francisco: Jossey-Bass.

Paul, J., & Strbiak, C. A. (1997). The ethics of strategic ambiguity. *Journal of Business Communication, 34,* 149–159.

Paulus, D. L., & Williams, K. M. (2002). The dark triad of personality: Narcissism, Machiavellianism, and psychopathy. *Journal of Research in Personality, 36,* 556–563.

Pearce, M. (2012, November 11). Unlikely allies, arguments lead voters to legalize pot. *Los Angeles Times,* p. A22.

Pearson, C. M., & Judith, A. C. (1998). Reframing crisis management. *Academy of Management Review 23,* 59–71.

Pearson, C. M., & Porath, C. L. (2004). On incivility, its impact and directions for future research. In R. W. Griffin & A. M. O'Leary-Kelly (Eds.), *The dark side of organizational behavior* (pp. 131–158). San Francisco: Jossey-Bass.

Pearson, C. M., & Porath, C. L. (2005). On the nature, consequences and remedies of workplace incivility: No time for "nice"? Think again. *Academy of Management Executive, 19,* 7–18.

Pearson, G. (1995). *Integrity in organizations: An alternative business ethic.* London: McGraw-Hill.

Peck, M. S. (1983). *People of the lie: The hope for healing human evil.* New York: Touchstone.

Pellegrini, E. K., & Scandura, T. A. (2008). Paternalistic leadership: A review and agenda for future research. *Journal of Management, 34,* 566–593.

Pellegrini, E. K., Scandura, T. A., & Jayaraman, V. (2010). Cross-generalizability of paternalistic leadership: An expansion of leader–member exchange theory. *Group & Organization Management, 35,* 391–420.

Perez, J. (2006, December 4). Yellow pad: What the milk companies don't want you to know. *BusinessWorld,* pp. 1–5.

Perrow, C. (1999). *Normal accidents: Living with high-risk technologies.* Princeton, NJ: Princeton University Press.

Peter, T. A., Ahmend, A., & Arnoldy, B. (2011, April 18). Greg Mortenson's "Three cups of tea": Will CBS report harm aid work? *The Christian Science Monitor.*

Peters, T. (1992). *Liberation management.* New York: Ballantine.

Peterson, C., & Seligman, M. E. P. (2004). *Character strengths and virtues: A handbook and classification.* Oxford, England: Oxford University Press.

Peterson, D. K. (2002). The relationship between unethical behavior and the dimensions of the Ethical Climate Questionnaire. *Journal of Business Ethics, 41,* 313–326.

Peterson, K. (2009, July 16). After injuries, college athletes are often left to pay the bills. *The New York Times,* p. A1.

Peterson, S. (2008, August 6). In K2 aftermath, lessons learned. *The Christian Science Monitor.*

Petit, V., & Bollaert, H. (2012). Flying too close to the sun? Hubris among CEOS and how to prevent it. *Journal of Business Ethics, 108,* 265–283.

Petrick, J. A. (1998). Building organizational integrity and quality with the four Ps: Perspectives, paradigms, processes, and principles. In M. Schminke (Ed.), *Managerial ethics: Moral management of people and processes* (pp. 115–131). Mahwah, NJ: Erlbaum.

Petrick, J. A. (2008). Using the business integrity capacity model to advance business ethics education. In D. L. Swanson & D. G. Fisher (Eds.), *Advancing business ethics education* (pp. 103–124). Charlotte, NC: Information Age.

Petry, C. (2010, January 22). Chicago locks will stay open, Supreme Court rules. *Metal Bulletin.*

Peus, C., Wesche, J. S., Streicher, B., Braun, S., & Frey, D. (2012). Authentic leadership: An empirical test of its antecedents, consequences, and mediating mechanisms. *Journal of Business Ethics, 107,* 331–348.

Pfeffer, J. (1992). Understanding power in organizations. *California Management Review, 34*(2), 29–50.

Philip, C. (2011, November 19). Ethical conflicts of killing without risk. *The Times,* World News.

Philips, R. (2003). *Stakeholder theory and organizational ethics.* San Francisco: Berrett-Koehler.

Pierce, J. L., & Newstrom, J. W. (2011). *Leaders and the leadership process: Readings, self-assessments and applications* (6th ed.). New York: McGraw-Hill.

Pierson, D. (2012, December 28). China closing loophole in nation's Great Firewall. *Los Angeles Times,* p. B2.

Piliavin, J. A., & Chang, H. W. (1990). Altruism: A review of recent theory and research. *American Sociological Review, 16,* 27–65.

Pittinsky, T. L. (2010). A two-dimensional model of intergroup leadership: The case of national diversity. *American Psychologist, 65,* 194–200.

Pittinsky, T. L., & Simon, S. (2007). Intergroup leadership. *Leadership Quarterly, 18,* 586–605.

Pless, N. M. (2007). Understanding responsible leadership: Role identity and motivational drivers. *Journal of Business Ethics, 74,* 437–456.

Pless, N. M., & Maak, T. (2009). Responsible leaders as agents of world benefit: Learnings from "Project Ulysses." *Journal of Business Ethics, 85,* 59–71.

Pless, N. M., & Maak, T. (2011). Responsible leadership: Pathways to the future. *Journal of Business Ethics, 98,* 3–13.

Podsakoff, P. M., MacKenzie, S. B., Moorman, R. H., & Fetter, R. (1990). Transformational leader behaviors and their effects on followers' trust in leader, satisfaction, and organizational citizenship behavior. *Leadership Quarterly, 1,* 107–142.

Pogatchnik, S. (2010, March 14). Abuse scandals hit Catholic Church across Europe. *The Oregonian,* p. A11.

Politics, power and sex. (2011, May 21). *Belfast Telegraph,* p. 20.

Pollack, A., & Tavernise, S. (2012, November 22). Oversight failures documented in meningitis outbreak. *The New York Times,* p. A27.

Pollard, C. W. (1996). *The soul of the firm.* Grand Rapids, MI: HarperBusiness.

Popper, N. (2012, June 16). C.E.O. pay is rising despite the din. *The New York Times.*

Porath, C. L., & Erez, A. (2007). Does rudeness really matter? The effects of rudeness on task performance and helpfulness. *Academy of Management Journal, 50,* 1181–1197.

Potter, R. B. (1972). The logic of moral argument. In P. Deats (Ed.), *Toward a discipline of social ethics* (pp. 93–114). Boston: Boston University Press.

Power, M. (2008, November). K2: The killing peak. *Men's Journal.*

Powers, C. W., & Vogel, D. (1980). *Ethics in the education of business managers.* Hastings-on-Hudson, NY: Institute of Society, Ethics and the Life Sciences.

Prati, L. M., Douglas, C., Ferris, G. R., Ammeter, A. P., & Buckley, M. R. (2003). Emotional intelligence, leadership effectiveness, and team outcomes. *International Journal of Organizational Analysis, 11,* 21–40.

Price, T. L. (2006). *Understanding ethical failures in leadership.* Cambridge, England: Cambridge University Press.

Puffer, S. M., & McCarthy, D. J. (2008). Ethical turnarounds and transformational leadership: A global imperative for corporate social responsibility. *Thunderbird International Business Review, 50,* 304–314.

Quenqua, D. (2012, October 21). Clinic raffles could make you a winner, and maybe a mother. *The New York Times,* p. A1.

Quigley, N. R., Sully de Luque, M., & House, R. J. (2005). Responsible leadership and governance in a global context: Insights from the GLOBE study. In J. P. Doh & S. A. Sumpf (Eds.), *Handbook on responsible leadership and governance in global business* (pp. 352–379). Cheltenham, England: Edward Elgar.

Rainey, M. (2012, April/May). Fired before you're hired. *INSIGHT Into Diversity,* pp. 18–21.

Raissman, B. (2008, March 21). Brackets of millions, players net nothing. *Daily News,* p. 93.

Ramesh, R. (2008, August 5). K2 tragedy: Death toll on world's most treacherous mountain reaches 11. *The Guardian,* Home Pages, p. 2.

Rampersad, A. (1997). *Jackie Robinson*. New York: Alfred A. Knopf.

Ramstack, T. (2008, May 21). U.S. web services misused by oppressors. *The Washington Times,* p. C08.

Ramzy, A. (2013, January 24). After successful missile launch, North Korea threatens new nuclear test. *Time.* Retrieved from http://www.time.com

Rancer, A. S., & Avtgis, T. A. (2006). *Argumentative and aggressive communication: Theory, research, and application.* Thousand Oaks, CA: Sage.

Randerson, J. (2006, December 6). World's richest 1% own 40% of all wealth. *The Guardian.*

Ransley, C., & Spy, T. (Eds.). (2004). *Forgiveness and the healing process: A central therapeutic concern.* New York: Brunner-Routledge.

Rapisarda, B. A. (2002). The impact of emotional intelligence on work team cohesiveness and performance. *International Journal of Organizational Analysis, 10,* 363–370.

Rasche, A., & Gilbert, D. U. (2012). Institutionalizing global governance: The role of the United Nations Global Compact. *Business Ethics: A European Review, 21,* 100–114.

Rath, T. (2007). *StrengthsFinder 2.0.* New York: Gallup Press.

Rath, T., & Conchie, B. (2008). *Strengths based leadership.* New York: Gallup Press.

Rawls, J. (1971). *A theory of justice.* Cambridge, MA: Belknap.

Rawls, J. (1993). Distributive justice. In T. Donaldson & P. H. Werhane (Eds.), *Ethical issues in business: A philosophical approach* (4th ed., pp. 274–285). Englewood Cliffs, NJ: Prentice Hall.

Rawls, J. (1993). *Political liberalism.* New York: Columbia University Press.

Rawls, J. (2001). *Justice as fairness: A restatement* (E. Kelly, Ed.). Cambridge, MA: Belknap.

Ray, D., & Bronstein, H. (1995). *Teaming up: Making the transition to a self-directed, team-based organization.* New York: McGraw-Hill.

Reave, L. (2005). Spiritual values and practices related to leadership effectiveness. *Leadership Quarterly, 16,* 655–687.

Reb, J., Goldman, B. M., Kray, L. J., & Cropanzano, R. (2006). Different wrongs, different remedies? Reactions to organizational remedies after procedural and interactional injustice. *Personnel Psychology, 59,* 31–64.

Reece, D. (2012, September 20). Ofcom delivers the final blow to James Murdoch's UK years. *The Telegraph.*

Reed, L. L., Vidaver-Cohen, D., & Colwell, S. R. (2011). A new scale to measure executive servant leadership: Development, analysis, and implications for research. *Journal of Business Ethics, 101,* 415–434.

Rego, A., & Pina e Cunha, M. (2008). Workplace spirituality and organizational commitment: An empirical study. *Journal of Organizational Change Management, 21,* 53–75.

Resick, C. J., Hanges, P. J., Dickson, M. W., & Mitchelson, J. K. (2006). A cross-cultural examination of the endorsement of ethical leadership. *Journal of Business Ethics, 63,* 345–359.

Rest, J. R. (1986). *Moral development: Advances in research and theory.* New York: Praeger.

Rest, J. R. (1993). Research on moral judgment in college students. In A. Garrod (Ed.), *Approaches to moral development* (pp. 201–211). New York: Teachers College Press.

Rest, J. R. (1994). Background: Theory and research. In J. R. Rest & D. Narvaez (Eds.), *Moral development in the professions: Psychology and applied ethics* (pp. 1–25). Hillsdale, NJ: Erlbaum.

Rest, J. R., & Narvaez, D. (1991). The college experience and moral development. In W. M. Kurtines & J. L. Gewirtz (Eds.), *Handbook of moral* behavior and development: Vol. 2. Research (pp. 229–245). Hillsdale, NJ: Erlbaum.

Rest, J. R., Narvaez, D., Bebeau, M. J., & Thoma, S. J. (1999). *Postconventional moral thinking: A neo-Kohlbergian approach.* Mahwah, NJ: Erlbaum.

Reynolds, S. J. (2006). A neurocognitive model of the ethical decision-making process: Implications for study and practice. *Journal of Applied Psychology, 91,* 737–748.

Reynolds, S. J. (2008). Moral attentiveness: Who pays attention to the moral aspects of life? *Journal of Applied Psychology, 93,* 1027–1041.

Richter, A. W., West, M. A., Van Dick, R., & Dawson, J. F. (2006). Boundary spanners' identification, intergroup contact, and effective intergroup relations. *Academy of Management Journal, 49,* 1252–1269.

Richter, J. (2001). *Holding corporations accountable: Corporate conduct, international codes and citizen action.* London: Zed.

Ricks, D. (2009, January 22). Salmonella scare spreads. *Newsday,* p. A10.

Riggio, R. E., Zhu, W., Reina, C., & Maroosis, J. A. (2010). Virtue-based measurement of ethical leadership: The Leadership Virtues Questionnaire. *Consulting Psychology Journal:*

Practice and Research, 62(4), 235–250.

Ritzer, G. (2004). *The globalization of nothing.* Thousand Oaks, CA: Pine Forge.

Roberto, M. A. (2005). *Why great leaders don't take yes for an answer.* Upper Saddle River, NJ: Wharton School Publishing.

Roberts, K. H. (2006). Some characteristics of one type of high reliability organization. In D. Smith & D. Elliott (Eds.), *Key readings in crisis management: Systems and structures for prevention and recovery* (pp. 159–179). London: Routledge.

Robins, F. (2006). The challenge of TBL: A responsibility to whom? *Business and Society Review, 111,* 1–14.

Rochlin, G. I., LaPorte, T. R., & Roberts, K. H. (1987). The self-designing high-reliability organization: Aircraft carrier flight operations at sea. *Naval War College Review, 40(4),* 76–90.

Rockness, H., & Rockness, J. (2005). Legislated ethics: From Enron to Sarbanes-Oxley, the impact on corporate America. *Journal of Business Ethics, 57,* 31–54.

Rogers, B. (2013, January 29). North Korea in the dark. *The New York Times,* Op-Ed.

Rogers, E. M., & Steinfatt, T. M. (1999). *Intercultural communication.* Prospect Heights, IL: Waveland.

Roloff, M. E., & Paulson, G. D. (2001). Confronting organizational transgressions. In J. M. Darley, D. M. Messick, & T. R. Tyler (Eds.), *Social influences on ethical behavior in organizations* (pp. 53–68). Mahwah, NJ: Erlbaum.

Roose, K. (2012, March 2). Wall St. bonuses don't shrink as much as bank profits. *The International Herald Tribune,* Finance, p. 23.

Rosanas, J. M., & Velilla, M. (2003). Loyalty and trust as the ethical bases of organizations. *Journal of Business Ethics, 44,* 49–59.

Rosenberg, T. (2011, November 24). An electronic eye on hospital hand-washing. *The New York Times,* Opinionator blog.

Rosenfeld, P., Giacalone, R. A., & Riordan, C. A. (1995). *Impression management in organizations: Theory, measurement, practice.* London: Routledge.

Ross, J., & Staw, B. M. (1993). Organizational escalation and exit: Lessons from the Shoreham Nuclear Plant. *Academy of Management Journal, 36,* 701–732.

Rowley, A. (2011, March 24). Fukushima Fifty: Japan's new heroes. *The Business Times Singapore.*

Royce, J. (1920). *The philosophy of loyalty.* New York: Macmillan.

Rubin, R. S., Dierdorff, E. C., & Brown, M. E. (2010). Do ethical leaders get ahead? Exploring ethical leadership and promotability. *Business Ethics Quarterly, 20,* 215–236.

Rubin, T. (2011, May 1). Waiting for author Greg Mortenson to explain himself. *Lewiston Morning Tribune.*

Ruschman, N. L. (2002). Servant-leadership and the best companies to work for in America. In L. C. Spears & M. Lawrence (Eds.), *Focus on leadership: Servant-leadership for the twenty-first century* (pp. 123–139). New York: John Wiley.

Rushton, K. (2012, December 2). Rupert Murdoch to split News Corp early to limit fallout from hacking. *The Telegraph.*

Russell, R. F., & Stone, A. G. (2002). A review of servant leadership attributes: Developing a practical model. *Leadership & Organization Development Journal, 23,* 145–157.

Sachs, J. (2007, May 27). Sharing the wealth. *Time,* p. 81.

Sack, A. (2008, March 7). Should college athletes be paid? *The Christian Science Monitor,* Opinion, p. 9.

Salmonella shipped. (2009, February 7). *Newsday,* p. A09.

Salvador, R., & Folger, R. G. (2009). Business ethics and the brain. *Business Ethics Quarterly, 19,* 1–31.

Samuelson, R. J. (2013, January 7). Can't we kill farm subsidies? *The Oregonian,* p. A9.

Sandin, P. (2009). Approaches to ethics for corporate crisis management. *Journal of Business Ethics, 87,* 109–116.

Sanford, N., & Comstock, C. (Eds.). (1971). *Sanctions for evil.* San Francisco: Jossey-Bass.

Sanger, D. (2013, February 26). Washington treads warily on Chinese cyberattacks. *The International Herald Tribune,* News, p. 3.

Santora, M. (2012, December 8). After radio prank, hospital chairman condemns Australian network. *The New York Times,* The Lede blog.

Saunders, D. (2012, April 25). Rupert Murdoch says sorry, but takes no blame for scandal. *The Globe and Mail* (Canada), p. A 3.

Sauser, W. I. (2011). Beyond the classroom: Business ethics training for professionals. In R. R. Sims & W. I. Sauser (Eds.), *Experiences in teaching business ethics* (pp. 247–261). Charlotte, NC: Information Age.

Savage, C. (2011, March 3). Soldier faces 22 new WikiLeaks charges. *The New York Times,* p. A6.

Savage, C. (2013, March 1). Soldier admits providing files to WikiLeaks. *The New York Times,* p. A1.

Savage, C. (2013, July 31). Manning found not guilty of aiding the enemy. *The New York Times,* p. A1.

Savage, C., & Baker, P. (2013, May 22). Obama, in a shift, to limit targets of drone strikes. *The New York Times,* p. A1.

Savage, D. G. (2010, January 13). Scanners put privacy against security. *Los Angeles Times,* p. A11.

Sawyer, K. (2003, August 24). Shuttle's "smoking gun" took time to register. *The Washington Post,* p. A1.

Schmit, J. (2009, April 27). Broken system hid peanut plants' risks. *USA Today,* p. 1B.

Schmit, J., & Weise, E. (2009, January 29). Peanut butter recall grows. *USA Today,* p. 1B.

Schrag, B. (2001). The moral significance of employee loyalty. *Business Ethics Quarterly, 11,* 41–66.

Schriesheim, C. A., Castor, S. L., & Cogliser, C. C. (1999). Leader-member exchange (LMX) research: A comprehensive review of theory, measurement, and data-analytic practices. *Leadership Quarterly, 10,* 63–114.

Schrotenboer, B. (2013, January 28). USADA leader says Armstrong might still be lying. *USA Today,* p. 8C.

Schubert, S., & Miller, T. C. (2008, December 21). Where

bribery was just a line item. *The New York Times*, p. BU1.

Schultz, B. (1982). Argumentativeness: Its effect in group decision-making and its role in leadership perception. *Communication Quarterly, 3,* 368–375.

Schwartz, M. S. (2011). *Corporate social responsibility: An ethical approach.* Peterborough, Ontario: Broadview.

Schwartz, S. K. (2010, April 20). Medical pot use can conflict with job rules. *USA Today*, p. 7A.

Schweiger, D. M., Sandberg, W. R., & Rechner, P. (1989). Experiential effects of dialectical inquiry, devil's advocacy, and consensus approaches to strategic decision making. *Academy of Management Journal, 32,* 745–772.

Seeger, M. W., Sellnow, T. L., & Ulmer, R. R. (2003). *Communication and organizational crisis.* Westport, CT: Praeger.

Seeger, M. W., & Ulmer, R. R. (2001). Virtuous responses to organizational crisis: Aaron Feuerstein and Milt Cole. *Journal of Business Ethics, 31,* 369–376.

Sendjaya, S., & Sarros, J. C. (2002). Servant leadership: Its origin, development, and application in organizations. *Journal of Leadership & Organizational Studies, 9*(2), 57–64.

Shane, S. (2010, December 12). Keeping secrets WikiSafe. *The New York Times*, p. WK1.

Shane, S. (2011, January 14). Accused soldier stays in brig as WikiLeaks link is sought. *The New York Times*, p. A1.

Shane, S. (2011, October 10). A world soon armed with drones. *The International Herald Tribune*, p. 8.

Shane, S. (2012, September 25). Report cites high civilian toll in Pakistan drone strikes. *The New York Times*, At War blog.

Shane, S. (2013, April 8). Targeted killing comes to define war on terror. *The New York Times*, p. A1.

Shared sacrifice? Not for these airline executives. (2006, February 2). *USA Today*, p. 14A.

Shaw, J. B., Erickson, A., & Harvey, M. (2011). A method for measuring destructive leadership and identifying types of destructive leaders in organizations. *Leadership Quarterly, 22,* 575–590.

Shockley-Zalabak, P., Ellis, K., & Cesaria, R. (2000). *Measuring organizational trust: A diagnostic survey and international indicator.* San Francisco: International Association of Business Communicators.

Shockley-Zalabak, P., Ellis, K., & Winograd, G. (2000). Organizational trust: What it means, why it matters. *Organization Development Journal, 18*(4), 35–48.

Shockley-Zalabak, P., Morreale, S. P., & Hackman, M. Z. (2010). *Building the high-trust organization: Strategies for supporting five key dimensions of trust.* San Francisco: Jossey-Bass.

Shriver, D. W. (1995). *An ethic for enemies: Forgiveness in politics.* New York: Oxford University Press.

Shriver, D. W. (2001). Forgiveness: A bridge across abysses of revenge. In R. G. Helmick & R. L. Peterson (Eds.), *Forgiveness and reconciliation: Religion, public policy, and conflict transformation* (pp. 151–167). Philadelphia: Templeton Foundation Press.

Shu, L. L., Gino, F., & Bazerman, M. H. (2009). *Dishonest deed, clear conscience: Self-preservation through moral disengagement and motivated forgetting.* Harvard Business School Working Paper 09-078.

Sides, H. (2011, May 2). Shattered faith: What the fall of Greg Mortenson tells us about America's irrepressible longing for heroes. *Newsweek*, p. 5.

Siemens settles World Bank with $100 million for anti-fight corruption. (2009, July 6). *Africa News.*

Silla, B., Knight, D., & Fang, B. (2006, February 27). Learning to live with big brother. *U.S. News & World Report.*

Silverman, R. E. (2012, February 4). Where's the boss? Trapped in a meeting. *The Wall Street Journal.*

Simola, S. (2003). Ethics of justice and care in corporate crisis management. *Journal of Business Ethics, 46,* 351–361.

Simola, S. (2005). Concepts of care in organizational crisis prevention. *Journal of Business Ethics, 62,* 341–353.

Simola, S. (2010). Anti-corporate anger as a form of care-based moral agency. *Journal of Business Ethics, 94,* 255–269.

Simons, T. L. (2002). Behavioral integrity: The perceived alignment between managers' words and deeds as a research focus. *Organization Science, 13,* 18–35.

Simonson, I., & Staw, B M. (1992). Deescalation strategies: A comparison of techniques for reducing commitment to losing courses of action. *Journal of Applied Psychology, 77,* 419–426.

Sims, R. L., & Keon, T. L. (1997). Ethical work climate as a factor in the development of person–organization fit. *Journal of Business Ethics, 16,* 1095–1105.

Sims, R. R. (2003). *Ethics and corporate social responsibility: Why giants fall.* Westport, CT: Praeger.

Sleesman, D. J., Conlon, D. E., McNamara G., & Miles, J. E. (2012). Cleaning up the big muddy: A meta-analytic review of the determinants of escalation of commitment. *Academy of Management Journal, 3,* 541–562.

Smith, C. M., & Tindale, R. S. (2009). Direct and indirect minority influence in groups. In R. Martin & M. Hewstone (Eds.), *Minority influence and innovations: Antecedents, processes and consequences* (pp. 263–284). Hoboken, NJ: Psychology Press.

Smith, D. H. (1993). Stories, values, and patient care decisions. In C. Conrad (Ed.), *The ethical nexus* (pp. 123–148). Norwood, NJ: Ablex.

Smith, J. Y. (2009, August 12). The Olympian force behind a revolution. *The Washington Post,* p. A07.

Smith, P. K., Jostmann, N. B., Galinsky, A. D., & van Dijk, W. W. (2008). Lacking power impairs executive functions. *Psychological Science, 19,* 441–447.

Smith, T. (1999). Justice as a personal virtue. *Social Theory & Practice, 25,* 361–384.

Smith, W. (2007). Cosmopolitan citizenship: Virtue, irony and worldliness. *European Journal of Social Theory, 10,* 37–52.

Smith-Spark, L. (2012, December 8). Hospital nurse found dead after taking prank call on Catherine. CNN. Retrieved from http://www.cnn.com

Smith-Spark, L., & Brocchetto, M. (2012, December 11). Prank call radio station to donate funds to nurse's family. CNN. Retrieved from http://www.cnn.com

Snow, N. E. (1993). Self-forgiveness. *Journal of Value Inquiry, 27,* 75–80.

Snyder, C. R., & Lopez. S. J. (2005). *Handbook of positive psychology.* Oxford, England: Oxford University Press.

Snyder, P., Hall, M., Robertson, J., Jasinski, T., & Miller, J. S. (2006). Ethical rationality: A strategic approach to organizational crisis. *Journal of Business Ethics, 63,* 371–383.

Solnik, C. (2012, November 13). Class action lawsuit filed against Long Island Power Authority, national grid. *Long Island Business.*

Solomon, C. M. (2001). Put your ethics to a global test. In M. H. Albrecht (Ed.), *International HRM: Managing diversity in the workplace* (pp. 329–335). Oxford, England: Blackwell.

Solomon, R. C. (1990). *A passion for justice: Emotions and the origins of the social contract.* Reading, MA: Addison-Wesley.

Solomon, R. C. (1992). *Ethics and excellence: Cooperation and integrity in business.* New York: Oxford University Press.

Spears, L. (1998). Introduction: Tracing the growing impact of servant-leadership. In L. C. Spears (Ed.), *Insights on leadership* (pp. 1–12). New York: John Wiley.

Spears, L. C. (2004). The understanding and practice of servant leadership. In L. C. Spears & M. Lawrence (Eds.), *Practicing servant leadership: Succeeding through trust, bravery, and forgiveness* (pp. 9–24). San Francisco: Jossey-Bass.

Squires, N. (2012, July 11). Costa Concordia captain: "I ****** up." *The Telegraph.*

Srivastva, S. (Ed.). (1988). *Executive integrity.* San Francisco: Jossey-Bass.

Stanley, D. J., Meyer, J. P., & Topolnytsky, L. (2005). Employee cynicism and resistance to organizational change. *Journal of Business and Psychology, 19,* 429–459.

Starmann, R. G. (1993). Tragedy at McDonald's. In J. A. Gottschalk (Ed.), *Crisis response: Inside stories on managing image under siege* (pp. 309–322). Detroit, MI: Gale Group.

Statman, D. (2006). Supreme emergencies revisited. *Ethics, 117,* 58–79.

Staw, B. M. (1981). The escalation of commitment to a course of action. *Academy of Management Review, 6,* 577–587.

Stein, M. (2003). Unbounded irrationality: Risk and organization narcissism at Long Term Capital Management. *Human Relations, 56,* 523–540.

Stein, R. (2009, September 26). Mandatory flu shots hit resistance. *The Washington Post,* p. A01.

Stein, Y., & Richter, E. D. (2010, Fall). Suspected mass killings—call them democide, politicide, or maybe genocide in North Korea. Genocide Prevention Now, no. 4. Retrieved from http://www.genocidepreventionnow.org

Sternberg, R. J. (2002). Smart people are not stupid, but they sure can be foolish. In R. J. Sternberg (Ed.), *Why smart people can be so stupid* (pp. 232–242). New Haven, CT: Yale University Press.

Stoda, G. (2012, August 25). Don't blame LeBron James for $300 sneaker. *Palm Beach Post.*

Stogdill, R. M., & Coons, A. E. (1957). *Leader behavior: Its description and measurement.* Columbus: Ohio State University, Bureau of Business Research.

Story, L. (2008, December 18). Wall St. profits were a mirage, but huge bonuses were real. *New York Times,* p. A1.

Stott, B. R. (2001, January–February). The great divide in the global village. *Foreign Affairs,* pp. 160–177.

Strauss, G. (2012, January 24). More CEOs rake in $50m and up. *USA Today,* p. 1A.

Street, M. D. (1997). Groupthink: An examination of theoretical issues, implications, and future research suggestions. *Small Group Research, 28,* 72–93.

Strom, S. (2013, January 5). F.D.A. proposes broad new rules on food safety. *The New York Times,* p. A1.

Sucher, S. J. (2008). *The moral leader: Challenges, tools, and insights.* London: Routledge.

Surico, J. (2012, December 27). The *Journal News* gun owner database debacle. *The Village Voice,* Guns blog.

Swardson, A. (2007, March 11). A tale of courage, told in a blink of an eye. *The Washington Post,* p. A01.

Tabuchi, H. (2011, April 11). Less pay, fewer benefits, more radiation; disaster in Japan. *The International Herald Tribune,* p. 6.

Talbot, M. (1999). Against relativism. In J. M. Halstead & T. H. McLaughlin (Eds.), *Education in morality* (pp. 206–217). London: Routledge.

Tangney, J. P. (2000). Humility: Theoretical perspectives, empirical findings and directions for future research. *Journal of Social and Clinical Psychology, 19,* 70–82.

Taras, V., Kirkman, B. L., & Steel, P. (2010). Examining the impact of *Culture's Consequences*: A three-decade, multilevel, meta-analytic review of Hofstede's cultural value dimensions. *Journal of Applied Psychology, 95,* 405–439.

Tavernise, S., & Pollack, A. (2012, October 27). F.D.A. details contamination at pharmacy. *The New York Times,* p. A1.

Tavis, T. (2000). The globalization phenomenon and multinational corporate developmental responsibility. In O. F. Williams (Ed.), *Global codes of conduct: An idea whose time has come* (pp. 13–36). Notre Dame, IN: University of Notre Dame Press.

Taylor, J. (2008, August 5). What makes K2 the most perilous challenge a mountaineer can face? *The Independent,* Comment, p. 30.

Taylor, J. (2012, September 26). Outrage at CIA's deadly "double tap" drone attacks. *The Independent.*

Tenbrunsel, A. E., Diekman, K. A., Wade-Benzoni, K. A., & Bazerman, M. H. (2009). *The ethical mirage: A temporal explanation as to why we aren't as ethical as we think we are.* Harvard Business School Working Paper No. 08-012.

Tenbrunsel, A. E., & Messick, D. M. (2004). Ethical fading: The role of self-deception in unethical behavior. *Social Justice Research, 17,* 223–236.

Tepper, B. J. (2000). Consequences of abusive supervision. *Academy of Management Journal, 43,* 178–190.

Tepper, B. J. (2007). Abusive supervision in work organizations: Review, synthesis, and research agenda. *Journal of Management, 33,* 261–289.

Terez, T. (2001, December). You could just spit: Tales of bad bosses. *Workforce,* pp. 24–25.

Thoma, S. J. (2006). Research on the Defining Issues Test. In M. Killen & J. G. Smetana (Eds.), *Handbook of moral development* (pp. 67–91). Mahwah, NJ: Erlbaum.

Thomas, G. (2000, January 10). The forgiveness factor. *Christianity Today,* pp. 38–43.

Thomas, R. J. (2008). *Crucibles of leadership: How to learn from experience to become a great leader.* Boston: Harvard Business Press.

Thompson, G. (2010, August 9). A soldier's path toward a leak investigation. *The New York Times,* p. A1.

Thompson, M. (2012, December 24). General disorders: Why some senior military officers are going off the rails. *Time,* p. 16.

Thoresen, C. E., Harris, H. S., & Luskin, F. (2000). Forgiveness and health: An unanswered question. In M. E. McCullough, K. I. Pargament, & C. E. Thoresen (Eds.), *Forgiveness: Theory, research,* *and practice* (pp. 254–280). New York: Guilford.

Thoroughgood, C. N., Padilla, A., Hunter, S. T., & Tate, B. W. (2012). The susceptible circle: A taxonomy of followers associated with destructive leadership. *Leadership Quarterly, 23,* 897–917.

Thoroughgood, C. N., Tate, B. W., Sawyer, K. B., & Jacobs, R. (2012). Bad to the bone: Empirically defining and measuring destructive leader behavior. *Journal of Leadership & Organizational Studies, 19,* 230–255.

Tileaga, C. (2006). Representing the "other": A discursive analysis of prejudice and moral exclusion in talk about Romanies. *Journal of Community & Applied Social Psychology, 16,* 19–41.

Timmons, H., Trivedi, A., & Gottipati, S. (2012, December 31). Six charged with murder in India as rape victim dies. *The New York Times.*

Timmons, M. (2002). *Moral theory: An introduction.* Lanham, MD: Rowman & Littlefield.

Tims, D. (2010, February 17). Bob gives Red Mill to workers. *The Oregonian,* pp. A1, A5.

Tivnan, E. (1995). *The moral imagination.* New York: Routledge, Chapman, and Hall.

Toffler, B. L., & Reingold, J. (2003). *Final accounting: Ambition, greed, and the fall of*

Arthur Andersen. New York: Broadway.

Toor, S. R., & Ofori, G. (2009). Ethical leadership: Examining the relationships with full range leadership model, employee outcomes, and organizational culture. *Journal of Business Ethics, 90,* 533–547.

Tourish, D. (2008). Challenging the transformational agenda: Leadership theory in transition? *Management Communication Quarterly, 21,* 522–528.

Tourish, D. (2013). *The dark side of transformational leadership: A critical perspective.* New York: Routledge.

Tourish, D., & Pinnington, A. (2002). Transformational leadership, corporate cultism, and the spirituality paradigm: An unholy trinity in the workplace? *Human Relations, 55,* 147–172.

Trevino, L. K., & Brown, M. E. (2005). The role of leaders in influencing unethical behavior in the workplace. In R. E. Kidwell & C. L. Martin (Eds.), *Managing organizational deviance* (pp. 69–87). Thousand Oaks, CA: Sage.

Trevino, L. K., Brown, M., & Pincus, L. (2003). A qualitative investigation of perceived executive ethical leadership: Perceptions from inside and outside the executive suite. *Human Relations, 56,* 5–37.

Trevino, L. K., Butterfield, K. D., & McCabe, D. L.

(1998). The ethical context in organizations: Influences on employee attitudes and behaviors. *Business Ethics Quarterly, 8,* 447–476.

Trevino, L. K., Hartman, L. P., & Brown, M. (2000). Moral person and moral manager: How executives develop a reputation for ethical leadership. *California Management Review, 42*(4), 128–133.

Trevino, L. K., & Nelson, K. A. (2004). *Managing business ethics: Straight talk about how to do it right* (3rd ed.). Hoboken, NJ: John Wiley.

Trevino, L. K., & Weaver, G. R. (2001). Organizational justice and ethics program "follow-through": Influences on employees' harmful and helpful behavior. *Business Ethics Quarterly, 11,* 651–671.

Trevino, L. K., & Weaver, G. R. (2003). *Managing ethics in business organizations: Social scientific perspectives.* Stanford, CA: Stanford University Press.

Triandis, H. C. (1995). *Individualism and collectivism.* Boulder, CO: Westview Press.

Tronto, J. C. (1993). *Moral boundaries: A political argument for an ethic of care.* New York: Routledge.

Tropman, J. (2003). *Making meetings work: Achieving high quality group decisions* (2nd ed.). Thousand Oaks, CA: Sage.

Troyer, J. (2003). *The classical utilitarians: Bentham and Mill.* Indianapolis: Hackett.

Tucker, E. (2012, May 7). Scandal highlights lack of women in US Secret Service. *The Nation.*

Turner, N., Barling, J., Epitropaki, O., Butcher, V., & Milner, C. (2002, April). Transformational leadership and moral reasoning. *Journal of Applied Psychology, 87,* 304–311.

Turning a blind eye to North Korea's "hidden gulag." (2012, April 12). *The Washington Post.*

The twilight zone. (2011, November 15). *The Economist,* pp. 49–50.

Ulmer, R. R., Seeger, M. W., & Sellnow, T. L. (2007). Post-crisis communication and renewal: Expanding the parameters of post-crisis discourse. *Public Relations Review, 33,* 130–134.

Ulmer, R. R., & Sellnow, T. L. (2000). Consistent questions of ambiguity in organizational crisis communication: Jack in the Box as a case study. *Journal of Business Ethics, 25,* 143–155.

Ulmer, R. R., Sellnow, T. L., & Seeger, M. W. (2008). Post-crisis communication and renewal: Understanding the potential for positive outcomes in crisis communication. In R. L. Heath & D. H. O'Hair (Eds.), *Handbook of risk and crisis communication* (pp. 302–322). Hoboken, NJ: Routledge.

United Nations. (1948). The Universal Declaration

of Human Rights. Retrieved from http://www.un.org/en/documents/udhr/index.shtmlUN Declaration of Human Rights

United Press International. (2009, April 24). Poll: U.S. split on torture.Retrieved from http://www.upi.com/Top_News/2009/04/24/Poll-US-split-on-torture/UPI-55341240631033

Upper 1 percent of Americans are rolling in the dough. (December 12, 2012). *The Oregonian*, p. A2.

Upton, J., & Berkowitz, S. (2012, May 15). Budget disparity growing among NCAA Division I schools. *USA Today*. Retrieved from http://www.usatoday.com

Upton, J., & Wieberg, S. (2006, November 16). Million-dollar coaches move into mainstream. *USA Today*, p. 1A.

U.S. Bureau of Labor Statistics. (2013). *Women in the labor force: A databook*. Retrieved from http://www.bls.gov

U.S. Department of Labor. (2010, July). Frequently asked questions (FAQs). Retrieved from http://dol.gov/dolfaq/dolfaq.asp

Usborne, D. (2012, June 7). Thin and fragile, America's public enemy No. 1 Bradley Manning in court. *The Independent*, Americas.

Useem, M. (1998). *The leadership moment: Nine stories of triumph and disaster and their lessons for us all*. New York: Times Books.

Valacich, J. S., & Schewenk, C. (1995). Devil's advocacy and dialectical inquiry effects on face-to-face and computer-mediated group decision making. *Organizational Behavior and Human Decision Processes, 63,* 158–173.

Valentine, S., & Barnett, T. (2003). Ethics code awareness, perceived ethical values, and organizational commitment. *Journal of Personal Selling & Sales Management, 23,* 359–367.

Van Vuuren, L. J., & Crous, F. (2005). Utilising appreciative inquiry (AI) in creating a shared meaning of ethics in organizations. *Journal of Business Ethics, 57,* 399–412.

Varachaver, N. (2004, November 15). Glamour! Fame! Org charts! *Fortune,* pp. 76–85.

Vecchio, R. P. (1982). A further test of leadership effects due to between-group variation and in-group variation. *Journal of Applied Psychology, 67,* 200–208.

Vega, G., & Comer, D. R. (2005). Bullying and harassment in the workplace. In R. E. Kidwell, Jr., & C. L. Martin (Eds.), *Managing organizational deviance* (pp. 183–203). Thousand Oaks, CA: Sage.

Velasquez, M. G. (1992). *Business ethics: Concepts and cases* (3rd ed.). Englewood Cliffs, NJ: Prentice Hall.

Verhovek, S. H. (1993, April 22). Death in Waco: F.B.I. saw the ego in Koresh, but not a willingness to die. *The New York Times,* p. A1.

Vetelson, A. J. (2005). *Evil and human agency: Understanding collective evildoing.* Cambridge, England: Cambridge University Press.

Victor, B., & Cullen, J. B. (1988). The organizational bases of ethical work climates. *Administrative Science Quarterly, 33,* 101–125.

Victor, B., & Cullen, J. B. (1990). A theory and measure of ethical climate in organizations. In W. C. Frederic & L. E. Preston (Eds.), *Business ethics: Research issues and empirical studies* (pp. 77–97). Greenwich, CT: JAI Press.

Viesturs, E., & Roberts, D. (2009). *K2: Life and death on the world's most dangerous mountain.* New York: Broadway.

Viswesvaran, C., & Ones, D. S. (2002). Examining the construct of organizational justice: A meta-analytic evaluation of relations with work attitudes and behaviors. *Journal of Business Ethics, 38,* 193–203

Vitell, S. J., Nwachukwu, S. L., & Barnes, J. H. (1993). The effects of culture on ethical decision-making: An application of Hofstede's typology. *Journal of Business Ethics, 12,* 753–760.

Waldman, D. A. (2011). Moving forward with the concept of responsible leadership: Three caveats to guide theory and research. *Journal of Business Ethics, 98,* 75–83.

Waldman, D. A., Bass, B. M., & Yammarino, F. J. (1990). Adding to contingent-reward behavior: The augmenting effect of charismatic leadership. *Group and Organizational Studies, 15,* 381–394.

Waller, J. (2007). *Becoming evil: How ordinary people commit genocide and mass killing* (2nd ed.). Oxford, England: Oxford University Press.

Waltman, M. A., Russell, D. C., Coyle, C. T., Enright, R. D., Holter, A. C., & Swoboda, C. M. (2009). The effects of a forgiveness intervention on patients with coronary artery disease. *Psychology and Health, 24*(1), 11–27.

Walumbwa, F. O., Avolio, B. J., Gardner, W. L., Wernsing, T. S., & Peterson, S. J. (2008). Authentic leadership: Development and validation of a theory-based measure. *Journal of Management, 34,* 89–126.

Walumbwa, F. O., Hartnell, C. A., & Oke, A. (2010). Servant leadership, procedural justice climate, service climate, employee attitudes, and organizational citizenship behavior: A cross-level

investigation. *Journal of Applied Psychology, 95,* 517–529.

Walumbwa, F. O., Luthans, F., Avey, J. B., & Oke, A. (2011). Authentically leading groups: The mediating role of collective psychological capital and trust. *Journal of Organizational Behavior, 32,* 4–24.

Walzer, M. (1977). *Just and unjust wars: A moral argument with historical illustrations.* New York: Basic Books.

Wang, Y.-D, & Hseih, J.-H. (2012). Toward a better understanding of the link between ethical climate and job satisfaction: A multilevel analysis. *Journal of Business Ethics, 15,* 535–545.

Waples, E. P., Antes, A., Murphy, S. T., Connelly, S., & Mumford, M. D. (2009). A meta-analytic investigation of business ethics instruction. *Journal of Business Ethics, 87,* 133–151.

Warnke, G. (1993). *Justice and interpretation.* Cambridge: MIT Press.

Washington, R. R., Sutton, C. D., & Feild, H. S. (2006). Individual differences in servant leadership: The roles of values and personality. *Leadership & Organization Development Journal, 27,* 700–716.

Wayne, L. (2005, March 8). Boeing chief is ousted after admitting affair. *The New York Times,* p. A1.

Wayne, L. (2012, March 11). Hits, and misses, in a war on

bribery. *The New York Times,* p. BU1.

Wayne, L. (2012, September 4). Foreign firms most affected by a U.S. law barring bribes. *The New York Times,* p. B1.

Weaver, G. R., Trevino, L. K., & Cochran, P. L. (1999). Integrated and decoupled corporate social performance: Management commitments, external pressures, and corporate ethics practices. *Academy of Management Journal, 42,* 539–552.

Weber, E. T. (2011). What experimentalism means in ethics. *Journal of Speculative Philosophy, 25*(1), 98–115.

Weber, J., & Wasieleski, D. (2001). Investigating influences on managers' moral reasoning: The impact of personal and organizational factors. *Business & Society, 40,* 105–107.

Weber, J., & Wasieleski, D. M. (2013). Corporate ethics and compliance programs: A report, analysis and critiques. *Journal of Business Ethics, 112,* 609–626.

Weber, J. A. (2007). Business ethics training: Insights from learning theory. *Journal of Business Ethics, 70,* 61–85.

Webley, K. (2013, January 21). The baby deficit. *Time,* pp. 30–39.

Webster, P. (1997, March 7). Memoir unlocks medical enigma. *The Guardian,* p. 15.

Weick, K. E., & Roberts, K. H. (2006). Collective minds in organizations: Heedful interrelating on flight decks. In D. Smith & D. Elliott (Eds.), *Key readings in crisis management: Systems and structures for prevention and recovery* (pp. 343–368). London: Routledge.

Weick, K. E., & Sutcliffe, K. M. (2001). *Managing the unexpected: Assuring high performance in an age of complexity.* San Francisco: Jossey-Bass.

Weiner, R. (2012, December 27). *Journal News'* gun-owner database draws criticism. Lohud.com. Retrieved from http://www.lohud.com

Weise, E. (2009, April 2). Nuts. *USA Today*, p. 1B.

Weise, E. (2012, January 12). Pythons strangling Everglades. *USA Today*, p. 3A.

Weise, E. (2013, February 26). Telecommuters to Yahoo: Boo. *USA Today*, p. 1A.

Weise, E., & Schmit, J. (2009, February 10). Health risks may reach far beyond reported victims. *USA Today*, p. 1A.

Wentling, R. M. (2004). Factors that assist and barriers that hinder the success of diversity initiatives in multinational corporations. *Human Resource Development International, 7,* 165–180.

Werhane, P. H. (1999). *Moral imagination and management decision-making.* New York: Oxford University Press.

West, H. R. (2004). *An introduction to Mill's utilitarian ethics.* Cambridge, England: Cambridge University Press.

White, B. J., & Prywes, Y. (2007). *The nature of leadership: Reptiles, mammals, and the challenge of becoming a great leader.* New York: AMACOM.

Whiteside, K. (2004, September 1). College athletes want cut of action. *USA Today*, p. 3C.

Whitney, D., & Trosten-Bloom, A. (2003). *The power of appreciative inquiry: A practical guide to positive change.* San Francisco: Berrett-Koehler.

Whoriskey, P. (2010, March 19). Toyota resisted government safety findings; automaker followed "game plan," escaped a broad early recall. *The Washington Post,* p. A01.

Why your negotiating behavior may be ethically challenged—and how to fix it. (2008, April). *Negotiation, 11*(4), 1–5.

William, J., & Blood, M. R. (2012, September 28). Arnold Schwarzenegger affair: Ex-governor says maid affair was "stupidest thing." Huffington Post.

Williams, G., & Zinkin, J. (2008). The effect of culture on consumers' willingness to punish irresponsible corporate behaviour: Applying Hofstede's typology to the punishment aspect of corporate social responsibility. *Business Ethics: A European Review, 17,* 210–226.

Williams, K. D., Harkins, S. G., & Karau, S. J. (2003). Social performance. In M. A. Hogg & J. Cooper (Eds.), *The Sage handbook of social psychology* (pp. 327–346). London: Sage.

Wilmers, R. G. (2009, July 27). Where the crisis came from. *The Washington Post,* p. A19.

Wilmot, W. W., & Hocker, J. L. (2001). *Interpersonal conflict* (6th ed.). New York: McGraw-Hill Higher Education.

Wilson, D. (2009, March 3). Patching a wound. *The New York Times,* p. B1.

Wilson, D. (2010, July 22). A tougher conflict of interest policy at Harvard Medical School. *The New York Times,* p. B4.

Wiseman, P. (2008, April 23). In China, a battle over Web censorship. *USA Today,* p. 1A.

Witt, J. L., & Morgan, J. (2002). *Stronger in the broken places: Nine lessons for turning crisis into triumph.* New York: Times Books/Henry Holt.

Wolff, L. (2012, October 17). Free to be a sexual predator? *The New York Times,* Op-Ed.

Wolff, M. (2012, November 26). Murdoch may not be out of the woods yet. *USA Today,* p. 1B.

Wolvin, A. D., & Coakley, G. C. (1993). A listening taxonomy. In A. D. Wolvin & C. G. Coakley (Eds.), *Perspectives in listening* (pp. 15–22). Norwood, NJ: Ablex.

Wong, E. (2011, April 24). Two schools, one complicated situation. *The New York Times,* p. WK5.

Woodruff, P. (2001). *Reverence: Renewing a forgotten virtue.* Oxford, England: Oxford University Press.

Woodzicka, J. A., & LaFrance, M. (2001). Real versus imagined gender harassment. *Journal of Social Issues, 57,* 15–30.

Wooten, L. P., & James, E. H. (2008). Linking crisis management and leadership competencies: The role of human resource development. *Advances in Developing Human Resources, 10,* 352–379.

Worthington, E. L., Jr. (2005). Initial questions about the art and science of forgiving. In E. L. Worthington (Ed.), *Handbook of forgiveness* (pp. 1–13). New York: Routledge.

Wright, D. K. (1993). Enforcement dilemma: Voluntary nature of public relations codes. *Public Relations Review, 19,* 13–20.

Wright, M. (2011, November 7). Success means telling people to buy less. *The Guardian.*

Wright, M. (2013, January 7). Google shows China the white flag of surrender. *The Telegraph.* Retrieved from http://www.telegraph.co.uk

Wu, A. (2008, January 3). Balancing rights and burqas. *The Washington Times,* p. A17.

Wyatt, E. (2012, March 20). Behind the blood money. *The New York Times,* p. B1.

Yen, H. (2011, July 26). Wealth gap between whites, minorities widens to greatest level in a quarter century. Huffington Post.

Yokota, T., & Yamada, T. (2012, March 12). Disposable heroes. *Newsweek* (international ed.).

Yunus, M. (1998, October 31). Banker to the poor. *The Guardian.*

Yurtsever, G. (2006). Measuring moral imagination. *Social Behavior and Personality, 34,* 205–220.

Zadek, S. (2004, December). The path to corporate responsibility. *Harvard Business Review,* pp. 125–132.

Zhang, U. (2009, February 14). Peanut corporation files for bankruptcy. *Wall Street Journal Abstracts,* p. A3.

Zhu, W., May, D. R., & Avolio, B. J. (2004). The impact of ethical leadership behavior on employee outcomes: The roles of psychological empowerment and authenticity. *Journal of Leadership & Organizational Studies, 11*(1), 16–26.

Zimbardo, P. G. (2005). A situationist perspective on the psychology of evil. In A. G. Miller (Ed.), *The social psychology of good and evil* (pp. 21–50). New York: Guilford.

Zimbardo, P. G. (2007). *The Lucifer effect: Understanding how good people turn evil.* New York: Random House.

Zinnbauer, B. J., & Pargament, K. I. (2005). Religiousness and spirituality. In R. F. Paloutzian & C. L. Park (Eds.), *Handbook of the psychology of religion and spirituality* (pp. 21–42). New York: Guilford.

Zuckerman, P., & Padoan, A. (2012). *Buried in the sky: The extraordinary story of the Sherpa climbers on K2's deadliest day.* New York: Norton.

Zyglidopoulus, S. C. (2002). The social and environmental responsibilities of multinationals: Evidence from the Brent Spar case. *Journal of Business Ethics, 36,* 141–151.

Index

Cynicism, 9
Czech Republic, xx

Dalai Lama, 170
Damon, William, 78, 92
Dana-Farber Cancer Institute, 441
Day, Louis Alvin, 205–210
Death
    denying, 44
    euthanasia, 391
    on the job, 328
    by peanuts, 68–71
    Rwandan genocide, 125–126,
        130, 133
    suicide, 145, 445–447
    See also Health care; School
        shootings
Deceit, 13, 377
Deception, evil as, 123, 127
Deceptive practices, 17–19, 377,
    380, 385
Decision making, 187–228
    altruism, 170–176
    case study method, 214–218
    components of moral action,
        189–200
    in crisis event, 429
    in culturally diverse settings,
        395–398
    dual-process approach, 187–189
    ethical judgment, 62
    ethical perspectives tools, 156
    faulty decision-making, 48–57
    formats, 202–218
    HKH model, 396–398
    justice as fairness, 162–164
    Kant's categorical imperative,
        159–161
    Kidder's ethical checkpoints,
        202–205
    moral disengagement, 54–57
    moral imagination, failure of,
        52–54
    Nash's 12 questions, 210–213
    in organizational climate, 339
    pragmatism, 165–169
    SAD formula, 205–210
    in small groups, 276, 297
    utilitarianism, 157–159

Deductive reasoning, 290
Deepwater Horizon oil spill in
    Gulf of Mexico, xvi, 417,
    427, 434
Defensive versus supportive
    communication, 282–283
Defining Issues Test (DIT), 195
Dehumanization and moral
    disengagement, 56
Deification, 14
Democratic societies,
    164, 165, 402
Denmark, 380, 383, 386
Denny's, 343
Denver International Airport, 299
Denying death concept, 44
Deontological ethics,
    159–160, 193
DePree, Max, 236
Derailed leaders, 7
Descriptive theories, 229
Destructive behaviors, 4, 6, 7
    zero tolerance for, 326–332,
        355–356
Destructive conflict, 287
Destructive leader behavior scale,
    34–35
Developmental schemas, 194
Devil's advocate technique, 297
Dewey, John, 165, 166, 167
Dialectic inquiry method, 297
Difference principle, 163
Dignity, 372–373, 374, 393, 394
Dimon, Jamie, 24
Dingell, John, 32
Disagreement, 9
Disasters. *See* Crisis
Discourse of renewal, 427–428
Discrimination, 327
Discriminative listening, 279
Disease
    AIDS epidemic, 3, 17
    food poisoning, 68–71, 433
    influenza, 206–210
    locked-in syndrome, xxiii–xxv
    meningitis outbreak, xvi,
        32–34
    See also Health care
Disgust, 192

Disregard, 14
Dissent, 9
Diversity, ethical challenges of,
    369–414
    cultural differences and ethical
        values, 381–390
    ethical choices in culturally
        diverse settings, 395–398
    ethical scenarios, 400–402
    leadership in global society,
        374–381
    moral common ground,
        390–395
    perceptions scale, 407–409
    promotion of diversity in
        organization, 369–374
Diversity management, 370
Diving Bell and the Butterfly, The
    (Bauby), xxiv
Donaldson, Thomas, 395–396
Dow Jones Sustainability World
    Index, 356
Downsizing, 97
Dramatic rehearsal, 165–166, 167
Dreadful pleasure,
    evil as, 120, 127
Drone warfare, 56, 181–183
Drugs
    clinical drug trials in
        developing nations, 377,
        400–401
    drug compounders, 32–34
    drug industry in medical
        school, 196
    marijuana in workplace,
        308–309
    performance
        enhancing, 147–148, 197
    See also Health care
Duchon, Dennis, 137
Dufresne, Ronald, 441
Dunfee, Thomas, 395–396
Dunlap, Al, 320
Duty, 160–161, 379

Eaton Corporation, 342
Ebbers, Bernie, 85, 89, 326
Economic values, 103
Ecoterrorists, 56

Perot, Ross, 174
Perseverance, 94, 180
Personal power profile, 36–38
Personal trauma, 96–97
Person, Julia, 262
Peru, 130, 373, 383
Peters, Tom, 232
Petraeus, David, 16
Petrick, Joseph, 61
Pharmaceutical
    industry, 32–34, 196
    See also Drugs
Philanthropy, 326, 340
Philippines, 255, 377, 387
Pinto Ford recall, 53–54, 190
Pittinsky, Todd, 302
Plato, 78, 248
Pless, Nicola, 250, 251, 253
Pluralism, facing evil, 127
Poland, 386
Political activity, 349, 350
Political apologies, 133–134
Political contributions, 21–22
Political people, 104
Porras, Jerry, 341
Portugal, 383
Positivity, 92
Posner, Barry, 102, 232
Posttraumatic stress disorder, 435
Potter, Ralph, 208
Poverty, 17, 166–167
Power
    classification systems of,
        10–11, 12
    deprivation, 15
    personal power profile, 36–38
Power distance, as value
    orientation, 382–383
Power, leader shadows of, 10–15,
    375–376
Powers, Charles, 189
PPG Industries, 349
Practical wisdom, 82–83
Pragmatism, 165–169
Praise, 140
Precrisis stage, 418–423
Prejudice, 370–371, 374
    implicit, 197–198
Pressure to maintain numbers, 324
Price, Terry, 52

Pride, 45
Prince, The (Machiavelli), 46
Principled reasoning, 193
Principle of equal liberty, 162
Priorities, 99
Privacy issues, 18
Privilege, leader shadows of,
    15–17, 376–377
Proactive leaders, 98
Problem-centered messages, 282
Problem employees, 97
Problem recognition, 190–192
Process focus, in organizational
    climate, 338
Prodromes, 421
Productive conflict, 286–288
Programmed value patterns,
    382–385
Project GLOBE. *See* Global
    Leadership and
    Organizational Behavior
    Effectiveness
Property principle, 393
Prototypes, 20, 103–104
Provisionalism, 283
Prudence, 82–83, 200
Pseudo-transformational
    leadership, 232–233, 235
Psychological ownership, 244
Psychological systems (of
    morality), 389–390
Public morality *vs.* private
    behavior, 88–89
Public *vs.* private spheres in ethic
    of care, 172
Pulley, Mary Lynn, 96
Purity, 389, 390
Purpose
    corporate, 343–345
    in mission statement, 101
    in servant leadership, 238
Putin, Vladimir, 13
Pythons, Burmese, 178

Qaddafi, Muammar, 211
al-Qaeda, 181–183
Qualcomm, 15
Questionable practice (QP)
    model, 396–398

Quisling, Vidkun, 22
Qwest, 335

Radio, 173–174
Ragghianti, Marie, 91
Raines, Franklin, 79
Rape, in India, 402–404
Rationality, ethical, 437, 439–440
Rawl, Lawrence, 431
Rawls, John, 162–164
Rawls' justice as fairness theory,
    162–164, 171
    in ethical decision making,
        193, 209
    promoting diversity in
        organization, 370
Reagan, Ronald, 261, 425
*Real Power: Business Lessons
    From the Tao Te Ching,* 254
Rea, Peter, 82
Reasoning
    logical, 290
    to solve ethical problems,
        187–189
Reave, Laura, 137
Receptivity, 140
Reciprocity, 389
Recognition
    in apology, 135
    of ethical problems (moral
        sensitivity), 62, 190–192
Recommendation for job, 400
Reconsidering structure, 427
Red Mill Natural Foods, xviii, 23
Reese, Pee Wee, 23
Reflective practice, 138–139
Relational transparency, 242
Relativism, ethical, 390
Reliability, 337, 393
Religious clothing, 370
Religious conflicts, and
    a global ethic, 392
Religious thinkers, 104
Religious wars, 175–176
Relin, David Oliver, 110
Remains of the Day, The
    (Ishiguro), 241
Remorse, in apology, 135
Renewal, discourse of, 427–428

About the Author

Craig E. Johnson (PhD, University of Denver) is professor of leadership studies at George Fox University, Newberg, Oregon. He teaches undergraduate and graduate courses in leadership, ethics, and management. Previously he served as director of the George Fox Doctor of Business Administration program and chair of the university's Department of Communication Arts. Johnson is the author of *Organizational Ethics: A Practical Approach* (also published by SAGE) and coauthor, with Michael Z. Hackman, of *Leadership: A Communication Perspective.* He has published research findings, instructional ideas, and book reviews in the *Journal of Leadership Studies,* the *Journal of Leadership and Organizational Studies,* the *Journal of Leadership Education, Academy of Management Learning and Education,* the *International Leadership Journal, Communication Quarterly, Communication Reports,* and other journals. Johnson has led and participated in service and educational trips to Honduras, Kenya, Rwanda, New Zealand, China, and Brazil and has held volunteer leadership positions in a variety of religious and nonprofit organizations. When not teaching or writing, he enjoys working out, reading, fly-fishing, watching sports, and spending time with family.